International business economics

a European perspective

second edition

Edited by

Judith Piggott
Mark Cook

LONGMAN

Addison Wesley Longman Limited
Edinburgh Gate
Harlow
Essex CM20 2JE
England
and Associated Companies throughout the world

Published in the United States of America
by Addison Wesley Longman Inc., New York

Visit Addison Wesley Longman on the world wide web at:
http://www.awl-he.com

© Longman Group Ltd 1993
This edition © Addison Wesley Longman Limited 1999

First published 1993
Second edition 1999

ISBN   0 582 305802

British Library Cataloguing-in-Publication Data
A catalogue record for this book is available from the British Library

Library of Congress Cataloging-in-Publication Data

International business economics : a European perspective / edited by
  Judith Piggott, Mark Cook, ––2nd ed.
       p.   cm.
   Includes bibliographical references and index.
   ISBN 0–582–30580–2 (pbk.)
   1. International business enterprises –– European Economic Community
   countries.   2. European Economic Community countries––Commercial
   policy.   I. Piggott,   Judith,   1956–   . II. Cook, Mark, 1954– .
   HD2844.5.I566   1998
   338.8'894––dc21   98–20729
                                                                   CIP

Typeset by 30 in 10/12 pt New Baskerville
Produced by Addison Wesley Longman Singapore (Pte) Ltd, Printed in Singapore

Contents

CHAPTER 1

Introduction 1

Judith Piggott and Mark Cook

CHAPTER 2

The changing nature of international business 5

Judith Piggott and Mark Cook

CHAPTER 5

The protection of trade 69

Mark Cook

CHAPTER 8
Industrial policy and competition policy 169

Alan Jarman

CHAPTER 9

The Single European Market and Beyond 201

Judith Piggott

CHAPTER 10

Multinational corporations 233

Alan Jarman

CHAPTER 13
International banking and capital markets 319

Mark Cook and Jon Stephens

CHAPTER 14
Central and Eastern Europe 367

Andrew Kilmister and Mark Cook

CHAPTER 15
Conclusion 408

Judith Piggott and Mark Cook

Tables and figures

Tables

Figures

MARK COOK BA MSc is a principal lecturer in economics at Nene University College, Northampton and was previously a research associate at the University of Leicester. He is author of a wide range of articles covering small and medium-sized enterprises and business economics, and is business section editor of the EBEA Journal. His authored works include *Growth and Structural Change* (with N. Healey – MacMillan, 1995), *Supplyside Economics* (with N. Healey – Heinemann, 1996) and *Business Economics: Applications and Strategy* (with C. Farquharson – Pitman, 1998).

ALAN JARMAN BA LLB MA Cert Ed is a principal lecturer in economics at Oxford Brookes University. He has worked for the Canadian government in the Fair Trading Office and has previously taught at Bristol University and Teesside Polytechnic, and undertaken some part-time work for the Open University, WEA and Durham and Oxford Universities.

ANDREW KILMISTER BSc MPhil is a senior lecturer in economics at Oxford Brookes University. He is an author of various articles on models of economic development, Central and Eastern Europe and on the motor industry.

JUDITH PIGGOTT MA (Cantab) MPhil is a senior lecturer in economics at Oxford Brookes University. She previously taught at Nene University College, Northampton and spent some years working in industry and local government.

HALUK SEZER BSc DipEconDev, MA is a senior lecturer in economics at Oxford Brookes University and was previously an Economics Lecturer at the Department of Economics of Leicester Polytechnic (now De Montfort University).

JON STEPHENS BA PGCE is a senior lecturer at Nene University College, Northampton. He specialises in European business policy and organisation studies and is a visiting lecturer at Poitiers and Trier Business Schools.

Acknowledgements

We are indebted to many individuals for their help in the preparation of this text. In particular, a major debt is owed to those who have contributed to chapters and without whom the text could not have been produced. Also thanks to those in the School of Business at Oxford Brookes (and Ann White in the Library) and Nene University College, Northampton, who have helped.

We would like to thank our respective families for their unfailing support and encouragement – in particular Jools, Helen and Joe, and Judith's Dad for all his help in checking the manuscripts.

We two, of course, bear the full responsibility for all errors and omissions.

We are grateful to the following for permission to reproduce copyright material: Table 2.2 from Competition and Integration, *European Economy* (1994), European Commission; Table 2.3 from Economic Evaluation of the Internal market, *European Economy* (1996), European Commission; Tables 2.5, 2.6, 2.7, 2.8, and 10.1 *Fortune*, Aug. 1997 and Tables 13.7 and 13.8 *Fortune* Global 500 (1997) © *Fortune Magazine*, Time Life International; Figure 3.5 Corporate Tax Rates 1996 from *European Policy Analyst*, 1st Qtr 1997 p 29, © The Economist Intelligence Unit Ltd., reproduced by permission of the Economist Intelligence Unit Ltd.; Table 5.3 from GATT and Multilateral Trade Liberalisation ... Economics, *Journal of the Economics Association*, Autumn, pp 103 (Greenaway, 1991); Table 6.3, Davenport, *The European Economy: Growth and Crisis* edited by Boltho (1982) and Table 7.1 CEC (1995:17), © Oxford University Press, 1982, reprinted with permission of Oxford University Press; Figure 9.1 from *The Big Question: The Cross Channel Trade in Beer*, CBMC and the European Brewers Association, 1997; Figure 9.2 from *Facing the Facts*, European Brewers Association, 1997; Table 9.2, 9.3 and 9.4 from *The Impact and Effectiveness of the Single Market*, European Commission, 1996; Tables 11.2 and 11.3 from UNCTAD (1996), World Investment Report 1996: *Investment Trade and International Policy Arrangements* p 4–5; Tables 11.4 and 11.5 from the European Internal Market Programme and Inbound Foreign Direct Investment: Part 1, *Journal of Common Market Studies*, tables 2 and 5 (Dunning 1997a), Blackwell Publishers reprinted with permission; Table 11.6 from The Growth of Foreign Direct Investment in Europe (Barrell & Pain 1997) and Table 11.7 from Regional Economic Investment in Europe (Pain & Lansbury 1996), *National Institiute Economic Review*, The National Institute of Economic and Social Research reproduced with permission; Tables 12.1, 13.2 and 14.11 *The Financial Times* reprinted with permission; Tables 12.4, 12.6 and 12.8 from *UK Balance of Payments Pink Book*,

Office for National Statistics, © Crown copyright 1998; Table 12.9 from *Convergence Situation of Potential EMU members,* 14th Sept. 1997, © *The Observer* reproduced with permission; Table 13.4 from Creditor countries, *The Journal of Development Studies,* Vol. 27, No. 3 (Griffiths-Jones, 1989), International Monetary Fund; Tables 13.5 and 13.6 from *World Bank Report,* 1997 International Monetary Fund; Table 14.2 from *The Independent on Sunday,* July 1991 reprinted with permission, Table 14.3 from *EBRD Transition Report* 1994, European Bank for Reconstruction and Development; Tables 14.5 and 14.6 *Transforming Economies and European Integration* p 118–19 (Dobrinsky & Landesmann, edited), Edward Elgar Publishing Limited, reprinted with permission; Tables 14.7 and 14.8 from Foreign direct investment ..., *Economic Policy,* 24, tables 1 and 2 (Sinn & Weichenrieder) © Centre for Economic Policy, Blackwell Publishers reprinted with permission; Table 14.9 and 14.10 from A Survey of Foreign Investment, © The Economist Newspaper Ltd., first published in *Business Central Europe,* April 1996; Table 14.3 *from The Economics of Transition* (Lavinge, 1995) from Macmillan Press Ltd, reproduced with permission; Tables 14.14, 14.15, 14.16 and 14.17 *Barclays County Reports,* data from IMF and World Bank Sources, permission to print from Barclays Bank Economics Dept.

The Financial Times Ltd for extracts from the articles 'Bittersweet taste of expansion' by G de Jonquieres in *The Financial Times* 2.10.95, 'Deutsche Telekom' in *The Financial Times* 18.12.95, 'Woven into the fabric' by S Wagstyl in *The Financial Times* 10.1.96, 'Jilted Chile hitches up to Mercosur' by D Pilling and I Mark in *The Financial Times* 25.6.96. 'World economy and finance: Prospects brighten' by G Bowley in *The Financial Times* 27.9.96, 'Mercosur trade group under fire' by G de Jonquieres in *The Financial Times* 24.10.96, "OECD air transport report angers the Japanese" by de Jonquieres in *The Financial Times* 20.1.97, 'UK Tractor Marker Fears EMU opt out' from *The Financial Times* 4.3.97, 'Feathers Fly' in *The Financial Times* 3.4.97, 'Commissioners square up for regional aid fight' by Barber in *The Financial Times* 28.4.97, 'Swedish Banking and Finance: Rivals merge for a competitive edge' by C Brown-Humes and G McIvor in *The Financial Times* 1..97, 'Farming reforms sow seeds of doubt: CAP changes are causing misgivings despite being 'step in right direction' in *The Financial Times* 18.7.97, 'Cornish fisherman on warpath: Outrage as Spanishquota-hoppers win compensation 'in principle' 'by G Mead in *The Financial Times* 1.8.97, 'Bulgaria 97: Privatisation Last attempt to dispose of assets' by K Hope from 'Survey of Bulgaria' in *The Financial Times* 21.10.97, 'Spain prepares to fight for EU grants: Madrid fears accession of new members will be paid for by cutting 'cohesion' funds' by D White in *The Financial Times* 18.11.97, 'Bigger EU a test for sugar' by G Mead in *The Financial Times* 26.11.97, 'Pulp Futures: Smoothing out the peaks and troughs' by G McIvor in *The Financial Times* 8.12.97; Guardian Newspapers Ltd for an extract from 'Unfair Aviators' in *The Guardian* 7.2.96; Time Warner Publishing BV for an extract from 'The Global 500' by Colby in *Fortune* Magazine, August 1997.

Whilst every effort has been made to trace the owners of copyright material, in a few cases this has proved impossible and we take this opportunity to offer our apologies to any copyright holders whose rights we have unwittingly infringed.

APC	Average propensity to consume
ASEAN	Association of South East Asian Nations
APEC	Asian Pacific Economic Cooperation
BAE	Bank for Agricultural Economics
BIS	Bank of International Settlements
BLRA	British Licensed Retailers Association
BSI	British Standards Institute
BTC	Bulgarian Telecommunications Company
CA	Comparative advantage
CAP	Common Agricultural Policy
CBOT	Chicago Board of Trade
CD	Comparative disadvantage
CEEC	Central and Eastern European Countries
CET	Common External Tariff
CEFTA	Central European Free Trade Area
CFC	Chlorofluorocarbon
CFP	Common Fisheries Policy
CITES	Convention on International Trade in Endangered Species
CM	Common Market
CME	Chicago Mercantile Exchange
CMEA/Comecon	Council for Mutual Economic Assistance
CP	Competition policy
CSE	Consumer subsidy equivalent
CTP	Common Transport Policy
CU	Customs Union
DC	Developed country
DG 4 or DG IV	Directorate General of the Commission for Competition
DIN	Deutsches Institut für Normung
EAEC	East Asian Economic Caucus
EAGGF	European Agricultural Guidance and Guarantee Fund
EBDR	European Bank for Reconstruction and Development
EC	European Community
ECJ	European Court of Justice
ECB	European Central Bank
ECR	European Court Reports (Law Reports)

ECSC	European Coal and Steel Community
ECU	European Currency Unit
EEA	European Economic Area
EEC	European Economic Community
EER	Effective exchange rates
EFTA	European Free Trade Area
EIB	European Investment Bank
EMS	European Monetary System
EMCF	European Monetary Co-operation Fund
EMU	European Monetary Union or Economic and Monetary Union
ERDF	European Regional Development Fund
ERM	Exchange rate mechanism
ESF	European Social Fund
ESI	Export Specialisation Index
EU	European Union
EUA	European Unit of Account
Euratom	European Atomic Energy Community
FDI	Foreign direct investment
FEOGA	Also EAGGF – European Agricultural Guidance and Guarantee Fund
FRN	Floating rate note
GATT	General Agreement on Tariffs and Trade
GDP	Gross Domestic Product
GM	General Motors
GMT	Greenwich mean time
GNP	Gross national product
GSP	General System of Preferences
H-O	Heckscher-Ohlin
IATA	International Air Transport Association
IBF	International Banking Facilities
IDO	Integrated development operation
IDP	Integrated development programme
IMF	International Monetary Fund
IOSCO	International Organization of Securities Commission
IRC	Industrial Reorganization Corporation
ISA	Internalization specific advantage
LDC	Less developed country
LIBOR	London Interbank Offer Rate
LIFFE	London International Financial Futures and Options Exchange
LSA	Location-specific advantage
M&A	Mergers and acquisitions
MCA	Monetary compensation amount
MEC	Marginal efficiency of capital
MFA	Multifibre agreement
MFN	Most favoured nation
MNC	Multinational company
MNE	Multinational enterprise

MYRA	Multi-year rescheduling agreement
NAFTA	North American Free Trade Area
NIC	Newly industrialised country
NIF	National investment funds
NTB	Non-tariff barrier
OECD	Organisation for Economic Co-operation and Development
OEEC	Organisation for European Economic Co-operation
OLI	Ownership, location and internalization advantages
OMA	Orderly marketing agreement
OPEC	Organisation of Petroleum Exporting Countries
OPT	Outward processing trade
OSA	Ownership-specific advantages
PPP	Purchasing power parity
PSE	Producer subsidy equivalent
R&D	Research and development
RER	Real exchange rates
RTP	Restrictive trade practice
SBA	Strategic business area
SCP	Structure–conduct–performance
SDR	Special Drawing Rights
SEA	Single European Area
SEM	Single European Market
SMEs	Small and medium-sized enterprises
SPD	Single programming documents
STRIDE	Science & Technology & Regional Industrial Development in Europe
TAC	Total allowable catch
TC	Trade creation
TD	Trade diversion
TEU	Treaty on European Union
TN	Transnationals
TNC	Transnational Corporation
TRIM	Trade-related investment measures
TRIP	Trade-related property rights
VAT	Value-added tax
VCR	Video cassette recorder
VER	Voluntary export restraint
WHO	World Health Organisation
WTO	World Trade Organisation

1 Introduction

This book has two basic aims: firstly to analyse the European business environment, and secondly to describe and explain the growth and impact of business, within both the European context and the wider international framework. It does contain a certain amount of theoretical discussion but its main emphasis is on applied analysis. It is hoped the book will encourage students, from the outset of their business courses, to gain a wider perspective of the European and international economy than they might derive from the more narrow, home nation view characteristic of traditional texts. *International Business Economics* has been developed for first and second year undergraduate students taking business studies courses and, in particular, those studying for European business degrees.

The structure of the book is such that the reader can dip into the text and select those chapters which are most appropriate to current needs without destroying the context of the book as a whole. There is a theme running through the text – starting with the business environment faced by European enterprises, then dealing with trade and its problems before considering the European Union (EU) framework. The growth, development and strategy of enterprises are then considered, and finally a chapter on Central and Eastern Europe and its impact economically in Europe and the world has been added to this new edition.

Chapter 2 provides an excellent starting point, with an overview of the nature and growth of international business as a preparation for subsequent chapters. It first describes both the internal and external factors that have resulted in the changes for international business, before investigating the ways in which firms can both expand and contract their boundaries. The question of how we judge which are the biggest firms, both in Europe and internationally, is then considered, as too are the major markets in which European multinationals are to be found. A number of examples are used to indicate the extent to which large firms in Europe are truly international. It analyses the areas where 'big business' dominates and the reasons for the growth of merger activity within Europe.

Chapter 3 outlines the general European environment within which international business works. It considers the effect of different European cultures, languages, lifestyles and tastes on this environment.

With business becoming increasingly international, trade between countries has expanded enormously. Chapter 4 reviews the various trade theories, from Adam Smith to the newer theories of Linder, Posner and Vernon. The usefulness of trade theory in practice is then considered in a discussion of world and

European trade patterns. The chapter concludes with a review of the strengths and weaknesses of EU trade, and an example of the importance of trade to various UK companies is used to supplement the analysis.

Trade in theory tells us many things but trade in practice is another matter. The benefits arising from the trade theories mentioned above rely on the assumption of free trade. Chapter 5 investigates the rise of trade protectionism in both its tariff and non-tariff forms. The main forms of this new protection – the quota, the voluntary export restraint (VER), the export subsidy, government procurement, plus other less direct non-tariff barriers (NTBs) such as red tape – are discussed in detail. A study of the General Agreement on Tariffs and Trade (GATT) and the new WTO is then undertaken, looking at their roles in reducing tariffs, plus the difficulties faced in controlling the 'new protectionism'.

Chapter 6 considers a further development in international trading relations since the Second World War, that of increasing economic integration. The chapter begins by examining the various types and extent of the levels of integration. The theory behind customs unions and free trade areas is then discussed, from both a static and a dynamic point of view. The chapter continues by examining economic integration in practice. The formation and development of the EC/EU are examined in detail and the EC/EU is compared with other examples of integration from outside Europe.

Chapter 7 concentrates on some key policies of the EU: the Common Agricultural Policy (CAP), European Fisheries Policy, regional policy, social policy and transport policy. The chapter begins with a section on CAP which explores the general problems facing agriculture before examining the general principles and objectives of the CAP and the EU's methodology in overcoming these problems. Following this, a discussion of the impact of the CAP on EU member countries and non-member countries is undertaken. This section finishes with a critical examination of the CAP, suggesting methods by which it can be reformed.

The chapter next considers fisheries policy in the EU. It charts its development alongside attempts at international regulation and considers the problems it has faced from widening EU membership and concerns from environmentalists. The area of quota-hopping is considered and current problems with the EU's fisheries policy are then developed.

Regional policy is the next policy area considered. The definition and need for such a policy opens the discussion. The European Regional Development Fund (ERDF) and its changing nature are examined with data on the recipients of this aid, being presented. The emphasis is on critical appraisal, addressing such questions as whether regional policy has worked and if it is cost-effective.

Related to the need for regional policy is the need for social policy. European social policy has evolved from social policies developed in the individual states. Thus EU social policy is a compromise, although the social issues to be overcome have received broad agreement. The chapter charts the development of EU social policy and the importance of the Social Charter/Chapter. The tension between social policy and the need for flexible labour markets is also considered.

The final section of this chapter deals with transport policy. It indicates the slow progress in this area, particularly up to 1985. From this date, activity towards developing a Common Transport Policy has quickened. The areas of road haulage, air transport, road passenger and rail transport are discussed in detail. Without a common transport mechanism in the EU, the full benefits from the SEM and EMU will not be fully felt. Nonetheless, national differences, state aid and the lack of full deregulation still hamper the development of a common view on transport.

Chapter 8 begins with a discussion of industrial policy. The various approaches to industrial policy are considered, and comparisons are made between industrial policy in the UK and in the EU. Questions relating to individual governments' attitudes to their national 'champion' companies are considered in the context of a section on state aid. The issue of public procurement is also examined – the ways in which governments conduct their own 'sourcing' systems, usually from home-based (or domestic) firms and not in line with the spirit of the SEM.

The second section of Chapter 8 concerns competition policy. After a brief historical introduction, the chapter examines Articles 85 and 86 of the Treaty of Rome, dealing with restrictive and collusive practices and the abuse of monopoly power. These are considered in detail and are compared with UK legislation. It is concluded that the interpretation of the EU articles is still unsettled, and this brings an undesirable element of uncertainty into the conduct of international business within the EU.

The shape of the Single European Market is the subject of Chapter 9. The historical movement of the EU towards the single market is considered. The barriers that legislation has attempted to remove are examined, together with the means of their removal. The benefits that have occurred, or are still expected and the possible recipients of these, together with the problems remaining to be faced, are also considered.

The actual extent, growth and strategies of international business, especially within Europe, are the focus of the next two chapters.

Chapter 10 outlines the structure of international business. It lists the top multinational companies, their country of origin and their effect on world trade. The general question is asked as to whether multinationals may be usefully categorised as 'benign' or 'malign' in their influence and, if the latter, whether agencies can control them. A consideration of the structure–conduct–performance paradigm then follows, focusing on its applicability to the analysis of multinationals. It is concluded that, if used with caution, this theoretical approach can be useful in the analysis of large international business organisations.

Why firms undertake foreign direct investment (FDI) is the question addressed in Chapter 11. Theoretical approaches which explain the magnitude and direction of such investment – such as the neoclassical theory and capital arbitrage hypothesis – are critically analysed together with the alternative theories of ownership-specific and location-specific advantages. The chapter then considers empirical evidence relating to FDI and the EU: both investment coming into the EU from outside and investment flows between EU countries. The distribution of FDI between sectors, countries and regions is considered, as well as the motives for FDI and its effects. In particular, the chapter considers the issue of whether FDI has been encouraged or discouraged by the development of European integration.

Chapters 12 and 13 look at the financial environment for European businesses. Chapter 12 explores the foreign exchange market. The two contrasting systems of fixed exchange rates and floating exchange rates are explained, with particular emphasis given to the Exchange Rate Mechanism (ERM) and the European Monetary System (EMS) of the EU. Having considered the mechanics of exchange rate determination, some discussion of the 'fundamental' determinants of exchange rates follows, e.g. the real exchange rate, purchasing power parity and monetary expositions. The chapter concludes with a discussion of the costs and benefits of a single currency in Europe.

Chapter 13 opens with a brief history of international banking and its growth. The chapter then proceeds to look at the activities and instruments of international banks and the extent of the involvement of European banks in the world debt crisis. The Eurocurrency markets are then considered in detail. Having identified the major borrowers and lenders and the differing motives for using the markets, the authors then discuss the main factors which have stimulated the Eurocurrency markets. This section concludes with an examination of the major factors that influence the relationship between Eurocurrency interest rates and equivalent domestic money market rates. The chapter concludes with a comparison of the financial systems of the UK, France and Germany with reference to the different regulatory structures and the likely effect of the single market on banking institutions.

Chapter 14 considers the changes that have taken place in Central and Eastern Europe. It draws upon the historic perspective from which the Central and Eastern European Countries (CEECs) have emerged and considers their development, particularly from the late 1980s. The chapter analyses the growth of FDI in CEECs and their trading relationships between each other and with the rest of Europe. The role of international debt and its influence on CEEC development is then considered before turning to the development of market forces within the CEECs through the privatisation of state assets. Finally, the important issue in the new millennium for the EU of widening EU membership to include the CEECs is looked at.

Chapter 15 draws together the themes of the earlier chapters and highlights developments such as financial crises within Asia, the role of labour markets in improving both European and international competitiveness, whether foreign ownership matters and whether globalised markets need globalised regulation, and how these changes may influence a possible future scenario for international business.

Introduction

The 1980s and 1990s have seen unprecedented growth in international business activities, which has been prompted by a number of factors. One such factor is changes in the market in which organisations operate, such as the development of the Single European Market (SEM) (see Chapter 12), and a further factor is the democratisation of Eastern Europe (see Chapter 14). Reductions in trade barriers (see Chapter 5), deregulation of markets and the development of trading blocs also provide further explanations of the internationalisation process. It is important for organisations to operate globally within the Global Triad of Europe, the Americas and East Asia. For the firms themselves, improving their competitive position has resulted in growing internationalisation. This has been established through the growth of multinational behaviour, the development of joint ventures and the move towards strategic alliances. Mergers and takeovers have also allowed firms to reap the advantages of economies of scale, as has the development of technology. At the same time, not all growth into international markets has been successful and the 1990s have witnessed a number of organisations demerging, selling off unwanted parts through management buy-outs, or divesting themselves of non-core business. This chapter, therefore, considers the changing boundaries of international business, and considers those sectors in which Europe may have a competitive advantage. Finally, the chapter examines the role of small firms in the European economy and their impact on the internationalisation process.

Growth of large firms

On a macro-economic level there are many factors which can be put forward to explain the growth of international business. International trading agreements such as the General Agreement on Tariffs and Trade (GATT) rounds offer one explanation. In these trade talks, tariffs on manufactured goods have been reduced markedly, and markets that were once highly protected have been opened up to trade. In particular, the reductions in barriers to trade in services at the eighth GATT round and subsequently through the World Trade Organisation (WTO) have opened up an even wider variety of markets to trade. These GATT rounds were paralleled by the increase in regional trade agreements. From a

European perspective the European Union (EU) is one of the oldest and best-known trading blocs, but more recently the North American Free Trade Area (NAFTA) has been developed to include the countries of Canada, the USA and Mexico. Trade agreements and trading blocs abound and Chapter 6 looks at these in more detail. Some of these trading blocs or areas are more important than others, and three (the EU and European Free Trade Area (EFTA) bloc, NAFTA, and Japan and the newly industrialised countries (NICs) of East Asia), known as the **Global Triad**, have come to dominate world trade. These three blocs account for 60 per cent of all world trade.

From an organisational point of view, barriers to trade within the blocs have been reduced and the example of the Single European Market (SEM) within the European bloc is an indication of this. At the same time, external barriers have not been reduced so easily. One response by international organisations to the relative strength of these external barriers is to have operations in all three regions. This strategy has a number of advantages for the international organisation:

- Organisations can avoid surprises from organisations and/or from domestic competitors by forming alliances with foreign companies.

- By being inside the Triad the organisation can ascertain the basic needs of Triad consumers and can then tailor its products to fit local requirements.

- With a presence in the three blocs the organisation can get its products to market very quickly.

- If a competitor develops a new product with great potential in one of the blocs then the international organisation can copy it very quickly and deprive the developer of the opportunity for sales in the other two markets.

Thus being in each of the Triad areas is important for international companies and such areas account for over 90 per cent of foreign direct investment (FDI) (see Chapter 11). The extent to which the Triad blocs will continue to influence the internationalisation of business behaviour depends upon the relationship between the members of the Triad and the degree to which they may attempt to bar non-Triad companies and countries.

Deregulation and the internationalisation process

Within the Triad, greater competition has also been achieved through the process of deregulation. Privatisation has played an important part in the questions of ownership, efficiency, and the performance of a number of industrial sectors not only in Western Europe, but also in South East Asia, Oceania and Central and Eastern European countries (see Chapter 14) during both the 1980s and 1990s. However, selling off state enterprises to the private sector is only one method by which state enterprises can feel the full effect of private sector forces. An alternative approach is **deregulation**. Deregulation allows private sector companies to compete in previously protected markets, sometimes with a public sector organisation, and at other times with a newly privatised company. Deregulation also has the effect of reducing differences between national regulatory systems, and thus previously regulated national markets become more international, deregulated ones. This process of deregulation is likely to lead to the growth and internationalisation of business. For example, in the UK, deregulation of the telecommunications market took place in 1981. The result was the establishment of a number of small new entrants, some of which were domestic firms whilst others were parts of large foreign telecommunications companies. The outcome has been that some of these companies have established a growing share of the UK telecommunications market, and in doing so they have threatened British Telecom's (BT's) dominant position.

Liberalisation in continental Europe has been slower; none the less, the result of the working through of the Single European Market (SEM) (see Chapter 9) has deregulated and opened up markets in banking (see Chapter 13), telecommunications and air transport. The result of the deregulation has been companies establishing **joint ventures and strategic alliances**, and increased merger activity as a means of enhancing their market position or to act as a protective measure. For example, Telecom Eireann has been in negotiation for some time to form a range of strategic alliances with BT, Cable and Wireless, AT&T, and Telia of Sweden to protect its domestic telecommunications industry. If these negotiations fail then it is likely that these other 'telecom giants' will 'cherry pick' the Irish Republic's telecommunications sector.

Impact of technology

In the case of telecommunications the boundaries between markets also have been reduced through the process of technology. Technology can have an impact on the growth of business in a number of ways. It allows countries to obtain **comparative advantages** in the production of a commodity, and based on these cost advantages previously unprofitable markets now become worth considering. As a result, organisations may export to new markets or expand into these markets via indigenous growth, or through mergers/takeovers/joint ventures. It is also possible that technology may provide organisations with products which are completely new and allow them to expand into new external markets. Technology also enables markets that were once believed to be separate to be joined together, and thus competition is increased.

The activity of **multinational companies** (MNCs) (see Chapters 10 and 11) can lead to the transfer of technology, which makes it possible for host economy firms to become more heavily involved in international markets. For example, the establishment of Japanese car manufacturers in the UK has resulted in car component suppliers increasing efficiency and quality. The result has been to create a strong positive externality, improving international competitiveness in the UK car-supply industry.

In terms of technological change, breakthroughs in basic science or the discovery of new innovations open large new markets. These new markets attract new investment and the entry of established and new companies. For example, in the semiconductor industry the breakthrough in logic and memory devices caused the rapid development of new applications in computers, telecommunications and other markets. These breakthroughs acted as structural breaks in the market and led to the development of new companies and the decline of others. Technological developments have also played their part in linking and integrating markets, while leading to increased heterogeneity and market fragmentation. Furthermore, the technological advances in communications have revolutionised business operations, allowing them to be managed on a wider geographical range. Global information systems have rapidly expanded and improved the coordination of global production and distribution logistics. Similarly, advances in telecommunications have enabled an organisation to monitor changes in consumer demand and competitors' behaviour, allowing a more rapid adaptation and response.

Companies that have played a great part in the growth of international business are the multinational enterprises (MNEs) (these are discussed in Chapter 10). Dicken (1998) suggests that not only has the world become more internationalised but it has also become increasingly globalised. He acknowledges that global corporations still have the objectives of increasing market share or becoming a market leader, but he also considers that the desire for global profit is the dominant motive. The extent to which these global companies can expand, imposing their strategies and going across boundaries (and thereby improving their profits), depends on the way governments behave. Governments can be supportive of their actions or can make conditions less conducive to the globalisation and enhancement of profits. Technology is one of the most important contributory factors underlying the internationalisation of economic activity, according to Dicken. He identifies advances in communications and transport as fundamental 'space-shrinking' technologies which have facilitated the development of the global organisation.

Escalating R&D costs can provide a strong incentive for boundary change, particularly in rapidly moving technological sectors. Industries such as pharmaceuticals and aerospace often require expansion to finance investment. This encourages them to look for exports and growth overseas. High R&D costs also encourage firms to collaborate, reducing investment costs and risk. This often leads to the establishment of joint ventures, although where collaboration is not possible, acquisition may be pursued in an attempt to reach a critical mass.

The route towards growth by organisations for a wide range of objectives can take many forms, such as mergers and takeovers, strategic alliances, and joint ventures.

Types of growth

There are a number of ways in which firms can grow but the single means of growth is usually classified in one of four ways: horizontal, vertical, lateral or conglomerate growth, and it is achieved through either organic (internal) growth or merger/takeover (external growth). With horizontal growth, firms expand within the same stage of production. Examples of such growth are the takeover of Rover by BMW, the Swiss drug makers Sandox and Ciba-Geigy merger to become Novartis, and the Glaxo and Wellcome proposed merger in

1997, plus the suggested merger with Smithkline Beecham in 1998. External horizontal integration often leads to the biggest threat to competition and increasing market power, so it is not surprising that the majority of mergers which are investigated under competition policy in the home country or EU are of this type.

Vertical growth involves the linking of successive stages of production within the same industry. Vertical growth may be forwards or backwards. Backwards is towards the earlier stages in the production chain, e.g. the purchase of an East German coalfield by Powergen in the UK and its US partner. Forward vertical growth would be towards the later stages in the production process; for example, the French Oil company Elf found that the only feasible way to develop retail outlets in the UK was to take over the independent VIP petrol retailing chain.

Lateral growth or integration involves the expansion of a firm into another industry. This action is seldom random; there are usually threads connecting the products or markets. They may employ similar raw materials or technology or both. The recent proposed merger of Guinness and Grand Metropolitan could be classified as this lateral growth: they are not in the same industry but the linkage could be that Guinness can use Grand Metropolitan outlets to boost its sales.

Finally, conglomerate growth or integration involves expansion into a totally unrelated area. The takeover of Inntrepreneur (a joint venture of Grand Metropolitan and Fosters and involving over 4000 British pubs) by Nomura Securities (a Japanese securities conglomerate) is an example of this kind of expansion.

This classification in terms of growth is inevitably oversimplified, since growth can involve elements of both horizontal and vertical integration. For example, Thomson-CSF, the French state-controlled defence electronics group, merged horizontally with other companies to achieve scale economies but this also gave Thomson-CSF access to their markets outlets and hence a rationale for vertical growth. Similarly, some would term the Grand Metropolitan and Guinness merger as more of a vertical merger, and the Nomura/Inntrepeneur takeover could be seen as lateral as Nomura has many property interests. Nevertheless it is useful to see how the different directions of growth contribute to achieving different objectives:

1 Horizontal integration contributes to economies of scale and market power.

2 Vertical integration contributes to the security of supply and outlets.

3 Diversification can spread risks and enable companies to escape from the constraints of a sluggish or a declining market.

Transaction cost theory also provides an explanation of organisational growth, particularly through vertical integration. The substitution of internal organisations in place of market exchange permits the internalisation of transaction costs and a subsequent reduction in contracting and monitoring. As Williamson (1985) notes, an advantage of the organisation is that intra-organisation activities are more easily and sensitively enforced than inter-organisation activities. An organisation is more able to evaluate performance than a buyer, and an organisation's reward and penalty instruments may be more refined than those that exist in the marketplace.

Economies of scope provide one of the drivers for the process of conglomerate growth or diversification. For example, an organisation may find that in the production of one product it has spare capacity that could be used in the production of another. Here the minimum cost of producing a combined unit of both products is less than if the two products were produced separately.

However, given all the advantages that could arise through mergers and takeovers, they do not all have successful results. It is possible for **diseconomies of scale** to set in, particularly if management struggles to keep control over a larger empire, and perhaps profit figures are much worse than expected after merger. Such problems have led to some famous demergers. For example, the Asda supermarket group in the UK acquired the MFI furniture chain but it later sold its interests to a management buy-out. Hanson Trust sold off parts of the Imperial Group, which did not fit the wider activities of the Hanson industries. In addition, problems with different organisational cultures, accounting practices and the like can contribute to disappointing performance from the newly merged organisation. Given these problems, what other methods are there of achieving a greater international presence?

Joint ventures

A joint venture is an arrangement under which organisations remain independent but set up a newly created organisation jointly owned by the parent companies. The reasons put forward to explain the development of a joint venture rather than other forms of expansion are as follows:

- economies of scale
- a desire to overcome barriers to entry
- the pooling of complementary pieces of knowledge
- a way for organisations to diversify
- to strengthen an organisation's market position
- to reduce the costs that may arise through R&D, production and marketing
- a way in which complementary products can be developed.

In addition, a joint venture may be preferred when the transaction costs are lower than those faced when establishing a wholly owned subsidiary. Joint ventures have become a popular form of growth in the 1990s, often used as a method to serve rapid expansion while at the same time reducing the financial risk of the partners. For example, they are currently the prime method of moving into the Chinese economy, where the government is keen to attract investment but wants to maintain some element of state control. Similarly, joint ventures can be pursued as a means of attaining a critical mass without the risks of acquisition, as was the case in the car industry with the joint venture between Renault and Matra to produce the Espace minivan. Renault benefited from Matra's knowledge of product concepts, design capability and manufacturing competence, while Matra gained access to Renault's marketing, distribution and service resources. A further example of this type of activity arose in March 1998 when GEC announced a £1 billion defence industry sales tie-up with Italy's Alenia Difesa in a 50:50 joint venture. However, not all joint ventures are successful as a means of organisational growth. There may be disagreements between partners about the objectives of the joint venture, contrasting organisational cultures may not gel, and technical know-how can be provided to potential future competitors.

Case study: Joint ventures in the commercial vehicles market

After a tough year in most markets, the outlook for the world's biggest commercial vehicle groups was looking up a little for 1998. But, just as the gloom was starting to lift in Europe and demand climbed even further than expected in North America, economic uncertainties in Asia and South America clouded the picture.

The new doubts caused by the crises of currencies and confidence in emerging markets mean analysts are downgrading their forecasts for world demand in 1998. And they are warning that the predicted climb in sales may not fuel higher profits as pricing may remain weak or even soften.

Such commercial uncertainties are likely to accelerate the two decisive trends driving the commercial vehicles industry. Manufacturers will redouble their efforts to reduce costs by developing more modular products, and they will work even harder on joint ventures.

Both tendencies have been unmistakable in recent months. Volvo has tightened its links with Mitsubishi, its partner in the Nedcar passenger cars joint venture, to include trucks. It is still unclear how far the relationship will go. However, Volvo has agreed to market a light Mitsubishi truck alongside its own 7.5-tonne model in Europe from January. The two will also develop a future generation of middleweight 7.5- to 18-tonne products. And Volvo may supply axles and gearboxes for Mitsubishi's heavy vehicles.

Daf and Renault have also announced plans to work together on developing shared parts for future 6- to 19-tonne vehicles. The deal is expected to involve cabs, but may include engines and axles. The move is telling for both manufacturers: it gives the first pointer to Daf's strategy following its purchase last year by Paccar, one of the biggest US truck makers. And it shows that Renault's commercial vehicles side is now belatedly striving to improve its lacklustre earnings by cutting costs. That strategy lay behind Renault's decision earlier this year to sell its exhaust parts and air tank operations to Nelson, a US specialist, and effectively divest some of its gearbox activities to ZF of Germany, its existing joint venture partner.

The French group is also trying to harness economies of scale in its light van business by working more closely with GM. Under their deal, GM will rebadge Renault's existing Trafic range – to be called the Arena by GM in Britain. At a later stage, the companies will launch two new vehicles, to be built in Britain by IBC, the GM–Isuzu joint venture, and by Renault in France.

Closer co-operation is also under way at Leyland Trucks, the independent UK truck maker, which produces the 45 and 55 light–medium weight range for itself and Daf. The signs are that Leyland Trucks is also strengthening its links with Isuzu, for which it is already building light trucks under contract, amid signs it will next launch a Leyland-assembled 7.5 tonner.

Other producers have been swallowing unpleasant medicine to improve their financial health. In May, Iveco closed its Langley truck plant in the UK, transferring production of the Cargo to its main Brescia factory. The group has also concentrated cab production at Brescia after closing the assembly unit at its Magirus-Deutz subsidiary in Germany.

Truck makers have also accelerated their efforts to develop more modular products. Virtually every new vehicle on the market has been designed to share components – and even body panels, such as cab doors – with other products in a manufacturer's range.

Mercedes-Benz, the world's biggest truck maker, expects to save about DM1 billion a year from simplifications to its Actros heavy range. The Actros requires far fewer parts, cutting inventories and money tied up in working capital. And it is much easier to build than its predecessor, increasing productivity at the Worth plant. Mercedes-Benz's strategy should emerge even more clearly with the launch of its new light–medium truck range next year. The new vehicle, called the Atego, is expected to share many features with the Actros.

Joint ventures and modularisation may not be enough, however, to see the industry through potential minefields ahead. Scania predicted big savings in assembly times for its new 4 Series heavy vehicle last year. In fact, the range has turned out to be significantly more expensive to produce than expected, partly explaining the sharp deterioration in Scania's profits since its flotation.

Volvo's plans to save money by developing a family of modular heavy trucks around the world have also been becalmed. The problem is not the product: the new US-built VN range shares much with the well-regarded FH family sold in Europe. Volvo's US problems, rather, have stemmed from its sliding market share, which has still not been fully reversed, in spite of the unexpectedly buoyant US market this year.

Whether more joint ventures and use of modules will be enough to improve truck makers' profits and maintain the industry's current structure remains uncertain, however. Much depends on demand in South America – where most of the big manufacturers build vehicles – and Asia, where they are less – but still significantly – exposed.

It is already clear that salvation will not come from any windfall rise in demand, or the surprise collapse of one manufacturer, helping to reduce the industry's chronic overcapacity. Daf, the smallest of the main European truckmakers and for years the weakest link, has found a strong new parent in Paccar. Attention has now turned to the future of MAN, the next-smallest brand, amid speculation it may be snapped up by Volkswagen. Even Scania's future has come into question.

External salvation has been no more apparent in North America. This year's widely predicted collapse in heavy truck sales turned into just the opposite and demand should recover even more next year. That has probably postponed any further rationalisation in the industry, in spite of the widely held belief that this year's decision by Ford to pull out of heavy trucks may not be the last of its kind.

Even Navistar, for many analysts a chronically weak producer, has gained a new lease of life in heavy trucks after a union deal, meaning that the company will invest in a new Class 8 product. The upshot of the changes is that while the pain in the world of commercial vehicles – especially heavy trucks – has not worsened significantly, it has not got any better either.

Source: Simonian, H. (1997) FT Automobile: European sunshine clouded by Asian Worries, *Financial Times*, 4 December.

Questions

1 What factors lie behind the growth in joint ventures in the commercial vehicles market?

2 Why might joint ventures not answer the problems faced by the commercial vehicles industry?

Strategic alliances

Whereas joint ventures may provide formalised arrangements between partners, networks are at the other end of the scale, providing for collaboration without formal relations through the process of mutual advantage and trust. In between these lie the more intermediate relationships. One of these is franchising. Here the developer of a business idea (the franchiser) enters into a relationship with the franchisee, who is responsible for delivering the good or service. Examples of this type of relationship can be seen with Coca-Cola, McDonald's and Telepizza of Spain. The reason for the franchiser not delivering the product or service may be that no economies of scope exist, or that the delivery of the product or service to the market requires skills or knowledge which the franchiser does not possess.

In addition to franchising, both licensing and subcontracting provide other forms of intermediate arrangements for organisations which allow them to expand into, or control, more markets. In the former, the right to manufacture a product is granted to a few producers, whilst in the latter a company chooses to subcontract particular services or part of a process. Having looked at the theoretical motives for growth and the ways in which organisations have sought to pursue the growth motive, what has been the aggregate result of this behaviour in Europe?

Merger and acquisition in Europe

Various explanations for merger and acquisition activity within the EU can be found (see Chapter 8). One major one has been the SEM, which has led to a major restructuring of European industry.

From Table 2.1 it appears the SEM has triggered a world-wide mergers and acquisitions boom involving European firms. Between 1985 and 1987, the value

Table 2.1 Share of worldwide mergers and aquisitions (%)

	1985–87	1988–90	1991–93
Intra-European	9.9	22.8	28.8
Extra-European	9.7	15.0	14.0
European total	19.6	37.8	42.8
US domestic	68.0	44.3	35.4
US cross-border	12.0	15.7	11.7
US total	80.0	60.0	47.1
All other	0.3	2.2	1.1
Global/Total	100.0	100.0	100.0

Source: EAG. Based on Smith and Walter (1994), *European Economy* (1996) page 117.

of mergers and acquisitions involving European firms accounted for approximately 20 per cent of the world total, but by the period 1991–93 this had increased to 43 per cent. The motives for merger activity are shown in Table 2.2.

Since the middle of the 1980s there has been a decline in the importance of mergers for 'rationalisation and synergy' and for 'diversification'. However, the growth in importance of mergers for both 'expansion' (17.1 per cent in 1985–86 to 32.4 per cent in 1991–92) and 'strengthening the market position' can be clearly seen (10.6 per cent in 1985–86 and 44.4 per cent in 1991–92), so illustrating the SEM effect.

Although there has been a rapid growth of European merger and acquisition activity generally, following the launch of the SEM, this has become increasingly focused on mergers which involve EU firms (accounting for 9.9 per cent in 1985–87 and 28.8 per cent in 1991–93 (see Table 2.1). However, although cross-border operations have been important, the national dimension has grown in emphasis, suggesting that the restructuring of EU industry has occurred in each member state in the domestic market possibly for defensive reasons (i.e. increased competition domestically from the SEM) or aggressive reasons (i.e. using the domestic market as a stepping stone to the EU market). This has been the case for mergers and acquisitions in the larger members of the Union and particularly so for Germany, Spain and Italy, as Table 2.3 indicates.

Table 2.2 Motives for European mergers and acquisitions (%)

	1985–86	1986–87	1987–88	1988–89	1989–90	1990–91	1991–92
Expansion	17.1	22.1	19.6	31.3	26.9	27.7	32.4
Diversification	17.6	5.8	8.3	7.1	3.0	2.8	2.1
Strengthening market position	10.6	11.5	25.4	42.2	45.3	48.2	44.4
Rationalisation and synergies	46.5	42.0	34.4	14.4	17.7	13.3	16.2
R&D	2.4	5.3	0.7	0.0	0.6	0.0	0.0
Other	5.9	13.3	11.6	4.9	6.4	8.0	5.0
	100.0	100.0	100.0	100.0	100.0	100.0	100.0

Source: European Commission (1994). Competition & Integration, *European Economy*, No. 57, table 1 page 48.

Table 2.3 Mergers and acquisitions in the EU, by nationality of partners (%)

| | Operations | | | | | | | |
| | National | | Community | | International | | Total | |
	1990–95	1986–89	1990–95	1986–89	1990–95	1986–89	1990–95	1986–89
Belgium	60.2	60.4	31.9	34.8	7.9	4.9	100.0	100.0
Denmark	67.0	41.7	22.0	40.6	11.0	17.7	100.0	100.0
Germany	79.5	72.9	12.3	18.7	8.2	8.4	100.0	100.0
Greece	73.1	0.0	19.2	0.0	7.7	100.0	100.0	100.0
Spain	80.9	74.6	11.5	23.9	7.6	1.5	100.0	100.0
France	66.0	60.7	24.5	26.7	9.5	12.6	100.0	100.0
Ireland	36.9	19.9	49.0	58.1	14.1	22.0	100.0	100.0
Italy	77.8	74.9	14.9	18.6	7.3	6.4	100.0	100.0
Luxembourg	2.0	5.3	86.1	89.5	11.9	5.3	100.0	100.0
Netherlands	57.9	57.0	30.5	30.1	11.7	12.9	100.0	100.0
Austria	22.4	30.4	65.7	56.5	11.9	13.0	100.0	100.0
Portugal	64.9	0.0	35.1	100.0	0.0	0.0	100.0	100.0
Finland	78.8	65.8	14.4	23.0	6.8	11.2	100.0	100.0
Sweden	56.8	47.2	29.4	34.9	13.7	17.9	100.0	100.0
UK	73.8	75.1	12.9	9.0	13.3	15.9	100.0	100.0
Total	70.8	70.1	18.7	15.5	10.5	14.4	100.0	100.0

Source: DG II AMdata, European Economy (1996) page 118.

The smaller open economies, such as those of Austria and Ireland, have been involved in a greater proportion of cross-border merger and acquisition activity, and these two countries, together with Sweden and the UK, have been the major centres of international merger and acquisition activity.

Within the Union the flow of merger activity has differed between the countries in the North and South. In the main it is the northern countries of the Union that have been bidders in terms of cross-border merger activity, while the main recipients have been Italy and Spain together with Germany (see Table 2.3). This flow of merger activity has also a sectoral bias. Whereas in the initial period prior to the SEM, merger activity was dominated by the manufacturing sector, the period after (between 1993 and 1995) has more of a service industry bias. In particular, domestic mergers and acquisitions have a service sector bias, possibly suggesting that a factor like the slow adoption of SEM regulations in services could have prevented some cross-border mergers taking place, or that a defensive position is being taken in the home market.

Table 2.4 Changes in concentration in selected European industries

NACE code	Industry type/Industry class	CR4 in 1987 (%)	CR4 in 1993 (%)	Change in CR4
	Unweighted average for total manufacturing*	20.5	22.8	2.3
	Conventional industries	13.2	14.4	1.2
	Advertising-intensive industries	22.3	23.6	1.3
	Technology-intensive industries	32.9	38.9	6.0
	Industries with both high advertising and high R&D expenses	30.1	32.4	2.3
326	Transmission equipment	30.6	64.1	33.5
418	Starch	19.4	50.1	30.7
346	Aerospace	47.7	64.3	16.6
374	Clocks and watches	17.2	31.7	14.5
341	Insulating wires and cables	34.7	48.9	14.2
346	Domestic electrical appliances	36.9	50.5	13.6
342	Electrical machinery	13.1	22.8	9.7
411	Oils and fats	21.7	30.2	8.5
423	Other foods	14.6	20.9	6.3
428	Soft drinks	25.8	31.8	6.0
371	Measuring instruments	9.3	15.3	6.0
417	Pasta	22.3	28.2	5.9
362	Rail stock	45.5	50.9	5.4
221	Iron and steel	34.5	39.8	5.3
372	Medical instruments	24.3	29.2	4.9

Source excluded for lack of data, 223, 224, 246, 255, 256, 259, 313, 314, 322, 328, 353, 373, 441, 442, 456, 461, 462, 463, 464, 465, 466, 467, 473, 481, 483, 492, 494, 495.

Total number of sectors included: 71.

* = NACE codes 2 to 4.

Source: EAG: data by Davies and Lyons, revising estimates published in Davies and Lyons (1996) *Industrial Organisation in the European Union: Structure, Strategy and Competitive Mechanism*, Clarendon Press, Oxford; *European Economy* (1996) page 120.

The major restructuring that has occurred within the EU has altered the concentration of European industry (Table 2.4). The most significant increases have taken place in industries related to public procurement (in telecommunications (wires and cables, transmission equipment) in transportation (aerospace and rail stock), in food sectors (especially those sectors sensitive to the SEM such as pasta, starch, oils and fats), and in other sectors such as electrical machinery, domestic electrical appliances and measurement equipment). Even though concentration rates have increased in many sectors, it still leaves concentration ratios behind those to be found in the USA (see Chapter 8).

The service sector concentration has been influenced by the nature of each service. Sectors such as distribution and road freight transport have been affected by high levels of restructuring, resulting in concentration levels increasing at both the domestic and EU levels, which is not surprising as this sector was expected to benefit greatly from the SEM and light regulation. Other areas of the service sector such as retail banking have exhibited smaller rises in concentration. This can be explained partly by institutional constraints and low adoption of the SEM regulations, and more alliances have been seen rather than mergers and acquisitions.

The shrinking boundaries of the firm

As noted earlier, some joint ventures do turn out to be failures and as a result the organisation diminishes in size. It is equally possible, however, that the organisation could follow a strategic path to reduce its international activities, through the process of **divestment, buy-outs and demergers**.

During the 1990s there have been moves by a number of large organisations to divest themselves of their non-core areas, both for defensive and offensive reasons. The offensive reasons might include the following:

- refocusing the total business and selling areas no longer required, even though they may be profitable;
- the need to raise extra money, e.g. British Aerospace's sale of the Rover Group to BMW or the sale of Falconbridge by Trellborg, the Swedish mining company, to raise money for its core operations;
- to improve the return on investment;
- the sale of a family company where there is no obvious succession.

Reasons for divestment for defensive reasons might include the following:

- a part of the organisation does not or is unable to meet profitability requirements, e.g. Philips, Europe's largest consumer electronics group, put its printed circuit board group up for sale in March 1997, as part of its strategy to sell off under-performing or non-core businesses;
- a means of avoiding acquisition (BAT divested itself of a number of businesses to avoid the unwanted attention of a predator);
- the organisation requires money to prevent it from collapsing;

- the organisation may be risk, averse and future projects in some areas of its business may be quite risky;
- it has become too difficult to manage a wide range of diverse activities;
- not being in control of a major source of earnings which could be lost in the future.

Divestment may also be forced on an organisation by regulators. For example, the Guinness and Grand Metropolitan merger was permitted provided that they gave up ownership of Dewar's Scotch whisky, sold Ainslie's Scotch whisky in Europe and withdrew from the distribution of gin, vodka and white rum in some countries.

Case study: Cable & Wireless divestment strategies

Cable & Wireless, the UK-based international telecommunications group, intends to raise £1 billion over the next 12 months by disposing of businesses where it has no operational control or influence.

The disposals are central to plans to transform C&W from what has been described as an 'investment trust with a ragbag of telecoms stocks' to an operationally active telecommunications company with a clearly defined international strategy driven from London.

Announcing the group's interim results ... Dick Brown, chief executive, said: 'If we can influence or control a business, we will stay in. Otherwise, we will get out.'

The group refused to speculate on likely disposals, arguing that the price obtained for any company named prematurely could be affected. C&W's international strategy covers the UK, the USA and Caribbean, the Asia Pacific region including Australia, and a small interest in the Middle East. Thus holdings in other areas such as Latin America and Eastern Europe could be put up for sale. A possible candidate for divestment is Bouygues Telecom, the third cellular operator in France, where C&W could realise £450 million for its 20 per cent stake. South Africa and Japan could also see disposals.

C&W's principal strength is in the Asia Pacific region and the UK. It holds 51 per cent of Hongkong Telecom, which provides 65 per cent of its world-wide profits.

Mr Brown has made it clear that he intends to reduce C&W's dependence on Hong Kong profits by investment in other parts of the group. He said £1.6 billion had been invested over the past six months in Cable and Wireless Communications, the group's UK subsidiary, together with operations in Panama and Australia. In each case, C&W had control over developments.

In the UK, One-2-One, C&W's cellular venture with US West, added 29 per cent of net new mobile customers in the past year, surpassing all other operators. 'We have not been passive owners,' Mr Brown said, while giving credit to One-2-One's management for turning round the operator.

He said the group had the strength to compete internationally but was talking to other operators about alliances, including Global One, owned by Deutsche Telekom, France Telecom, and Sprint of the USA.

It was an attractive partner because of its substantial global assets, strength in China and strong cash flow. Mr Brown said he had not been approached by British Telecommunications with a view to reopening merger negotiations, which were abandoned last year just when it seemed possible that a UK-owned super carrier could be created. Observers believe such a merger is still possible.

Source: Cane, A. (1997) Cable and Wireless set to raise £1bn in asset sell-off programme, *Financial Times*, 13 November.

Questions

1 Why has Cable & Wireless opted for the strategic option of divestment?

● ●

Management **buy-outs** and **buy-ins** are also ways of restructuring and altering the boundaries of the organisation. The former occurs when the ownership of an organisation is transferred to a new range of shareholders, of which the current management team make up a significant element and are often the ones who initiate such a move. A buy-in, on the other hand, is where an external management team, sometimes with the help of existing internal managers, executes a transfer of ownership. Part of the reason for the growth in both of these activities has been the privatisation process in the UK. In Europe, however, the level of buy-out and buy-in activity has been much less. This can be partly explained by the greater proportion of family-owned firms and legal and tax frameworks, but none the less, activity in France, the Netherlands and Sweden has been growing. It is interesting to note that most of the buy-outs in continental Europe have been the result of divestments by foreign investors.

A further driver in altering the size of international firms has been the process of demergers. Demerger activity often follows unsuccessful merger activity (as seen earlier). Demergers may also take place as a way of deflecting a takeover bid. Both Hanson and Courtaulds have gone down this route. In 1996, Hanson chose to break itself up into more discrete parts. Courtaulds turned its textile division into an independent business, concentrating management effort on its chemical and industrial activities. In fact, Courtaulds had a number of options. It could have sold one of its areas as a management buy-out, it could have sold some of its sectors to another organisation, or it could have floated off the other company on the stock market. It chose to do the last of these. The problem with any of the three approaches, and one that Thorn-EMI faced during 1997, is that demerging leads to smaller core business units, which make the new companies vulnerable to predators.

Such has been the popularity of demerging that it has affected all segments of production/services during the 1990s, from investment banks, telecommunication firms, chemical companies and clothing companies (such as the break-up of Coats Viyella), to insurance companies (such as the demerger of Ina, Italy's third largest insurer).

Thus the 1990s have witnessed major changes in both international and European business. Some companies have divested and demerged to concentrate on their core business activities as a means of improving their organisation's performance, whilst at the same time other companies have preferred to merge and takeover other organisations as a means of strengthening their market position. It is against these two backgrounds that this chapter now considers Europe's service and production sectors and considers their current strengths and weaknesses.

Europe's best?

How do we measure which are the most successful firms in Europe? There are a number of possible criteria: they could be determined by greatest sales, or highest profitability, or largest number of employees. Each measure, however, has its own problems. If we use the highest number of sales then this would disadvantage the service industries. Some would argue profits are more important but this measure is biased against trading companies. Given the state of unemployment in Europe, it may be that the largest employer should be seen as very important. Other measures of success also could be used, such as the changes in profits or the growth of sales, and these would highlight companies not seen in the other measures. How to judge success is therefore very debatable.

Furthermore, it must be remembered that the data are far from perfect. There are differences in data collection within countries, and changes in this can affect the figures vastly; for example, changes in Japanese accounting rules adversely affected the sales revenue of the large Japanese trading firms in 1996 and therefore reduced their standing in the world's top companies. The figures are also all denominated in US dollars and it could be argued that when looking at European companies only (with no Japanese and US involvement), ECUs may be a better currency for comparison.

With the above in mind we should now look at which are arguably the most successful European businesses. In August each year, *Fortune* magazine sets out the top 500 companies in the world and ranks them in terms of sales revenues, profits, assets, stockholders' equity and employees. It also notes the changes in sales revenue and profits from the previous year. The criteria that this chapter will concentrate on are sales, profits and employment.

In 1996, according to sales revenues, 171 of the top 500 companies were European, as compared with 162 US firms and 126 Japanese. In Europe, France has the most companies in the top 500 with 42, followed by Germany with 41, then the UK with 34. Also of note is the increasing presence of the newly industrialised countries (NICs) in world MNCs, including South Korea (13), Brazil (5) and China (3).

Taking a closer look at Europe, Table 2.5 gives the top ten European companies ranked according to sales. Shell is the largest European company, with $128.2 billion in sales; the next has only just over half the sales of Shell, i.e. Daimler-Benz with $71.6 billion. It is noticeable that the tenth European company is ranked only 36th in the world, and that many of these ten companies are connected to the oil, petroleum and car industries.

Table 2.5 Europe's largest corporations according to sales revenue, 1996

Rank	Company	Country	$millions in 1996	World ranking 1996	$millions in 1995	World ranking 1995
1	Royal Dutch/Shell Group	UK/Netherlands	128174.5	6	109833.7	10
2	Daimler-Benz	Germany	71589.3	20	72256.1	17
3	British Petroleum	UK	69851.9	21	56981.9	27
4	Volkswagen	Germany	66527.5	23	61489.1	24
5	Siemens	Germany	63704.7	25	60637.6	25
6	Allianz	Germany	56577.2	28	n/a	n/a
7	Unilever	UK/Netherlands	52067.4	31	49738.0	38
8	Fiat	Italy	50509.0	32	46467.6	41
9	IRI	Italy	49055.7	35	n/a	n/a
10	Nestlé	Switzerland	48932.5	36	47780.4	39

Source: *Fortune,* August 1997.

Profits could be seen as a better measure of success. The picture changes with this measure, as seen in Table 2.6. Shell still tops the list and in fact was the most profitable company in the world in 1996, but apart from Shell only Nestlé and Unilever remain in the list from top ten sales. The service sector also shows its profitability, with HSBC Holdings, Barclays and BT in the top ten in Europe. However, in the world rankings only Shell and HSBC would be in the top ten profitmakers. The top profit-makers are also less dominated by the car and petrol industries; in fact it is much more of a 'mixed bag'.

The biggest employers in Europe are shown in Table 2.7. Unilever and Nestlé still appear in the top ten; in fact these two companies are the only ones which appear in all three measures of success. As with profits, more service-type industries appear (e.g. La Poste, Deutsche Bahn and Deutsche Post), which is not surprising given the labour-intensive nature of services in general. Now, however, Europe has only one in the world top ten employers, and this is Siemens.

However, it is important not to look just at the best performers but to look at in which industrial sectors Europe is most competitive. Where do these large firms

Table 2.6 Europe's largest corporations according to profit, 1996

Rank	Name	Country	Profit $millions	World ranking 1996
1	Royal Dutch/Shell Group	UK/Netherlands	8887.1	1
2	HSBC Holdings	UK	4859.7	9
3	BP	UK	3985.2	12
4	BT	UK	3295.3	19
5	Roche Holding	Switzerland	3154.0	20
6	Glaxo Wellcome	UK	3118.5	21
7	ENI	Italy	2885.1	28
8	Nestlé	Switzerland	2751.2	35
9	Barclays	UK	2559.5	41
10	Unilever	UK/Netherlands	2499.7	42

Source: *Fortune,* August 1997.

Table 2.7 Europe's largest corporations according to employment, 1996

Rank	Name	Country	Number Employed	World ranking 1996
1	Siemens	Germany	379 000	6
2	Unilever	UK/Netherlands	306 000	11
3	Daimler-Benz	Germany	290 029	12
4	La Poste	France	289 050	13
5	Deutsche Bahn	Germany	288 768	14
6	Deutsche Post	Germany	284 889	16
7	Philips Electronics	Netherlands	262 500	20
8	Volkswagen	Germany	260 811	21
9	Fiat	Italy	237 865	23
10	Nestlé	Switzerland	221 144	26

Note: Rao Gazprom (Russia) ranked no.5 in the world with 336 000 employees.

Source: Fortune, August 1997.

have a substantial presence and where does the rest of the world dominate? Table 2.8 gives us some indication. It shows that Europe has a strong presence, compared with Japan or the USA, in banking, chemicals, electronics, food, mining, insurance, metals, motor vehicles, petrol refining, pharmaceuticals and telecommunications. These sectors will be looked at in a little more detail.

Banking (commercial)

Although the top commercial and savings bank in the world is Japanese (the Bank of Tokyo-Mitsubishi) in terms of sales, Europe dominates this sector with 37 of the top 69 companies. The largest European bank is Deutsche Bank of Germany (second largest in the world), closely followed by Credit Agricole of France. The most profitable company in this sector is also European – HSBC Holdings of Britain with profits of $4860 million. This is encouraging for Europe, especially given the fact that the SEM in the financial services sector is still to take full effect.

Chemicals and pharmaceuticals

There were 24 chemical or pharmaceutical companies listed in the top 500 companies world-wide in 1996. In the chemical sector, four are from the USA, one is from Japan and the other eight are European. The largest company, however, is EI du Pont de Nemours from the USA, with $39 689 million in sales and with the highest profit of $3636 million. The next three in ranking of sales are German (Hoechst, BASF and Bayer), with Rhône-Poulenc of France and ICI of Britain coming sixth and seventh in the ranking of the world's top chemical companies. The highest-ranked Japanese company is next, Mitsubishi Chemical, although this recorded far lower profits in 1996 than the rest of the group.

The pharmaceutical sector includes ten companies that are in the top 500 but this sector is dominated by the USA, with six out of the ten top companies. The most profitable company is also from the USA (Merck), although the

Table 2.8 Top 500 corporations by industry and country

Industry	Total	US	Jap	Eur	European country	Other
1 Aerospace	8	6	–	2	1F/1UK	
2 Airlines	7	4	1	2	1D/1UK	
3 Apparel	0	–	–	–		
4 Beverages	4	2	–	1	1UK	1
5 Building materials, glass	3	–	1	2	1F/1UK	
6 Chemicals	14	4	2	8	3D/2F/1UK/1NW/1NL	
7 Commercial banks	69	9	15	37	9D/7F/6UK/2NL/3CH/1B/2E/7I	8
8 Computers, office equipment	9	6	3	–		
9 Diversified financials	5	4	–	1	1F	
10 Electric, gas utilities	14	2	6	5	2F/1I/1UK/1D	1
11 Electrical equipment and electronics	26	7	9	7	1D/1N/1CH/2F/1SW/1UK	3
12 Energy	3	1	–	1	1E	1
13 Engineering, construction	13	1	9	3	3F	
14 Entertainment	6	4	–	1	1F	1
15 Food	12	7	1	4	1UKN/1F/1CH/1I	
16 Food services	2	2	–	–		
17 Food, drug stores	27	8	3	12	4UK/2CH/1B/4F/1N	4
18 Forest, paper products	7	4	2	1	1FN	
19 General merchandise	14	7	4	3	1D/1UK/1F	
20 Health care	2	2	–	–		
21 Hotels, casinos, resorts	2	1	1	–		
22 Industrial, farm equipment	9	2	4	3	1UK/2D	
23 Insurance (mutual)	21	7	12	2	1CH/1UK	
24 Insurance (stock)	36	11	4	19	2N/4F/1NB/4UK/3D/3CH/1I/1SW	2
25 Mail, package, freight delivery	8	3	2	3	1D/1UK/1F	
26 Metal products	3	1	1	1	1F	
27 Metals	14	1	6	5	3D/1F/1UK	2
28 Mining, crude oil production	3	–	–	2	1D/1NW	1
29 Motor vehicles, parts	27	6	10	9	4D/1I/2F/1SW/1TK	2
30 Petroleum refining	31	12	5	7	1UKN/1UK/2F/1I/1B/1E	7
31 Pharmaceuticals	10	6	–	4	2CH/2UK	
32 Publishing, printing	4	–	2	2	1D/1F	1
33 Railroads	7	2	3	2	1D/1F	
34 Rubber, plastics	3	1	1	1	1F	
35 Scientific, photo control equipment	3	2	1	–		
36 Securities	4	3	–	–		
37 Shipping	2	–	1	1	1UK	
38 Soaps, cosmetics	3	1	–	2	1D/1F	
39 Specialist retailers	5	3	–	2	1D/1UK	
40 Telecommunications	22	11	1	9	1D/1F/2UK/1E/1CH/1N/1I/1SW	1
41 Tobacco	3	1	1	1	1UK	
42 Trading	22	–	13	3	3D	4
43 Transportation equipment	0	–	–	–		
44 Wholesalers	9	7	–	2	2D	
45 Misc*	6	1	4	1	1UK	

Key: A = Austria; B = Belgium; CH = Switzerland; D = Germany; F = France; FN = Finland; I = Italy;
LUX = Luxembourg; N = Netherlands; NB = Netherlands and Belgium; NW = Norway; P = Portugal;
E = Spain; SW = Sweden; TK = Turkey; UK = United Kingdom; UKN = UK and Netherlands;
•travel, real estate, advertising, transportation equipment, waste management, entertainment, textiles, pipelines, hotels.

Source: Fortune, August 1997.

second most profitable is Britain's Glaxo Wellcome with $3119 million in profits. Similarly, the largest company in terms of sales is Novartis (the combination of Sandox and Ciba-Geigy) with $29 310 million in sales.

Electronics, electrical equipment

The electronic and electrical engineering sector is a highly globalised sector: 26 of the top 500 companies are in this sector; seven are from Europe, seven from the USA and nine from Japan. The largest player is General Electric (US) with sales of $79 179 million and profits of $7280 million. Hitachi of Japan, however, has sales just slightly lower ($75 669 million) but profits considerably lower ($784 million). In fact, the US companies General Electric and Intel (14th in terms of sales with $20 847 million, but with $5157 million in profits) have considerably higher profits than the rest of the sector in general. The highest-placed European company is Siemens (fourth in terms of sales and third in terms of profits), followed by Philips Electronics of the Netherlands (eighth and 26th, respectively) and ABB Asea Brown Boveri (ninth and fifth, respectively). There appears to be little change in the major players over time, but in Europe their rankings have changed according to whether they are producers for either consumer or producer markets.

Food and drug stores and beverages

The food and beverages sector has been a rapidly growing sector in terms of share of the total turnover of the world's largest companies. Two reasons for this appear to be important. Firstly, the sector is less cyclical than equipment sectors, and secondly, the major firms have been involved in external growth strategies, especially those in Europe. For example, in 1993, BSN, Grand Metropolitan and Cadbury Schweppes undertook acquisitions in India and China; Grand Metropolitan has also merged with Guinness.

In 1996, the world's largest food and drug stores organisation (in terms of sales) in this sector was Metro Holding of Switzerland, followed by Carrefour of France and Ito-Yokado of Japan. The most profitable one was Tesco of Britain with $21 942 million. Of the top 500 companies, 27 are in the food and drug stores sector, and Europe, with 12 of these, exceeds the combined strength of both the USA and Japan in terms of numbers of firms (with 11). A couple of Australian firms (Coles Myer and Woolworths), plus Jardine Matheson of Hong Kong and George Weston of Canada, also appear in the top 27 of the food and drug stores sector.

In the beverages sector, four companies appear in the top 500; the largest of these is Coca-Cola, which is also the most profitable. Grand Metropolitan of Britain appears as second in terms of sales but fourth in terms of profits (perhaps due to its growth strategy – see above). No other European firm appears in this group. In Europe, most of the sector's production is accounted for by small and medium-sized enterprises.

Insurance

Insurance can be divided into stock and mutual. Given that there are only two mutual insurance companies in the world, both US, we shall concentrate on stock insurance. Some 36 insurance companies appear in the world's top 500 companies, and 19 of these are European – outnumbering Japan and the USA, together (with 15). The top company in terms of sales is Allianz of Germany, with $56 577 million, followed by Union Des Assurances (France), AXA (France) and Zurich Insurance (Switzerland). The most profitable, however, is the American International Group (US) with $2987 million, although this lies only sixth in terms of sales. As with banking, the full effect of the SEM is still to be felt in this sector.

Metals

There has been intense restructuring in the metals sector amongst the largest firms as competitive pressures have increased both because of the entry of Central and Eastern European producers into this market and due to the weakening of demand in the early 1990s. The larger companies in the West have also diversified away from basic metals production and moved upstream in their product lines. Of the top 14 firms (in the top 500) in terms of sales, there is only one US firm (Alcoa), with Nippon Steel (Japan), NKK (Japan), Fried.Krupp Ag Hoesch-Krupp (Germany), Broken Hill Proprietary (Australia) and Usinor (France) filling the top five places. The European metals sector is still dominated 'by national champions', even though the major players have been involved in cross-border mergers and acquisitions. Amongst the top European producers, three are German, one is British and one is French.

The motor vehicle sector

The traditional Triad of Europe, the USA and Japan, which has dominated this sector, is now beginning to be under threat from the NICs. The sector accounts for 27 of the world's top 500 companies and within this, Daewoo and Hyundai Motor of South Korea now appear in sixth and nineteenth places (with regards to sales). General Motors is the company with greatest sales and profits in the sector in 1996 ($168 369 million and $4963 million respectively). However, Japan has nine of the 27 compared with the USA's six.

The largest European producer is Daimler-Benz, which is ranked fourth but which has a turnover of less than half that of General Motors. It is followed by Volkswagen (fifth), Fiat (ninth) and Renault (11th). In total, Europe has nine of the 27 in terms of sales in this sector but they generally have done less well in terms of profit, with Volvo being the most profitable European company (ranked sixth) and Daimler-Benz ranking only seventh in the world.

Telecommunications

The telecommunications sector is in the throes of liberalisation and this is transforming the key national players. The largest companies are seeking to become more global players not only through acquisitions but also through joint ventures. The largest company in this sector is Nippon Telegraph & Telephone with sales of $78 321 million, followed by AT&T of the USA (second but most profitable). Within Europe, IRI of Italy was the largest organisation in 1996, with a turnover of $19 056 million (third worldwide in terms of sales), followed by Deutsche Telekom with $41 911 million (fourth), France Telecom (fifth) and BT (sixth).

The picture painted above indicates that the European Union has a number of large companies in many industrial sectors. None the less, member states have been concerned about the general weak performance of the EU economy and that in a number of sectors, European conglomerates are not performing as well as their Japanese or US competitors. In particular, the EU has seen its unemployment levels rising over time, unlike in the USA. As a response to these problems the European Commission produced a White Paper on Growth, Competitiveness and Employment in 1993. In this paper much attention was given to the job-creating capacity of small and medium-sized enterprises (SMEs) and it is to an overview of this sector that this chapter now turns.

Small and medium-sized enterprises in Europe

Small and medium-sized enterprises can be defined in a number of ways. This chapter uses the definition of the European Commission:

- micro-enterprises: less than 10 employees
- small enterprises: between 10 and 99 employees
- medium-sized enterprises: between 99 and 250 employees
- large enterprises: more than 250 employees

Within the EU, SMEs comprise 99.9 per cent of the total number of enterprises and account for approximately 80 per cent of employment. Micro-enterprises comprise the biggest group, with 93.3 per cent of all enterprises having less than ten employees. There are differences in the distribution of SMEs between the various industrial sectors. Micro-enterprises dominate the retail distribution and personal services sector, while micro- and small enterprises are the dominant production units in the construction and wholesale sectors. Although producer services such as communications, supporting services to transport and R&D are dominated by large-scale enterprises, micro-enterprises account for a relatively large part of such sectors.

Taking the EU as a whole, the average enterprise employs six persons (including the entrepreneur), although there are differences between the individual member states. Enterprises in the southern countries generally are smaller than those in the north. This can be partly explained by GDP per capita and the level of population density. Thus countries such as Germany, Luxembourg and the Netherlands have a higher than average enterprise size.

Comparing the EU with the USA indicates that the EU has a greater proportion of micro-enterprises than the USA, but with other size bands there are no great differences, although the USA does have a greater proportion of large-scale enterprises. In Japan, the proportion of micro-enterprises is smaller than in both the EU and the USA. However, Japan does possess a greater proportion of small enterprises.

Within the EU, Directorate General XXIII is responsible for policies for SMEs. The focus of policies from this directorate has been to reduce the burdens on SMEs arising from European legislation, provide help in the late payment of debts, improve the information flow to SMEs, promote SME co-operation across borders through the Business Consortium Network (BC-NET), and provide a better structural and financial environment for SMEs. Within the EU therefore, SMEs are the main size for enterprises, and the perception that they have created more jobs during the last decade than the large enterprises indicates why the EU considers this sector to be the important generator of growth during the next decade.

Conclusion

There have been both internal and external forces in play which have led to the growth of international business. Markets have become increasingly dominated by a few major organisations. However, for organisations, size is not necessarily correlated with performance and the 1990s have witnessed a number of organisations divesting themselves of areas that do not fit in with their core philosophy or portfolio.

During the 1970s and 1980s, few changes occurred in the make-up of the top 20 or top 50 firms, but the business world has become more dynamic during the 1990s. Mergers and acquisitions, changes in technology, the emergence of companies from newly industrialised countries (NICs) and the impact of the Single European Market have led to continual change in the ranking of dominant companies. There are concerns, however, about the degree to which the EU is falling behind some of its main competitors, and an indication of this is the gradual and long-term increase in the levels of unemployment the EU has experienced. The promotion of the SME sector has been seen as one solution to this growing problem of unemployment within the EU.

Having gained an overview of European business, its strengths and weaknesses and its trends, the next chapter considers the environment in which firms either thrive or decline.

Questions for discussion

1 List the sectors where Europe has a large presence in the world market. Consider why Europe appears to have an advantage in these sectors compared with the USA and Japan.

2 Similarly, look at where Japan and the USA dominate and consider why they appear to have an advantage in these sectors.

3 Bearing in mind your answers to 1 and 2 above, consider the sectors where the NICs are likely to make the biggest impact on the world market and why.

4 Do you think the SME sector will provide Europe with the investment and employment it needs? What are the problems with putting so much hope in this sector?

5 Why do companies prefer to grow by merger rather than by internal growth?

6 Why have joint ventures proved to be a popular route to organisational growth during the 1990s?

7 Why have some companies sought to reduce in size during the 1990s? What are the problems with this strategy?

8 Using examples, consider the ways in which organisations have strategically reduced in size.

Main reading

Dicken, P. (1998) *Global Shift: Industrial Change in a Turbulent World*, 3rd edition, Paul Chapman, London.

European Economy (1996) Economic Evaluation of the Internal Market, No. 4, European Commission.

Fortune (1997) The top 500 corporations in the world, 4 August.

Additional reading

Cane, A. (1997) Cable and Wireless set to raise £1bn in asset sell-off programme, *Financial Times*, 13 November.

The Economist (1991) Riding the wave, 28 September, p. 104.

European Commission (1996) The world's top 200 companies, *Panorama of EC Industry*.

European Commission (1996) Small firms in Europe, *Panorama of EC Industry*.

Financial Times (1991) European investment locations, July.

Lloyds Bank Economic Bulletin (1991) February, pp. 1–2.

Simonian, H. (1997) FT automobile: European sunshine clouded by Asian worries, *Financial Times*, 4 December.

Williamson, O. E. (1985) *The Economic Institutions of Capitalism*, Free Press.

The environment of international business

Introduction

At a time when more and more businesses are anticipating further development in overseas markets, particularly the European market, it is becoming increasingly important for businesses to develop their awareness of the environment in which they operate. This chapter will focus on assessing the business environment and its strategic significance for businesses within a European context. Particular attention will be paid to government policies and to issues that would affect firms seeking to develop in Europe, using selected examples from throughout Europe. The issue of national cultural differences will also be looked at together with its significance for business, and finally the issue of the impact of the EU on the business environment will be evaluated.

Business in Europe and the world

If the 1980s were characterised by an increased awareness of the meaning and potential of the Single European Market (SEM), the 1990s have been a time when the SEM has come into fruition and Europe has begun to grapple with the issues of a single currency, which would take the concept of a single market one stage further. At the same time, the 1990s saw rapid changes in the Central and Eastern European states, with them experiencing the pain of political and economic transformation but beginning to achieve high rates of economic growth by 1997 (e.g. Poland). All these factors have led to more and more businesses seeking to take advantage of market opportunities through developing links with other countries, which in turn has led to increasing contact with different business environments and cultures. The extent to which businesses actually move into a more international environment will largely be conditioned by their current structure and outlook.

The 1990s have also seen a continuation of the globalisation of business. Although Europe remains the world's biggest market, it exists within a global perspective, especially that of the Triad, which represents the continuing battle for world business supremacy between East Asia, the Americas and Europe. The Asian economies experienced sustained high levels of economic growth throughout the 1980s and 1990s despite the economic crisis which hit certain of these countries towards the end of 1997. Although Japan remains a dominant economic power in the region, this has been augmented by the success of the 'tiger' economies such as South Korea, Hong Kong (despite its return to China in 1997), Singapore, Taiwan and Malaysia. Furthermore, China is developing rapidly and drawing significant amounts of foreign direct investment from both the United States and Europe. In the Americas the development of NAFTA (North American Free Trade Area) has seen increasing links between the United States, Canada and Mexico as they develop their potential as a trading bloc.

One particular feature of the 1990s has been the increased rate of change in the European and global environment. This is leading to increased turbulence in business environments, with the consequence that companies that have existed in fairly stable environments hitherto are having to make radical strategic shifts in order to maintain a competitive advantage in their markets. This in turn has often led to significant changes in the company structure, with increased decentralisation and downsizing and even a shift towards flexible organisations which have a minority 'core' workforce that is fully employed, but also a range of people on temporary or short-term contracts, which enables the company to expand or contract quickly in a turbulent environment and thus remain flexible. An example of how a business environment can suddenly become more volatile can be seen in the case study on the telecommunications industry later in this chapter.

However, the extent to which businesses are likely to move into a European or international environment will to a large extent be conditioned by their current structure and outlook.

Local companies

Local companies tend to be primarily concerned with local or regional markets and thus would tend to show little interest in developing markets overseas. This would apply primarily to small and medium-sized enterprises (SMEs), which are defined as businesses with up to 250 employees, although this is even more significant for micro-enterprises, which have up to nine employees. One of the problems faced by such companies is lack of information about market opportunities, partly because of short-term objectives by the entrepreneurs and also a lack of a strategic perspective, especially when there are resource constraints (primarily finance and labour), which would hinder any international expansion. Thus SMEs have not made effective use of EU-funded information sources such as European Reference centres, BC-NET and Europartenariat. At the same time such companies may well find in the 1990s that their previously secure local markets may be threatened by overseas competitors, especially given the reduction of trade barriers resulting from the Single European Market.

If such companies are seeking to expand or distribute their product abroad, the most likely route is through an agent, who will seek to find the most appropriate distribution source for them and will help market their product or service in the target country or countries.

National companies

National companies also have the vast bulk of their business located in the home market and yet may be seriously considering developing abroad, especially in terms of opening up selling and distribution channels in new markets. For many of these companies the initial step will be to develop links in a specific country before moving on to a wider front; they will seek to do this before considering direct investment through either production or retail units and they might stop short of direct acquisition at this stage. Thus an increasing trend has been towards the use of joint ventures or strategic alliances as a means of making this first step.

A joint venture is where two (or more) companies create a new, shared enterprise without affecting their own share ownership, and the strategic alliance can take on a number of forms, which could involve an exchange of shares, although the figure is usually a minimal one. This is a useful way of building up networks in hitherto closed markets, e.g. by opening up distribution channels to each other or by sharing research and development (R&D) or know-how.

European companies

European companies are those which have steadily developed links within Europe to the extent that they have started to develop manufacturing and retail outlets in other countries. However, they are not yet big enough to really call themselves multinational companies (MNCs). Very often this has been done by direct expansion as opposed to takeover, as this route may encounter fewer legal and organisational problems, although it might take longer to build up distribution and retail outlets.

Being already established in Europe, they might be seeking to develop their operations into new countries in the EU or Eastern Europe, building on their expertise and core competencies.

Such companies often have a greater appreciation of national cultural differences and adapt their operations accordingly. However, they are not at this stage looking to operate in other areas of the Triad.

Multinational companies

Multinational companies are already well established throughout Europe and may often originate from outside Europe, predominantly from the United States and from Japan and the Pacific Rim, and thus are best placed to take full advantage of market developments there. They have usually developed a more international corporate culture and make full use of nationals of the countries where they operate.

Thus it could be said that the multinationals are already better informed about the business environment at a European level as they have been treating Europe as a single market for some time previously and thus may have developed marketing and human resource strategies at that level and so again can respond more rapidly to changes in the European business environment.

They can also adjust their production outlets overseas to take into account factors like generous taxation laws or the availability of cheaper labour supplies than in their home market.

Global companies

Global companies are very similar to multinationals but perhaps the main difference is that they are not so closely linked in organisational or cultural terms to the 'home country'; they see themselves as truly global without a 'headquarters mentality', which may be conditioned by a particular national culture (see Ohmae 1989). These companies would operate effectively at the European level but would be focusing on future investment on a global basis, which may or may not include a European dimension.

Thus one can identify a spectrum of companies, ranging from the small micro-company to the giant global companies such as Shell and IBM. Some of these, such as the global companies, will be very tuned to their business environment, whereas others will have a very limited information base and will be slow to respond to environmental changes. However, given the trends of increasing development and integration at European and international levels, few companies can afford to ignore the business environment in which they will be operating and thus there is a need for a greater understanding of this.

Analysing the business environment

The key objective in analysing the business environment for a company is to identify factors in the company's external environment that are likely to present potential threats or opportunities to it in order that it can adjust its strategy accordingly. If a company begins to lose track of changes in its environment, a phenomenon known as strategic drift, then there is a risk that its strategy will not be relevant to the current state of the environment and so dramatic shifts in strategy may be called for in order to bring it into line.

Most companies would, to some extent, be aware of factors that are changing in their national environment but the effects of these external changes become even more significant when the company is thinking of moving into a new business environment by developing into another country.

The most common form of business environment auditing is through a model known as LEPEST-C, which gives a framework in which the company can evaluate a range of factors that will influence its environment and from which key opportunities and threats might be identified. This in turn would enable the company to avoid strategic drift. LEPEST-C refers to the broad legal, economic, political, ecological, socio-demographic and technological factors, and the 'C' refers to the competitive factors for the company. It makes use of Porter's (1980) five-forces model. The range of the impact of these factors can be seen in Fig. 3.1.

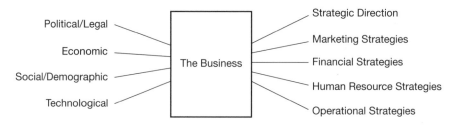

Figure 3.1 The impact of environmental factors on business strategy

Political and legal factors will have a major impact on the company's environment, both in terms of the political nature of the government in power and in terms of the various types of legislation passed by the state that will have a bearing on the operations of the business. In the event of a general election, there may well be changes of government policy, which will lead to new legislation or the repeal of existing legislation which may be of significance to the company; for example, the election of 'New Labour' in the UK in 1997 has led to the adoption by the government of the Social Chapter, which will be significant for companies affected by legislation on paternity leave and atypical worker rights.

At a wider level, political change can lead to economic and societal instability, as has been seen in the Russian Federation since 1989, where one of the consequences of the rapid change in the country has been the increased role played by the Russian mafias, which have a very large stake in both illegitimate and, increasingly, legitimate businesses, with all the consequences that this brings.

Companies should be monitoring the various types of legislation that will have a bearing on their operations. Areas such as company law, competition law and laws governing employment, the environment and health and safety will have to be taken into account, especially where a proposed or new piece of legislation will have an impact on business operations. Whilst the company may be aware of legislation affecting it nationally, it will need to research these areas in more depth when planning to operate in another country (see later in the chapter). The issue gets even more complicated when EU legislation is taken into account, and a separate audit of current and proposed EU legislation may be needed in its own right.

Social factors will also be of consequence when planning to have dealings with other countries. These could include issues such as social mobility, attitudes to leisure, differing lifestyles and traditions and consumer attitudes. These may be of great concern when considering marketing a product or service in a different country. One example would be that a company manufacturing toasters in the UK may have to rethink its product design or marketing strategy considerably given that the British habit of having pre-sliced bread that fits easily into toasters may not be found in other countries such as France and Italy, and toast may not be heard of in China. These aspects of a country are sometimes the hardest to find information on and may lead to culture clashes (see later in the chapter).

One area that is usually included with social factors is demographic trends. Information on this is more readily available and an awareness of population growth and structure may highlight opportunities for the business. For example, the German and Italian populations have shown a clear trend towards an ageing population with an ever-increasing number of people over 60 and relative declines in birth rates. This, together with the move towards earlier retirement, imposes increased burdens on those remaining in the working population. At the same time, these older people are healthier than ever before and also have considerable spending power. One consequence of this has been the market opportunity for travel firms to develop package tours exclusively aimed at this age group.

Economic factors are of critical importance to a business and may well be the prime consideration when considering development. One of the most critical factors will be the state of the economy, and whether it is entering a recessionary or a growth phase. If the home economy shows signs of poor growth compared to other economies then this may act as a considerable spur to companies planning investment in other countries. The economic policy of the government should also be taken into consideration, as should all the leading indicators such as inflation, unemployment, wage rates, the exchange rate and interest rates (especially if the business is going to borrow in order to expand). These factors will have strategic implications for all businesses: high interest rates will affect the costs of borrowing for the company; if wage rates are high it could affect the company's labour costs; and movements in the exchange rate could affect the raw material costs and export prices. Most economic data are published, together with predictions into the future, and so companies can start to make an economic evaluation when looking at a foreign market as a potential source of growth.

Technological factors are of importance to most businesses, whether they are to do with information technology, which is critical in service industries, or manufacturing technology, where developments of new products or processes can be critical in giving a company a competitive advantage over its rivals. This is more significant for some businesses than others and is usually reflected in the amounts spent on R&D. A successful new drug can give a pharmaceutical company substantial advantages until its patent expires. One sector where continuous adaptation of products in response to fast technological change has been necessary is the personal computer market, where product life-cycle times have been reduced considerably.

Of all the factors, technology is probably of least significance to a company when it is considering the potential of the environment in a new country, primarily because technology is a global phenomenon and there may well be few differences between developed markets and industries.

To illustrate the above let us imagine a toy company in the UK which is considering entering the Italian market and which decides to carry out some analysis of the business environment in Italy. Figure 3.2 shows some of the issues that could emerge from a LEPEST-C analysis and some of the possible strategic implications that it might pose for the company when it is considering whether to expand into this market.

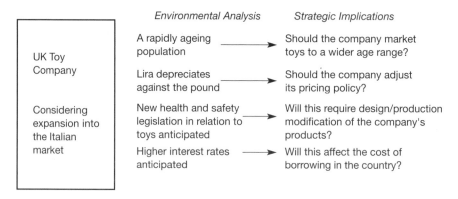

Figure 3.2 Example of strategic responses to hypothetical environmental changes

Another analysis which the company could carry out is an analysis of its competitive environment, in terms of either its current competitive environment or the competitive environment it might encounter if it was to enter another geographical market. Porter (1980) developed a useful model to analyse this, which he called 'The five-forces model' (Fig. 3.3).

The model shows a range of factors in the competitive environment that might be significant for the company in its current or intended market. One issue will be the threat of entry into the market in which the company operates and to a large extent this will depend upon barriers to entry into the market. Such barriers could include extensive economies of scale (e.g. in the motor industry), patent barriers (e.g. in pharmaceuticals) or lack of distribution networks (e.g. in retailing) and thus could prove a real barrier for the company seeking European expansion. The threat of substitutes will also affect the competitive position of the company: its home market could be threatened by substitute products from other countries or its product or service may have unique factors which could be a means of entry into a new market by acting as an effective substitute in the foreign market. The power of sellers could be significant in a sector such as food and drink, where retail chains have significant selling power, and thus it would be hard to enter such markets unless the company could get its goods distributed by a powerful retail chain. The power of buyers may also be significant in some sectors and refers to the state of competi-

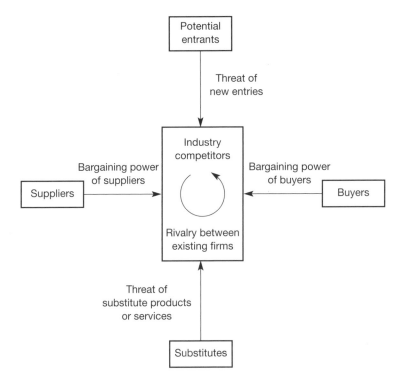

Figure 3.3 Porter's five-forces model

tion in the market where the producers have to use intermediaries to get their product on the market. Competitive rivalry refers to the state of competition within the market, i.e. is the market a very competitive one or is there an element of monopoly or oligopoly power? For a company seeking to develop into another country the existence of strong monopoly or oligopoly power may be a deterrent to market entry because of the potentially high entry costs. If we go back to the UK toy company seeking to enter the Italian market then we might get the situation shown in Fig. 3.4.

The example of the toy company in Figs 3.2 and 3.4 shows that by carrying out an effective business environmental audit, the company is able to pick up potential opportunities for development but may also pick up possible or actual threats of which it had previously been unaware. Once these have been identified, the company can develop either defensive strategies where there is a potential threat, or offensive strategies where there are potential opportunities. In the example of the toy company already mentioned, the company may decide to increase the range of its toys in response to the high birth rate in Italy, or even opt for more European-orientated toys if it sees a gap in the Italian market where it would be an effective substitute product.

It is also useful for the company to determine whether it is in a rapidly changing or dynamic environment as opposed to a slowly changing or static environment, as this will influence its need to respond to strategic drift. One feature of the 1990s has been a trend towards more dynamic environments, either driven by government policies such as privatisation and deregulation or because of the increased globalisation of business driven by rapid technological development.

This is significant in that the firm that considers itself in a static environment tends to rely on historic information (e.g. previous sales trends) and will make its future forecasts in its business plan based on previous behaviour. When such a firm moves into a more dynamic environment, these previous patterns may be much less significant and the firm has to focus as much on guessing future trends as on relying on past ones. It may have to respond much more quickly to change if it is to survive, which may mean the use of techniques such as scenario planning and planning alternative contingencies, together with a much more flexible

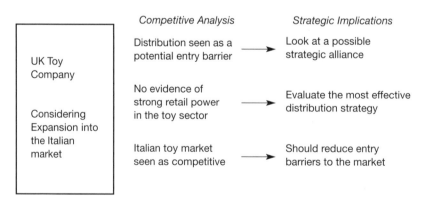

Figure 3.4 Possible strategic responses to the competitive environment

organisational structure that can respond quickly to these changes. Failure to do so may well mean that it loses its competitive advantage to its rivals, and the key to avoiding this is successful auditing of the business environment.

Let us imagine three rival toy companies, which operate in a very dynamic market, with all three seeking to export their product throughout Europe. At the same time the European Commission is proposing a directive to cover safety in toys, which could directly affect their main product lines. Company A (the proactive company) immediately obtains information from the EU and other sources about the proposed directive and may even seek to influence the directive in its planning stage when the Commission seeks opinion from interested parties. Company A is therefore well informed about the directive and when it finally comes out has already adjusted its strategy, e.g. by adjusting its design specifications to meet the directive's needs, and is able to develop its exporting to Europe without any interference from the directive.

Company B (the reactive company) only picks up the directive once it has been passed but, having identified the directive as a potential threat to export sales. It then sets in train the various modifications needed to adjust its toy products, and once this has been done it can develop its export markets, although note that it may have lost important time in getting its products onto the market compared with Company A (especially in dynamic environments, where time can be seen to be a form of competitive advantage).

Company C (the non-reactive company) does not carry out business environment audits and thus is totally unaware of the directive which has been passed and which will affect its products. It is surprised when it finds out at a trade fair that its products no longer measure up to European specifications on safety and thus it will not be able to sell its products in the European market without modification. It then has to find out what the directive entails before seeking to make the relevant modifications, by which time it will be difficult for the company to make up lost ground on companies A and B.

For all these reasons the concept of business environment auditing can be of great significance to businesses, especially when they are thinking of entering a new geographical market.

A further example of LEPEST-C can be seen in the telecommunications case study, which illustrates the rate of change that is affecting international business and suggests some of the strategic responses by companies.

Case study: The telecommunications industry

The telecommunications industry has become a massive global industry and yet is one where changes have been sudden and dramatic with differing consequences for consumers and producers. In most countries (with the exception of the USA) there have been state-run monopolies in telecommunications, such as France Telecom used to be.

If we are looking at the LEPEST-C model we could probably identify two major factors that have forced radical change on the sector. The first of these would be that of technology in that telephone systems have developed with improved technology in the transmission of information. There are now cellular (mobile) phone networks, electronic and voice mail, electronic data interchange, videotext and data communications, and digital radio and television are likely to appear at the end of 1998. These developments have given new companies the chance to enter markets by using the latest technologies, often picking niche markets. Under the old system of state monopolies there would have been few if any new entrants because of the legal barriers that existed – but this is where the second major change occurred.

The second major change was in the area of legislation on telecommunications. The European Union started to try to liberalise the market in 1984 but this process accelerated in the 1990s, for example in countries like the UK, where privatisation had successfully taken place and the benefits to consumers were being seen through lower prices. The EU's aim was to have the European market totally deregulated for the end of 1997. Although some countries still have some way to go (e.g. Deutsche Telekom still controls 75 per cent of the market in Germany) there has been a dramatic change in many others, with the advent of new competitors coming into the market. At the same time, the World Trade Organisation (WTO) has signed an agreement with 69 countries for market liberalisation to commence from January 1998 and many countries are following this (e.g. Brazil has agreed to privatise its telecommunications sector by June 1998).

The results of this have been that barriers to entry have been reduced, with more new entrants coming into the market using the latest technology to gain some competitive advantage. Consumers have generally benefited from this as the dual impact of new technology and competition has led to a greater choice of products, lower prices (the average cost of delivering a telephone call fell by 25 per cent in 1997) and finally increased customer care. As for the producers, many of them are seeking to develop new global alliances in order to improve their global presence. Examples of these include Global One, which is made up of Sprint (USA), Deutsche Telekom and France Telecom; and ATT Unisource, which is made up of AT&T (USA), Telia (Sweden), Telecom Italia and Swisscom. Perhaps the biggest of these alliances was to have been Concert, which would have consisted of MCI (USA), British Telecom, Telefonica (Spain) and Portugal Telecom. Up to date (March 1998) none of these groupings has been particularly successful, possibly because of cultural problems, and Concert fell apart in November 1997 when MCI pulled out and agreed to be taken over by another American company called Worldcom in a $37 billion merger which in turn is under investigation by the Justice Department in the USA.

• •

In the next section some of the critical areas affecting businesses when they seek to expand into Europe will be examined. The areas covered are by no means exhaustive but do give a flavour of some of the practical areas from the business environment that would have to be addressed when a company comes to the point where it seeks to develop within the European market. The same issues would have to be developed if the company was moving into a wider international market.

Key issues in the business environment

Government policies

In whichever country a business decides to operate, it is bound to be highly influenced by the nature of government policies therein.

In France there has been a long tradition of state intervention in industry and business. This is reflected by the fact that alongside the public utilities, such as telecommunications (France Telecom) and electricity (Electricité de France), there are a number of firms which are directly owned by the state or where the state has a partial shareholding such as Renault (motor vehicles), Rhône-Poulenc (chemicals) and Thomson (electronics and defence). There are also a number of state-owned banks and insurance companies (see Chapter 13). There has been a gradual movement towards more privatisation and greater private holdings in these firms and industries but the change has been erratic, and whereas there has been a substantial move towards privatisation with France Telecom, attempts to privatise parts of the the railway system have been met with paralysing strikes, despite the government taking over a large portion of the company's debts in a restructuring package in 1996.

In Germany there is a social market economy built around the two key objectives of a low inflation rate and a strong trade balance. There are a number of public monopolies such as telecommunications, radio and TV, railways and airports and, as with France, the government has substantial shareholdings in a number of companies, such as Lufthansa. Again the progress towards privatisation has been slow and hampered by the absorption of the East German states.

In Italy there is perhaps the highest level of government involvement in industry and business, characterised by the large state holding companies such as IRI (Instituto per la Reconstruzione Industriale), which controls shipbuilding, shipping and a large part of the construction industry in Italy. Another area of strong government control can be seen in the financial sector. This large state intervention comes at a price, in that many of these companies are permanently in debt and a large proportion are overstaffed. The overall effect is that Italy has a substantial public sector debt requiring a continually high level of public sector borrowing to service it, which restricts growth in the economy – a problem it shares with Belgium.

Company taxation

Another aspect that will be of great importance to businesses seeking to expand into other countries, especially into Europe, is the relevant system of taxation and especially the rate of company taxation, as this will have a significant impact on a company's earning potential.

Figure 3.5 shows the different rates of company taxation that are found throughout Europe. From this it can be seen that a UK company is almost certain to face higher company tax when developing operations in the European environment than is the case for companies developing operations in the UK. Another factor to take into consideration in many countries is the existence of local taxes or state taxes, which add considerably to the basic company taxation.

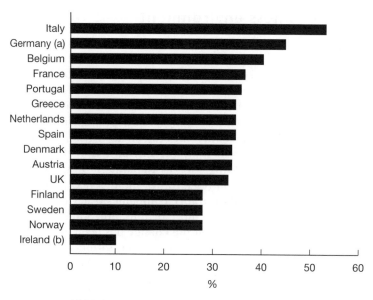

(a) 30% for distributed profit. (b) For manufacturing and certain specific activities

Figure 3.5 European company tax (reprinted with permission from Economist Intelligence Unit Ltd)

Company law

If a company is seeking to set up a physical presence in another country then it will have to pay attention to the company law of the relevant country. For example, if it is a private limited company in the UK, it would seek to become a *Société à Responsabilité Limitée* (SARL) in France, a *Società a Responsabilità Limitata* (SRL) in Italy or a *Gesellschaft mit Beschränkter Haftung* (GmBH) in Germany. The corresponding forms for a public limited company (plc) in the UK are a *Société Anonyme* (SA) in France, a *Società per Azioni* (SpA) in Italy and an *Aktiengesellschaft* (AG) in Germany.

Under German company law a company has to have both a management board (*Vorstand*) and a supervisory board (*Aufsichsrat*), together with mandatory works councils if there are regularly more than 20 employees. The *Aufsichsrat* is meant to exercise supervision over the *Vorstand* on behalf of the shareholders, who appoint all the members if fewer than 500 people are employed. This moves to a situation described in Fig. 3.6 where, if there are over 2000 employees, the *Aufsichsrat* is divided equally between shareholders' representatives and workers' representatives, although the shareholders do retain a slight edge through the chairperson's casting vote. In addition, the arrival of the European Works Council Directive, which came into force in 1997, will have significant impacts on larger companies that operate throughout the EU.

Regional policies

If our UK company is envisaging setting up production or retail facilities in other European countries, then the choice of its location might be affected by

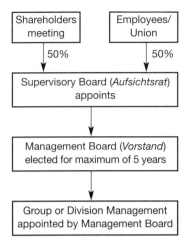

Figure 3.6 Control in German companies with over 2000 employees

the various regional incentives which are offered by national governments throughout Europe, mainly in the form of financial and tax incentives.

In France the main regional body is DATAR, which offers a range of incentives for foreign companies, including a range of grants for investment into buildings and machinery, often backed up by incentives from local authorities and chambers of commerce. Although Paris still dominates France in both governmental and commercial terms, there are significant developments elsewhere, most notably in the attraction of high-technology companies to southern locations and the redevelopment of the north-east with the opening of the Channel Tunnel and the redevelopment of Lille as a communications hub for the development of the region.

In Italy there are batteries of incentives, especially if a company is thinking of locating in the less developed Mezzogiorno and the south. Substantial grants of up to 40 per cent of costs, low-interest loans and tax holidays on both company and local taxation will be available. These incentives have been successful to some extent, notably in the Lazio region around Rome, but against this the company will have to weigh issues such as lower productivity, weaker infrastructure and certain cultural problems.

By contrast, if our company is thinking of locating in the Netherlands, it will find a government that has reduced financial supports, preferring instead to rely on the country's reputation for a skilled workforce, good industrial relations and excellent communications.

Infrastructure

Whilst regional incentives may entice companies away from the main market centre of Europe (sometimes known as 'The Golden Triangle', bounded by London, Frankfurt and Turin), another important factor that would determine their location would be the local infrastructure, especially in terms of transport communications, telecommunications and local business services.

Communications are especially important when the business has a wide distribution network, and the availability of a good communications network may enable the business to locate further away from its prime markets and possibly take advantage of regional incentives or other factors. France has shown through its heavy investment in its railway network, and through its high-speed TGV (*trains à grande vitesse*) system, that a high-speed network can considerably reduce travel times between major centres and thus make some of the more peripheral regions more attractive. As well as trains, a good motorway network is crucial as most freight still goes by road and it is here that Germany has an advantage in terms of having the most kilometres of motorway per inhabitant.

One of the prime needs of a company that is operating in several other countries is the need for quick and effective communications between the headquarters and the various branches of the company, and thus the role of telecommunications becomes crucial. Many countries in Europe still have state-run telecommunications systems which, it is argued, have hindered competition and innovation. The lowest costs are usually found where privatisation has led to increased competition, such as in the UK and Denmark, although the move to increased global competition in the industry is leading to a range of strategic alliances.

Human resource factors

When a company decides to establish itself in a new country then a number of human resource issues will come into play. One of the key issues will be the availability of labour. Both Italy and Germany (at least before its unification) face rapidly ageing workforces, and Italy (which has the lowest birth rate in Europe) faces an actual fall in its population, leading to potential labour shortages in the future. More important for the company may be the skill base of the labour force and the ability of the company to acquire the specific skills needed for its operations. This is where a country that has invested heavily in developing vocational skills, such as Germany, may well prove attractive to a potential industrial investor.

Labour costs will also have to be taken into account, especially if the company is contemplating a labour-intensive operation, or will need high skill levels from its workforce. Table 3.1 shows labour costs measured in ECU in relation to the average for the European Union. This would indicate to a company that labour costs are relatively high in countries such as the Netherlands and Germany in relation to some other countries such as the UK, Ireland and some of the Mediterranean countries. Attention should be paid, however, to how the pattern changes once productivity is taken into account; in other words a labour force with high unit costs need not be a hindrance if there is high productivity, thus reducing unit labour costs. Another issue to take on board is the amount of flexibility in the labour force; for instance, wage levels may become rigid in certain countries, especially when statutory holidays, the existence of statutory minimum wages and the tradition in many countries of paying for 'the thirteenth month', wherein a bonus equivalent to one month's pay is given either in summer or at Christmas (indeed some countries even have 'the fourteenth

Table 3.1 Hourly labour costs in industry in the EU (measured in ECU)

Country	1984	1992	1994
Austria	10.99	19.84	22.87
Belgium	13.40	21.27	24.26
Denmark	11.95	19.28	21.07
France	12.37	19.12	n.a.
Finland	n.a.	17.56	17.82
Germany	14.24	23.14	26.14
Greece	5.85	6.97	7.64
Ireland	10.73	18.09	n.a.
Luxembourg	11.07	17.16	19.29
Italy	10.73	18.09	n.a.
Netherlands	13.68	19.27	21.33
Portugal	2.38	5.55	5.53
Spain	n.a	15.11	14.13
Sweden	11.89	19.02	16.05
United Kingdom	9.04	13.11	12.65

Source: adapted from Eurostat, 1993, pages 181–2.

month' so that both options can be covered!). Indirect labour costs may also be significant in some countries, such as Italy, where an employer has to pay high pension contributions as well as contributions to the Cassa Integrazione Guadagni, which makes up most of the wages of workers who are laid off through no fault of their own.

Finally, a company might also consider the industrial relations climate and may resist investing in countries where industrial relations are poor or complicated. Germany has long benefited from a stable industrial relations climate, which might prove an attraction to companies that have experienced severe industrial relations problems in their own countries.

Cultural differences

An area which is being seen to be of increasing importance for companies operating within the European environment is that of national cultures. National culture is affected by a number of factors, some of which are suggested in Fig. 3.7.

Language is becoming increasingly important as more and more companies operate in a wider European market and find the need for effective communication between different parts of the organisation or for the need for members of the organisation from different countries to work in teams together. A company may have to decide whether to put home country managers in the senior positions in other European subsidiaries or whether to appoint managers from the home country. The former would guarantee clear communications between the head office and its subsidiaries but the latter approach may mean a better understanding of attitudes of customers and the organisation's workforce and management. Sometimes companies make a strategic decision to adopt a particular language as the company language to avoid confusion, an example of this being Asea Brown Boveri (ABB), which, although its headquarters are in

Figure 3.7 Cultural factors affecting business organisations

Zurich, uses English as the company language for senior meetings and reports. Languages have traditionally been a weakness of UK companies. A study by Price Waterhouse which looked at over 6000 EU companies' attitudes to training found that less than half the British employers provided, or were willing to provide, language training, compared with nearly 70 per cent of Spanish companies and 75 per cent of French companies.

Some of the most interesting work on national culture has been done by Dutch writers, most notably Hofstede and Trompenaars. Hofstede (1984) based his research on cultural differences of people working for IBM in over forty countries, which has led to some criticism that the findings may have been influenced by the corporate culture of IBM. Moreover, it also means that there are no data for Eastern European countries as IBM did not operate in these areas at the time of the research.

However, the model is still used extensively and can be of value to businesses seeking to understand the culture of a country in which they are seeking to expand. Hofstede used four criteria to assess the national business culture. The first of these is the concept of *power distance*, which looks at power relationships, especially at work, and looks at issues such as subordinates' attitudes towards disagreeing with a superior and how significant hierarchies are seen to be in the organisation. Thus France has a relatively high score here (see Table 3.2), reflecting the superior role of the **cadres** (managers who have emerged from the top management schools) and the significant gap there would be in power terms between the top managers and lower-level managers in a French organisation. A second area is that of *uncertainty avoidance*, which reflects the difference between cultures where uncertainty is tolerated, with a greater degree of risk-taking and a greater willingness to accept ambiguous situations. Other cultures show the need for a high degree of uncertainty avoidance in that managers will be expected to give very clear directions and there tends to be a higher emotional resistance to change. Thus it can be seen from Table 3.2 that Danish managers operating in Greece might have to change their management approach in their Greek subsidiary. *Individualism* is the third of Hofstede's criteria and this relates to the preference for individual behaviour as opposed to a more collective, group-based approach to work and relations within the organisation. Thus many of the 'Anglo-Saxon' cultures have a strong level of individualism inherent within them where individuals will be expected to take decisions and live by them. A more collectivist culture such as is found in parts of Asia would see individuality to some extent subsumed within the overall corporate culture – the idea that the company looks after you from cradle to grave, which used to be identified with Japan, although this has changed in recent years. Many of the European countries have a significant level of individualism, as can again be seen from Table 3.2. The final element is *masculinity/femininity*, which basically contrasts the emphasis on work goals (high masculinity) with personal goals (femininity). Thus in a masculine culture there is a greater likelihood that roles will be accorded to gender, such as in Japan, where there are significantly fewer female manager roles than in more feminine-type cultures such as in Scandanavia.

Further work on national business cultures was carried out by Fons Trompenaars in 1993 which, developing Hofstede's work, identified seven dimensions of culture, based on research involving questionnaires to over 15 000 managers. Some of these dimensions reflect those of Hofstede but additionally there is *neutral versus affective relationships*, which looks at how emotions are expressed in different cultures. He contrasts those where emotion would be used as a natural part of business relationships, as in Italy and Russia, with those societies where the open expression of emotion would be more frowned upon within the organisation, such as in the UK and Japan. There is also *specific versus diffuse relationships*, which reflects the extent to which private life is distinct from life in the organisation, e.g. there can often be great formality amongst working colleagues in Germany who have known each other for many years.

Table 3.2 Hofstede's cultural analysis (selected countries)

Country	PD score	UA score	IDV score	MAS score
Austria	11	70	55	79
Belgium	65	94	75	54
Denmark	18	23	74	16
Finland	33	59	63	26
France	68	86	71	43
Germany	35	65	67	66
Greece	60	112	35	57
Ireland	28	35	70	68
Italy	50	75	76	70
Netherlands	38	53	80	14
Norway	31	50	69	8
Portugal	63	104	27	31
Spain	57	86	51	42
Sweden	31	29	71	5
Switzerland	34	58	68	70
UK	35	35	89	66
Hong Kong	68	29	25	57
Japan	54	92	46	95
USA	40	46	91	62

IDV = individualism; PD = power distance;
MAS = masculinity/femininity; UA = uncertainty avoidance.
Source: adapted from Hofstede (1995).

The impact of the EU on the business environment

The final area where businesses can examine their business environment within a European context relates to current and proposed legislation emanating from the EU to the extent that the business could carry out an EU audit to identify which pieces of current or proposed legislation are most likely to affect them. The objective would be that the company could undertake a more proactive approach as mentioned before and thus gain some competitive advantage over its rivals. A mass of legislation has come from the EU which has gradually been enacted into national law in areas such as social policy, competition policy, technical harmonisation, regional policy, environmental policy and many other areas, several of which are covered in more depth later in this book. This has led to a significant increase of lobbying at a European level, where industries cannot only lobby to influence legislation, but can also pick up advance information of any proposed legislation. Although not exhaustive, Fig. 3.8 gives an idea of some of the main areas that would need monitoring.

Some issues that might concern a company in response to EU legislation could be as follows:

1 Have there been any changes in the technical standards relating to the company's products?
2 Will the opening up of public procurement lead to potential new contracts or business with government departments in the country?
3 What would be the implications for the company of increased tax harmonisation in VAT, excise duties or company taxation?
4 Will new legislation from the Social Chapter have any impact on the company's wage structure and costs?
5 Would any changes in the EU's Regional Policy affect future location decisions in the EU?
6 Will directives establishing equivalence of vocational qualifications make it easier for the company to assess its human resource needs in each country?
7 Will the advent of European Monetary Union have any impact on the company's foreign exchange transactions with its European subsidiaries?

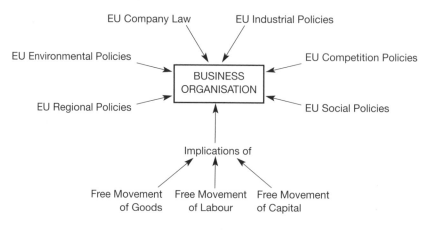

Figure 3.8 European Union environmental audit

As can be seen from the small selection of examples above, the legislation at European level will have an impact upon strategy, both in the short run and the long run, and failure to identify the key policy areas which affect the company may lead to problems when competing at the European level with those proactive companies that have anticipated the changes.

Conclusion

The objective of this chapter has been to indicate the importance of company awareness of the European and international business environment in which it operates, especially when the company is seeking to expand from its familiar national environment and enter new ones. This whole process has been thrown into sharp focus by significant developments in the European Union such as the development of the Single Market and the Maastricht Treaty and thus the potential threats and opportunities these developments pose for businesses all over Europe, including Central and Eastern Europe. In addition, the increased push to globalisation has meant that companies have to look at developments in America and Asia and consider their impact on their business environment. By focusing on some of the areas discussed in this chapter, companies can avoid a number of problems that might follow from either entering a new market without adequate research or not identifying threats within the home market from potential competitors.

Finally, a good awareness of the business environment, whether it is in the company's home market or the European and international markets into which it is seeking to expand, will enable the company to adopt a proactive position and adjust its strategies to give it a degree of competitive advantage over its rivals, and hopefully flourish in the European and international business environment of the future.

Questions for discussion

1   Give a profile of the types of business that you feel are most likely and least likely to benefit from the development of the Single European Market.

2   Identify reasons why it might be strategically unsound for a business to ignore developments in Europe, America and Asia.

3   Identify an industry with which you are familiar and carry out a LEPEST-C analysis. On the basis of this can you identify any threats or opportunities facing the industry?

4   Identify business areas where a static environment has suddenly changed to a more dynamic one and discuss the possible strategic consequences for companies in that business area.

5   Compare and contrast the extent of government intervention in the UK with that of other European countries and assess whether this has been a hindrance or a help to British industry.

6   Pick an Asian country, a North or South American country and a European country and identify some of the key issues that might influence a company's decision when it is assessing the three countries as potential sites for manufacturing or retail investment.

7   How might a small or medium-sized enterprise approach developing internationally, as opposed to a larger firm ?

8   What sort of cultural problems might a European firm face when it is considering expansion into Hong Kong, Japan or the USA?

9   Making use of Table 3.2, identify the main cultural problems that would be likely to occur with the merger of a UK and French firm and the development of joint management teams in the newly merged company.

10 Carry out an EU business environmental audit on a company of your choice. How significant are EU developments in affecting the company's environment?

Main reading

Johnson, G. and Scholes, K. (1997) *Exploring Corporate Strategy*, 4th edition, Prentice-Hall.
Swann, D. (1992) *The Single European Market and Beyond: A Study of the Wider Implications of the Single Europe Act*, Routledge.
Welford, R. and Prescott, K. (1996) *European Business*, 3rd edition, Pitman Publishing.

Additional reading

Brooks, I. and Weatherston, J. (1997) *The Business Environment*, Prentice-Hall.
Eurostat, Statistics, various issues.
Gatley, S., Lessem, R. and Altman, Y. (1996) *Comparative Management*, McGraw-Hill.
Hoecklin, L. (1995) *Managing Cultural Differences*, Addison-Wesley.
Hofstede, G. (1984) *Culture's Consequences: International Differences in Work-Related Values*, Sage Publications.
Ohmae, K. (1989) Managing in a borderless world, *Harvard Business Review*, Vol. 67(3).
Porter, M. E. (1980) *Competitive Strategy and Techniques for Analysing Industry and Competitors*, Free Press.
Randlesome, C. *et al.* (1990) *Business Cultures in Europe*, Heinemann.
Rugman, A. M. and Hodgetts, R. M. (1995) *International Business*, McGraw-Hill.
Tsoukalis, L. (1993) *The New European Economy*, OUP.
Trompenaars, F. (1993) *Riding the Waves of Culture*, London Economist Books.

4 International trade

Introduction

Home producers gain in many ways from trading. Raw materials and semi-manufactured goods can be obtained at lower cost, and exporting brings higher profits and large-scale production (so reducing costs again). Exports and imports can smooth demand fluctuations in the domestic economy, and growth via exports could increase competition at home.

Escaping the domestic market could therefore reduce costs, improve quality and lead to higher sales and profits. As the advantages have become increasingly obvious and transport and distribution have improved so markedly, so trade has grown.

Given the importance of trade to businesses, this chapter will look at how trade theory attempts to explain why countries trade, in which goods and with whom. It will consider both 'traditional' and more recent theories and look at how their predictions relate to trade in practice. The real beginning of trade theory is usually seen as Adam Smith's basic principle of exchange, but the mercantilist theory of trade predates this.

Mercantilism

The major school of thought from the 16th to mid-18th century was called mercantilism. Mercantilists believed that the more gold and silver a country had, the richer and more powerful it was. Exports were seen as 'good' since they brought in gold and silver (i.e. wealth) and stimulated industry to produce more. Imports, on the other hand, were 'bad' since they reduced demand at home and led to gold and silver flowing out of the country. Basically the mercantilists encouraged countries to export more than they imported. It was proposed, therefore, that exports should be encouraged using such things as state subsidies, and imports discouraged by means of tariffs and quotas.

Under this theory, trade could be advantageous to one party alone. As the supply of precious metals was relatively fixed, a nation could only increase its stock of gold at the expense of other nations. Moreover, it was impossible for all countries to possess trade surpluses.

The mercantilists' theory did little to explain the basic questions of international trade, i.e. questions such as which goods are exported and imported, and by whom. There was also no consideration of what determines the prices at which exchange of exports and imports takes place, i.e. the terms of trade. Adam Smith was the first to address these questions and in doing so attacked the mercantilist view of trade. Taking the arguments he had formulated regarding specialisation and division of labour, he applied them to international trade, producing the principle of absolute advantage.

Absolute advantage

In essence, the principle of absolute advantage suggests that some countries are better, or more efficient, at producing certain commodities and less efficient at producing other goods when compared with other countries. In theory, all will gain if they specialise in the product that they produce efficiently (in which they have an absolute advantage), and trade for the other products (in which they have an absolute disadvantage).

For example, if we assume Belgium is more efficient at producing chocolates than the UK but the UK is more efficient in the production of cheese, then Belgium should produce chocolates and trade these with the UK in exchange for cheese; similarly the UK should produce and trade cheese for chocolates. Such international specialisation and exchange will increase output of both chocolates and cheese, thereby allowing both countries to enjoy a higher standard of living.

Smith also stressed that the greater resources achieved would be allocated efficiently by the market. Any interference in this process would reduce these gains. Accordingly, therefore, all countries would benefit from free trade and a policy of **laissez faire**.

At the root of Smith's theory of trade can be found the **labour theory of value**. In a closed economy, with labour the only factor of production, goods exchange according to the relative amounts of labour embodied in them. If it takes twice as much labour to make a TV than to make a vacuum cleaner, then one TV should exchange for two vacuum cleaners.

Obviously this is an oversimplification; labour is not homogeneous, due to different labour skills, and it is not the only relevant factor of production. However, as will be seen later, to discard this assumption has little effect on the conclusion of the theory; it is merely a simplifying factor. Bearing this assumption in mind, therefore, how does Smith's theory actually work?

Let us assume there are only two countries – France and Germany; two goods – clothing and beer; perfect competition; and one factor of production – labour. As it is homogeneous, labour can be used to produce either clothing or beer in both countries. Let us assume both countries can produce clothing or beer in the quantities shown in Table 4.1.

From Table 4.1 we can see that Germany has an absolute advantage over France in producing beer but France has an absolute advantage in clothing. Without international trade, one unit of beer will exchange for two units of clothing in Germany and one unit of beer for six units of clothing in France.

Table 4.1 Example of absolute advantage

	Output per unit of labour (per day)	
	Beer (B)	Clothing (C)
France	2	12
Germany	4	8

It can also be seen that beer is relatively cheap in Germany (1B = 2C) and expensive in France (1B = 6C). The opposite exists for clothing: in Germany, 1C = $\frac{1}{2}$B but in France, 1C = $\frac{1}{6}$B. Obviously it would be profitable to buy at a low price and sell at a high one; therefore it pays to buy German beer and sell this in France and to buy French clothing and sell in Germany. Let us assume the terms of trade settle at 1B = 3C: if Germany exports two units of beer to France, it will receive in exchange six units of clothing. Domestically Germany can only exchange 2B for 4C, thereby it gains 2C. Similarly, France gains 1B because domestically 6C can only exchange for 1B, not 2B. Both countries benefit from trade.

Absolute advantage, however, can really explain only a small proportion of world trade today. Even at the beginning of the 19th century problems with the theory were becoming obvious and out of these grew Ricardo's theory of comparative advantage.

Comparative advantage

The theory of comparative advantage showed that, even if absolute advantage did not always exist, all countries could benefit from trading as long as a comparative advantage existed. Suppose we have the situation shown in Table 4.2.

Germany has an absolute advantage in both commodities. Without trade, 1B will again exchange for 2C in Germany and 1B for 6C in France. Again, would trade still benefit both countries now? According to Ricardo, yes. Comparative advantage is all that is necessary for both to benefit.

A country has a comparative advantage in a commodity when it has a higher degree of superiority in its production and it has a comparative disadvantage in a commodity when its degree of superiority is lower, relative to another country. In our example, Germany's degree of superiority in beer is 8B:2B, which is greater than its superiority in clothing, 16C:12C. Germany thus has comparative advantage in beer and comparative disadvantage in clothing. France has comparative advantage in clothing because 12C:16C is greater than 2B:8B.

Table 4.2 Example of comparative advantage

	Output per unit of labour	
	Beer	Clothing
France	2	12
Germany	8	16

So we get the law of comparative advantage: each country should specialise in producing the good in which it has a comparative advantage and total world output of all goods will increase. All countries will gain.

How does this work? Let us say the terms of trade are 1B = 3C: then Germany sells 4B for 12C. Germany gains 4C as it would only get 8C at home; France gains 2B because it would only get 2B not 4B for 12C at home. So as long as comparative advantage exists free trade will benefit all. On the very rare occasion when a comparative advantage does not exist then there is no gain from trade.

The above system, however, is based on **barter**. How does this change when we bring in money? World trade is then determined not by differences in labour costs but by differences in money prices. We now need to transform these labour cost differences into money price differences.

We have seen above how France has a comparative advantage in clothing, but the problem we face now is, if Germany is more efficient absolutely, how can the cost of clothing be lower in France than in Germany in money terms? Wages are the key. When French wages are sufficiently below those of Germany this is a possibility. For example, if the German wage is DM120 per day, the average cost of producing one unit of beer will be DM15 (DM120/8 units) and the average cost of clothing per unit, DM7.5 (DM120/16 units). If we also assume the French wage is Ffr180 per day, the average cost of production in France is Ffr90 per unit of beer (180/2) and Ffr15 per unit of clothing (180/12). Is beer cheaper in Germany or France?

To consider this we need to express prices in terms of the same currency; we need the exchange rate. Table 4.3 assumes DM1 = Ffr3.

Beer is cheaper in Germany in both currencies, but clothing is cheaper in France. As we have seen above, each country will specialise accordingly and relative prices determine trade.

Given the wage rates of DM120 and Ffr180, this pattern of specialisation will remain, provided the exchange rate remains favourable (between DM1 = Ffr2 and DM1 = Ffr6). Above DM1 = Ffr6, both commodities are cheaper in France; for example, if DM1 = Ffr7, we get the situation shown in Table 4.4.

Both commodities are cheaper in France, so there is no basis for trade. If the exchange rate was 1DM = Ffr1.5, the situation shown in Table 4.5 would result. Both commodities are cheaper in Germany, so there would be no gain for Germany in trading. Obviously, the nearer the exchange rate is to DM1 = Ffr6, the more Germany will gain from exchange, and the nearer to DM1 = Ffr2 the more France would gain.

Table 4.3 Example of comparative advantage – money prices 1

| | Germany | | France | |
	DM*	Ffr	Ffr	DM*
Beer	15	45	90	30
Clothing	7.5	22.5	15	5

* DM1 = Ffr3.

Table 4.4 Example of comparative advantage – money prices 2

	Germany		France	
	DM*	Ffr	Ffr	DM*
Beer	15	105	90	12.9
Clothing	7.5	52.5	15	2.1

*DM1 = Ffr7

Table 4.5 Example of comparative advantage – money prices 3

	Germany		France	
	DM*	Ffr	Ffr	DM*
Beer	15	22.5	90	60
Clothing	7.5	11.25	15	10

*DM1 = Ffr1.5

As already pointed out above, the theory depends on the assumption of the very questionable labour theory of value. If we use Haberler's (1936) theory of **opportunity costs** then we can drop this assumption but still keep its results.

Opportunity costs are the costs of opportunities given up. In our example Germany must give up 2C in order to produce one more unit of beer – the opportunity cost of beer is 2C. In France the opportunity cost of beer is 6C. Therefore Germany has a comparative cost advantage in beer as it is cheaper (2C < 6C). The lowest-cost producer of beer has a comparative advantage in beer. The opportunity cost of clothing compared with beer is merely the reciprocal of the opportunity cost of beer compared with clothing. The opportunity cost of clothing is $\frac{1}{2}$B in Germany and $\frac{1}{6}$B in France, and as $\frac{1}{2}$B > $\frac{1}{6}$B France has a comparative cost advantage in clothing.

An empirical study of comparative advantage

As part of his study 'Gains and Losses from 1992', Neven (1990) calculated the revealed comparative advantage (CA) between EC countries for products using various factors of production – labour, capital, human capital and natural resources.

Table 4.6 shows that the CA of Portugal and Greece lies in labour-intensive goods, and these are exchanged for goods intensive in human capital. Similarly, Italy has a CA in labour-intensive goods but does not have a comparative disadvantage (CD) in goods using human capital intensively as do Portugal and Greece.

A CA in natural resource-based industries seems to exist in Ireland, Denmark and to a lesser extent in Portugal, the Netherlands and Belgium. Germany and France seem to have some CA in industries using human capital. Furthermore Belgium, and to a lesser extent Italy, have a CA in capital-intensive products.

Finally, the figures suggest that the UK, and to a slightly lesser extent France, has no clear CA or CD in any category of products within the EC. This suggests its stocks of factors of production are probably in line with the community aver-

Table 4.6 Revealed comparative advantage: net exports/domestic output (adjusted for overall trade balances) (%)

	Natural resources	Average capital/ average labour	High labour	High capital	High human capital
Belgium	7.5	8.4	−91.8	18.3	−10.3
Denmark	28.5	−11.6	−26.5	−9.1	n/a
France	1.7	−2.6	−9.8	0.2	1.4
Germany	−4.0	−0.4	−26.2	−20.0	5.8
Greece	−1.7	7.0	80.0	−1.3	−98.7
Ireland	16.5	−9.1	−61.3	−9.5	11.2
Italy	−14.9	6.1	36.1	3.1	−5.2
Netherlands	12.0	n/a	−74.4	−17.2	−10.1
Portugal	12.2	4.4	79.4	10.2	−35.8
Spain	0.6	2.4	8.7	2.4	−6.6
UK	−0.8	1.0	−2.2	2.8	−4.8

Source: Neven (1990) p. 26.

age. 'They are not particularly good at anything but they are not particularly bad either, relative to their EC partners' (Neven 1990).

Neven concludes, therefore, that specialisation within the EC occurs between North and South, not North and North, and the factors of production which appear to give strong advantage and disadvantage are labour and human capital, respectively; physical capital appears to give little CA.

Criticisms of the comparative advantage theory

Criticisms mainly surround the sweeping assumptions on which the theory is based, especially those regarding technology. For example, CA assumes perfect substitutability of labour and capital, yet this is not always possible. There is a limit to the transferability of factors of production from one use to another – eventually the costs will outweigh the benefits of specialisation. For example, if highly skilled agricultural workers were transferred to high-technology computer industries, it is likely that efficiency would decline quite quickly. Ricardo and Smith also ignored transport costs, yet high transport costs could rule out theoretical comparative advantage. A further, and more obvious, criticism concerns full employment – a not very realistic assumption.

Other criticisms could be made of the assumptions, but a more basic problem is that comparative advantage suggests that trade is based on different costs, but it does not explain what leads to these differences in comparative costs. A suggested solution to this question came about a century afterwards in the **Heckscher–Ohlin theory**.

Heckscher–Ohlin theory

The Heckscher–Ohlin theory assumes that not only was there more than one factor of production (e.g. land, labour and capital), but also that different goods require different proportions of the various factors of production. Basically, some goods are labour-intensive, some land-intensive and some capital-intensive.

Furthermore, different countries have different amounts of factors of production (or endowments) and these result in different relative factor prices. This means that if a country has a great deal of land, land-intensive goods (i.e. agricultural goods) should be relatively cheap to produce and the country will have a comparative advantage in land-intensive products. According to this theory, Argentina, Australia and Canada, with plenty of land, should export land-intensive goods such as meat, wheat and wool. The same can be argued for labour-intensive and capital-intensive countries. For example, labour-abundant countries such as India, Korea and Taiwan should export labour-intensive goods such as footwear, rugs and textiles, whereas capital-intensive countries such as Germany and Japan should export capital-intensive goods such as computers and cameras. This leads to the basic Heckscher–Ohlin conclusion – that countries should specialise in the goods which use intensively the factor of production which they have in abundance.

The Heckscher–Ohlin theory is based on a number of assumptions. It is a two factors of production–two goods–two countries model. There is no product differentiation, only that one good is capital–intensive and the other is labour-intensive, and production functions are identical in each country. In addition there are constant returns to scale, and all countries are assumed to have access to the same technology. Factors of production are perfectly mobile inter-country, but they are immobile outside countries. All consumers have the same tastes and all product and factor markets are assumed perfectly competitive, with no transport costs or barriers to trade. Finally, neither country, it is assumed, will specialise completely in the production of one commodity but produce both to some extent. Many criticisms surround these assumptions, but the biggest problem for the Heckscher–Ohlin theory came with the Leontief paradox.

The Leontief paradox

Leontief (1954) tried to apply the Heckscher–Ohlin theory to reality. He used US data for 1947, at which time the USA had higher capital per head than all its trading partners. According to the Heckscher–Ohlin theory, therefore, the USA should export capital-intensive goods and import labour-intensive goods. Leontief attempted to prove this.

Leontief estimated the capital and labour requirements needed to produce a representative bundle of $1 million of US exports and $1 million US home import-competing commodities. His study showed that the capital:labour ratio was approximately $14 000 per worker year in the export industries and $18 100 for import-competing industries. Therefore the USA import-competing production required 30 per cent more capital than its exports. Exports from the USA were, therefore, more labour-intensive than imports into the USA – the opposite prediction to Heckscher–Ohlin. The world's most capital-intensive country was exporting labour-intensive goods. Why? Was the Heckscher—Ohlin theorem wrong? Perhaps factor endowments do not determine trade. This is one conclusion which could be drawn.

Many alternative explanations have been suggested, however. One such suggestion is that Leontief picked unrepresentative data as 1947 was a period of post-war reconstruction. The exercise was, however, repeated in 1951 and the same results were obtained. Later work has suggested that 'the paradox' disappeared by the early 1970s, although this does not dismiss the early problem. There is little reason to doubt that capital-abundant countries sometimes, temporarily, export labour-intensive goods.

Furthermore, the USA was highly protected against trade in 1947. If these **tariffs** were aimed at labour-intensive goods then the only chance of exporting to the USA would be by selling capital-intensive goods. Baldwin (1971) showed both tariff and non-tariff barriers operated in the direction of the Leontief paradox but these can only partly explain it.

An alternative explanation is that of factor intensity reversal. Heckscher–Ohlin suggests that one commodity is capital-intensive (cars) compared with the other (furniture) in all countries all of the time. However, cars could be capital-intensive in some countries but labour-intensive in others. This is referred to as factor intensity reversal. If cars are capital-intensive in Spain, but labour-intensive in Germany, and then labour-abundant Spain exports furniture (its labour-intensive commodity) to Germany. To pay for it, Germany must export cars, but cars are labour-intensive in Germany. So Germany is both importing and exporting labour-intensive products. So we get the Leontief paradox. In reality, however, there is little evidence to suggest this is commonplace.

Heckscher–Ohlin is, however, purely a supply-side theory – demand conditions are totally ignored. The Leontief paradox could, therefore, be explained by demand conditions in the USA. There may be strong preferences for capital-intensive goods in the USA and such demand could exceed domestic supply, therefore it must import such goods. Various studies suggest, however, that there is considerable similarity in demand functions between countries and this consumption bias cannot account for much of the Leontief paradox.

Leontief proposed his own answer to the paradox. He suggested that US workers were three times more productive than workers in other countries and, if this was taken into account, the USA was really a labour-abundant country. This suggestion was supported by Kreinin's (1965) study but to nowhere near the extent. Kreinin found an approximately 20–25 per cent superiority, not the 300 per cent that Leontief claimed. This would not make the US a labour-abundant country.

Finally, Heckscher–Ohlin ignored certain factors of production. Vanek (1963) pointed out that natural resources were not considered, yet in 1947 the USA was importing a lot of metals and minerals which it had previously exported (especially oil) and the production of such resources needs considerable capital. When it began importing such products, the USA began importing a great deal of capital – hence the Leontief paradox. If natural resources are included, some of the paradox disappears (Baldwin 1971) but not all of it.

Similarly, Leontief did not include human capital in his notion of labour – all labour has the same skill. It is argued, therefore, that the USA was a skill-abundant country, with a comparative advantage in skill-intensive, not in labour-intensive, commodities, so explaining the Leontief paradox.

Having looked at 'traditional' theories, and before looking at the newer theories, we should now ask what the facts are concerning international trade in the 1980s and early 1990s.

World trade flows

As can be seen in Fig. 4.1, a high percentage of trade takes place within the industrialised countries. This has been a feature of trade which has been increasing since the Second World War. For example, $2667.3 billion of world trade comes from the developed country sector; however, only $92.9 billion and $417.2 billion comes from the Eastern European and less developed country (LDC) sectors. The growing sector of the world economy, South East Asia, still accounted for only $490.2 billion of trade in 1992.

If we look more specifically at the EU we can see the same sort of pattern. Figure 4.2 shows that most (63.2 per cent) of EU trade occurs within the union.

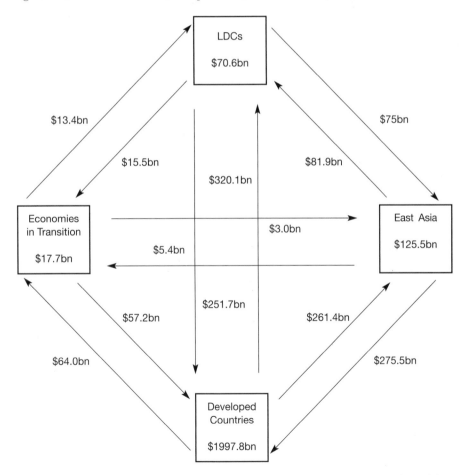

Figure 4.1 Direction of world trade: the annual average of exports, 1992 (adapted from *OECD Economic Outlook* No. 59, June 1996)

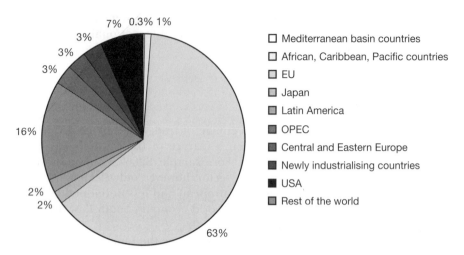

Figure 4.2 World trade with the EU: the annual average of exports, 1992 (adapted from *OECD Statistics,* various editions)

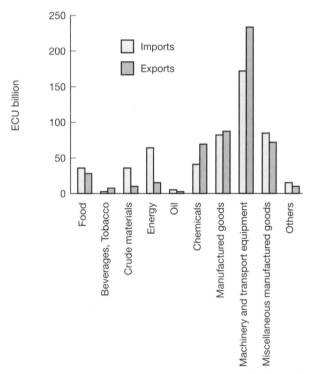

Figure 4.3 EU imports and exports by product (in ECU billion) (adapted from *Eurostat External Trade Statistics*)

It is interesting, however, to break down these figures and see what commodities are traded by the EU. We can see that in many commodity groups the EU exports and imports similar amounts (Fig. 4.3). There is no sign that some goods are imported and others exported. This type of trade between countries

Table 4.7 Average intra-industry trade indices (%)

	UK	Ger	Bel	Fra	Neth	Ita	Den	Spa	Ire	Por	Gre
UK	–	73	73	79	77	64	63	57	70	40	41
Germany	73	–	74	74	63	58	71	58	59	36	35
Belgium	73	74	–	72	77	54	55	59	50	40	36
France	79	74	72	–	63	63	50	63	48	40	36
Netherlands	77	63	77	63	–	41	67	53	52	39	37
Italy	64	58	54	63	41	–	46	60	47	39	44
Denmark	63	71	55	50	67	46	–	39	55	47	31
Spain	57	58	59	63	53	60	39	–	40	29	28
Ireland	70	59	50	48	52	47	55	40	–	46	19
Portugal	40	36	40	39	39	47	29	46	25	25	25
Greece	41	35	36	37	44	31	28	19	25	31	–

Source: Neven (1990) page 21.

producing similar products is referred to as intra-industry trade. Obviously this contradicts the Heckscher–Ohlin theory.

The study by Neven (1990) mentioned earlier attempted to measure intra-industry EC trade. Neven worked out an index for 29 industries representing the whole manufacturing sector and trade flows within the EC. The results are shown in Table 4.7, which gives the average intra-industry trade indices as percentages.

It can be seen that both Greece and Portugal have lower percentages of bilateral EC trade compared with other EC countries. This could be due to their later entry into the EC (although Spain seems less affected) but it also suggests that the two countries have different factor endowments leading to the production of different goods compared with the other EC countries. At the other end of the spectrum, Germany, France, the UK, the Netherlands and Belgium show signs of very high levels of intra-industry trade, mainly with each other. The results for Ireland, Spain and Italy are less decisive.

Finally, in the post-war period, two other possibly contradictory features in international trade have occurred. Firstly, there has been increasing liberalisation of trade (see Chapter 5) but secondly there has also been a growth of economic integration or intra-bloc trade (see Chapter 6).

The growth of trading blocs is shown by Fig. 4.4, where the number of regional agreements is seen to have increased dramatically between 1990 and 1994 (as notified to GATT). Similarly, the percentage of merchandise trade (exports and imports) to trade in specific regions has grown: 69.9 per cent in Western Europe in 1993 compared with 52.8 per cent in 1958; 33 per cent in North America compared with 31.5 per cent in 1941 and 16.8 per cent in Latin America, and 41.11 per cent to 49.7 per cent in Asia. The growth of trading blocs in Western Europe shows the effect of the EU.

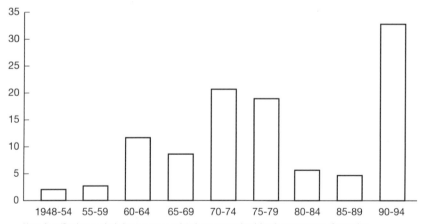

Note: A notification may include one or more related agreements involving the same group of countries. Figures include agreements which are not currently in force.

Figure 4.4 Regional agreements 1948–94 (adapted from WTO 1993, page 9)

This, of course, links up with our first feature of trade – the growth of trade between industrialised countries – and can be a partial explanation for this. However, even given this fact, we can see that traditional theories have been found somewhat wanting. The result has been a plethora of new theories to explain the post-war modern 'facts' of international trade.

Case study: Automobile and clothing trade

The structure of automobile trade in the world strongly reflects the dominance by developed countries of world trade. Approximately 95 per cent of world automobile trade comes from three areas: North America, Europe and Asia. In fact, 36 per cent of world exports come from Germany and Japan alone. Furthermore, intra-regional trade comprises 76 per cent of Western European trade, 74 per cent of North American but only 26 per cent of Asian trade.

In clothing exports, however, the picture is different. Here the developing world has increased production greatly in the 1980s – especially the so-called 'second generation' newly industrialising economies. The Philippines, Malaysia and Indonesia have especially grown into this area, but China's growth here has also been substantial. Italy and Germany, however, were pulling out of this sector in 1995. The destinations of these exports are dominated by Western Europe and North America; in fact, 50 per cent of EU imports and almost 66 per cent of US imports come from Asia. 'It is in the clothing sector that the greatest degree of penetration of developed country markets by developing country producers has occurred' (Dicken 1998). However, there is still a substantial amount of trade between the developed world as well.

Source: Dicken, P. (1998) *Global Shift*, Paul Chapman Publishing.

Questions

1 Can comparative advantage explain either or both automobile and clothing trade patterns?

2 Why do you think so little of Asian trade in automobiles is intra-regional?

3 Why has China grown so substantially in the clothing sector?

Increasing returns and imperfect competition

One explanation of intra-industry trade has been that modern industries tend to be dominated by large industrial units and thereby gain various economies of scale. This obviously means that modern industry is typified by increasing, not constant returns to scale – the assumption of both Ricardo and Heckscher–Ohlin theories.

If firms concentrate on the domestic market then there will be limited economies of scale. Trade, as we have seen already, allows specialisation in a narrower range of products, and production can exceed that necessary for the domestic market, thereby allowing further economies of scale to be reaped through larger plants and larger production runs. A good example of this is through a comparison of Europe before and after the formation of the EEC. Before the formation, EEC industrial plants tended to be small and catered for the domestic market. The EEC allowed firms to expand and trade; they grew in size, their costs fell and there was an increase in efficiency (see Chapter 6).

These reduced costs due to economies of scale are a reason for, or determinant of, trade in itself. Normally, however, a situation where scale economies exist will also be one of imperfect competition. This is where firms have some power over the price charged – it is not totally determined by the market. This usually occurs because the goods are made to be different (e.g. via packaging, adverts, etc.) and this differentiation prevents substitution. Alternatively, we could see economies of scale, which mean lower costs per unit, as bringing imperfect competition in that they give large firms an advantage over smaller firms and consequently market power.

Trade will enlarge the domestic market to an international market so increasing the number of firms, but at the same time, each can produce on a greater scale so reducing average costs.

Trade, therefore, allows increased competition and economies of scale and enables countries to gain a greater variety of goods at lower prices. Basically, as Krugman (1987) summarises it, 'the presence of increasing returns increases rather than reduces the gains from international trade' and 'by creating larger, more competitive markets, trade may reduce the distortions that would have been associated with imperfect competition in a closed economy.' Such a view supports the traditional belief that free trade is best. What it also suggests, however, is that free trade is best in a second-best world (i.e. an imperfectly competitive world). Such a view has serious implications for trade policy as it does not totally reject interventionist policies.

Linder's preference similarity hypothesis

The preceding theory of increasing returns is not the only explanation of post-war trade patterns. Linder (1961) put forward another explanation. He said a country will export the manufactured products for which it has a good domestic market. Why? Three reasons lie behind this conclusion:

1 A good domestic market gives producers a greater awareness of the opportunities for profit with their product.

2 Any research and development undertaken by firms is aimed at satisfying obvious needs – usually made obvious through the domestic market.

3 Even if a firm recognises the profitable opportunities within the foreign market, it is often expensive to develop or adapt a product to fit an unfamiliar market.

It therefore follows, according to Linder, that the range of products which a country exports will be a subset of the range supplied and consumed in the domestic market. Similarly, the products which a country imports will have a close resemblance to the products it already consumes. Whether these products are imported or produced domestically depends on the relative price of imports compared with domestic goods. This suggests that trade will take place between similar countries in similar products.

Linder also asked what determines the demand structure. The most important influence is per capita income. The higher the per capita income, the higher the demand for high-quality and luxury consumer goods and more sophisticated capital goods. Lower per capita income means more demand for necessary consumer goods and less sophisticated capital goods. So if a country is rich, it will have a comparative advantage in quality goods for the above reasons and will therefore export them to other rich countries, where their big export markets are (due to their overlapping demand structure).

There will be some overlapping demand with some poor countries and rich ones due to unequal distribution of income, so the richer sections of the populations in LDCs will buy luxury goods from developed countries. Therefore income, taste and demand patterns generally determine trade. This leads to the conclusion that the closer the overlap between two countries' consumption patterns, the higher the potential for trade.

It should perhaps be stressed at this point that Linder's theory is an attempt to explain the trade in manufactured goods; it does not cover primary product trade. For this, Linder suggested that the basic nature of primary products ensures the export potential is easily recognisable. However, it is often foreign entrepreneurs who provide the initial impetus to these exports, possibly because they are more aware of the demand for these products in their home country.

Linder's theory, therefore, explains intra-industry trade from a demand side point of view. It does ignore the supply side, however (the opposite problem to the Heckscher–Ohlin theory). We must also question whether it is realistic to assume that countries cannot appreciate foreign demand and respond to it, or that a country's natural advantages in some goods will not be exploited due to limited demand from the home market. There are also a number of cases which do not fit in with Linder's theory. For example, why does South Korea export Christmas ornaments to the UK when there is little to no domestic market for them? One explanation could lie in Linder's explanation of primary product trade, i.e. that foreign importers, aware of demand at home, look for low-cost sources of supply and encourage production abroad in places such as Hong Kong. If we accept this view the reason for trade lies in the lower cost element, not only demand.

Finally, two other models attempting to explain empirical evidence on trade are based on the question of technology. These models attempt to make traditional theory more dynamic.

Posner's technological gap theory

Posner's (1961) technological gap theory suggests that innovation and imitation are especially important for exports. New products are developed, they become profitable, thereby giving firms a temporary monopoly, and this leads to easy access to foreign markets. Initially, the level of exports grows, but growing profits bring imitation elsewhere, gradually eroding the comparative advantage. Once this has been lost the firm or industry will search for another new product and so a new cycle of innovation and imitation begins. The innovating country will continue to develop new products and to have temporary absolute advantage in these, but eventually other countries will produce them more efficiently. Therefore Posner's explanation of patterns of trade is based around different innovations occurring through time.

Posner's theory, however, fails to explain why this technological gap exists and the size of the gap. A generalised version of this theory was suggested by Vernon (1970) in the context of a product's life-cycle.

Vernon's product-cycle model

Vernon (1970) stressed how some countries have better access to technology than others – they have a comparative advantage in 'high-tech' goods. Without such technology a country could not compete in this market. There is a link to Linder's theory in the first stage, as the producers become more aware of using technology through its possible use in the home market.

Vernon suggests that a product goes through three stages: it starts off as a new product, then becomes a maturing one and finally a standardised one. In the new product stage the product is produced in response to domestic demand and marketed in the domestic market, thereby allowing the production techniques and the product itself to be tested. It also requires more skilled labour in this development stage.

In the maturing stage the product gradually becomes standardised and mass production begins to take place. Less skilled labour is necessary and capital becomes more important. At this stage the product will be marketed internationally; producers will look for similar markets in other similar countries as export markets. As exports increase, producers will then start to look at the possibility of locating nearer, or in, these markets. The final stage is one of more advanced standardisation. Factors such as production and location costs are more important in location decisions and it is more likely that the product will be made in other countries and imported into the original producing country. Gradually production in, and export from, the original market ceases and production is shifted elsewhere, often to LDCs. It should be pointed out that this process will vary according to the product considered.

The conclusions reached by this theory are that different countries will export different products over time; similarly, different countries will export the same good as it moves through its life-cycle.

An example of Vernon's theory is seen in the market for colour TV receivers (Baker 1990). The market started in 1954 in the United States, and in the early years the market for receivers was dominated by domestic producers. In 1967, imports were 6 per cent of the market but only three years later these amounted to 19 per cent (over 90 per cent of which were from Japan). Later, as the technology spread to other countries, imports from Taiwan and Korea began to challenge the Japanese imports and these fell to 80 per cent of the imports by 1977 and 50 per cent a year later.

A further, more long-term example of the product life-cycle theory is the textile industry. Britain at first had a technological advantage (at the time of the Industrial Revolution). Gradually the technology spread to the USA and production moved accordingly. Then, as production became increasingly standardised, costs became more important and production moved towards LDCs, especially Asia. Even within Asia, production is now shifting from the higher wage centres of Hong Kong and Singapore towards the lower wage centres of Malaysia, the Philippines and China (Yarbrough and Yarbrough 1997).

The usefulness of Vernon's theory to modern times has, however, been questioned. It sees producers as operating in their home markets and responding initially to this market, which is separate from other national markets. The growth of multinational companies catering for a global market has brought the relevance of the theory into question. It does, however, still have relevance for the inventive and innovative small firms. These may begin by concentrating on the home market but they eventually begin to export to find new markets for their goods. Similarly, we can also relate LDC trade to this theory. Moreover, it does have important points to make: that it is unwise for countries to attempt always to remain competitive in products in which they initially had an advantage; and that an element of a country's success in international trade could be how mobile its resources are between sectors: the more mobile, the more successful.

European trade

The importance of trade to EU countries is shown in Table 4.8, which illustrates the dependence of various EU countries on trade, as shown by exports as a percentage of GDP.

Table 4.8 Exports as a percentage of GDP, 1994

EU		Other Europe (1991)		Others	
Belgium	75.2%	Norway	45.0%	Hong Kong	141.0%
Denmark	30.7%	Switzerland	35.0%	Singapore	185.0%
Germany	25.8%			India	9.0%
Greece	11.7%			China	20.0%
Spain	16.0%			Japan	10.0%
France	21.6%			USA	11.0%
Ireland	69.5%				
Italy	18.1%				
Netherlands	53.7%				
Austria	28.0%				
Portugal (1993)	27.5%				
Finland	25.5%				
Sweden	29.2%				
UK	21.3%				

Source: Husted and Melvin (1995) *International Economics*, 3rd edition pages 5–6; Eurostat (1994) *External Trade*.

These figures show a very varied dependence on trade within the EU. It is not really surprising that the smaller countries, such as Belgium, Ireland and the Netherlands, should exhibit such a high reliance on trade within their economies. The table also shows, however, that trade is highly important to the larger economies of France, Germany and the UK – all with over 20 per cent of their GDP relying on external trade.

Case study: European trade

A study undertaken by the European Commission into the competitiveness of European industry with regard to trade concluded with the following results.

Generally the EU was less specialised than Japan and the USA, and there were a number of weaknesses sectorally and geographically. Sectors which accounted for over 3 per cent of total world exports represented only less than 30 per cent of EU total manufacturing exports, whereas the equivalent figures were 51 per cent for USA and 62 per cent for Japan. Exports were more uniformly spread in the EU.

Mechanical engineering was found to be the largest export sector (16 per cent total EU exports), automotive equipment was second with 8.7 per cent, and food third with 6.5 per cent. Chemicals (especially speciality chemicals), pharmaceuticals and electrical engineering (especially industrial electrical equipment) were also prominent. However, most sectors where the EU had a strong competitive advantage had below 3 per cent EU manufacturing exports, whereas Japan's strong sectors accounted for over 8 per cent of its exports.

Furthermore there were worrying weaknesses in the EU's largest export sectors – mechanical engineering and automotive equipment – where import share was falling and costs development was poor.

Similarly the geographical structure of trade was weak, with less specialism in the fast-growth areas (1987–93) of NICs, China, Central and Eastern Europe and Latin America. These accounted for 23 per cent of EU, 35 per cent of US and 42 per cent of Japanese, exports in 1993, whereas the four slow-growth areas, EFTA, rest of the world (e.g. OPEC, Africa) and other Asia accounted for 40 per cent, 27 per cent and 27 per cent in the EU, USA and Japan, respectively.

Finally, the EU took clear technical dominance in research and development, ,and traditional areas were being challenged.

Source: adapted from: European Commission (1995) *Panorama of EU Industry.*

Questions

1 How serious is the above for EU trade?

2 What can the EU do to overcome this?

The importance of trade to companies – a study of some European companies

Trade is obviously important to most European countries and therefore is likely to be important to most European firms, but how important? We can see this through a sample of major UK companies. Guinness, Cadbury Schweppes, Grand Metropolitan, Body Shop and BP, for example, had over 50 per cent of their sales in export markets in 1995/96. Other firms such as Bass, Hillsdown and Laura Ashley rely more heavily on the domestic market, although overseas sales are still a substantial element of total sales.

It is also interesting to note the destination of the goods. Europe is an obvious market for many companies but for others (such as Cadbury Schweppes, Grand Metropolitan, Body Shop and Laura Ashley) North America is also a vital market. However, the Asian market is less significant in many instances – although still very important to Unilever, Guinness, Thorn EMI and BICC.

The pattern of trade for companies obviously varies but, not surprisingly, most UK companies find their main market in Europe and to some extent the USA, mirroring the patterns of countries seen earlier. Asia, Africa and Australia are less important.

Conclusion

Trade is a vital part of all EU economies and companies, and is becoming a very important feature in Central and Eastern Europe also. Various theories have attempted to explain why trade occurs, between which countries and in which goods. Each has played its part in contributing to our knowledge of the pattern of trade. Each, however, assumes that free trade exists. As the next chapter shows, this is a huge assumption.

Questions for discussion

1 How useful is the theory of comparative advantage to our understanding of international trade in reality?

2 Assume that the production capacity of the Netherlands and Denmark in two goods – bacon and lager – is as follows:

	Lager (000s barrels/day)	Bacon (000s rashers/day)
Netherlands	20	50
Denmark	100	80

(a) Which country has a comparative advantage in which product? Explain your conclusion.

(b) What rate of exchange would Denmark prefer and why?

(c) What rate of exchange would the Netherlands prefer and why?

(d) What rate of exchange is likely?

(e) Prove that both will gain if they follow the principle of comparative advantage. Use the example of Denmark selling 30 000 barrels of lager and a rate of exchange, or terms of trade, of 1L = 1.5B (L = lager and B = bacon).

3 The Netherlands exports Heineken beer and imports Lowenbrau. What sort of trade is this an example of?

4 Using Fig. 4.1, work out the various percentages of trade within and between the areas. Which theories explain these best?

5 What differences has the growth of trading blocs had on world trade patterns?

6 Can you apply Vernon's product cycle theory to a particular product?

7 How important is trade to companies in your country?

Main reading

Chacholiades, M. (1990) *International Economics*, McGraw-Hill.
Hudsted, S. and Melvin, M. (1995) *International Economics*, 3rd edition. Harper & Row.
United Nations (1995) *World Economic Survey.*

Additional reading

Baker, S. A. (1990) *An Introduction to International Economics*, Harcourt Brace Jovanovich.
Baldwin, P. E. (1971) Determinants of the commodity structure of US trade, *American Economic Review*, Vol. 56 (June), pp. 466–73.
Donnelly, G. (1987) *International Economics*, Longman.
European Commission (1995) *Panorama of EC Industries*.
Eurostat (1996) *External Trade Statistics*, June.
Grimswade, N. (1989) *International Trade*, Routledge.
Harberler, G. (1936) *The Theory of International Trade*, W. Hodge & Co.
Kreinin, M. E. (1965) Comparative labour effectiveness and the Leontief scarce factor paradox, *American Economic Review*, Vol. 55 (March), pp. 131–40.
Krugman, P. R. (1987) Is free trade passé?' *Economic Perspectives*, Vol. 2.
Krugman, P. R. and Obstveld, F. (1991) *International Economics – Theory and Policy*, 2nd edition, HarperCollins.
Leontief, W. N. (1954) Domestic production and foreign trade: the American capital position re-examined, *Economic Internazionale*, Vol. 7 (Feb.) pp. 3–32.
Milner, C. and Greenaway, D. (1979) *An Introduction to International Economics*, Longman.
Neven, D. J. (1990) Gains and losses from 1992, *Economic Policy*, April, pp. 13–62.
Posner, M. V. (1961) International trade and technical change, *Oxford Economic Papers*, Vol. 17, p. 323.
Vanek, J. (1963) *The Natural Resource Content of Foreign Trade, 1870–1955*, The MIT Press, Cambridge, Mass.
Vernon, R. (1970) *The Technology Factor in International Trade*, Columbia University Press.
WTO (1995) Focus no. 3, May–June.
Yarbrough, B. V. and Yarbrough, R. M. (1997) *The World Economy*, 4th edition, Dryden Press.

The protection of trade

Introduction

One of the rationales for the formation of the EU in 1958 was a desire to transform several national markets into a single market, thereby increasing competition, fostering trade and economic welfare (see Chapter 9). Nevertheless, as in the rest of the world, trade within the EU has never been 'free'. Although members of the GATT/WTO, the European nations have used a number of protectionist measures relying historically on **tariffs**, although subsequently these have been replaced by **non-tariff barriers** to trade. In this chapter we examine the effects of tariffs on trade, discuss the role of the GATT/WTO in reducing this type of trade barrier, consider the development of GATT into the World Trade Organisation (WTO) and chart the growth of non-tariff barriers. Finally we look at the role of the WTO as a means of conducting orderly trading relations between the EU and the rest of the world, and examine the outcome of the last round of GATT trade talks – the Uruguay Round.

Arguments for free trade

In theory, international trade increases world efficiency by specialisation in production and exchange according to comparative advantage, given certain assumptions (see Chapter 4). In other words, a country that engages in international trade enjoys the benefits in terms of both immediate improvements in standards of living and economic growth. The standard of living that can be obtained exceeds that which would be available to a competitive economy which operates without trade (**autarky**). In addition, there may be political and economic benefits, in that as countries become more economically independent, they are less likely to undertake hostile actions. Nevertheless, countries still apply a variety of measures aimed at controlling the amount of free trade. Why then do countries ignore the obvious benefits of free trade policies?

In developed industrial economies, arguments for intervention in free trade include the following:

1 the danger of over-specialisation in a narrow range of products that follows from comparative advantage;

2 the preservation or encouragement of traditional industries;

3 strategic reasons, e.g. defence;

4 the protection of special interest groups such as agricultural sectors;

5 the protection of an infant industry;

6 the improvement of the terms of trade;

7 a countermeasure against dumping;

8 revenue reasons;

9 strategic trade policy;

10 gaining externalities (see Chapter 4).

In monetary terms the costs of protection are not always obvious. In the case of Argument 2 above, in the United States for example, the cost of protecting each job in the textile industry has been calculated to be roughly four times the average wage of a textile employee. In the case of Argument 5, the automobile industry in Korea, the production of commuter airplanes in Brazil, and the EU's protection of its video and compact disc markets, can be termed as successes in the protection of 'infant industries'. Such successes are rare and failure is all too common. Moreover the 'infant industry' argument as a form of protection has a number of problems:

1 The main beneficiaries of the import-substitution (infant industry) process in developing countries have been foreign firms which were able to locate behind tariff walls.

2 Often the process of attracting firms has involved heavy government-subsidised importation of capital goods and intermediate products by foreign and domestic companies. In response to this problem the developed countries, and the EU in particular, have specified **local content** factors, forcing many foreign firms to use a high proportion of domestic intermediate products in the production of a foreign firm's final product. Without such conditions foreign companies may simply be '**screwdriver operations**', importing the majority of their parts from abroad and merely putting them together in the country.

3 Many industries do not grow up and are content to hide behind protective tariffs with governments loathe to reduce tariffs.

> Countries therefore face a dichotomy. On the one hand free trade maximises efficiency, economic welfare, and provides the possibility of economies of scale ... Whilst on the other, some level of protection may be 'rational'. Furthermore, that which is economic fact may not be politically expedient ... for example, the impact of the liberalisation of trade may not affect all parties equally. Consumers may benefit from a £2–£3 reduction in prices but this may result in the loss of an entire industry. Trade barriers, it can be argued, can be justified politically if not on economic grounds.
>
> (Cook 1990, page 95)

Tariffs as a barrier to trade

Historically, the main form of trade protection has been the tariff. This can be levied as an **ad valorem** percentage of the value of imports or as a specific duty, (e.g. as so many pounds per tonne) or as a mix of both. The effect of a tariff on output and price is relatively simple to demonstrate.

In Fig. 5.1 the standard domestic demand and supply curves for an industry when there is no international trade are shown as D and S, respectively. The equilibrium home price and quantity are P_1 and Q_1. If our economy now indulged in international trade and is assumed to be small relative to the rest of the world, then it would face a horizontal or perfectly price-elastic demand curve for its product (i.e. it could buy or sell all it wanted at the world price without causing the world price to change). In such a situation domestic consumers would benefit from the lower price of imports, increasing their demand for the goods (from Q_1 to Q_3), whilst domestic producers would clearly be undercut and start losing business (from Q_1 to Q_2). The difference between the amount domestic producers are willing to produce and what domestic consumers wish to consume is made up by imports – the distance ab or $Q_2 - Q_3$. This detrimental effect may force the government to impose a tariff on imports in order to protect domestic producers.

The effects of a tariff (equal to t_0) are shown in the lower half of the diagram. The tariff leads to the domestic price being raised from P_2 to P_t. Domestic consumers reduce their demand for the commodity given the price rise from Q_3 to Q_5, whilst domestic producers expand output from Q_2 to Q_4. The area $cdfe$ measures the amount of revenue accruing to the government following the tariff. The imposition of a tariff imposes a cost on society. Consumer surplus is reduced from gbP_2 to gdP_t, and producers' surplus is increased by the area P_tcaP_2.

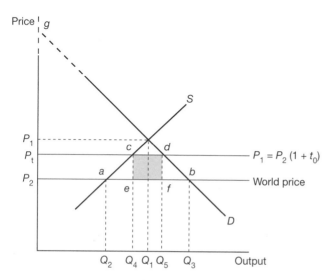

Figure 5.1 Effect of tariff on output and price

The resource misallocation costs of the tariff (called the deadweight loss of the tariff) are shown by the triangles *ace* and *dfb*. *ace* is the cost of supporting inefficient domestic industry, and *dfb* is the cost to consumers of paying a higher price. In the long run, because the domestic industry can grow behind the tariff barrier, it can achieve economies of scale and the increased supply will push down the world price.

Tariff protection is a familiar barrier to trade, and Table 5.1 shows the level of tariffs for a selected range of products for the USA, Japan, EU and EFTA countries.

Table 5.1 Tariff rates for selected countries and products, 1987 (percentage: weighted by own-country imports, excluding petroleum)

	Australia[a]	Austria	Benelux	Canada[a]	Denmark	Finland	France	West Germany	Ireland
Textiles	21.2	15.9	7.2	16.7	8.7	22.5	7.3	7.4	7.8
Wearing apparel	61.8	36.2	13.4	24.2	13.2	35.5	13.2	13.4	13.2
Leather products	20.3	7.7	2.5	6.3	1.8	9.3	1.6	3.2	1.8
Footwear	33.8	23.4	11.4	21.9	11.5	17.4	11.3	11.7	11.9
Wood products	12.5	3.7	2.4	3.2	3.4	0.4	2.4	2.9	2.5
Furniture and fixtures	31.2	22.1	5.6	14.3	5.5	5.5[b]	5.6	5.6	5.7
Paper and paper products	7.1	12.3	6.9	6.7	7.9	4.5	5.5	5.2	8.0
Printing and publishing	1.8	1.5	1.5	1.0	2.8	1.1	2.2	2.1	1.5
Chemicals	5.4	4.7	8.0	7.5	8.5	1.8	7.6	8.0	7.6
Rubber products	11.2	9.9	4.2	6.7	4.4	13.5	3.5	3.8	3.7
Non-metal mineral products	11.5	5.9	3.7	6.4	5.0	2.9	4.7	3.6	4.5
Glass and glass products	15.2	12.9	8.0	7.2	7.5	22.3	7.4	7.9	7.3
Iron and steel	10.8	5.8	4.6	5.4	5.5	4.2	4.9	4.7	5.9
Non-ferrous metals	4.2	3.3	1.6	2.0	6.6	0.8	2.6	1.9	6.5
Metal products	23.7	10.4	5.4	8.5	5.5	7.7	5.4	5.5	5.4
Non-electrical machinery	13.9	6.4	4.3	4.5	4.4	6.1	4.4	4.5	4.3
Electrical machinery	21.6	14.7	7.4	5.8	7.1	6.0[b]	7.7	8.3	7.2
Transportation equipment	21.2	22.1	7.9	1.6	7.2	3.8[b]	7.9	7.7	10.2
Miscellaneous manufactures	12.8	8.7	3.0	5.4	6.1	12.6	5.8	5.6	6.5
All industries	16.5	12.1	5.9	5.2	6.6	7.1	6.0	6.3	6.9

	Italy	Japan	Netherlands	New Zealand	Norway	Sweden	Switzerland	UK	USA	All
Textiles	5.6	3.3	8.5	12.3	13.3	10.3	6.6	6.7	9.2	8.5
Wearing apparel	13.2	13.8	13.5	58.5	21.7	14.2	12.4	13.3	22.7	17.5
Leather products	0.7	3.0	3.0	15.3	5.8	4.0	2.1	1.2	4.2	3.0
Footwear	10.4	15.7	11.2	40.7	21.7	13.7	9.0	12.5	8.8	12.1
Wood products	0.8	0.3	2.8	11.4	1.6	0.7	3.2	3.1	1.7	1.9
Furniture and fixtures	5.6	5.1	5.6	38.3	5.1	4.0	9.2	5.6	4.1[b]	7.3
Paper and paper products	2.6	2.1	6.2	20.5	1.9	2.4	4.3	4.9	0.2	4.2
Printing and publishing	1.8	0.1	2.2	1.1	4.3	0.2	0.7	2.1	0.7	1.5
Chemicals	8.1	4.8	8.1	8.1	6.2	4.8	0.9	7.9	2.4	6.7
Rubber products	2.7	1.1	4.1	9.5	6.6	6.1	1.7	2.7	2.5	4.1
Non-metal mineral products	2.8	0.5	3.3	12.7	2.4	2.8	2.5	2.4	5.3	4.0

Table 5.1 (Contd)

	Italy	Japan	Netherlands	New Zealand	Norway	Sweden	Switzerland	UK	USA	All
Glass and glass products	7.6	5.1	7.5	13.5	8.0	7.1	3.1	7.9	6.2	7.9
Iron and steel	3.5	2.8	5.6	5.2	1.7	3.7	1.7	4.7	3.6	4.4
Non-ferrous metals	1.8	1.1	3.6	4.1	0.9	0.7	2.4	1.7	0.7	1.6
Metal products	5.5	5.2	5.4	26.5	4.4	4.0	2.8	5.6	4.8	6.3
Nonelectrical machinery	4.5	4.4	4.3	22.1	5.2	3.5	1.2	4.2	3.3	4.7
Electrical machinery	8.0	4.3	7.8	19.6	6.9	4.5	1.6	8.1	4.4	7.1
Transportation equipment	8.8	1.5	9.0	26.8	2.2	5.1	6.1	7.2	2.5	6.0
Miscellaneous manufactures	5.8	4.6	5.2	18.2	7.4	4.6	1.1	3.0	4.2	4.7
All industries	5.4	2.9	6.8	16.7	5.2	5.0	3.1	5.2	4.3	5.8

[a] Prevailing rates, which include unilateral reductions in post-Kennedy Round tariff rates.
[b] Estimated from incomplete data.
Source: Alan Deardorff and Robert Stern, 'The Economic Effects of Complete Elimination of Post-Tokyo Round Tariffs', in William Cline, ed., *Trade Policy in the 1980s*, Washington D.C.: Institute for International Economics, 1983, Table 20.1, pp. 674–75. Reprinted by permission.

Source: adapted from Husted and Melvin (1990) *International Economies*, table 4.9, page 191.

Table 5.1 indicates that tariffs tend to differ by product and, some would say, increase as the product is refined, a process called **tariff escalation**, which will be considered later in this chapter. Nevertheless, the average tariff levels tend to be fairly low at around 6 per cent for developed countries, but the level is somewhat higher for developing countries.

The problem with the analysis outlined above is that the impact of a tariff has been discussed under rather strict assumptions. Two such assumptions are those of the 'small country' and perfectly competitive markets. Krugman (1987) has argued that because trade does not occur in perfect markets, but in markets where imperfections and possible **increasing returns to scale** exist, it is possible for governments to intervene in free trade via a tariff to increase the welfare of that country (see also Chapter 4). This tariff, known as the optimal tariff, is one which raises a country's welfare by more than the losses caused by protectionism (see earlier in Fig. 5.1). The ability of a country to impose an optimal tariff may arise where a country is an important participant in the world market. It would therefore have market power and can affect the world price of the good through an import tariff if it is a large consumer, or through an export tariff if it produces a large amount. In addition to this, the more elastic demand and supply conditions are in home markets, and the more inelastic in foreign markets, the greater the ability of the home country to impose an optimal tariff.

To see how this optimal tariff might work, let us take an example suggested by Krugman (1987). Assume there are two regions, the USA and Europe, each of which has a firm capable of producing a particular good. Suppose this is a 200-seat passenger aircraft, so the two firms could be Boeing and Airbus Industrie. We further assume that the good is produced only for export, and that the market can support only one firm, not two. Finally, the firms only face a choice of whether to produce or not to produce.

From the above information, a possible payoff matrix can be constructed as shown in Fig. 5.2. Boeing's choices are given in upper case letters and those of Airbus are in lower case. The lower left number shows Boeing's profit (greater than 'normal' profit) and the upper right number represents the figure for Airbus.

If we assume that Boeing has acquired some sort of lead over Airbus then the result will be Pn (the upper right-hand cell): Boeing's profits are £100 million and Airbus receives nothing.

Such a scenario is not one to be favoured by the Europeans. Suppose the Europeans subsidise Airbus Industrie by £10 million before Boeing gains the early advantage. The payoff matrix would then be as shown in Fig. 5.3.

Boeing now knows that Airbus will produce irrespective of what Boeing does. As the market can support only one firm, Boeing will probably make losses. It could be persuaded, therefore, not to produce, changing the outcomes from Pn to Np. A subsidy of £10 million raises profits from zero to £110 million for Airbus – £100 million being a transfer from the USA to Europe. Europe raises its welfare at the expense of the USA, since if trade was really free, that is without government intervention, Boeing would produce the 200-seater aircraft.

It is unlikely that if one country imposes an optimal tariff others will sit idly by. If country A's welfare has been increased, it must be at the expense of, say, country B, which then imposes a retaliatory tariff. Such is the beginnings of a tariff war and everyone is worse off. It has also been argued by Bhagwati (1987) that governments do not possess the information to intervene correctly in the market. They are unable to know for certain the position of the market without intervention and if this information is not known with certainty, intervening may make the country worse off. Even if the government thinks it knows every-

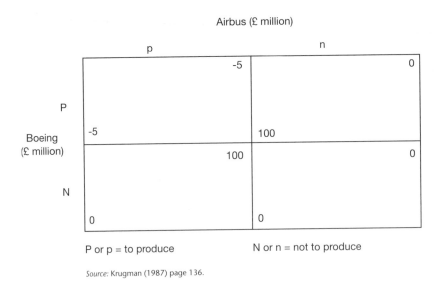

Airbus (£ million)

Source: Krugman (1987) page 136.

Figure 5.2 Hypothetical payoff matrix: Boeing/Airbus example before subsidies

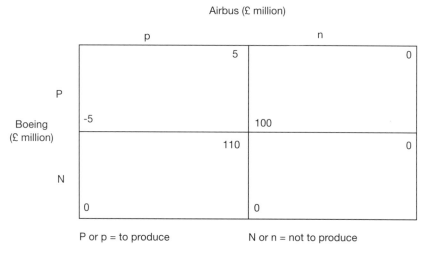

Airbus (£ million)

	p		n	
		5		0
P				
	-5		100	
		110		0
N				
	0		0	

P or p = to produce   N or n = not to produce

Source: adapted from Krugman (1987) page 136.

Figure 5.3 Hypothetical payoff matrix: Boeing/Airbus example after European subsidy

thing about the market, Krugman (1996) argues that there is a big difference between knowing lots of facts and really knowing how a market works. Furthermore, even if you can understand the market for aircraft (as described above), it is possible that very little of that knowledge generalises to the market for computers, which is in turn very different from telecommunications. He further argues that 'even if you understand an industry well enough to devise an activist policy, or are willing to assume that your model is really good enough, estimates of the gains from strategic trade policies are almost always very small' (Krugman 1996, page 24).

Moreover, trading relations are not just between two countries, as the models of 'new international trade' describe, and therefore the outcome once again is uncertain. It is the danger and uncertainties of this intervention in either the perfectly competitive or the imperfectly competitive market that led to the establishment of GATT, whose major role has been to reduce the overall level of tariffs between countries.

Tariff escalation and graduation and LDCs

Tariff escalation is the practice of setting higher tariffs on manufactures than on raw materials, a feature noted earlier in Table 5.1. For example, a tariff may be higher on groundnut oil than on groundnuts and higher on shirts as opposed to raw cotton. Products for which the escalation is more pronounced include rubber, tobacco, leather, paper and jute. For the LDCs this tariff escalation obstructs the way for them to add value to their exports and prevents their industrialisation.

The purpose of this protection is to retain high value-added processing in the developed countries. If tariff escalation could be substantially reduced it would be easier to diversify away from producing primary commodities. A study cited in the *World Bank Report 1990* suggests that the removal of all industrial country tariffs on various processing would increase such activities in developing countries by almost 80 per cent in the case of coffee, 76 per cent for wool and 52 per cent for cocoa.

Non-tariff barriers to trade

GATT, as we shall see later, appears to have been a success in reducing tariffs. However, little has been done to take account of the various forms of non-tariff barrier (NTB), the so-called '**new protectionism**', which have been rapidly replacing tariffs as instruments of commercial policy. Pelkmans and Winters (1988) and Cecchini (1988) have outlined the benefits to be gained by the EU by the reduction in these barriers following completion of the SEM (see Chapter 9). The social gain from reducing these types of barriers would be the area *acdb* of Fig. 5.1. In other words, there are very significant gains available in the EU by the reduction of **intra-industry trade** barriers, particularly when we realise that the figure for this type of trade exceeds ECU 500 billion per year.

Non-tariff barriers in the wider sense are barriers to trade which are not tariffs.

Quotas

The motives for quantitative restrictions, such as **quotas**, are similar to those used for the imposition of tariffs, that is, to be protective of trade and for fiscal motives. They are protective in the sense that quotas restrict the quantity of imports, and give fiscal gains through the raising of revenue – the licences to import can be auctioned off in a competitive market.

The economic effects of quotas for a small open economy, in which the domestic producers can also supply the good involved as a perfect substitute for the imported good, are shown in Fig. 5.4.

The domestic supply curve is drawn as S_d and since this cuts the vertical axis at P_o, then under free trade the domestic producers do not supply any units. If the price rises above P_o, the domestic suppliers will begin to provide goods. The foreign supply curve becomes inelastic at Z, i.e. it is $P_o Z Q^*$, since the world price of the good is P_o and the quota set by the home economy is $0B$. Without the quota in place $0A$ units are imported and sell on the domestic market at price P_o. A quota $0B$ is now introduced. The imposition of the quota restricts imports to FB. Domestic producers now provide $0F$ and consumer surplus falls by $c+d+a+b$; a is redistributed to importers, producers' surplus increases by area c and the net welfare loss is therefore $d+b$.

Examples of quotas in practice are the US and EU quota arrangements with Japan regarding cars, due to be phased out during 1998, and the **MFA** with many Asian nations covering textiles and fibres. Apart from quotas that exist at an EU level, countries within the EU have also been able to negotiate their own

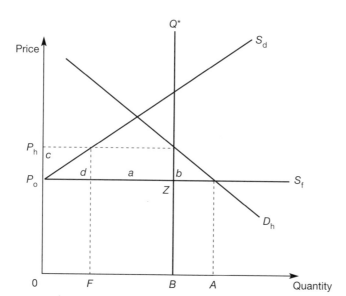

Figure 5.4 Effect of quotas for a small economy

quota arrangements. These nationally imposed quotas were phased out entirely on 1 January 1993.

Although quotas are outlawed under the GATT, certain exceptions are allowed: for example, with agricultural products, and in cases where governments need to impose temporary protection to aid locally distressed industries, or when a country has a balance of payments problem. Quotas can, therefore, be used by one country in a discriminatory way to prevent imports from specific countries. Whereas global quotas are relatively uncommon, country to country quotas are more common. In addition, countries have found ways of imposing quotas indirectly on others by obtaining agreements from exporting countries to 'voluntarily' limit exports.

Voluntary export restraints

A second type of quantitative restriction is the **voluntary export restraint** (VER) or orderly marketing agreement (OMA). Here the exporting firm or country agrees with the importing country to restrict the volume of its exports to a specified amount, over a given period of time. Such an arrangement used to exist between Japanese car makers and the UK government, but Japan's agreement is now with the EU. Other examples of UK VERs have been on footwear from Taiwan, Korea and Poland, and cutlery from Korea and Japan. The MFA operated in much the same way. Many countries have been involved with the imposition of VERs, as Table 5.2 shows.

To be more specific, the EU has negotiated such VERs for steel, electronics, automobiles, textiles and especially agricultural products. From the UK's point of view, the VER arranged with Japan over car imports during the early 1980s appears to have made little difference to overall car imports, as Japanese cars

Table 5.2 Voluntary export restraint arrangements: 1987

Product	Importing countries	Exporting countries
Steel	European Union	Australia, Brazil, Bulgaria, Czech Republic, Finland, Hungary, Japan, Poland, Romania, Slovak Republic, Sweden
Machine tools	European Union	Japan
	United States	Japan, Taiwan
Motor vehicles	Canada	Japan[a]
	European Union	Japan
	United States	Japan[b]
Televisions	European Union	Japan
	United States	South Korea
Video tape and cassette	European Union	Japan, South Korea
recorders	United States	South Korea
Footwear	Canada	South Korea, Taiwan
	European Union	South Korea, Taiwan
	France	China
	Ireland	South Korea
	United Kingdom	Czech Republic, Slovak Republic, Romania
	United States	
Textiles and apparel[c]	Austria	Singapore, South Korea
	Canada	Maldives, Pakistan, Vietnam
	European Union	Bulgaria, former Soviet Union, Cyprus, Egypt, Malta, Morocco, Tunisia, Turkey, former Yugoslavia
	United States	El Salvador, Fiji, Haiti, Mauritius, Nepal, Taiwan, United Arab Emirates
Agricultural products	European Union	Argentina, Australia, Austria, Brazil, Bulgaria, Canada, Chile, Korea, China, New Zealand, Norway, South Africa,
	United States	Uruguay
Stainless steel flatware	European Union	Japan, Australia, New Zealand
	Belgium	South Korea
	Netherlands	South Korea

[a]Formal agreement ended in 1987. An informal understanding with regular bilateral consultations still exists.
[b]Formal agreement ended in 1985. Japan still sets export restraints.
[c]Excludes VERs negotiated under a multifibre arrangement.
Sources: General Agreement on Tariffs and Trade, *Trade Policy Review: The United States, 1992, The European Communities, 1991, Canada, 1992, Japan, 1992, and Republic of Korea, 1992.*
Source: Husted and Melnin (1995) *International Economies,* 3rd edition table 4.9, p. 191.

were merely replaced by imports from the EU, which were not restricted. As an illustration of the level and impact of the VER on Japanese cars into the EU, in 1994, 990 000 units were imported. This was equivalent to approximately 8.1 per cent of the total car sales within the EU. Although this suggests some success in keeping Japanese cars outside of the EU, the response by the Japanese has been to establish car plants within the EU, chiefly in the UK, and there have been calls from other member states of the EU to have these also set against the VER negotiated with Japan. The argument has abated somewhat following local content rules applied to Japanese cars and the phasing out of the VER on Japanese cars by the late 1990s. Many other countries have volunteered to be involved in this type of restriction to trade, including many poorer countries such as Brazil, Mexico and Poland. Members of the EU have also joined this 'club' by agreeing to restrict exports of steel to the USA.

We can analyse the impact of a VER thereafter by using Fig. 5.4. Here the VER restricts the volume of imports to Q^*. The overall effects on price and quantity are the same for the VER as for the imposition of a quota. Consumer surplus falls by $a+b+c+d$. d and b are deadweight losses, d being the production deadweight loss (i.e. the inefficient use of domestic economic resources to produce a good which could be produced more efficiently abroad), and b being the consumption deadweight loss (because home consumers must buy at the higher price if they want the good).

The main difference between a VER and a quota, however, is in the area a. VERs are administered by the exporting country and if, after the imposition of the VER, there is a rise in the domestic price then foreign suppliers will also raise their price from P_o to P_h. In other words, foreign producers gain an economic rent – a net transfer from domestic consumers to overseas producers. Therefore, with a quota importers receive a, and with a VER foreign suppliers receive a. Of course, offsetting the impact of this loss to the domestic consumer is the impact of increased employment and output in the domestic economy; although whether this is the most efficient way of achieving these gains, if there are any, is a moot point.

A further point to consider is the balance of payments effect. A quota should reduce foreign exchange requirements as long as the international price ratio remains unchanged or moves in the favour of the importing country. Under a VER the foreign exchange requirements may well rise if the price elasticity of demand for the good is less than one. That is, if the demand for a good is price-inelastic and we restrict the supply of the good arriving on the market, then price increases by a greater proportion than quantity demanded falls, and total revenue spent on the good rises. Since this expenditure is on a foreign import, total foreign exchange requirements rise.

VERs tend to be less effective than quotas in restricting trade because it is easier to control imports rather than exports. In addition, VERs usually cover only major suppliers, so suppliers from other countries can still gain access to the market, e.g. Japanese cars. VERs, therefore, are discriminatory and a violation of the non-discrimination rule embodied in GATT's/WTO's MFN principle. Another implication that follows from a quota or VER constraint is that if there is a limit on the amount that can be exported, then higher-quality exports tend to be sent so as to enhance the profit on each unit, thereby causing a loss to the consumer and having a greater impact on the balance of payments.

Moreover, since a VER is source-specific, we may run into the following problem. Suppose both country A and country B can supply the UK with a good more cheaply than the UK can produce it but that country B is a more expensive producer than country A: then a VER is arranged with country A. This will simply result, however, in part of the domestic demand being switched to country B, and costs are higher than if we bought all our goods from country A. UK producers do not benefit, and UK consumers now end up paying more for their goods. A National Consumers Council survey of the effect of early EU–Japanese VERs on cars suggested that losses to the consumer exceeded gains for producers by around £9 billion (National Consumers Council 1993). This translates into the EU consumer paying £700 more for each imported Japanese car.

So why the proliferation of VERs? Perhaps one reason is paramount: with a VER the costs of government involvement are hidden and less affected by changes in government expenditure patterns. Secondly, if the domestic market is expanding, domestic producers know they will be able to provide the extra goods at the higher price without any alteration in the supply by foreign companies. VERs are also contracted for a fixed term and therefore can be reviewed. Such a process is more difficult with subsidies and cannot occur with tariffs under the regulations of GATT/WTO.

For the government, a VER shows that it is proactive on behalf of industry; the impact is hidden, particularly from consumers; the budgetary implications are minimised; and of course you can get away with these measures under GATT. For foreign producers the VER may be the least damaging of a number of measures that could be taken against them.

The amount of trade affected by VERs is difficult to quantify, but it is suggested that about 38 per cent of EU imports from Japan and 33 per cent of US imports from the same source are affected. By product, 80 per cent of all trade in textiles and 20 per cent of world trade in steel is regulated by this type of restriction. VERs have become a popular way of restricting trade, with over 150 such arrangements in place in the early part of the 1990s (Griffiths and Wall 1997).

Under the fiscal intervention instrument of non-tariff barriers there are other direct means of restricting trade.

Discriminatory government procurement

Most governments discriminate in favour of their domestic producers, perhaps for strategic and employment reasons (e.g. the purchase of arms and defence equipment by domestic governments). Furthermore, the government may instruct certain industries in the home economy to buy their raw materials or semi-manufactured goods from other companies in the domestic economy. An example of this used to be the arrangement between the Electricity Board in the UK before privatisation and the British coal industry, where the Electricity Board bought more expensive coal from British Coal rather than imported coal, in order to safeguard the coal industry. As a further example, it is interesting to note that in 1990 less than 10 per cent of local authority contracts for street cleaning, waste disposal and the like had found their way to firms in other EU countries. This type of discrimination is really a subsidy paid to domestic firms, which would be undercut by foreign firms in a free-market situation.

In 1979 the GATT was amended to incorporate restrictions on local preferences by government purchasing agents. It was agreed that countries would grant each other equal access to government contracts, though countries would be free to exclude certain agencies from the agreement. Most governments therefore exclude part, if not all, of contracts for defence, energy, postal services and so on. One estimate is that only 1 per cent of public contracts are placed outside of the country of origin (Griffiths and Wall 1997).

Production subsidies

Domestic producers may be encouraged by a production subsidy reducing costs rather than raising the price faced by domestic producers.

In Fig. 5.5 the impact of the subsidy shifts the domestic supply curve down from S_h to S_h^{sub}. Domestic suppliers now supply $0C$ but domestic consumers still pay P_w. Since domestic demand is unaltered, there are no losses in consumer surplus; however, area a is again the increase in producer surplus and b is the deadweight production loss, or the net loss to the economy.

Export subsidies

The impact of an export subsidy is the opposite to that associated with a tariff. With a tariff the domestic price of the imported good is pushed above the world price. With an export subsidy the domestic price of exports is pushed below the world price.

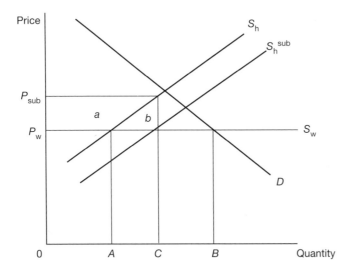

Figure 5.5 Effect of production subsidies

Price discrimination of this type in international markets is thought of as a form of **dumping** and countries that believe that the price of the exported good is lower than the price of the good in the exporter's domestic economy often impose penalties such as border taxes to remove any advantages that these goods may obtain. There has been a large increase in the number of anti-dumping cases initiated by the WTO, increasing from 176 in 1983/84 to 226 in 1993/94 (Grimwade 1996). In fact, a World Bank study in 1995 suggested that the average tariff on imports into the USA for manufactured goods was really 23 per cent rather than 6 per cent if dumping was taken into account. The Europeans are also not averse to instigating dumping actions and in the EU in 1997 there were 56 goods, including CD players, photocopiers and printers, that were subject to dumping duties.

Unlike a tariff, where there is a revenue gain to the government, here there is a revenue loss. Not all export subsidies are easy to recognise. For example, it is possible to give exporting companies preferential low rates of interest on any money borrowed, or for these companies to offset more items against tax; it is also possible for governments to subsidise wages through increased transfer payments so that the workforce keeps its wage demands low, leading to competitive export prices.

As with quotas, export subsidies on manufactured goods are not allowed under the GATT/WTO. However, the GATT did allow export subsidies on primary products, and the USA and the EU are just two of a whole range of countries which subsidised most, if not all, of their agricultural products. As we shall see later, the final round of GATT trade talks has tackled this issue, though not removed it. The cost of export credit (money loaned by the government to help exports, on which an interest rate is charged) as a means of supplying an export subsidy has received agreement by the OECD countries, which are now supposed to have set a minimum rate of interest to be charged. However, some industrial countries mix development grants with export credits, concealing the attractive credit terms under the disguise of development assistance.

Tariff quotas

A tariff quota is defined as a tariff on imports which increases with the amount imported. For example, imports of a commodity are free of tax up to a specified amount, but beyond that point a tariff is imposed.

Multiple exchange rates

Monetary authorities may sell foreign currency at different rates of exchange depending on the use to which the currency is being put. This can have effects similar to a tariff (see Corden 1971). Within this category we should also include the case where trade in one commodity takes place at a different exchange rate to the market rate. See Yeager (1976) for a discussion of trade when countries deal with the 'black' or 'underground' market rate rather than the official exchange rate.

Indirect non-tariff barriers

The previous types of direct non-tariff barrier or new protectionism have advantages over the indirect methods that follow, in that it is possible to deduce, through a system of economic analysis and use of diagrams, the burden of these. Indirect measures of non-tariff barriers, it is argued, are far more pervasive and they are more difficult to identify. Such indirect measures raise costs and reduce competitiveness and would include customs valuation procedures which are made sufficiently complex to add to the uncertainty of importers; for example, the French system for the importation of VCRs made them all enter the country through Poitiers. Environmental measures will also prevent the free flow of goods: for example, if all new cars must run on lead-free petrol or have catalytic converters and if a car manufacturer has its manufacturing process set up for leaded petrol, then it will need possibly expensive alterations to produce the lead-free engine.

Other possible sources of trade restraint are that some items (e.g. exhausts or biscuits) must be of the correct diameter, or that lights may need to be a certain distance apart. On health and safety grounds countries may prevent the importation of goods; for example, livestock or milk may be prevented from entering a country because the former may have too large a quantity of hormones (e.g. the EU ban on US beef or the EU ban on British beef due to BSE), whilst the latter may not be processed in a plant which satisfies the health grounds of another country. In a more recent case, health and safety matters have been brought to the fore in the dispute between the USA and the EU in the market for chickens.

Case study: Feathers fly

It is faintly absurd that European objections to the American way of slaughtering chickens have brought the two sides to the brink of a trade war this week. The retaliation threatened by both sides appears out of proportion to the dispute which provoked it. But behind the grandstanding lies a serious issue, with important implications for efforts to open world agricultural markets.

Ironically, the two sides have fallen out over an attempt to free transatlantic trade by accepting each other's food safety and inspection standards. They have already struck such mutual recognition deals for a variety of agricultural products. But their talks have stumbled largely because the EU deems US hygiene regulations for processing poultry to be inadequate. Brussels has reacted by halting US exports of the products in dispute, prompting the USA to block EU meat exports.

The USA accuses the EU of outright protectionism. But the story in this case is more complex. A series of scares, notably over BSE, has aroused deep public concern in Europe over food safety. The EU has responded by tightening its hygiene rules, while there is growing pressure in several member states for more effective and accountable regulation at national level.

The dilemma is how to reconcile genuine public interest with free trade. Understandably, consumers are concerned that imported foods should meet the same standards as home-grown ones. In theory, mutual recognition agreements should provide that assurance. In practice, as the USA–EU dispute shows, there is scope for endless argument between trading partners about whether differing standards are applied with equal effect.

World Trade Organisation rules offer no satisfactory answer, requiring mutual recognition but giving no guidance on how to achieve it. The WTO needs to tackle this problem if efforts to free global agriculture markets are to succeed. Otherwise, progress in lowering classic trade barriers, such as tariffs and quotas, risks being frustrated by the growth of incompatible national hygiene regulations – whether their intent is protectionist or not.

Longer term, the only solution may be to move towards regulatory harmonisation around internationally agreed norms – a course which the EU has already found necessary to create in its internal market. That would involve a formidable negotiating challenge, not least because, to be effective, it would require some countries to raise their national standards above their current levels. But it is much preferable to the alternative of trade conflict.

Source: Financial Times, 3 April 1997.

Questions

1 Can the EU's hygiene arrangements be construed as a barrier to trade?

2 Should the WTO consider international hygiene arrangements?

. . . .

In other areas of the market it is not hygiene factors that are important but safety factors. In recent years Japan has announced that foreign-made skis would not be allowed into their country because they were unsafe, citing the reason that the snow in Japan differed from the snow in Europe and the USA. Even within the EU such barriers exist, with different countries having different requirements for tractors (some require a cab, others do not). It is also possible for tax regimes to deter the entry of some goods into a market. The French domestic tax on cars is positively related to a car's horsepower; as such, it raises the prices of American cars relative to their own cars since US cars have more horsepower, and can be regarded as discriminatory. The UK and Italian governments have sometimes required importers to deposit, at their government's treasury, a sum equal to half the value of the import of a commodity for six months at no interest.

Apart from the 'goods' side of the market, services have become of increasing importance in trade. Wide price differentials are noticeable for some services in different EU countries and these are usually the result of barriers to trade. These barriers would include national regulations preventing foreign banks and insurance companies from soliciting for business, restrictions on the acquisition of banks by foreigners, discriminating tax regimes, restrictions on financial instruments and restrictions on facilities. Moreover, the separate national systems of accounting, corporate law and taxation, as well as differing industrial policies between EU members, have prevented some firms from setting up in other EU countries. France, for example, limits foreign equity in accounting firms, and the EU restricts or excludes foreign vendors from its data communications network. Standards, such as BSI in the UK or DIN in Germany, are important in restricting trade, particularly emphasising the consumer's point of view of quality. In addition, testing and certification procedures involve duplication or even exclusion from a national market; an example would include the definition of what exactly constitutes chocolate. Japan still continues to approve foreign truck imports on an 'individual' basis and not by type of truck. The Japanese argue that such an approach is necessary to meet quality standards, but it can be viewed as a clear non-tariff barrier.

Border measures and frontier formalities

Border measures and frontier formalities add to the bureaucracy at external borders, due to such things as the different VAT rates, excise duties, monetary compensation amounts, bilateral trade quotas, veterinary checks, different regulations and standards. Low staffing at checkpoints also delays entry and adds to costs (see Chapter 9). As we have seen, NTBs are used by most countries as a method of restricting trade, but within the EU, as with other customs unions, we could point to additional methods.

Cartels and concentrations

It is possible for the nature of competition in markets and the restrictions that might flow from these to inhibit free trade. These are either restrictive arrangements between otherwise independent firms, or the practices of dominant firms coupled with merger behaviour. In the case of the former, price agreements may exist whereby firms in one member state, when selling to another, agree on the prices they will charge for inputs, or even set up a separate company – called a common selling syndicate – which will conduct the exports sales of all the participants. These dominant firms could be in a powerful position to persuade domestic firms to deal exclusively with them, and imports and exports could be severely restricted.

Differences in VAT and other indirect taxes

Although all countries in the EU at the present time use value-added tax (VAT) as their main source of indirect taxation, the coverage of VAT has differed considerably between countries, even though a banding system for VAT rates currently exists, and also in terms of exemptions (see Chapter 8). The exact importance of this as a non-tariff barrier is open to question, yet VAT distorts prices and requires a large level of bureaucracy. Excise duties also differ between countries, often discriminating against country of origin on imported goods. For example, the UK has a greater duty on wine than on beer and the

Italians charge a greater duty on imported spirits compared with home-produced ones.

The EU's common commercial policy

The EU is founded on the principle of free trade between member countries, but there are a number of exceptions. The notion is that the Union members abolish all customs duties, charges of equivalent discriminating effect and quantitative restrictions on trade between them and apply a common customs tariff (Common External Tariff or CET) on trade with non-member countries.

Although the member states allow the EU to negotiate international trade agreements, import policies and so on under Articles 91, 99 and 113, the members have retained some measure of autonomy in external trade policy using Article 115, to restrict or control specific products subject to national import restrictions originating from within or from outside the EU. Recourse to Article 115 for intra-EU trade, however, is made impossible by the SEM legislation, whereby border customs checks are removed within the EU.

On the whole, EU policy on trade is similar to, although some would say, harsher than that which existed under GATT. By adopting the New Commercial Policy instruments in 1984, the EU sought to tighten up some of the 'grey areas' that existed under the GATT rules. Many saw this as a means by which the EU could issue anti-dumping writs more easily, and some have fears that the anti-dumping actions for tackling post-1992 adjustment problems has imposed the costs of adjustment on the outside world (see Chapter 4). This fear can be seen in the growth of intra-EU trade, which has outstripped the growth in world trade.

Adopting the CET does not mean that this applies equally to all goods. Agriculture is highly protected in the EU as it is in the USA. The steel industry was highly protected during the 1970s and 1980s, with VERs in place with a number of countries. It is said that 'approximately three-quarters of all VERs known to exist world-wide in April 1988 originated from the EU and the US' (Hitiris 1991).

One important aspect of trade, however, is the special arrangements made between developed and developing countries to stimulate exports from the latter. The main such arrangement is the Generalised System of Preferences (GSP). With some exceptions, these schemes have done little to offset the damage done by the broader range of overtly protectionist devices, with the benefits from the scheme being concentrated in a few middle-income countries leaving the poorer developing countries as the losers in the area of trade.

Why the growth of non-tariff arrangements?

All these non-tariff barriers may be difficult to quantify, but why were they introduced in the first place? It is not sufficient to say that they have simply replaced tariff barriers. Perhaps we need to look at the conditions under which tariffs were reduced.

The period up to the mid-1970s was one of general world expansion and in this sense it was easier for the developed nations to reduce tariffs. Since then we have seen three world recessions, in 1974–75, 1980–81 and 1990–92. When economies experience slow-downs in world growth they are, on the one hand, more loathe to reduce tariffs, and on the other hand they may seek to further protect their domestic economies through non-tariff barriers. The 1980s also witnessed the growth of some of the LDCs into NICs; thus the Western developed nations felt threatened in their traditional markets and in their domestic markets. A response was to protect these through non-tariff barriers. There is also evidence that products which face a high incidence of non-tariff barriers also tend to be products which face high tariffs, i.e. non-tariff barriers and tariffs are complements rather than substitutes. To make matters worse, non-tariff barriers are often not imposed singly but piled upon a single commodity. Thus a country which faces a non-tariff barrier such as a quota on a particular product may also face health and safety restrictions on the same product.

This growth in the non-tariff barrier (or new protectionism) can be clearly seen in Fig. 5.6. The figures exclude health and safety and other regulations. If these were included the figures would obviously be worse. Non-tariff barriers are also product-specific.

Furthermore, the original GATT rules were set in a world that was far different from the one we have now, in terms of both financial markets and trading groups, and the life-cycle of high-technology products.

GATT

The General Agreement on Tariffs and Trade (GATT) evolved after the Second World War as a means by which the high levels of protectionism that appeared between the wars could be reduced. Formed in 1947 in Geneva by 23 nations, its charter contained 38 articles with three overriding aims:

1 to provide a framework for the conduct of orderly trading relations;
2 to encourage free trade and reduce the possibility of countries taking unilateral action against others;
3 to reduce tariffs and quantitative restrictions.

Articles I and II relate to the basic obligations of all contracting parties. Articles III to XXIII are the code for fair trade, including the rules for anti-dumping, and protection for balance of payments difficulties. Articles XXIV to XXV concern the procedures for application and conditions for the amendment of articles. Articles XXXVI to XXXVIII, produced in 1965, deal, in the main, with trade of less developed nations.

Although GATT may not appear to affect individual countries directly, it has a number of indirect effects. In particular, by encouraging countries to lower their trade restrictions with other member countries of the GATT, it enables some organisations to achieve greater cost competitiveness and widen their markets. In addition, it provides companies with consistency since they realise that they can undertake longer-term trading contracts without them being disrupted on the whim of a country's government.

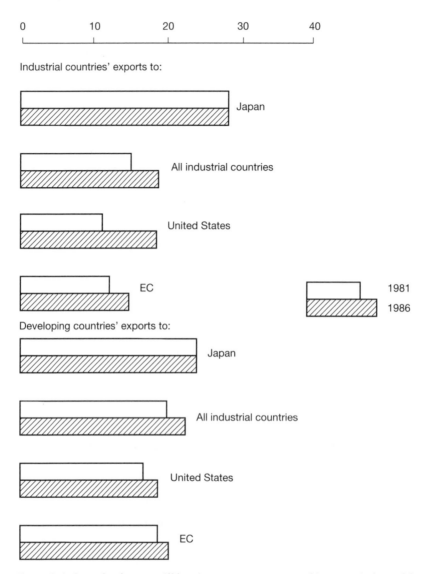

Figure 5.6 Growth of non-tariff barriers as a percentage of imports (adapted from *The Economist* (1987) page 187)

The GATT agreement embodies three main principles: non-discrimination, reciprocity and transparency.

1 **Non-discrimination**: countries should treat all their trading partners the same way; for example, if the UK puts a tariff of 40 per cent on an Australian import, it should not put a higher tariff on a similar good imported from India. This is known as non-discrimination or most favoured nation (MFN) treatment. Similarly, if the UK agrees a tariff reduction with Australia, bilaterally, then this tariff concession should be extended to all other countries. Any tariff reduction gained can almost certainly be expected to be

permanent. Therefore, the advantages of the MFN treatment is that two countries, in bargaining for tariff reductions, know that a later deal between one of the countries and a third party will be passed on. The process also helps small countries, which may have little bargaining power. The growth of non-tariff barriers, as we shall see later, has been an attempt to overcome the non-discrimination principle.

2 **Reciprocity**: if country A makes a 10 per cent reduction in tariffs on an import from country B, country B should make a corresponding reduction in tariffs on imports from country A. The MFN rule would then enable these reductions to be transmitted between all GATT nations. Reciprocity recognises the existence of the 'free-rider' problem inherent with trade liberalisation.

3 **Transparency**: countries should replace disguised and less quantifiable protectionism with more visible tariffs. This includes quotas which, as a type of non-tariff barrier, generate uncertainty, which then acts as another non-tariff barrier.

GATT also realises that there may be occasions, such as temporary balance of payments problems and the need to protect a domestic industry, when short-term trade measures might be allowed. Additionally, discrimination is also allowed against countries that 'dump' goods onto another country's home market.

Furthermore, Article XXIV allows for the establishment of free-trade areas and customs unions, within which the parties receive preferential treatment. A special place is made within GATT for less developed countries (LDCs), which may benefit from MFN tariff reductions without the necessity for reciprocation. Nevertheless, the extent to which an LDC remains an LDC or becomes a newly industrialised country (NIC), and thereby loses some of its tariff protection, has come under close scrutiny by the developed nations.

The GATT rounds

The Uruguay Round was the eighth round in the GATT trade negotiations. The previous seven rounds can be split into two unequal groups: the rounds of trade negotiations in Geneva (1947), Annecy (1949), Torquay (1950–51) and Geneva (1955); and the Dillon Round (1959–62), and the Kennedy Round (1963–67), which were almost exclusively concerned with tariff liberalisation. Following the conclusions of the Kennedy Round the tariff cuts affected around $40 billion worth of world trade – approximately 75 per cent of total trade, with an average reduction of 36–39 per cent.

Three factors were important in the outcome of the first six rounds. First, the tariff reductions noted above applied mainly to industrial goods. The developed economies still protected their agricultural sectors. Second, one important sector of manufacturing – textiles – was exempted. Third, industrialised countries tended to reduce tariffs on primary commodities and raw materials to a greater extent than those on finished goods.

The major difference between the Tokyo Round (1973–79) and the previous rounds was that it examined a much wider set of issues apart from tariff reductions, such as non-tariff barriers (subsidies and quotas) and trade in agricultural goods. The Tokyo Round led to average tariff reductions of between 33 and 38 per cent, with higher average tariff countries conceding higher than average cuts. Altogether around $112 billion of trade in industrialised products (at 1976 prices), or around 20 per cent of the value of trade in industrial products, was affected.

The Uruguay Round

GATT was particularly successful in dealing with tariff barriers to trade, especially those associated with industrial products. Nevertheless, as this chapter has shown, the fall from grace of the tariff has occurred at the same time as the rise in the popularity of the NTB as a trade impediment. The situation had gradually been getting worse with regard to NTBs. More and more the EU and the USA had resorted to anti-dumping and anti-subsidy measures to keep out imports. Moreover, the slow-down in the growth of world trade and the move by many industrialised countries towards more of a service-orientated economy, and the role of agriculture within trade relationships, meant that the last round of GATT talks had a much wider range of issues with which to deal.

The eighth round of GATT talks began in Uruguay in 1986 and finished in Marrakech in 1993. It had a much wider portfolio to consider and, as Table 5.3 indicates, many of the key parties had certain objectives and certain concessions they were willing to offer.

Its conclusion involved 28 separate accords devised to extend fair trade rules to agriculture, services, textiles, intellectual property rights and foreign invest-

Table 5.3 Uruguay Round trade-offs

Country	Targets	Concessions
United States	Agriculture	Textiles and clothing
	TRIPs	Tariffs
	Services	CVDs/AD
	TRIMs	NTBs
European Community	TRIPs	Textiles and clothing
	TRIMs	Agriculture
	Services	Safeguards
	Tariffs	CVDs/AD
Japan	NTBs	Agriculture
	TRIMs	Services
	CVDs/AD	TRIPs
	Safeguards	
Developing countries	Textiles and clothing	Services
	NTBs	TRIPs
	Safeguards	TRIMs
	Agriculture	Tariffs
	Tropical products	
	Natural resource-based products	

Source: Greenaway (1991), page 104.

ment. Tariffs on industrial products were cut by more than one-third and were eliminated entirely in 11 sectors. Many non-tariff barriers were to be converted into tariff barriers and these would then subsequently be removed.

More specifically, in the agricultural sector it was agreed that access was to be improved with non-tariff barriers being replaced by tariff barriers (the **tariffication** process) and these tariffs being reduced on average by 36 per cent in the case of developed countries and 24 per cent in the case of developing countries. Members were also required to reduce the value of mainly direct export subsidies to a level 36 per cent below the 1986–90 base period over a six-year implementation period.

In the area of textiles and clothing, the Uruguay Round secured the eventual integration of the textiles and clothing sector – where much of the trade is currently subject to bilateral quotas negotiated under the Multifibre Agreement (MFA) – into the GATT on the basis of strengthening GATT rules and disciplines.

There has been an agreed list of trade-related investment measures (TRIMs) and all non-conforming TRIMs needed to be eliminated within two years of the start of the Uruguay Round. TRIMs refer to performance requirements imposed on multinational firms that engage in foreign direct investment (see Chapter 11). Governments may impose local content rules on these companies or specify that a certain proportion of output is exported. As these actions have trade effects, a negotiating group has had the responsibility of evaluating current GATT disciplines to consider whether changes are required.

The new agreement also provided greater clarity and more detailed rules in relation to the method of determining when a product has been dumped, and the action of the injured party. The area of services was considered in detail under five 'Parts'. Part I described the scope of services, i.e. the type of trade in services. Part II set out general obligations and principles; on the whole the most favoured nation (MFN) principle that had been applied to goods was to be applied to services. However, it was recognised that MFN treatment would not be possible for every service activity and, therefore, it was envisaged that parties should indicate specific MFN exemptions. Part III contained provisions on market access and national treatment which would not be general obligations but would be commitments made in national schedules, i.e. there is an obligation to treat both foreign services suppliers and domestic services suppliers alike. Part IV of the agreement established the basis for progressive liberalisation in the services area through successive rounds of negotiations. It also permitted parties to withdraw or modify commitments after a period of three years. Finally, Part V contained institutional provisions, including consultation and dispute settlement and the establishment of a council on services. There were various annexes attached to the services agreement covering the areas of financial services, telecommunications and air transport services. These annexes reduced the barriers to market access, and encouraged co-operation and competition.

Agreement was also reached on trade-related aspects of intellectual property rights, including the trade in counterfeit goods. The agreement recognised that widely varying standards in the protection and enforcement of intellectual property rights and the lack of a multinational framework of principles, rules and disciplines dealing with international trade in counterfeit goods had been a growing source of tension in international economic relations. In this regard, the agreement addressed the applicability of basic GATT principles and those of relevant international intellectual property agreements; the provision of adequate intellectual property rights; the provision of effective enforcement measures for those rights; multilateral dispute settlement; and transitional arrangements.

A provisional analysis of the Uruguay Round on market access for goods suggests that world income should gain by $235 billion annually, and trade by $755 billion annually, by 2002. These figures should increase substantially when gains from increased trade in services, strengthened rules and dynamic effects are allowed for (see Fig. 5.7).

At the same time as the Uruguay Round was being finalised/ratified the members of GATT agreed to establish a new trade body, the **World Trade Organisation** (WTO), which came into operation on 1 January 1995. This new body is in charge of administering the new global trade rules agreed in the Uruguay Round and reflects a widespread desire to operate in a fairer and more open multilateral trading system for the benefit and welfare of all countries.

The WTO is different from GATT in a number of respects:

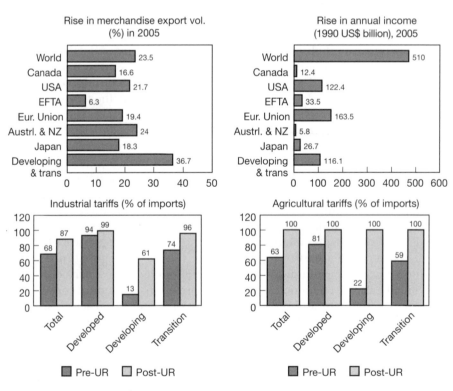

Source: Focus, GATT NEWSLETTER, No. 112, Page 3, Nov 1994, Pub. The Information and Media Relations Division of GATT

Figure 5.7 The effects of the Uruguay Round

- The WTO is more global in its membership than GATT. Its membership already comprises over 150 countries and territories, with many more considering accession.

- It has far wider scope than GATT, bringing into the multinational trading system, for the first time, the trade in services, intellectual property protection, and investment.

- It is a fully fledged international organisation in its own right, while GATT was basically a provisional treaty by an *ad hoc* secretariat.

- It will administer a unified package of agreements to which all members are committed, whilst GATT included a number of side issues, such as anti-dumping measures and subsidies, whose membership was limited to a few countries.

- It contains a much improved version of the original GATT rules plus a lot more. In other words, it uses the 1994 GATT rules, which were a large improvement on the original rules.

- It reverses policies of protection in certain 'sensitive' areas, which had become tolerated under the old GATT system, such as export restraints on textiles and clothing, and voluntary export restraints.

- The WTO's objectives are to oversee the tariff cuts (averaging 40 per cent) and the reduction of non-tariff measures agreed at the Uruguay Round. It is to be the guardian of international trade, examining on a regular basis the trade regimes of individual members. In this respect it will examine proposed trade measures and proposals by countries which could lead to trade conflicts. Members of the WTO are also required to supply a range of trade statistics, which will be kept on the WTO data base.

It is recognised that there will be issues that arise that could lead to trade disputes. Thus the WTO provides a whole range of conciliation services and also a disputes mechanism for finding an amicable solution to the problems. If trade disputes cannot be solved through bilateral talks, then the dispute will be adjudicated under the WTO dispute settlement 'court'. Here panels of independent experts are established to examine disputes in the light of WTO rules and provide rulings. This tougher, streamlined procedure ensures equal treatment for all trading partners and encourages members to honour their obligations. The whole programme of dispute settlements is far more streamlined than the old GATT system and will encourage parties to seek independent jurisdiction of their case rather than resorting to individual pieces of domestic legislation. In addition, the WTO is a forum where countries continuously negotiate exchanges of trade concessions to further lower trade barriers. Table 5.4 indicates an overview of the disputes settlement in the WTO as of April 1996.

This speeded-up disputes settlement appears to be achieving results. For example, in Table 5.4 the dispute between the USA and Japan regarding 'Measures concerning sound recordings' was resolved in March 1997. The USA had complained in February 1996 that copyright should exist over the protection of past performances and existing sound recordings in Japan under the

Table 5.4 Dispute settlement in the WTO, April 1996

Complainant	Subject of complaint
On Appeal	
Venezuela, Brazil	United States – Standards for reformulated and conventional gasoline
Active Panels	
Canada, Chile, Peru	European Communities – Trade description of scallops
European Communities, Canada, United States	Japan – Taxes on alcoholic beverages
Philippines	Brazil – Measures affecting desiccated coconut
Costa Rica	United States – Restrictions on imports of cotton and man-made fibre underwear
Panel Requested	
India	USA – Measures affecting imports of women's and girls' wool coats
India	USA – Measures affecting imports of woven wool shirts and blouses
Consultations	
United States	Korea – Measures concerning the testing and inspection of agricultural products
Thailand	EC – Duties on imports of rice
Canada	Australia – Measures affecting the importation of salmon
India	Poland – Import regime for automobiles
United States	Australia – Measures affecting the importation of salmonids
Uruguay	European Communities – Implementation of Uruguay Round commitments concerning rice
United States	European Communities – Measures affecting meat and meat products (hormones)
Ecuador, Guatemala, Honduras, Mexico, USA	European Communities – Regime for the importation, sale and distribution of bananas
United States	Japan – Measures concerning sound recordings
Hong Kong	Turkey – Restrictions on imports of textile and clothing products
Sri Lanka	Brazil – Countervailing duties on imports of desiccated coconut and coconut milk powder from Sri Lanka
United States	Canada – Certain measures concerning periodicals
India	Turkey – Restrictions on imports of textile and clothing products
Argentina, Australia, Canada, New Zealand, Thailand, United States	Hungary – Export subsidies in respect of agricultural products

Source: WTO (1996) page 6.

TRIPs agreement. The US complaint was based on the belief that the agreement obligated WTO members to grant protection to past performances undertaken in a WTO member state and existing sound recordings for a term of at least 50 years from the end of the calendar year in which the performance took place or the sound recording was made. In December 1996, Japan amended its copyright law to provide this 50-year protection to past performances and existing sound recordings. The USA has now withdrawn its WTO complaint. The case study indicates how the WTO is tackling disputes.

Case study: WTO attacks EU banana licensing arrangements

•••••••••••••••••••••

The World Trade Organisation has found that the European Union's controversial banana import regime violates free trade rules on 19 counts, it emerged yesterday with publication of the WTO's final ruling. The final report on the banana regime was sent confidentially to governments involved at the start of May, after an interim report found against the EU regime in March.

The trade organisation backed complaints by five countries – the USA, Honduras, Guatemala, Ecuador and Mexico – that the EU's preferential treatment of bananas from African, Caribbean and Pacific countries discriminated against their growers and marketing companies.

The 395-page report, which has just been made public, found the regime contravened both the General Agreement on Trade and Services and the General Agreement on Tariffs and Trade on 19 counts.

The main EU measures criticised included distribution of import licences for Latin American bananas to French and British companies, which took away a large part of the US banana distribution business.

Distribution of import licences for Latin American bananas to European banana ripening companies also took away US business, the WTO found, while licensing requirements for imports from Latin America were more severe than for other countries.

The report also accused the EU of 'discriminatory' allocation of access to the EU market. But, importantly, the report focuses on the EU licensing regime and does not target tariff preferences for Caribbean banana producing countries in the EU.

Caribbean countries say their economies face disaster if the EU regime is dismantled.

The USA hailed the report as an 'important precedent for all US exporters of services and agricultural goods'.

Mr Alfredo Pinoargote, Ecuador's ambassador to the EU, said Ecuador, the world's largest exporter of bananas, had been 'badly hurt' by the EU regime. 'I hope now that the damage done to our banana industry can be put right,' he added.

The European Commission was not available for comment last night, but is known to be considering an appeal against the WTO ruling.

Mr Franz Fischler, agriculture commissioner, told the European Parliament last week that the EU firmly believed its regime was non-discriminatory. But he warned European MPs that launching an appeal risked ending up with an even more onerous judgment.

European MPs have called for a consumer boycott of Latin American bananas in favour of Caribbean producers.

Source: Buckley, N. (1997) *Financial Times*, 24 May.

Questions

1 Why might the EU discriminate in favour of certain Caribbean countries?

2 How could EU consumers benefit from the WTO ruling?

• •

All the members of the old GATT (128 countries) automatically became members of the WTO on acceptance of the Uruguay Round agreements and submission of commitments on trade in goods and services. Given that there are currently a further 20 countries seeking admission to the WTO then it will cover virtually the whole of the world. Whether the WTO will promote or retard trade is open to question. Certainly, it encompasses a wider array of products and services than GATT; this may encourage greater trade, but it also allows for greater cross-retaliation, bringing unrelated businesses into trade disputes.

Whilst GATT and now the WTO have been moving the international community towards free trade, at the same time there have been moves over the past 40 years to develop trading blocs. These trading blocs, such as the EU and NAFTA (North American Free Trade Area), have reduced the barriers to trade between member countries whilst at the same time erecting external barriers to countries outside the trading bloc. This suggests a two-speed situation: liberalising world trade by WTO but constraining it through the development of trading blocs. However, a study undertaken by the WTO in 1995 suggested that the dichotomy between free trade and trading blocs may be overstated. The WTO noted that 'The legal foundations for more open trade have been laid by the multilateral trading system – global in its coverage – with regional integration agreements serving to deepen relations with neighbouring countries. Thus the regional and multilateral initiatives are complements rather than alternatives in the pursuit of open trade' (WTO 1995, page 3). In fact, the WTO argues that there are some areas where global actions are better placed. For example, few regional agreements cover services, agriculture and the protection of international property rights, whereas the World Trade Organisation has provided an integrated system of rights and obligations at the multilateral level in all these areas as well as merchandise trade in general.

Green trade issues

The move towards free trade has led both markets and organisations to become increasingly globalised. Many proponents of free trade argue that environmental regulations are often used as new barriers to trade, reducing the efficiency of the global economy and slowing down the process of technological change. Those who support the protectionist view of limiting trade argue that free trade enables multinational enterprises to shift their polluting activities to less well-regulated countries, thereby perpetuating the use of inefficient technologies and harming the world's poor. Thus trade barriers are an important part of sustaining and protecting the environment.

Both sides of the argument can be seen in the use of the EU's **eco-labelling system**. Eco-labels indicate the most environmentally friendly way of producing a product. The eco-label for tissue paper, for example, is intended as a means of informing European consumers which tissue products are environment-friendly. It sets standards for air and water emissions and for resource usage. These standards are consistent with the conditions that exist within Europe, but they are not consistent with the conditions in Brazil, the USA and Canada. Thus, this eco-label discriminates against products from the Americas. Thus the governments of the Americas see it as a means of protecting the European producers of tissue paper, whilst the European governments see it as a method of environmental protection. As Morris (1996) notes, since governments are beginning to include environmental considerations in their procurement policies, eco-labels are a new form of protectionism.

However, there are other environmental regulations that clearly impede free trade, such as the Convention on International Trade in Endangered Species (CITES), which, for example, prohibits the importation of ivory, and the Basel Convention on Transboundary Movements of Hazardous Wastes and their Disposal, which rules out trade in certain substances. The Montreal Protocol added a further twist. This protocol was concerned with ozone depletion and initiated the phasing out of CFCs. The treaty, however, also allowed member countries to implement trade sanctions against non-member countries. In addition, the convention prohibits imports of all products which use CFCs in their production processes, such as computer components cleaned with CFC-based solvents. Other examples of the use of environmental protection to restrict trade include the USA's efforts to protect dolphins by banning Mexican tuna, which tended to be caught in nets which also caught dolphins, and Denmark's efforts to protect its refillable bottle system by requiring all beer and soft drinks to be sold in refillable bottles.

The problem for the WTO is that multilateral environmental agreements such as the Basel Convention or the Montreal Protocol state that countries can restrict trade on environmental grounds, whereas the WTO is trying to remove all trade restrictions. Therefore, there is a conflict between the two. Efforts are under way, however, to 'green' the WTO. The tension between **multinational enterprises**, governments and free trade therefore needs to be reconciled, and at the first Ministerial Conference of the WTO in December 1996 the WTO

Committee on Trade and the Environment attempted to move this issue forward, through bringing both environmentalists and those who believe in free trade together.

But are free trade and the environment in conflict? It is possible to argue that free trade is a prerequisite for environmental improvement rather than a threat. Free trade can improve economic growth and wealth, and Grossman and Kreuger (1991) have indicated that economic growth begins to alleviate air pollution when per capita income reaches $4000–$5000 per year. Material poverty, not economic trade, is the single greatest threat to environmental quality.

Within Europe, even though many barriers to trade have been removed by the development of the Single European Market (see Chapter 9), eco-taxes can be used as a barrier to the free flow of trade. During 1997, DG XI started to draft documentation to distinguish between those taxes which are in accordance with EU law and those which are not.

What DG XI is doing is getting individual states to describe the timing and the manner of their plans for environmental taxation, so as to promote transparency and avoid future problems. In addition, the EU countries will be asked to specify the environmental objective to be pursued and the manner in which it would be promoted by the tax or levy, the impact on the internal market and selection of the instrument which achieves the environmental goal with the least limitation on the free movement of goods.

Although the Fifth **Environmental Action Programme** encourages environmental taxation, the problem has been that individual EU states want control over fiscal matters.

Conclusion

Trade barriers will always exist; the question is how hidden are they and to what degree do countries wish to reduce them. Historically trade barriers were tariffs but GATT and now the WTO have been fairly successful in reducing these. However, as tariff barriers have fallen, so they have been replaced by other forms of new protectionism. Included here would be quotas, VERs, health and safety regulations and red tape. The protracted last round of trade talks took seven years to complete and indicated the growing complexity of matters in the international trade arena. There are now more countries, more issues, and a wider variety of trade barriers to consider. Although the talks appeared to be stalled on a number of occasions, a final satisfactory conclusion was reached in 1993. The Uruguay Round boosted world trade, which for the global economy may have been all the better considering the dampening effect on total world activity that has taken place as many of the EU countries attempt to achieve the criteria for monetary union (see Chapter 12). The Uruguay Round also highlighted that the GATT, which may have been the appropriate organisation for discussing trading relations in the three decades after the Second World War, needed changing. Its development into the WTO has heralded a new approach to trade. The arrival of the WTO has added impetus to trade negotiations and the belief in free trade, as can be seen from the rise in membership. Moreover it has a much more appropriate and speedy disputes mechanism, which has encouraged countries to seek help from the WTO rather than for individual countries to undertake direct reprisals. The world is unlikely to get less complex and the WTO faces some interesting times ahead, particularly in bringing environmentalism and free trade together as well as considering the growth in power of trading blocs.

Questions for discussion

1 As instruments of protection go, a tariff is less harmful than a quota, and a quota is less harmful to a country than a VER. Discuss.

2 Protection is an expensive and inefficient way to create jobs. Discuss.

3 To what extent has GATT been successful in combatting tariffs?

4 Can environmental concerns be justified as barriers to trade?

5 The Multifibre Agreement represents a good way of organising international trade. Discuss. Should similar agreements be arranged for other sectors?

6 How did the growth of GATT membership hinder the talks on reducing trade barriers?

7 What are the main forms of non-tariff barriers to trade? Can countries be justified in imposing these types of trade restriction?

8 What are the potential problems and benefits to trade if the world breaks into three major trading areas, the Americas, the EU and the South East Asian zone?

Main reading

Artis, M. J. and Lee, N. (1994) *The Economics of the European Union*, Oxford University Press.

Bhagwati, J. (1987) *Protectionism*, MIT Press.

Cecchini, P. (1988) *1992: The European Challenge*, Gower.

Greenaway, D. (1991) GATT and multilateral trade liberalisation: knocked out in the eighth round, *Economics*, Journal of the Economics Association, Autumn.

Greenaway, D. (1994) The Uruguay Round of trade negotiations, *Economic Review*, November.

Grossman, G. and Kreuger, A. (1991) *Environmental Impacts of a North American Free Trade Agreement*, Princeton University, November.

Krugman, P. (1987) Is free trade passé?, *Economic Perspectives*, Vol. 1 (2).

Krugman, P. (1991) The move towards free trade zones, *Federal Reserve Bank of Kansas Economic Review*, November/December.

Krugman, P. (1996) Making sense of the competitiveness debate, *Oxford Review of Economic Policy*, Vol. 12 (3), pp. 17–25.

Morris, J. (1996) *Green Goods? Consumers, Product Label and the Environment*, Institute of Economic Affairs, London.

Additional reading

Cook, M. (1990) The rise of new protectionism: Is there still a role for GATT? in Cook, M. and Healey, N. (eds) *Current Topics in International Economics*, Anforme.

Cook, M. (1991) GATT: Can it control the New Protectionism? *UK Economic Studies*, Spring, Vol. 2, p. 14.

Corden, M. (1971) *The Theory of Protection*, Oxford University Press.

The Economist (1987) The World Economy Survey, 26 September.

The Economist (1992) Japan's troublesome imports, 11 January.

Financial Times (1992) US chipmaker leads drive for tougher tariffs, 11 March.

Greenaway, D. (1983) *International Trade Policy: From Tariffs to New Protectionism*, Macmillan.

Greenaway, D. (1985) New ways of restricting imports, *Economic Review*, November.

Griffiths, A. and Wall, S. (1997) *Applied Economics: An Introductory Course*, Longman.

Grimwade, N. (1996) Anti-dumping policy after the Uruguay Round, *National Institute Economics Review*, February.

Guieu, P. and Bonnet, C. (1987) Completion of the internal market and indirect taxation, *Journal of Common Market Studies*, Vol. 25 (3).

Herin, J. (1986) Rules of origin and differences between tariff levels in EFTA and in the EU, mimeo, Occasional Paper No. 13, European Free Trade Association, Geneva, February.

Hindley, B. (1980) Voluntary export restraints and Article XIX of the General Agreement on Tariffs and Trade, in Black, J. and Hindley, B. (eds) *Current Issues in Commercial Policy and Diplomacy*, Macmillan.

Hindley, B. and Greenaway, D. (1985) *What Britain Pays for Voluntary Export Restraints*, Thames Essays No. 43, Trade Policy Research Centre.

Hitiris, T. (1991) *European Community Economics*, 2nd edition, Harvester Wheatsheaf.

Husted, S. and Melvin, H. (eds) (1990) *International Economics*, Harper & Row.

Kostecki, M. (1987) Export restraint arrangements and trade liberalisation: the world economy, in Husted, S. and Melvin, M. (eds) (1990) *International Economics*, Harper & Row, p. 198.

National Consumers Council (1993) *International Trade: The Consumer Agenda*.

Pelkmans, J. and Winters, L. A. (1988) *Europe's Domestic Market*, Routledge.

World Bank (1990) *World Bank Report 1990*.

World Trade Organisation (1995) Regionalism and the world trading system, in *WTO Focus*, May–June, No. 3, p. 6.

Yeager, L. B. (1976) *International Monetary Relations: Theory, History and Policy*, 2nd Edition, Harper & Row.

6 Economic integration

Introduction

Economic integration is a term which encompasses different forms of economic co-operation between the independent nations of a particular region, such as NAFTA or the EU. These forms range from the minimum co-operation, i.e. free-trade areas, to the maximum, which is economic union or complete integration. In fact it is customary in the literature to refer to at least four different categories of co-operation: **free-trade areas** (FTAs), **customs unions** (CUs), **common markets** (CMs) and **economic unions** (EUs).

Forms of economic integration

FTAs involve the elimination of tariffs between the member countries but each country applies its own tariff policy to non-member countries. CUs are the same as FTAs except for the presence of a **common external tariff** (CET), which is applied to trade with non-members. In a CM not only do the commodities move freely between the member countries but so do the factors of production, such as labour and capital. An economic union is a common market but in addition it involves a high degree of integration of fiscal, monetary and commercial policies. In fact a complete economic integration would mean the unification of economic policies. Table 6.1 indicates the degree of co-operation for each category.

Economic co-operation beyond an FTA requires policy compatibility, which involves the imposition of constraints on policy objectives and, ultimately, the creation of supranational institutions. Progress towards integration depends on the willingness of national governments to relinquish some of the traditional national legislative and executive powers in favour of these supranational authorities. If this is lacking, it is conceivable that the economic co-operation between all or some of the members may cease to exist altogether.

Table 6.1 Forms of economic integration

Features	FTA	CU	CM	EU
1 Free trade between the members	*	*	*	*
2 CET		*	*	*
3 Free movement of factors of production			*	*
4 Harmonisation of economic policy				*

Many suggest that economic integration has its own dynamics. A CU would be under pressure to progress to higher forms of economic integration. This arises from the increasing political and economic interdependence between the participants, which tends to create policy conflicts between the members, which in turn necessitates either a forward step towards deeper integration or a backward step towards a looser form of international co-operation. Others point to historical examples where such moves have not occurred. The EU has gradually moved towards closer integration within Europe. It never really was a free-trade area, but certainly was a customs union until recently with a common external tariff and no tariff barriers between member states. The SEM legislation, however, made it more of a common market as legislation to encourage the free movement of goods and services, people and capital across frontiers was enacted. Further elements of an economic and monetary union have also been put in place in the Maastricht Treaty.

The theory of customs unions

Although the literature on the subject goes back to the classical economists, it has generally been accepted that the real theory of CUs goes back only as far as 1950 with Jacob Viner's theory. The pre-Vinerian view was that since free trade maximises world welfare and a CU is a move towards free trade from protectionism, then a CU would increase world welfare, even if it does not maximise it. Viner showed that this was not necessarily the case. He suggested that CUs combine elements of free trade with greater protectionism, so it is not clear whether such arrangements increase or decrease welfare.

Customs unions have two opposing tendencies: they will increase trade within the union but reduce trade with the rest of the world. This is the basis of Viner's central concepts: trade creation and trade diversion.

Trade creation (TC) is when a country starts to import a good previously produced at home, because it is now cheaper to import from inside the union. Basically the nation is changing from a higher-cost domestic producer who was protected by a tariff to a lower-cost producer from within the union/FTA. This represents a positive welfare effect on the economy as the price is now lower and a more efficient producer is being used.

Trade diversion (TD) occurs when a country starts to import from a member of the union/FTA a good which previously had been imported from outside the union. So a switch is made from a lower-cost producer outside the union (but with a tariff imposed) to a higher-cost producer inside the union (without tariff), giving a negative welfare effect, as a less efficient producer is being used.

To illustrate this, a fictional example can be used. Assume the home country is Sweden and the product concerned is camcorders. The free trade price of such camcorders is ECU300 for Sweden. Other producers and traders are Spain and South Korea, which have free-trade prices of ECU250 and ECU180, respectively. These prices reflect the costs of production and therefore show the level of economic efficiency. Say Sweden, to protect its camcorder industry, places a 100 per cent tariff on camcorders. The effect would be as shown in Table 6.2a. With a 100 per cent tariff, Sweden would produce camcorders domestically.

Table 6.2 Example of trade creation and trade diversion effects

	Price of camcorders (ECU)		
	Sweden	Spain	South Korea
Free trade price	300	250	180
(a) Price + 100% tariff	300	500	360
(b) Price with customs union between Spain and Sweden	300	250	360
(c) Price with 50% tariff	300	375	270
(d) Price with customs union	300	250	270

If Sweden then agrees a customs union with Spain, it will drop the tariff from Spanish camcorders (see Table 6.2b). Spain is now the cheaper producer and Sweden will now import from Spain at the price of ECU250 rather than produce at home for ECU300. This is an example of trade creation. Trade has occurred where previously it did not and production is being undertaken by a more efficient producer (Spain's prices and costs are lower than those in Sweden). It should be noted, however, that Spain is not the lowest cost producer – this is South Korea. Therefore, although a positive move has been made towards more efficiency, it is not as good as free trade would be.

However, if the tariff was originally set at 50 per cent, the picture would be different (Table 6.2c). The cheapest producer would now be South Korea, and Sweden would therefore import from there. However, if Sweden forms a CU with Spain, the result will be that again Spain becomes cheaper (Table 6.2d) and Sweden will import from Spain, but this time trade will be diverted from South Korea to Spain – an example of trade diversion. Trade has been diverted from the most efficient producer to a less efficient producer and the effect is negative on world welfare.

Therefore trade creation occurs when the formation of a CU means that the country in question starts trading from a cheaper union partner and produces less domestically; trade diversion occurs when the formation of the CU means that the country starts to trade with a higher-cost partner within the union and stops trading with a lower-cost (but tariff-affected) country outside the union.

The economic welfare effects of a CU can be neutral, detrimental or beneficial. In short, trade creation is good as it tends to increase welfare, while trade diversion is bad because it decreases welfare. The net effect depends on whether TD is greater than TC (leading to a fall in welfare) or TC is greater than TD (leading to an increase in world welfare).

Partial equilibrium theory of customs unions

Using the example above let us start from the idea that Sweden has a common tariff of 50 per cent on both Spain and South Korea (Fig. 6.1). The situation is as follows: the price of South Korea with a tariff ($P_{SK}{}^*$) is lower than the Swedish price without a tariff (P_{SW}).

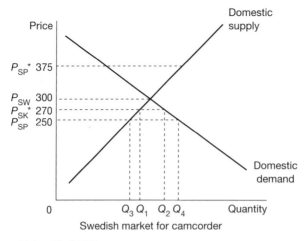

* With tariff of 50%

Figure 6.1 Welfare effects of a customs union

Sweden will import Q_1–Q_2 from South Korea and produce 0–Q_1 at home, and nothing is imported from Spain. Then Sweden forms a customs union with Spain. The price of camcorders falls to ECU250 and the level of imports increases to Q_3–Q_4. Both trade creation and trade diversion can be seen in this example. Trade has been diverted from South Korea to Spain of Q_1 to Q_2. However, the price has fallen again, which has encouraged domestic consumption but discouraged domestic production. Trade creation of Q_3–Q_1 has occurred (production has moved from Sweden to Spain). The area Q_2 to Q_4 is not strictly trade creation as this area did not previously exist before the price reduction; it is more **trade expansion**, which is an increase in trade due to lower prices.

Thus a CU reduced the price, but still not as low as the free-trade price. This is better for consumers than when there were tariffs on all countries, but is not as good as free trade. It is good news for the consumer but bad news for the inefficient producer, who was previously protected by tariff barriers. The net effect on the world economy, however, depends on the extent of trade creation and diversion.

Conclusions from Viner's analysis

Some generalisations can be drawn from the analysis so far:

1 The scope for trade creation is larger if the foreign trade sector is small relative to the domestic economy. This is because the scope for distortions in trade would be relatively small and creation greater.

2 A country's benefits from a CU will be larger the higher the proportion of trade with the country's union partner; that is, countries heavily dependent on each other should integrate with each other. If the trade between countries A and B constitutes a small proportion of total trade of A, it will not bring many gains for A to form a CU with B.

3 A CU is more likely to bring gains the higher the initial tariffs between the union partners. Conversely, the lower the tariffs with the rest of the world, the smaller the welfare losses arising from trade diversion.

Although still the basis of CU theory, Viner's analysis has been extended in certain vital areas, i.e. the **terms of trade** effects and dynamic effects of economic integration.

The terms of trade effects

An important assumption made above was that the home country is small in relation to both its partners and the rest of the world and thus the formation of a CU would not have any effect on the terms of trade. Clearly, this is very unrealistic. A large CU like the EU must have some effect on terms of trade. Once the assumption is dropped, the welfare effects are harder to distinguish in simple TD and TC terms – the welfare of the CU and the rest of the world will not necessarily move in the same direction.

The terms of trade effect also focuses attention on the importance of a CU in enhancing the bargaining power of its members in negotiations with the rest of the world. Thus, the higher the number of member countries in the union, the stronger the bargaining position of the union will be. However, the higher the membership, the less likely the union is to achieve consensus on the precise nature of the concessions desired from the rest of the world.

Dynamic consequences of economic integration

The static consequences of economic integration have been concentrated upon so far. However, the dynamic effects must also be considered: positive dynamic effects could be sufficient to outweigh some negative trade diversion. Dynamic effects embrace a whole category of factors which influence growth and improve efficiency, including external **economies of scale**, 'learning by doing', capital accumulation, technical progress, training and **market concentration** (competition levels). These are difficult to analyse within a conventional economic framework, with the exception of external economies of scale. However, they can be discussed in general terms.

Two possible dynamic consequences of integration can be taken to illustrate their possible effects: economies of scale and market concentration. Balassa (1961) suggested that customs unions expand the market facing domestic producers and present further opportunities for gaining economies of scale. A movement to a common market, with its removal of internal barriers, would have a similar effect (see Chapter 9). These economies of scale could/should result in higher growth, which will lead to possibly more investment and technical progress. Such growth could also reduce uncertainty and improve expectations, so boosting investment again – a virtuous circle.

The removal of barriers through a FTA, customs union or common market should lead, initially, to greater competition or at least potential competition. Monopolistic and oligopolistic structures within the domestic economies become exposed to much greater outside competition. This should bring greater efficiency and possibly higher levels of research and development, and technical change. Again this should bring higher investment and economic growth. This, of course, assumes that a domestic monopoly does not become a union monopoly!

Empirical studies

The economic theories above have suggested various factors which lie behind the emergence of free-trade areas and customs union formation. Let us relate these concepts more closely to Europe. Various studies have been undertaken to see the net effect of setting up the EU by attempting to measure the trade creation/diversion that might have occurred. (Most of these studies measured the effect after the EU had existed for 10 years.)

Table 6.3 summarises many of these and most show trade creation exceeding trade diversion, indicating a net positive welfare effect. Only one study suggests that the effect was negative and these figures are much smaller than the others. One might also observe that the differences between 'manufactures' and 'all goods' are very small, which might suggest that most of the effect regarding trade creation and diversion was felt in manufacturing.

As an example of how such studies were undertaken, one often-quoted study by Balassa (see El-Agraa 1989) used the changes in the ratio of the average annual change in imports to that of GNP as an indicator of the effect of integration. The assumption was that the ratio would remain constant if there were no

Table 6.3 Estimates of trade-creating and trade-diverting flows in the EC[a]

	Date	Coverage	Trade creation ($ billion)	Trade diversion ($ billion)
Truman	1968	Manufactures	9.2	1.0
Balassa	1970	Manufactures	11.4	0.1
Balassa	1970	All goods	11.3	0.3
Verdoorn and Schwartz	1969	Manufactures	11.1	1.1
Aitken	1967	All goods	9.2	0.6[b]
Kreinin	1969–70	Manufactures	7.3	2.4
Truman	1968	Manufactures and raw materials	1.8	3.0

Notes: [a]Original six only. [b]Diversion from EFTA only.
Source: Davenport, in *The European Economy: Growth and Crisis* edited by Boltho (1982)
© Oxford University Press 1982. Reprinted by permission of Oxford University Press.

integration, so an increase in the ratio for intra-area trade is supposed to indicate gross trade creation. The same increase in trade with all sources of supply would point to net trade creation. Conversely, a decrease in the ratio for extra-area trade would mean trade diversion. Balassa found evidence of trade creation and external trade creation but not of trade diversion for manufactured commodities within the EC in the early years.

The welfare implications in terms of income gains of these studies were also similar but they were rather small, varying between 0.15 and 1.0 per cent of the combined GNP. However, the method of estimating the welfare effect was rather crude and involved multiplying the volume of trade created or diverted by half of the tariff.

A later, similar but more sophisticated study by Winters (1987) found that, on average, external trade creation outweighed trade diversion within the EC, that trade creation internal to the UK was substantial, and that the UK exports to EC countries increased considerably at the expense of exports to elsewhere. However, although UK imports from the EC increased even more rapidly, with the result that the UK incurred considerable deficit in manufacturing trade with the EC, the increase was not at the expense of imports from elsewhere, which indicated that there was no trade diversion as a result of British accession to the EC.

The overall picture appears to be that the EC has had a considerable impact on the pattern of trade in Europe in general but the welfare effects of the EC have not seemed significantly large. However, it should be noted that these studies are concerned mainly with the static resource-allocation effects of integration. Studies on the dynamic effects are less easy to find but the theoretical analysis suggests that the dynamic effects would be much more beneficial to the EC, although the distribution of these benefits might be less than desirable. Moreover, nearly all the studies are based on the assumption that the main objective of integration in Western Europe is to remove discriminatory tariffs. This is unsatisfactory, since the EU has been guilty of discrimination in its tariff policy, for example regarding textiles from Turkey, India and Pakistan, and by forcing Japan to adopt voluntary export restraints (see Chapter 5). Furthermore, at the time of the formation of the EC and EFTA, certain changes in the pattern of trade were already beginning to emerge, such as reduction in the discrimination against the USA. Such developments are bound to have influenced the trade patterns.

It should be noted that the impact of integration on the manufacturing sector only has been considered (largely because the agricultural sector is dealt with in Chapter 7). Moreover, economic integration may have had a negative impact on the member economies apart from the trade-diversion effects on welfare. These negative effects include the influence that a CU might have on regional and interpersonal inequalities for example (see Chapter 7).

The adjustment costs of integration and implications for distribution

Clearly the impact of economic integration will not be felt equally by all groups or individuals within a particular country. There are two main issues to be considered here: firstly, the long-term effects of integration, and secondly the **adjustment costs** of integration. These are the costs involved in moving from one situation, e.g. tariff barriers, to another, such as a free-trade area; such costs are associated with the process of transition rather than the final outcome.

With regard to the first issue, we can measure the distributional effect of integration in a number of ways. One approach is to concentrate on factors of production such as land, labour and capital and look at the impact of changes in trading arrangements on these. This involves, for example, asking whether the move to integration favours workers more than the owners of companies, or vice versa. Alternatively, we can look at the impact of integration on sectors or industries, defined more or less broadly. A general approach would be to look at the relative impact of free-trade areas or customs unions on agriculture, manufacturing and services. More specifically, we could examine the effect of integration on particular industries within these broader categories. A third approach is to look at the way in which integration changes the relative position of particular regions; either within country boundaries or spanning borders. More recently, feminist writers have looked at the effect of the European Union on the relative position of women. It is possible to extend this list of approaches to distribution to encompass a wide range of other categorisations.

Clearly, the approaches listed above are not independent of each other, although they are distinct. The decline or rise of certain industries, for example, can have pronounced regional impacts and also alter the industrial relations climate.

In addition to looking at the long-term effect of integration, it is also important to look at the transition process between different stages of integration and the associated costs. In a textbook example of a freely adjusting market such costs are relatively minor. As openness to trade causes industries where there is a comparative disadvantage to decline, new industries open up. Similarly, if regions experience economic difficulties, labour and other costs will tend to fall, making investment more attractive and attracting new flows of capital. In practice, however, there may be significant costs if either labour or capital is immobile. Such a situation might arise if there are difficulties for workers in moving geographically or between sectors requiring differing skills, or if there are problems for companies in raising the finance to move into new areas of production.

The number of different issues involved makes it impossible to formulate a general theory covering the adjustment costs and distributional implications of the formation of the European Union, or a similar regional arrangement. It is necessary to analyse these questions concretely by focusing on the experience of particular groups, industries or regions. One example of this is Milward's detailed study of the impact of the EEC on the Belgian coal industry in the

1950s and 1960s (Milward 1992). Milward shows both how the particular position of the industry affected the negotiations which led up to the Treaty of Rome in 1957, and how in turn the process of integration affected the industry and the region, the Borinage, where it was primarily located.

Finally, one should remember that a CU is only one form of economic integration. Higher forms of integration might bring far more benefits than a CU at relatively low costs. For example, with respect to the EU, some argue that real benefits and substantial gains can be achieved only after the establishment of a single market or currency.

The advantages and disadvantages of customs unions and economic integration cannot be evaluated simply by examining the theory of integration. It is also necessary to look at the experience of movements towards regional integration in practice. In the remainder of this chapter we shall look at this, focusing on the growth of the European Union but also comparing the EU with other regional groupings.

Economic integration in practice

Economic integration and customs unions are not a new development in historical terms; in the 19th century for example there were the Austro-Hungarian customs union and the 'zollverein' – the Prussian-led customs union beginning in 1834, which helped to begin the process of German unification. However, regional integration declined in the period between the two world wars as both European and Latin American countries responded to recession by imposing tariffs and other controls on trade. Further, the concept of regional blocs was put into question somewhat by, on the one hand, the use of colonial possessions as an alternative trading area by Britain and France, and on the other, the attempt to impose regional domination through force by Germany and Japan. Finally, the inter-war period was typified by an isolationist mood in the USA, which weakened the interest of that country in forms of economic integration.

The period since 1945, however, has seen a resurgence of regional blocs. Between 1992 and 1996 the number of regional trading arrangements in the world nearly doubled to over 100 (Boscheck 1996). Almost all the members of the **World Trade Organisation (WTO)** belong to some kind of regional arrangement. Among these various groupings the EU is unique in the level of integration that has been achieved; in terms of unifying trading policies with the rest of the world, dismantling non-tariff barriers, enforcing common policies in areas like competition and agriculture, and moving towards further integration in areas like the common currency. The EU has also been in existence for considerably longer than many of the new trading arrangements. In order to understand the process of economic integration then it is necessary to look at two main questions: firstly, that of why the EU has taken integration so much further than other groups of countries and whether this is likely to continue; and secondly, whether the experience of the EU provides a useful model of integration for other regional blocs.

Origins and nature of the EU

The European Economic Community (EEC) and the European Atomic Energy Community (Euratom) came into being with the signing of the Rome Treaties in March 1957. The countries involved at this stage were Belgium, France, Luxembourg, Italy, the Netherlands and West Germany. The combination of the EEC and Euratom brought about the European Community (EC), which became the European Union (EU) on 1 January 1994, following the ratification of the Maastricht Treaty. By January 1973, Denmark, Ireland and the UK had expanded the Community to nine members, and these were joined by Greece in January 1981 and by Spain and Portugal in January 1986. In October 1990, the five Eastern *länder* of the newly united Germany became part of the EC. Austria, Sweden and Finland joined the EU in January 1995, yielding a total of 15 members.

The process of the formation of the EEC is quite controversial, because of what it tells us about the nature of the grouping and the intentions of its founders. The Treaty of Rome followed some ten years of discussions concerning various forms of closer co-operation in Western Europe, including the Benelux customs union of Belgium, the Netherlands and Luxembourg, which was founded in October 1947; the formation of the **Organisation for European Economic Co-operation (OEEC)** (later to become the Organisation for Economic Co-operation and Development (or OECD) with the addition of the USA and Canada) in April 1948; the Council of Europe in April 1949; and the **European Payments Union** in September 1950. The immediate predecessor of the EEC was the **European Coal and Steel Community (ECSC)**, originally proposed by the French foreign minister Robert Schuman in May 1950, embodied in the Treaty of Paris in March 1951 and taking effect in July 1952. The proposal for the ECSC (often referred to as the 'Schuman Plan') was prepared within the French Planning Commission by staff under the direction of Jean Monnet, and it is on the basis of this that Monnet and Schuman are sometimes regarded as the originators of the EU. A notable fact about the ECSC is that it was never simply a free-trade area; proposals for liberalising trade went together with a supra-national arrangement for regulating the market under a 'High Authority', including rules for pricing, subsidies for firms hurt by the new trading arrangements (in particular the Belgian coal mines; see Milward 1992), and funds for retraining workers. In this way the ECSC foreshadowed a number of later developments in the EU.

Some writers have seen the formation of the EEC as the culmination of this period of increasing interest in integration and as the launching pad for future developments in this area after 1958. In this way the Treaty of Rome becomes part of a gradual movement towards closer and closer integration. These writers differ about what exactly is the cause of this process. It has variously been seen as resulting from the federalist ideas of Monnet and his circle, from the increasing integration of the world economy and the growth of multinational companies, and in its most sophisticated form, from the logic of institutional developments. The so-called '**neo-functionalist**' analysts of the EEC, such as

Ernst Haas, stressed 'the additive logic of institutional development: that is, the way modest functional changes tended to lead to complementary alterations along an extending path of often involuntary integration' (Anderson 1996a, page 13; see also Haas 1958).

This whole approach to economic integration and the formation of the EEC has been questioned by Alan Milward, who has presented a very different account of the developments (Milward 1984, 1992). For Milward, the EEC and the ECSC were not the end-point of the discussions of integration that had taken place in the 1940s; rather they represented a very different view of what the nature of integration should be. The attempts at integration in the 1940s, especially the negotiations that led to the OEEC, were largely encouraged by the USA and linked to the programme of 'Marshall Aid' for Western Europe. The aim of the USA in these discussions was to encourage a form of integration that would weaken the nation-state in Western Europe, and eventually lead to a United States of Europe, which would be a global ally for the USA. According to Milward, this concept of integration was successfully resisted by the Western European countries, and the institutions created in the 1950s were designed to promote a very different approach. The idea of integration behind the ECSC and the EEC was one which would strengthen rather than weaken the nation-state. In particular, by adopting an international approach to a limited number of key questions (notably agriculture, employment protection and the management of trade), Milward argues that the Western European governments created a situation that would enable them to adopt nationally based policies in other areas which would reassert and protect the authority of the nation-state in the region, following the traumas of the 1930s and the Second World War. Key to these policies were the maintenance of high wages and demand and the establishment of the welfare state in Western Europe. Milward claims that the ECSC and EEC were instrumental in providing a stable international environment that would permit national renewal; but international arrangements were generally designed to serve national goals rather than the reverse.

The importance of the approach to integration proposed by Milward is that, if it is correct, there is no reason to suppose that integration has an inherent tendency to increase and deepen:

> the ECSC, the Common Agricultural Policy and the Common Market were indispensable pillars of Europe's reconstruction. But each was and is designed to resolve a particular and limited, not a generalised and universal, problem. There was no necessary implication in any of these carefully controlled acts of economic integration that the supersession of the nation state was an inevitable continuing process. The process of integration is neither a thread woven into the fabric of Europe's political destiny nor one woven into the destiny of all highly developed capitalist nation states.
>
> (Milward 1984, page 493)

The '**neo-realist**' view of integration put forward by Milward and others has been challenged, notably by Perry Anderson (Anderson 1996a; see also the wider range of articles on this debate in Anderson and Gowan 1997). Anderson argues that Milward cannot explain the scope of EU institutions simply by appealing to national interests: 'A customs union, even equipped with an agrarian fund, did not require a supranational Commission, a High Court capable of striking down national legislation, a Parliament with nominal rights of amendment or revocation. The limited domestic goals Milward sees as the driving-force behind integration could have been realised inside a much plainer framework' (Anderson 1996a, page 14). He claims that it is also necessary to consider a number of other factors driving integration: the federalist views of Monnet and others, the desire of the USA to create a strong West European counterweight to the Soviet Union, the aim of the French government to limit German power and the German objective of returning to the established community of nations and keeping open the possibility of eventual reunification. These international issues, for Anderson, have to be linked with the domestic concerns emphasised by Milward, in order to explain European integration.

While Anderson is critical of the framework proposed by Milward, he does not state explicitly the extent to which he sees European integration as a process which has an inbuilt tendency to deepen. In a later article he argues that the combination of the plans for monetary union, the unification of Germany and the collapse of the Soviet bloc necessitates a radical reconsideration of the whole basis of the European Union (Anderson 1996b). It is not clear, however, whether this reconsideration will lead in the direction of closer economic integration. To analyse this would require looking not just at the formation of the EEC but also at developments since 1958, as well as attempts at integration elsewhere.

The development of the EU

The development of the EU has often been divided into four main periods (see e.g. Middlemas 1995). The first, from 1958 to 1973, saw the removal of internal tariffs and the accession of three new members. The relatively optimistic atmosphere of this period saw a number of new proposals for further development of the Community, for example in the area of monetary union. The second period, from 1973 to the early 1980s, was a less happy period for the Community. Middlemas refers to it in a chapter headed 'The Stagnant Decade' though this judgement is qualified somewhat in his text. Economic crisis and internal disagreement led to something of a paralysis of decision-making within the Community, and the ambitious schemes of the late 1960s were not carried out. However, the early 1980s saw the opening of a more positive third period in the Community's development, leading up to the Single European Act of 1986 and the preparations for the Single European Market and involving renewed interest in monetary union. The fourth period begins with the Maastricht Treaty of 1991 and unsurprisingly is the most ambiguous and difficult to interpret of the subdivisions. It has involved a determined effort on the part of almost all the EU member states to achieve the criteria for monetary union, as well as the expression of a strong commitment towards expansion towards the east in the future. However, the uncertainties mentioned by Anderson above lie in the background, and there is evidence both of increasing public disquiet at the economic sacrifices seen as involved in monetary union and of a loss of popular enthusiasm for further integration. Consequently, the conclusion of the Inter-Governmental Conference initiated by the Maastricht Summit, at the Amsterdam Summit of July 1997, was rather muted and the Treaty of Amsterdam did not extend the integration process in as many directions as some had hoped that it would.

In order to explain why the EU has taken the process of integration further than other regional groupings in the world, it is especially important to analyse the developments in the 1980s. At the start of that decade it appeared quite possible that the EC would remain simply as a customs union. In particular, the Community faced major problems in the areas both of fiscal policy and the budget and of monetary co-operation.

There were recurrent disagreements over the EC budget. Caught between the insistence of the British and German governments in particular on budgetary restraint, and the French and German agreement to maintain the Common Agricultural Policy (CAP) with consequent escalating costs of farm support, the budget was progressively squeezed. This in turn limited the effectiveness of other areas of Community expenditure such as the Social Fund, European Investment Bank and the European Regional Development Fund, which was agreed on in 1974 and established in 1975. The UK, which was the member state most unhappy with the budgetary position, actually found these latter funds more attractive than the CAP, but by targeting the CAP expenditure via renegotiating its budgetary commitments the UK was squeezing expenditure other than agricultural support (Swann 1988).

The attempt to formulate a common monetary policy was equally problematic. The Hague summit of December 1969 endorsed the idea of Economic and Monetary Union (EMU) for the Community and set up the Werner Group to report on the matter. The Werner Report of October 1970 called for complete and irreversible convertibility, closely aligned exchange rates, full liberalisation of capital movements and a common central banking system within a decade. In the wake of this approach the EC members formed the 'Snake' in 1972. EC currencies were to be kept within a margin of fluctuation of 2.25 per cent on either side of the dollar's value. Within this margin they could float up and down in value, hence the name of the arrangement. However, the Snake was a victim of the increased instability in world exchange rates after the floating of the dollar in 1971, particularly the frequent rises in the value of the German mark. Sterling left the Snake in June 1972, the Italian lira in February 1973 and the French franc in January 1974. By the end of 1977, only five EC members – West Germany and those most closely economically linked to it, the Benelux countries and Denmark – remained in the Snake. Further, the hoped-for effect of exchange rate discipline in encouraging the co-ordination of EC members' economic policies had not materialised (Swann 1988; Middlemas 1995).

A key question in explaining the development of the EU is thus that of why the 1980s saw a resurgence of interest in integration after the disappointments of the 1970s. A number of reasons have been put forward for this development. The following four seem especially important.

Firstly, there is the issue of the economic problems faced by Western Europe in the 1980s. Lawrence and Schultze write that:

> In the early 1970s, however, Europe's economic performance began to deteriorate on almost every count: GNP growth, productivity, unemployment and inflation. Although performance also deteriorated elsewhere in the industrial world, the difference was that in Europe unemployment kept on rising all through the 1970s and early 1980s not with a cyclical rhythm but monotonically. Indeed, unemployment accelerated its upward move after 1980. By 1986 unemployment among the European members of the OECD stood at over 11 per cent, 2 percentage points higher than it had been at the height of the 1982 recession, and 4 per cent higher than it was in the United States ... both left and right agree that Europe faces a serious economic problem.
>
> (Lawrence and Schultze 1989, page 251)

In particular, Western Europe appeared to be falling behind one of its major competitors, the USA. Between 1960 and 1973 the USA grew at an average of 4 per cent per annum, while Western Europe grew at 4.8 per cent. Between 1982 and 1990 the positions were reversed, with the US growth rate at 3.6 per cent and that of Europe at 2.8 per cent (Glyn 1992). The EU has also tended to lose ground in a number of key industries with high rates of growth. Martin Wolf quotes research showing that the research and development intensity of US exports of manufactures to the EU in 1987 was almost twice as high as that of EU exports to the USA. Of the US exports to the EU, 51 per cent were labelled 'high technology', compared with only 23 per cent of EU exports to the USA (Wolf 1994). The European share of the output of the world's 12 largest companies in the dynamic industry of computers and office equipment between 1980 and 1990 was just 7 per cent (Wolf 1994).

This relative economic failure was often attributed to institutional problems in the European economies and given the name 'Eurosclerosis'. Economic integration was widely seen as a potential cure, especially as the performance of the US economy became more widely admired in the late 1980s and early 1990s.

A second factor that has been seen as encouraging the rejuvenation of European integration was the influence of the European Commission and in particular its president, Jacques Delors. George Ross writes that 'two processes interacted to get the EC up and moving after 1985. The first was a changing political opportunity structure, itself connected to broader contextual changes as impinging on EC institutions and policy legacies. The second was successful strategising and resource mobilisation by agents for change, the Commission in the first instance, along with its key member state allies, to capitalise upon these prospects' (Ross 1995, page 12). Against those who argue that integration arose naturally from economic problems, Ross stresses that business leaders in Europe had widely divergent views on integration, and that consequently the Commission played a key role in unifying different perspectives and outlining a way forward: 'Institutions and politics count a great deal at historical turning points, and in the mid 1980s it was the decisive action of the European Commission that pointed Europe in new directions' (Ross 1992, page 56).

A third approach stresses the growing convergence in terms of ideas among the European governments and policy-makers in the 1980s. Kenneth Dyson has traced the importance of ideas about 'sound money' in creating the movement towards European Monetary Union in the late 1980s (Dyson 1994). Dyson does not argue that these ideas caused the movement towards integration in themselves. Rather, they provided a framework within which the different governments could reach the kind of compromises that allowed the movement towards integration to proceed. For example, the growing consensus around the need for strong anti-inflationary policies enforced by credible monetary policy authorities meant that in the Maastricht negotiations the EU member states accepted a set of convergence criteria and a proposed constitution for a European central bank which allayed many of the fears that the German Bundesbank had previously expressed about monetary union. Another key development in terms of ideas was a growing scepticism about the possibility of an individual European country maintaining an effective independent economic policy. The key development here was the experience of the French socialist government in the early 1980s. After its election in 1981 the Mitterrand government tried a policy of economic expansion, which triggered a balance of payments crisis and the devaluation of the franc and was abandoned in 1983. Ross writes that 'its failure was symbolic. Mitterrand's subsequent turn towards austerity moved French policies closer to those of Germany and brought renewed French commitment to the Community' (Ross 1992, page 56).

The fourth set of reasons for increased movement towards integration in the 1980s centre on institutional developments within the Community. A number of developments can be highlighted here. First, the Community expanded with the joining of Greece, Spain and Portugal. This was by no means a development without problems (see Swann 1988), but by the same token the ability of the Community to bring negotiations concerning the accession of relatively poor countries with substantial agricultural sectors to a successful close enhanced its prestige. Second, the EC began to have more success in the area of exchange rate policy with the formation of the European Monetary System (EMS) in 1979. The first few years of the EMS were fairly cautious, following the experience of the Snake, with frequent realignments of currencies; however, after 1983, realignments became fewer and from 1987 until 1992 there were no realignments (Gros and Thygesen 1992). The convergence of European inflation rates in the 1980s was widely attributed to the effect of the EMS, though this is difficult to prove. The seeming success of the EMS played a large role in encouraging the movement towards monetary union.

The third institutional development was the decision in 1976 to institute direct elections to the European Parliament. The first such elections took place in 1979. The powers of the Parliament remain limited, but direct election has played a role in increasing popular interest in, and involvement with, the EU. Finally, the June 1984 Fontainebleau Summit provided agreement both on budgetary reform and on a commitment to reform the CAP. Again, this did not solve all the problems in these areas, but it did lessen the previous arguments over the budget.

In addition to these particular institutional developments which encouraged further integration, Dyson makes a more general point about what he calls the 'rules of the game' (Dyson 1994). He looks in particular at the influence of the functioning of the EMS on the movement towards a single currency. His argument is that the institutional structure provided by the EMS provided an important background stability and context within which debates about further integration could evolve: 'The institutional evolution of the EMS shows that history matters, but that historical change has an inbuilt tendency to follow the admittedly not always well-defined contours provided by institutional regulation' (Dyson 1994, page 227). Further, 'institutions impart a self-reinforcing character to change. Reflecting the structural power of the anchor currency, they also provide a context of predictability in which the complex bargaining relations that comprise the EMS and EMU policy process evolve' (Dyson 1994, page 227; the 'anchor currency' referred to here is the Deutschmark).

These four reasons for increased interest in economic integration within Europe are not mutually exclusive. On the contrary, to a large extent they reinforce one another. Many of the converging ideas in Europe about policy resulted from the economic difficulties the EU was facing. The ability of the European Commission to play an active role depended on the institutional context within the Community. The desire of the Commission to play this role was in turn influenced by high unemployment and slow growth in Europe, and so on.

The extent to which these various factors imply that there is a continuing pressure for further integration is not clear. It could be argued that the role of institutional factors in promoting integration lends credence to an 'evolutionary' view in which, as institutions evolve, so integration follows. In addition, to the extent that economic difficulties and changes in policies reflect long-run problems in the European market, they may be expected to generate continuing pressure for further moves towards union. On the other hand, the stress placed on the role of the European Commission indicates that integration depends to a large degree on conscious policy choices as well as structural factors. Further, if economic circumstances or policy ideas change it may well be that the momentum towards integration will reverse. Both Dyson and Ross indicate that this has happened in the 1990s. For Ross the key changes were the collapse of the communist system and German reunification: 'Dramatic changes in the EC's backyard introduced political complexities that, in turn, could create new risks for the very delicate political equations upon which Delors's strategy was premised ... With the coming of new international problems, there was danger that the EC might sink under a load of too many priorities, there was great danger of institutional and political overload' (Ross 1995, pages 47–48). For Dyson, the key issue, related again to German reunification, is the increasing instability in currency markets, as shown by the ERM crises of September 1992 and June 1993, and by growing divergencies in monetary policy among the major world economies. Neither writer argues that integration is bound to fail to proceed; however, they do stress that further progress in these more difficult circumstances cannot be assumed but depends upon political judgement and priorities.

It is also important not to regard integration simply as a package, but to look separately at the different aspects contained within it, since the relative weight of different factors affecting each aspect may alter. For example, the influence of the European Commission appears to have been especially important in the case of the Single European Market. In the movement towards monetary union institutional factors such as the role of the EMS and the influence of ideas appear to have played a more decisive role, with the Commission in large measure reflecting these: 'The crucial fact is that the victory of sound money in the Treaty on European Union was the product of forces of which the EC Commission and Delors were largely a reflection' (Dyson 1994, page 256).

In order to investigate the forces leading towards economic integration in more detail it is necessary to look beyond developments in the EU and investigate some of the other regional trading agreements which have emerged in recent years.

Economic integration outside the EU

Until recently, regional trading agreements took two main forms. Firstly, there were arrangements which in large measure were responses to European developments and to the formation of the EU. Relevant examples here are the European Free Trade Association (EFTA), which groups those Western European countries that are not members of the EU, and the Council for Mutual Economic Assistance (Comecon), which involved the old communist states of Eastern Europe and the USSR. These agreements did not lead to any more general moves towards integration. Comecon was dissolved in 1991, while the majority of EFTA members have joined the EU and the remaining countries are linked to the EU through the European Economic Area (EEA), with the exception of Switzerland.

The second kind of arrangement was that between groups of developing economies; for example, the Andean Pact in South America, the ASEAN Free Trade Area in South East Asia, the West African Economic and Monetary Union (including former French colonies using the franc as the national currency), and the Caribbean Community. The extent to which such groupings could become truly integrated was rather limited, since trade relations with dominant partners from the industrialised countries (the USA, France, Japan) tended to take precedence over regional objectives.

The recent rebirth of widespread interest in regional integration began with the North American Free Trade Agreement (NAFTA), concluded in 1991 and ratified in 1993, which involves the USA, Canada and Mexico. This agreement built on the earlier free-trade agreement between Canada and the USA implemented in 1989, and on a decade of trade liberalisation between the USA and Mexico, including Mexico's accession to the General Agreement on Tariffs and Trade (GATT) in 1986. The importance of NAFTA lay not just in the trading arrangement itself but in the debate which it provoked about future integration in both North and South America.

NAFTA is simply a free-trade area at present with no common external tariff, and so discussion of its effects has focused very much on internal trade within the region. The central debate has been over the possibility of companies moving from the USA and Canada to Mexico, where wages are lower and environmental and labour laws are less strict, with consequent job losses in North America. This fear mirrors that expressed in Canada when the initial free-trade agreement with the USA was signed, since union membership and social benefits are higher in

Canada than in the USA. NAFTA has been criticised by trade unions and environmentalists for favouring big business. On the other hand, the defenders of the
agreement argue that following the principle of comparative advantage will benefit all countries in the agreement, and that companies are not just concerned with
wages but with the productivity of workers, which is higher in the USA than in
Mexico. They also argue that 'NAFTA probably goes further to recognise environmental concerns than any previous international trade package. Its arrangements
include the provision of money to clean up the heavily polluted
Mexican–American border, and a commission to monitor compliance with
national environmental laws and pursue governments for persistent breaches'
(*The Economist* 1993, page 26). However, trade relations within NAFTA are highly
asymmetrical: 80 per cent of Canadian export earnings come from the USA and
the USA takes 70 per cent of Mexican exports, while only 25 per cent of USA
exports go to Canada and less than 10 per cent to Mexico.

The record of NAFTA has been mixed. Initial effects appeared positive. In
the first six months of the agreement US exports to Mexico increased by 16.7
per cent and to Canada by 9.6 per cent. Mexican exports to the USA increased
by 20.3 per cent and Canadian exports by 10.2 per cent. It was estimated that
100 000 new jobs were created in the USA in this period because of NAFTA, and
direct investments of $9 billion flowed into Mexico in 1994 (Boscheck 1996).

However, the adjustments required by NAFTA for the Mexican economy proved
very difficult to make. By mid-1994, unemployment had risen by 3.7 per cent, inflation rose from 7 per cent (at the beginning of 1994) to 45 per cent, and interest on
industrial loans tripled. The Mexican peso dropped in value by 53 per cent in late
1994, money flowed out of the country and the Mexican crisis required a $50 bil-
lion international loan, largely organised by the USA. The terms of this loan
committed Mexico to a tighter money supply policy and used Mexican oil revenues
as collateral. This led to a fierce debate in Mexico about the impact of NAFTA on
national sovereignty, and the government used NAFTA emergency clauses to
impose special duties on imports in threatened sectors (Boscheck 1996).

The devaluation of the peso led to a $10 billion trade deficit for the USA with
Mexico in the first eight months of 1995. The view that NAFTA threatened US
jobs became more widely heard, and disputes between the three countries over
protective duties and subsidies became more widespread. NAFTA has no supranational institution to supervise such disputes. It does provide for a judicial
review by a bi-national panel, but this only covers anti-dumping and countervailing duty proceedings.

While NAFTA played an important role in generating renewed interest in
regional integration, the Mexican crisis of 1994 has removed some of the impetus
from the process. The USA government, mainly because of problems with con-
gressional approval, has delayed opening up the agreement to new members,
although Chile is keen to join. Discussion of possible free-trade agreements across
the Americas, or of links between the EU and NAFTA, have remained at a very
general level, with few concrete initiatives. To a large degree the US government
has preferred to pursue trade liberalisation on a global scale through the World
Trade Organisation (WTO). However, the formation of NAFTA did influence a
number of other regional agreements in the first half of the 1990s. Two contrasting examples are discussed in the case studies on Mercosur and APEC.

Mercosur (or Mercosul in Portuguese as opposed to Spanish) was formed in 1991 by Brazil, Argentina, Paraguay and Uruguay. The aim of Mercosur is to create a customs union.

In the first stage of Mercosur, from 1991 to 1994, members cut tariffs on trade with one another. However, tariff reduction is not universal. Cars and sugar are subject to special arrangements. Each country is also allowed to maintain tariffs on a list of products which are deemed 'sensitive' (950 items for Uruguay, 427 for Paraguay, 221 for Argentina and 29 for Brazil). The members are committed to removing all internal tariffs by the year 2000 and to bringing cars and sugar into the agreement. However, unlike NAFTA, the agreement does not extend to services, and does not cover intellectual property or government procurement.

From 1 January 1995 Mercosur embarked on a second stage of integration. A common external tariff was applied to most imports into the region. This tariff is set at 11 different levels, ranging from zero to 20 per cent, with a trade-weighted average of 14 per cent. Each country, except Paraguay, was allowed to exempt 300 items from this tariff until January 2001, when tariffs must converge at the common level. Paraguay, which has low tariffs and will have to raise them in order to converge with other member countries, has been allowed to exempt 399 items from the common tariff until January 2006. There are special arrangements for telecommunications equipment and for capital goods.

In 1996 Chile became an associate member of Mercosur. It joined an extended Mercosur free-trade zone but will act unilaterally in trade arrangements with countries outside the agreement. It was decided that Chile's uniform 11 per cent tariff was too difficult to incorporate into the varied external tariff structure of Mercosur. However, the agreement with Chile was viewed as extremely significant by Pilling and Mark (1996) in the *Financial Times*, where it was reported that 'From Mercosur's perspective, getting Chile on board goes far beyond the limited commercial advantages of incorporating 14m more consumers. Fundamental was bridging what Mr Klaus Schwab, president of the World Economic Forum, calls the "missing link" between Mercosur and Asia. "Mercosur now has access to the Pacific Ocean and Chile has access to the Atlantic Ocean", says Mr Jorge Campbell, Argentina's secretary of international economic relations. "This accord has united us in a bi-oceanic bloc"' (De Jonquieres 1996, page 5).

Mercosur has appeared to be strikingly successful in a number of ways. Trade among the four original members grew from $4 billion in 1990 to $14.5 billion by 1995. Outside direct investment in Mercosur also grew, totalling around $6 billion in both 1994 and 1995. The decision to make democracy a formal condition of membership is widely credited with helping to forestall the attempted military coup in Paraguay in April 1996. In December 1995 Mercosur signed a framework agreement with the EU, with a tentative target of free trade by 2005. Japan has expressed interest in dialogue with Mercosur. Peru and Bolivia have indicated that they would like to join the agreement.

However, Mercosur does also face a number of problems. Firstly, the disruption caused by the Mexican crisis affected Mercosur as well as NAFTA. In particular, the Argentinian financial system was put under strain, and Argentina imposed a general duty of 3 per cent on imports from outside Mercosur and raised its tariffs on capital goods and telecommunications equipment in response. Brazil also increased its list of products exempt from the common external tariff by 150 for a year and raised tariffs on consumer electronics and cars.

Secondly, there are some doubts about the importance of Mercosur for Brazil, which is the largest economy in the grouping. In the first half of 1996 trade with Mercosur amounted to just 15 per cent of Brazil's trade, as compared with 28 per cent for Argentina; while in 1995, 27 per cent of Brazilian exports went to the EU, 21 per cent to NAFTA and 18 per cent to Asia. Brazil has sometimes taken trading decisions unilaterally. In 1995 Brazil, worried by a rising trade deficit, raised tariffs to 70 per cent on cars imported by firms without manufacturing plants in Brazil; firms with such plants could continue to import at a tariff rate of 35 per cent. This measure applied to Mercosur members as well, notably to Argentina, and appeared to be an attempt to concentrate the growing motor industry foreign investment in the Mercosur grouping within Brazil. Similarly, in July 1995 Brazil temporarily raised tariffs on toys from 20 per cent to 70 per cent without consulting Chile, despite the importance of toy exports for that country.

While these decisions have caused considerable strain for the Mercosur agreement, it is also true that Brazil did compromise over cars, exempting Mercosur-made imports from the tariff rise (to the displeasure of some Japanese motor industry investors in Brazil). Brazil has also compromised on a lower common external tariff in Mercosur than it originally wanted, and has maintained the agreement even though its former trade surplus with the Mercosur countries became a deficit following the 1995–96 recession in Argentina.

A third potential problem for Mercosur is raised by Richards (1995). He argues, in a similar way to North American critics of the NAFTA agreement, that the relatively high wages in Argentina will be threatened by free trade with Brazil. Manufacturing production will migrate to Brazil, where trade union bargaining is more fragmented, leading to a greater concentration in Argentina on agricultural production and related industries, where the position of Argentinian workers is weaker. It is certainly true that the summer of 1997 saw increased worker unrest in Argentina, including a general strike, though the extent to which this is linked to Mercosur remains controversial.

Perhaps the most serious criticism of Mercosur results from its very success in increasing regional trade. A World Bank study in October 1996, by Alexander Yeats, argued that the grouping was distorting international trade flows and discriminating against other countries' exports. In other words, trade diversion was exceeding trade creation. Yeats found that intra-Mercosur trade had expanded most rapidly in capital-intensive products, which are most heavily protected under the external tariff rules. Mercosur members have had little success in selling such products in third markets, suggesting that regional integration was hindering competitiveness in the area. While intra-Mercosur trade in motor vehicles more than doubled between 1990 and 1994, analysts found the quality of vehicles produced inside the region to be lower than elsewhere.

Sources: *The Economist* (1996) Survey on 'Mercosur' (12 October). Pilling D. and Mark I. (1996) Jilted Chile hitches up to Mercosur, *Financial Times* 25 June. De Jonquieres G. (1996) Mercosur trade group under fire, *Financial Times* 24 October.

Questions

1 How serious do you think the criticisms that have been made of Mercosur are? What actions might the governments of the Mercosur countries take to answer these criticisms?

2 What are the main differences between the approach to integration followed by the NAFTA countries and that followed in Mercosur? How would you explain these differences?

3 Chile originally wanted to join NAFTA but has negotiated an agreement with Mercosur following the slow progress of NAFTA in accepting new members. What are the advantages and disadvantages for a country like Chile in joining each of these groupings? Do you think that Chile is better or worse off in its arrangement with Mercosur than it would have been in an agreement with NAFTA?

• •

Case study: APEC

• •

The Asia-Pacific Economic Co-operation was founded in 1989. It currently has 18 members: the six ASEAN countries of Brunei, Indonesia, Malaysia, the Philippines, Singapore and Thailand; the three NAFTA countries; Australia, New Zealand, Papua New Guinea, Chile, Japan, Taiwan, South Korea, China and the autonomous region of Hong Kong, which maintains a separate membership of APEC. Negotiations under way for Vietnam, Cambodia and Burma to join ASEAN may well add more members to APEC as well.

APEC is clearly a much larger grouping, both in terms of population and numbers of countries, than NAFTA or Mercosur, or even the EU. Consequently, it is more loosely structured than these groupings. While it is concerned with intra-regional issues, APEC also attempts to act as a pressure group in global trade negotiations.

Yoichi Funabashi states emphatically that:

> APEC was born out of fear – fear of a unilateralist or isolationist America, fear of a balkanization of the world into competing economic blocs, and fear of the potential death of the GATT-centred world trading system. It was no coincidence that the strongest initiatives for APEC's founding came from Japan and Australia. Both countries faced similar threats from the emerging forces at the end of the Cold War. Both nations also traditionally relied politically, militarily and economically on the United States, making them especially vulnerable to an aggressive or inward-focused America.

(Funabashi 1995, page 105)

As a result of this the APEC countries developed a philosophy of 'open regionalism'. The objectives of the grouping included encouraging the Uruguay Round of GATT trade negotiations; discouraging the formation of regional blocs in Europe, North America and East Asia; defusing trade friction between the USA and Japan; involving China as a partner within the Asia Pacific region and maintaining US commitment to the region.

APEC appears to have had some success in these objectives. Funabashi reports Australian prime minister at the time of the GATT negotiations, Paul Keating, as saying of the preceding APEC summit, 'if it weren't for the Blake Island meeting, we wouldn't have got the GATT signed.' German GATT negotiator Lorenz Schomerus said that 'the chief determinant of the successful conclusion of the Uruguay Round was the APEC summit in Seattle; they sent us a clear message. You had an alternative and we did not.' APEC has also been successful in heading off the proposal floated under the Reagan administration in the USA that individual countries in the Asia Pacific region might join NAFTA. This caused great concern in Asia at the time, because of the possibility that trade would be diverted away from non-member countries and because of the pressure this would cause for a countervailing East Asian regional bloc. The Malaysian prime minister Dr Mahathir Mohammed was particularly active in floating the idea of an East Asian Economic Caucus (EAEC). Funabashi (1995) comments that 'some speculate that the EAEC proposal led Washington to change its focus from NAFTA extensions toward a more comprehensive open regionalism through APEC' (page 110).

However, while APEC has had some success in promoting these more general objectives, there is some concern about what are the most appropriate concrete measures that can be taken by such a large and potentially unwieldy grouping. There has been disagreement between the United States on the one hand and China and Indonesia on the other over issues of human rights and labour regulation, with pressure from the USA for the adoption of common minimum standards for labour conditions. *The Economist* magazine criticised the 1995 APEC summit in Osaka for avoiding real commitments. It commented that 'the Osaka summit adopted an Action Agenda. But it avoided real action, and "agenda" is a flattering word to describe the vague programme that the delegates agreed upon. The forum's propagandists cite its commitment to "free and open" trade and investment ... But there is a catch. APEC's members do not agree on what "free and open" means' (*The Economist* 1995, page 125).

C. Fred Bergsten, the chairman of the main advisory group to APEC from 1992 to 1995, replied to this criticism one month later. He pointed to the way in which the grouping had resisted protectionist views from Japan and South Korea on agriculture, and had reached agreements on customs harmonisation and simplification, product standardisation, mutual recognition agreements for product testing and certification, as well as the commitment by a number of member countries to reduce tariffs more quickly or more than required by the WTO. He stressed the commitment to consensus in APEC and argued that it could now move on to take the lead in the movement towards the global liberalisation of trade.

Sources: Funabashi, Y. (1995) *Asia Pacific Fusion: Japan's Role in APEC*, Institute for International Economics. *The Economist* (1995) Trade in the Pacific: no action, no agenda, 25 November. Bergsten, C.F. (1996) The case for APEC, *The Economist*, 6 January.

Questions

1 In what ways do you think that APEC differs from other regional trading arrangements? How would you account for these differences?

2 How justified do you think the criticisms that have been made of APEC are? What problems would the grouping face in changing its approach to emphasise firmer commitments by member countries?

3 What obstacles do you think that APEC might face in the future in putting its philosophy of 'open regionalism' into practice?

Questions for discussion

1 Assume that Austria, Hungary and Turkey all produce refrigerators and the domestic price per refrigerator in Austria is £600, in Hungary £500, and in Turkey £360.
   (a) Suppose Austria imposes a 100 per cent tariff on refrigerators. What are the trading options open for Austria?
   (b) If Austria then formed a CU with Hungary with a common external tariff of 100 per cent how would Austria's options change?
   (c) How would you describe the situation in (b)?
   (d) If the tariff rate in Austria in (a) were 50 per cent instead of 100 per cent how different would your answers to (a), (b) and (c) be?

2 Would it be, in general, better for a country like Austria to form a CU with a country like Switzerland instead of Hungary? Why?

3 To what extent are the Vinerian concepts of trade creation and trade diversion relevant today?

4 Which group of countries would have lost out most by the UK's membership of the EC in 1973?

5 Turkey has had an arrangement of CU with the EU since the beginning of 1996. What will the effect of this arrangement on (a) the Turkish car industry, and (b) the Turkish textile industry?

6 How convincing do you think that Milward's view that the formation of the EEC was mainly determined by national economic priorities is? What other factors do you think might have had an influence on the formation of the Community?

7 How would you account for the relatively poor economic performance in Western Europe in the 1970s and 1980s? In what ways might the revival of European integration help this performance?

8 Can you think of any factors that might have encouraged the revival of interest in European integration in the 1980s which are missing from the account given above?

9   To what extent do you agree with the view put forward by Ross that the European Commission and Jacques Delors played a crucial role in restarting the process of European integration in the 1980s? Can you think of any arguments that might suggest that their role was not so important?

10   Why do you think that the momentum of European integration has slowed down in the 1990s, so that the Amsterdam Summit produced less dramatic results than the Maastricht Summit?

Main reading

Anderson, P. and Gowan, P. (eds) (1997) *The Debate on Europe*, Verso.

Husted, S. and Melvin, M. (eds) (1995) *International Economics*, 3rd edition, HarperCollins.

Tsoukalis, L. (1997) *The New European Economy Revisited*, OUP.

Winters, A. L. (1987) Britain in Europe. A survey of quantitative grade studies, *Journal of Common Market Studies*, Vol. 24 (4) pp. 315–35.

Additional reading

Anderson, P. (1996a) Under the sign of the interim, *London Review of Books*, 4 January.

Anderson, P. (1996b) The Europe to come, *London Review of Books*, 25 January.

Artis, M. J. and Lee, N. (eds) (1994) *The Economics of the European Union*, OUP.

Balassa, B. (1961) *The Theory of Economic Integration*, Richard D. Irwin Inc.

Bergsten, C. F. (1996) The Case For APEC, *The Economist*, 6 January.

Boscheck, R. (1996) Managed trade and regional choice, *Financial Times: Mastering Management Supplement*, International Macroeconomy and Competitiveness section.

Chacholiades, M. (1990) *International Trade Theory and Policy*, McGraw-Hill.

Corden, W. M. (1972) Economies of scale and customs union theory, *Journal of Political Economy*, Vol. 80, pp. 465–75.

De Jonquieres, G. (1996) Mercosur trade group under fire, *Financial Times*, 24 October.

Dyson, K. (1994) *Elusive Union: The Process of Economic and Monetary Union in Europe*, Longman.

El-Agraa, A. M. (1989) *The Theory and Measurement of International Economic Integration*, Macmillan & St Martins.

El-Agraa, A. M. (ed.) (1994) *The Economies of the European Community*, Harvester Wheatsheaf.

The Economist (1993) NAFTA: the showdown, 13 November.

The Economist (1995) Trade in the Pacific: no action, no agenda, 25 November.

The Economist (1996) Survey on Mercosur, 12 October.

Funabashi, Y. (1995) *Asia Pacific Fusion: Japan's Role in APEC*, Institute for International Economics.

Glyn, A. (1992) The costs of stability: The advanced capitalist countries in the 1980s, *New Left Review*, Vol. 195, September/October.

Gros, D. and Thygesen, N. (1992) *European Monetary Integration: From the European Monetary System towards Monetary Union*, Longman.

Haas, E. (1958) *The Uniting of Europe: Political, Social and Economic Forces 1950–1957*, Stevens.

Hitiris, T. (1988) *European Community Economics*, Harvester Wheatsheaf.

Johnson, H. G. (1965) An economic theory of protectionism, tariff bargaining and the formation of customs unions, *Journal of Political Economy*, Vol. 73, pp. 256–83.

Johnson, H. G. (1974) Trade diverting customs unions: a comment, *Economic Journal*, Vol. 84.

Lawrence, R. and Schultze, C. (1989) Barriers to European growth: An overview, in Jacquemin, A. and Sapir, A. (eds) *The European Internal Market*, OUP.

Lipsey, R. G. (1960) The theory of customs unions: a general survey, *Economic Journal*, September, pp. 496–513.

Middlemas, K. (1985) *Orchestrating Europe: The Informal Politics of the European Union 1973–95*, Fontana.

Milward, A. (1984) *The Reconstruction of Western Europe 1945–51*, Methuen.

Milward, A. (1992) *The European Rescue of the Nation State*, Routledge.

Pilling, D. and Mark, I. (1996) Jilted Chile hitches up to Mercosur, *Financial Times*, 25 June.

Richards, D. (1995) Regional integration and class conflict: the Mercosur and the Argentine labour movement, *Capital and Class*, No. 57, Autumn.

Robson, P. (1987) *The Economics of International Integration*, Allen & Unwin.

Ross, G. (1992) Confronting the new Europe, *New Left Review*, No. 191, January/February.

Ross, G. (1995) *Jacques Delors and European Integration*, Polity.

Swann, D. (1988) *The Economics of the Common Market*, 6th edition, Penguin.

Viner, J. (1950) The customs union issue, in Robson, R. (ed.) *International Economic Integration*, Penguin, 1972, pp. 31–47.

Wolf, M. (1994) A relapse into Eurosclerosis, *Financial Times*, 24 February.

7

Introduction

This chapter considers a number of the salient areas of EU policy. In particular it focuses on areas which have led to much public and political debate. The areas of agriculture, fishing, regional, social and transport policy show important inter-linkages as well as highlighting the development and growth in some of these areas during the 1990s. In addition, the five areas chosen are likely to play an even greater part in the development of the EU as it comes to terms with monetary union and its further expansion.

The problems of agriculture

Government intervention in agriculture is a common feature of most economies. This is due partly to the economic characteristics of agriculture, and partly to historical and political factors. However, the form of government intervention varies widely between countries. Intervention by the EU in agriculture via the Common Agriculture Policy (CAP), established in 1962, has not satisfied all member states in its attempt to create a single market for agricultural goods and to bring stability to the agricultural sector. It has been one of the most controversial and problematic issues within the EU.

It might seem paradoxical that while food is a necessity of life, agriculture, as a sector, is on the decline in relation to other economic activities. Moreover, while certain parts of the world are suffering from starvation and malnutrition, there is a crisis of overproduction of food elsewhere, such as the 'grain mountains' and 'milk lakes' of the EU. Why has agriculture been beset with such problems?

Short-term factors

The actual output of many agricultural goods diverges from planned levels as a result of factors beyond the control of farmers. Drought, floods, epidemic diseases, etc. can cause agricultural output to decline, while favourable conditions can lead to excess production, resulting in wide fluctuations in agricultural prices and incomes even in the short term. What effect does this have on the agricultural market? Firstly, unplanned fluctuations in supply will cause the price to vary in the opposite direction to output. However, the extent of the price change will depend upon the **price elasticity of demand:** the higher the price elasticity of demand, the lower the price fluctuation, and vice versa. Furthermore, the actual output and revenue will move in the same direction (with price-elastic demand), and in the opposite direction with price-inelastic demand.

Long-term factors

In addition to short-term factors, there are long-term factors which work against agriculture. Firstly, empirical observations indicate that the **income elasticity of demand** for agricultural goods is low. This fact, coupled with a low price elasticity of demand for agricultural products, has meant that as economies grow, agricultural incomes lag behind non-agricultural incomes (El-Agraa 1994). Furthermore, agricultural productivity growth has not been as high as that of the industrial sector. Consequently, there is a long-term tendency for farm incomes to decline.

Another long-term consideration which militates against agriculture is that agricultural products have a relatively low elasticity of supply. Therefore, as demand fluctuates its impact is that much greater on agricultural prices. When demand falls in a general recession, prices tend to follow suit in a dramatic fashion in agriculture, whereas the impact on industrial prices is cushioned by a fall in output.

The above analysis provides economic reasons for the instability in agricultural prices and incomes and shows why many industrialised economies have given support to agriculture. However, it must be stated that there are also historical, political, strategic and emotional reasons for adopting agricultural support policies.

Objectives of the CAP

At the time of the formation of the EU the relative importance of agriculture in terms of labour employed was, on average, just over 20 per cent within the original six countries.

The main objectives of the CAP, as set out in Article 39 of the EEC Treaty, were as follows:

1 to increase agricultural productivity by promoting technical progress and by ensuring the rational development of agricultural production and the optimum utilisation of all factors of production, in particular labour;
2 to ensure a fair standard of living for the agricultural community, in particular by increasing the individual earnings of persons engaged in agriculture;
3 to stabilise markets;
4 to assure the availability of supplies;
5 to ensure that supplies reach consumers at reasonable prices.

The Treaty also sets out in general terms in Articles 40–47 the principles and the policies by which the above objectives would be achieved, although specific details were left to the relevant organisations.

From its inception the CAP was committed not only to the establishment of a single market by abolishing all barriers to trade, but also to the structural change in farming throughout the EU by the common organisation of agriculture. New objectives also emerged during the operation of the CAP which reflected the inadequacies of the existing policies in the face of new trends and developments. Thus, in recent years new policy initiatives have underlined the problems of regional inequalities and the concern about the links between agriculture and environmental protection.

The operation of the CAP

The policies of the CAP are implemented by an executive body called the European Agriculture Guidance and Guarantee Fund (EAGGF), better known by its French acronym FEOGA (Fonds Européen d'Orientation et de Garantie Agricole). As its name indicates, the FEOGA has two main functions: to implement the common prices and trading policies of the EU, and to implement the common structural policy in order to shape the future of agriculture within the Union. The former is known as the guarantee (support) function, and the latter as the guidance function. The FEOGA is financed from the general budget of the EU. Originally it was thought that the revenue from the duties on the agricultural imports of the EU would be sufficient to finance the expenditures of the FEOGA. However, the increase in agricultural output within the EU, which reduced the revenue from the import duties, together with the increase in the cost of the support system, has necessitated additional sources of finance as well as a radical rethinking about the CAP. It suffices to note that the EU budget for the financial year 1994 was just over ECU33 billion, with agricultural expenditure accounting for around 52 per cent of total spending (Artis and Lee 1997).

If Table 7.1 is compared with Table 7.2 it may be noted that agricultural expenditure as a percentage of the total overall budget is set to decline by the end of the decade.

The method of support for agriculture within the EU varies from product to product. However, in the literature the support system for cereals has been regarded as 'the model', mainly because it contains most of the basic characteristics of the CAP system. Farm incomes within the EU are supported by maintaining a high enough domestic price, partly by preventing cheap imports exerting influence on the domestic price and partly by support buying to eliminate the excess supply encouraged by the guaranteed price level. The excess supply is either stored, disposed of by being destroyed, exported, given away or converted into another product that is not in direct competition with the original (e.g. using eggs to make egg powder). 'The model' can be illustrated by referring to Fig 7.1, which relates to the market for an agricultural product.

A target price is set annually based on the cost (including a profit mark-up) of producing the commodity in the most inefficient area in the EU. The target price, P_r, is allowed to vary monthly. A guaranteed price is set at about 7–8 per cent below the target price. Thus, there are as many target and corresponding guaranteed prices, P_g, in the designated areas for the product (there are 11 such areas in the UK). If the price of the commodity tends to fall below the guaranteed price, the

Table 7.1 Payments made in 1994 by sector and recipient member state (ECU million)

Member state	EAGGF Guarantee	EAGGF Guidance	ERDF	ESF	Admin	Other	Total
Belgium	1174.4	42.8	77.9	87.3	600.5	529.8	2512.8
Denmark	1287.9	66.6	14.8	38.7	2.7	85.4	1496.1
France	8048.8	384.1	460.8	453.3	23.0	554.6	3924.5
Germany	5271.6	476.0	726.8	611.9	24.0	619.0	7729.2
Greece	2723.5	332.4	912.0	444.6	3.1	428.7	4844.2
Ireland	1527.1	128.9	213.3	339.8	2.6	179.1	2390.0
Italy	3481.4	328.3	665.1	385.8	17.7	341.0	5219.2
Luxembourg	12.7	6.6	3.0	4.0	303.6	89.2	419.1
Netherlands	1935.9	31.3	60.0	173.1	17.1	198.6	2416.0
Portugal	713.3	450.0	1120.7	260.8	2.4	496.4	3042.6
Spain	4426.9	527.4	1361.2	660.2	5.3	853.7	7834.7
UK	3001.9	121.4	788.6	685.4	46.7	614.7	5258.6
Misc.	–	–	6.6	–	2515.9	4695.1	7217.7
Total	33605.4	2893.9	6410.8	4144.8	3565.6	9684.3	60304.8

Source: CEC (1996) page 305. Reprinted with permission © Oxford University Press.

relevant national intervention agency enters the market to buy the product so as to keep the price at or above P_g. As long as the equilibrium price, P_e, happens to be above the guaranteed price, P_g, farmers will sell their product at P_e. Therefore the guaranteed price is the minimum below which P_e will not be permitted to fall. For the system to work, farmers must also be protected from imports. Naturally, if the import price, P_w, is above the guaranteed price, P_g, there is no need to do anything. However, P_w is more likely to be below P_g (see Fig. 7.1). In such a case an appropriate tariff, $P_w P_r$, would be required to bring the price of imports up to P_r. In practice, however, the actual tariff does not have to be equal to the difference between P_w and P_r, since importers need to pay transport costs within the EU; it would be less than $P_w P_r$, for example $P_w P_t$. Thus, the world price plus the actual tariff, i.e. $0P_w + P_w P_t$, will give the threshold price, $0P_t$, for the product. In other words, the difference between the target price and the threshold price is equal to the transport costs. If farmers want to export, they would obtain only $0P_w$ per unit of the product. Thus an export subsidy or restitution of $P_w P_g$ is paid to the farmer to make up the difference between the world price and the guaranteed price.

Green currencies

An interesting aspect of the CAP is the common pricing system for agricultural products. The various agricultural support prices are expressed in terms of ECUs. Prices expressed in ECUs are then converted into national currencies. The rate at which 1 ECU exchanges for the national currency regarding agricultural goods is called the '**green rate**'. For instance, if the common price for milk were set at 1 ECU per litre, and the green rate for the pound were £1 = 2 ECU, then a dairy farmer in the UK would receive 50p per litre of milk. If the green pound were to be devalued to £1 = ECU 1, then the farmer would receive 100p = £1. Thus devaluation of the green pound would increase the incomes of UK farmers, and its revaluation would decrease them.

Table 7.2 Financial perspective for 1993–99, as agreed at the Edinburgh Summit (appropriations for commitments, ECU million 1992 prices)

Year	Common Agricultural Policy	Structural operations			Internal Policy	External action	Reserves			Total appropriations			Own-resources ceiling (as % of GNP)
		Structural funds	Cohesion fund	Total			Monetary reserve	Guarantee reserve	Total reserves	For commitment	For payment	For payment of GNP	
1993	35 230	19 777	1500	21 277	3940	4150	1000	300	1300	69 177	65 908	1.20	1.20
1994	35 095	20 135	1750	21 855	4084	4200	1000	300	1300	69 944	67 036	1.19	1.20
1995	35 722	21 480	2000	23 480	4323	4580	500	300	800	74 485	69 150	1.20	1.21
1996	36 364	22 740	2250	24 990	4520	4860	500	300	800	75 224	71 290	1.21	1.22
1997	37 023	24 026	2500	26 526	4710	5130	500	300	800	77 987	74 491	1.23	1.24
1998	37 697	25 690	2550	28 240	4910	5580	500	300	800	80 977	77 248	1.25	1.26
1999	38 389	27 400	2600	30 000	5100	5900	500	300	800	84 089	80 114	1.26	1.27

Source: CEC (1993) page 382.

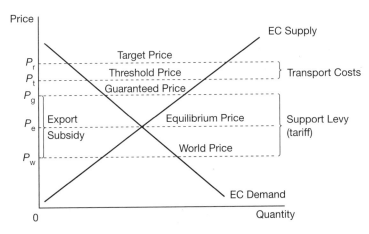

Figure 7.1 The market for an agricultural product

It would be natural to expect the green rate to change as the exchange rate of the country's currency (*vis-à-vis* other currencies) changes. However, this would disturb agricultural prices and incomes in the EU. For this reason the EU employs the system of **monetary compensation amounts** (MCAs) to accommodate **devaluations** and **revaluations** rather than changing the green rates. It has been stipulated in the Maastricht Treaty, which has been ratified by all the member states, that a single currency for the EU will be introduced by 1999. When that happens there will be no need for green currencies or the MCAs.

Assessment of the CAP

Has the CAP been successful in achieving its objectives? In answering this question it is necessary to reconsider the objectives of the CAP. It can be said that the CAP has achieved self-sufficiency in farm products within the EU, although the desirability of the objective itself is questioned by many. The general aim of creating a single market with common policies has also been achieved, although some would argue that the system is far too complicated and costly (see below). There has also been considerable technical progress and rationalisation in EU agricultural markets. As for the objective of market stability, increases in agricultural prices have, by and large, been lower than the EU inflation rate. However, EU prices must also be compared with the world prices for agricultural products. Such a comparison reveals that world market prices for most agricultural goods are much lower than those of the EU. Thus, price stability and the self-sufficiency of the EU seem to be achieved at a cost. However, it should be noted that the CAP itself is responsible for depressing the world prices for agricultural products since it has increased the supply and diverted the exports from non-EU countries.

The CAP has also succeeded in increasing the average farm size as well as in reducing the total number of farm businesses. Coupled with the reduction in the total area of cultivated land, it is possible, therefore, to claim that the CAP has achieved partial success in the objectives of rationalisation. Finally, some people claim that the CAP has made a positive contribution to the growth of the economies of the EU with the exception of the UK, West Germany and Italy. However, critics of the CAP point to a number of weaknesses or failures:

- it has failed to achieve the objective of shifting some of the farm labour to alternative uses;
- it has created embarrassing surpluses such as the butter and beef mountains and the wine and milk lakes, although the significance of these surpluses has been exaggerated;
- it has mainly benefited the rich farmers and the big farms, but has not done much for the poorer farmers;
- it has increased inter-country and inter-regional inequalities;
- it has transferred incomes from consumers in one member country to producers in another;
- it has failed to provide reasonable prices for the consumer, since it has kept prices above world prices;
- it has generated considerable financial expenditures and inter-member financial transfers;
- finally, the CAP has undermined the interests of the less developed countries (LDCs), mainly by allowing the EU to compete unfairly against imports from these countries, and also by encouraging the EU to indulge in 'dumping', which deprives the LDCs of potential export earnings.

The impact of the CAP on the EC/EU

The estimation of the cost of the CAP to the EU is a complicated matter. The most obvious cost of the CAP is the budgetary cost because it is relatively easy to measure (Barnes and Barnes 1995). However, the total cost of the CAP also includes payments from the EAGGF by the Guidance Section for structural improvement; support by national governments for research, infrastructure and advisory services; and transfers from consumers to producers in terms of high food prices.

Costs of the CAP

Initially, the EC budget was specific in that expenditures were directed towards particular activities and the revenues consisted of predetermined financial contributions made by the member states. Although it is still specific with respect to expenditure, it has been self-financing since 1970: the financial contributions of member states have been replaced by 'own resources', which the EU has the right to collect directly. The EU budget is required to be in overall balance annually, which distinguishes it from national budgets. Another characteristic of the EU budget is that its size still remains insignificant. For example, in 1995 the central EU expenditure per head was £104, compared with the UK government expenditure of £3800 per head (Griffiths and Wall 1997), and it is only around 2 per cent of the combined GDPs of the EU countries.

The main spending areas of the EU budget are the CAP, the regional fund and the social fund. Total spending in 1997 was ECU74.5 billion (1 ECU was around £1.44 in 1997). Over 50 per cent of this amount was absorbed by the CAP, while the structural and cohesion funds together accounted for around 35 per cent (CEC 1997).

There is inequity in the distribution of the budgetary burden between the partners of the EU. Germany, the UK, Luxembourg and Belgium have been net contributors, while the other members have been net recipients. There are two reasons for this: the fact that the CAP has accounted for around two-thirds of total funds, and the way in which revenues are collected and funds are disposed of. A high proportion of the FEOGA expenditure – which is itself a high proportion of the EU budget – is directed towards countries with relatively large agricultural sectors having large surpluses and exports. Countries with relatively small agricultural sectors and thus small exports receive relatively little, and yet these are the main contributors to the EU budget. This is why the UK and Germany were net contributors. However, what made the situation with respect to the UK 'unfair' was the fact that the UK, unlike Germany, was a relatively poor member of the Union (the ninth poorest), and yet it was the second largest net contributor. Consequently, the UK argued for a review of its contributions and, after rather prolonged negotiations, succeeded in persuading the Community to accept the principle of compensation for the UK in 1980. In the early 1980s the UK received *ad hoc* payments as part of this compensation, but the Fontainebleau Summit in June 1984 agreed to a more permanent solution: any member with a disproportionate budgetary burden may receive an appropriate correction at the time. In the case of the UK this has meant receiving 66 per cent of the difference between what it pays in VAT and what it receives from the Community budget.

As has already been stated above, the budgetary costs constitute only a part of the total cost of the CAP. **Producer subsidy equivalent** (PSE) is a measure of the total payments made to the farmer as part of the agricultural support system. An OECD study indicates that total help given to the farmer is well in excess of that indicated by the EU budget. The consumer subsidy equivalent (CSE), on the other hand, measures the burden of agricultural support schemes on the consumer from higher prices. This constitutes a tax on the consumer and is estimated to be around 40 per cent for the EU in the early 1990s (Barnes and Barnes 1995). It should also be borne in mind that the CAP operates in a highly regressive way since the above-said tax mainly falls on the poor as they pay a higher proportion of their income on food.

The problems of inequity and high cost regarding the CAP have been the subject of discussion for a long time. More recently, the budgetary problems of the EU have reached crisis point and thus the reform of the CAP itself has become a matter of urgency.

The impact of the CAP on the rest of the world

What about the impact of the CAP on the rest of the world? It has depressed the prices of agricultural products in general. This has important implications for the

LDCs. It has also been claimed that the CAP has insulated EU markets from external price effects and thus magnified the price fluctuations outside the EU. These price effects are supposed to harm mainly the exporters of CAP substitute commodities, i.e. the USA and the developed countries in the British Commonwealth such as Canada, Australia and New Zealand. The LDCs as a group would gain in so far as they are net importers of agricultural products. However, the CAP penalises the poor outside the EU by depressing world prices and hence depriving some LDCs of important foreign exchange. Dumping of sugar by the EU has had a devastating effect on the Philippines and hurt other sugar exporters such as Brazil, Cuba and the Dominican Republic. In addition to sugar, the EU is also a major exporter of food in general. In this capacity it competes with many LDCs, which depend on agriculture for their survival.

The CAP has accelerated the race in agricultural protection. The losers in this race are the poorer farmers in the LDCs, where the government cannot afford to support them. The increased price instability due to the CAP also has discouraged agricultural investment in the LDCs. Thus the CAP has contributed to the general neglect of agriculture in poor countries. The combination of (misguided) domestic policies which support the industrial sector and the protectionist policies of the EU and other industrialised countries resulted in lower agricultural productivity in many African countries and led to reliance on food imports and, for the very poor countries, on food aid. The LDCs became net food importers in the mid-1970s from a position of net food exporters in the previous two decades, and the deficit has been increasing.

The reform of the CAP

Obviously some serious problems with the CAP still remain: low farm incomes; growing agricultural surpluses in an increasing number of commodities; rapid growth of agricultural spending; high agricultural prices within the EU; detrimental effects on poor countries outside the EU; and negative environmental impacts.

Some of these problems are more serious than others. Attempts to reform the CAP go as far back as 1968, when the so-called Mansholt Plan proposed to reduce agricultural employment by 50 per cent and farmland by 7 per cent. In addition, it recommended the nationalisation of agricultural production to achieve economies of scale and liberalisation of agricultural trade. However, it failed in the face of political opposition.

In 1981 the Commission published a memorandum called *Guidelines for European Agriculture* in which a mixture of quotas and price costs were proposed in order to reduce agricultural production. The memorandum was in addition to *Reflections of the CAP* (EC Commission 1980) which elaborated on the theme of producer co-responsibility, whereby producers share the cost of disposal of excess supplies by means of a co-responsibility levy.

The measures, however, failed to bring a 'permanent' solution to the fundamental problems of the CAP. Production continued to outgrow consumption by 300–400 per cent. The problem became critical when budgetary funds were exhausted and expenditure was getting out of control in relation to resources. A solution was announced at the Agricultural Council meeting in March 1984, later to be adopted at the Fontainebleau Summit in June of that year. The package included the following measures:

1 The system of quotas was extended to milk. Dairy products were taking up more that 25 per cent of total FEOGA expenditure. Thus, the new system was intended to reduce milk production from 103 million tonnes in 1983 to 98 million tonnes in 1985.

2 A system of '**super levy**' was introduced to penalise those who overran their quotas.

3 The common farm prices were reduced by 0.5 per cent.

4 In order to reduce wine production, new wines were banned until 1990.

5 To alleviate the financial crisis the ceiling on VAT contributions was raised from 1 per cent to 1.4 per cent.

These reforms did not achieve the expected results. The quota system did not constitute a permanent solution to the problem, since it dealt with the symptom not the cause, which was overpricing. Moreover, the quotas set were well above the self-sufficiency level and thus surpluses continued to accumulate: milk production exceeded the official quota by one million tonnes. The situation was similar with respect to butter. Part of the problem was the loopholes in the system which, with the tacit approval of governments, allowed farmers to avoid the punitive 'super levy'.

The effect of the 0.5 per cent price cut which was expressed in ECU was to increase prices on average by 3.2 per cent in national currencies because of the operation of the MCAs discussed earlier. However, it should be noted that, because of inflation, real farm incomes actually fell. Paradoxically the agreed package did not reduce the cost of the CAP; in fact, the cost increased by ECU 2.3 billion between 1984 and 1985.

In July 1985 the Commission published a Green Paper entitled *Perspectives for the CAP*, in which it reviewed the problems of the CAP and made recommendations to solve them. The Commission recognised that cutting production was absolutely essential in order to reduce surpluses, and that farm incomes could no longer be supported by open-ended price guarantees. The *Perspectives* also stressed the links between agriculture and the protection of the environment. As a result, certain steps were taken in 1986 towards reforming the CAP. Milk quotas were adjusted to reduce output by 9.5 per cent over two years and to prevent further addition to the butter mountain. It was also decided that the unconditional support for beef and veal should be dropped; instead intervention should be related to certain quantitative and qualitative conditions. However, the agricultural ministers of the Community failed in 1987 to agree on how these policies should be implemented. Without agreement to implement reforms, the CAP began to expand rapidly and the financial crisis deepened. Farm spending overshot the 1987 budget by more than 15 per cent and the EU Council had to agree to introduce a series of supplementary budgets, and to postpone in 1987 some ECU 4 billion of agricultural spending until 1988.

Eventually the EC agreed on a package of reforms for the CAP endorsed by the Council on 29–30 June 1987 and refined in February 1988. It was a compromise. The expenditure on the CAP in future was to be limited to around 75 per cent of the average rate of growth in the Community's GNP. A ceiling of 160 million tonnes was introduced on cereal production. Similar quotas were set for oil seeds and protein products, and the quota system for milk extended for another three years. A new 'co-responsibility levy' of 3 per cent was introduced on larger farmers. Significantly the Council agreed to reduce agricultural output by withdrawing agricultural land from production. Funds were allocated for a compulsory and voluntary '**set-aside**' policy, which aimed to reduce agricultural land by 20 per cent over five years. All these measures meant extra spending, at least in the short run. Thus, to ease the financial burden a new source of finance was introduced in the form of an extra payment by each member state to the EC budget, a sum equivalent to up to 1.2 per cent of GNP.

In spite of the measures above, food mountains continued to grow. In July 1991 these amounted to 20 million tons of cereal, 750 000 tons of beef and 900 000 tons of dairy products (*The Guardian* 1991). Additionally, Community expenditure on market support had increased by 50 per cent from £16.8 billion to £24.7 billion between 1989 and 1992, but because of stock costs and export refunds this increase was having little impact on farm incomes. Thus, pressure for a radical reform package to alleviate the problems associated with the CAP was mounting. The situation was aggravated by the urgency for new initiatives to bring the negotiations in the much troubled Uruguay Round of the GATT to a successful conclusion (see later in this chapter). Consequently, on 1 February 1991 a formal document of reforms was published and submitted to the Council, which has come to be known as the MacSharry Plan. The document stressed the problems faced by the CAP, particularly the imbalance between production and consumption resulting in an increase in stocks. It pointed out that the CAP encouraged intensive farming systems, giving rise to environmental concerns. It recognised the unfairness in the support system, stating that 80 per cent of the support was devoted to 20 per cent of farms. It also pointed out that despite ever-increasing budgetary costs, real farm incomes improved very little between 1975 and 1989.

The MacSharry Plan

The reform package produced by the Agriculture Commissioner, Ireland's Mr Ray MacSharry, had four main objectives: competitiveness via reduced guaranteed prices; market balance through production controls via compensation through acreage payments; compensation to producers in a modulated form, with small farms receiving full compensation while big farms receive only partial compensation; and sensitivity to environmental requirement via the set-aside scheme.

The cost of the package led to an increase of £2.6 billion in the EU budget in 1992. However, it was anticipated that the EU budget would be significantly lower in the following years than it would have been in the absence of these reforms. The reform package implied that there would be a fundamental shift in the source of support for farmers, i.e. from consumers to taxpayers.

Big farm lobbies criticised the modulation of the compensation scheme (and in the July 1991 session of the Commission which endorsed the MacSharry proposals, they managed to extract a better deal on the issue of compensation for big farms). Particularly the National Farmers Union of the UK considered the MacSharry Plan as being damaging to UK farming and farmers, not surprisingly since UK farming is based on large units. In fact, in July 1991, the UK agriculture minister, John Gummer, attacked the reform package claiming that it would penalise efficient producers, discriminate against Britain and hamper the EC's ability to compete on world markets against other food exporting countries (Hornsby 1991). On the continent, however, there was opposition to direct payments from taxpayers via the government to farmers, partly because these payments were regarded as social security handouts based not on what the farmer produced but on what the authorities thought the farmer ought to receive.

Despite the above sentiments the compensation plan was, in fact, linked to acreage and thus encouraged at least the legal, if not the actual, fragmentation of farms to maximise receipts. It also maintained high land prices. As high land prices encouraged heavier use of fertilisers and agro-chemicals, the environmental pressures would be greater than they might otherwise have been. The MacSharry Plan was further criticised for being too difficult to police and thus open to fraud.

Arguably the most significant aspect of the MacSharry reform package was its implication for the Uruguay Round of the GATT. There was great pressure on the EU to come to a compromise with the USA and the other members of the GATT regarding the reform of trading relations in farm products in order to aid a successful conclusion to the Uruguay Round. The MacSharry reform was not the first reform of the CAP but it was the first reform that was not specifically aiming to reduce the budgetary implications of the CAP. In fact it resulted in higher FEOGA expenditure, at least initially. Thus it is possible to argue that the main motive for the MacSharry reform was to make the CAP consistent with international agreements on agriculture and not to sabotage the Uruguay Round (Tangermann 1996).

Case study: Reform of the CAP

Reform of the European Common Agricultural Policy, which has been a looming but indistinct spectre for some years, has at last taken definite shape with the publication this week of the Agenda 2000 proposals by the European Commission.

Farmers, consumer groups and environmentalists now have detailed plans to examine. Initial reactions from most in the UK are the reforms are 'a step in the right direction'. But there are misgivings.

British farmers fear their incomes will fall and limits on the aid to individual farms will hit them harder than farmers in other member states. Consumer groups say food prices will fall little, and not for some years. Environmentalists complain that proposals to increase spending on conservation are vague.

All are worried the reforms will be watered down during the wrangling in Brussels. That process has already started. For instance, Mr Jochen Borchert, the German federal agriculture minister, said the reforms, which could cut German farmers' incomes by 15 to 20 per cent, were not necessary.

The Commission aims to cut the aid farmers receive through the intervention system – where the European Union sets a floor price at which it buys surplus production – and phase out methods of limiting production, such as set-aside – where land is taken out of use – and quotas.

In return farmers would receive direct aid payments, while some spending would be diverted to agri-environment schemes and rural development. Mr Ian Gardiner, policy director of the National Farmers Union, welcomed the thrust of the proposals. He said farm incomes would fall sharply, with cereal farmers losing £330m, beef farmers £90m and dairy farmers £20m. But, he said, that was not a fair comparison. Farm profits were destined to fall anyway because the EU would have been forced to restrict production to meet world trade commitments.

Farmers would gain in the long term by being free to grow what the market wanted and to export their products, he said. 'Nevertheless, we have substantial reservations,' Mr Gardiner said. The first is the proposal to put a limit on the aid an individual farm can receive.

The proposals gave scant details of how this would work. But, Mr Gardiner said, such a limit would 'be bad for British agriculture and bad in principle.' UK farms are on average larger than those in other EU countries. 'The aim of the reform is to make European agriculture more competitive, so why penalise the more efficient farmers?' he said.

Another of the farmers' concerns is that many decisions on rural development spending will be left to 'the initiative of member states'. Mr Gardiner said farmers were worried because the previous government did not participate in voluntary measures to the same extent as other member states. Consumer groups also have their doubts about the proposals. Ms Ruth Evans, director of the National Consumers Council, said the CAP cost the average family £20 a week through taxes and high prices. 'The new system could end up just as wasteful and expensive as the current CAP,' she said.

Mr Stephen Crampton, at Consumers in Europe, reckoned the subsidy cuts would 'do no more than cut the price of a 250g pack of butter by 5p by 2005.' Environmental groups are the most critical of the proposals. The Royal Society for the Protection of Birds said the package 'will do nothing to promote better management of the rural environment' and that 'wildlife will be devastated by the abolition of set-aside.'

Source: Atkins, R., Buckley, N. and Urry, M. (1997) Farming reforms sow seeds of doubt: CAP changes are causing misgivings despite being 'step in right direction', *Financial Times*, 18 July.

Questions

1 Why are there misgivings about new reforms to the CAP?

2 Why might farmers benefit from the new reforms in the long run?

However, the problems for the agricultural sector never seem to end. It is true that the beef and wheat mountains have disappeared as a result of the 1992 reforms, and that farm incomes rose by 4.5 per cent per annum after the reforms – faster than before. However, the basic structure of the CAP is still the same and therefore the 'mountains' and 'lakes' could return in the near future and would be more difficult to get rid of since the Uruguay Round makes export subsidy illegal. Thus the EU Commission wants to introduce further reforms in the form of further substantial cuts in the guaranteed prices and direct compensatory payments to farmers, thus decoupling support from production. The long-term aim is to reduce the EU's guaranteed prices to the level of world prices and to give farmers direct aid should it be needed (*The Economist* 1997). These reforms would go a long way towards reducing the risk of costly surpluses but, more importantly, they would seem to be a priority in the light of the proposed enlargement of the EU, since the agricultural sector is more important in the prospective member countries than it is for the present members. However, there is a problem with direct compensatory payments: they are determined and financed by Brussels. This not only violates the principle of subsidiarity but also makes little economic sense since they treat a Greek farmer the same as a German one in terms of income expectation. They also make budgetary discussions more difficult. The recipient countries want to increase spending while the net payers want to cut it. One way around this would be a quasi-nationalised support system whereby the EU finances an agreed minimum income support and the member countries are allowed to top it up if they so desire.

Furthermore, a potentially explosive issue developed in the UK in the 1990s in the form of a contagious disease called BSE, more popularly known as mad cow disease, which mainly affects cattle. It would appear that ignorance, negligence and complacency turned what was a reasonable health hazard into a major disaster when in March 1996 it transpired that humans could also contract BSE with fatal consequences (the human version being known as CJD). The reluctance of Europeans to import British beef then became an official EU ban on British beef, with the prospect of hundreds of thousands of British cattle being destroyed. The situation eased slightly during 1997/98 with the Labour government attempting to negotiate the lifting of the ban by the EU on British beef exports. However, the situation has been complicated by recent scientific evidence that beef on the bone might present a greater risk than was previously thought.

The Common Fisheries Policy (CFP)

The common policy for agriculture developed under the Treaty of Rome is defined to include not only the products of the soil and stock-breeding, but also fisheries. This is not surprising when one considers the fact that even in its initial stage the EU included member countries with coastlines in the Mediterranean, the Adriatic and the North Sea. Moreover, the fisheries industry has many features in common with agriculture, such as a highly inelastic supply in the short run, low price and income elasticities of demand, and the specialised nature of its capital and labour. All these characteristics give rise to potential price instability. Additionally, the fisheries industry is susceptible, like farming, to natural random shocks such as bad weather; and it is, also like farming, made up of a large number of small enterprises. However, the fisheries industry also has its own special characteristics. Fishing is an example of market failure in that fish can be considered as a '**common good**'. This means that it is not possible to exclude anyone from consuming (in this case catching fish), but there is rivalry in consumption. That is, the more one individual consumes fish, the less there is available for others. In the past the stock of sea fish was thought to be inexhaustible; however, modern technology has made it possible to catch fish in such quantities that an enormous but finite resource is in danger of being depleted completely. The inability of the market to solve the problem has opened the door for regulation and control. Moreover, since fish move about in the open ocean, regulation and control necessitate international co-operation. It is not surprising, therefore, that fisheries happen to be an obvious area for the EU policy-makers. However, due to a combination of monitoring difficulties and conflicting national interests, developing an appropriate fisheries policy has proved to be rather difficult.

Rationale for a policy

It could be argued that a common policy for fishing makes more sense than that for agriculture, since fishing is an activity which transcends national boundaries. For instance, a vast majority of the codfish in the North Sea start their lives in the coastal waters of Germany, the Netherlands and Denmark, but by the time they are three years old, and therefore profitable to catch, most of them have 'emigrated' to the territorial waters of the UK (Nevin 1990). Thus, fishing activity in one country often has an important impact on the fishing industry in another country.

On the demand side, fish is regarded as a valuable part of the human diet and an essential part of healthy eating. It has also been a useful source of animal feed and fertilisers. Thus there is a continuous demand from the industry as well as from the direct consumers of fish.

On the supply side, the most problematic area in the subject of fisheries is overfishing. This is not a particularly new problem. It is possible to find examples of particular types of fish stocks being depleted as far back as the 19th century. However, modern technology has enabled the fishing industry to increase its catching capacity enormously. Even without any increase in tonnage, better-designed vessels can lead to an annual increase of 2 per cent in catching capacity (Barnes and Barnes 1995).

Overfishing is closely related to the biological constraints on fish stocks. It takes time for the fish stocks to replenish themselves. However, due to the existence of the **free-rider** problem, one individual's reduction in fishing means increased benefits for others. Consequently, in the absence of agreed rules or management, it is perfectly rational for individuals to maximise catches, which reduces the total stock for everyone. Thus, collective action is necessary to effect conservation by taking proper account of biological constraints. Nevertheless, why has there been so much discussion and controversy about fishing in the EU? After all, the total number of people engaged in the fishing industry, including the ancillary sectors of processing, transport, ship maintenance, etc., constituted approximately 1 per cent of the total workforce of the EU in the early 1980s (Nevin 1990). However, fishing is a politically sensitive issue, partly because it is one of the most dangerous occupations and thus attracts disproportionately large popular sympathy, and partly because fishing communities are highly concentrated geographically without many economic alternatives so that downturns in the fishing industry have major local impacts.

Attempts at international regulation

There have been several international attempts to regulate sea-fishing activities. The 1958 Geneva Convention on the High Seas, which was adopted by the First United Nations Conference on the Law of the Sea (UNCLOS I), established the general principles of fishing in open seas. Accordingly, fish were regarded as common property which did not become the property of any state until actually caught. No state could be excluded from such fisheries without agreement. Thus even under the extended coastal state fisheries jurisdiction, fish did not become the property of the state concerned until the point of capture. The convention also recognised the special position of the coastal states and encouraged them to adopt conservation measures. At that time the customary international law required that coastal states confine their exclusive fishing zones to narrow limits. However, there was no uniformity in practice regarding exclusive jurisdiction over fishing zones. For example, the UK claimed three-mile territorial waters although it had accepted the concept of additional fisheries zones, while some countries such as Chile, Ecuador and Peru claimed sovereignty and exclusive jurisdiction over 200-mile zones. UNCLOS II tried to solve the problem in 1960 by getting the member states to agree on a proposal for a six-mile territorial sea with a further six-mile fisheries zone, but the proposal was rejected by one vote.

Following the failure of UNCLOS II to agree upon limits for territorial waters or for fisheries, 17 states of Europe signed the European Fisheries Convention in 1964, which was ratified by all the member states of the EEC except Luxembourg. The convention allowed coastal states to have the exclusive jurisdiction over fisheries in a six-mile zone from the baselines of the territorial sea. However, by the mid-1960s it was clear that competition for open sea fishing was severe; fish stocks were being depleted and in some cases were in danger of disappearing. Moreover, some countries were threatening to impose 200-mile exclusive fishing zones. The Third United Nations Conference on the Law of the Sea (UNCLOS III) began discussing these issues from 1969 onwards and some of the sessions were allocated to the issue of exclusive economic zones (EEZs). The conference, with the support of the EU, resisted the idea of EEZs until 1973. Some countries strongly opposed the concept of EEZs. The UK was particularly against Iceland's declaration of a 50-mile zone in 1972 being extended to a 200-mile zone in 1975. In fact, the UK threatened to institute proceedings against Iceland before the International Court of Justice during the so-called 'Cod Wars' in 1972. However, during the 1974–76 session of UNCLOS III, Britain announced that it would be prepared to consider a 200-mile jurisdiction over fisheries on the condition of an acceptable package of agreement being reached at the conference. Unfortunately, the conference failed to reach an agreement in that session. It was not until 1982 that UNCLOS III agreed on the 200-mile exclusive economic zones, which was, in fact, the legitimisation of a *de facto* situation.

The development of European policy on fishing

By 1966, fish production in the original six of the EU began to stagnate and the EEC ceased to be self-sufficient in the major fish species. Additionally, some non-member countries began to complain about the restrictiveness of the existing fishing limits. Consequently, certain proposals, which contained the basic ingredients of the 1983 CFP, were submitted to the relevant authorities of the Community in June 1968. These proposals were adopted by the Council in October 1970, and came into force in February 1971. The most important feature of the proposals was that the six members of the EU accepted the principle of 'equal access' for all fishermen to the territorial waters of the EU. Thus even before Britain, Ireland, Denmark and Norway were due to start negotiations to join the EU, some elements of fisheries policy had been decided and their agreement meant a *fait accompli* for those countries seeking entry into the EU. It is worth noting that the combined catch of the UK, Ireland and Denmark fishing fleets was twice as big as the combined catch of the original six. Thus there existed a conflict of interest in the field of fisheries in the Community as early as the 1970s. (In fact, Norway eventually refused to join, arguably based upon this issue.)

In more detail, the proposals contained two main elements. One concerned the structure of the industry and related to rules for conservation comparable to the guidance section of the CAP. According to the proposals, the Commission would draw up conservation rules – the duration of the fishing season, minimum mesh size for nets, minimum sizes of fish to be landed and so on – to be applied to all members. The most important issue here was the total allowable catch (TAC), which is defined as the maximum number of fish that can be caught without threatening the maintenance of the total fish population. This total was to be specified by the Commission based on biological criteria advised by scientists, and to be varied from year to year according to the natural variation in the size of the fish stock (Nevin 1990). The allocation of this yearly total between the member states would be decided by periodic discussion and agreement. This was to be one of the most controversial aspects of the proposals.

The second element of the proposals was the creation of a common marketing organisation in fishing products operated by 'recognised producers' in each member country. The main principle was similar to that of the CAP. There would be an official guide price for each species of fish and a lower intervention (withdrawal) price. However, unlike the CAP, the guide price was to be realistic related to the market price. Thus the very high costs of operating the CAP were to be avoided.

There was a long process of negotiations, which were very tense and difficult, before a policy in any shape or form emerged. The first detailed proposals for a

CFP reached the Council in September 1976 but the CFP itself was not finalised until January 1983.

The CFP covered four broad areas regarding fishing and aquacultural activity. Firstly, it created a system for conservation of sea resources. The policy established a system in which measures are taken to limit fishing activity, to set rules for coastal fishing and to set specific TACs and quotas for individual countries and fish types. More specifically, it established a conservation box around the Orkney and Shetland islands and limited the number of licences to be offered to EU fishermen so as to protect endangered species. This involved the thorny dual issue of 'access' and the TACs. Different members argued for different criteria to be applied in the allocation of TACs. For example, Britain argued for allocation based on ownership (not surprisingly, since around two-thirds of the Union's waters in the Atlantic and the North Sea were British territorial waters) and that it should receive at least 45 per cent of the TAC; whereas other countries, while accepting that 60 per cent of the fish caught had come from British territorial waters, argued that the fish had originated elsewhere. France and the Netherlands, on the other hand, which had been fishing in the territorial waters of other Union members for decades, argued that the geographical distribution of quotas was as important as their overall tonnage (Nevin 1990).

Secondly, the CFP created a common organisation for the market in fishing. It aimed to facilitate trading between members in frozen and preserved as well as fresh fish products. The ultimate objective was to provide an adequate income for producers, to achieve flexibility in supply, to promote standardisation, and to guarantee reasonable prices for consumers.

Thirdly, there was the introduction of structural measures, including those which aimed to make rational use of the sea resources; to ensure equal treatment of all fishermen/women from different members; and to reduce overcapitalisation. In this respect special measures designed to rationalise vessel capacity, to aid exploratory fishing and joint ventures with non-EU members, and to aid the construction and modernisation of fishing vessels were agreed by the Council in January 1983. These measures were to apply for three years and were to qualify for ECU250 million of EU funding. Britain was to be the main beneficiary of this funding arrangement since it favoured projects designed to help fleets to adjust from long-distance fishing to nearer-water fishing following the loss of rights in faraway places (El-Agraa 1994).

Finally, the fourth area was that of negotiating agreements with non-EU countries. Fisheries agreements were signed with many countries outside the EU covering the north-east and north-west Atlantic, the Antarctic, the Baltic and the south-east Atlantic.

Like the CAP, the CFP has proved to be controversial. There has been friction between the fishermen of different countries, particularly those of Spain, Ireland and the UK. However, the main difficulty with the CFP is that of implementation, since monitoring of activities is rather problematic.

The problems with the CFP

The experiences of the CAP enabled the CFP to avoid some of the chronic problems associated with the former. While the CAP encourages farmers to indulge in unlimited production due to its support price system, the CFP is based on restriction of output and realistic price policy and thus does not result in excessive burden on the EU budget.

Important developments in the CFP followed from the accession of Portugal and Spain in 1986. These two countries increased the number of larger vessels (over 500 tonnes) within the EU by more than 100 per cent, increased fish consumption by 50 per cent, and raised the number of fishermen by 90 per cent. The integration of the Iberian Peninsula into the EU has been achieved, though not without a certain degree of pain.

There still remain, however, some very serious problems with the CFP. The most important problem is the depletion of fish stocks and the related issue of the determination and the allocation of TACs. Firstly, there is the issue of the absolute size of TACs. Conservation suggests the acceptance of reductions in TACs. However, such an action would threaten the livelihood of many fishing families in the community. The second problem is the necessity to negotiate TACs every year, which means variations in production from year to year resulting in variations in capacity utilisation. Thirdly, the process of allocation of TACs, which is based on political criteria, generates a tense bargaining atmosphere for it involves a kind of free-rider problem.

Another problem is the related issue of 'access'. An EU agreement in 1994 allowed Spanish and Portuguese fishermen to have access to waters to the west of the British Isles. This created great controversy since the Labour Party (then in opposition) and some Tory MPs felt at the time that this presented a threat to the long-term economic viability of British fishing communities (*Financial Times* 1995). The issue is further complicated by 'quota-hopping', which refers to a situation where foreign-owned fishing boats can buy up British boats, and thus can operate under British licences, and therefore catch fish under the UK quota since quotas are attached to the vessels. Some people feel that quota-hopping should be banned, while others argue that banning would violate the EU provision on freedom of movement. The British government is not considering a ban on quota-hopping, as these British boats were bought on the open market. Currently there are around 150 Spanish- and Dutch-owned fishing boats operating under UK licences (*Financial Times* 1997). However, it is possible to restrict quota-hopping by imposing conditions when fishermen register in another member state. For example, they may be required to land part of their catch in a particular port, or may be obliged to apply UK social security rules, and so on.

A third problem facing the EU fishing industry, also related to TACs, is that of overcapacity. Since 1991, member countries have been required to reduce the capacity of their fishing fleets by 20 per cent since too many vessels were chasing too few fish. Few members states have managed to achieve anything close to this reduction. It is possible to let the market mechanism sort this problem out. Fleets would be naturally depleted as the profitability in fishing activity declined and bankruptcies increased. However, market solutions would result in socio-economic hardship for some fishing communities. It would also aggravate the problem of conservation as it would encourage cheating on quotas. Thus planned decommissioning of vessels seems to be a more sensible approach. However, this requires funding, which brings its own problems such as the problem of free-riding. Funding to reduce fleet sizes must be collective, i.e. all members must fully participate in the scheme, otherwise non-participants will benefit, at the expense of others. Reducing fleet size might also increase catching capacity by encouraging efficiency.

Finally, there is a conflict between the structural aspect of the CFP and its market organisation. The former encourages conservation but the latter encourages larger catches by giving price support based on the size of the catch.

Case study: Quota-hopping

Mr Jim Portus, chief executive of the South Western Fish Producers Organisation, said he was 'gutted' by yesterday's High Court ruling that Spanish fishermen are entitled 'in principle' to claim millions of pounds in compensation for the period they were excluded from fishing against UK quotas.

His anger reflects growing bitterness over the thorny issue of 'quota-hopping', which occurs when Spanish vessels are registered in the UK or British-registered vessels are bought by Spanish owners.

According to Mr Portus there are now 160 such boats and they have established themselves as 'significant catchers' of UK quota fish. 'In 1996 they caught fish with a value of £43m. In volume terms, their catch last year was 13 per cent of the total UK quota.'

According to government figures, the quota-hoppers target six key species: monkfish, megrim, plaice, hake, pollack and Dover sole. In 1996, they took 53 per cent of the UK quota for plaice and 49 per cent of the hake. Mr Barry Deas, chief executive of the National Federation of Fishermen's Organisations, was equally angry.

'The Spanish quota-hoppers have won another round, simply by pursuing these legal loopholes,' Mr Deas said. 'But it does not detract from the fact that it is nonsense to have a system of national quotas which you cannot enforce on behalf of your own fishing industry,' he added.

For Mr Mike Townsend, who as chief executive of the Cornish Fish Producers Organisation represents 300 vessels, the High Court's decision could hardly come at a worse time. Fishing in the UK has been hit hard by low domestic prices and the strength of sterling. 'Fish prices are extremely depressed right now. At Newlyn 80 per cent of our catch is exported and with the strong pound we're having real problems,' said Mr Townsend. 'We're getting less today for megrim – which underpins our trawling fleet – than we did 20 years ago,' he added. UK fishermen had hoped the EU summit in Amsterdam might have brought them better news. But it 'was a lost opportunity', said Mr Deas. 'Unlike other commodities such as gas or minerals, fish is treated as a common resource.'

He said: 'The Common Fisheries Policy has become utterly discredited. It has failed to achieve a management system guarding against stock depletion, and has failed at the level of fairness, which the original agreement in 1983 – which established the principle of quotas across the EU – was meant to safeguard.'

Mr Portus is due to meet agriculture ministry officials on Monday. Quota-hopping will be top of the agenda. Mr Portus and his colleagues are hoping the government will deploy more effectively a requirement that quota-hopping vessels plough a significant portion of their profits back into the local communities from where they sail. 'I'm optimistic that things will change for quota-hoppers, and that the requirement that there is a genuine economic link between the boats concerned and the flag they fly under is enforced much more tightly,' he said.

Source: Mead, G. (1997) Cornish fishermen on warpath: outrage as Spanish quota-hoppers win compensation 'in principle', *Financial Times*, 1 August.

Questions

1 From the case study, what are the problems with quota-hopping?

2 What impact is quota-hopping having on fish prices?

●●●

Thus, like agriculture, a common fisheries policy has been hard to achieve and the approach adopted so far has been slow due to the differing importance of the fisheries industry for the different member countries.

Regional policy

Theories behind the need for a regional policy

In neo-classical theory, the free movement of capital tends to equalise factor earnings between participating countries or regions, leading to convergence. A critique of neo-classical theory, however, suggests that no such convergence will take place, but instead the free movement of capital will exacerbate national and regional differences in real income and welfare, with the well-off regions gaining at the expense of the poorer ones. Myrdal (1957) held that this free movement of capital would lead to 'polarisation' effects through a process of 'cumulative causation', i.e. the inflow of capital goes to where its marginal productivity is greatest and sets in motion dynamic processes that reinforce the attractiveness of these host areas; they then grow in prosperity attracting even more capital. Similar arguments exist for labour, and although a movement towards less prosperous areas may occur due to lower labour costs, less congestion, less pollution and so on, this is insufficient to offset the polarisation effect described above.

If Myrdal's view is to be believed and capital and labour are not completely mobile, persistent discrepancies between regions may exist. In other words, on its own the move towards equalisation between the regions may not work as quickly as neo-classical theory predicts. Moreover, it is not obvious that the process is a convergent one, since the wealthier regions may benefit more from new investment. In addition, the movement of labour and capital in response to market forces will be determined by private rather than social costs, which, if they differ appreciably, can lead to a serious misallocation of resources. Finally, there may be a lack of knowledge of other regions and constraints on wages, such as minimum wage legislation, which may prevent the flexibility required.

Thus some regions may always have advantages over others. In this case new industry and trade will be attracted to where it already exists, and where the infrastructure is already in place. Governments may also be 'prodded into action' on this regional issue not only on economic grounds but also on political ones. Regional inequalities are felt to be a political problem chiefly because large sections of the population feel that unequal access to wealth and opportunity is morally unjust as well as socially unacceptable. This call for 'equity' is supported from an economic standpoint in that regional disparities prevent optimum use of resources and thus keep total wealth below its maximum potential.

Why the need for a European regional policy?

In terms of the EU the following factors are suggested as important:

Disparity of income

Levi Sandri (1965) showed that the per capita income of the most favoured region in the Community (Hamburg) was about seven times that of the least well-off area (Calabria). It is argued that without the development of the **European Investment Bank** (EIB), with its provision of loans for the less developed regions in the Community, Italy would not have been so eager to become one of the original six members of the EU. In addition, as the Community has grown over time from six to 15 members, income disparities have been further highlighted. Denmark and Germany have per capita incomes which easily exceed the EU average, whilst Ireland, Spain, Portugal and Greece all have per capita incomes below the average. These poor regions tend to fall into one of two categories: they are either areas with a traditional dependence on small-scale agriculture and which have never developed the infrastructure for industrial development, or they are regions which have been heavily dependent on traditional industries, such as steel, textiles or shipbuilding, e.g. southern and eastern Belgium, the Ruhr and Saar in Germany, and west central Scotland, Wales and Northern Ireland in the UK. The decline could have been the result of a loss in comparative advantage, a decrease in demand for a region's output, shifts in technology, and so on (Table 7.3).

Their difficulty is in attracting investment in modern, productive industrial activities. For the first group, their lack of infrastructure is the major problem; for the second group, infrastructure is in place, but it is often in a poor condition and the workforce has inappropriate skills.

Union membership

If a country, on membership of the EU, has to adopt less strict restrictions on imports from non-EU countries, and so forth, then there may be structural changes in the country's economy leading to regional difficulties. Non-tariff protection against other members of the Union may also be dropped over time and this can further exacerbate these problems. These regional impediments may manifest themselves in a decline in the balance of payments, which could be compensated for by a depreciation in the country's currency under a flexible exchange rate regime. However, under the fixed European Exchange Rate Mechanism and the move towards monetary union, such a procedure is not an option and regional disparities may continue to exist.

External/internal borders

Armstrong and Taylor (1985) suggest that countries may lose out after a union is in place because the internal border will not profit from border activities. The same applies to an external border. Thus, a country which was previously outside the union and obtained finance from external trading activities with another non-union country will lose these once it becomes a member of the union, as trade gets redirected within the union.

Gravitation principle

Attention has been drawn to the possible tendency for industrial activity to gravitate towards the centre of the community – the so-called '**Golden Triangle**' of London, Frankfurt and Turin – to the exclusion of the other regions. Reasons for this are potential economies of scale, closeness to markets, and **agglomeration economies**, which occur through concentration in one area, such as transport and telecommunications facilities. However, diseconomies may also emerge due to pollution, for example, leading to companies moving out of an area. An example of a 'congested region' would be the area around Paris, which consists of 2 per cent of French territory, contains 20 per cent of the population and 25 per cent of the total employment, and produces 30 per cent of the national output. Similar congested areas would be the Rhine–Ruhr area of Germany, London and greater Athens. The regional problem here is how to divert activity away from these regions to the peripheral areas.

Changes in other Union policies

Alterations in the Common Agricultural Policy (CAP) mechanism or attempts at an overall energy policy may, as by-products of these policies, cause regional problems. For example, reducing milk subsidies may hit some countries harder than others, and some regions within these countries more than others.

Other factors

A Union regional policy can also be justified on the grounds that it may make national policies more effective; for example, it can prevent competition between member states in the giving of state industrial aids. A Union problem may also cut across national boundaries, requiring Union action rather than individual action.

These regional disparities (as depicted in Table 7.3) are large in some countries and do not appear to be diminishing. The knock-on effects from this are

Table 7.3 Regional economic disparities in the EU

Member state	Output per capita 1994 (EU = 100)			Unemployment 1994 (%)			Participation rate 1994 (%)		
	National average	Regional maximum	Regional minimum	National average	Regional maximum	Regional minimum	National average	Regional maximum	Regional minimum
Germany	113.2	212.9	55.8	10.5	19.8	5.8	47.2	54.5	41.0
France	116.2	178.5	79.3	12.8	17.4	8.6	43.9	50.0	34.8
Italy	96.7	123.4	54.0	12.5	24.5	4.0	39.7	45.4	32.9
Netherlands	104.3	150.8	70.3	9.0	12.4	6.7	47.8	51.2	43.3
Belgium	101.8	163.8	73.8	12.9	25.7	7.4	42.3	45.0	37.4
Luxembourg	121.9	–	–	2.7	–	–	45.2	–	–
UK	103.7	135.9	77.1	9.8	15.0	5.0	48.2	60.0	39.4
Irish Republic	81.3	–	–	15.6	–	–	39.2	–	–
Denmark	129.4	131.7	118.2	11.5	13.7	11.2	56.0	56.7	54.3
Greece	37.8	49.6	25.6	9.6	11.9	3.8	40.3	45.4	29.3
Spain	62.4	83.6	44.1	23.6	34.2	13.8	40.3	43.7	34.6
Portugal	31.6	45.6	18.8	7.1	11.3	4.1	48.5	49.9	39.8
Austria	112.6	159.5	72.0	6.7	8.5	4.2	40.9	53.1	29.9
Sweden	144.0	173.4	119.3	8.0	11.3	5.7	48.4	52.2	44.7
Finland	116.0	148.0	93.8	19.9	26.7	15.6	48.6	52.6	44.4

Note: The regional maximum and minimum values were calculated from NUTS2 level data using the EU's standard system of Nomenclature des Unités Térritoriales Statistiques. Output per capita is measured by gross value added (GVA), since this provides the most up-to-date measure of output per capita at regional level. GVA is measured in purchasing power parities (PPPs) and is defined as gross domestic product plus value-added tax plus import taxes.

Source: European Regional Database, April 1996, Cambridge Econometrics and Artis and Lee (1997) page 174.

social unrest, moves towards devolution and other social and political issues. Moreover, regional imbalances in unemployment can lead to a mismatch between labour supply and labour demand, the increasing tendency for inflationary pressures to be built up in one region of a country before being transmitted elsewhere – even though these other regions could have relatively high levels of unemployment and the social costs that can occur through regional disparities in terms of increased pollution, loss of social capital and the like.

Thus regional policy seeks to reduce disparities between regions, reduce the loss that might occur in social capital, improve overall growth performance and achieve a more equitable distribution of income.

The EU states' approach to regional policy

Regional policy in the individual European countries existed in its many guises long before the setting-up of regional policy at EU level. It could operate to induce inward investment via some form of carrot and stick policy. During the 1980s this policy was to change, focusing on stimulating indigenous growth rather than encouraging inward investment. Part of the explanation for this change was due to the growth in interest in small and medium-sized enterprises as job creators (see Chapter 2), and through the notion of entrepreneurship and the 'rolling back' of the state. None the less, the individual member states continued to seek to attract large overseas companies. Regional policy in the individual states, however, has also been used to counteract social issues in their deprived areas by improving infrastructure, educational facilities and the like.

Within these broad policy areas of regional policy there have been a number of notable similarities in the way regional policy has been pursued by the member states but also some important differences. Germany's approach to regional policy is somewhat similar to that adopted by the Netherlands. Regional policy has been used as a means of diffusing inflationary pressures and to maximise national economic growth as well as to deal with comparatively poor regions. The UK's regional policy has been set against an economy which has a worse performance record than that of its main Northern European competitors. In the post-Second World War period through to the mid-1970s, UK regional policy concentrated on inward investment into declining areas. From the mid-1970s, regional policy was formulated alongside that of dealing with ever-increasing economic crises. The financial constraints faced by governments at that time also led to cuts in regional policy. The 1980s saw government relying more on market forces. Regional policy which took place was more related to encouraging indigenous firms to develop rather than encouraging inward investment, though FDI was still courted.

In France, regional policy was set against more distinctive regional problems than other countries within the EU. There were major discrepancies between the region around Paris and other rural areas, and regional policy was used up to the 1960s as a means of reducing social inequalities. In the 1960s regional policy switched to maximising economic growth from all the regions, but by the 1970s global economic crises meant that regional policy appeared to become less effective. On the whole, French regional policy appears to be of a very *ad hoc* nature.

In Italy, regional policy has been dominated by the problems of the south – a strongly based but backward rural economy with comparatively low GDP per capita. The emphasis on helping the south was to some extent clouded by the need to improve overall economic growth, the major generator of which was in the north of Italy. Given the economic pressures that built up in the north during the latter part of the 1960s, Italy's strategy for the regions shifted more towards a set of balanced economic policies similar to those adopted in other countries.

Comparing the EU regional approaches

As noted above, regional policy in the different EU countries shows both similarities and differences. The instruments used can be grouped into those aimed at influencing the labour market, those aimed at industry and those concerned with improving infrastructure. However, rarely have they been integrated in the way adopted by the French.

Labour policy has rarely been to encourage labour mobility. In general, regional policies concerning labour have focused more on general training programmes. The focus of regional policy to help industry has been to encourage new industries into deprived regions as well as making it more difficult for industries to set up in prosperous regions. This was an approach adopted by the UK's Industrial Development certificate scheme, France's Agreements mechanism and the Selective Investment levy of the Netherlands. Governments have also used the public sector as a means of locating industry in deprived areas. For example, Italy used its state corporations to direct 60 per cent of new investment to the south of the country. The main approach to industry, however, has been to use financial incentives to encourage private sector companies to move towards depressed areas. This approach has been used by Italy, France, the UK and the Netherlands. Financial incentives can be discretionary and/or automatic. The 1980s saw the UK switch from automatic to discretionary incentives. Other countries such as the Netherlands continued with a combination package of the two, although the general trend for most countries has been towards **discretionary financial regional support** and away from automatic incentives.

These financial incentives can also be capital- or labour-related, with the former taking precedence. In addition, they can be available nationally, as in Italy, or regionally, as in the Netherlands. Moreover, the financial incentives can be targeted at particular sectors. Manufacturing has been well supported but in both Germany and the Netherlands the service sector has also been well favoured. In general, the service sector in all EU states has become increasingly encompassed in regional support programmes and at the same time 'special' sectors have also been targeted such as small firms and high-technology companies.

Infrastructure development has also been a means for regional development and support. This began with the development of trading estates but has since moved on to the development of office and science parks. In this respect the development of growth centres has played a part in regional development in Germany, France, Italy and the Netherlands. Such centres constitute a concentration of state investment in particular locations with the aim that the linkages between the investment improve the growth potential effect from the region and lead to spillover effects into surrounding areas.

Assessing regional policy at the member state level

A question often asked about regional policy is whether or not organisations would have naturally gone to a certain region without such a policy? When organisations in declining or lagging regions were asked about regional policy as a push factor it did not feature highly compared with other competitive factors. It has also been said that restricting development in one area does not necessarily mean that organisations will set up in declining or lagging areas; they may just move to areas fringing the most prosperous area. When organisations do move to poorer areas it may be through a branch plant of the main organisation and as such this does not develop any major inter-regional linkages with other existing firms. These branch plants may be more akin to 'screwdriver' plants rather than using a large proportion of localised production and parts. Growth centres as an aspect of regional policy may also develop without much reference to other areas of the region therefore, the spillover effects being minimal. With regard to the switch of regional support to small firms, some of the jobs created are low-quality and Mason and Harrison (1990) note that small firms may have limited innovation potential.

European regional policy

This section is not meant to be a list of the various attempts at developing a regional policy in the Union but an overview of policies to tackle regional disparities. (For a closer look at the development of regional policy, see Vanhove and Klaassen (1987) or Artis and Lee (1997).) EU regional policy has been developed alongside that of the member states and since 1989 has been strengthened appreciably. One important question to consider is whether a separate EU regional policy is needed given the move to subsidiarity in the member states following on from the Treaty on European Union (1992). The reasons why a Europe-wide approach to regional policy might be needed is for reasons of social cohesion – the disparities between countries can be reduced. This problem concerning regional disparities will become increasingly important when the full repercussions of the SEM feed through into the member state economies and after the completion of European Monetary Union. In addition, the widening of membership (see Chapter 14), is likely to lead to the greater use of regional transfers. One approach to the latter issue is for the current member states to delay entry of their Eastern European neighbours in particular so that both regional and national disparities are reduced.

There are other reasons, too, why an EU-wide regional policy should be strengthened. Firstly, one source of the regional disparities that have occurred in the EU is the EU itself through its process of the SEM and Monetary Union.

Secondly, as stated above, if the full benefits of the SEM and European Monetary Union are to be felt then a strong regional policy is required. Moreover, it is likely to take a long time for poorer regions to attract resources away from their richer neighbours, and in the interim, their richer neighbours are likely to become even more wealthy. There are also issues which affect a number of member states (e.g. transportation issues) where a common regional policy could cut across country discrepancies and enable the whole EU to benefit from a particular element of regional policy. Coordination of policy is also needed as a way of getting different decision-making bodies to integrate better and to make sure that domestic regional policies are not used as a means to improve one country's competitiveness in comparison with another's.

Current regional policy in the EU

The last major reform of regional policy took place in 1989. This revised the three major sources of structural funds, the ERDF, the European Social Fund (ESF) and the Guidance section of the European Agricultural and Guarantee Fund (EAGGF). The co-joining of two other sources of funding, the European Investment Bank (EIB) and the European Coal and Steel Community (ECSC), with the three earlier structural funds was seen as imperative if the SEM was not to lead to wider economic disparities between member states. As a result of this process and a further reworking of regional funding in 1993, there are a number of common objectives for structural funding.

- Objective 1. These are regions whose development is lagging behind other regions. Such regions would have their GDPs under approximately 75 per cent of the EU average. This would include a large section of the Mediterranean South, East Germany, Ireland and parts of the UK. Money for Objective 1 regions comes from all three structural funds as well as from the EIB.

- Objective 2. These are regions suffering from declining industrial areas. Certain parts of the UK, France, Germany, Spain, Sweden, Finland and Italy fit into this category. The ERDF, EIB, ESF and ECSC provide funding for these regions. Initially the regions designated for Objective 2 funding were to receive money until 1996, but this has now been extended until 1999.

- Objective 5. Objective 5 regional funding is split into two parts. Objective 5a is concerned with structural or regional problems that occur through changes in the Common Agricultural Policy and this is funded through the EAGGF. Objective 5b is concerned with rural areas which require development and structural adjustment. Parts of the UK, Sweden, France, Germany, Austria, Spain and Finland qualify for this type of funding and the money comes from the three structural funds together with the ERDF.

- Objective 6. These are regions where the population density is low and there is a need to make sure that they obtain an equitable distribution of the wealth of the EU. These regions include the sub-arctic regions of both Sweden and Finland.

Both the reforms of regional policy and the need to expand its role because of the SEM and the Single European Currency have led to regional policy as a proportion of total expenditure by the EU to grow immeasurably. From constituting only around 5 per cent of the annual EU budget in the early 1980s, it is expected to account for approximately 35 per cent in 1999. In addition, the funding will be biased towards the most disadvantaged regions, i.e. those designated under Objective 1.

Of the five funds involved with regional funding, the three designated as structural funds (the ERDF, ESF and EAGGF) supply grants, whilst the EIB and ECSC supply loans. Before the 1989 reforms of regional policy, the assistance required to gain ERDF funding and the type of funding given required extensive work by the European Commission to ascertain detailed knowledge of plans and to gain expertise on projects. Gathering such information was particularly time-consuming and since 1989 the approach has been to streamline regional funding through a process of *planning, partnership, subsidiarity* and *additionality*.

The individual member states in consultation with regional and local organisations draw up plans for the various objective regions and submit them to the European Commission. Once discussion has taken place between the individual member states and the Commission, single programming documents (SPDs) are produced. The SPDs specify how much of the regional plan will be paid for by regional funding, by the member state, and by other regional and local partners. Implementation of the SPDs is aided through financial assistance from the Commission, but the actual implementation is left to the individual member state. The SPDs are evaluated before and after implementation and are also regularly monitored. The 1989 new guidelines also allowed the EU to consider regional projects which encompassed a number of members states, as it had done before 1989. These larger projects make up less than 10 per cent of all the regional funding available. Thus it is the individual states' SPDs which are the driving force behind the success or failure of EU regional policy.

One feature of the SPD programme is the concept of additionality. It has been suggested that EU regional funding has become 'instead of' rather than 'in addition to' a member state's regional funding. For some member states this appears to be true. It is also possible that some member states have not taken up their full quota of EU regional funds since they may have faced fiscal constraints in their own economy and cannot afford to match domestic funding with European funding.

Case study: Regional aid

Mrs Monika Wulf-Mathies, EU commissioner for regional policy, will this week reject calls for a big increase in aid to rural areas aimed at cushioning farmers against the coming shake-up in the Common Agricultural Policy.

The proposals were the centrepiece of a plan put forward last year by Mr Franz Fischler, EU agricultural commissioner. He wanted to direct EU regional aid to help farming communities cope with reductions in subsidies from Brussels.

Mrs Wulf-Mathies, a former German trade union leader, says she is not opposed to helping the countryside; but regional aid – or 'structural funds' – should be targeted toward poor areas with a view to strengthening economic and social cohesion in the EU.

'I don't want structural policies linked to the CAP,' she says in an interview, adding pointedly: 'Rich farmers get 80 per cent of the EU farm subsidies.'

Mrs Wulf-Mathies will launch the debate over the future of EU regional aid today at a three-day conference – European Cohesion Forum – in Brussels. The main protagonists, including Mr Fischler, will be present.

In practice, a battle over the direction of policy has been going on for months inside the Commission. President Jacques Santer is preparing to unveil proposals this summer for the reform of the CAP, regional aid, and a new seven-year EU budget to prepare for the EU's planned enlargement around the turn of the century.

Late last year Mr Fischler tried to seize the initiative at a conference in Ireland. He pressed the idea of amalgamating the regional and CAP funds, which together comprise more than two-thirds of the total EU budget. His proposal reflected pressure on the CAP from the next round of world trade talks at the end of the century, which will force further cutbacks in subsidies to EU farmers.

Other factors include the entry into the EU of farm-intensive economies such as Poland and Hungary; and growing calls to lower the CAP's share of the overall EU budget, which, many believe, will most likely remain at 1.27 per cent of EU gross domestic product between 2000 and 2006.

Mr Padraig Flynn, EU social affairs commissioner, added to the debate this year when he said that the ECU38bn (£26.6bn) annual regional aid budget was over-complex, inefficient and spread over too many EU objectives and initiatives.

Mr Flynn's intervention was partly viewed as a defence of the European Social Fund, which supports worker training. But it also gave Mrs Wulf-Mathies a useful ally in her campaign to prevent regional aid being skewed toward rural development and the farmer.

In the interview, Mrs Wulf-Mathies sets out her priorities for reform. First, it is vital to shrink the regional aid map. At present, just over half of the EU receives some form of hand-out from Brussels. 'Aid is spread widely but thinly, which gives a kind of "sprinkler effect".' Second, the Commission should 'define and apply' stricter criteria for poorer regions. The real need is to help industries restructure, to strengthen small businesses, and fight long-term unemployment. Third, the Commission should simplify procedures for assessing projects eligible for aid and avoid duplication with DG 4, the competition directorate. Brussels should deal with big projects such as dams and railways, but otherwise the regions should have more responsibility for management.

Finally, it is wrong to single out the countryside for special treatment at the expense of the cities. 'Links between rural areas and the cities are being developed. You cannot have a development strategy which leaves out the cities.'

Mrs Wulf-Mathies says the CAP has not helped economic and social cohesion in general in the EU: most of the aid went to farmers in rich countries such as Denmark and France, rather than poorer countries such as Portugal.

'The CAP has created the development of industrialised farming which depends less on natural resources and people,' she says, echoing concern about innovations such as genetically engineered soyabeans. 'I want the broadest possible partnership.'

She also argues it is time to clamp down on sharp practices by private companies exploiting the regional aid market.

She cites the case of Renault, the French car maker, which this year shut down its plant in Vilvoorde, near Brussels, while standing to gain from EU aid for opening a factory in Spain. 'There should be spin-offs from regional investment, like organising a chain of suppliers in the region – not just the big shot bringing over his own supply chain. We need companies rooted in the area.'

Source: Barber, L. (1997) Commissioners square up for regional aid fight, *Financial Times*, 28 April.

Questions

1 Why is there a desire to keep regional aid separate from the CAP?

2 What are the priorities for reform of the regional aid programme?

• •

EU regional funding, therefore, has taken on a much larger profile during the past decade. This can be partly explained by the impact of the SEM and the expected impact of monetary union. However, the balance between member states' regional policy and the role played by the EU is a reflection of the tight fiscal positions many of the states have found themselves in. Moreover, the EU has taken a more central role in identifying pan-European issues. The move towards widening membership of the EU will see regional policy playing an ever-increasing role in EU affairs. None the less, the important feature of regional policy is one of partnership, and in particular the view of subsidiarity with the individual states deciding regional priorities and then carrying out their own plans. It waits to be seen whether the size of any regional funding is large enough for the challenges ahead and whether over the longer term regional disparities are reduced.

EU social policy

EU social policy could be viewed as the 'poorer sister' relative to regional policy in the early years of the EU yet the later development of the **Social Charter** and the **Social Chapter** within the Maastricht Treaty has seen social issues take a stronger profile in terms of the current policy debate.

The remit of social policy can be quite broad, covering areas of the labour market such as industrial relations, the terms and conditions of work, and anti-discrimination behaviour, as well as considering areas of the welfare state such as social services, social insurance and family policy. If the remit of social policy is fairly consistent between countries their approach is somewhat different. Social regimes differ from the liberal to the conservative and social democratic approaches. If these approaches are coupled with the different economic circumstances in which the member states find themselves such as population growth, unemployment and the like then it is not surprising that the EU has found it difficult to operate an EU-wide social policy.

The origins of social policy can be found in the Treaty of Rome, where there are a number of references to social issues. Articles 48–51 refer to the free movement of workers, and Articles 52–58 refer to the rights of freedom of establishment. Articles 117–128 also relate to social issues. Articles 117 and 118 encourage the promotion of improved standards of living and working conditions. Articles 119–122 deal with equal pay for equal work, whilst Articles 123–128 provide the legal basis for the setting up of a European Social Fund (ESF), which was mainly focused on improving worker mobility.

Despite all this, the bulk of legislation on social issues remained a national affair and the various strands described above had little impact. One reason for the slow progress in the field of a common social policy was that it was assigned a minor role since the EU was initially envisaged as an economic union. In addition, changes in social policy required absolute majority voting and the differences in member states' approaches to social policy meant that to move rapidly forward at an EU level was just not possible.

During the 1970s and 1980s there was some improvement in terms of achieving free movement of labour, although Straubhaar (1988) noted that the actual flows were fairly limited and actually reduced as economic conditions improved in countries that had traditionally been net exporters of labour. However, as in the 1960s there was little concerted social action. There was some increased funding given to the ESF, where the emphasis shifted more to the issues of youth and long-term unemployment but it remained limited in comparison with regional funding. Moreover, social policy was not well integrated with other policy areas – certainly not until the structural reforms of 1988, when regional and social funds were linked to tackle specific unemployment issues. Like regional policy, the social fund suffered from the problem of additionality whereby countries were using the social funds to replace national expenditure instead of using them in addition to national expenditure.

A major shift in social policy came with the proposals for the development of the Single Market (see Chapter 9). This was an attempt to kick-start the European economy from its period of '**eurosclerosis**' in order to compete more effectively with the United States and Japan. If the Single Market was going to stimulate greater linkages and co-operation between European companies then there was a need for some closer linkage of workers' conditions and rights across Europe. This theme was enunciated in Stockholm in May 1988 by the then President of the European Commission, Jacques Delors, who called for a European Charter of Fundamental Social Rights to protect workers at a European level, which became known as the **Social Charter**. In fact, the Social Charter originally constituted 47 different areas of legislation which covered social issues. Some of these were fairly non-contentious, such as the rights of men and women to equal treatment, the rights of the elderly and the disabled, the right to protection in the workplace and the right to freedom of movement, but others were to be resisted, especially by the UK, as they were seen to be threatening the flexibility of the labour market. The UK opposition was such that it negotiated an opt-out from the Social Provisions within the Maastricht Treaty so that what remained was the Social Protocol between the remaining members of the EU, which sought to develop the social provisions begun by the Social Charter. It must be said that many of the less contentious areas were accepted by the UK, which had one of the best records of implementation of the EU legislation into national legislation. This situation was to change in May 1997 with the election of the Labour Party headed by Tony Blair, one of whose first acts was to sign up for the Social Chapter, thus ending the UK's exclusion.

One issue that emerged during this debate was that of **social dumping**. Countries with lower wages (which did not have a minimum wage, for example) were attracting foreign direct investment (FDI) away from countries with more rigid wage structures and thus 'dumping' unemployment on them. In addition, lower wages reduced export prices with the same effect. Conversely, it has been argued that there are a number of factors affecting decisions to invest and that the effect of the social dumping argument could not be fully substantiated. There is, however, a tension between having a flexible labour market with an increasing number of part-time jobs and increasing legislation that will tend to add more rigidity in the market, and it is against this background that there are a number of current areas of discussion on social issues concerning current or proposed directives.

One of the important areas developed under social policy was that of **minimum wage legislation**. A minimum wage is set in many countries but the proposal is for a European-wide minimum wage to act as a 'safety net' for lower-paid workers. The counter-argument is that minimum wages can be set too high, above the market clearing wage in some sectors, and this increases rigidity and costs, which in turn may lead to greater unemployment and may even increase poverty. On the other hand, there have been studies (e.g. Card and Kreuger 1994) which suggest that the imposition of a minimum wage can lead to increased productivity and increased employment. Much of the debate will centre around the level at which the minimum wage will be set. Although the UK in 1997 accepted the need for a minimum wage, it also decided on a lengthy period of consultation with no decision before mid-1998.

Another current area of development within both social policy and part of the Social Chapter is to do with **worker councils**. There has long been a tradition of worker councils in many countries such as Germany (see Chapter 3) and the trend towards these has been growing given the advantages of greater communication and involvement of all the stakeholders in an organisation, rather than the confrontational approach that was more familiar in countries such as

the UK. Under the Works Council Directive every company in the EU employing 1000 workers, with at least 150 or more of them working in at least two
member states, must establish an information and consultation committee by
the end of the century. Most of the larger European companies have long since
adopted this and although the Conservative government under John Major
adopted a hostile stance to this programme, by the end of 1996 55 UK companies had set up European works councils. With the UK's 'opt-in' to this directive
in 1997, it is estimated that the number will grow to at least 240.

Another significant directive is that associated with '**working time**'. This sought
to establish some control on the maximum number of hours worked per day and
per week and also to establish minimum holiday provision. The first draft suggested a maximum 48-hour week and a minimum of four weeks annual holiday.
This was challenged from a number of directions, in particular where long hours
were part of the job, and a number of derogations have been made, exempting
certain categories of workers. The Conservative government in the UK brought a
court action against the directive, challenging the legal basis of the directive and
the extent to which it could be decided by a qualified majority on the grounds of
being a health and safety issue. This was despite the fact that the basic working
week in the UK is little different to that in the rest of the EU. In the event, the
case was rejected and the UK government now recognises the directive.

Parental leave has been another area of recent interest following the adoption
of the Framework Directive in June 1996. This had been negotiated between representatives of employers' organisations and trade unions at European level on
the basis of the Social Protocol in the Maastricht Treaty. The directive gives all
employees (men as well as women) the right to a minimum of three months of
unpaid leave following the birth of their child. Many countries had already introduced this measure following the development of the Maternity Leave Directive,
although some countries such as Greece and Ireland had no such earlier legislation. Again the UK originally chose to opt out of this directive but is now likely to
legislate towards such provision by mid-1998 at the earliest.

The **atypical worker directive** was first introduced in draft form in 1990 and
relates to the right of part-time and casual workers in terms of giving them similar
rights to full-time workers, although this was again resisted by the UK government
and also by European employers' organisations. This was finally resolved in June
1997 when European trade unions and employers signed an agreement to support atypical worker rights in the fields of non-discrimination against part-time
employees (both male and female). It gives equal access to pay, bonuses and shift
work and will ensure equal contractual terms in connection with occupational
sick leave schemes and paid holiday leave. It will also give equal access to share
options and occupational pensions. This is important given the shift throughout
Europe to more flexible organisations, which, by their nature, will employ more
workers on a part-time or very short contract basis. In the UK alone this will affect
5.7 million part-time employees, although the measure was watered down to
exclude casual workers from coverage under this directive.

A recent area of legislation is with **disability discrimination**, where it is now
illegal to discriminate on grounds of individual disability, although there are
some exemptions for certain jobs.

Thus it can be seen that there are a number of significant measures now affecting businesses all over Europe as a result of directives at a European level. There still remains the issue of implementation of these directives as they are translated into national law, as this is by no means a straightforward process and sometimes the implementation of these measures can be delayed for years.

However, it can be seen that many of the ideas introduced with the Social Charter are now leading to legislation to protect workforces across Europe, and that the Social Fund acting as part of the overall structural funding is much more effectively aimed at youth and long-term unemployment. It remains to be seen how this legislation can be implemented without making the labour market too rigid and expensive in relation to Europe's major trading partners.

Transport policy

Although the Treaty of Rome established the idea of a common transport policy (CTP) under Articles 3e and 74–84, the move towards developing a common transport policy within the EU has been very slow. The basic principles of a common transport policy were set out in the Schaus Memorandum of 1961 and the measures suggested were incorporated into the Commission's First Action Programme of 1962. The measures suggested could be incorporated under the following headings:

- Liberalisation measures: carriers were to be allowed greater access to supply services across national boundaries within the EU.

- Anti-discrimination measures: it was intended that discrimination between member states and between different modes of transport should be eliminated.

- Harmonisation measures: items such as the weights and dimensions of road vehicles, and the taxation of vehicles, amongst other items, were to be standardised.

The reason why progress was slow in developing the above lies in the distinctive nature of transport systems in the member states and their desire to move transport policy forward along one, not necessarily the same one, of the approaches above. For example, the peripheral countries of the Union wanted a move towards the liberalisation of transport, whilst Germany and Italy wanted more emphasis on harmonisation. Moreover, the relative shares of the different transport modes differ markedly between member states. Inland waterway traffic is more important in the Netherlands than in the UK, whilst in terms of freight haulage the use of roads is more important in Spain than in the Netherlands. The transport of freight by rail is more important in Germany than in the Netherlands. Despite these differences there are some common problems to be faced within the transport sector of the EU. Firstly, there has been increasing pressure on transport infrastructure as passenger traffic, particularly on roads, has increased, which may lead to lost resources, congestion, pollution and safety issues. Secondly, there has been increasing pressure on public provision for transport as car ownership has continued to rise.

The lack of action towards a common transport policy was to change. In 1985 the European Court of Justice was successful in convicting the Council of Transport Ministers for its 'failure to act' upon its duty to set up a common transport policy. Such a policy was needed if the full benefits from a single market were to be established. The Commission thereafter put forward a series of proposals for harmonisation of road haulage, road passenger transport, civil aviation, rail, sea transport, and for structural improvement in inland waterways. The following section concentrates on the first four in particular.

Road haulage

Following the 1985 changes in transport policy, certain minimum levels of harmonisation in road haulage were developed, concentrating on technical requirements such as weight and length of vehicles, as well as on social aspects such as the number of driving hours. In 1988 the Council adopted its regulation on access to the market for the carriage of goods by road. The regulation required the abolition by Community hauliers of all Community quotas, bilateral **quotas** between member states and quotas for transit traffic to and from non-member countries by 1 January 1993. Access to the market for cross-border carriage of goods by road within the Community was now governed by a system of Community licences. There were still, however, a number of major sticking points in the road haulage sector, particularly in the area of taxation and user charge and **cabotage**.

Some countries in the more central region of the EU are more likely to have their roads used by other countries' hauliers. One way to overcome this problem was through a system of tolls. In the north-western EU countries an alternative system – the residence principle – was adopted, which meant that the individual country taxed the carrier. Cabotage, on the other hand, permits non-domestic freight hauliers to provide haulage services in the domestic market of a member state. If this is coupled with the better use of technology, which can allow a home office to trace trucks at all times, then this allows international hauliers to compete with domestic hauliers. Cabotage is to be fully liberalised within the EU by July 1998. Although liberalisation of the road haulage sector has progressed fairly quickly, there is still the problem of differences between member states in road user charging systems to rectify.

Air transport

Initially, air transport remained outside of the influence of EU regulation. In 1974, however, an ECJ ruling brought it under the general rules of the Treaty of Rome with regard to the free movement of services and competition rules.

The market for air transport can be broken down into three parts: charter, cargo and scheduled passenger traffic. Both cargo and charter traffic are subject to light regulatory regimes and are on the whole competitive; however, it is in the passenger aircraft market that complications can be found.

The lack of competition in this market arose from the Chicago Convention of 1944. This convention permitted each state to have its own flag-carrying airline and these were usually in public ownership. Thus they could receive state aids (see Chapter 8). States had bilateral agreements with each other about landing rights and flight routes between the two countries. Often the flights between two carriers were shared on a 50:50 basis. Fare levels were negotiated within the framework of the International Air Transport Association (IATA), though they were subject to government approval. The result of the Chicago Convention was that air fares were likely to be higher than truly competitive air fares, cost levels were higher due to the lack of competition, and consumer choice was limited. In addition, whilst the bilateral arrangements placed restrictions on existing carriers, they virtually excluded new entrants from international markets. By the mid-1980s there were about 200 bilateral agreements providing air transport services between 22 countries in Europe. The right of a Community carrier to offer services between two other member states, the '**Fifth Freedom**' rights, were almost prohibited, being offered on only 44 of the 400 routes. The 1985 White Paper on transport liberalisation set about altering this, expressing a need for the Community to liberalise its air transport services, particularly with respect to tariffs, capacity control and access to the market.

In December 1987, the Council adopted measures to regulate air fares, capacity sharing and the application of competition rules to civil aviation. Although the first package of proposals did little to liberalise the market, it did set in train important developments of liberalisation.

The third package of measures was a major turning point in liberalising the air transport market. It covered scheduled, non-scheduled and cargo services and came into force on 1 January 1993. This package made it easier to get an EU operator's licence, the great majority of intra-EU air routes were to be opened to recognised EU operators, cabotage restrictions were reduced with full cabotage rights (with some minor restrictions) established by April 1997, and airlines were free to determine their own scheduled passenger fares, subject to certain safeguards. In addition, all restrictions on charter fares were removed and cargo rates continue to be unregulated.

Although the liberalisation of the air transport sector has come a long way since 1985, there are still further difficulties to resolve. Some exemptions still apply, such as the allocation of landing and take-off slots: notice the difficulty in which British Airways is currently finding itself as it tries to divest itself of lucrative landing slots at Heathrow as a way of placating the European authorities with regard to its alliance with American Airlines. Secondly, state aid continues to be given. Thirdly, making airlines compete against one another could result in the market becoming more oligopolistic in the long term.

Case study: Air transport

Japan has publicly attacked a report by the Organisation for Economic Co-operation and Development which calls for further liberalisation of international air transport. Japan also says the OECD should make no further studies of policy in the sector.

This is believed to be the first time any member government has failed to endorse an OECD report. The organisation, whose 29 members include the world's richest economies, normally operates on the basis of full consensus.

The report, to be issued next month, was written by the OECD secretariat with input and advice from about 30 public and private sector participants drawn from the airline, aircraft manufacturing and tourism industries, which also financed the project.

Among the companies involved were eight international airlines, including Air France, Alitalia, American Airlines, British Airways, SAS and Singapore Airlines. Manufacturers included Boeing of the USA, Europe's Airbus Industrie, Deutsche Aerospace of Germany and Bombardier of Canada.

However, Japan's ministry of transport, which represented its government in the project, says in a dissenting annex that the report's analysis and recommendations are 'based not upon the reality of today's international air services but upon misconceptions.'

Japan accuses the OECD of exaggerating the benefits of airline liberalisation and undervaluing the role of the bilateral government agreements which have governed international aviation since the 1940s. Japan says these arrangements should continue to determine the industry's development. The ministry says it 'strongly objects' to the report's proposals that governments relax restrictions on foreign ownership of airlines and apply competition rules more firmly to international air transport.

The Japanese ministry also makes a thinly veiled attack on domestic airline deregulation in the USA. It suggests the policy has achieved an unfair advantage for national airlines and has been used to pressure other countries into opening their markets against their will.

'One country should never impose "liberalisation", which is apt to create a monopoly or oligopoly and has a risk of loss of effective international participation in international air transport of the other side, while leaving a vast domestic market reserved to the national carriers of the other side,' it says.

The ministry says it does not oppose liberalisation, but that the pace must be determined and agreed by governments. It says many countries share its view, and that any further industry studies should be undertaken in a broad international forum, such as the International Civil Aviation Organisation.

Japan's attack is the more striking because the OECD report is cautiously worded. It suggests that further liberalisation should be put into effect gradually and should take account of different attitudes and conditions in countries around the world.

Source: De Jonquieres, G. (1997) OECD air transport report angers the Japanese, *Financial Times*, 20 January.

Question

1 What arguments have been put forward to suggest that liberalisation of the airline sector has not led to expected benefits to both EU countries and Japan?

Road passenger transport

The road passenger transport sector of the market has been paid much less attention than other areas of the transport system, the reason being that much of the bus and coach travel that occurs within the EU is regional or rural in nature. Different countries have operated different regimes for their coach and bus traffic. In many countries the level of public ownership is high and a certain degree of state subsidy is attached. In the UK the market is somewhat different, with much coach and bus transport having been privatised.

The main emphasis of EU transport policy in this area covers the liberalisation of the coach market for inter-member state traffic. Changes in regulations have made it possible for a limited amount of cabotage in the inter-member state coach market and a reduction in the authorisation for certain inter-member state coach services.

Rail transport

Although rail transport accounts for a significant part of both passenger and freight transport, its importance has been declining. One objective of a CTP has been to enable the various systems of transport to compete more effectively with one another. In this respect it was important to reduce the distortions in competition that could arise from state intervention in railway operations. Moreover, there was a need to separate the public-service element of rail from the commercial-service element. In addition, the building of the Channel Tunnel throws up further difficulties and at the same time opportunities. Although the UK has the same track gauge as other member states, it has a different loading gauge. Thus many continental trains are wider and this has implications for tunnels, stations, etc., in the UK.

Towards the end of 1989 the European Commission called for the establishment of a high-level working group on the development of a European high-speed rail network. At the same time, the Commission adopted a set of proposals on relations between states and their railways. The proposals were developed to ensure greater integration and the strengthening of the railways position in the single market. The proposals were based on the following principles:

- autonomy and commercial management of the railways;
- separation of the infrastructure ownership and railway operating functions, with the financial responsibility of the former being borne by the member states and the railways paying for the use of the facilities, which could mean that the rail infrastructure could remain in public hands or it could be privatised;
- re-organisation of the financial situation of the railways and commercial management backed up by contracts between railway companies and the public authorities.

By 1995 a review of these proposals revealed that progress had been patchy. This led the Commission to propose further measures to assist in achieving the 1991 directives.

The EU has now produced a common transport action programme for 1995–2000. There are three main objectives to the programme:

- improving the quality of transport systems in terms of competitiveness, safety and environmental impact;
- improving the functioning of the Single Market to promote efficiency and choice;
- broadening the external dimension by improving links with third countries.

In terms of improving quality, the Commission seeks to develop the system by providing better links between the different modes of transport. New technologies and applications of these need to be stimulated. In the light of this a Trans-European Network policy was developed to improve the efficiency, integration and interconnectedness of the transport systems across the internal borders of the EU. Public transport was to be put forward as an attractive alternative to the private car and intermodal freight transport promoted. To help the environment all forms of transport were to be encouraged as a means to shift more freight traffic off the roads. The Commission has considered also the ways in which the external costs of the different modes of transport are charged. At present, differences in charging systems in different member states can distort competition, even within a single mode of transport, giving some national industries competitive advantage. In its Green Paper of 1995 (Towards Fair and Efficient Pricing in Transport) the Commission has explored ways of making transport pricing fairer and more efficient, with the aim of using price signals to curb congestion, accidents and pollution.

EU transport policy might be considered in three phases. The period up to 1985 was one where progress towards a CTP was extremely slow. The period up until the mid-1990s was one where the Commission was forced to push forward in the area of a CTP in the light of the development of the SEM and the TEU. However, many of their proposals have not had much time to feed through and exemptions still occur in some sectors. The third phase will be for a CTP to address other issues, including the continued differences in transport arrangements between countries, the widening of transport policy to include third countries, addressing even more vigorously the issue of state aids, and the problems that can arise through transport liberalisation from the development of oligopolistic behaviour through the process of merger behaviour.

Conclusion

The continued evolution of the member states has led to the EU to examine, modify and develop new policies to cater for the changing nature of international competition and for the development of closer harmonisation of policy by the individual member states. From its position of taking the majority of expenditure of the EU budget, agricultural support by the EU has been reduced to 50 per cent of the total EU budget. Part of the reduction can be explained by pressure from the EU states themselves that expenditure on agriculture needed to be controlled, but the role of Uruguay GATT trade talks, the need to expand other areas of expenditure, such as social and regional policy, and changes that will come about through the admission of the new CEECs in the next decade have all played their part in addressing some of the problems with agricultual expenditure and support. The reduction in agricultural funding has allowed the funding for both social and regional funding to be increased. Both areas have become more prominent in the EU during the past decade through the development of the SEM, and it would be expected that their role will take on greater significance as the EU heads for monetary union and widening its boundaries once more. In the area of social policy, the problems raised by the Social Charter appear to have been resolved, with the UK signing up to the agreement along with its fourteen partners.

The issues raised by fisheries have become more prominent following the widening of membership to include Spain and Portugal. Its efforts are very localised and have strategic importance for some regions as well as having general importance for environmentalists. A common fisheries policy still appears to be a long way off, and its relative lack of importance for some member states suggests that problems for the maritime nations will remain well into the future.

With regard to transport policy within the EU, there was a distinct lack of action until 1985. Since then transport policy has been taken on greater emphasis because the EU has perceived that the barriers that have existed in transport markets can result in increased cost to industry. Transport policy cuts across competition policy and state aid. There are also environmental reasons as to why there has been renewed activity in this area; nonetheless, there is still a long way to go to make the transport sectors truly competitive and to establish a common transport policy.

The policy areas above indicate major changes and revisions by the EU over the past decade. Sometimes the EU is proactive in these policy areas following an overall aim to improve EU competitiveness; at other times, however, the EU has followed a more piecemeal appraoch. In some of these policy areas more changes have taken place in the past decade than in the previous thirty years, and it would be expected that further changes will take place in the new millennium.

Questions for discussion

1 What have been the objectives of the CAP? Have they been achieved?

2 How far have the reforms of the CAP addressed its weaknesses?

3 Does the EU require a Common Fisheries Policy?

4 In what ways can the UK overcome quota-hopping?

5 Has regional policy within the EU reduced regional disparities?

6 Why has regional policy become more important since the development of the SEM and the proposals for monetary union?

7 Why has it been difficult to produce a common social policy within the EU?

8 What factors suggest that social policy will take on a greater role within the EU during the next decade?

9 How can a common transport policy improve the competitiveness of EU industry?

10 Although transport policy within the EU has come a long way, it still has a long way to go. Discuss.

Main reading

El-Agraa, A. M. (ed.) (1994) *The Economies of the European Community*, 4th edition, Harvester Wheatsheaf.

Barnes, I. and Barnes, P. M. (1995) *The Enlarged European Union*, Longman.

Artis, M. J. and Lee, N. (1997) *The Economics of the European Union*, OUP.

Additional reading

Ackrill, R. (1992) The common agricultural policy – its operation and its future, *Economics*, Spring, p. 5.

Atkins, R., Buckley, N. and Urry, M. (1997) Farming reforms sow seeds of doubt: CAP changes are causing misgivings despite being 'step in right direction', *Financial Times*, 18 July.

Armstrong, H. and Taylor, J. (1985) *Regional Economics and Policy*, Philip Allen.

Barber, L. (1997) Commissioners square up for regional aid fight, *Financial Times*, 28 April.

Buckwell, A. E., Harvey, D. R. Thomson, K. J. and Partan, K. A. (1982) *The Cost of the German Agricultural Policy*, Croom Helm.

Card, C. and Kreuger, A.(1994) Minimum wages and employment – a case study in the fast food industry, *American Economic Review.*

CEC (1997) Commission of the European Communities, *Financial Report for the European Community*, CEC, Brussels, p.17.

Comfort, A. M. (1988) Alternatives to infrastructure? Possible ways forward for the ERDF: a perspective from Luxembourg, *Regional Studies*, Vol. 22.

Committee for the Study of Economic and Monetary Union (1989) *Report on Economic and Monetary Union in the European Community*, EEC.

Cutler, T., Haslam, C., Williams, J. and Williams. K. (1989) *1992: The Struggle for Europe*, Berg.

de Joniquieres, G. (1997) OECD air transport report angers the Japanese, *Financial Times*, 20 January.

EC Commission (1969) Memorandum on regional policy, *Bulletin of the European Communities*, No. 12.

EC Commission (1973) Report on the regional problems in the enlarged community, *The Thompson Report*, EC.

EC Commission (1980) *Reflections of the CAP.*

EC Commission (1981) *Guidelines for European Agriculture.*

EC Commission (1985) *Perspectives for the CAP.*

EC Commission (1990) *Background Report, A Community Transport Policy.*

EC Commission (1996) *Background Report, European Transport Policy.*

EC Commission (1996) *Employment in Europe*, European Commission, Brussels.

The Economist (1987) Beyond mountains and lakes, 3 October, p. 18.

The Economist (1997) Leaders' and wanted: a farming revolution, 6 September, p. 37.

El-Agraa, A. M. (1989) *The Theory and Measurement of International Integration*, Macmillan and St Martins.

Eurobarometer (1988) *Europeans and their Agriculture*, Commission of the European Communities, February.

Fennell, R. (1987) Reform of the CAP. Shadow or substance? *Journal of Common Market Studies*, Vol. 26 (1).

Financial Times (1990) French and German opposition to reforming the CAP, 24 October, p.16.

Financial Times (1991) The final showdown, 1 November, p. 20.

Financial Times (1992a) Some progress in EC–US talks says MacSharry, 12 March, p. 6.

Financial Times (1992b) Farm subsidies accord urged, 13 April, p. 3.

Financial Times (1995) Government staves off defeat over fisheries policy, 19 January.

Financial Times (1997) Commissioner hopeful of swift fisheries deal, 16 June.

Griffiths, A. and Wall, S. (1997) *Applied Economics*, 7th edition, Longman.

The Guardian (1991) EC plans to slash farm gate prices, 10 July, p. 8.

Gupta, S., Lipschitz, L. and Meyer, T. (1989) The CAP of EEC, *Finance and Development*, Vol. 26 (2), p. 37–9.

Hitiris, T. (1991) *European Community Economics*, 2nd edition, Harvester Wheatsheaf.

Hornsby, M. (1991) Gummer attacks EC farm reforms, *The Times*, 15 July.

International Management (1991) EC Dateline, November.

Levi Sandri, L. (1965) The contribution of regional action to the construction of Europe, *Third International Congress on Regional Economics*, Rome.

Lipsey, R. G. (1983) *An Introduction to Positive Economics*, 6th edition, Wiedenfeld & Nicolson.

Mason C. M. and Harrison, R. T. (1990) Small firms: phoenix from the ashes, in Pinter, D. (ed.) *Western Europe: Challenge and Change*, Belhaven, pp. 72–90.

Mead, G. (1997) Cornish fishermen on warpath: outrage as Spanish quota hoppers win compensation 'in principle', *Financial Times*, 1 August.

Mendes, A. J. M. (1986) The contribution of the EC to economic growth, *Journal of Common Market Studies*, Vol. 24 (4).

Myrdal, G. (1957) *The Theory of Underdeveloped Regions*, Duckworth.

Nevin, E. (1990) *The Economics of Europe*, Macmillan.

Padua-Schioppa, T. (1987) *Efficiency, Stability and Equity: A Strategy for the Evolution of the Economic System of the European Community*, EEC.

Pratten, C. (1988) *Research on the Cost of Non-Europe. Basic Findings, EC*, HMSO.

Roarty, M. (1987) The impact of the CAP on agricultural trade and development, *National West Bank Quarterly Review*, February.

Schumpeter, J. A. (1954) *Capitalism, Socialism and Democracy*, 4th edition, Allen & Unwin.

Spaak, P. H. (1957) *The Spaak Report*.

Straubhaar, T. (1988) International labour migration within the Common Market, *Journal of Common Market Studies*.

Swinbank, A. (1992) The MacSharry reforms and the future of the CAP, paper delivered at conference at the University of Warwick, 26 March 1992.

Tangermann, S. (1989) Evaluation of the current CAP reform package, *World Economy (UK)*, June, pp. 175–88.

Tangermann, S. (1996) An ex-post review of the 1992 MacSharry reform, paper delivered at the Credit Conference on 'CAP Reform: What Next?' Coventry, 26 March 1996.

Thomson, K. (1996) The CAP and the WTO after URAA, paper delivered at the Credit Conference on 'CAP Reform: What Next' Coventry, 26 March 1996.

The Times (1992) Jobs on the line, 1 April, p. 15.

Tyers, R. and Anderson, K. (1986) Distortions in world food markets: a quantitative assessment, *World Development*, background paper, The World Bank.

Vanhove, N. and Klaassen, H. (1987) *Regional Policy: A European Approach*, 2nd edition, Gower.

Welford, R. and Prescott, K. (1996) *European Business*, 3rd edition, Pitman.

Whitley, R. (ed.) (1994) *European Business Systems*, Sage.

Winters, L. A. (1987) The economic consequences of agricultural support: a survey, *OECD Economic Studies*, Vol. 9, Autumn, pp. 7–54.

8

Industrial policy and competition policy

Introduction

This chapter first considers some definitions and discussion of **industrial policy**, including its significance as indicated by the European Commission and others. The rationale for, and scope of, industrial policy is examined, always bearing in mind the highly politically charged context in which it is conducted. The current state of industrial policy in the EU is also considered before looking at two aspects of these policies in some detail: **public procurement** and **state aid**. Both public procurement and state aid involve very considerable resources and funds within the EU; the conclusion reached for both of these is that the situation is something less than ideal, and that further ongoing reform is necessary.

There is a somewhat arbitrary division between industrial policy and **competition policy** because they are closely linked aspects of both governmental and EU activity. They are treated separately here in line with their usual treatment in other texts and by the Commission, and because topics *have* to be taken in a sequence. The second part of this chapter then considers the theoretical basis of competition policy in the EU, its applications and current status.

Industrial policy

What is industrial policy? 'Industrial Policy means the initiation and co-ordination of governmental activities to leverage up the productivity and competitiveness of the whole economy and particular industries within. Above all it means the infusion of goal-oriented strategic thinking into economic policy' (Van Zon 1996, page 119). This definition is rather too wide in its description of what industrial policy involves. Van Zon's approach could include most (if not all) micro- and macro-economic government activities that influence industry and business. The focus of EU industrial policy is, however, predominantly about trying to coordinate policies – the policies of the member states – if not necessarily the initiating of them. The EU budget for the sort of activities (interventions, supports, subsidies, grants, cheap loans) involved in industrial policy is very small – especially in comparison with the amounts spent in these areas by member states. The role of the EU is primarily that of trying to set a framework in which private economic activity can flourish and especially one in which international competitiveness can be encouraged and enhanced. The European Commission regards industrial policy (and its concomitant, competition policy) as vital for the success of the Single European Market (SEM). A vital part of this drive for success is to make the new single market more efficient and competitive with respect to competition from beyond the single market; international competitiveness now becomes the key factor. The future prosperity of the 15 member states is declared to be crucially linked with maintaining and increasing international competitiveness – the debate for industrial policy is how best to achieve this objective. Indeed Martin Bangemann, the Industry Commissioner, once stated 'I understand "industrial policy" to mean creating international competitiveness. There is no simple way to do this' (Barnes and Barnes 1995, page 226).

The Commission issued a White Paper in 1994 entitled 'Growth, Competitiveness, Employment – the Challenges and the Way Forward into the 21st Century'. The White Paper recognised the slippage in the EU's relative position in the world economic tables (particularly in comparison with the USA and Japan) in the previous two decades with respect to growth rates, unemployment levels, investment ratios, new product development, research and development, and export performance.

> It was clear that national solutions to economic crisis simply did not work … the Commission blamed 'eurosclerosis' on the folly of national solutions … Although the Community had emerged as the largest market in the world, it was still becoming less and less competitive in a global sense. It could not ascribe its failings to world-wide recession. There was something wrong structurally.
>
> (Ward 1996, page 107)

Something had to be done.

Amongst the areas needing special attention, according to the White Paper on industrial competitiveness, were the following:

- the need to promote research and development and intangible investments such as intellectual property;
- the need to develop industrial co-operation, including strategic alliances and co-operation with countries beyond the EU;
- the need to promote competition policy within the EU, and to simplify rules on 'public procurement' and state aid.

A global approach and attitude is recognised as a vital prerequisite for future trading prosperity, based on internal EU cohesion and co-operation to face the challenges from the USA, Japan and the Pacific Rim tigers. Thus the sorts of policy area that could be viewed as coming within the range of EU industry policy might include the following:

- regional policy
- enterprise policy
- research and development
- transport
- tourism
- Maastricht implementation and the SEM generally

- co-operatives
- public procurement
- state aid and subsidies
- mergers and alliances
- competition policy in general.

The relevant Directorates of the EC could, therefore, include the following:

- DG I External Economic Relations
- DG II Economic and Financial Affairs
- DG III Industry
- DG IV Competition
- DG V Employment, Industrial Relations and Social Affairs
- DG VII Transport
- DG XII Science, Research and Development
- DG XV Internal Market and Financial Institutions
- DG XXIII Enterprise Policy, Distributive Trades, Tourism and Co-operation.

From this list of some of the main relevant Directorates General, it can be seen that the objective of promoting cohesion and co-ordination in member states' business and economic activities may need to start with efforts to co-ordinate policy-making amongst these overlapping DGs and the activities of their Commissioners – perhaps easier said than done. In an effort to combine the co-ordination policies effectively, the President of the Commission, Jacques Santer, has recently set up working parties of groups of the various DGs to try to avoid duplication and ensure consistency of approach. Whatever may be argued about the nature of industrial policy and how it works in practice, it must be recognised that this is a very political arena. It is often said that right from the early days of the EEC, and indeed before even the signing of the Treaty of Rome, the economic rationale of the EEC was a very unlikely mixture of neo-classical market economics and Keynesianism. A classic example is that the SEM relies heavily on competitive markets for best results (the neo-classical approach), yet long-term measures dating back to the Treaty of Paris in 1951 in the steel industry show many signs of EC/EU intervention and will continue to do so until at least 2002.

Individual member states have for many years practised various degrees of intervention and support of their own industries and companies, regions and sectors at the expense, if need be, of other 'partner' states' interests, and certainly at the expense of the 'level playing field' ideal. The language of 'dirigisme' and national 'champions' sets the tone here. France, Germany and Italy are all seen as major spenders in the defence of national champions. Similarly Thatcherite Britain is sometimes said to have turned its back on state intervention on behalf of its national champions, though 'sweeteners' were paid, for example, to BAe to help it purchase Rover. A recent and detailed unpublished thesis suggests that UK policy towards the shipbuilding industry in the 1980s and 1990s represented little more than pragmatic politics, with little or no theoretical consistency of approach (Kean 1996).

Barberis and May (1996) similarly argue that industrial policy is fundamentally and inevitably a mixture of ideology, technical realities, pragmatism and politics – indeed that industrial policy is in fact really 'just politics'. Whilst this may appear to be an extreme position it is by no means a lone view: 'the economic rationale has always been subservient to the demands of the various nation states, and not vice versa. Ideology always gives place to political expedience and accommodation' (Ward 1996, page 101).

What is the theory behind and the rationale for industrial policy?

Whatever the theory or ideology behind any particular policy might be, two general observations may be made. Firstly, there is widespread agreement that no interventionist policies should be pursued unless there is a clear expectation that benefits will significantly exceed costs. Secondly, as a corollary, any policy involving resource allocation decisions involves opportunity costs: resources used in accordance with policy directives are not available for other uses. Here are encountered elements of the 'crowding-out' argument, i.e. government expenditure has to come from somewhere. It may well deprive private sector enterprises of these resources, and at the same time *may* lead to higher interest rates, adding further costs to the private sector at large.

If, as has been suggested above, industrial policy is about politics, defending national interests and governments seeking the approval of their electorates, it will be difficult to discern much theoretical support for these policies. If we are prepared to consider that *not all* such policies are solely politically motivated, some general objectives of industrial policy may be identified. Clearly the sort of objectives of any policy will depend upon the nature of the policy. Ferguson and Ferguson (1994) have a useful taxonomy of possible forms of industry policy (Table 8.1).

The *laissez faire* approach implies a 'hands-off' government, with a minimum of government activity intervention in economic business affairs. According to Milton Friedman (1962), *laissez faire* would involve the government only in establishing a legal system, **anti-trust** agencies and control of the money supply and very little else. Thus this policy approach is about setting up a framework in which private enterprise free markets can flourish, with the minimum of regulation and intervention by governments.

The supportive approach is broadly similar to *laissez faire* but admits more instances when some government involvement may be desirable, for example

Table 8.1 Possible forms of industrial policy

Policy approach	Policy form
Laissez faire	Very limited intervention through neutral policies
Supportive	Neutral policies
Active	Accelerative and/or decelerative policies
Planning	Accelerative and/or decelerative policies

Source: adapted from Ferguson (1994) page 151.

'to improve the allocation and enforcement of property rights, to encourage education and entrepreneurship in order to foster the process of economic change [and] to adopt [retaliatory] protectionist measures [when appropriate]' (Ferguson and Ferguson 1994, page 149).

The active approach sees a much more involved role for government and government agencies and supports for selected industries and possible protectionist measures, not necessarily retaliatory.

The planning approach 'is a more extreme version of the active approach. Its rationale is that welfare can be improved through centralised planning' (Ferguson and Ferguson 1994, page 149). In terms of the policy form that may be taken, accelerative policies aim to promote economic growth by providing financial support to the most promising firms, markets or technologies. (Ferguson and Ferguson 1994, pages 150–1). Perhaps the best-known example of these sorts of initiatives are those of the Japanese MITI (the Ministry of International Trade and Industry).

Decelerative policies are aimed either at temporary support for firms in trouble, or at helping a dying firm to phase out with a minimum of disruption to the local and national economies. In general, EU industry policy may be classified as being 'a supportive approach to industry policy' (Ferguson and Ferguson 1994, page 189).

> This is significant as such an approach has often been rejected in favour of more active involvement in industry. Even in the USA ... industry policy [relies] on active intervention by the government. The industry policy of the EC is the most promising. It is closer to the requirements of a supportive policy ... the EC sets an example by showing that a common policy framework can be devised to ensure consistency and coordination between policy elements.
>
> (Ferguson and Ferguson 1994, page 193)

But does the evidence really support this very positive appraisal of EU industrial policy as given by Ferguson and Ferguson? The Belgians, for example, have been slow to recognise many training qualifications from other countries, as required by the mutual recognition directives. The Germans have the worst record (bar the Austrians, who have only recently joined) of translating single-market regulations into national law, with Denmark and the Netherlands topping the list for the enactment of single market laws by national governments. However, Germany and France each accounts for approximately one-fifth of the complaints against countries for flouting trade rules each year (50 out of 250 in 1995) whereas the UK prompted only ten such complaints, Denmark five, and Ireland none.

Public procurement and state aid to industry provide two illustrations of individual nation-states pursuing their own economic and political objectives and treating foreign suppliers unfairly.

Public procurement

Public procurement is the purchase of goods and services by governments and state-owned companies, usually by contract or tender. The EU estimates the value of public procurement purchases at between 12 and 16 per cent of the total GDP of the member states (see Chapter 9). The problem is that nearly all governments tend to be highly nationalistic in the conduct of their public procurement. Member states may be paying as much as 25 per cent extra as a result of supporting national companies and industries through this process, and as much as ECU20 billion (a conservative estimate) could be saved if tendering was done on a (more) competitive basis (Ward 1996). The EU believes in liberating markets and encouraging competition, and Commission directives on the opening up of public procurement have been issued periodically since 1977 (see Chapter 9).

The directives are also supported by international agreements. In 1979 the EC countries plus EFTA members and the USA, Canada, Japan and others signed an **Agreement on Government Procurement** (GPA), proposing to open procurement processes to international competition. This was reinforced by a new GPA with similar signatories.

Most recently, the Commission has set about 'initiating a debate on ways to improve public procurement in the EU'(EC 1996a). Interested parties were invited to submit comments by 31 March 1997. This Commission briefing went on to say 'the Directives that form the legislative framework have not been fully transposed by all Member States ... and their impact is still relatively small. Discussion is needed on ways to improve implementation, facilitate access by suppliers, link procurement to other EU policies, and on access to other countries' procurement markets.' Monitoring and proving bias is difficult, however (see Chapter 9).

The continuing presence of non-tariff barriers in the public procurement area may also inhibit competitive tendering. *European Parliament News* (1996) noted that of 376 British companies surveyed, 83 per cent had never bid for any of the contracts put out for public tender in the EU: these were contracts worth £453 billion in 1995. This could be indicative of British business apathy towards European opportunities; but it could be associated with the difficulties of engaging in public procurement abroad. The Commission has urged all public authorities and others to use a **common procurement vocabulary** (CPV) when drafting public procurement notices, in an attempt to make them easier for potential suppliers to understand. To appreciate the complexities of these processes we can note that the CPV lists 6000 terms used in the procurement process in all 11 EU official languages! The importance for business of these imperfections in the market for public purchases can hardly be overstated, with business in excess of £400 billion to be competed for.

State aids

The anticipated and expected gains from the SEM can only be realised if markets are as open and competitive as possible. However, most governments use aid in one form or another to protect state and private industries from home and international competition for various political, social, regional or defensive reasons. In the late 1980s and early 1990s total state aids within the EU have been at very high levels, amounting to ECU44 billion in 1994 (*The Economist* 1997). The Commissioner, Karel Van Miert, has said that the bulk of this money goes not into new industries with a future but to old and dying industries like shipbuilding and coal. Typically, Italy, Germany and France have been 'leaders' in the granting of state aids, with Germany spending over 5 per cent of its total public expenditure on state aid in 1994; the poorest countries in the EU (including Greece and Portugal) put 2–3 per cent of their total public spending on state aid in 1994. Van Miert describes France and Germany as 'drug addicts that cannot kick their habit' (*The Economist* 1997, page 107) and has suggested two new rules to further limit and regulate payment of state aid. Firstly he wants to concentrate on the large cases of aid, giving block exemptions to smaller cases, and secondly he seeks to extend the state aid rules to cover tax breaks, which can have similar effects to aid. State aids allow inefficient firms to reduce costs and neo-classical or 'free market' economics argues that such state aids, grants and subsidies distort the workings of free markets. The EU 'official line' on state aid is fairly clear:

> Aids are prohibited in principle as they distort competition in the free market. Exceptions may be allowed by the Commission. If an exception is granted by the Commission it is done so to pursue the general objectives of the European Union, such as economic integration and cohesion, social welfare and environmental protection.
>
> The aim of these regulations is to create a level playing field for all industries in the Union and to stop companies gaining unfair competitive advantage due to government assistance. Regulations are essential as Aid can strain National Budgets and impede economic convergence. Aid to inefficient firms, which should restructure or disappear, prejudices the functioning of viable enterprises.
>
> (European Commission 1995, page 3)

State aid – the legal framework

State aids are dealt with in EC Treaty Articles 92–94, and ECSC Treaty Article 67. The basic prohibition is set out in Article 92(1):

> Save as otherwise provided in this Treaty, any aid granted by a Member State or through State resources in any form whatsoever which distorts or threatens to distort competition by favouring certain undertakings or the production of certain goods shall, in so far as it affects trade between Member States, be incompatible with the common market.

There are, however, some clear and important exceptions to this blanket prohibition. The main discretionary exceptions are in Article 92(3). This covers the following:

- regional aid to areas with abnormally low standards of living;
- projects of common European interest;
- the development of certain economic activities [*sic*];
- the promotion of culture and heritage conservation.

Amongst the most commonly granted discretionary aids are those called 'rescue aids' and 'restructuring aids'. The guidelines for these aids were set out in a 1979 directive. Rescue aid must:

- consist of guarantees or loans bearing normal commercial interest rates;
- be restricted to the amount needed to keep the firm in business;
- be paid as part of a feasible recovery plan;
- have no adverse effects on the industrial situation;
- be a one-off operation.

Restructuring aid must meet five conditions:

- the *sine qua non* is that a restructuring plan must be capable of restoring long-term viability of the enterprise within a reasonable time scale;
- measures must be instituted to offset as far as possible adverse effects on competitors: if there is overcapacity the aid recipient must cut capacity on a proportionate basis; if there is no overcapacity the aid recipient may not increase capacity;
- the amount of aid must be the minimum needed to enable restructuring to be undertaken;
- specific conditions and obligations are laid down;
- detailed reports are required.

The Commission, however, does not always seem to apply its own rules. In 1994, aid was granted to the Hualon Corporation in Northern Ireland. Davison *et al.* (1995) noted that the £61 million aid was approved to assist in the construction of a new £157 million synthetic fibres plant. Europe had overcapacity in this industry; there seemed little economic sense in increasing this overcapacity, and it violated a critical principle of the restructuring policy. The aid was allowed, however, because it would create direct employment for 1800 people and a further 500 jobs indirectly.

Procedures for supervision of state aid

The procedures by which state aid is supervised are contained in Articles 93 and 94. In Article 93:

- The Commission shall keep under constant review all systems of aid existing in Member States.
- If the Commission finds that aid is not compatible with the common market, or that such aid is being misused, it shall decide that the aid shall be abolished or altered.
- The Commission shall be informed of any plans to grant or alter aid.

In Article 94:

- The Council, acting on a proposal from the Commission, may make any appropriate regulations for the application of Articles 92 and 93.

From Articles 92–94 and the relevant directives, it would appear that the definition of state aids is open and transparent with clear formal procedures for monitoring and control. As with many other aspects of business and economic life in the EU, the reality is not so straightforward. In November 1996 the

Directorate General for Competition, DG IV, put forward proposals for a radical revision of state aids. These new proposals had been prompted by a significant increase in levels of state aid in the mid-1990s and a number of high-profile and controversial cases. The new proposals included the following:

- raising the threshold above which state aid cases are examined. Currently this is ECU100 000 (about £70 000). Raising the threshold would let the Commission concentrate on big cases with a large potential impact;
- introducing a timetable for notification and investigation;
- strengthening the role of third parties in the investigation process;
- establishing a register of decisions on state aid, so as to make the decisions more generally accessible.

The Volkswagen case study gives an indication of the closer scrutiny under which state aid is being examined. However, anomalies still appear to exist, as the Credit Lyonnais case illustrates.

Case study: State aid for Volkswagen and Credit Lyonnais

German state aid for Volkswagen

The German car maker Volkswagen yesterday shelved all investment plans in eastern Germany after the European Commission slashed a state aid package for a car plant by DM241m (£102m).

Brussels cleared DM539m under rules allowing state subsidies to be paid in European Union regions with low living standards and high unemployment, but it blocked the rest of the package. It said only part of VW's investments at its plants at Mosel and Chemnitz in Saxony could be regarded as greenfield developments, for which more state aid is permissible. The German authorities had proposed DM780m of regional aid to the project, split into grants, income tax refunds and special depreciation. Half of the proposed aid has already been paid.

Brussels' decision has caused outrage in eastern Germany, where it is seen as a serious blow to economic reconstruction. Mr Kajo Schommer, Saxony's economics minister, said: 'I fear the decision will be seen potentially as a signal for investors to bypass Saxony and the other East German states.' He said that 'decisions by the Commission, which so clearly hinder economic reconstruction, will not exactly strengthen the European ideal among eastern Germans.'

VW said that the 'rejection comes against a backdrop of a real unemployment rate in eastern Germany of 25 per cent and is especially surprising considering that Volkswagen had planned to help reconstruct Saxony and create 2200 new jobs, including 1200 in supplier industries.'

A spokesman for Mr Karel Van Miert, the EU competition commissioner, said that 'part of the investment, and part of the aid supporting the investment, could not be accepted by the Commission using the normal rules, because part of it could not be claimed to be a greenfield concept.'

Any expansion of Volkswagen's capacity would have a 'negative impact' on the car market in Western Europe, already suffering from overcapacity. The Commission had therefore decided not to allow any state aid in the car sector unless it was strictly necessary to compensate for problems in disadvantaged regions.

The two German commissioners, Mr Martin Bangemann and Mrs Monika Wulf-Mathies, are understood to have delayed a decision on the case last week, but to have been unable to persuade other commissioners to reject the competition directorate's advice this week. Commission officials also hinted that Bonn had applied heavy pressure for the aid to be allowed.

Volkswagen said it 'considers the investment in Saxony clearly as new investment, a judgement that was shared until recently even by EU experts.' The company declared that the investment plans were shelved 'as a consequence of the negative decision from Brussels, with immediate effect.' At Mosel, VW is already producing its Golf series car and had hoped to expand the site between 1997 and 1999 to a capacity of 750 cars a day. Capacity at the Chemnitz plant was also to be increased through a new engine production facility.

Source: Munchau, W. and Buckley, N. (1996) VW halts investment in East Germany, *Financial Times*, 27 June.

More recently it has been reported that 'the eastern German state of Saxony paid more than DM91 (£37 million) to two profitable Volkswagen plants, ignoring a Commission ruling that the payment would be illegal' (*Financial Times* 1996). 'After a long row the Commission has insisted that [the] illegal subsidy paid to Volkswagen by the state of Saxony, must be paid back' (*The Economist* 1997).

The Credit Lyonnais case

There was a whiff of theatrics about yesterday's announcement that the European Commission had approved FFr3.9bn (£490m) in 'emergency' aid from the French government to the disaster zone known as Credit Lyonnais.

It has been clear for months that the state-owned bank would need another substantial injection of funds from its long-suffering shareholder. It has scarcely been a better-kept secret that the shareholder was prepared to stump up. It is less comprehensible why the Commission has been prepared to nod through another huge subsidy without extracting further significant concessions from the state or the bank.

Admittedly, Mr Karel Van Miert, competition commissioner, emphasised yesterday that this was a holding operation and that he would take a very tough line in negotiations on the overall re-rescue package for the bank in coming months. But he was also more conciliatory than he needed to be about the difficult conditions facing the bank in its home market, the need to fatten it up for eventual sale, and the danger it would have been in without yesterday's lifeline. The obvious effectiveness of the French government's lobbying thus far does not engender confidence that Brussels will translate rhetoric into action.

The truth is that there is no justification for pouring in further subsidies without a complete overhaul of the government's and Commission's approach. First, Paris needs to be held strictly to the commitments it made when last year's bail-out was approved. Progress has been too slow on divestments the bank promised to make outside France. Worse, there are signs that Credit Lyonnais was allowed earlier this year to buy back a former subsidiary at well below market terms. The Commission is already looking into this case. It should broaden its inquiry to cover the whole relationship between the bank and the supposedly separate holding company set up to contain a large chunk of its rotten assets.

Second, the Commission should rapidly spell out its conditions for a further rescue. These must include a rapid acceleration in asset sales, including substantial divestments outside France and a shrinking of the bank at home. France would be overbanked even without the distorted competition created by Credit Lyonnais. If the French taxpayer – sheltered from the latest bail-out because the government has dipped into privatisation receipts – is not prepared to cry enough, then the task must fall to Brussels.

Source: Financial Times, 26 September 1996

Note. This approved French government payment was in addition to FFr45 billion (£5.6 billion) paid to Credit Lyonnais in 1995 – the biggest state aid payment ever approved by Brussels.

Questions

1 To what extent do the two cases suggest that state aid policies are still ambiguous in the EU?

• •

The two following cases – German shipbuilders Bremer Vulkan and Iberia – illustrate further difficulties faced by state aid policy. In November 1996, Bremer Vulkan, the largest shipbuilder in Germany, had switched DM700 million of approved state aid for its failing shipyard in East Germany to the profit-making West German parent. This ignored a Commission ruling that using the aid for any purpose other than to support the ailing East German operation, in an area of high unemployment, would be illegal. The outcome of this apparent blatant flouting of the Commission's authority is not yet known. Regardless of the eventual outcome, this case aptly illustrates the willingness of some governments to ignore (or even treat with contempt) Commission rulings. Another of the rules of Commission aid policy is the 'one time, last time' principle. This is to say that aid may be allowed (as above) for 'rescue' and/or 'restructuring', but *not* as ongoing support. This 'one time, last time' rule seems particularly feeble in the aviation context, as shown in the case of Iberia, the Spanish national airline.

In 1992, the Commission approved nearly £700 million of state aid to Iberia, on certain conditions:

- that the one time, last time rule would have to apply;
- and that restructuring would take place.

However, in January 1996 the Commissioner for Transport, DG VII, decided that Iberia could receive a further government hand-out of £460 million. The Commissioner's decision was unanimously adopted on the rather dubious grounds that the cash for the struggling airline was not aid 'in the traditional sense', and should be treated as an investment, justifiable on commercial grounds. Not surprisingly this decision caused some strong responses. The British transport secretary commented that the decision taken in the case of Iberia would 'undermine all our efforts to establish fair competition in the community aviation market' (*The Guardian* 1996a, page 5).

So where does this leave EU industrial policy? To what extent can the European Commission operate this independently and without accountability either to the European Parliament or to the parliaments of the member states – the so-called 'democratic deficit'? Although boosted somewhat by new provisions in the SEA and also in the Maastricht Treaty, the role and powers of the European Parliament are still heavily circumscribed (Tsoukalis 1993). This concept of the democratic deficit is in contrast to the view of national governments' relatively independent position *vis-à-vis* industrial policy. However, it can be seen that Commissioners can make decisions with a good deal of autonomy and little real accountability on behalf of the EU, assuming that the approval of the other Commissioners is forthcoming. However, we may also be able to identify, rather paradoxically, an element in the democratic deficit which actually strengthens the ability of national governments to influence Brussels and, in so doing, to circumvent the rules and the spirit of the *aquis communautaire*.

Philip (1996) suggests that the need to satisfy 15 EU viewpoints often leads to 'legislation' by government-to-government negotiation (or civil service to civil service) or government to Brussels dealings (government civil servants and Brussels bureaucrats making decisions themselves). Seen in this light it could be suggested that decisions like that for Iberia should be seen as the result of intensive lobbying of DG VII (Transport) administrators by enthusiastic Spanish bureaucrats, rather than as a real policy decision by the Commissioner himself.

A second problem for industrial policy is, can governments 'pick winners'? The history of governments' attempts to pick winners is mixed. In the UK the aid to de Lorean, in the late 1970s, was an extreme example of active policy failure. John de Lorean, once a top US auto industry executive, received many millions of pounds from the UK government to build a totally new factory, for a totally new car, near Belfast. The scheme failed – though some 'de Loreans' were made. (One can be seen as the time machine in the *Back to the Future* films.) A 1996 survey, compiled by the EU's statistical office in Luxembourg (*The Guardian* 1996b), indicated a very poor track record for EU-funded new businesses in Eastern Europe. Some £7 billion was invested by the EU in Eastern Europe in 3.4 million companies in the two years between 1992 and 1994 (the latest data available). Of these companies, more than one million have already failed and two-thirds of the remaining operations are in danger of bankruptcy. Finally, can regulation actually promote good economic performance? Koedijk and Kremers (1996) have studied the effects of government regulation of economies. The performance (as measured by growth rates of per capita GNP) of 11 EU economies (excluding Luxembourg, Austria, Finland and Sweden) was plotted against the level of regulation in those economies. Clearly measuring 'regulation' is not easy. However, even after recognising the measurement problems there seems to be a fairly clear inverse relationship between levels of regulation and levels of growth. The least regulated economies of the EU (Ireland, Britain and Denmark) were also those with the highest growth rates; Greece, Italy and France, amongst the most highly regulated economies, showed the poorest growth performance. Whilst this is a relatively simplistic correlation study it might be argued that less regulation would be good for Europe. Similar conclusions had been reached in an OECD study two years earlier (OECD 1994), and by a McKinsey report of the same year (McKinsey Global Institute 1994).

Thus we may observe that the democratic deficit may lead to policy decisions being taken by unaccountable bureaucrats; that policy-makers are unlikely to be good at picking winners (they are after all bureaucrats, not entrepreneurs); and that highly regulated economies seem likely to perform less well than free-market economies. If these points are valid an active industrial policy will be in difficulties. Even if EU and EU member states' industrial policy is only supportive, the prospects for a successful industrial policy are not good. It appears that the 'integrated' EU can still be described as a loose grouping of nation-states whose governments are likely to pursue their own national and political interests first, and that the objectives of co-operation, cohesion and integration, are still to be achieved. Does EU competition policy work in a more coherent and consistent way to contribute to the achievement of the aims and objectives of the EU and the SEM? It is to this area that the chapter turns next.

Competition policy

What is meant by 'competition policy'?

Competition policy (CP) is open to several interpretations. It can be interpreted as any activities or rules designed either to promote 'competitive' economic or business behaviour or to inhibit the restriction of competitive forces. By this interpretation economic policies, directives and initiatives of individual governments and the EU *could* be included. This is too wide, thus the focus here will be to consider the laws and regulations directly relating to monopoly, merger, acquisition, restrictive practices and the like. In the EU this stems mainly from Articles 85 and 86 of the Treaty of Rome and is the responsibility of the Directorate General of the Commission responsible for competition, usually called simply DG 4 or DG IV. As was noted earlier there is a distinct overlap between areas designated as 'industrial policy' and 'competition policy', and their effects on companies may also overlap and intertwine.

The objectives of competition policy

There is considerable debate as to the objectives and the efficacy of CP, whether in the UK or in the EU. The USA has the oldest system of CP rules (or 'anti-trust' legislation) in the world, dating back to 1890. In the EU the SEM has a very strong presumption that competition is a 'good thing', and that the 'restructuring' of industry anticipated as a result of the SEM and the enforcement of EU CP will give rise to substantial efficiency gains.

Neo-classical theory tells us that welfare is optimised (the Pareto optimum) when perfect competition prevails in all markets. The welfare gains from competition paradoxically may be easier to illustrate in reverse by consideration of the situation where welfare is forfeited due to elements of monopoly being present.

Figure 8.1 shows an industry operating both under perfectly competitive conditions and where an element of monopoly is present. In perfect conditions the competitive price is set equal to marginal cost, at P_c, and output is Q_c. If the industry is monopolised overnight, price will be set above P_c at, say, P_m and output will fall to Q_m. This is the 'classic case' against monopoly: so long as cost conditions stay the same, the price is higher, and output lower, under monopoly than under competitive conditions.

Under competitive conditions the area above the line $P_c dc$, and below the demand curve (i.e. triangle $P_c ac$), is **consumer surplus**. Under monopoly conditions consumer surplus is reduced to triangle $P_m ab$. The rectangle $P_c P_m bd$ represents an income or welfare redistribution from consumers to producers. Some argue that this redistribution represents a welfare loss to society, being a transfer to the few (producers) from the many (consumers). This, however, involves a value judgement that producers' welfare is less worthy than consumers' welfare. Even if we do not make this value judgement we still have the triangle *bcd* to consider. This triangle measures the so-called 'deadweight loss'

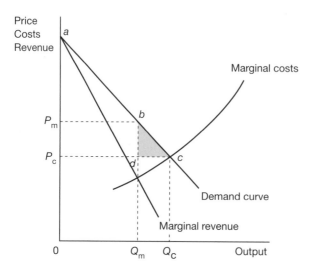

Figure 8.1 The deadweight loss of welfare due to monopoly

caused by monopoly pricing and output, in contrast with what would happen under competitive conditions. Output has fallen from Q_c to Q_m. The consumer surplus, *bcd*, is simply lost to society; not transferred to producers, but lost. Monopoly therefore leads to social welfare losses, and is a 'bad thing'. This in essence is the rationale behind most variants of CP.

Attempts have been made to estimate the extent of the loss of GNP attributable to the output-restricting effects of monopoly. The seminal work on this question was undertaken by Harberger (1954) who suggested that for the USA the loss, depending on the nature of the various elasticities and other estimates, would be only about 0.1 per cent of GNP per year. If Harberger's estimate is reliable, this would suggest that monopoly power is a fairly trivial matter as far as society's welfare is concerned, and that CP would hardly be necessary. If the losses to monopoly are trivial it might also be argued that the potential gains from an increase in competition may have been hitherto overstated. Many other analysts have considered this question of the costs of monopoly. Cowling and Mueller (1978) reworked the figures and assumed a high degree of monopoly control over prices; on their various assumptions they estimated the losses at around 10 per cent of GNP. The 'true' estimate, if there can be such a figure, is probably somewhere between the two extremes of Harberger and of Cowling and Mueller. Critics argue that in this line of analysis the attempt to measure welfare loss or resource misallocation is merely static analysis based on the price and output of firms and industries at different points in time, without consideration of their 'performance' over time. If the behaviour of firms and industries is viewed as a dynamic process through time, however, the role of research and development (R&D) becomes critical. Schumpeter (1954), Galbraith (1963) and others argue that competitive or oligopolistic 'big business' most effectively promotes R&D, and that technical progress arising from R&D is of such significance in the overall development and success of firms, industries and economies that the benefits from technically progressive big business outweigh any possible costs. There is a paradox here: big business is likely to be technically progressive, but only if competitive.

This is the situation that Cecchini (1988) envisaged in terms of the SEM. Furthermore, the Cecchini Report suggested that the restructured economies which would follow from the SEM would also lead to substantial efficiency gains from economies of scale. Critics of Cecchini argued that the anticipated economies of scale were greatly exaggerated. Neuberger (1989), for example, declared that the claims made for economic benefit were not supported by the evidence in the report; Pratten (1988) could find no clear evidence of the claimed scale economy gains and Cutler *et al.* (1989) added the argument that the real point of the SEM was to move the EU inexorably along the road to political union rather than looking for gains in efficiency. However, regardless of this body of criticism, the Cecchini Report *is* important as an indicator of attitudes within the EU towards CP. The position taken by Cecchini is that competition is good and that more competition is better than less. Therefore, how can competition be encouraged?

Competition, which is usually associated with free markets, may require government intervention to encourage and ensure its success. That is, effective competition requires some active form of competition policy.

The purpose of EU competition policy

The main elements of the law relating to CP in the EU are stated in Articles 85 and 86 of the Treaty of Rome. However, even before the drawing up and signing of the Treaty of Rome (in March 1957), the concept of competition had figured prominently in the deliberations of the original six member states. The foreign ministers of the six states met at Messina in Sicily in 1955 to produce a **declaration**, a key phrase which referred to the vital role to be played by the forces of unfettered competition in the Community. Following on from this declaration came the Spaak Report (1957), which declared that

> The object of the European Common Market should be to create a vast zone of common economic policy, constituting a powerful unit of production permitting continuous expansion and increased stability and accelerated raising of the standard of living ... (in) Member States ... These advantages of a Common Market cannot be obtained unless ... practices whereby competition between producers is distorted are put to an end.
>
> (Spaak 1957, page 10)

The report went on to give clear and detailed requirements of the CP to be incorporated in the Treaty.

> It will be necessary to prevent
>
> - a division of markets by agreement between enterprises, since this would be tantamount to re-establishing the compartmentalization of the market;
> - agreements to limit production or curb technical progress because they would run counter to progress and productivity;
> - the absorption or domination of the market for a product by a single enterprise, since this would eliminate one of the essential advantages of a vast market, namely that it reconciles the use of mass production techniques with the maintenance of competition.
>
> (Spaak 1957, page 13)

The Spaak Report provided the seed not only for Articles 85 and 86 but also for key parts of the Cecchini analysis, in particular the linking of large economic enterprises and operations with efficiency through economies of scale, *provided they operate in a competitive environment.* Following in the tradition of the very pro-competition statements made in the Messina Declaration and the Spaak Report, the Commission has continued, more recently, to make its feelings on the importance of competition and competition policy well known.

Each year since 1972 the Commission has published a report on competition policy. The first report (1972) contains a very clear statement of the benefits of competition:

> Competition is the best stimulant of economic activity since it guarantees the widest possible freedom of action to all. An active competition policy pursued in accordance with the provisions of the Treaties establishing the Communities makes it easier for the supply and demand structures continually to adjust to technological development. Through the interplay of decentralized decision-making machinery, competition enables enterprises continuously to improve their efficiency, which is the sine qua non for a steady improvement in living standards and

employment prospects within the countries of the Community. From this point of view, competition policy is an essential means for satisfying to a great extent the individual and collective needs of our society.

(European Commission 1972, page 12)

In the Ninth Report on Competition Policy (1980), the Commission took the argument a step further:

It is an established fact that competition carries within it the seeds of its own destruction. An excessive concentration of economic, financial and commercial power can produce such far-reaching structural changes that free competition is no longer able to fulfil its role as an effective regulator of economic activity.

(European Commission 1980, page 3)

The Commission argued, here, that any genuine competition by its very nature must have winners and losers. The winners may be expected to go from strength to strength, ultimately achieving a position of some dominance. It is in this sense that 'competition carries within it the seeds of its own destruction', and competition policy has a vital role to play in ensuring and maintaining competitive market structures.

This view of the importance of competitive market structures, to be maintained by competition policy, is at odds with the Chicago School view. These theorists assume that if barriers to market entry are typically low, any excess or monopoly profit will quickly attract new entrants, thus driving down profit rates to something approaching 'normal' profit levels. Competition policy administrators should therefore intervene only in those cases where price/cost margins are abnormally high (as the result of cartels or other collusive behaviour). The Commission is clearly unwilling to accept this reliance on market forces.

The Commission further developed its position on competition policy and market structure (abuse of dominant firm position), as well as in the policing of restrictive practices, in the Seventeenth Report on Competition Policy (1988):

As the completion of the internal market by 1992 gathers pace, competition policy is coming more to the fore ... There is an increasing awareness amongst the general public that the absence of an effective competition policy entails substantial costs since it is always the taxpayer who pays for unjustified State subsidies and the consumer who pays through higher prices and lower efficiency due to cartels, price fixing, abuses by dominant firms and other restrictive practices ... The overall economic policy of the Community has the threefold aim of promoting a co-operative strategy for the creation of employment, of strengthening economic and social cohesion and of achieving an internal market ...

Thus the task of Community competition policy is to determine how best to contribute to the achievement of these major economic objectives:

The future growth of the Community economy entails improving the allocation of production factors, increasing market profitability and boosting innovation, in order to increase the international competitiveness of Community undertakings. Dynamic growth of supply is precisely the contribution policy can bring to the economy of the Twelve.

(European Commission 1988, page 7)

The Commission continues to state its commitment to a vigorous and effective CP. Guidelines on CP issued on 10 September 1996 stressed the Commission's ongoing conviction that CP has a vital part to play in developing the international competitiveness of the EU as the millennium approaches, and that national CP authorities could and should play a part in monitoring compliance with EU rules on competition. The Commission should be able to concentrate on cases with more of a European dimension and on the more effective enforcement of competition rules. Again in October 1996 the Commission declared that the single market had produced some very satisfactory results (see Chapter 9) but that results could have been even better if competition policy rules had been more diligently applied and enforced by member states. Further, in *The Week in Europe* of 23 January 1997, the Commission stated its intention to reform the rules on vertical restraints to make markets freer and more competitive in accordance with Article 85.

Thus CP is seen as vital and has a key role to play in ensuring that the gains from the SEM are realised. But how do these very clear and strong 'mission' statements fit with the practice of competition policy within the EU?

The practice of EU competition policy

As noted earlier, the rules of EU CP are set out in Articles 85 and 86. Article 85 deals with agreements that may restrict competition in inter-state trade. Article 86 refers to the abuse of a dominant position.

Article 85

Article 85 of the CP rules prohibits agreements that restrict competition and threaten the unity of the common market. To come within the scope of Article 85 there must be three factors present: (a) an element of collusion between 'undertakings' which could (b) affect trade between member states, thus (c) restricting trade in the common market.

The text of Article 85 provides that:

1 The following shall be prohibited as incompatible with the common market: all agreements between undertakings, decisions by associations of undertakings, and concerted practices which may affect trade between Member States and which have as their object or effect the prevention, restriction or distortion of competition within the common market, and in particular those which:

   (a) directly or indirectly fix purchase or selling prices or any other trading conditions;
   (b) limit or control production, markets, technical development, or investment;
   (c) share markets or sources of supply;
   (d) apply dissimilar conditions to equivalent transactions with other trading parties, thereby placing them at a competitive disadvantage;
   (e) make the conclusion of contracts subject to acceptance by the other parties of supplementary obligations which, by their nature or according to commercial usage, have no connection with the subject of such contract.

2 Any agreements or decisions prohibited pursuant to this Article shall be automatically void.

3 The provision of paragraph 1 may, however, be declared inapplicable in the case of:

> any agreement or category of agreements between undertakings;
> any decision or category of decisions by associations of undertakings;
> any concerted practice or category of concerted practices;

which contributed to improving the production or distribution of goods or to promoting technical or economic progress, while allowing consumers a fair share of the resulting benefit, and which does not:

(a) impose on the undertakings concerned restrictions which are not indispensable to the attainment of these objectives;
(b) afford such undertakings the possibility of eliminating competition in respect of a substantial part of the products in question.

Thus, the first paragraph of the Article sets out the prohibition of concerted action, the second paragraph mentions automatic nullity as the sanction of the violation of the prohibition, and the third paragraph provides for an exemption from the prohibition should certain conditions be met. 'Agreements' have included both horizontal and vertical mergers (see Chapter 2 for more detail). It has been argued that Article 85 should distinguish between horizontal and vertical agreements, as horizontal agreements could be seen as more directly anti-competitive. 'Concerted practice' has been taken to include something less than a formal agreement or contract, but which none the less is designed to replace competition by co-operation. The phrase 'which may affect trade between member states' is also an important part of Article 85. If there is no effect, actual or potential, on inter-member trade then Article 85 does not apply – but individual national CP rules could still operate. 'Affect' has been interpreted by the European Court of Justice (ECJ) to mean activities which undermine the unity of the market, irrespective of whether the activity actually increases or decreases trade. Thus it is the distortion of the conditions of, and for, competition and not the consequences which are vital. Furthermore, agreements may be caught by Article 85 if they 'may' affect competition, i.e. potential restrictions on competition may be enough for an agreement to be prohibited, as illustrated in the well-known Pronuptia case (1986 ECR 353), where a potential limitation on the franchisee's areas of operation was enough for the ECJ to condemn the agreement (Korah 1994, page 54). Indeed, even 'the term competition has been interpreted as referring not only to actual but also to potential competition ... [in one case] the Court ruled that a commitment not to manufacture a product, undertaken by a firm not presently capable of manufacturing such product, constituted a restriction of competition' (Van Bael and Bellis 1989, page 33).

Thus Section 1 of Article 85 prohibits collusion and generally leads to prohibition. There are, however, possibilities for exemptions: common restrictive agreements may benefit from a 'block exemption' from Article 85 (1) for agreements in categories such as patent and know-how licensing, franchising and research and development. Section 3 outlines further exemption opportunities. When an agreement falls outside the terms of a block exemption, or is in an area where there is no block exemption, Article 85(3) exemptions can still be granted in cases where agreements contribute to improving the production of goods or promote technical progress and allow consumers a fair share of the resulting benefits. Such exemptions can only be granted by the Commission, thus inevitably slowing the whole process down. Thus a whole range of 'restrictive practices' are outlawed in Section 1a–1e. This is similar to the 1956 Restrictive Trade Practices (RTP) Act in the UK. Both Article 85 and the RTP Act are designed to curtail collusive activities which reduce, obstruct or eliminate competition. Here, however, the comparison ends. The UK law requires all restrictive agreements, as defined in the legislation, to be registered (with the Registrar of Restrictive Trade Practices). They are all deemed void and unlawful unless the parties to the restrictive agreement can successfully plead some public benefit which accrues from the restriction(s) within the agreement. The emphasis in the UK is on the form of the agreement, in the first place, and its 'economic impact' second. Article 85 does not separate the economic consequences, or the analysis, and legal form in this way.

Section 2 of Article 85 provides that activities or agreements which infringe the Article are void (unenforceable). Thus national courts cannot require the fulfilment of contracts which infringe section 1 of Article 85 (where there is conflict, EU law takes precedence, so a contract which is valid in a member state, by its national law, may be unenforceable by Article 85 rules.). This uncertainty is not good for business, especially as the uncertainty is partly due to the law being unsettled, but also because of the time and cost of litigation. This is contrary to the basic concept of competition-enforcing rules; that business should be inhibited (and competition potentially reduced) whilst the process of adjudication takes place. Sometimes the Commission takes a rather benign approach. In the Interbrew case of 1994, the Belgian brewer had negotiated rights to be the sole distributor in Belgium of two luxury lagers – the Danish brands Tuborg and Carlsberg. The Commission first said that this sole distributorship was against the public interest. Tuborg and Carlsberg then entered into a **joint venture** for the distribution of their products with a second Belgian distributor. The Commission was satisfied with this result as it increased competition in this market. The Commission also approved an agreement to reduce capacity in the Dutch brick-making industry, designed to reduce capacity by 30 per cent. This could be considered as collusive practice; however, the Commission sanctioned the proposal, seeing it as a constructive reorganisation of the industry which would surely reduce costs and hopefully lead to lower prices to the end-consumer. In accordance with Article 85(3) approval was given.

In October 1996 the Commission announced some substantial fines on five cross-Channel companies that were deemed to have violated Article 85. The five companies had been operating a cartel inasmuch as they had raised prices in an agreed and collective manner (in October 1992). The companies argued in their own defence that the price rises (a surcharge on cross-Channel freight shipments) were necessary to maintain a reasonable level of profits and to compensate for the effects of the devaluation of the pound (at that time). The Commission dismissed this 'defence' and declared against the cartel: it was a 'concerted practice' coming within the scope of Article 85.

Article 86

Article 86 provides that:

> Any abuse by one or more undertakings of a dominant position within the common market or in a substantial part of it shall be prohibited as incompatible with the common market in so far as it may affect trade between Member States.
>   Such abuse may, in particular, consist in:

(a) directly or indirectly imposing unfair purchase or selling prices or other unfair trading conditions;
(b) limiting production, markets or technical development to the prejudice of consumers;
(c) applying dissimilar conditions to equivalent transactions with other trading parties, thereby placing them at a competitive disadvantage;
(d) making the conclusion of contracts subject to acceptance by the other parties of supplementary obligations which, by their nature or according to commercial usage, have no connection with the subject of such contracts.

Thus the first paragraph of the Article sets out the prohibition of any abuse of a dominant position within the common market and its possible affects on trade between member states. The second paragraph gives some illustrative examples of abuse of a dominant position. In the Continental Can case (1973, ECR 215) the ECJ made it clear that Article 86 would cover not only practices which cause damage to consumers directly, but also those which are detrimental to consumers' interests through their impact on effective competitive structures, as in sections (b), (c) and (d) above. In any action under Article 86, two elements must be present: the existence of a 'dominant position' and 'abuse' of the dominant position.

The 'dominant position' argument

In the Sirena case (1971, CMLR 260) dominance was stated as a position which could prevent effective competition within an important part of the market. The wording did not clear matters. In the case of United Brands (1978, ECR 207) it was stated that a dominant position is 'A position of economic strength enjoyed by an undertaking which enables it to prevent competition being maintained in the relevant market by giving it the power to behave to an appreciable extent independently of its competitors, customers and ultimately of its consumers' (Van Bael and Bellis 1989, page 49). But how is the 'relevant market' defined? Over the years many aspects of the relevant market have been considered in various 'test' cases. The degree of interchangeability, or substitutability, has been used as an attempt to define the relevant market. Thus in United Brands the banana was considered to be sufficiently different from other fruits as to constitute a market on its own; in Hoffman-LaRoche (1979, 3 CMLR 211) it was held that vitamins for industrial and bio-nutritive uses were in different product markets; whilst in Michelin (1983, ECR 3461), it was held that the market for replacement tyres for trucks and buses was different from the market for the supply of tyres to original vehicles!

The relevant *geographic* market also needs to be defined. Article 86 refers to dominance 'within the common market or in a substantial part of it'. On the whole, the Court is willing to define relevant geographic markets quite narrowly, even going as far as the smallest of member states. Having determined the relevant market, the Court then has to consider whether a company is indeed dominant within it – the concept of market power. In Hoffman-LaRoche, the Court referred to a number of elements comprising market power: market share, and the share of competitors, the company's technical lead, its highly developed sales network and the absence of potential competition. Barriers to entry and vertical integration have also been considered in the market power context. Thus it can be said that the Court typically tries to define relevance quite narrowly, thus making it easier for the Court to establish dominance.

'Abuse' of a dominant position

In contrast with the narrow definitions of the market, abuse of a dominant position has been construed widely. In Hoffman-La Roche an objective test was used. Are methods 'different' from those which exist under conditions of normal competition? The sorts of behaviour which may be considered 'different' include excessive prices, discriminatory prices, predatory pricing, refusal to supply and so on. Thus it seems that the Court is willing to try to extend the scope of Article 86, and that the abuse of monopoly power will be condemned by the court. As Ward notes, 'this area of law is riddled by the inconsistencies which beset any jurisprudence which is decided on an essentially ad hoc basis' (Ward 1996, page 130).

Again, as with Article 85, it is far from easy to predict what the Court or Commission's view is likely to be in any given case, adding uncertainty and increased transaction costs to the firm's wish to find out where it stands *vis-à-vis* the CP rules. This is far from satisfactory.

Overall, Articles 85 and 86 of the Treaty of Rome appear to give the Commission wide powers of enforcement and prohibition in competition policy. The way in which competition policy is used and applied is not always consistent and is surrounded by complexity and uncertainty. The merger provisions of EU competition policy are not significantly better.

The conflict between domestic and EU competition rules

In addition to the EU rules on competition policy, most member states have their own competition laws. If there should be a conflict of laws, EU law takes precedence. This was established as far back as 1964 (*Costa* v. *ENEL* (1964) ECR 585). The situation is not quite so clear where there is an overlap of the law, or concurrent jurisdiction. However, in the Bundeskartellamt case (*Wilhelm* v. *Bundeskartellamt* (1969) ECR 1) the ruling was made that it was quite feasible and permissible for there to be parallel actions under both EU and national law.

Regardless of the rules and their application, the enforcement of CP by the Commission has so far been a rather slow and cumbersome process. The Commission is divided into 25 directorates general (DGs), each rather similar to a ministry within the UK government. The Commission, acting through the 25 DGs, develops policy proposals, which must then go through a process of deliberation and discussion involving the Council of Ministers and the European Parliament. When policies have been decided upon the Commission then implements the policies as directives, decisions and regulations. All three have the force of law. Directives act through national legislatures, requiring legislation to be developed appropriate to each country. Decisions normally affect a specific company, person or country. Regulations have general applicability throughout the Community. The Court of Justice has a wide jurisdiction, including the interpretation of, and adjudication on, disputes arising from Community legislation. The Court has taken a number of decisions which have altered or extended Community laws. In addition to the Court of Justice, another court, the Court of First Instance, was established in 1989. This court has a more limited jurisdiction but can deal with actions initiated by Commission officials, damages cases and competition cases.

Both the Court of Justice and the Court of First Instance have a considerable volume of work to handle. The Court of Justice has a backlog that increases by approximately 50 cases a year, and even the new Court of First Instance began with a deficit.

Competition rules become part of the law of all member states, and in the spirit of the *aquis communautaire* it is assumed that all member states will comply. Any agreements or arrangements that infringe these rules are prohibited, and national courts will not enforce contracts that infringe the rules. The interaction between national courts and the EU courts can and does give rise to considerable complexities. In January 1997 a situation arose indicating the tensions between national and EU authorities. The UK government and the Commission disagreed about a proposed merger of BA (British Airways) and AA (American Airlines), the US airline. The Commission felt it had authority to challenge the proposal, as it had a potential 'EU dimension' (in that BA's strengthened position would change the balance of competition within the EU), whereas the UK government refused to refer the proposal to the UK Monopolies Commission, and disagreed that the Commission had any jurisdiction. DG IV and the Commission successfully argued that the merger was a EU matter, and the merger was delayed. In July 1998, the merger was allowed to proceed provided that BA surrender one-third of its slots at Heathrow.

Thus it may be very important for companies to consider the implications of CP when planning marketing and production activities. Fines can be levied on companies that are deemed to have violated Article 85 or 86 (as high as 10 per cent of the previous year's turnover) and contracts which violate the rules are void and unenforceable. To put it another way, 'The EC competition rules are of wide application and enforced by important sanctions. It may be costly to remain ignorant of them' (Korah 1994, page 26).

Some heavy fines have been imposed, and the existence of the rules and the threat of substantial fines have had a real deterrent effect on the behaviour of organisations. On the other hand, there is no doubt that DG IV is under-resourced in its budget and its staffing. It is a familiar part of the critique of CP in the UK, USA and Canada as well as the EU, that the strong words of the legislation and regulations do not tally with the power of the bureaucrats to 'make things happen'. Sampson (1983) has written extensively on the interconnections between government, civil service and business in the UK. Sampson argues that the sort of people who are expected to 'police' the system of monopoly in capitalism are of the same socio-economic elite within society as the directors of the companies they are to 'control'. This holds just as markedly for other countries in Europe – there is a very close socio-economic class linkage between governments, civil servants (i.e. European Commissioners and their staffs) and business executives. It is simply not in their view of reality, he says, to see the operation of business in general as likely to be against the public interest. From this point of view it should not really be surprising if CP is not vigorously enforced, or adequately resourced. A parallel argument here is that made in relation to the role of the regulators of privatised industries. Regulatory 'capture' can take place, i.e. the regulators and the industries they are supposed to regulate by the very nature of their activities are bound to be closely connected, and there is a distinct possibility that the regulators simply become the puppets of their industrial charges. The recent case (in September 1997) of Ms Spottiswood, the regulator for the electricity industry in the UK, may fall into this category, where earlier announcements of relatively large reductions in electricity charges were reduced after further consultation with the electricity generators. Furthermore, it is often argued that the good intentions of CP may be thwarted by the promotion of national rather than EU interests, as in the de Havilland case. In October 1991 the Commission refused to allow France's state-owned Aerospatiale and Italy's state-owned Alenia jointly to purchase the de Havilland aircraft company, a division of the American Boeing company. This proposed joint venture would have given the French and Italian consortium approximately 65 per cent of the EU production of small commuter aircraft (20–70 seaters). Two privately owned EU companies, Fokker of The Netherlands and British Aerospace, were concerned that this new Franco–Italian group would represent unfair competition and would have a dominant market position, restricting potential competition. Enormous political pressure was put on Jacques Delors, the French President of the Commission, to support the consortium proposal. In the end the bid was vetoed. An article in *The Economist* (1991) argued: 'The EC will never have a coherent competition policy without an independent agency, similar to Germany's Federal Cartel office, to act as a watchdog. In the end, all competition decisions are subject to political debate' (*The Economist* 1991, page 18).

The comparisons with industrial policy are plain. There is a very strong argument that industrial policy, both of the EU and of member states, is primarily driven by political considerations, dirigisme, and defending national champions. To the extent that this is true of industrial policy, it is surely likely to be similarly so in the CP arena.

Mergers and joint ventures

A **merger** (or acquisition) is usually taken to mean the situation where two or more independent businesses come together to form one new organisation, usually a new legal entity. This may be done by mutual consent, or it could be an aggressive act by one firm – a 'takeover', possibly by means of a 'dawn raid' in the stock market. This can be differentiated from a **joint venture**, which is an agreement between two or more companies to co-operate in some way(s), which may be fairly trivial, or fundamental to the operation of either or both or all of the parties involved, but each company will maintain its own separate legal identity. Joint ventures could also involve the creation of a new company jointly owned by the co-operating parties. Both mergers and joint ventures could be seen as methods of 'integration' and of 'diversification'.

The rationale for mergers and joint ventures

The rationale for mergers and joint ventures can be judged from two very different perspectives: that of the companies involved and their commercial objectives, and that of 'the public interest'. Integration may be undertaken by management as a matter of fashion or fancy, whether the expansion be at home or abroad. Under these quite common circumstances it would be expected, as Porter (1987) has argued, that the performance of the diversified operation would be largely determined by luck. If, however, an 'expansion decision' (whether at home or abroad) has been undertaken after some serious consideration, success is a good deal more likely.

> Whilst market entry is not, by itself, a source of competitive advantage, it can unlock the value of the competitive advantages that either of the firms may have, by enabling the advantages to be extended to new markets. In this respect, mergers motivated by the desire to enter new markets appear to be directed more toward the exploitation of potential synergies than their domestic counterparts.
>
> (Davis *et al.* 1991, page 67)

Thus from the companies' perspectives it can be seen that either a merger or a joint venture could be an attractive strategy, under suitable conditions. But from whose perspectives should these be judged?

Public policy and mergers

The joint venture as a route to growth appears to have a number of specific advantages and it appears also that both UK and EU legislation may be reasonably well disposed to this form of company expansion. How does this compare with the alternative of a merger, and how does public policy treat this approach to corporate growth and development?

Much of the early empirical work done in the UK on post-merger performance has been highly critical. From Meeks' (1977) investigation to Newbould and Luffman (1978) and Dutton (1980), the conclusions have been broadly similar: mergers did not seem to give rise to obvious or clear efficiency or performance gains. More recently, similar doubts have been expressed as to the efficacy of merger as a strategy. Bruton *et al.* (1994) identified the importance of firms having some prior experience of the merger process, and the general observation that any financial advantages to acquiring firms may take some time to show up was made by Loderer and Martin (1992).

Regardless of the **synergy** and related arguments in favour of acquisition and merger, the impact of merger may be to the detriment of the bought firm, its shareholders, their employees and customers. When the added complexities and transactions costs associated with cross-border merger are taken into account, further doubts creep in as to the post-merger performance of international acquisitions. Only in the case of the genuinely 'failing firm', rescued by the optimistic acquiring purchaser, may the public interest be expected to be served in the majority of cases.

What has been the attitude of EU legislators towards mergers?

The Treaty of Rome did not deal specifically with mergers and takeovers. However, the Treaty of Paris, 1951, which set up the ECSC (European Coal and Steel Community), did contain powers to prevent mergers in those industries. The ECSC agreement expires in 2002, and there is some debate as to whether it will be renewed along with its anti-merger clauses. Mergers are a very sensitive area in EU political and economic circles. Concentration levels and attitudes to mergers and big business vary from country to country. Denmark, for example, has a very high standard of living coupled with a low level of business concentration; this, they argue, is not coincidental. The Danes have no affection for mergers and the increase in market and/or aggregate concentration levels that follows. On the other hand, some countries which, like Denmark, also have relatively small-sized business units (e.g. Greece and Portugal) may resist moves to restrict mergers. These countries argue that the 'restructuring' advantages expected to flow from the SEM should not be inhibited by unnecessarily stringent anti-merger rules. The Continental Can case of 1973 established that Article 86 could apply to mergers, but since then the Commission has rarely used Article 86 to prevent a proposed merger, although a number of market concentrations have been considered by the Commission with a view to action under Article 86. The EU's position on mergers appears to be somewhat confused and uncertain. After protracted debate the Council of Ministers eventually adopted a regulation to bring some mergers – those with a 'Community dimension' – within the scope of its powers. This came into force as 'The Merger Control Regulation' in September 1990. A merger is deemed to have a Community dimension, and so to be subject to the regulation, if it leads to concentration and passes three tests:

- that the aggregate worldwide turnover exceeds ECU5 billion;
- that the aggregate EU turnover of each of at least two firms involved exceeds ECU250 million and;
- that none of the firms has two-thirds of its EU-wide turnover in one member state (Merger Control Regulations, September 1990).

Criticism of the new regulation has so far hinged mainly on the magnitude of the thresholds, and the small number of eligible 'concentrations' which get referred. For example, a giant firm could buy up one competitor or potential competitor after another, year after year, without falling foul of the regulations, as long as each purchase was below ECU250 million. These high thresholds are much more likely to catch conglomerate than horizontal or vertical mergers. Conglomerate mergers, of course, may be viewed with some suspicion, bringing as they do an increase in aggregate concentration and the threat of an increase in the general power of 'big business'. However, conglomerates are not the forms of business which most competition legislation tries to monitor and/or control. There is no reference in the Merger Regulation as to the markets in which the companies operate; the thresholds are in terms of total size, not of share (or implicit power) within industries or markets (horizontal) or within production stage processes (vertical). It is the horizontal and vertical mergers which give rise to theoretical and empirical concerns about abuse of power and are a detriment to the public interest, but these may escape the Regulation.

The Commission's recent proposal to reduce the ECU5 billion threshold to ECU2 billion has also run into opposition from the three most merger-active member states, the UK, France and Germany. 'Politically, it is not so easy to effect what competition lawyers and economists might perceive to be the neatest solution to the present uncertainty' (Ward 1996, page 132).

EU merger policy has therefore received a certain amount of criticism: thresholds are said to be too high and activity levels too low, some inconsistency of approach has been noticed and too much politics is in evidence – particularly national politics of the sort which clouds and confuses industrial policy too (see above). However, Art and van Liedekerke (1996) have suggested that change may be afoot in EU merger policy. In support of their contention they indicate an increased willingness to act, at least in certain industries. In 1995 'the Commission dealt with a record number of individual merger notifications. It received 114 notifications and adopted 109 final decisions. Sectors with high M&A (merger and acquisition) activity which resulted in a substantial number of notifications were telecommunications, financial services, media and pharmaceuticals' (Art and van Liedekerke 1996, page 740).

Controlling joint ventures

The EU's position with respect to joint ventures is unclear. In the case of conflict between domestic and EU laws with regard to joint ventures, then EU law takes precedence. This would seem to be a very clear position. However, in one of the cases that established this precedence rule (Bundeskartellamt 1969, ECR 1) the position was rather special in that here was the possibility of both EU and domestic law applying to the case. Under these circumstances it was made clear that EU law 'rules'. There has been some debate since, however, as to whether this necessarily applies in all cases: for example, the situation could arise in which EU law might permit a merger which some domestic law might prohibit. In particular, Germany and the Netherlands have laws relating to the ownership and holding of shares, which could rule out contested takeovers which EU law might be willing to allow.

In EU law, joint ventures could come under either Article 85 or 86 or the merger regulations. Article 86 – abuse of a dominant position – could clearly be applicable, but has been little used. A distinction is also made between 'concentrative' joint ventures and 'co-operative' joint ventures. It might be expected that 'concentrative' ventures would be treated more harshly than 'co-operative' activities. However, the opposite is the case. If a joint venture is of the type where the parties set up a new company jointly owned to fulfill the joint purpose, then the merger regulations apply – with their very high thresholds, etc. In this case very few, if, any concentrative joint ventures would be stopped (by the merger regulation). However, 'co-operative' joint ventures arise where the parties simply collaborate – to test the situation and to see if the joint endeavour 'works' – and these are likely to fall under Article 85 and to be prohibited as limiting competition like any cartel. Thus what might seem like a sensible approach to a new arrangement – try it and see ('collaborative') – is likely to be condemned, whereas the full blown intervention of a new 'concentration' is likely to be permitted as too small to worry the merger watchdogs. Even when the 'parents' of a joint venture are not actually in competition, it may still be possible for a joint venture to come within the scope of Article 85(1) if it has an adverse effect on *potential* competition. This might seem to raise matters of 'justiciability', i.e. to question the fitness or ability of the legal process to judge the *possible* economic consequences of business behaviour. If it is felt that the partners to the potential joint venture might be reasonably expected to enter the market separately and as competitors in the not too distant future, then the planned joint venture could be deemed to be a restriction on potential competition and be disallowed.

In Vacuum Interrupters (OJ 1977, L 48/32), the damage to potential competition was widely interpreted. In this case, two UK firms started to develop a new form of switch gear – the vacuum interrupter. Each abandoned the research on the grounds that the risk in the competitive nature of the research made it not worth continuing. The two companies then decided to collaborate. The Commission declared that this would restrict competition between the two (parent) companies, as naturally they would not wish to compete with the joint venture. This was considered likely to affect trade between member states, and might discourage other firms from starting research in this area. Exemption was granted, none the less, as it was considered that technical and economic progress would be enhanced by the joint venture. However, regardless of how widely Article 85(1) may be interpreted, there is always Article 85(3) to follow. Article 85(3) allows exemption to be granted under a wide range of circumstances. In fact, in nearly all cases considered by the Commission the exemption clause has been used. This section has a strongly worded presumption that joint ventures are likely to bring forth all sorts of economic benefits, such as rationalisation and innovation. Thus if joint ventures come under Article 85, they are quite likely to be condemned; if they come under Article 86 or the merger regulations, they may well be allowed.

Conclusion

The EU approaches to industry and competition still seem far from unified or unifying areas of policy. National interests seem to play a large part in the actual practice of what goes on; however, this does not mean that we should be too dismissive of attempts to regulate, co-operate and integrate industry and competition policies across the 15 member states. The SEM and EMU initiatives are often described as elements in an attempt to create the 'United States of

Europe' to match the economic advantages of the USA, and the instances of local lobbying for federal contracts, and in furtherance of local interests, are all too common there. Examples can be given (see above) which seem to give evidence of the role of national rather than European interests being served, but this may also reflect different national attitudes, rather than real anomolies. When BMW bought Rover some elements of the British press fumed angrily and asked the rhetorical question of whether the government in Bayern or in Bonn would have stood by and watched Rover take over BMW. To the President of the Board of Trade (then Michael Heseltine) it was simply a matter of 'doing business'. Similarly, in late 1997 the possibility arose of the takeover by a German car manufacturer of the UK's prestige engineering firm, Rolls Royce. The British government (now Labour) once again did not wish to intervene.

The European administration of both industrial and competition policy is much criticised. High case loads lead to backlogs and delays in decision-making; worries persist about the processes involved, and the associated democratic deficit, and politics rather than policy seems to work too often (e.g. the second Iberia handout, as above). However, there is without doubt a greater degree of transparency in the procedures and processes than hitherto. Slowly the SEM becomes more of a reality; the first 11 members of EMU were declared in the spring of 1998 (the 15 EU countries less Greece, Denmark, Sweden and the UK) and EMU is likely to start on target in 1999. Industrial policy and competition policy will continue to play important, and developing, roles in this ongoing integration process.

These rules are not unambiguous. There may be inconsistencies between one member state and another, and between national and EU regulations. If conflict should occur between a member state's rules and EU rules, then EU rules prevail. The real problem from a firm's point of view, however, is that competition policies and rules throughout the EU and the 15 member states are uncertain. Since the law is uncertain this adds costs which business could well do without. The public too are not immune from this uncertainty. If there is a real case for the promotion of competition and the restriction of monopoly power to promote the public interest then lack of clarity in the contents and direction of the policies is a thoroughly bad thing.

Questions for discussion

1 Many critics have argued that the EC Merger Regulations of 1990 have set the thresholds far too high; smaller mergers should be included, it is said. What are the arguments for and against widening the scope of the merger regulations, by reducing the thresholds?

2 What are the theoretical grounds for expecting monopolistic market structures to lead to poor economic performance?

3 The Cecchini Report on the benefits that were expected to flow from the SEM assumed as a prerequisite a strongly competitive economic and

trading environment. Would you agree that a vigorous EU CP is a necessary condition if these anticipated gains are to be achieved and the EU is to enter the late 1990s and the next century able to compete with Japan and the USA?

4 How could the operation of UK competition policy law and the EU rules, in Articles 85 and 86, be improved to reduce the uncertainty associated with them?

5 Do you think that the benefits from CP are likely to outweigh the costs? (The costs include both the administrative expenses and costs to the firms involved.)

6 It is sometimes argued that CP is a mere sop to public opinion, rather than a serious attempt to influence business behaviour. Would you agree? Argue your case carefully.

Main reading

Ferguson, P. R. and Ferguson, G. J. (1994) *Industrial Economics, Issues and Perspectives*, 2nd edition, Macmillan.
Korah, V. (1994) *EEC Competition Law and Practice*, 5th edition, Sweet & Maxwell.
Tsoukalis, L. (1993) *The New European Economy*, 2nd edition, Oxford University Press.
Ward I. (1996) *A Critical Introduction to European Law*, Butterworths.

Additional reading

Art, I. Y. and van Liedekerke, D. (1996) Developments in EC competition law in 1995: an overview, *Common Market Law Review*, Vol. 33 (4).
Bangeman, M. (1992) *Meeting the Global Challenge*, Kogan Page.
Barberis, P. and May, T. (1993) *Government, Industry and Political Economy*, Open University Press.
Barnes, I. and Barnes, P. M. (1995) *The Enlarged European Union*, Longman.
Barrass, R. and Madhavan, S. (1996) *European Economic Integration and Sustainable Development*, McGraw-Hill.
Bruton, G., Oviatt, B. and White, M. (1994) Performance of acquisition of distressed firms, *Academy of Management Journal*, Vol. 37 (4).
Cecchini, P. (1988) *The European Challenge, 1992: The Benefits of a Single Market*, Wildwood House.
Cowling, K. and Mueller, D. (1978) The social costs of monopoly, *Economic Journal*, Vol. 88, pp. 727–48.
Coutler, T., Haslam, C., Williams, J. and Williams, K. (1989) *1992: The Struggle for Europe*, Berg.
Davis, E., Shore, G. and Thompson, D. (1991) Continental mergers are different, *Business Strategy Review*, Spring, pp. 49–69.
Davison, L., Fitzpatrick, E. and Johnson, D. (1995) *The European Competitive Environment*, Butterworth-Heinemann.

Department of Trade and Industry (1988) *Policy and Procedures of Merger Control*, Mergers Policy, HMSO.

Dutton, P. (1980) *Mergers and Economic Performance*, Cambridge University Press.

The Economist (1991) War by competition policy, 12 October, pp. 17–18.

The Economist (1996a) Is the single market working? 17 February.

The Economist (1996b) Two rules good, four rules bad, 12 October.

The Economist (1997) State aid: the addicts in Europe, 22 November.

European Commission (1972) *First Report on Competition Policy*, Luxembourg.

European Commission (1983) *Thirteenth Report on Competition Policy*, Luxembourg.

European Commission (1985) *Fourteenth Report on Competition Policy*, Luxembourg.

European Commission (1988) *Seventeenth Report on Competition Policy*, Luxembourg.

European Commission (1992) *Twenty-First Report on Competition Policy*, Luxembourg.

European Commission (1994) *Growth, Competitiveness, Employment, The Challenges and the Way Forward into the 21st century*, Luxembourg.

European Commission (1995) *Background Report – State Aid*, ISEC/B3/95, March 1995.

European Commission (1996a) *The Week in Europe*, WE/42/96, 28 November.

European Commission (1996b) *The Week in Europe*, WE/30/96, 5 September.

European Commission (1997) *The Week in Europe*, WE/04/97, 23 January.

European Parliament News (1996) December.

Financial Times (1996) The Aidbuster's Charter, 14 November.

Friedman, M. (1962) *Capitalism and Freedom*, University of Chicago Press.

Galbraith, J. K. (1963) *American Capitalism*, revised edition, Penguin.

Galbraith, J. K. (1974) *The New Industrial State*, 2nd edition (revised), Penguin.

The Guardian (1996a) Unfair aviators, 1 February.

The Guardian (1996b) EU sponsors a million failures, 31 October.

Harberger, A. (1954) Monopoly and resource allocation, *American Economic Review*, Vol. 44, pp. 77–87.

Kean, A. R. (1996) *An analysis of UK industry policy with particular reference to shipbuilding*, unpublished dissertation, Oxford Brookes University.

Koedijk, K. and Kremers, J. (1996) Market opening, regulation and growth in Europe, *Economic Policy*, October.

Loderer, C. and Martin, K. (1992) Post-acquisition performance of acquiring firms, *Financial Management*, Vol. 21 (3).

McKinsey Global Institute (1994) *Employment Performance*.

McShane, D. (1995) Europe's next challenge to British politics, *Political Quarterly*, Vol. 66 (23).

Meeks, G. (1977) *Disappointing Marriage: A Study of the Gains from Merger*, Cambridge University Press.

Neuberger, H. (1989) *The Economics of 1992*, Socialist Group of European Parliament, Labour Group, London.

Newbould, G. D. and Luffman, G. A. (1978) *Successful Business Policies*, Gower Press.

OECD (1994) *The OECD Jobs Study: Evidence and Explanations*.

Philip, A. B. (1996) *Accountability in the European Union*, John Stuart Mill Institute, London.

Porter, M. E. (1980) *Competitive Strategy*, The Free Press.

Porter, M. E. (1985) *Competitive Advantage*, The Free Press.

Porter, M. E. (1987) The state of strategic thinking, *The Economist*, 23 May, pp. 21–28.

Pratten, C. (1988) *Research on the Cost of Non-Europe. Basic Findings*, EC, HMSO.

Roney, A. (1998) *EC/EU Fact Book*, 5th edition, Kogan Page.

Sampson, A. (1983) *The Changing Anatomy of Britain*, Coronet.

Schumpeter, J. A. (1954) *Capitalism, Socialism and Democracy,* 4th edition, Allen & Unwin.

Spaak. P. H. (1957) *The Spaak Report.*

Van Bael, I. and Bellis, J. F. (1989) *Competition Law of the EEC,* CCH Editions.

Van Zon, H. (1996) *The Future of Industry in Central and Eastern Europe,* Avebury Publishers, Aldershot.

Whish, R. (1993) *Competition Law,* 3rd edition, Butterworths.

9

The Single European Market and beyond

Introduction

It was always the aim of the European Union to become a **common market**. The Treaty of Rome in 1957 intended Europe to be more than a **customs union**; its ultimate aim was the establishment of **economic union** between the members of the EEC. The Single European Act was a move towards this goal.

Attempts to build a more unified Europe have been tried in the past. For example, the Fouchet Plan in 1961 attempted to create a joint foreign policy but the fear of a loss of **sovereignty** prevented its success. Similarly, the Werner Plan of the early 1970s put forward the idea of economic and monetary union by 1980, but again this met with little response due to concern for independence.

Why then did the concept of the single market and unified Europe 'take off' in the mid-1980s? Five principal reasons exist:

1 Part of the explanation lies in the recent past (see Chapter 6). The earlier period of the EC (1958–72) saw very fast growth rates (faster than the USA) as **customs duties** were cut. Gradually, however, as **tariffs** were reduced, other less visible non-tariff barriers began to take their place. The 1970s and its oil crisis slowed down world trade and brought worldwide recession but the response to this by the various member countries of the EC was very much on an individual basis. Many short-term measures were taken to protect national markets against not only non-member countries, but also co-members of the EC in order to protect jobs and strategic industries. The result was a rapid slowdown in the growth of the EC, with higher unemployment and inflation, and lower productivity and innovation. Community action was needed and the French experience of 'going for growth' in 1981–83, with its resulting higher inflation and balance of payments crisis, showed that attempts to 'go it alone' were doomed to failure. The response of the EC was to press for more unification. In Copenhagen in 1982 EC heads of state agreed to make this a high priority; a pledge repeated in 1984. In 1985 the White Paper, 'Completing the Internal Market', was issued, giving details of the proposal for the single market. Subsequently, the 1986 Single European Act (SEA) was adopted by all the then 12 members, so committing themselves to market unification by the end of 1992.

2 The actual construction of the White Paper helped with its acceptance. The Act agreed on a programme containing 300 separate pieces of legislation (subsequently reduced to 279) which would bring about a single market by

the end of 1992. These directives were basically statements of the required outcome, and how this outcome could be achieved, but the legislation necessary for this was left to the individual members. For example, in the UK, the Product Liability Directive was enacted by the 1987 Consumer Protection Act.

No attempt was made to develop EC-wide targets, which had hampered such attempts in the past, and the idea of 'sufficient harmonisation' was put forward and extended to the concept of 'mutual recognition' and 'approximation', thereby giving national governments some room for manoeuvre.

Furthermore, the acceptance of the legislation was made much easier by the change in the process by which legislation was adopted. In the past, legislation required a unanimous vote to be adopted. The changes involving procedure allowed adoption by a qualified majority on many items, with some exemptions such as fiscal policy, which still requires unanimous voting. Without majority voting there would have been no hope of achieving the task in time.

3 The aim of the SEA was to create one large market with common policies and uniform legal frameworks to cover the internal trade of the EC. To put it in the White Paper's own words, the objective was the 'welding together of the 12 individual markets of the Member States into a Single Market of 320 million people' (paragraph 8). Furthermore, the objective of the SEA was to create an area without internal frontiers, allowing the free movement of goods and services, capital and people, as foreseen by the original Treaty of Rome. To achieve this, non-tariff barriers to trade within the EC had to be demolished, enabling countries to reap the benefits of free trade and take full advantage of their comparative advantage in certain goods. All would then gain.

The ideological basis of this was right for the time. The philosophy underlying it was that of market liberalisation, with the market achieving optimality and efficiency and being beneficial, eventually, for all. The philosophy appealed to the liberal–conservative governments in the UK, Germany and, to some extent, France.

4 It appeared to steer clear of the political issues of sovereignty and to be based more in economics.

5 It had a very strong backing from the industrialists within the EC as it was seen as a way of increasing profits and cutting back the lead of the USA and Japan in the high-tech industries. A large domestic market was considered a necessary prerequisite for EC firms to compete.

What exact benefits were anticipated? Basically the EC was trying to bring about freer trade by removing the barriers to trade (see Chapters 4 and 5), so reducing costs and thereby prices. It was also hoped that the elimination of barriers would bring greater competition and new patterns of competition, as markets were no longer so protected by national barriers. Old cartels would be threatened, and ossified industries 'woken up' by new forces of competition. Rationalisation would then occur and costs would be reduced. Also firms would be encouraged to go out and attack the European market and more innovation in processes and production would also occur. Firms would grow and gain greater efficiency through the exploitation of potential economies of scale by serving a much greater 'domestic EC' market. Costs would again fall, prices follow and both consumers and producers gain.

To summarise, the constraints of the non-unified market were preventing companies from achieving their potential. To remove these constraints would improve the competitive environment and allow exploitation of new opportunities. This would then make the EC industries more competitive and better equipped to compete against the USA, Japan and the newly industrialised countries.

The Cecchini Report (1988) into the costs of a non-united Europe suggested that such a supply-side shock to the European economy could trigger a boost to economic activity in the medium term of, on average, 4.5 per cent to the EC's GDP, and that the cost of maintaining the barriers to free movement of people and capital could be in the region of ECU200 billion at constant 1988 prices. It is also estimated that prices to consumers could be deflated by an average of 6.1 per cent, and some 1.8 million new jobs could be created.

Gains in output and competitiveness and the reduction of inflation would ease the pressure on governments, allowing more space for action on growth. So if the EC governments pursued relevant macro-economic policies, in the long run it was estimated that the EC economy could grow by up to 7.5 per cent in GDP and gain approximately five million new jobs without the risk of higher inflation.

Some criticisms of Cecchini's figures should be noted, however:

1 They were very optimistic. It was assumed that all the proposals would be carried out on time and in a world and European economy that was expanding, not one of recession and unemployment.

2 They also assumed that labour made redundant by rationalisation due to restructuring would be successfully re-employed – again, a very optimistic view.

3 They ignored the distributional aspect by not looking at the possible detrimental effects on some states compared with others. No account was made of the adjustment costs of firms, regions and even governments to the single market.

4 It assumed states would adopt similar economic policies and trade policies.

5 The estimates were only approximate.

6 It was a report commissioned by the EC and one has to question its neutrality.

Having said this, however, the possible gains could also have been underestimated as certain dynamic consequences were ignored; for example:

1 There is evidence to suggest that technical innovation increases with the presence of competition. Therefore a more open, integrated market should increase such innovation.

2 Also ignored are learning **economies of scale**, which are especially important in high-tech industries.

3 No account was made for the changes of business strategies that occurred after 1992, and these could boost the gains.

So far we have been referring to 'the barriers' to trade but what were or are these barriers exactly? At what was the SEA aimed? The barriers to a unified Europe are usually summarised into three types: physical, fiscal and technical.

Physical barriers

Physical barriers were the most visible representation of the divisions within the EC, and their elimination became a symbol of the 'new' European Community, or European Union as it later became. Removal, however, has proved much more problematic than first thought.

Duties and import restrictions between EU countries had long been abolished but customs controls and formalities still persisted. Internal EU frontiers were used for various controls: the control of terrorism, drugs trafficking, immigration control, checks on plants and animals, inspection for the adherence to technical and health standards, collection of statistics on intra-EU trade, collection of various duties and taxes (such as VAT), and checks on regulations for vehicles and drivers.

These barriers were a symbol of a disunited Europe and a strong psychological barrier. They were furthermore a costly barrier. Queuing, and filling out and dealing with the various administrative documents all took time and money and increased prices. For example, lorry drivers taking a commercial load from Rotterdam to Naples could spend 10 hours of the 26-hour journey at customs posts. Delays were also increased by masses of documentation; for example, lorry drivers could be required to fill out as many as 70–80 different forms. Governments also had to incur substantial costs in running these frontier posts. The costs of administering such frontiers were estimated by the Commission to be in the region of $670 million per annum, although they varied; for example, they were five times more in Italy than in Belgium.

Finally, there was a further, less obvious cost – the loss of trading opportunities. The barriers were an especially significant deterrent for small–medium companies, which could not afford the delays or administration costs of exporting. The possible gain from such new trade was estimated at £10 billion.

The aim of the White Paper therefore was to ease these border formalities and to take many of them inland. Harmonisation means that plant and animal checks have now changed to place of departure and destination. Technical and health and safety standards have been increasingly recognised or standardised. VAT has moved towards a new system of collection and harmonisation and EU statistics are now obtained from these VAT statistics (see later in this chapter).

Worries still remain concerning terrorism, drugs trafficking and immigration. There is little evidence, however, that physical customs barriers alone have had that much success in these areas; usually if offenders are caught, it has been the result of tip-offs and police co-operation, rather than just random checking at ports. There is probably some psychogical barrier but most major drugs hauls, for example, are at lonely airstrips, not frontier posts, and heavily guarded frontier posts rarely catch terrorists. Really these are international problems not national ones and the answers may lie in more police co-operation internationally.

The free movement of people has been achieved between seven EU members under the **Schengen Agreement**. In July 1995, the Benelux countries, Germany, France, Spain and Portugal signed this agreement, but France has since reinstated its northern border controls temporarily. Eventually it is hoped that Austria, Italy and Greece will also sign. However, amongst the other EU states such areas exist already: Denmark, Sweden and Finland (plus Norway) have a Scandinavian passport area and UK and Ireland have a common travel area; therefore these countries are reluctant to sign Schengen.

The legality of keeping such barriers, however, is questionable, and the European Parliament has asked the Commission to seek their removal. Some, especially the UK, do not accept the need to abolish them and the UK negotiated an opt-out from this at the Amsterdam Summit in June 1997.

The problems of law enforcement and immigration without frontiers has led to calls for the introduction of an EU identity card, thereby allowing immigration controls to be moved inland. Many EU countries already have these but those without, such as the UK, the Netherlands and Ireland, strongly resist such a move.

The streamlining of customs procedures has been especially appreciated by firms. The savings for a typical 1000 km road journey have been estimated as 2 per cent of total costs for road hauliers. Futhermore, in a Eurostat business survey, 60 per cent of firms surveyed had gained from changes in documentation and 56 per cent from the opening of frontiers (European Commission 1997). A Price Waterhouse study (1996) also suggested that reductions in frontier delays had brought additional savings of approximately ECU400 million to EU firms.

Fiscal barriers

The main fiscal barrier lay in the lack of harmonisation of VAT rates and excise duties, and attempts to eliminate these barriers have been difficult to achieve.

Before looking at the problems which have been encountered, why is fiscal harmonisation actually necessary? To abolish border controls without fiscal harmonisation could lead to major distortions in trade and increased fraud. For example, with different rates of taxation and no frontier controls, it would be increasingly profitable to buy goods in low-tax countries and transport them to higher-tax countries for sale. The highly taxed country would lose trade and revenue, and low-cost producers in a high-VAT country would become less competitive compared with high-cost producers in a low-VAT country. These different rates could also be used in a discriminatory way by various governments. For example, if the UK taxes beer at a lower rate than wine, it encourages beer sales and discourages wine sales; as a result, beer sales should rise and wine sales fall. As wine is mostly imported, the effect would be to discriminate against French, German, Italian and Spanish wine imports.

Such distortions lay at the basis of the EU proposals for fiscal harmonisation. The actual overall structure of VAT was harmonised in the Sixth VAT Directive of 1977, which laid down the method of assessment and the range of goods on which it should be applied. This harmonisation was, however, far from complete. Members could still choose their own rates and could place a zero rate on goods considered essential. The result was a vast number of different rates on different goods in different countries.

At the time of the White Paper all member states had lower VAT bands (ranging from 0 to 17 per cent) and standard bands (ranging from 12 to 23 per cent), but six countries had a further higher-rate band (ranging from 25 to 38 per cent tax rate). These overlapped: what was a lower band in Belgium (17 per cent) was higher than the standard in the UK (then 15 per cent). Also, an inconsistency of which goods were in the various bands existed, especially regarding food, fuel and transport, which were in a variety of bands. Gaining agreement on VAT has proven one of the most problematic areas of SEM legislation but EU finance ministers finally agreed to set a *minimum* rate for VAT of 15 per cent on all goods and services from January 1993 for a six-year period with no upper limit. There were exceptions for those goods already listed at a reduced rate of 0–5 per cent for special social or cultural reasons.

VAT was collected and refunded at borders but this was replaced in January 1993 by a temporary system where VAT was collected by the state where the good was bought (Barnes and Barnes 1995). This change to the transitional VAT system was greeted with much protest by firms as it involved them in compliance costs. Now, however, many see it as an improvement (according to a survey by Price Waterhouse 1996). The Commission suggests that the transitional procedures themselves have produced savings of approximately ECU5 billion per annum, or 0.7 per cent of intra-EU trade. The aim is still to move to an origin system where VAT is collected in the country of origin and the firm reclaims it as national VAT; for example, to send goods from London to Paris will be the same 'VAT-wise' as sending goods from London to Manchester.

Linked to the debate regarding VAT has been the question of harmonisation of excise duties. The coverage of such duties had already been mainly standardised – covering such goods as beer, wine, cigarettes and petrol – but the rates varied enormously across EU countries. Although minimum rates for tobacco, alcohol and mineral oils now have been set, these are the only products with such restrictions and excise duties can be imposed provided they do not distort trade or require frontiers.

There is therefore still little harmonisation and to increase the divergencies, many goods have **specific tax** plus an *ad valorem* element, and different VAT rates as well. The Commission has estimated that indirect taxes could differ by up to 5 per cent without increasing cross-border shopping. All but one border (Germany–Denmark) has VAT rates within this range, so showing sufficient convergence to prevent such moves. However, this cannot be said for excise duty. Such goods, especially alcohol and tobacco, attract more tax in some European states than in others and so have increased cross-border shopping. The effect of this can be seen in the case study on the effect of the SEM on UK brewers.

The brewing industry in the UK has been one of the first industries to experience the effect of increased competition brought about by the SEM. However, the brewers would claim that they are facing this greater competition handicapped by much higher indirect taxes, and that the failure to harmonise such taxes under the SEM legislation has adversely affected their business. The extent of the difference in taxes is shown in Fig. 9.1.

The result has been a massive increase in both legal and illegal purchases of beer from across the Channel. It is estimated that 'more than 1 100 000 (duty paid) pints a day are coming across the Channel,' and about a third of these duty-paid imports are made in large quantities and carried in many cases in vans. Some will be for personal use, but we can assume a lot will not be, but rather will be illegally resold. This is referred to as 'the van trade'. The possible growth of this van trade can be shown be comparing 1995 surveillance operations with those in 1994. Some areas show outstanding growth; for example,

> the number of vans from Truro doubled over the period and the number from Carlisle increased by a staggering 250%, so proving that distance from Calais is no object to a smuggler. Furthermore and ironically, the van trade through Calais also increased to Ipswich (+30%), Portsmouth (+22%) and Hull (+15%), despite the fact that these are ports with continental links themselves. Leicester (28 vans per week) and Swindon (19 vans per week) also were both spotted as destinations for such vans for the first time in 1995. Finally among destinations noted in 1994, the biggest increases in the van trade in 1995 were to Guildford (+85%), Oxford (+54%), Peterborough (+53%), and Northampton (+36%).

The Brewers and Licensers Retail Association (BLRA) states that the effect can be calculated as follows:

> At £1.60 a pint, the van trade is costing every pub in the UK approximately on average £3,225 in lost retail sales. The impact of all duty paid imports (at £1.60 a pint) could cost British pubs the equivalent of £10,600 a year in lost beer sales.

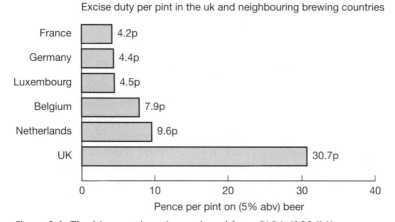

Excise duty per pint in the uk and neighbouring brewing countries

Country	Pence per pint on (5% abv) beer
France	4.2p
Germany	4.4p
Luxembourg	4.5p
Belgium	7.9p
Netherlands	9.6p
UK	30.7p

Figure 9.1 The big questions (reproduced from BLRA (1996b))

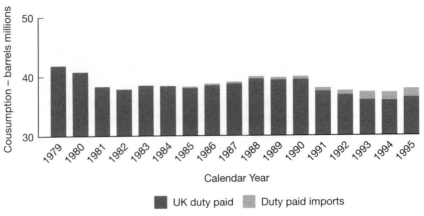

Figure 9.2 Sales of beer, 1979–1995 (reproduced from BLRA 1996a)

> The van trade alone is the equivalent to annual beer sales of every pub in North Yorkshire or Derbyshire or Staffordshire.

The effect can also be seen in the sales of beer in the UK generally and on duty-paid imports. Figure 9.2 shows that these imports apparently substitute for UK beer consumption rather than complement or increase it.

Finally, apart from smuggling and other forms of duty fraud, the illegal sale of duty-paid imports damages other aspects of society. For example, the need to safeguard young people in relation to the sale of alcoholic drinks. 'Smugglers do not observe liquor licensing laws.'

Source: adapted and quoted from VBLRA (1996) *Facing the Facts,* Memorandum to HM Treasury, July. BLRA (1996) *The Big Question: The Cross-Channel Trade in Beer.*

Questions

1 Does the above show that the SEM does not work for the beer trade?

2 If left to the market with present tax levels, what will happen?

3 What if anything can be done to ease the situation of UK brewers?

To some extent market forces have been left to bring about harmonisation, but in the short run, as shown in the case study above, there will be substantial exporting from high-tax to low-tax countries. High-tax states may want to keep prices high for health reasons and will want to resist their markets being swamped by low-tax imports. The budgetary effects of tax harmonisation on the various EU countries could also be significant. For example, Denmark has a high rate of duty on most of the products and to reduce this to the EU average level would mean a significant reduction.

Another area of tax harmonisation that has achieved little progress is company tax. The Ruding Committee reported in 1992 that there were significant differences in company taxes across the EU in terms of rates, base and treatment of cross-border flows. These could influence decisions regarding where to set up business and attract firms to different EU states. The report encouraged the EU to think about removing such discriminatory company tax systems, setting minimum levels of tax, and increasing transparency. Some efforts have been made to reduce discrimination for mergers and prevention of double tax for companies operating across states but progress has been slow (Barnes and Barnes 1995).

Tax harmonisation in terms of **direct taxes** such as income tax is not part of the SEM legislation. This, however, could be seen as one of the main factors which affects labour mobility and therefore is an important omission. It must be said that given the problems in agreeing on harmonisation of VAT such a move would be very difficult to achieve.

Technical barriers

Technical barriers can be considered under five headings:

1 obstacles to free movement of goods
2 obstacles to free movement of services
3 obstacles to free movement of labour
4 obstacles to free movement of capital
5 public procurement.

Obstacles to free movement of goods

Many of the barriers to free movement of goods took the guise of regulations on health, safety, consumer or environmental protection – such things as regulations on noise levels, food additives and exhaust emissions. Most EU members have had their own standards and laws set up by national standards bodies such as the BSI in the UK, AFNOR in France and DIN in Germany and these standards have represented significant barriers in the past. It has been estimated that there were something like 100 000 different technical regulations and standards in the EC/EU and with the increasing emphasis on the environment and consumer protection, these were still growing in number.

An example of the problem of such standards can be found in the food and drink industry. Different EU members had different regulations regarding the level of vegetable fat used in ice cream and chocolate, or the different amounts of additives in beer. The Cecchini Report found that in only ten food and drink products, and in only the five largest states, 200 such technical or standard barriers existed.

Such barriers fragmented and segmented the market, with companies having separate production lines for different markets, or having to modify their products to suit the standards of the other markets. Inventory, distribution and

marketing costs rose. Furthermore, companies had to undergo different procedures in different countries in order to sell abroad, with consequent duplication
of testing. All increased costs to the producer and prevented them gaining
economies of scale. To quote the European Commission (1996), 'Technical
trade barriers therefore strike at the heart of business operations, affecting pre-
production, production, sales and marketing policies' (page 19).

They also cost the relevant governments significant amounts in setting up
and running such procedures. Ultimately the consumer paid with higher prices
and taxes. Moreover, these barriers forced producers to aim at a narrower
national basis and discouraged firms from seeking business outside their country of origin. Finally, policies discriminated against small or newer firms,
compared with the relatively large and established firms, and undermined the
incentives to innovate and co-operate on a European scale.

How significant were these barriers in the goods market? A Commission
study of 20 000 EU businesses showed that they rated technical and administrative barriers as the second most important barrier. The significance of such
barriers furthermore could be seen in such areas as the telecommunications
equipment, cars, food and building product industries and the associated costs
were estimated in the region of ECU3.5 billion for telecommunications, ECU2.6
billion in the car industry, between ECU500 million and ECU1 billion in foodstuffs, and ECU1.7 billion in building products, causing significant cost
increases (Brearley and Quigley 1989). Other studies suggested that such barriers were also important in the electrical, engineering and precision, and
medical equipment sectors. Generally the costs of differing national standards
added at least 10 per cent to production costs (European Commission 1996).

The basic EU approach via the SEM has not been to harmonise standards
generally, but to bring recognition of differing national standards. This principle of 'mutual recognition' of standards was established in the Cassis de Dijon
case (see Appendix), and once a good meets the conditions of the national
standards in the country where it was made, it must be accepted throughout the
EU. There are exceptions where goods are considered to affect public morality,
the health of humans, plants or the environment, or the protection of national
treasures. Examples include the case of British beef, which was banned in continental EU countries on grounds of health. Similarly, the Danish bottles legal
case argued, for environmental reasons, that all beverages (including imports)
should be sold in specified returnable bottles and the Court accepted this as an
environmental measure.

This principle is 'relied upon to overcome technical trade barriers affecting
25% of intra EU trade' (European Commission 1997, page 19), although the
figure tends to understate the coverage. This means all the EU must have confidence in the adequacy of others' testing and certification arrangements and
results. The Commission has been active in enforcing this principle, with 1230
cases being undertaken up to the end of 1996. For example, it brought an
action against Italy, which refused to let other EU members sell their beers in
Italy as the manufacturing methods did not comply with Italian regulations, and
the Court ruled against this ban.

There are, however, some problems or concerns about the concept of mutual recognition. Firstly, sometimes regulations are so different they are impossible to apply across the board and some harmonisation in the area of 'permissible products and their composition and labelling may be needed' (European Commission 1997, page 21). Furthermore, it is sometimes very difficult for health and safety inspectors to judge whether the products actually do meet the home specifications. Even when technical barriers have been overcome, the consumer may still prefer or trust their home-produced products which meet voluntary local specifications. It has also been difficult at times to enforce acceptance of standards where there is a particularly high risk to the user.

Moreover, for some goods, this principle was not considered sufficient; for example, where equivalence of differing national technical regulations cannot be assumed, and the need to develop European standards was called for. Under Article 100a a common set of regulations could be agreed upon by member states and such legislation has had two distinct approaches: detailed harmonisation measures and the 'new approach' legislation. The former concerned products where the risk is such that detailed legislation is required product by product. Such an approach can be seen in the motor vehicle, chemical, pharmaceutical and foodstuff industries. The latter 'new approach', introduced in 1985, took a different stance in that the EU legislation set prescribed essential requirements (gaining the CE mark) but details are set by standardisation bodies nationally. These details are, however, voluntary; producers have only a legal responsibility to ensure products comply with the essential requirements set by the EU. Certificates given by one member state showing that a product conforms to the code of essential requirements (CE) must be accepted elsewhere in the EU. This approach has been applied to a range of products such as consumer goods like toys and producer goods such as machines. Seventeen new approach directives have been adopted so far (representing 17 per cent of intra-EU trade), 5000 European standards have been produced already, and 16 000 work items are foreseen. This shows a rapid expansion of European standardisation. The effect of this 'new approach' according to the European Commission (1996) is to 'have contributed to enhanced safety and performance of products by allowing more rapid integration of innovation and quality improvements' (European Commission 1997, page 24).

Finally, in order to prevent new and differing standards being formulated in the EU, in 1983 the Commission set up a new mutual information directive. Member states, and now EFTA states, must inform the EU in advance of any new regulations or standards they intend to set up, and these are widely publicised. If the EU feels these could provide a barrier to intra-EU trade, it has the power to 'freeze' these standards for up to a year, in order to develop European standards to take their place. Many felt this directive was effective, with only 30 of the 450 notifications being frozen between 1983 and 1989, and it was extended in January 1989 to include previously excluded areas of agricultural products, food, pharmaceutical and cosmetics to make it more effective.

Furthermore, 90 per cent of new regulations by member states are still in the sectors where EU legislation has already been adopted (i.e. foodstuffs, transport equipment, chemicals, pharmaceuticals, telecommunications, construction and mechanical engineering), suggesting some problems in these areas. However, from January 1997 member states were required to inform the EU of any products where they are withholding the benefits of mutual recognition. This should aid the situation as any product not so notified should circulate freely without further regulations being imposed.

Obstacles to free movement of services

The aim of the SEM was to open and liberalise service sectors, leading to lower prices, greater efficiency and more adaptation to customer needs. Barriers in the service industries generally differ from those affecting goods. The need for more contact between buyer and seller (a feature the service industries usually exhibit) gives more scope for a high degree of government interference, often on the grounds of consumer protection. Furthermore, for some time services were seen as non-traded activities and resulted in national restrictions. The importance of the restrictions depended on the sector. For some, such as telecommunications and audio-visual services, the restrictions were based on access to networks. In other areas, such as road and air transport, restrictions were on scope and volume. In finance, discrimination conditions and rules regarding establishment and doing business increased costs prohibitively. Finally, in professional services the obstacles were more in the form of recognition of qualifications (see later in this chapter).

The White Paper aimed at liberalising services by providing freedom of establishment and freedom to provide cross-border services. There was some delay but most measures regarding service liberalisation were in place by 1993–94. In terms of transport, liberalisation was undertaken firstly internationally and then nationally (via cabotage). For audio-visual services liberalisation only concerned the opening up of international broadcasting services and full liberalisation of telecommunication services is now complete.

One service sector which has been highly regulated and opened up by the SEM is the financial service sector and this will be considered in further detail as an illustration of the SEM's stance with regard to services, and due to its importance generally.

In the 'higher'-level markets of the financial services sector, such as the **Eurobonds** market and foreign exchange markets, there were already highly developed international markets for financial services. However, in the 'middle-level' or retail side of the financial services sector, such as insurance services, provisions tended to be at a more national level.

The type of barriers faced by the SEM legislation have been of two types, technical and fiscal. Technical barriers have tended to restrict the right to set up in other EU states and restrict products offered. Moreover, different capital requirements imposed on financial institutions have acted as a barrier, as have actual restrictions on the movement of capital (see later in this chapter). Fiscal restrictions have been mainly in the form of differences in taxation of savings, tax relief on different transactions, double taxation in death duties and inheritance tax. The technical barriers have been tackled fervently whereas little progress has been made concerning the fiscal type of barrier.

The general aims of the SEA with regard to this sector were as follows:

1 to harmonise the standards set for prudential supervision, e.g. capital and solvency requirements and monitoring;

2 to protect investors, depositors and customers;

3 to establish the principle of mutual recognition of the application of such standards;

4 to give home control and supervision of institutions operating in member states;

5 to establish minimum European regulatory standards.

Basically, it was felt that if sufficient harmonisation could be achieved, the European market for financial services would operate on mutual recognition of control and supervision. This would open up an EU-wide investment market, making finance available to industries from anywhere in the EU. Such proposals were ambitious. The single licence and home country control would mean that a member state must allow a company, over which it has little supervisory control, to import a financial product or service which it does not allow its own companies to produce.

Such liberalisation, according to the Cecchini Report (1988), could increase the GDP of the EU by 1.5 per cent, have a deflationary effect of 1.4 per cent and improve public finances by 1 per cent of GDP. This would occur mainly because prices to customers in the sector would be reduced due to increased competition. Similarly, lower interest rate charges (caused by the same factors) should encourage investment and greater consumption. Finally, credit could be made more widely available, increasing domestic demand and further encouraging investment.

Looking in detail at the three main areas in this sector – banking and credit, insurance and securities markets – the strategy for the single market in financial services will unfold.

The main piece of the SEM legislation affecting banking has been the Second Banking Coordination Directive. This confers a 'passport' to credit institutions. It allows a member to establish branches and subsidiaries elsewhere in the EU, and supply services to other EU states across the borders. The licence covers those whose business is to grant credit, receive deposits or make investments, and covers such activities as lending, leasing, trading, participation in share issues and portfolio management. Non-EU banks are granted the same rights within the EU as were granted to EU banks in that country.

This directive put forward the principles of home country control and mutual recognition of regulatory systems: once authorised at home, institutions have the right to provide services in all the EU. Home country control can be overruled, however, if the monetary policy of the host country becomes adversely affected, and it does not apply to the monitoring of liquidity in banks and securities activities.

The directive has been in force since January 1993 and covers the EEA. However, in a study by the Bank of England in 1994, which asked institutions their opinions on the effect of SEM, its impact was considered limited. There had been some increased competition but domestic retail markets were still well protected by cultural and structural barriers – people preferred using banks from their own countries. Such barriers were seen as more insuperable than the technical or legal barriers which still existed. As a result, the response by most European banks has been to form alliances or mergers across borders in order to access markets. There has also been an effect on non-EU institutions, especially those from the USA, which have reorganised their European activities and in many cases ensured they were present in at least one member state.

Furthermore it is clear that there still exist product restrictions here which affect cross-border supply. These fall into two main categories. Firstly, there are the restrictions of free provision by a 'general good' clause. Examples of this can be found in mortgage credit law in Belgium and consumer law in France, ,where these laws are seen as part of the 'general good' and companies must comply. Secondly, notification requirements in the Second Banking Directive are interpreted in a restrictive way and throw into doubt the legal status of some transactions and services (European Commission 1997).

The effect on wholesale banking has been minimal as this had been international for many years. If anything, the new legislation has been seen as more restrictive; for example, the new notification arrangements for the 'passports' tended to constrain rather than liberalise in the opinion of UK banks surveyed.

With regard to the insurance sector, before the White Paper, the EC had legislation in force coordinating national legislation concerning the establishment and operation of insurance companies. It covered such things as the setting up of businesses, branches and agencies, plus the supervision of **reserve assets**, solvency margins and minimum guarantee funds. However, many obstacles still existed to the ability of a company in one EU state to cover risks in another EU state.

The general principles of harmonisation, mutual recognition and home control were also applied to the SEM insurance legislation. The Second Non-Life Insurance Directive was adopted in June 1988. This enforced a liberal regime but only for large risk insurance, i.e. that covering large amounts of insurance usually for sizable companies. During 1990 the Commission proposed a new Non-Life Framework Directive. However, it was the 'Third Generation Directives' which came into force in July 1994 that really opened up the insurance market. This allowed insurance companies to compete across EU borders on the same basis as home institutions via the adoption of a single licence. People can now compare and buy insurance policies across the EU. To show the differences, the example of car insurance is often quoted. The differences between the cost of car insurance in various EU countries in 1994 is illustrated in Table 9.1.

It can be seen that one of the most expensive places to insure your car in 1994 was Ireland – especially if you were a young driver! Although the legislation should reduce these differences in the prices on such a market and create an open market for consumers, they are likely to continue due to differences in taxation, and such 'variables in road safety, the cost of compensating victims, the level of service offered, traditional methods of selling insurance products … cultural factors, such as a distrust of foreign insurance products' (Barnes and Barnes 1995, page 61).

Table 9.1 The cost of car insurance in various EU countries in 1994

Country	Average insurance for an experienced driver of a Peugeot 405 (ECU)	Average premiums of a young driver of a SEAT Ibiza 1.2 (ECU)
Greece	127	155
UK	134	687
Portugal	157	285
Netherlands	159	473
Denmark	192	446
Spain	212	718
Italy	219	375
France	237	806
Germany	304	957
Luxembourg	367	372
Belgium	394	480
Ireland	585	1821

Source: Financial Times, 1 July 1994, page 19, quoting Bureau Européen des Unions de Consommateurs, and Barnes and Barnes (1995) page 61.

The Commission report on the SEM in 1996 (European Commission 1997) also pointed out that there had been persistent delays in transposing insurance legislation into national legislation. By the end of 1995, however, Greece was the only member left which had not done this, and had been taken to the Court of Justice for its tardiness. Having said this, the report also pointed out that some transpositions had been incorrect or infringed, so delaying an open insurance market in the EU.

The insurance market is therefore ready to be opened up and some increase in competition has been noted. A Eurostat survey in 1996 showed that 42 per cent of insurers felt that competition had increased and only 4 per cent disagreed. However, the full effect is still to be felt.

A Bank of England report (1994) pointed out that the general view of insurers sampled was that the directives on non-life insurance would have some effect but those regarding life insurance would not. Local presence in markets was felt to be essential, especially for consumers and small business policies, but there were still significant barriers in terms of national contract law and tax treatment. These meant policies had to be 'tailored to each market' (1994, page 345).

Furthermore, differences in the means of selling insurance and the way margins for solvency were calculated made it hard to enter new markets, and in the case of life insurance, conservatism was a huge barrier. The UK market was seen to be particularly open (and attractive from a tax of dividend policy viewpoint), and French, German and Swiss insurers had been very active in the UK. Some considered the benefits of opening up the insurance market to be more likely in the long term and via direct insurance companies. Insurance brokers are still in an uncertain position as rights of establishment have not yet been given.

The ultimate aim of the SEM legislation in the securities market sector was to create a European securities market, removing the barriers between national stock markets and creating an EU-wide trading system. As a result of the linking of the stock exchanges in the EU, brokers can offer the best conditions for clients from any EU stock exchange, increasing the liquidity of the Union and allowing more effective competition with Japan and the USA. In an attempt to achieve the above, various directives were adopted to set out the listing and disclosure requirements for securities in order to improve information across Europe.

An important directive in this area has been the Investment Services Directive, which came into effect on 1 January 1996 and which set standards for authorising investment firms. Once one EU state gives its authority, other states must also allow it to provide services or establish a branch there on the strength of this. Home states are again responsible for setting prudential rules. Similarly the UCITS Directive provides minimum requirements for authorisation for investment funds which invest in listed securities, e.g. unit trusts. Those which comply can market freely throughout the EU. This latter directive, however, had little impact and is at present being amended to liberalise it further.

Effects on services generally

As service liberalisation has tended to occur later than that of the goods market, few studies of its effectiveness, in general, have been undertaken. One of the first assessments was undertaken by Eurostat and its results are summarised in Table 9.2.

The figures are weighted according to size of firm and are average figures covering a wide range of services, e.g. hotels, transport, finance and business services. The most positive response (30 per cent) has been towards the freeing of cross-border operations. The figures, however, rise to 69 per cent when air transport and 39 per cent when land transport are taken separately. The second most positive area (25 per cent) is that of capital movement liberalisation (see later in this chapter) and again this figure rises to 55 per cent when financial services are looked at separately. The survey also showed that the SEM is seen more positively by the larger firms than by the smaller/medium-sized enterprises (SMEs). As with the goods market, a reason for this could be that larger firms are more able to grasp the opportunities and fight off new competition than the SMEs (European Commission 1997).

The study further summarised the differing sectors' feelings regarding the various measures, and their findings are summarised in Table 9.3.

Table 9.2 Service industries' assessment of the effectiveness of measures aimed at eliminating various barriers to the free movement of services (%)[a]

Measures	Opinions		
	Positive	Neutral	Negative
Harmonisation of licences	20	66	5
Recognition of licences	17	71	3
Facilitation of cross-border operations	30	60	4
Facilitation of physical establishment	17	74	1
Public procurement liberalisation	16	68	6
Capital movements liberalisation	25	66	1
Direct double taxation	18	67	1

[a]The sum is not equal to 100, the remaining percentage having no opinion on the issue.

Source: Eurostat survey, EU member states excluding Germany and European Commission (1996) page 29.

Table 9.3 Effectiveness of single market measures in removing barriers to the free provision of services (as perceived by economic operators)

	Barriers					
	Cross-border service restrictions	Restrictions on establishment	Restrictions on factor flows	Regulatory/technical barriers[a]	Fiscal issues	Others
Banking	✓✓ Discriminatory conditions for cross-border sale of services ✓ Restrictions on marketing and service content	✓✓ Discriminatory conditions for licences	✓✓ Capital controls	✓✓ Prudential requirements ✓ Conditions for sales	✗ Tax on savings ✗ Investment income tax ✗ Death duties	—
Insurance	✓✓ Discriminatory conditions for cross-border sale of services ✓ Restrictions on marketing and service content	✓✓ Discriminatory conditions for licences	✓ Capital controls	✓ Consumer protection ✗ Conditions for sale	✗ Taxation of reserves ✗ Taxation of premiums	✗ Contract Law
Road freight transport	✓✓ Bilateral quota restrictions on the access to other EC markets ✓✓ Price restrictions	✓✓ Discriminatory licensing conditions	✓ Cabotage restrictions ✓✓ Recognition of diplomas	✓✓ Weights and dimensions ✓ Road safety rules ✓ Speed limiters ✓ Resting hours	✓✓ Excise duties	✓✓ Border formalities for goods
Air transport	✓✓ Bilateral restrictions on free access to other EC markets ✓✓ Price restrictions ✗ Slots allocation	✓✓ Exclusive rights for licensing of air carriers ✗ Ownership rules in third country bilaterals	✓ Cabotage restrictions ✓✓ Designation and capacity restrictions	✓✓ Conditions for sales ✓✓ Security and safety rules ✗ Airport charges	✓ VAT	✓ Border formalities for passengers ✓✓ Access to computer reservation systems ✓ State aids, unfair pratices
Telecoms liberalised services	✓ Discriminatory conditions for access to network	✓✓ Exclusive rights on mobile, data and satellite services	✓✓ Exclusive rights to sell equipment	✓ Technical conditions for use of networks	—	✗ Fair access to networks
TV broadcasting services	✓ Restrictions on cross-frontier broadcasting ✓ Rental and lending rights ✓ Term of copyright protection ✓ Copyright applicable to satellite and cable	✗ National licensing rules for broadcasters ✗ Media ownership restrictions	—	✓ Technical conditions for use of networks	—	
Distribution (fast-moving consumer goods)	No restrictions	No restrictions	✓✓ Restrictions on free movement of goods	—	✓ VAT	✓✓ Border formalities for goods ✓ Technical barriers on products
Advertising	✗ Types of products and media ✗ Comparative advertising	No restrictions	✓ Restrictions on media	✓ Misleading advertising ✗ Content restrictions	—	

[a] These types of barriers tend to increase the cost of supplying services internationally and could be considered equivalent to technical barriers in maufacturing.
✓✓ Barrier effectively removed; ✓ barrier partially removed; ✗ Remaining barrier – not relevant.
Source: European Commission 1996, page 31.

Generally, the most visible barriers seem to have been removed (columns 1, 2 and 3). Less effective have been the harmonisation measures.

Obstacles to free movement of labour

Through the need to eliminate obstacles to the free movement of people, workers and their rights to residence, the SEM has helped both business and worker. Based on legislation, much of which predated the SEM, workers could become residents in other member states and have equal access to employment in all sectors (with exceptions such as the judiciary, police and diplomatic services). Migrant workers could also continue with their rights in social security regimes (i.e. pension rights) across borders. However, obstacles still existed and included incompatibility of education and vocational training; national requirements for many public sector jobs; and differences between taxation and social security systems.

There are hundreds of qualifications within each EU nation alone, awarded by different professional and vocational bodies. Added together over 15 countries, the size of the problem can be appreciated. Diplomas and professional qualifications should now be recognised, although sometimes conditions can be imposed to account for differences in training.

The procedure of recognition, however, has been slow. In the late 1970s and in the 1980s a number of directives were agreed giving mutual recognition to various professionals such as doctors, lawyers, nurses, architects and pharmacists, but rights of establishment of architects took 17 years to establish, and 16 years for pharmacists. To speed up the process the Community proposed recognising higher education diplomas awarded once three years of professional education and training at university or equivalent level had been completed, and this General Directive on Higher Education and Diplomas was adopted in December 1988. It applied to 'regulated' professional occupations (where there is a legal or administrative obstacle) not covered by earlier directives, and members had to arrange for the relevant qualifications to be acceptable to others, with perhaps an extra test or period of supervised practice to prove competence, should the qualification be substantially different from that required for the profession in the host state, e.g. professions such as law and accounting.

During 1991–94, approximately 10 000 EU citizens had their qualifications recognised under the official general system and nearly 5000 doctors, dentists, vets, nurses (general), midwives, pharmacists and architects per year sought recognition of their professional qualifications. In fact, this suggests a fairly low level of mobility (less than 2 per 1000 of the professional population) (European Commission 1996).

Recognition of craft-type certificates has been more problematic. A major obstacle in this for the UK, for example, is that a British craft certificate is not generally as rigorous as in the rest of the EU. There have been, however, various attempts to provide some sort of comparison between occupations and their training requirements. A study by Cedofop, the European Centre for vocational training, has been gathering and comparing job descriptions and their vocational qualifications in various EU countries as part of the groundwork for this, although many problems, such as how to define occupations and how tasks are divided into occupations, have been encountered.

This whole problem of training and qualifications has now been taken up by the Social Chapter (see later in this chapter). If successful, the recognition of diplomas and awards could result in increased mobility within the EU but the cost barrier of looking for work in another EU country, and the linguistic barriers, will still continue to some extent. Despite this, however, the prospect of increased labour mobility has brought with it a concern over the effect of such movement on the regions (see Chapter 7).

Case study: The Bosman case and its effect on UK football clubs

The Bosman case must be the most famous case concerning the free movement of people within the EU to date.

Jean-Marc Bosman is a Belgian soccer player who had reached the end of his contract at RFC Leige and wanted a free transfer to another club, Dunkerque in France – a cross-border transfer. When Bosman's contract expired, his old club cut his wages by three-quarters and set a very high transfer price on him. This effectively prevented his move to Dunkerque. Bosman therefore took the European soccer authorities to the European Court of Justice, claiming they had 'prejudiced his right to free circulation' as an EU worker. The Court found in his favour; that the imposition of such fees, across borders, was contrary to the rules in the Treaty of Rome concerning the free movement of labour.

The result was that UEFA has now decreed that cross-border transfers for players, out of contract, should not carry a fee to the previous club. This, however, does not apply to the individual EU domestic market transfers, only cross-border transfers.

The rule was greeted with gloom by the media, and various fears were expressed. Firstly, the fear was there would be a negative impact on youth training schemes, especially in smaller clubs. To keep a promising young player will mean tying them into contract in order to gain a good fee when they reach their peak. However, the risk is that promise may not be fulfilled and they could be left with a long contract and a below-standard player. Yet not to take the risk could mean a massive reduction in income. Most smaller clubs rely on such fees. For example, most English second and third division clubs receive more from players than they spend on new talent – an increase in net income. The importance of this income is shown by the fact it is estimated that 40–50 of the 92 English Football League clubs are kept in business by such income.

The other major effect of the ruling was on the 'three foreigner' rule, which restricted the freedom of footballers to move across borders. This was also removed following the Bosman ruling. The effect has been very visible. More top-class European and non-European players are in the UK leagues (Scottish and English). These provide, arguably, more entertaining, creative soccer and good role models for young potential footballers. The possible negative impact, however, could be on the development of talented indigenous players. The development of UK youngsters could be seen as too much of a long-term risk. Furthermore, the richer EU clubs like Ajax in the Netherlands, AC Milan in Italy and Manchester United in the UK can afford to buy a greater number of talented foreigners and so gain competitive (unfair) advantage over other, poorer clubs.

Obviously it is too early to judge the full impact on soccer in Europe, but this is an area where the SEM has had an immediate visible impact of great controversy.

Source: Football Association Information and *Financial Times*, various issues in 1995 and 1996.

Questions

1 Can you think of another EU country where foreigners have played a strong role in football in recent years? How did it affect the domestic talent?

2 Do you think this change will have a positive or negative net effect on British football?

3 Choose a UK team and look at the impact of this ruling in light of the above information.

Obstacles to the free movement of capital

It is very difficult to distinguish between the free movement of capital and the liberalisation of financial services (see above). These two areas should therefore be read in conjunction with each other.

One obvious barrier to the free movement of capital, which had to be removed before any progress could be made in other areas, was the existence of **exchange controls**. At the time of the White Paper, various countries had these in force but the Capital Liberalisation Directive in 1988 required them to be abolished by July 1990. Greece, Spain, Portugal and Ireland had additional time to achieve this, but by 1994 all were abolished.

Such freedom brought economic benefits by allowing more efficient allocation of capital and resulted in lower costs within the Union but it was also a necessary condition for freeing the opportunities in the financial services sector. Research by the European Commission, gained from a survey of EU financial institutions and OECD information, suggested success in this area with respondents giving 8.5 out of 10 for capital market freedom in 1996 (compared with 6.5 in 1990). The survey also pointed to certain factors inhibiting capital movements still, the most important being insufficient liquidity in local markets, non-residents' tax treatment, exchange rate risk, local prudential and incorporation requirements, and national differences in company law and accounting frameworks. Especially problematic was the withholding taxes and non-recoverability of tax credits. It was also felt by those surveyed that local restrictions on institutional investors' portfolios generally favoured the domestic government bond market and so distorted domestic equity and private sector bond markets (European Commission 1997).

As seen above, there are still barriers to the movement of capital but generally the legislation is seen as successful. A new directive to speed up and reduce the costs of cross-border transfers should be in force by July 1999 and the allowing of pension funds to invest across borders is currently in debate (some members do not allow pension funds, for example, to invest in foreign securities).

Steps have therefore been, and are being, taken to establish a free capital market. Progress has been slower than expected but the relevant steps are now well under way.

A further barrier which can be considered under this section of free capital movement is the company law barrier. This can be summarised by the fact that it is still not possible to form a European company. Companies must be registered for legal and tax purposes in some national state. Furthermore, there are many legal problems involved in undertaking cross-border operations and co-operation between EU enterprises. Apart from the operation of EU competition policy (see Chapter 8) tending to hinder mergers and co-operative agreements within the EU, there has been no actual legal framework to cover such operations and the result has been that many intra-EU projects have been unable to be established.

The SEA recognised that changes should be made to enable the establishment of subsidiaries, and encourage mergers and the restructuring of businesses across EU frontiers without meeting legal barriers. To aid cross-frontier co-operation, the EU has set up a new form of association called the European Economic Interest Grouping (EEIG) designed to encourage co-operation between small and medium-sized firms. It gives companies the chance to co-operate without having to meet the laws of the other member states. The aim of this is to ease the chance of setting up joint activities without merger or setting up a jointly owned subsidiary with uniform legislation throughout the EU.

Public procurement

Public procurement was and still is another form of technical barrier, often one imposed by the national government for political, social or defensive reasons (see Chapter 5).

It concerns the buying policies of local and national governments. Public procurement concerning work, supplies and services involved 11.5 per cent of EU15 GDP in 1994 and measured the size of the Belgium, Danish and Spanish economies taken together (European Commission 1997). However, in the past, only 0.14 per cent of the contracts were awarded to firms from other EU states outside the actual purchasing state. Furthermore, according to the Commission, in 1982 every penny of government spending in Italy went to Italian suppliers, and figures for France, Germany and the UK were 99.91, 99.7 and 98.3 per cent, respectively. Admittedly, 50 per cent of such spending could not go outside nations for geographical reasons, but this tradition within the EU of favouring home suppliers is a significant and a costly one. Cecchini's report estimated that the cost of such buying policies was in excess of ECU20 billion per annum. Such nationalistic public policies not only added to the fragmentation of the EU market, but they also meant that national governments were paying more for their goods and services than necessary, and were often protecting inefficient businesses. To open up the public procurement market would therefore reduce the governments' costs and create savings which could be passed on to the taxpayer in terms of either less taxation or better services.

Such procurement policies were against the spirit, and the letter, of the Treaty and since 1957 two directives have been specifically aimed at dealing with this problem: the 'Works' Directive (93/36) and the 'Supplies' Directive (93/37). These contain detailed rules regarding the advertisement of contracts, technical specifications and tendering procedures for contracts, criteria for disqualifying applicants and awarding contracts for all those contracts above a certain value, and closing many loopholes. They also stressed that the award should be given solely on the basis of the lowest price or the most economically advantageous tender, and banned discriminatory technical standards in the tendering processes.

Initially these seemed to have little effect for a variety of reasons:

1 The Treaty and directives excluded certain key sectors – defence, transport, water, energy and telecommunications – which covered something like 80 per cent of all public purchasing contracts in the EU. These are now covered by a separate directive, the Utilities Directive, which is more flexible and was extended in 1994 to cover water and energy utilities plus transport and telecommunications.

2 Only 25 per cent of contracts were advertised correctly – most were not published in the EU official journal. A popular way to avoid advertising such contracts was to split them up to reduce their value below the set threshold, despite the fact that this practice is prohibited under the 'Works' Directive. A study in the UK suggested that of the 45 000 public contracts which met the directives' criteria, only 500 were officially advertised. However, the total number of contracts advertised did rise from 12 000 in 1987 to 90 000 in 1995, suggesting some success. Nevertheless, it is estimated that 86 per cent of projects covered by the legislation are still not published.

3 Public sector contracts are often used by governments as part of their regional policy and to reduce recession.

Monitoring and proving bias has been difficult, however. There are basically two types of contract. With those for standard goods provided by normal competitive markets, for things like desks, chairs and vans, it is fairly easy to detect bias, and increasing levels of imports have been noted in this area since the SEM. With the second type of contract, the 'one-off' special purchase, it is much harder. Usually these contracts are in sectors with few competitors, with possibly high pre-contract costs in research and development, and often entailing close connection between buyer and seller. It is not really surprising that the award of such contracts to domestic firms is easy to justify.

A further directive – the Compliance and Remedies Directive – has also been adopted to allow suppliers to challenge purchasers who they believe have not kept to the rules. Under this directive, national review bodies are created which can take interim measures to put matters right and set aside unlawful purchasing decisions and award damages. Conciliation procedures have also been set up. The Commission can draw members' attention to breaches of the rules and require a response within 21 days, but it cannot take action itself.

The new directives, however, are based purely on cost factors and ignore the non-financial side. Important in such contracts are questions of reliability, security of supply, and nearness to site. In some industries, the uncertainty brought by competition could be unacceptable and may mean favouring domestic suppliers.

These new regulations attack the discrimination by public authorities and their consequent anti-competitive effect. The increase in the publication of contracts is a good sign and there are some positive signs for those tendering for jobs:

> Of companies submitting tenders in response to newly identified cross-border opportunities, 44% reported that they had won new business. Some 31% of companies reported that they were selling to partner country authorities ... 36% of respondents also reported increased competition in their domestic markets, although this contrasts with perceptions of purchasing authorities that new tenderers have not increased since the introduction of the legislation.
>
> (European Commission 1997, page 43)

However, there does seem less evidence of the expected increased competition and consequent price reductions. It is still fairly early to judge but the fact that more are publishing contracts (although still a small percentage) is a positive one. This however is an area which needs constant monitoring.

The single market measures involving the government sector must cover the question of state aid to industry as well. Aid is often used to protect state and private industries from home and international competition for social, regional or defensive reasons (see Chapter 5). This area is covered extensively in Chapter 8 and so will not be discussed here.

Regional matters

Few question the actual benefits of integrating markets, but there is little consideration of how the gains are distributed amongst the different regions of the EU. This is reflected in the Cecchini Report, which made no reference to the distribution of the welfare gains expected.

The single market's aim is to bring economies of scale, but unless the market grows significantly, greater concentration of production may occur. The process of concentration could mean that some areas are likely to lose their industries while other areas gain. This regional impact of the SEM is discussed in Chapter 7.

Social Charter

Social policy has been acknowledged by most as being an integral part of the SEM unification process. 'The European Council stresses the importance of the social aspects of progress towards the 1992 objective ... the internal market must be conceived in such a manner as to benefit all our people' (Barnes and Barnes 1995, page 325).

To deal with this social element of the SEM programme, a social charter was drawn up and the preliminary draft, in the form of a declaration, was issued in May 1989. The Charter was approved in December 1989 by 11 of the EU states – the UK alone did not support it.

The Charter put forward basic employment rights concerning free move-ment of labour within the EU; 'fair' remuneration in employment; improvement and approximation of conditions of employment EU-wide; collec-tive bargaining and freedom of association; the right to training; equal opportunities for women, disabled people and racial minorities; information, consultation and participation arrangements for workers; health and safety pro-visions and protection of young people at work; minimum wage provision; and the right to transfer pensions and social security provisions.

This Charter caused controversy and much argument leading to pressures to 'water down' the original proposal. Thus the new Charter still covered the same points, but changed emphasis somewhat. The final version stressed the impor-tance of present national practice and the limited role of the Commission in implementing the Charter. For example, regarding the right to strike, the origi-nal Charter stressed that the right was 'unqualified'; this was replaced by the right 'subject to the obligations arising under national regulations and collec-tive agreements.' Similarly, the concept of a 'decent wage' being established across Europe was replaced by 'an equitable wage, i.e. a wage sufficient to enable them to have a decent standard of living.'

This final draft was followed by a social action programme issued in November 1990 with some 48 measures to implement the Charter. The initiative included a directive on typical employment contracts; a directive on minimum requirements regarding duration of work, rest periods, holidays, night work, part-time work, weekend work and systematic overtime; a communication on collective bargaining; an instrument on procedures regarding worker participa-tion; and a directive on young people at work. Some directives were agreed easily, e.g. those aiding the handicapped (HORIZON) and vocational training for women (NOW). Others, however, were strongly disputed, especially by the UK, e.g. those regarding a maximum working week and guaranteed holiday, and protection for part-time and temporary workers. Given that the UK had large numbers of part-time and temporary workers and the fact that it had no law concerning maximum working hours, its opposition was not surprising. It did, however, argue that this would undermine existing arrangements and impose high costs on employers, as much as £2 billion for the working time directive alone. This would affect companies' ability to compete and reduce employment. The UK therefore opposed such moves. It also felt that such mea-sures would further inhibit the flexibility of companies in their use of labour, and they argued that the Social Charter was not necessary – opening up of the European market would eventually raise wages in the poorer economies via the market mechanism.

The UK was not the only state to fear the Social Charter. Some of the less industrialised EU states feared it would increase their employment costs and reduce their comparative advantage over the more advanced nations, especially in labour-intensive industries. The major advocates of the Social Charter were the more advanced industrialised nations such as France and Germany, which were worried that vast differences in health and safety provisions, unemploy-ment pay, social security benefits and employment legislation, for example, would disrupt the single market. They feared that businesses would exploit such differences during the restructuring brought about by the SEM and move to the EU states where employment conditions were less costly. Alternatively, domestic firms in states with lower safety standards or below-minimum wages would have lower production costs and undercut those with higher standards. 'Social dumping' of this kind could result in employment conditions in the EU falling to the lowest level in the Union and significantly reduce standards in the more advanced EU economies.

The Charter was originally intended as part of the Maastricht Treaty but the UK's opposition led to it becoming an annex to the treaty signed by all but the UK. This, however, has since been reversed by the present Labour government, which has now agreed to join with the 14 signatories (Austria, Sweden and Finland signed on joining the EU). At the time of writing, only two elements of the Chapter have been implemented: those concerning works councils and parental leave. Elements concerning things like maximum working time have controversially been dealt with by health and safety legislation and **qualified majority voting.**

The EU's SEM therefore has finally acquired a social dimension covering all 15 countries, although the strength and effect of this is still to be felt.

The impact of the SEM

As already seen, in many areas there has been substantial progress in, and positive effects from, the implementation of the SEM. However, in some areas the effects have been less than expected and there is still obviously more to do.

A survey of opinions within the manufacturing industry towards the SEM was recently undertaken by Eurostat (European Commission 1997). Figure 9.3 illustrates the results of this survey.

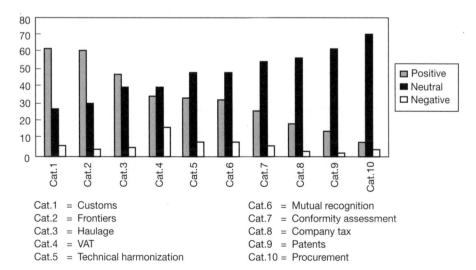

Cat.1 = Customs
Cat.2 = Frontiers
Cat.3 = Haulage
Cat.4 = VAT
Cat.5 = Technical harmonization

Cat.6 = Mutual recognition
Cat.7 = Conformity assessment
Cat.8 = Company tax
Cat.9 = Patents
Cat.10 = Procurement

Figure 9.3 Manufacturing industries' assessment of the effectiveness of measures for free circulation of products (reproduced from European Commission (1996))

It can be seen that the streamlining of customs posts and frontier opening plus the liberalisation of road haulage are seen by business as very positive moves. Following closely behind, with 30–40 per cent ratings, are moves to harmonise VAT, technical harmonisation and mutual recognition. The areas which point to negative or neutral assessment are company tax, patents and public procurement. These are all areas where legislation is either incomplete, not transposed or implemented, or covers a limited number of firms.

In order to try to evaluate what has already been achieved and problem areas still existing, a report on 'The Impact and Effectiveness of the Single Market' was issued by the European Commission in October 1996. This report makes a useful framework for analysing the SEM.

Obviously it has to be borne in mind when looking at this report that some legislation did not come into force until 1994 or 1995 and that some will not be implemented until the year 2000. Similarly, many firms are still adapting and restructuring to take account of the SEM; many of these firms delayed in this due to the impact of the early 1990s recession in Europe. To see the true effects of the SEM will therefore need a much longer time period.

Having said this, certain elements can be pointed at to illustrate its impact.

The impact on trade

The SEM appears to have boosted not only **intra-EU trade** but also **extra-EU trade**. Intra-EU manufacturing imports increased from 61.2 per cent in 1985 to 67.9 per cent in 1995 and for services the figure rose from 46.9 per cent to 50 per cent over the same time. Extra-EU manufacturing imports increased as a share of consumption between 1980 and 1993 from 12 to 14 per cent (European Commission 1996), and the market share rose by 2.5 per cent in the manufacturing sector between 1991 and 1994. The growth of EU trade therefore has not been at the expense of those outside the EU. A further interesting factor regarding trade is that of the nature of trade product flows. The SEM has accentuated intra-industry trade and countries are specialising in certain price–quality niche ranges, so increasing the range of products available. Such price–quality differences have led to more converging EU industrial structures, which augers well for the future and EMU.

The impact on industrial concentration and market structure

The impact on industrial concentration and market structure is considered in more detail in Chapter 8; however, the SEM does appear to have led to substantial restructuring of industry and thereby increased mergers and acquisitions, especially across borders between EU firms (18.7 per cent of all mergers and acquisitions). Between 1986 and 1995 the number of mergers and acquisitions increased from 720 to 2296 in manufacturing and from 783 to 2602 in services. However, 63.5 per cent of these mergers and acquisitions in manufacturing and 70 per cent in services were domestic, suggesting that maybe the domestic market has been restructuring due to the greater competition nationally. This is supported by the fact that in manufacturing between 1987 and 1993 the share of the four largest firms increased as a percentage of European turnover from

20.5 per cent to 22.8 per cent, whilst this figure declined nationally. It also suggests that some sort of pan-European strategy is being undertaken. The extent of restructuring, however, has differed across countries: it has been especially important for the UK but less so for Italy and Spain. Further, firms in the Nordic countries, the Netherlands, France and the UK have been more likely to be the acquirers, and those from Italy, Spain and Germany the targets.

Has this restructuring led to changes in industrial concentration? In manufacturing there does seem to be some increase in concentration. On average, the share of total sales of the top four companies rose from 20.5 to 22.8 per cent between 1987 and 1993. However, in France, Belgium and the UK the opposite was the case. Many industries have seen significant concentration increases (greater than 5 percentage points), especially those related to public procurement, some food sectors and in electrical appliances. Generally, those in technolog-intensive sectors have seen rising concentration. However, an interesting feature of European industry (especially manufacturing) is the difference in average firm sizes in different EU states. For example, in 1985 gross value added per firm in Germany was ECU7.4 million (1990 prices). This was 33 per cent higher than in France and the UK. Between 1985 and 1992 this increased by 8 per cent in France and 15 per cent in Germany. In the UK there was no increase. So the different structure of EU industry appears to have been reinforced rather than equalised by the SEM.

The growth of concentration shown above could suggest less competition and therefore fewer gains to consumers in terms of price reductions, or it could suggest greater potential for economies of scale and lower prices. Evidence suggests the latter has been more the case – showing lower price–cost margins of 1 per cent per annum from 1986–87 onwards. There also appears to be growing price convergence across the EU, especially in the consumer goods sector.

The impact on FDI

The effect on FDI of the SEM appears even more positive than that on trade. Some 44.4 per cent of world FDI came to the EU in the 1990s compared with 28.2 per cent in the mid-1980s and this is especially strong in the service industry. Furthermore, FDI between EU countries increased four times faster than intra-EU trade between 1984 and 1992.

Macro-economic effects

The study undertaken by the European Commission (1996) also suggested that certain macro-economic effects have become apparent. Investment is estimated to have increased by 1 per cent more than it would have done without the SEM, and inflation by between 1 and 1.5 per cent less. Income is estimated to have been 1.1 and 1.5 per cent higher in 1994 than it would have been (amounting to ECU60–80 billion extra).

Half of this greater income was seen as coming from increased competition and efficiency and the rest from improved technological progress associated with the SEM. Employment, furthermore, is estimated to be between 300 000 and 900 000 greater in the EU. It is interesting to compare these with the very optimistic figures in the Cecchini Report at the beginning of this chapter.

Finally, there does seem to be greater regional convergence, with Ireland, Portugal and Spain moving towards the EU average growth, due partly to the impact of the SEM and partly to regional policy (see Chapter 7).

The impact on business

The Commission Report (1996) suggested that, based on two major surveys, European business felt the SEM had removed obstacles to cross-border transactions and greater opportunities were apparent. The level of approval was greater in manufacturing than in services, and larger companies (over 1000 employees) liked the SEM more than smaller firms (20–49 employees).

However, having said that businesses feel positively about the SEM, the reaction of UNICE, the Confederation of European Industries, has been interesting. It strongly urged the Commission to take note of the fact that the report points to areas where the SEM is not complete and that Brussels should follow this report with a new white paper to deal with this. The areas pointed to are as follows:

1 **Company law**. As seen previously, there is still no legal framework for European Company law. Two directives which exist but remain unadopted – the 10th Directive and the European Company Statute – would complete this framework and greatly simplify life for European firms. This area is viewed as of high priority.

2 **Adoption, implementation and enforcement of legislation**. Most of the directives have now been implemented and become national law. The problem is that not all this legislation is applied effectively and fairly. Obviously one way to deal with it is for tougher infringement procedures to be in place; however, the real solution is for nations to take the relevant actions. The effect of such differences in implementation is that they distort competition and reduce the protective effect of the EU legislation.

3 **Taxation**. As seen earlier, there is no harmonisation of VAT and the delayed move towards an origin-based VAT system has greater problems for many businesses. The various special arrangements concerning **derogations** and implementation have also created problems. Furthermore, there is a lack of a coherent approach to the tax treatment of company income and the elimination of double taxation. This is felt to be a great disincentive for trans-European business.

Finally, a further obstacle which still exists, and may in the future be removed, is that of differing national currencies. Fluctuations in currencies can have, and recently have had, major effects on export prices and thereby profitability in the various countries. EU studies have shown that over the period 1992–95 firms with appreciating currencies have found it hard to enter markets of countries with depreciating currencies. Whilst those with depreciating currencies have not gained any advantage within EU markets, some have gained in non-EU markets. However, it is obvious that strategic decision-making, especially regarding pricing and sourcing, has been affected by exchange rate changes, and some sectors have experienced an adverse impact (see Table 9.4).

Table 9.4 Sectoral impact of currency fluctuations between 1992 and 1995

Motor vehicles	Improved export performance by the devaluing countries is explained by better export performance to non-EU countries. This is particularly true for Italy and Spain, which did not perform much better in countries whose currencies appreciated but substantially improved their export performance to non-EU countries. This poor performance on the EU market is explained by higher unit price increase (in national currency and ECUS) for intra-EU markets than for non-EU markets. On the other hand, countries whose currencies appreciated experienced more difficulties in penetrating other EU markets, while their performance on non-EU markets slightly improved.
Textiles	There has not been any such clear-cut differentiation. German reunification and EU enlargement to Spain and Portugal seem to have played a more important role. French manufacturers experienced some difficulties in penetrating the Italian market, while Italian, Spanish and Portuguese manufacturers improved their export performance to countries whose currencies appreciated. Some trade diversion from depreciating countries to appreciating countries has also been noticed.
Clothing	No clear trade diversion has been experienced. Operators in weak countries have increased profit margins by raising export prices in ECUs while decreasing production prices in ECUs.
Footwear/shoes	This is another example of discriminatory pricing policies where operators from depreciating countries have been reluctant to reduce prices in foreign currency, with a view to increasing profit margins in national currencies. German exports grew above the average in all weak markets, while Italian firms experienced some recovery in their exports to both EU and non-EU markets. Italian, Spanish and Portuguese producers increased their profit margins.

Source: *European Commission* (1996) page 66.

Chapter 12 considers the costs and benefits of a single currency for business, but in the context of the SEM, the lack of one currency across Europe is businesses' most often stated barrier not yet tackled by the SEM. A logical next step in completing the single market is a single currency.

Conclusion

The SEM has had a major impact on European businesses and on international business. All have been forced, some more reluctantly than others, to face the opportunities and threats the SEM has posed.

There are still gaps in the legislation – the Single European Market is far from complete – but further significant legislation is unlikely in the near future. To quote a Commission official 'Our message is no longer about legislation – it is about going out and making the most of what is there' (*Financial Times* 1996, page 15).

Brussels now has its attention very much diverted and focused on EMU. EMU is an obvious next step. Like the SEM it may be costly to implement and may challenge many businesses but to achieve a true European market, it may also be a necessity.

Questions for discussion

1 What factors have prevented countries from signing the Schengen Agreement? How important are these?

2 What are the benefits of moving towards an origin-based VAT system?

3 Why do you think car insurance is so expensive in Ireland (Table 9.1)? Will the SEM legislation deal with this?

4 Is there such a things as a 'Euroconsumer' for any type of good? If not, what are the implications of this?

5 Identify the various factors not covered by the SEM and consider their importance to European business.

6 Does a 'true' single market require a single currency? Consider the implications for the SEM if a single currency either does not occur or occurs only in certain countries.

Main reading

Barnes, I. and Barnes, P. (1995) *The Enlarged European Union*, Longman.

Emersen, M. (1992) *One Market, One Money – An Evaluation of the Potential Benefits and Costs of forming an Economic and Monetary Union*, Open University Press.

European Commission (1996) *The Impact and Effectiveness of the Single Market*, Communication to the European Commission, EU.

European Commission (1997) *The 1996 Single Market Review*, EU.

Additional reading

Bank of England Quarterly Bulletin (1994) The developing single market in financial services, November.

Barnes, I., Campbell, J. and Pepper, C. (1989) Local authorities, public procurement and 1992, *Local Government Studies*, November/December.

BLRA (1996a) *Facing the Facts*, Memorandum to HM Treasury, July.

BLRA (1996b) *The Big Question: The Cross Channel Trade in Beer*.

Brearley, M. and Quigley, C. (1989) Completing the internal market of the European Community, in *1992 Handbook*, Graham and Trotman.

Brittan, L. (1990) *Single Market News*, Winter, p. 9.

Cecchini, P. (1988) *The European Challenge, 1992: The Benefits of a Single Market*, Wildwood House.

Clarke, W. M. (ed.) (1989) *Planning of Europe*, Waterlow.

Dale, R. (1994) Regulating investment business in the single market, *Bank of England Quarterly Bulletin*, November 1994.

Department of Trade and Industry (1990) *The Single Market News*, Summer.

Department of Trade and Industry (1990) *The Single Market News*, Autumn.

DIHT (1995) *Survey among 733 German Companies*, September.

Dudley, J. W.(1993) *1993 and Beyond*, Kogan Page.

Dynes, M. (1989) When a barrier is not a fortress, *The Times*, 6 December.

The Economist (1990) Sticking together a United States of Europe, 1 December, pp. 63–5.

The Economist (1990) Europe's companies after 1992 – don't collaborate, compete, 9 June.

The Economist (1990) Europe's Horn of Plenty, 2 June, pp. 71–2.

The Economist (1991) Dutch treat, 14 December, pp. 13–14.

The Economist (1991) The deal is done, 14 December, pp. 55–8.

The Economist (1991) Financially sound, socially insecure, 14 December, pp. 84–90.

The Economist (1995) Soccer in the dock – the Bosman trial promises to change the face of European football, 17 January.

The Economist (1995) Foul! European Court gives ruling on soccer transfer fees, 23 September.

El-Agraa, A. M. (ed.) (1990) *The Economies of the European Community*, 3rd edition, Philip Allan.

Emerson, M. *et al.* (1988) *The Economics of 1992, the EU Commission's Assessment of the Economic Effects of Completing the Internal Market*, Oxford University Press.

European Commission (1988) *Completing the Internal Market, A Common Market for Services*, EU.

Evans, R. (1989) 1992: The bad news, *Geographical Magazine*, September, pp. 13–14.

Financial Times (1990) 1992 Redrawing the map of Europe, 2 July.

Financial Times (1996) Business and the law: football fees contrary to European Court, 16 January.

Football Association (1996) Letter to J. Piggott.

Gleed, R. and Baker, A. (1989) *Deloitte's Guide*, Butterworths.

Hall, M. (1990) UK employment practices after the Social Charter, *Personnel Management*, March, pp. 32–5.

Hamilton Fazey, I. (1996) Soccer's minnows survive by feeding the big fish, *Financial Times*, 11 January.

Hill, G. (1989) Backs to the future, *The Times*, 20 February, p. 13.

Holmes, P. (1987) Real and imaginary barriers to trade within the EEU and economies of scale, Mimeo, Discussion Paper, International Economics Research Centre, University of Sussex, September.

Johnson, R. (1990) Are the British qualified to join Europe?, *Personnel Management*, May, pp. 50–3.

Kuper, S. and Buckley, N. (1996) UEFA abolishes fees for cross border transfers, *Financial Times*, 5 March.

London Business School (1989) *1992 Myths and Realities*, Centre for Business Strategy.

Madhavan, S. (1996) *European Economic Integration and Sustainable Development: Institutions, Issues and Policies*, McGraw-Hill.

McDonald, F. E. (1988) Completing the internal market: or making the European Community a common market, *Economics*, Spring.

McKenzie, G. and Venables, T. (1989) The economics of 1992, *Economic Review*, May.

Palmer, J. (1989) *1992 and Beyond – EU Commission Deadline 1992 Document*, EU Commission.

Pelkmans, J. and Winters, A. (1988) *Europe's Domestic Market*, Routledge.

Political Quarterly Supplement (1990) The politics of 1992 beyond the single market.

Price Waterhouse (1996) *Customs and Fiscal Formalities at Frontiers*.

Pryce, V. and Sherlock, N. (1990) How far to 1992? *Economic Affairs*, April/May, pp. 22, 24–7.

Raven, J. (1987) Are Young's amateurs fit to take on EEU professionals? *The Times*, 17 October, p. 27.

The Times (1989) 1992: new frontier, a special report, 30 January, pp. 26, 28.

Tucker, E. (1996) No appetite to change the mix, *Financial Times*, 31 October.

Whynes, D. K. (1990) After 1992: the political economy of the Single European Act, *Economics*, Spring.

Wistrich, E. (1989) *After 1992: The United States of Europe*, Routledge.

Appendix: The importance of Cassis de Dijon

A (West) Germany company, Rewe Zentral AG, wanted to import a liqueur called Crème de Cassis into Germany. This liqueur was also called Cassis de Dijon. However, according to German regulations the product could not be imported into German because its alcohol content was too low to be deemed a 'liqueur' by German standards, which require at least 32 per cent alcohol content. The Germany authorities claimed that the import ban should be upheld as there was no discrimination between German and outside producers. No product with a lower than standard alcohol content could be sold as a liqueur in Germany, wherever it was made. The Court of Justice did not accept this argument. Thus member states may regulate the marketing of domestically made products, but they cannot regulate goods imported from other member states, as long as the production is lawful by general EC rules and the goods are produced and sold legally in the country of origin. For potential exporters into Germany or any-where else in the EC this case was of vital importance. An exporting firm may now be confident that if its output is legally satisfactory at home then it must be able to get access to markets in all the other member states.

10

Multinational corporations

Introduction

Trade and the effects of economic integration have been looked at in Chapters 4, 5 and 6. What now has to be considered is investment and the growth of multinational corporations (MNCs). These are looked at from the perspective of the company in this chapter and from the perspective of the economy in Chapter 11. The size and growth of MNCs are considered first. Arguments suggesting that the MNC is a benign influence spreading knowledge (technology transfer), increasing employment opportunities and raising living standards around the world are contrasted with the view that sees MNCs as agents of control rather than of change, exploiting markets, governments and employees in home and host societies to the benefit of the MNC alone. Differing opinions are discussed with relation to the desirability and efficacy of governments' attempts to regulate the activities of MNCs, particularly within Europe. Finally, MNC operations are analysed using a standard neo-classical model, which may seem inappropriate at first, but which yields some recent and rather promising analyses.

What are MNCs and why are they important?

Dunning and Sauvant (1996, page 11) tell us that:

It is not difficult to understand why so much attention has been given to TNCs and their activities:

- At least 37,000 TNCs operate more than 200,000 affiliates in virtually all countries of the world.
- The value of the production of these affiliates exceeds that of world exports.
- For most of the past three decades, FDI flows have been increasing at a higher rate than both the world's GNP and world exports.
- TNCs account for between 25 per cent and 30 per cent of the world's GNP, about three-fifths of non-agricultural trade and around three-quarters of the world's stock of privately generated innovatory capacity.
- TNCs employ directly some 73 million people or 10 per cent of employment in non-agricultural activities world wide.

These enormous commercial organisations are clearly factors of some significance in modern life – not just in business, but for society at large. Dominating world culture as well as world commerce, MNCs are a remarkable and significant feature of our lives. Of these corporations operating world-wide and loosely defined as multinationals, very many have EU-based operations and include such organisations as British American Tobacco (BAT), Philips, Siemens and Hanson Trust. But what leads us to define a firm or organisation as a multinational?

At its simplest, an MNC can be thought of as a company which operates in more than one country and is engaging in the company's main lines of business – not merely selling abroad. Some, however, prefer a broader definition that includes all 'income-generating assets', e.g. sales subsidiaries (Hood and Young 1979), whilst others have a much stricter approach, where the firm is considered an MNC only if it is located in more than two countries. In an interesting historical view of 'the corporate economy', Hannah (1983) discussed the seemingly irresistible trend towards larger and larger business units. He suggests that not only has British industry become increasingly concentrated into larger units but that 'large corporations themselves have been no respecters of national boundaries, but have expanded overseas as well as in the domestic economy' (page 2). These firms are the MNCs of today. How big are these organisations and where are they based?

The largest companies in the world

In Chapter 2 the largest EU companies were considered, but now, given the very nature of MNCs, a more global viewpoint will be taken. Table 10.1 shows the world's 50 largest corporations in 1996.

It can be seen that GM tops the list in terms of revenues, with Ford Motor second. These have displaced the giant Japanese trading companies that have dominated the list for the past two years. They are still represented in the top ten; in fact, six out of these ten are Japanese companies, with only three US and one European. The reasons for the change this year lie in the restructuring wave being led by US corporations, and the fact that accounting changes in Japan have reduced revenues by approximately 2 per cent for the top trading companies.

This restructuring trend globally has meant 'the big didn't get bigger last year; they got richer. Just look at the dazzling profit gains the streamlined 500 squeezed out from basically flat sales' (Colby, page F1). Only 50 are listed in Table 10.1 but the trend can still be seen. The percentage change from 1995 under the revenue section shows the dormant sales gains and sometimes falls; the profit figures, however, are far healthier.

It is interesting to compare the top profitable companies with those of sales. The top ten in terms of profit are Shell (6), Exxon (8), General Electric (20), Philip Morris (30), AT&T (5), IBM (15), Intel (161), GM (1), HSBC Holdings (96) and PDVSA (73) (the revenue rating being given in brackets). The Japanese trading companies as usual do not figure (being ranked in terms of profit at between 200 and 400 generally) but the top two companies show how profitable the oil/petrol industry is, and the appearance of services companies (AT&T and HSBC) is notable.

Table 10.1 The world's largest corporations in 1996

Rank	Company	Country	Revenues ($million)	% change from 1995	Profit ($million)	Rank	No. of employees	Rank
1	General Motors	USA	168 369.0	(0.3)	4 963.0	8	647 000	3
2	Ford Motor	USA	146 991.0	7.2	4 446.0	11	371 702	7
3	Mitsui	Japan	144 942.8	—	321.9	292	41 694	276
4	Mitsubishi	Japan	140 203.7	—	394.1	271	35 000	308
5	Itochu	Japan	135 542.1	—	110.9	411	6 999	470
6	Royal Dutch/Shell Group	UK/Netherlands	128 174.5	16.7	8 887.1	1	101 000	98
7	Marubeni	Japan	124 026.9	—	178.6	370	65 000	175
8	Exxon	USA	119 434.0	8.6	7 510.0	2	79 000	141
9	Sumitomo	Japan	119 281.3	—	(1 292.8)	491	26 200	354
10	Toyota Motor	Japan	108 702.0	(2.1)	3 426.2	18	150 736	51
11	Wal-Mart Stores	USA	106 147.0	12.0	3 056.0	22	675 000	2
12	General Electric	USA	79 179.0	13.1	7 280.0	3	239 000	22
13	Nissho Iwai	Japan	78 921.2	—	136.9	395	17 497	407
14	Nippon Telegraph & Telephone	Japan	78 320.7	(4.4)	1 330.3	100	230 300	25
15	Intl. Business Machines	USA	75 947.0	5.6	5 429.0	6	268 648	19
16	Hitachi	Japan	75 669.0	(10.1)	784.2	186	330.152	10
17	AT&T	USA	74 525.0	(6.4)	5 908.0	5	130.400	65
18	Nippon Life Insurance	Japan	72 575.0	(12.8)	2 799.1	33	86.695	126
19	Mobil	USA	72 267.0	8.3	2 964.0	24	43 000	272
20	Daimler-Benz	Germany	71 589.3	(0.9)	1 776.1	73	290 029	12
21	British Petroleum	Britain	69 851.9	22.6	3 985.2	12	53 150	218
22	Matsushita Electric Industrial	Japan	68 147.5	(3.2)	1 223.9	112	270 651	18
23	Volkswagen	Germany	66 527.5	8.2	437.9	257	260 811	21
24	Daewoo	South Korea	65 160.2	27.2	468.3	250	186 314	38
25	Siemens	Germany	63 704.7	5.0	1 877.1	66	379 000	6
26	Chrysler	USA	61 397.0	15.4	3 529.0	16	126 000	67
27	Nissan Motor	Japan	59 118.2	(5.5)	690.2	203	135 331	61
28	Allianz	Germany	56 577.2	1.9	1 096.3	131	65 836	171
29	US Postal Service	USA	56 402.0	3.9	1 567.2	82	887 546	1
30	Philip Morris	USA	54 553.0	2.7	6 303.0	4	154 000	48
31	Unilever	UK/Netherlands	52 067.4	4.7	2 499.7	42	306 000	11
32	Fiat	Italy	50 509.0	10.0	1 470.1	88	237 865	23
33	Sony	Japan	50 277.9	5.7	1 238.1	109	163 000	46
34	Dai-Ichi Mutual Life Insurance	Japan	49 144.7	(15.3)	1 941.3	59	66 953	166
35	IRI	Italy	49 055.7	17.1	279.4	313	132 489	64
36	Nestlé	Switzerland	48 932.5	2.4	2 751.2	35	221 144	26
37	Toshiba	Japan	48 415.8	(8.7)	595.5	222	186 000	39
38	Honda Motor	Japan	46 994.5	6.7	1 963.6	57	101 100	97
39	Elf Aquitaine	France	46 818.0	7.6	1 363.7	97	85 400	129
40	Tomen	Japan	46 506.3	—	42.2	448	11 500	455
41	Bank of Tokyo-Misubishi	Japan	46 451.0	42.0	361.6	281	19 304	398
42	Veba Group	Germany	45 246.2	(2.2)	1 633.2	75	122 110	69
43	Tokyo Electric Power	Japan	44 735.0	(14.6)	724.5	201	43 166	268
44	Texaco	USA	44 561.0	21.1	2 018.0	55	28 957	336
45	Sumitomo Life Insurance	Japan	44 063.3	(13.1)	1 858.4	69	67 027	164
46	Sunkyong	South Korea	44 031.0	—	313.0	294	33 299	320
47	NEC	Japan	43 932.7	(3.6)	813.1	180	151 966	50
48	Électricité De France	France	43 658.7	0.3	209.4	351	116 919	77
49	State Farm Insurance Co.	USA	42 781.2	4.8	2 567.9	40	71 612	154
50	Deutsche Telekom	Germany	41 910.7	(9.2)	1 168.1	123	201 000	32

Source: Fortune, August 1997, pages F2–11.

It is possible to derive a list of the very largest industrial MNCs over time, based on Table 10.1 and similar information for earlier years. This has to be limited to industrial corporations as service corporations were not included in the listings until recently. The 'membership' of this group of companies, shown in Table 10.2, remains fairly stable over time, especially at the very top.

Table 10.2 The very largest industrials, ranked by sales

Company	Ranking by sales			
	1996	*1990*	*1984*	*1978*
General Motors	1	1	3	1
Royal Dutch/Shell	3	2	2	3
Exxon	4	3	1	2
Ford Motor	2	4	5	4
IBM	7	5	8	10
Toyota Motor	5	6	–	–
BP	10	8	6	7
Mobil	8	9	4	5

Source: Adapted from *Fortune* (various issues).

The largest of the giant corporations have annual sales far greater than the GNP of many countries. The importance of such firms in the world can be seen by considering the relationship between size of country, measured by GNP, and sales of MNCs – using the example of General Motors, the largest of Table 10.1's corporations. France's GNP is eight times the annual sales of GM but Venezuela's is only half, whilst the annual sales of GM are 50 times as great as the GNP of Zambia, and more than 100 times as large as the smallest and poorest 70 countries in the world. This does not give us any detail of actual relationships and trading patterns between any specific MNCs and particular countries, but we can see that they often have a great deal of power. As an example of MNC strength, in 1989 the government of Zimbabwe introduced a new 'investment code' giving foreign companies improved taxation terms and increased rights to repatriate profits made in Zimbabwe back to their home base. The government of Zimbabwe, under Robert Mugabe, was not particularly enthusiastic about this but feared a 'pull-out' by MNCs. The threat of 'pull-out' is a very real one for small economies, but to the large MNCs such location decisions are far less important.

MNC research

Much research and empirical work in relation to the performance of multinational, transnational and international businesses has been undertaken. Such research and results are not always easy to interpret, however. This is hardly surprising, given some of the parameters of this area of research, not least the political aspects of any such studies. This area is inherently a very complex and 'untidy' one for research: MNCs come from a very wide variety of countries and cultures, industries and technologies, and operate in host situations similarly varied. The categorising of firms, industries, markets, cultures and so on, in order to set up research studies, can yield endless permutations. Ambiguous results are not really surprising. In addition we cannot ignore the nationalistically focused or country-centred perspective which may infiltrate analysis in this area. For example, an early study by Hymer and Rowthorn (1970) cited studies of European and US MNCs undertaken on both sides of the Atlantic in the 1960s and indicated that the role of the MNCs differed from the two cultures' perspectives. During the 1960s there appeared to be a strong feeling amongst European commentators that US MNCs were battling vigorously to penetrate European markets. They were doing this by FDI as well as by exporting, in an attempt to gain dominant positions in some European industries, or sections of them, such as motor manufacture. American commentators, on the other hand, saw US firms taking a long-term view of their European activities, as defensive strategies to try to maintain their share of world trade in the face of rapidly growing European firms. How did such a 'misunderstanding' arise? Hymer and Rowthorn argued that this was partly because of a conundrum in the 'evidence'. US operations in Europe typically exhibited faster growth rates than comparable European firms in the same sectors, whilst at the same time the European companies were growing more quickly than the combined (parent and subsidiary) US firms. So both points of view can be explained – 'a firm can be challenging and challenged at the same time' (Hymer and Rowthorn 1970) – but the differences in explanation surely also stem from the different country perspectives of the commentators. Even accepting the problems of conducting this sort of empirical research, it must be said that much of the work on the scope and size of MNCs, and their impact on home and host economies, is far from conclusive.

By penetrating foreign markets, particularly if doing so by FDI, MNCs could be said to be inhibiting the growth of indigenous firms, exporting profits and thereby retarding the growth of output and employment in the affected industries. But many accounts of MNC growth rates, profit rates and impact on host industries' performance levels have given rise to indeterminate findings. As suggested above, there are many possible reasons for the ambiguity of such findings: politics is one, and the sheer variety and complexity of the studies is another. A further difficulty could also be the lack of consensus on an adequate theoretical framework or 'paradigm' in which to conduct enquiries into the operations and outcomes of international business. The 'missing consensus' may reflect the varieties of situation in which MNCs act, the huge range of contexts within which, and as parts of which, they function, and the near impossibility of fitting the giant corporations into neat 'neo-classical boxes'. Vernon (1994) recently commented on the nature of research into MNCs. In his early book (Vernon 1971), he introduced the idea of an imbalance of power between some of the largest MNCs and some 'host' governments. More recently he discussed the failure of MNC research, in particular economic research, to deal adequately with MNCs. He describes economists as being stuck in a neo-classical paradigm and unable to break free. Thus economists often study MNCs just as if they were 'ordinary' firms, and consider their conduct as cost-minimising or profit-seeking, in line with typical neo-classical assumptions. What is needed, Vernon suggests, is to break away from this neo-classical constraining mind-set, and to think of MNCs in terms of their strategic competitive behaviour, more in line with **the prisoner's dilemma** and **game theory**. The analysis of MNCs could then begin to take account of the fact that MNCs are not just firms, in 'a market', but may be uniquely powerful players in a multifaceted environment, where politics, management and organisational culture, and sheer animal spirits of the executives, may be more significant explanators than the quantifiable factors like minimising transaction costs.

Krugman's contributions to international trade theory are considered in Chapters 4 and 5 but these have also had their effect on MNC research (Krugman 1987). Strategic trade theory now considers the ways in which firms themselves behave as key factors in the outcome. The larger, more powerful and independent-minded some of the trading organisations are, then the more the need to consider strategic and game-theoretic models of firm behaviour in this context.

Amongst the many aspects of the debates and disagreements about MNCs some areas of particular importance can be identified, e.g. the positive and negative effects of MNCs plus the possible regulation of them. The theory behind some of these arguments may be rather thin, but the ideas come thick and fast and the controversy about the role and operation of MNCs rages on.

The positive and negative effects of MNCs

It has been argued that MNCs are the ideal medium for spreading the advantages of modern technology and business methods world-wide. However, it has also been suggested that MNCs own huge resources and power, and with this comes the potential abuse of that power. The question then arises as to whose interest do MNCs serve? From a 'positive' or optimistic perspective, the following might be argued (Freeman 1981, pages 13–14).

1 MNCs serve the interests of the people who work for them; they are major employers who have increased employment and real wages at home and around the world substantially more quickly than non-international companies.
2 MNCs serve their shareholders.
3 MNCs serve their customers, by developing mass markets and thereby increasing efficiency, lowering costs and selling prices.
4 MNCs take technology to poorer countries; they are the equivalent of workhorses for the world.

The optimistic viewpoint of MNC behaviour can be seen within the arguments provided by Freeman. The companies are 'seeking the most efficient combinations of technology, people and resources to produce and distribute at the lowest possible cost to the consumer and with the highest profit to the shareholders' (Freeman 1981, page 15). Moreover, he claims that for MNCs, 'more and more companies are developing a global social conscience as their shares spread around the world and top management reflects the nationalities of the countries where they do business' (Freeman 1981, page 16). We could also add that **direct investment** can be advantageous to the host countries themselves as it provides new techniques of production, physical and financial capital, employment opportunities, social capital (e.g. roads) and external economies to other industries of the host economy.

This is a very optimistic viewpoint. A more critical view is to be found in Galbraith (1980). He notes:

A benign providence ... has made the modern industry of a few large firms an excellent instrument for inducing technical change ... Not only is development now sophisticated and costly but it must be on a sufficient scale so that successes and failures will in some measure balance out ... he power that enables the firm to have some influence on prices insures that the resulting gains will not be passed on to the public by imitators before the outlay for development can be recouped. In this way market power protects the incentive to technical development.

(Galbraith 1980, page 100)

A different approach to the behaviour of MNCs would look at some examples of unethical behaviour by some of the world's biggest MNCs. A few examples give the flavour of the argument.

The Swiss-based pharmaceutical giant Hoffman-LaRoche was brought to the attention of the European Commission for engaging in market-sharing and price fixing-activities which violated parts of the EC competition policy, and it was fined DM1 million for its breaches of these rules. Hoffman-LaRoche some-how found out the identity of the man from whom the information had been obtained, leading to his arrest under the Swiss industrial secrecy laws and ulti-mately a prison sentence. The questions raised by this case centre on the role played by Hoffman in generating huge profits from its illegal anti-competitive activities and in, apparently, pressurising EC officials to give up highly sensitive and confidential information (in this case on the informant). Deeper questions also arise. How typical is this example? Can the power, influence and financial 'muscle' of giant corporations be used to circumvent or subvert the proper process of regulation?

Another example of where an MNC's 'social conscience' has been ques-tioned is given by Nestlé, the Swiss confectionery giant, with its marketing of baby foods, especially powdered milk, in East Africa, despite the fact that the World Health Organisation and others have advocated that breast milk is far better than processed milk because of disease-resistance properties. Preparation of such milk also needs regular supplies of good drinking water, sterile bottles, teats and mixing equipment – conditions unlikely to prevail in most LDCs. Yet Nestlé still continues with its sales. When the first edition of this book was writ-ten, this example of the Nestlé baby food could have been considered as rather an old and tired accusation against Nestlé. However, the controversy is as flour-ishing today as it ever was. A WHO report which came out in the spring of 1997 severely criticised Nestlé for continuing to supply Third World families with baby formula, and Nestlé had to spend large sums defending itself.

Finally, one of the most tragic examples is that of the terrible accident at the US-owned Union Carbide plant at Bhopal in December 1984. On the tenth anniversary of the disaster, *The Economist* pointed out that it occurred 'as a result of slipshod management and a breakdown of safety procedure, water got into a tank of methyl isocyanate (MIC), a deadly cyanide gas, heating it and causing it to escape as a gas. It killed in the end almost 3,000 people; this was the worst ever industrial disaster' (*The Economist* 1994, pages 78–79). The tragedy of the deaths is shocking, but almost as shocking was the behaviour of Union Carbide in its attempts to avoid legal liability. In the end a settlement with the Bhopal victims 'for $470 million was reached, far less than even Carbide expected' (*The*

Economist 1994, page 78–9). This general critical stance suggests some of these huge and powerful organisations may simply see themselves and the pursuit of their corporate objectives as 'above the law' and may thus operate in ways which many find distasteful and unethical. Furthermore, their market power and relative size in comparison with some LDCs, plus their concentration, has led many to suggest that MNCs need to be monitored and regulated. There are only about 450 MNCs of significant size in the world but they almost entirely dominate 15 or so crucial industries such as petroleum, motor vehicles, electronics, electrical engineering, computers, aerospace, soaps and cosmetics, food, tobacco, beverages, rubber and paper.

Governments and MNCs – a case for action?

Many economists and business commentators would accept that some public policy is needed to monitor monopoly power and its abuse. Since 1890, when the US Congress passed the Sherman Act (the first legislation of its kind in the world), most industrialised societies have introduced some form of anti-trust or competition policy (see Chapter 8). To the extent that some government action is required to protect the public interest against potential abuse of power by 'domestic' monopolies and cartels, the argument for protection against those companies working across national economic boundaries (MNCs) would seem self-evident. A key myth about the MNCs is that they are like all other business enterprises in a market environment, in that they are subject to the disciplines of the market and in the fact that consumer sovereignty holds sway.

If MNCs are not subject to the 'normal' disciplines of the market, this may have crucial implications for the EU and especially the SEM. The advantages claimed from the SEM (see Chapter 9) hinge to a large degree on assumptions about efficiency gains to be achieved through rationalisation, restructuring and economies of scale, which are then expected to be passed on to consumers in improved quality and/or lower prices. European markets are characterised, at least in part, by the presence of many indigenous and foreign MNCs and, because of their size, doubts have been expressed about the ability of EU competition policy to control these. In other words, to ensure that firms across the whole of Europe enjoy the benefits of the new, freer, single market, competition is a prerequisite rather than monopoly power, which could be used and abused if uncontrolled.

Both Articles 85 and 86 (see Chapter 8) of the Treaty of Rome spell out the fundamentals of the EU's approach to promotion of competition and the regulation of anti-competitive elements. They stress that activities which would (adversely) 'affect trade between member states' are to be condemned. This adverse effect can be fairly narrowly construed – specifically to mean a reduction in the competitve conditions under which such trade is conducted – to judge whether or not such arrangements actually lead to an increase in trade or not. So a key factor in the EU policy *vis-à-vis* the conduct of businesses from the member states is that competition should not be compromised. It seems almost axiomatic that some of the operations of some of the world's very largest business organisations (i.e. the MNCs), would 'affect trade' in ways unacceptable to EU competition policy legislators and administrators. Moran (1996) states this point clearly: 'Not only do governments have to worry about economic distortion as a result of the behaviour of transnational corporations (TNCs), but they confront legitimate concerns about the impact of TNCs on national power and national autonomy, in particular in small and medium-sized countries.'

However, there is a different view of the role of MNCs *vis-à-vis* competition policy. Lecraw (1994) has suggested that the presence or arrival of 'foreign' MNCs could be highly beneficial for competition in domestic markets previously dominated by 'home-grown' monopolists, or colluding oligopolists. Lecraw even suggested that allocative efficiency in the 'host' economy might best be achieved by attracting more than one 'foreign' MNC and from different countries.

Frischtak (1994) further stresses the importance of entry barriers. Tariff and non-tarriff barriers exist in the EU for MNCs. This could well have an adverse effect on EU industrial efficiency as some vigorous newcomer MNCs could unsettle some complacent markets, so increasing general economic welfare.

Arguably there may be a case for governments to encourage the entry of 'new blood' MNCs. Perhaps a critical factor would be the relationship between the MNC and the host country government. Three 'great historical paradigms' are referred to by Moran (1996) concerning this: 'liberalism, neo-mercantilism and neo-imperialism' (page 418). The liberal tradition favoured market solutions to economic questions and relied on MNCs to deliver positive aspects (*cf.* Freeman (1981), cited above). Neo-mercantilists favoured government action to support domestic firms only, and subconsciously adhered to '**beggar-thy-neighbour trade policies**'. The neo-imperialist approach stressed the government's role in protecting domestic citizens and the nation's wider interests from exploitation by MNCs.

Using the neo-imperialist approach Sunkel took the Spanish word '*dependencia*' to describe the relationship between powerful developed and rich country-based MNCs and the exposed and exploitable developing world. He developed the thesis of Third World underdevelopment in the context of development for the visiting MNCs. The outcomes of the tensions between the powerful, and possibly disinterested, MNC and the weak but anxious-to-please developing country host government raises many disturbing questions.

The debate about government and MNC relations in developed countries is rather different. Here the neo-mercantilist paradigm arises again. Moran says there is a fundamental question here: 'What are the consequences for national power and national autonomy of allowing the globalization of the domestic market to proceed if globalization means a growing reliance on inward investment by foreign TNCs and increasing levels of outward investment by indigenous companies striving to become TNCs themselves?' (Moran 1996, page 426). In this context some of the issues raised in Chapter 8 are relevant – especially the question of whether governments can 'pick winners', and of the appropriate model of industry policy (see the Ferguson typology, Chapter 8).

Vernon (1971) argued that governments were increasingly feeling helpless in the face of raw MNC strength, but that the outcome could be a pooling of interests and autonomy between home and host governments in dealing with MNCs. Servan-Schreiber (1993) took the argument a stage further. Vernon had suggested that modern corporations could become more and more 'a-national', or stateless, in their pursuit of business objectives, whereas Servan-Schreiber thought it much more probable that MNCs would retain home links, and serve home country needs first and foremost. If European governments could not, or would not, encourage and support European MNCs then the new Europe could simply become a 'playground' for MNCs from other countries, notably the USA and Japan. The French, in particular, have sought to help their national 'champions' in just the way Servan-Schreiber outlines.

Most member states in fact have some interventionists, or *dirigistes*, who would build 'Euro-champions' through subsidies and mergers. EU Commissioner Leon Brittan's former department was quite forthright in its view of such subsidies and mergers. For example, British Aerospace was ordered to pay back the £44 million of government 'sweeteners' it received in connection with the purchase of Rover in 1988. Renault also had to hand back £600 million of French government aid, and Leon Brittan condemned Italian government aid for Fiat and French assistance to its national computer firm Bull. Given that the companies themselves are hardly likely to complain when they are given grants, hand-outs, subsidies or tax advantages by their home governments or any other government, it becomes clear that the task of trying to maintain 'proper' competitive behaviour among the giants is likely to be extremely problematic.

Moreover, there is another side to this question. Not only is there the difficulty of governments knowing which companies (as potential 'champion') to support, but the subsequent behaviour of the supported company could become problematic. 'The startling fact [is] that succesful national champion firms, once launched, exhibited a tendency to behave like their international competitors' (Moran 1996, page 427). Examples are many. Having accepted financial supports, Fiat then refused to co-operate with the Italian government in its expansion plans for the Mezzogiorno, the poor southern part of Italy, and built extra capacity in Brazil; Michelin similarly expanded outside France; and Philips ignored the Dutch government's pleas to help it alleviate Dutch unemployment and instead created more capacity in Asia, specifically in Singapore and Malaysia.

Governments and MNCs – is action possible?

There is obviously a good deal of concern at the possible ways in which MNCs may behave, and many calls for control over them to be exercised. However, even a stern critic of the abuse of MNC power like J. K. Galbraith recognised that sometimes giant firms are needed; large tasks, he has argued, require large organisations to undertake them, especially in the vital area of R&D.

In this respect there have been a number of international initiatives to exchange information and co-operate in the control of MNCs, such as the

OECD guidelines in 1976, the International Labour Organisation's declaration in 1977, and the UN code of conduct (abandoned in the late 1980s). These were all rather vague, with no binding elements in them, and not surprisingly they had little effect. 'It seems a plausible generalization from the record of the past four decades that intergovernmental agreements substantially affecting TNCs are unlikely to see the light of day unless they have the support of these firms themselves' (Vernon 1994, page 570).

Given this, what intervention is possible within the EU? Cowling and Sugden (1987) have suggested policies, some of which seem feasible, and others that seem impractical in the context of the SEM. MNCs which conduct a substantial amount of business, producing, selling or sourcing within a country could be controlled by host governments with threats to exclude the MNC from that country. Even to '**footloose**' giants this could possibly give governments very real leverage if, for example, the threat was to prohibit access to markets. The 'terms of trade' in such a relationship would depend upon the volume, value and significance to the company of the operation or activity being threatened, the sort of compliance required, and the importance of the company to the host economy. For example, a confectionery manufacturer in an EU member state might be in a weak bargaining position *vis-à-vis* the host government, if threatened by market exclusion. Hardly of strategic or other key importance to the host, the threat of lost sales could put the confectionery manufacturer in a weak position. On the other hand, an **inward direct investor** in a high-technology industry in a less developed or developing economy would, presumably, be in a much stronger bargaining position. To pull out of a country is always a possibility, but then clearly sales are lost. MNCs, however, are willing to pull out if they think fit. Coca-Cola, for example, has in the past ceased dealing in India, Nigeria and elsewhere to avoid host country interference, and the demand to disclose the secret formula to local partners.

For EU member states acting together, this 'denial of access' could be a very powerful threat indeed. Within the EU, Cowling and Sugden (1987, page 152) suggest:

> an international approach to the regulation of the transnationals is obviously desirable ... It is clear that a voluntary code of conduct for the transnationals is insufficient ... within the EC concern about de-industrialization could be used as a platform from which to advance a policy for effectively regulating the production and investment policy of the transnationals.

It is possible that the EU member states, acting in concert and with genuine commitment, could have the requisite economic and market muscle (countervailing power) to enforce appropriate MNC regulation. Establishing commitment to such a programme might be far from a simple process, let alone achieving consensus on the policies themselves. Should this agreement occur, however, the opposition of 'offended' MNCs would also come into the reckoning. Cowling and Sugden (1987) suggest that with strong, stable, growing domestic economies, governments can exercise some control over MNC management. Clearly the force of regulation outlined above and based on market access denial would be the more efficacious the larger, more stable and more attractive those markets were. So is such a policy occurring at least in part?

Dunning states:

> The European Commission does not have a policy towards MNE activity *per se*....The 'revealed' philosophy of its Secretariat is to downplay the significance of the nationality of ownership as a factor influencing the efficiency of intra-EC resource organisation and utilisation. [For example very little is said about inward or outward direct investment in Cecchini]. But through its various economic and social programmes, as agreed by the member countries, it can and does greatly influence the conditions affecting MNE activity.
>
> (Dunning 1993, page 398)

Thus the elements in the environment of business which the Commission may affect, the following may be included:

1 consumer protection

2 the protection of workers' interests

3 the maintenance of competition

4 acquisition and takeover rules

5 relations with developing countries

6 information release requirements.

Vernon and Dunning are probably both correct: Vernon in asserting that 'control' of MNCs can probably only exist with their cooperation, and Dunning in that the Commission can have a good deal of influence. The 'Vredeling' proposal could be a good example of the Commission learning that it needs MNC co-operation if 'controls' are to be accepted and to function sensibly.

The 'Vredeling' directive or proposal appeared in the early 1980s. Henk Vredeling, then Commissioner for Social and Labour Affairs, proposed that workers in MNCs should have some formalised rights to be consulted about decisions which directly concerned their jobs. As originally proposed, the directive suggested that any companies with more than one workplace, whether multinational or not, and with more than 100 employees, would be required to notify the workers' representatives of any changes involving working practices or closures at least 30 days in advance. Employers' organisations in Europe, and beyond, strongly objected. The case was made that such rules infringed management's right to manage, would damage industrial relations in the EU irreversibly, and might even 'choke off' some inward foreign direct investment, for example from Japan or the United States. These proposals, however, did not in fact suggest very much 'power sharing' in the decision-making processes of the companies to whom they would apply; the idea was more of a rather low level of 'information sharing'. Any decisions to close a plant in whole or in part, or plans to switch production entirely from one country to another, would remain as the prerogative of management alone. Such was the opposition to the proposals, however, that first they were 'revised' and subsequently 'buried'. Few now doubt that it was pressure from the MNCs that 'killed off' the Vredeling plans.

The Social Chapter has superseded the Vredeling proposals – but only partly. Key aspects of the Social Chapter, which would affect all businesses in Europe and not just MNCs, relate to conditions of service and not information disclosure. The Social Chapter does not, however, impose upon the management of Europe's

MNCs to anything like the extent that the Vredeling proposals would have done. Perhaps that is why MNC opposition to the Social Chapter, though vigorous, was much less determined than against Vredeling. We can reiterate Galbraith's paradoxical inquiry: how can MNCs be regulated if they control the regulators?

Another example of the influence of MNCs in national politics is given in Tolchin and Tolchin (1988). They refer to the actions of a group of foreign MNCs, including Sony, to get changes made in the tax rules of both Florida and California. Both states had introduced so-called 'unit taxation' to try to prevent MNCs from avoiding their true tax liabilities by the use of transfer pricing. After much hard lobbying and campaigning by the MNC consortium, the unit taxation schemes faded out. If the control of MNCs in the EU and USA can only be done 'by consent' it is not difficult to believe that in less developed economies the consent may be withheld, so that MNCs may effectively govern themselves.

The EU is both home and host to many multinationals. The Commission estimates that about one-third of the world's 200 largest MNCs have their headquarters in the EU. EU member states' attitudes and legislation show clear signs of conflicting views on MNC 'control', which arise from diverse economic, national, political and institutional factors. Their different attitudes may affect politically sensitive areas like wider employee participation and information, job protection and corporate disclosure. Generally the more open the economy the more friendly the approach by national governments to MNCs. Belgium is a favoured host of MNCs with its 'open' economy; nevertheless, union pressure makes Belgium a supporter of MNC legislation. The UK and Germany have adopted a more *laissez-faire* approach, particularly as the UK has much to lose if FDI is curbed, whilst France has been in favour of legislation against foreign MNCs but is not anxious to support legislation that might harm its own 'champions'. Ireland has pursued a policy of encouraging MNCs into its country and has often opposed EU legislation on international tax evasion and corporate group disclosure. The success story of the Irish economy in the 1990s owes a good deal to its long-standing policy of welcoming FDI with all sorts of incentives, not least in the boom area near Galway, and Shannon Airport (Chick 1990).

Finally, with regard to MNCs it could be argued there is a 'natural' contradiction in the EU's attitude to MNCs. The SEM (Chapter 9) and competition policy (and indeed the EU Industry Policy – see Chapter 8) all seek to ensure that the forces of competition can flourish in free markets. However, perhaps the greatest exponents of free-market behaviour – the MNCs – are limited by various directives. Is this another paradox, rather like that in competition policy; namely that competitive 'free' markets may require some government intervention if they are to function properly?

A paradigm for MNC analysis?

The orthodox or standard paradigm in the fields of industrial organisation and industrial economics is the so-called 'structure–conduct–performance' (SCP) model and this is derived directly from neo-classical theory.

In one of the earliest stages of the development of this approach, Berle and Means (1932), in their study of share ownership in large US companies, found evidence of widely 'scattered' share ownership, or 'divorce' of ownership and control. This led them to conclude that the managers of these companies would be able to exercise considerable discretion over the courses of action they would follow, their owners being at a long arm's length away. Specifically, they suggested managers might not seek to maximise profits. Attention thus was centred on the conduct of managers in their real rather than theoretical context. Although now many years old, Berle and Means' ideas can be seen to have potential applicability to MNC analysis – the managers of MNCs being arguably so powerful, and distant from their shareholders, that they may be almost laws unto themselves. The essence of the SCP model is summarised by Caves (1974):

> Elements of market structure constrain the behaviour of buyers and sellers in the market. Conduct comprises a systematic description of the ways sellers form their individual strategies and reconcile them in the market place ... performance refers to our normative appraisal of the resource allocations affected by market conduct subject to the constraints of market structure.

The full model is shown in Fig. 10.1, taken from Scherer and Ross (1990). In its original, 'basic' version the model assumes direct one-way causality. Structure affects conduct which then determines performance. Concentration and barriers to entry, usually seen as the two most important elements of structure, critically influence the conduct of firms – particularly price, output and promotion, which in turn affect price–cost margins and profitability.

The most fundamental criticism of this basic version of the model is the assumed directionality of causality, from structure to conduct to performance. It has been forcibly argued that causality may work in reverse too. A market structure including, for example, high barriers to entry is likely to promote at least some monopoly profit, which in turn may lead to higher advertising expenditure, and perhaps greater brand proliferation and consequently yet higher barriers. Conversely, market structures conducive to higher prices might attract new entrants, thus changing the structure. Reverse causality can occur, as shown in Fig. 10.2. Further, quite naturally, MNCs, with their extra degrees of market and political power, may be able to affect environmental/structural conditions significantly, particularly where the MNC is large relative to the host economy, such as a small LDC or NIC (see Fig. 10.3).

The agreement that the company makes with the host government can determine the firm's business environment within that country. If, for example, agreement can be reached to allow no competition from within, and absolute barriers (import restrictions and/or prohibition of rival FDI) also negotiated, then the business environment could be very 'relaxed' for the MNC. Even if the MNC or international business is thinking of expanding or diversifying into a mature developed industrial economy, the strategic thinking may well be along the lines of negotiating an operating environment that is as comfortable and convenient as possible. The FDI of Japanese companies around the world in the last two decades could be seen as illustrative of this. For example, Nissan, in seeking access to the UK and EC markets through its expansion in the north-east of England, obtained financial assistance and trade union support in the shaping of their commercial environment.

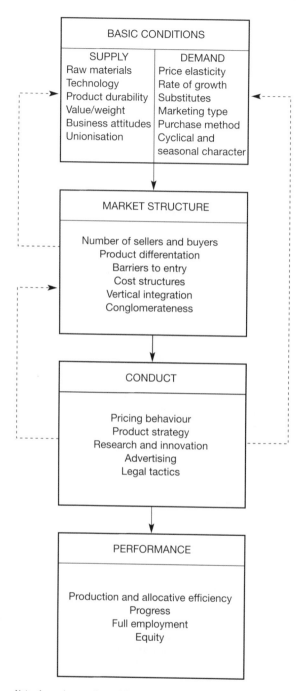

Note: As can be seen the model does include some reverse causality arrows; however, they are deemed to be weak relationships and, furthermore, do not go backwards from performance, which perhaps should be the case.

Figure 10.1 General version of SCP model (adapted from Scherer and Ross 1990)

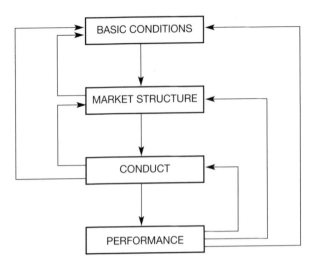

Figure 10.2 Revised model showing potential links backwards from performance (adapted from Scherer and Ross 1990)

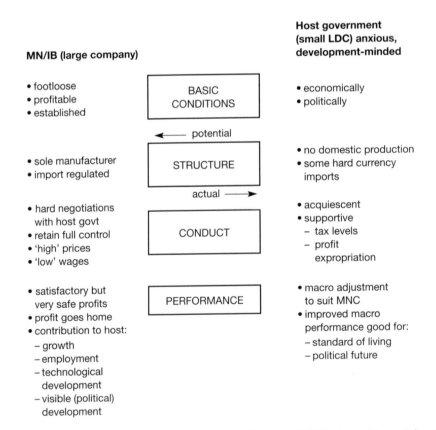

Figure 10.3 Model for an industrial MNC going to an LDC (adapted from Scherer and Ross 1990)

Frischtak and Newfarmer (1996) have developed a number of hypotheses relating to MNC performance, within the framework of the SCP model. They examine a number of hypotheses. The first of these hypotheses is that 'the distribution of benefits from FDI between host countries and TNCs depends fundamentally on the competitive structure of markets in the host country'(page 296). Their findings suggest there is a close correlation between FDI and host economy market concentration. However, they cannot decide whether this is because MNCs are attracted to highly concentrated markets, or because the arrival of large MNCs will naturally increase concentration levels. The assets that the MNC has typically make it more likely than national firms to engage in non-competitive conduct.

They further observe that many MNCs advertise more than their national counterparts. Is this an attempt to establish greater barriers to entry (the 'non-competitive behaviour referred to above), or are newly arriving firms naturally disposed to advertise more? On mergers and acquisitions, Frischtak and Newfarmer observe that contrary to some expectations, acquisition by foreign MNCs does not lead to more than usual asset stripping, and that MNC-acquired subsidiaries appear to perform as well as or better than other firms in their markets.

Frischtak and Newfarmer (1996) conclude their summary study with: 'a definitive assessment of the impact of TNCs on economic performance is not easy and perhaps not possible because the determinants of performance are multi-dimensional and complex' (page 310).

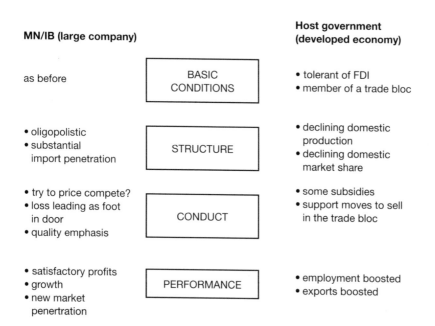

MN/IB (large company)   **Host government (developed economy)**

as before — BASIC CONDITIONS — • tolerant of FDI / • member of a trade bloc

• oligopolistic / • substantial import penetration — STRUCTURE — • declining domestic production / • declining domestic market share

• try to price compete? / • loss leading as foot in door / • quality emphasis — CONDUCT — • some subsidies / • support moves to sell in the trade bloc

• satisfactory profits / • growth / • new market penertration — PERFORMANCE — • employment boosted / • exports boosted

Figure 10.4 Model for an industrial MNC (e.g. Nissan) moving to an advanced economy (e.g. England) (adapted from Scherer and Ross 1990)

Conclusion

This chapter has considered the size and importance of MNCs in international trade and the debate aired as to their role and impact. Some optimistic attitudes towards MNCs have been contrasted with a more 'suspicious' approach and the ethics of MNC behaviour were questioned. There do seem to be grounds for suggesting that attempts should, and could, be made to regulate or control the operations of multinationals in the same way as monopolies and cartels are controlled by competition policy legislation.

The evidence from empirical work on the growth and profitability of MNCs is very mixed. The standard model used in industrial economics and industrial organisation studies for analysing company performance is the SCP paradigm. This is an applied version of the neo-classical theory of the firm. An adaptation of the SCP to include reverse causality links, whereby firms may affect their operating environments, is particularly important in the MNC context. Power of this type is open to potential abuse and may make it necessary for regulatory mechanisms to be put in place, either by individual governments or, even better if possible, by groups of governments working together. Within Europe, multinationals are clearly seen within the EU Commission, by the Secretariat, and by member states' governments as organisations that must operate within the standard rules of conduct.

Case study: Sports/training shoes

The UK consumer market for sports shoes has grown dramatically over the past 15 years and was worth nearly £1.5 billion in sales in 1994. Many people now own a pair of these shoes either for fitness or fashion purposes. However, the companies which market them (the five market leaders being Adidas, Hi-Tec, Nike, Puma and Reebok) do not actually make them. Instead they subcontract manufacture to LDCs: 99 per cent of such footwear manufacture, according to Nike, now takes place in Asia. For example, three countries – China, Thailand and the Philippines – sent £27 million worth of exports of such shoes to the UK in 1994.

This industry employs hundreds of thousands of workers, many young women – 75 000 are employed by subcontractors in Asia to make Nike shoes alone. One of the major reasons for subcontracting to these areas is the cheapness of the labour. According to Christian Aid calculations on a £50 pair of shoes, £1.50 would be paid as labour costs. This average, however, covers up the fact that the labour cost would be only £0.46 in China, £1.08 in the Philippines and £1.17 in Thailand. Furthermore, the Christian Aid report has suggested that there are other worrying factors in the treatment of labour in the production of such shoes: forced overtime, poor health and safety conditions, long hours and insufficient rest periods, lack of job security and discrimination against trade unions.

The response of the 'market leaders' to Christian Aid's concerns has been along three main lines:

1 'the workers are lucky',

2 'it is not the company's business' and

3 'they are dealing with the problem.'

Concerning (1), the Christain Aid report quotes Nike as saying, 'Nike impacts the lives of its subcontracted workers twice: as a client of their employer and as a participant in their country's economy. And in both roles, Nike's presence is a positive one' (Brookes and Madden 1995, page 19).

Regarding (2), Adidas explained, 'Today these products are manufactured by a large number of sub-contractors and licencees across the world, which most of the time do not have legal or financial ties with the Adidas Group. The absence of these ties limits the possibilities of intervention within these subcontracting companies.' Nike similarly replied, 'Well I think you should be asking that question of the United Nations ... I don't think it's something you can lay at a shoe company and say "You must accept responsibility for improving the social and living condtions of all employees".'

Finally, the following quotes are the response to (3). Reebok states, 'With large businesses you have the opportunity to change the way you operate and truly have an effect. As large companies you have the muscle to do it.' Nike points out, 'Nike expatriates investigated when they noticed a high number of workers being paid a training wage in Nike's Indonesian factories ... When the factories were questioned, there was a significant drop in the number of those employees.'

According to Christian Aid, 'Hi-Tec favours the first approach, Adidas the second and Reebok the third. Nike tends to use all three arguments simultaneously.'

Source: Brookes, B. and Madden, P. (1995) '*The Globe Trotting Sports Shoe*', 4 December, Christian Aid.

Question

1 Consider the responses of the various companies to points 1, 2 and 3 and comment on how well you feel they deal with the points raised in this case study.

Questions for discussion

1 Draw up a short list of reasons why the government of an advanced industrial economy would wish to encourage the growth of very large home-based companies, and another list of why they might wish to discourage the growth of such firms.

2 Cowling and Sugden (1987) suggest that governments could influence the behaviour of 'visiting' MNCs by threatening to deny them access to the host market for potential sales. Consider some companies for whom such restrictions could be effective and others for which such attempts at control would constitute idle threats.

3 Do you think MNCs increase or decrease levels of employment in countries

into which they move?

4 What impact has the Nissan plant near Sunderland had on employment in that area and on employment in the motor industry elsewhere in the UK?

5 Draw a chart along similar lines to Figs 10.3 and 10.4 to illustrate the possible impact of a large EU-based tractor manufacturer setting up in Zambia and one of a US-based high-tech company setting up in Spain.

6 One of the main rationales for MNCs as an organisational format for a company is to avoid the transaction costs of doing business through markets. Using the example of the motor industry, explain this proposition.

7 How might the provisions of the Social Chapter influence the decision of a TV manufacturing company based in Munich and thinking of setting up production facilities in the Netherlands and the UK?

8 Some argue that the study of large MNCs and their power is not really suitable for economic analysis. Would you agree or disagree and why?

Main reading

Dunning, J. H. (1993) *The Globalization of Business*, Routledge.

Ferguson, P. R. and Ferguson, G. J. (1988) *Industrial Economics: Issues and Perspectives*, 2nd edition, Macmillan.

Hay, D. A. and Morris, D. J. (1991) *Industrial Economics and Organization*, 2nd edition, Oxford University Press.

Hood, N. and Young, S. (1979) *The Economics of MNE*, Longman.

Additional reading

Berle, A. A. and Means, G. C. (1932) *Modern Corporation and Public Property*, MacMillan.

Caves, R. E. (1974) Industrial organization, in Dunning, J. H. (ed.) *Economic Analysis and the Multinational Enterprise*, Allen & Unwin.

Cecchini, P. (1988) *The European Challenge, 1992: The Benefits of a Single Market*, Wildwood House.

Chichilnisky, G. and Heal, G. (1986) *The Evolving International Economy*, Cambridge University Press.

Chick, M. (ed.) (1990) *Governments, Industries and Markets*, Edward Elgar.

Coase, R. (1937) The nature of the firm, *Economica* 4, pp. 386–405.

4Cowling, K. (1982) *Monopoly Capitalism*, Macmillan.

Cowling, K. and Sugden, R. (1987) *Transnational Monopoly Capitalism*, Wheatsheaf Books.

Dunning, J. H. and Sauvant, K. P. (1996) Introduction: transnational corporations in the world economy, in UNCTAD, *Transnational Corporations and World Development*, ITB Press.

The Economist (1994) Bhopal, ten years On, 3 December, pp. 78–9.

Fortune Magazine (1997) The Fortune global five hundred – the world's largest corporations, 4 August.

Freeman, O. L. (1981) *The Multinational Company: Instrument for World Growth*, Praeger.

Friedman, M. (1962) *Capitalism and Freedom*, University of Chicago Press.

Frischtak, C. R. (1994) From monopoly to rivalry: policies to realize the competitive potential of transnational corporations, in Frishtak, C. R. and Newfarmer, R. S. (eds)

Transnational Corporations: Market Structure and Industrial Performance, Vol. 15, UNLTNC, Routledge.

Frischtak, C. R. and Newfarmer, R. S. (1996) Market structure and industrial performance, in UNCTAD, *Transnational Corporations and World Development,* ITB Press.

Galbraith, J. K. (1974) *The New Industrial State,* 2nd edition, Penguin.

Galbraith, J. K. (1980) *American Capitalism,* new edition, Blackwell.

The Guardian, (1997) Shareholders shame Shell, 6 May.

Hannah, L. (1983) *The Rise of the Corporate Economy,* 2nd edition, Methuen.

Hymer, S. and Rowthorn, R. (1970) Multinational corporations and international oligopoly: the non-American challenge, in Kindleberger, C. P. (ed.) *The International Corporation,* MIT Press.

Krugman, P. R. (ed.) (1987) *Strategic Trade Policy and the New International Economics,* MIT Press.

Lecraw, D. (1994) Performance of transnational corporations in less developed countries, in Frischtak, C. R. and Newfarmer, R. S., (eds) *Transnational Corporations: Market Structure and Industrial Performance,* Vol. 15, UNLTNC, Routledge.

Moran, T. H. (1996) Governments and transnational corporations, in UNCTAD, *Transnational Corporations and World Development,* ITB Press.

Scherer, F. M. and Ross, D. (1990) *Industrial Market Structure and Economic Performance,* 3rd edition, Houghton Mifflin Co., Boston.

Servan-Schreiber, J. J. (1993) The American challenge, in Moran, T. H. (ed.) *Governments and Transnational Corporations,* UNLTNC, Routledge.

Sleuwagen, L. (1988) Multinationals, the European Community and Belgium; the small country case, in Dunning, J. and Robson, P. (eds) *Multinationals and the European Community,* Blackwell.

Tolchin, M. and Tolchin, S. (1988) *Buying into America: How Foreign Money is Changing the Face of Our Nation,* Times Books.

UNCTAD (1996) *Transnational Corporations and World Development.*

United Nations (1988) *Transnational Corporations in World Development,* UN.

Vernon, R. (1971) *Sovereignty at Bay: The Multinational Spread of US Enterprises,* Basic Books, New York.

Vernon, R. (1994) Research on transnational corporations: shredding old paradigms, *Transnational Corporations,* Vol. 3.

Williamson, O. E. (1963) Managerial discretion and business behaviour, *American Economic Review,* Vol. 53, pp. 1032–57.

11

Foreign direct investment

Introduction

Many see both trade and foreign investment as being all about markets. A local market can be serviced by local investment, production and sales, or by imports. A foreign market can be serviced either by investing and producing domestically and then exporting or by investing, producing and selling directly into that market. In practice, international firms utilise different combinations of these two possibilities. Thus trade and FDI are sometimes competing and sometimes complementary ways of servicing a foreign market (Julius 1993). Others consider that reasons for FDI are far more complex.

Foreign direct investment (FDI) by multinational companies (MNCs) is one of the most controversial subjects within economics (see Chapter 10). The less developed countries (LDCs) seem both to oppose and to flirt with it, and the developed countries (DCs) try to limit its outflow sometimes and its inflow at other times. Some see FDI as the key to various global problems such as famine, starvation and environmental damage; yet others regard FDI as the very instrument through which these disasters are globally inflicted. This chapter looks at all these questions.

Definition

It is difficult to provide a comprehensive definition of FDI. Some authors define it in terms of its international characteristics and contrast it with **portfolio investment**; others express it in terms of the activities of MNCs. Most definitions, however, seem to have two common elements. One is that FDI involves at least two countries. This criterion relates to the multinational character of FDI. The other is the issue of ownership and control, which distinguishes FDI from portfolio investment. Foreign portfolio investment is a simple transfer of financial capital – equity or loan – from one country to another, whereas FDI involves the ownership and control of production activities abroad. Needless to say, what constitutes ownership and/or control is itself a controversial issue.

FDI is more complex in nature than portfolio investment since it often involves the transfer of inputs such as technical know-how, managerial and organisational ability, and so on. Moreover, when the necessary finance is raised locally there is no capital flow at all, at least not in a strict sense. Finally, FDI is embodied in the activities of MNCs. Therefore the definition of FDI cannot be practically considered in isolation from the definition of a MNC, which is also difficult to establish (see Chapter 10).

Despite these difficulties it is necessary to define FDI one way or another partly for theoretical clarity and partly for empirical necessity. For our purpose it is sufficient to define FDI as the acquisition, establishment or increase in production facilities by a firm in a foreign country. What distinguishes FDI from portfolio investment – in the case of acquisition – is that the investing firm acquires enough equity to exercise control over the capital invested (Baker 1990). What proportion of equity is needed to have control is, of course, a matter of judgement. Outward FDI implies an increase in the overseas operations of MNCs, e.g. British firms investing abroad. Conversely, inward FDI also means an increase in the business activities of foreign MNCs in the host country, e.g. foreign firms expanding business into the UK.

Historical pattern of FDI

The analysis of the role of foreign investment becomes increasingly difficult as we go back in time. However, despite the difficulties, it is clear that the role of foreign investment has been important since the Industrial Revolution.

The pre-First World War period

In the period before the First World War there was considerable movement of capital investment and, until recently, it was thought that most of this consisted of portfolio investment. However, more recent research indicates that the role of direct investment was much more important than assumed previously. FDI from the UK amounted to approximately 7 per cent of its national income. The other important capital-exporting countries of Europe were France and Germany, and to a lesser extent Italy, the Netherlands, Sweden and Switzerland. A substantial amount of UK capital went into railways and government securities in the countries of the Americas and Australasia, and was mainly in portfolio investment. However, by 1914, 40 per cent of British overseas investment in the LDCs and America was direct investment (Hood and Young 1979).

It has been estimated that, by 1914, the cumulative FDI in the world was at least $14 billion, which represented around 35 per cent of the world's long-term debt. Table 11.1 indicates that in 1914 the UK was by far the largest exporter of FDI with 45.5 per cent, followed by the USA with 18.5 per cent.

The share of the European countries, not including the UK, was over 30 per cent. Europe including the UK accounted for more than three-quarters of the total FDI in the world in 1914. This was the heyday of European imperialism! What is not clear from Table 11.1 is that Europe concentrated on venture capital, i.e. foreign production activities were controlled by acquiring sufficient equity capital. European countries were already the main source of portfolio capital outflows. In contrast, US companies used their comparative advantage in technology and management skills to establish affiliates of the home MNC

Table 11.1 Percentage shares of cumulative FDI outflows by country

	1914	1938	1960	1971	1981–88[a]
UK	45.5	39.8	16.2	13.8	21.4
Germany	10.5	1.3	1.2	4.2	8.5
France	12.2	9.5	6.1	4.2	7.2
Belgium	–	–	1.9	1.4	n.a.
Italy	} 8.9	} 13.3	1.6	1.7	2.4
Netherlands			10.5	8.0	6.6
Sweden			0.6	1.4	2.0
Switzerland			3.0	5.5	1.6
Australia	1.3[b]	1.1[b]	2.2[b]	1.4[b]	3.1[b]
Japan	0.1	2.8	0.7	4.4	16.7
USA	18.5	27.7	49.2	48.1	21.6
Other	3.0	4.5	6.8	5.9	8.9
Total	100.0	100.0	100.0	100.0	100.0

[a] OECD total.
[b] Includes New Zealand and South Africa.

Sources: Dunning (1983), page 87; OECD (1989) *International Direct Investment and New Economic Environment*, page 60.

overseas. Another point worth noting is that FDI was largely concentrated in capital-intensive primary product and technology-intensive manufacturing sectors. More than 80 per cent of this investment went to what would be considered as LDCs by contemporary criteria; by 1978 this figure was less than one-third (Dunning 1983). However, the bulk of FDI in the LDCs was in the extractive and agricultural sectors, such as rubber, tea, coffee and cocoa plantations, as well as in cattle raising and meat processing. A single cash crop which dominated a country's economy was a particular favourite with the MNCs of the time, e.g. sugar (Cuba), bananas (Costa Rica), tea (Ceylon) and rubber (Liberia). Thus it is possible to observe a parallel between the pattern of FDI and that of colonialism. For example, 72 per cent of US investment was in the American continent, and much of British, French and Dutch investment in the extractive and agricultural sectors was in their respective colonies. In contrast, the breakdown of manufacturing subsidiaries of MNCs by country of location before 1914 indicates that around 80 per cent of the subsidiaries established by US, UK and continental European-based MNCs was in the developed countries (Dunning 1983).

The inter-war period

The inter-war years witnessed a slowdown in the expansion of international business, including capital exports. Britain was still the main creditor country, but continental Europe changed from net creditor to net debtor status by the 1920s because of war debts and reconstruction costs after the First World War. Conversely, the US position was reversed from that of a debtor to that of a creditor. During the 1930s, capital flows in general reduced drastically following the collapse of international capital markets in the late 1920s and early 1930s.

Nevertheless, the FDI of the USA increased its share of the world total because it was in the form of branch plant activities by MNCs as opposed to equity capital. Thus the US share of the world capital stock rose from 18.5 per cent in 1914 to 27.7 per cent in 1938, as can be seen from Table 11.1. In fact FDI overall increased in the inter-war period, in contrast to portfolio investment. There were also some quantitative changes. Firstly, the LDCs increased their share of FDI slightly, with Asia and Africa increasing their shares at the expense of Latin America. However, the latter was still by far the largest recipient of FDI. Secondly, there was a noticeable amount of new MNC activity in the LDCs, in such sectors as oil (Gulf of Mexico, Dutch East Indies and Middle East), copper and iron ore (Africa), bauxite (Dutch and British Guiana), nitrate (Chile), precious metals (South Africa), and most noteworthy, non-ferrous metals (South America). Indeed, according to some observers most of the mineral resources in South America were owned by US interests. Finally, FDI between the DCs was gaining in importance. There were substantial flows of US capital into Canada and Europe in addition to South America. Indeed, investment from continental European firms went mainly to the other parts of Europe and the USA, and the first four manufacturing affiliates of the largest Japanese MNCs existing in 1970 appeared in this period (Dunning 1983).

The post-war period

After the Second World War, FDI dominated capital movements. The dominant position of FDI was mainly due to the increase in US capital outflows up to the 1960s, after which FDI from Europe, Japan and the newly industrialised countries (NICs) began to play an increasingly important role. In the 1950s and the 1960s, the Marshall Plan, the formation of the EEC, the IMF, the GATT, and the revolutionary developments in communication and transport, such as the computer and the jet aircraft, were all contributory factors for the phenomenal increase in FDI from the USA. Of about a $40 billion increase in total FDI world-wide between 1938 and 1960, the USA accounted for about two-thirds, which increased its cumulative share of world capital stock from 27.7 per cent to 49.2 per cent, whereas the share of Western Europe declined from 63.9 per cent to 41.1 per cent (see Table 11.1).

However, some radical changes had also taken place in the composition of FDI in the aftermath of the Second World War. In 1914, nearly two-thirds of new FDI was still going to the LDCs; by 1938 this had fallen to 55 per cent; and in 1960 it was around 40 per cent. This was mainly due to another structural change in FDI: in 1914 only 15 per cent of the US and UK accumulated investment was in manufacturing, but by 1960 this had risen to 35 per cent. By contrast, the proportion of UK and US FDI going to agricultural and public utility activities declined drastically between 1914 and 1960. It should be noted, however, that investment in non-ferrous metals by UK and US MNCs was an exception to this trend, since investment in, for example, copper (Chile and Peru), bauxite (in the Caribbean) and particularly oil (in the Persian Gulf) grew very rapidly (Dunning 1983).

Recent developments

Recent years have witnessed increased globalisation of the world economy, helped by technological development as well as the liberalisation and privatisation policies followed by many governments in the 1980s. In parallel, MNCs have assumed an increasingly important role in the global economy, accounting for some 80 per cent of world trade and an equal proportion of private R&D expenditure (Dunning 1993). Consequently, FDI has grown dramatically in recent years, reaching unprecedented levels in 1995 (see Table 11.2). In addition to this quantitative increase, the composition and the geographical distribution of FDI has also changed in recent years. One significant development regarding FDI is the increase in its relative importance in national economies in both capital-exporting and capital-importing countries.

Two measures of the importance of inward FDI to an economy are the ratio of FDI to the gross domestic product (GDP) and the ratio of FDI to gross fixed capital formation (GFCF). From Table 11.3 we can see that both FDI inflows and outward stock have grown much faster than either the GDP or GFCF, which indicates an increase in the two ratios concerned, which in turn implies an increase in the relative importance of FDI.

Table 11.3 indicates that the FDI inflow in the world increased on average by 29 per cent per annum in the 1983–87 period. This growth slowed down substantially in the 1988–92 period, going down to 1 per cent mainly due to the recession, but picking up again to increase to 24 per cent in the following period of 1993–95 and reaching a staggering 40 per cent in 1995. A similar picture can be observed regarding outflows. The table shows that around two-thirds of FDI inflows and four-fifths of outflows are accounted for by developed countries. However, the importance of developed countries is decreasing and that of developing countries is increasing. This is reflected in the declining shares of developed countries in both inflows and outflows from 76 per cent and 95 per cent, respectively, in 1983–87 to 62 per cent and 85 per cent in 1993–95. The corresponding shares of developing countries have increased

Table 11.2 The importance of FDI

Item	Value at current prices, 1995 ($ billion)	Annual growth rate (%)	
		1986–90	1991–94
FDI inflows	315	24.7	12.7
FDI outward stock	2730	19.8	8.8
GDP at factor cost	24948[a]	10.8	4.3
Gross fixed capital formation (GFCF)	5681[b]	10.6	4.0
Exports of goods and services	4707[c]	14.3	3.8[d]

[a]1994
[b]1994
[c]1993
[d]1991–93

Source: UN: *World Investment Report* (1996), table 1.1, page 4.

Table 11.3 FDI inflows and outflows 1983–95

	Developing countries		Developed countries		Central and Eastern Europe		All	
	Inflow	Outflow	Inflow	Outflow	Inflow	Outflow	Inflow	Outflow
Value ($ billion)								
!983–87	58.7	72.6	18.3	4.2	0.02	0.01	77.1	76.8
1988–92	139.1	193.3	36.8	15.2	1.36	0.04	177.3	208.5
1993	129.3	192.4	73.1	33.0	5.59	0.20	207.9	225.5
1994	132.8	190.9	87.0	38.6	5.89	0.55	225.7	230.0
1995	203.2	270.5	99.7	47.0	12.08	0.30	314.9	317.8
Share in total (%)								
1983–87	76	95	24	5	0.02	0.01	100	100
1988–92	78	93	21	7	0.77	0.02	100	100
1993	62	85	35	15	2.70	0.09	100	100
1994	59	83	39	17	2.60	0.24	100	100
1995	65	85	32	15	3.80	0.09	100	100
Growth rate (%)								
1983–87	37	35	9	24	–7	68	29	35
1988–92	–4	3	15	16	298	46	1	4
1993	13	6	45	52	46	99	24	11
1994	3	–1	19	17	7	179	9	2
1995	53	42	15	22	106	–45	40	38

Source: UN: World Investment Report, (1996) Table 1.2, page 4.

from 24 per cent and 5 per cent in 1983–87 to 35 per cent and 15 per cent in 1993–95. There has been a similar increase in the shares of Central and Eastern European countries as well. This means that there has been a widening of participation of source countries as far as the stock of outflows is concerned.

As for the geographical distribution of inward FDI within the developing world there has been a shift away from Latin American, the Caribbean and most African countries in favour of East and South Asia. It has also become highly concentrated. The ten biggest FDI recipients received 68 per cent of the total in 1995, whereas the share of the 100 smallest recipients has remained at only around 1 per cent in the same period (UN 1996).

The structure of FDI has also changed profoundly in recent years. There has been a considerable shift in FDI stock away from natural resources towards services. In 1970, only 31 per cent of the world FDI stock was in services, compared with 23 per cent in natural resources. The share of services rose to 50 per cent and that of natural resources declined to 11 per cent in 1990 (UN 1996, page 10).

Finally, an important feature of FDI in recent years has been that its pattern has started increasingly to resemble that of international trade. On the one hand, many countries, particularly the Triad countries (the EU, the USA and Japan), are engaging in both inward and outward investment in a more balanced way, and on the other hand, FDI and trade are becoming more and more complements for each other rather than substitutes (Dunning 1993).

Theories of FDI

The complexities of FDI make it rather difficult to fit it into one neat theory. Firstly, there is the problem of definition, as discussed above. It is necessary to know exactly what is to be explained before a rigorously testable hypothesis can be developed. Secondly, any theory of FDI is almost inevitably a theory of MNCs as well, and thus inseparable from the theory of the firm. Thirdly, the nature of FDI makes it a multidimensional subject within the sphere of economics as well as an interdisciplinary one. It involves the theory of the firm, distribution theory, capital theory, trade theory and international finance as well as the disciplines of sociology and politics. Consequently, there have been many explanations of FDI, but it is not possible to identify any single theory of FDI.

Neither is it easy to classify these explanations into distinct and neat groups, because there is substantial overlapping between some of the explanations. Nevertheless, it is possible to group these theories into three broad categories: traditional theories, modern theories and radical theories. Traditional theories are based on neo-classical economic theory and explain FDI in terms of location-specific advantages. Modern theories emphasise the fact that product and factor markets are imperfect both domestically and internationally, and that considerable transaction costs are involved in market solutions. They also acknowledge that managerial and organisational functions play an important role in undertaking FDI. Radical theories, however, take a more critical view of MNCs. Before considering the theories of FDI it is useful to examine ownership, location and internalisation advantages, which are sometimes referred to as the paradigm of OLI in the literature.

The paradigm of ownership, location and internalisation (OLI)

There are three different types of advantage which are assumed by some to be necessary to explain the activities of MNCs: ownership advantage, location advantage and internalisation advantage.

Ownership-specific advantages (**OSA**) refer to certain types of knowledge and privileges which a firm possesses but which are not available to its competitors. These advantages arise because of the imperfections in commodity and factor markets. Such imperfections in commodity markets include product differentiation, collusion, and special marketing skills, and in factor markets appear in the form of special managerial skills, differences in access to capital markets, and technology protected by patents. Imperfect markets may also arise from the existence of internal or external economies of scale or from government policies regarding taxes, interest rates and exchange rates, for example. These market imperfections give rise to certain ownership-specific advantages, which can be grouped under the following headings:

1 *Technical advantages* include holding production secrets such as patents, or unavailable technology or management–organisational techniques.

2 *Industrial organisation* relates to the advantages arising from operating in an oligopolistic market such as those associated with joint R&D and economies of scale.

3 *Financial and monetary advantages* include preferential access to capital markets so as to obtain cheaper capital.

4 *Access to raw materials* if a firm gains privileged access to raw materials or minerals then this becomes an ownership-specific advantage (Hood and Young 1979).

Location-specific advantages (LSA) refer to certain advantages which the firm has because it locates its production activities in a particular area:

1 *Access to raw materials or minerals* this normally represents an LSA. This advantage, however, applies to all the firms established in the locality and is not sufficient to explain FDI in itself.

2 *Imperfections in international labour markets* these create real wage-cost differentials which provide an incentive for the MNC to shift production to locations where labour costs are low. An example of this is electronics component firms using South East Asian locations for assembly production.

3 *Trade barriers* these provide an incentive for MNCs to set up production in certain locations. For example, Japanese MNCs may wish to produce in Europe to avoid the CET. Similarly, high Canadian tariff barriers have been used in the past to attract US direct investment.

4 *Government policies* such as taxation and interest rate policies can influence the location of FDI.

Internalisation-specific advantages (ISA) occur when international market imperfections make market solutions too costly. The idea is that the market is too costly or inefficient to undertake certain types of transaction, so whenever transactions can be organised and carried out more cheaply within the firm than through the market they will be internalised and undertaken by the firm itself.

The benefits of internalisation can be grouped under three headings:

1 The advantages of vertical integration cover such things as exploitation of market power through price discrimination and avoidance of government intervention by devices such as transfer pricing.

2 The importance of intermediate products for research-intensive activity: the firm appropriates the returns on its investment in the production of new technology by internalising technology.

3 The internalisation of human skills keeps the benefits of training, etc., particularly in high-return areas such as marketing and finance, within the firm.

However, internalisation is not entirely costless. It creates communication, co-ordination and control problems. There is also the cost of acquiring local knowledge.

The various theories of FDI in relation to the paradigm of OLI can now be examined.

Traditional theories of FDI

Capital arbitrage theory

This theory was developed in parallel with orthodox trade theory and eventually integrated with it by Samuelson. It states that direct investment flows from countries where its profitability is low to countries where it is high. It follows the same pattern as portfolio investment, which flows from low-interest countries to high-interest countries. The theory therefore assumes that capital is mobile both nationally (across industries) and internationally (across national boundaries).

Some interesting implications follow from the above hypothesis. Firstly, capital-abundant countries should export capital and capital-scarce countries should import capital. Secondly, if capital arbitrage were all there is to FDI then one would expect large financial intermediaries to be prominent among MNCs. Thirdly, given the link between the long-term interest rate and return on capital, portfolio investment and FDI should be moving in the same direction.

The reality, however, suggests differently. Firstly, some countries, such as the UK, are both a source of, and a host to, FDI. This could be explained by the different rates of return on capital between industries within the country; that is, FDI flows into some industries and out of others. This, however, would require segmentation of capital markets to an unrealistic degree. Secondly, most MNCs are non-financial companies, and their profits do not seem to be related to the long-term rate of interest. Thirdly, portfolio investment and FDI do not always move in the same direction. For example, the USA is well known to have been a net exporter of FDI at the same time as being a net importer of equity capital.

FDI and international trade theory

Orthodox theory of trade originally did not have much to say about FDI. In fact, the theory of capital movements was developed in parallel with the trade theory. For example, the Heckscher–Ohlin (H–O) model (see Chapter 4), does not deal with the subject of FDI in any explicit way. The model established the proposition that countries will specialise in the production of, and export, those commodities which make intensive use of the country's relatively abundant factor. One of the assumptions of the model is that factors of production are mobile across industries within the country but immobile across national boundaries.

Thus FDI is ruled out in the model. Indeed, there is no need for FDI, since international exchange of commodities renders international movements of capital unnecessary. It is interesting to note that if the assumption is reversed and it is assumed instead that factors are internationally mobile but commodities are not, we would be back in the realm of the capital arbitrage hypothesis.

Modern theories of FDI

Quite independently from these developments in the theory of international trade, some researchers were concentrating on FDI investment from a different perspective. Hymer's (1976) pioneering study, and others that followed, focused on particular kinds of ownership advantages. These developments took place in parallel with the dramatic increase in the activities of MNCs in the decades that followed the Second World War.

The Hymerian view

Hymer (1976) was one of the first authors to bring together both the LSAs and OSAs in an explanation of FDI. Hymer saw the MNC as a monopolist/oligopolist in product markets, investing in foreign enterprises in order to eliminate competition. The MNC was able to compete in a foreign market because it possessed an advantage over the domestic firms. Such an advantage could arise from imperfections in commodity or factor markets. The presence of OSAs to compensate for the LSAs of domestic firms explains foreign involvement, but not why it is in the form of FDI. The answer is that FDI is preferable to exports because of tariff barriers and transport costs. It is also preferable to licensing because the franchisee is a potential competitor and because the franchiser loses some control.

Hymer's approach is particularly useful in explaining the pattern of 'defensive' investment. Large companies seem to establish subsidiaries, often not so profitable, with the sole purpose of shutting competitors out. For instance, Pepsi-Cola might open up factories in a country because if it does not, Coca-Cola will.

The Hymerian interpretation is that FDI is an instrument for MNCs to exercise oligopolistic power and to manipulate the market. In fact, Hymer suggested that the MNC is an instrument through which wealth and power are channelled away from 'peripheral' to 'central nations', i.e., from the 'Southern' to the 'Northern' nations. The policy implication of this view is that the governments of host countries should take the necessary steps to prevent MNCs from such manipulation and exploitation (see Chapter 10).

The product-cycle model

Another theory of FDI that shows the interactions between the OSAs and the LSAs is the product-cycle theory of Vernon (1966) (see also Chapter 4). New products appear first in the most advanced economy – the USA – in response to demand conditions. The 'maturing product' stage is characterised by standardisation of the product, increased economies of scale, high demand and low price. At this stage other advanced economies also start producing the commodity, partly via US FDI. The 'standardised product' stage is reached when the commodity is sold entirely on the basis of price. Thus the main concern is now to produce it as cheaply as possible, and this is when the production moves to the LDCs, where labour is relatively cheap.

This theory explains well the US 'offshore production' in low labour-cost countries. However, the validity of this theory has somewhat declined. One reason is that the USA no longer has the totally dominant position regarding FDI. The MNCs of Europe, Japan and the NICs also require explanation. Moreover, MNCs are now capable of developing, maturing and standardising products almost simultaneously. Thus Vernon modified his earlier model mainly to overcome the first criticism; in this modified version, MNCs adapt in order to prevent entry into the industry by new firms.

The internalisation theories of FDI

Although the concept of internalisation was first introduced by Coase in the 1930s, Buckley and Casson (1985) were the first to incorporate the ISAs into the main analysis of FDI in the 1970s. It was no coincidence that at the time FDI was growing in high-technology-intensive manufacturing industries, where the integration of R&D with production and marketing is crucial. Buckley and Casson emphasised the importance of imperfections in the intermediate product markets, particularly those of patented technical knowledge and human capital. Such imperfections provide an incentive for the firm to internalise, say, the knowledge market. The incentive to internalise depends on the relationship between four groups of factors:

1 Industry-specific factors, e.g. economies of scale, external market structure, etc;
2 Region-specific factors, e.g. geographical distance and cultural differences;
3 Nation-specific factors, e.g. political and fiscal conditions (leading to possible transfer pricing);
4 Firm-specific factors, for example, management expertise.

Clearly, internalisation is as much a characteristic of a multiplant uninational firm as of a multinational firm.

The second theory which makes use of the concept of internalisation is the theory of appropriability. In this theory the key firm-specific advantage which results in FDI occurs in a key input market, such as its managerial excellence or a patent on an invention. Such an advantage does not provide any monopoly power in the product market, but it enables the firm to acquire economic gains. The firm decides to engage in FDI because the best way of appropriating the potential gains from its advantage is to keep control and ownership of the advantage to itself. This theory explains why there is a strong presence of high-technology industries among MNCs. The policy implication of the theory is that host countries should either leave FDI alone or positively encourage it.

The eclectic theory of FDI

Dunning's (1981, 1983) eclectic theory attempts to integrate the Hymerian view with the concept of internalisation and claims that all three types of advantage are required for MNCs to exist. Many theories of FDI start with the question: why does a firm extend its activities to other countries? Dunning's answer to this question is that there are LSAs to be enjoyed in the host country. The second question is how could a foreign firm compete with the domestic firms of the host country? Dunning's answer to this question is the OSAs. These answers inevitably lead to a third question: why should the firm choose FDI instead of exporting or licensing? The answer, of course, is the ISAs.

It is clear that the three advantages are sufficient to explain FDI. However, are they necessary? The answer seems to be no, because the LSAs and the ISAs seem to be sufficient to explain MNCs, thus rendering the OSAs redundant. In fact, some people claim that the concept of internalisation alone is sufficient to explain MNC activity, and indeed the theory of internalisation is the theory of FDI.

The radical explanations of FDI

Unlike orthodox economists, who view the MNC as the most efficient vehicle for both the optimal allocation of resources and the efficient distribution of products internationally, radical economists view MNCs as instruments of economic exploitation, political instability (in the LDCs), and environmental damage due to their relentless search for profits and enormous economic and political power (see Chapter 10).

It is easy to see the reasons for such concerns. Although the bulk of the activities of the MNCs takes place among the developed countries and only a small proportion relates to the LDCs, the former is a two-way whereas the latter is a one-way relationship. In other words, inflows and outflows of the developed countries more or less balance each other out, whereas the inflows of FDI to the LDCs are well in excess of the outflows from these countries. Yet there seems to be a net transfer of resources from the LDCs to the DCs.

FDI in the European Union

FDI in Western Europe is part of a complex world-wide network of FDI, involving investments originating outside the European Union, for example covering the USA, Japan and South Korea (referred to as **extra-EU FDI**); Western European investments outside the EU; and flows of investment within the European Union (referred to as **intra-EU FDI**). This network is growing with bewildering speed, and data on FDI are imperfect, especially for Europe as compared with the USA and Japan. What follows then is very much an introduction to a rapidly changing scene.

Scope of FDI in Western Europe.

The first main source of FDI in Western Europe was the USA (see earlier). US investment started to be significant in the inter-war period (for example Ford's factory at Dagenham in the UK) but really grew in the 1950s and 1960s, partly due to the formation of the EC. Although this caused a great stir at the time, Europe was not the major recipient of US investment. In 1960, for example, 57.4 per cent of US direct investment in industrial countries went to Canada and only 34.2 per cent to Europe (Sleuwagen 1988). By 1985, 55 per cent of US investment was going to Europe, but the USA was now a net recipient of European investment and the stock of European investment in the USA exceeded that of US investment in Europe by 1985.

In recent years the role of the USA in foreign direct investment in the EU has been taken over to some extent by other countries; notably Japan, but also increasingly by other East Asian countries such as South Korea and Taiwan. The stock of Japanese FDI in the EU grew from $712 million in 1971 to $26957 million in 1993 (Dunning and Cantwell 1991; Dunning 1997a). Europe still represents, however, a comparatively small part of Japanese investment abroad. In 1987 only 14.1 per cent of Japan's stock of outward FDI consisted of investment in the European Union. In 1988 the estimated value of sales of Japanese manufacturing affiliates in the EU was only about 20 per cent of direct exports from Japan to Europe (as compared with a figure of 500 per cent for US affiliates) (Dunning and Cantwell 1991). An indication of the relative importance of investment in the European Union for different countries is given in Table 11.4, adapted from Dunning 1997a).

Note that the **intensity ratio** is defined in this context as the ratio of the share of the EU in the total FDI coming from another region to the share of the EU in total world FDI (excluding that coming from the investor region). If the ratio is more than unity it means that the investor region is investing more intensively in the EU than in other areas; if it is less than unity the reverse is the case.

It can be seen from Table 11.4 that the 1980s saw a tendency for countries to invest relatively more in the EU compared with other areas of the world. This tendency applies to both EU countries and to the USA and Japan. However, Japanese

Table 11.4 Intensity ratios of selected foreign investing countries in the EU, early 1980s–92

Investor country	Year	Intensity ratio
Belgium/Luxembourg	1980	1.65
	1988	n.a.
Denmark	1982	1.31
	1991	1.42
France	1982	1.00
	1991	1.37
Germany	1980	1.02
	1992	1.19
Italy	1980	n.a.
	1992	1.52
Netherlands	1984	0.89
	1992	1.03
United Kingdom	1981	0.50
	1992	0.58
Portugal	1985	1.23
	1988	n.a.
Spain	1984	n.a.
	1989	1.39
United States	1980	0.60
	1990	0.73
Canada	1980	0.45
	1990	0.45
Japan	1980	0.30
	1990	0.38

Source: Adapted from Dunning (1997a) table 5, page 18.

investment is still significantly less centred on the EU than US investment. For example, the intensity ratio for Japanese investment in North America rose from 0.98 in 1980 to 1.26 in 1990 (Dunning 1997a). Both figures were considerably more than the equivalent ones for the EU shown in the table.

Distribution of investment within the European Union

An important question is whether FDI is concentrated in a relatively small number of favoured EU countries, or whether it is distributed more widely. Table 11.5 provides some information relating to this for the 12 EU member countries prior to 1995.

It can be seen that inward investment is concentrated very much in the countries that Dunning refers to as the '**core countries**', which in general are those with the highest incomes in the EU. This concentration actually increased in the late 1980s, although this trend was reversed in the 1990s, largely because of a large increase in investment in Spain.

This concentration of investment held for investment from both the USA and Japan. From 1991 to 1993, for example, 20.3 per cent of Japanese FDI was directed to the then 12 members of the EU. Of this, 18.8 per cent went to the core EU countries. The corresponding figures for US investment were 44.2 per cent and 40.1 per cent (Dunning 1997a). The UK was the most favoured EU location for both Japanese and US investors, followed by the Netherlands for Japan, and Germany and France for the USA.

The one country from among the EU members outside the core to gain significant US FDI has been the Republic of Ireland. The role of FDI in the Irish

Table 11.5 The geographical distribution of changes in the inward FDI stock within the EU, 1980–85 to 1991–95 (%)

	1980–85	*1986–90*	*1991–95*
Core countries			
Belgium/Luxembourg	4.1	5.9	16.4
France	28.6	11.3	26.1
Germany	0.8	15.8	7.8
Italy	26.8	8.3	2.3
Netherlands	15.4	10.4	10.0
UK	2.7	32.8	8.9
Total	78.4	84.5	71.5
Non-core countries			
Denmark	–1.5	1.2	4.3
Greece	10.1	1.2	1.8
Ireland	2.4	0.1	1.8
Portugal	0.6	0.8	0.6
Spain	10.1	12.2	21.5
Total	21.7	15.5	28.4

Source: Dunning (1997a) table 2, page 14.

economy is shown clearly by the significant difference between gross national product (production carried out by Irish nationals) and gross domestic product (production carried out in Ireland). For 1989, Irish GDP was IR£23918 million while Irish GNP was IR£20879 million – a 13 per cent difference (Datastream). Furthermore, about one-third of Irish manufacturing employment is in multinationals (Jackson and Barry 1989). In comparison, the relative importance of US multinational production in a number of EU countries is shown in Table 11.6.

There has been some controversy about the most recent trends in the distribution of inward investment in the EU. United Nations figures suggested that France overtook Britain in the first half of the 1990s to become the largest recipient of inward investment in Europe. However, OECD figures released in July 1997 painted a rather different picture. These showed Britain receiving about 40 per cent of EU inward investment in 1996 – almost double its share for the preceding year and more than twice as much as France. The OECD said that, with a total inflow of investment of $81 billion between 1991 and 1995, Britain was in third place in the world ranking of host countries after the USA and China, with France in fourth place with inflows of $63.5 billion (de Jonquieres 1997).

The role of FDI in different sectors

Data on the sectoral distribution of FDI are rather limited. Dunning (1997a) presented figures for the growth of sales by US affiliates in Europe. Over the period 1982–93 by far the largest growth was in the category of finance (excluding banking). This was followed, in descending order, by household appliances, drugs, other food products, beverages, electronic components, business services and office and computing equipment. However, these aggregate figures concealed some fairly striking shifts over time. Dunning looked at two sub-periods; 1982–89 and 1989–93. The strong performance of finance, office and computing equipment and to some extent household appliances was very much concentrated in the first of these periods. On the other hand, beverages and business services showed especially strong growth in the second period.

Table 11.6 Gross product of US majority-owned non-bank foreign affiliates for 1994 (% of host country GDP)

Host country	All sectors	Manufacturing
UK	5.9	2.5
Germany	2.8	1.8
France	2.4	1.2
Belgium	5.1	3.0
Netherlands	4.3	2.3
Italy	1.8	0.8
Spain	1.6	1.1
Ireland	11.9	8.8

Source: Barrell and Pain (1997) table 3, page 68.

Davies and Lyons (1996) and their co-workers found that the industry with the greatest non-EU presence for 1987 (measured by share of production) was computers and office equipment, at 54 per cent. They attribute this in large measure to the role of IBM. This industry was followed by tobacco at 34 per cent, soap and cosmetics at 31 per cent, scientific and photographic equipment at 28 per cent, toys and sporting goods at 27 per cent, food at 20 per cent, motor vehicles at 19 per cent, and industrial and farm equipment at 18 per cent. In all of these cases the non-EU share of production was higher than that of EU-owned multinationals. Industries with very little non-EU-owned production included iron and steel, non-metallic mineral products, metal products, other transport equipment, aerospace, textiles, clothing and wood. In all of these the non-EU share was less than 7 per cent. However, they are also industries in which there is little EU-owned multinational production. On the other hand, in electrical engineering and electronics and in telecommunications, non-EU firms held a modest share of production, while EU-owned multinationals accounted for a much larger proportion of output (Davies and Lyons 1996, page 133).

Davies and Lyons and their collaborators went on to look at the extent to which US and EFTA investment in the EU was based on home country comparative advantage, again using 1987 figures. Their results are shown in Table 11.7.

For those industries in the first group, where home country comparative advantage holds, it was generally the case that the EU was not strong. The exceptions here were machinery and food, and this suggested that EFTA companies were attracted to the EU market not just by locational advantages but also by the opportunity of using EU entrepreneurial skills (Davies and Lyons 1996, page 140). In pharmaceuticals and soaps and cosmetics, the EU, while not demonstrating global comparative advantage, did have a strong export performance, indicating locational advantages that might well attract FDI.

Table 11.7 Comparative advantage and foreign presence in the EU, 1987

USA	EFTA
Industries in which strong foreign presence is based on home country comparative advantage	
Soap and cosmetics	Machinery
Computers	Food
Scientific and photographic equipment	Pharmaceuticals
Tobacco	Electronics
Industries in which there is low foreign presence despite home country comparative advantage	
Food	Minerals
Pharmaceuticals	Metal products
Drink	Wood
Aerospace	Other transport
Wood	
Clothing	

Source: Pain and Lansbury (1991) table 6, page 96.

The second group of industries show cases where FDI has not taken place even though foreign producers were strong. In pharmaceuticals, aerospace and wood this may have been because of alternative strategies such as exports or alliances. In food and minerals, on the other hand, the strength of EU companies was likely to have played a role in deterring investors.

Overall there has been a trend towards more FDI in services as opposed to manufacturing for the EU in recent years, though this was interrupted in the late 1980s. With regard to extra-EU FDI, the share of manufacturing rose from 28.7 per cent in 1984–86 to 38.2 per cent in 1987–89 before falling back to 28.6 per cent in 1990–92 (Dunning 1997a). The corresponding figures for services show a fall from 54.4 per cent to 51.9 per cent, followed by a rise to 61.8 per cent. The main Japanese FDI has been in the area of services. In 1987 services constituted 75.5 per cent of the Japanese FDI stock in Europe, with 49.9 per cent of Japanese FDI in finance and insurance; however, it is argued by Dunning and Cantwell (1991) that this may have been an overestimate.

Patterns of intra-EU FDI

So far we have concentrated on investment originating outside the EU; however, intra-EU FDI is also important. The most comprehensive early analysis of intra-EU FDI flows is that by Molle and Morsink (1991). They looked at data from 1975 to 1983, finding that investment flows were heavily concentrated among the most industrialised countries (with the UK, the major recipient of FDI, also being the main investor). They also found that investment from and to the rest of the world was more than that within the EU for this time period: intra-EU FDI amounted to ECU30.7 billion, with investment from the EU to the rest of the world at ECU77.8 billion and investment coming into the EU from outside at ECU48.4 billion. The EU was thus a net capital exporter at this time.

Molle and Morsink (1991) define the following indicator as a measure of the direction of FDI for any country, i:

$$\text{INVCRO} = \frac{\text{Outward investment from } i - \text{Inward investment in } i}{\text{Outward plus inward investment for } i}$$

The following categories are defined:

investor country (I):   INVCRO > 0.33
crossroad country (C):   −0.33 < INVCRO < 0.33
recipient country (R):   INVCRO < −0.33

They used this indicator to categorise their world data and found that four EU countries (Greece, Portugal, Spain and Ireland) were recipients of FDI; two (the Netherlands and West Germany) were investors; the rest were crossroad countries. Using intra-EU data, Italy became a recipient rather than a crossroad country.

In recent years there has been a dramatic rise in the importance of intra-EU FDI for the European Union countries, as opposed to investments made by these countries in other regions.

The share of EU FDI directed to the EU itself rose from 30.6 per cent in 1985–87 to 57.7 per cent in 1991–93 (annual averages, taken from Dunning 1997a). Within this general trend it is notable that FDI was more decentralised than in the case of extra-EU FDI. The role of the UK was less dominant; in 1991–93 for example, more EU FDI was directed to Belgium/Luxembourg, Germany and the Netherlands than to Britain. The 'non-core' countries played a larger role; the proportion of EU FDI directed to Greece, Spain and Portugal rose from 4.2 per cent in 1985–87 to 12.5 per cent in 1991–93. Table 11.4 shows the relatively high, and increasing, FDI intensity ratios for a number of European Union countries with the EU, indicating the importance of intra-EU FDI. It also shows a certain amount of detachment of the UK from this process; the intensity ratio here remains comparatively low.

The rise in intra-EU FDI was partly the result of a decline in EU investment in North America. The share of EU FDI directed to the United States, for example, fell from 48.1 per cent in 1985–87 to just 15.9 per cent in 1991–93 (Dunning 1997a). Intra-EU investment exceeded EU investment in North America in 1988 and has remained above it thereafter (Pain and Lansbury 1997).

Trade, investment and European integration

A central issue when analysing FDI in the EU is the relationship of FDI flows to trade flows and to the process of European integration with regard to both widening and deepening the EU. There are two alternative views that suggest themselves concerning this relationship. If FDI is viewed as an alternative to exporting, then a decline in investment as barriers to trade are reduced would be expected. In this case the process of European integration would lead to less intra-EU FDI. Extra-EU FDI might well increase, however, as US, Japanese and other companies attempt to produce inside the EU Common External Tariff and take advantage of the more unified European market.

The problem with this view is that, as seen above, the acceleration of European integration in the late 1980s associated with preparations for the Single European Market was associated with both a relative and an absolute *increase* in intra-EU FDI. This suggests that the relationship between trade flows and FDI flows may be complementary, rather than one between substitutes. Various explanations have been put forward for this, mostly centring on the restructuring of European businesses and the development of new strategies in preparation for the single market.

Cantwell (1992) has distinguished between two main kinds of FDI taking place in the world today. Firstly, there is FDI *within* regions. This, he argues, is mainly about restructuring and reorganising multinational companies into what he describes as 'corporate networks'. Such networks can be organised horizontally, with plants in different countries specialising in different parts of the product range, or vertically with foreign components being shipped to assembly plants elsewhere. Secondly, there is FDI between regions. This, according to Cantwell, is 'motivated, in large part by defensive considerations: wishing to avoid being closed out of markets and to take advantage of the opportunities for the formation of local networks in the other integrating regions' (Cantwell 1992, page 9). In this case the formation of the single market would be expected to stimulate both extra-EU and intra-EU FDI but for very different reasons.

Empirical evidence on FDI and the EU and the role of the SEM

There have been a number of studies which have attempted to investigate the determinants of investment flows in the EU. These have been reviewed by Dunning (1997b).

The first study was one by UNCTAD. This found 90 per cent of the fluctuations in FDI in the EU to be explained by four factors: the level of GNP in the preceding year, the growth rate over the preceding year, the ratio of domestic investment to GNP for the preceding year, and a measure of exchange rate volatility. Of these, the level of GNP was the most important, and much more important for the EU than for other developed countries. However, this study did not go beyond 1988 and so was unable to assess the full impact of the single market, though it did suggest that any rise in output caused by European integration would in turn raise FDI.

Srinivasan and Mody looked at Japanese and US investment into the EU (see Dunning 1997b). They found the size of the market and the cost of labour to be important, as well as 'agglomeration' factors (in other words, factors resulting from previous investment which made future investment more attractive; the production of electricity per head, and the number of telephone lines per head were considered). Their data covered the period 1977–92; however, when they looked at three sub-periods separately they could find no evidence that the single market significantly improved the EU's share of either US or Japanese FDI. In fact, in the case of Japanese FDI the share of FDI directed to the EU, as compared with that directed to East Asia, fell during the 1987–92 period.

Clegg conducted a long-term study looking separately at US FDI in each of the original six EU member states from 1951 to 1990 (see Dunning 1997b). He found that FDI depended on market size and growth, exchange rates, relative interest rates and a trade discrimination variable. Interestingly, while market size was positively related to FDI in the first two decades of his time period, it later showed a negative relationship to FDI. Dunning reports:

> Clegg suggests the reason for this was that, whereas in the 1950s and early 1960s, most US FDI was defensive and was directed to the larger local markets in Europe, in the later years, particularly after the UK joined the EC, it was more of an efficiency or strategic asset-seeking kind, and intended to exploit the EC market as a whole
>
> (Dunning 1997b, page 193)

This raises the general issue of the importance of seeing FDI in a dynamic context, rather than simply viewing the determinants of investment as fixed for all time. Agarwal (1997) makes the point that when a country's stock of outward FDI is small, such FDI may well be a substitute for domestic investment. However, as the stock is built up and earnings are repatriated home, they may well contribute positively to domestic capital formation.

Clegg found little evidence for a strong effect on FDI coming from the single market programme. However, Dunning argues that this may result partly from the changes mentioned above, which obscured the effect of the single market variable, and partly from the fact that an aggregate variable did not capture industry-specific effects.

Buigues and Jacquemin looked at the relationship between extra-EU FDI (from the USA and Japan) and exports to the EU, and at the significance of trade barriers between the EU and the rest of the world as a determinant of FDI (see Dunning 1997b). They found that FDI and trade appeared to be very much complementary to one another, and that while non-tariff barriers were important in determining FDI from Japan, they played only a minor role in influencing US FDI.

The most detailed study reviewed by Dunning is one by Pain and Lansbury carried out for the European Commission. The importance of this study was firstly that it distinguished between the relative importance of the single market programme in some industries as compared with others, and secondly that it looked at intra-EU FDI. To be more precise, the scale of non-tariff barriers, and thus the potential impact of the single market, was ranked for various industries along a scale from 1 to 3. The study looked in particular at the outward intra-EU FDI of the UK from 1981 to 1992 and Germany from 1980 to 1992.

Pain and Lansbury found that host country output was an important determinant of FDI, although less than in the UNCTAD study. They also found that data on the US-registered patents of UK and German firms played a significant role. The argument was that this would capture some of the internalisation-specific advantages of FDI mentioned earlier.

The single market indicator mentioned above had a significant role in determining FDI, somewhat more so for the UK than for Germany. Including this variable reduced the impact of output and patents on FDI, demonstrating that, in the absence of a variable capturing the effect of the single market on FDI, some of its effects are captured by other variables. Pain and Lansbury then considered the impact of the single market programme on the value of FDI. Dunning reports their results as follows:

> Pain and Lansbury calculated that, by the end of 1992, the IMP may have raised the constant price stock of UK FDI by $15 billion (or 31 per cent of the capital stake at that date) and the stock of German FDI by $5 billion (or 6 per cent of the aggregate stock level). In both instances, the prime gainers were shown to be the financial and other service sectors and the electronics sector (which also includes telecommunications equipment). For the UK, major gains were also recorded in the distribution and food, drink and tobacco sectors, in both of which the UK has a comparative advantage.
> (Dunning 1997b, page 197. Note that IMP refers to Internal Market Programme)

The main beneficiary of the single market programme in terms of attracting German FDI was Britain, according to Pain and Lansbury. They estimated the German stake in the UK as $4.3 billion in 1992, or a third higher than it would have been without the SEM. Other gainers were Italy, the Netherlands and Portugal, with France and Belgium losing German investment. They found that intra-EU FDI from Germany due to the single market appeared to have diverted investment away from Austria and the USA. By way of contrast, the increase in intra-EU FDI from the UK did not appear to have diverted investment flows from the USA.

In a later study (Pain and Lansbury 1997), they developed this approach further, and obtained similar results for the German case. The main difference between this and the earlier work was that when considering German investment outside the EU, they paid more attention to the distinction between manufacturing and services. Table 11.8 shows some of the key results.

The decline in investment in France resulted in large part from the important role played by German chemicals and mechanical engineering investment there. Pain and Lansbury argued that labour market factors played a role in attracting German investment to the UK. However, similar factors (relative labour costs and low levels of strike activity) also attracted German investment to France, Austria and Italy, despite very different institutional structures in the labour market to those in the UK. On the other hand, labour costs and labour relations had an effect on limiting German investment in Spain between 1986 and 1992. The importance of patent activity by German firms was significantly greater in encouraging FDI than that of labour market factors, however, for all the countries studied.

It seems, then, that in contrast to developments in FDI immediately after the formation of the EEC in 1957, when investment from outside Europe was more significantly affected than investment within Europe (Dunning 1997a), recent moves towards European integration have encouraged intra-EU FDI. However, the precise extent to which integration affects both intra-EU and extra-EU FDI

Table 11.8 The impact of the internal market on the location and composition of German FDI in the EU ($ billion, 1990 prices)

	1992 Stock	IM effect
Country		
Belgium/Luxembourg	21.9	2.1
United Kingdom	12.2	4.9
France	13.7	−0.5
Italy	9.0	2.5
Netherlands	9.5	3.0
Spain and Portugal	10.1	1.7
Sector		
Chemicals	9.5	−0.1
Mechanical engineering	2.4	−0.3
Electrical	4.8	1.0
Transport equipment	4.0	0.4
Other manufacturing	7.1	0.9
Distribution	17.3	2.9
Financial and other services	31.3	8.9
Total	76.4	13.7

Source: adapted from Anderson and Norheim, table 2.2, page 29–30.

remains controversial. In particular, the effect of integration on FDI appears to differ substantially across industries. It also works at least in part through its effect on other variables, such as output or market size. Results for the effect of integration on extra-EU FDI vary considerably. While a number of the studies show that this effect is limited or negligible, other studies are more encouraging. Aristotelous and Fountas found that the level of inward investment by US and Japanese firms has been significantly higher than might have been expected since 1987 without the SEM (see Dunning 1997b). Agarwal (1997) also makes the point that economic integration cannot be seen as a sufficient condition for increased FDI. For example, flows of investment from EU member countries into Greece remain subdued. In the case of the North American Free Trade Area (NAFTA), despite the free-trade agreement, Canadian and Mexican shares in the total outward FDI stock of the USA fell from 19 per cent in 1990 to 13 per cent in 1995; while in 1994 the US share in Canadian FDI stock was 5 per cent lower than in 1991 (Agarwal 1997).

FDI in the European Union and industrial restructuring

It may be possible to obtain a clearer picture of the relationship between FDI and European integration by looking at particular industries and companies and at their responses to the single market programme. Among the many examples of decisions relating to FDI emerging from this, four types of investment appear to be especially common (these categories are not intended to be exhaustive). Firstly, there is investment motivated by the desire to cut costs. For example, Thomson was attracted to produce TV tubes in Italy by low labour costs and government incentives. It then closed its German and French factories to achieve economies of scale by centralising production (Savary 1992). Secondly, there is investment motivated by market location, in particular centrality to the European Union marketplace. Belgium has been a favoured location for investment from the northern part of the EU for this reason. An example of this is the 1988 acquisition of Société Générale de Belgique by Suez of France. At the same time, Belgian companies have invested in southern Europe and outside the EU (Van Den Bulcke and De Lombaerde 1992). Similar motives connected to market location appear to be behind German investments in France, such as those by BASF and Hoechst in chemicals and pharmaceuticals, and Daimler-Benz's purchase of a stake in the software house Cap Gemini Sogeti.

A third motivation for investment is technological considerations. Cantwell and Sanna Randaccio (1992) argued that in industries where there is a significant amount of intra-industry FDI there is also a significant amount of intra-industry technological activity. Examples are in chemicals and electrical equipment. They looked at British and German companies in the chemicals area. Their findings were that German companies investing in Britain appear to do so in order to benefit from those specific areas where British companies are strong, such as pharmaceuticals. Consequently, their technological activity follows the pattern of the British companies. British chemical companies in Germany, however, tended to follow their own previous lines of business, but to try to benefit from the generally high level of scientific expertise in Germany.

Finally, FDI can arise out of the workings of strategic alliances. An example is BSN, the French company, which formed an alliance in the late 1980s with the Agnelli group in Italy, partly because the 5.12 per cent Agnelli holding in BSN helped to protect it from takeover. Together the two companies went on to acquire a wide range of Italian food companies (Savary 1992).

An example of foreign investment strategies of European companies is considered in the case study of Volkswagen's investment in Spain and Portugal.

Case study: Volkswagen in Spain and Portugal

The most important direct investment by Volkswagen in the European Union has been its purchase of the Spanish subsidiary SEAT. SEAT was acquired in 1986, having previously produced Volkswagen cars under licence. The company was making losses, and the Spanish government asked Volkswagen to take a majority stake. The company agreed to take a 50 per cent stake, which was raised to 100 per cent in 1990, for a total of Ffr4.3 billion. In return, the Spanish government agreed to retire the company's debt and provide a cash infusion of Frf817 million. By 1988 SEAT had returned to profit.

SEAT was quite attractive for Volkswagen because it fitted into the model range of the group as a whole. The mid-range models (the Polo, Golf, Passat, Jetta and Corrado), which were the best sellers, were made under the Volkswagen marque; while luxury cars were made by the Audi subsidiary and SEAT produced a range of cars for the lower end of the market under its own name. Labour conditions also made Spanish production attractive. In 1992, employees at Volkswagen's Spanish plants worked 1500 hours a year on the production line, as compared with 1200 hours for German employees. However, in 1990 there were fears in Spain that Volkswagen would shift investment from SEAT to its newly acquired Czech subsidiary Skoda, and to other developments in Eastern Europe. Volkswagen attempted to calm these fears, raising its stake in SEAT to 99.98 per cent in December 1990 and planning an increase in SEAT production by a third to 600 000 by 1994. The SEAT Pamplona plant was to become the main assembly plant for the Polo, and SEAT would also export components for Polo production in East Germany.

Unfortunately, the recession of the early 1990s and increased global competition in the motor industry forced Volkswagen to scale back its investment plans and rationalise production methods across the whole group. This period also saw mounting losses at SEAT (DM180 million in 1992). With a further loss of about Pta100 billion forecast for 1993, a rescue package was agreed for SEAT by Volkswagen in September 1993. This involved Volkswagen directly taking over the Pamplona plant and the finance company Fiseat. In return, SEAT was expected to take measures to return itself to profit. SEAT suggested a recovery plan which depended on future increases in volume sales and a medium-term cut of 5000 of the workforce, to a level of 18 000. This was rejected by Volkswagen, and the SEAT chairman, Jose Antonio Diaz Alvarez, resigned.

Volkswagen then decided to close the SEAT plant at Barcelona and shed 9000 jobs. In return, it offered a cash injection for SEAT of DM1.5 billion without taking the Pamplona factory into Volkswagen ownership.

The proposed closure sparked off strikes and riots in Barcelona and the Catalan regional government intervened. A settlement was reached, with trade union agreement, according to which SEAT was committed to re-employing within two years 4600 workers with fixed employment contracts and making up unemployment benefit to ensure that laid-off workers would receive at least 80 per cent of their take home pay. The settlement was costed at Pta30 billion for SEAT. The company planned to create a 'supplier park' at the closed Zona Franca plant in order to encourage components suppliers to take on some of the surplus labour. The aim was to increase the share of components bought in Spain from 54 per cent to 67 per cent by 1996.

Volkswagen then started negotiations with the Spanish government for state aid for SEAT. In July 1994 it reached agreement on a figure of Pta40 billion (about two-thirds of its original request). The Spanish government was reluctant to provide aid, in part because of the possibility of similar requests from other companies, such as Suzuki, which had a troubled plant in southern Spain. However, it faced strong pressure from the Catalan Nationalist Party, which runs the regional government in Barcelona, and which at the time was supporting the minority Socialist government nationally. The aid was conditional on its being invested in technology, not redundancies; on SEAT being maintained as a separate trade mark within the Volkswagen group; on SEAT retaining a design and technology centre and the capacity to produce new models; and on any new manufacturing plants opened by SEAT in the future being located in Spain.

In October 1994, Werner Schmidt, Volkswagen's finance director, who had been in charge of the SEAT supervisory board during the events of 1993, was dismissed. In June 1995 the European Commission announced an investigation into the state subsidies being paid to SEAT. It was thought that the payments might be illegal under EU competition rules. In November 1995 the Commission approved the aid package, but only after the Spanish government had explicitly stated that the aid would go towards shrinking and restructuring SEAT and not towards technological developments. In 1994 SEAT net losses were reduced by nearly 80 per cent to Pta29.4 billion, and by 1996 SEAT had returned to profit.

SEAT was not Volkswagen's only investment in the Iberian Peninsula during this period. In June 1991 a £1.5 billion joint investment bid by Ford and Volkswagen was announced for an assembly plant in Portugal to produce 'multi-purpose vehicles' or 'people carriers'. This project was desired also by Ireland and Spain, although Portugal offered an incentive package of Es120 billion, including an Es80 billion cash grant. In July 1991 the French producer Matra took unsuccessful legal action against the European Commission's approval of the project, claiming that EU aid of 70 per cent of the investment for the project violated competition policy.

Source: Financial Times, various dates.

Questions

1 For the case study above, list the various factors that affected the investment decisions of Volkswagen in Spain and Portugal. Try to classify them using the OLI framework. Are there any factors that do not fit easily into this framework?

2 How well do you think that Volkswagen managed the process of foreign investment in Spain and Portugal in the early 1990s? Are there any ways in which it could have changed its approach for the better?

•••

The impact of FDI

The impact of FDI is very hard to measure, since we do not know what would have happened if the investment had not taken place. The orthodox and most widespread view is that FDI will, in general, have a positive impact through economic integration and consequent specialisation according to comparative advantage. The ability to exploit increasing returns to scale and the benefits to the consumer of increased competition are also cited (Julius 1990). However, more particular issues are also often discussed and are more controversial. These include the impact of FDI on employment, technological change, management techniques and the balance of payments.

FDI is often advocated as a way of providing jobs, but obviously it will fail to do this if it simply displaces domestic production. Buckley and Artisen (1988) examined the employment effects of intra-EU investment in Greece, Portugal and Spain. They studied 19 particular cases using a questionnaire survey, and found that FDI almost always had a positive effect in the host country. Impacts on the source country were smaller and the overall effect of the two taken together was generally positive. FDI donors did, however, experience job losses in several cases.

Sleuwagen (1988) argued that FDI in Belgium was a complement to, rather than a substitute for, domestic production. However, his evidence for this – that FDI in Belgium had occurred mainly by setting up new companies rather than by takeover, and that multinationals in Belgium concentrated on product differentiation and exploiting technological differences – did not seem conclusive. There were also questions about the kinds of jobs provided by FDI and about the permanence of such jobs.

Both of these issues for the Irish case were discussed by Jackson and Barry (1989). They argued that FDI in Ireland failed to improve the segregation of women into low-paid, low-skill jobs. In addition, the jobs were not always secure; the Dublin magazine *Business and Finance*, for example, examined the employment record of 13 multinational companies employing 7631 people up until 1982. Layoffs and closures reduced employment in these companies by 54 per cent between the time of setting up and the end of the period in 1982.

FDI has been seen, nevertheless, as a way of encouraging technological change. However, the European reality might be more complex. In innovative and competitive industries foreign investors established local R&D facilities to gain access to local expertise, and by doing this further increased the rate of innovation. In declining sectors, investment would be in assembly production with R&D located abroad. FDI production in such cases competed with domestic producers, who had to cut back their R&D even further as a cost-saving measure and thus entered a vicious circle of decline (Cantwell 1988). Cantwell supported this argument with two case studies of the impact of FDI in the UK; the pharmaceuticals sector was seen as the first kind of industry, the motor vehicles sector as the second.

A third possible impact of FDI is on management styles. In particular, Japanese investment is often seen as bringing new innovations in management techniques (Oliver and Wilkinson 1992). The link between such changes and foreign investment is not always clear. In addition, these new techniques might not be an unalloyed benefit for workers in the companies concerned. They could increase stress and the pace of work and decrease effective union representation (Garrahan and Stewart 1992). A particularly notorious case occurred when in December 1984 Hitachi invited all workers over 35 at their factory in Hirwaun in South Wales to take voluntary retirement. The argument was that older workers are more prone to sickness, are slower, have poorer eyesight and are more resistant to change (Pearson 1989).

Barrell and Pain (1997) agreed that inward FDI can raise productivity through its effect on technology and management styles in manufacturing but in their studies of the UK and Germany they found that 'there did not appear to be any discernible effect from FDI in non-manufacturing industries on labour productivity in the non-manufacturing private sector' (page 71). This is particularly significant in that about two-thirds of inward investment in the UK is in sectors outside manufacturing.

FDI has also been seen as a way of improving the balance of payments for host countries. Again, however, the picture is more complex. Foreign-owned firms may import inputs and components rather heavily from abroad, as Japanese plants in the USA have tended to do (Graham and Krugman 1989). More fundamentally, FDI might lead to the shifting of low value-added production abroad, freeing up resources for higher-value production at home, and thus worsening the balance of payments in the host country (Thomsen and Nicolaides 1991).

Conclusion

Both intra-EU and extra-EU FDI are certain to play a significant and continuing role in shaping the landscape of European business. However, their determinants and effects are different in important ways. While investment from outside continues to flow into the European Union, and is heavily concentrated in particular countries, perhaps more significant in recent years has been the increase in investment within the EU. This has been more widely dispersed than extra-EU investment, and shows the importance of the single market programme in stimulating a wide range of approaches to restructuring and strategic change among businesses in the European Union. The key question for the future is that of whether the rise of intra-EU FDI is a temporary phenomenon, sparked off by the upsurge in European integration in the late 1980s, which will eventually give way to a reassertion of the greater role of extra-EU FDI; or whether, on the other hand, it indicates a continuing increased role for FDI in altering and developing production strategies within the European Union.

Questions for discussion

1 From Table 11.2 determine whether the growth of the ratio of FDI outward stock to GDP was higher during 1986–90 or 1991–94?

2 Repeat the exercise for the ratio of FDI inflows to the exports of goods and services.

3 Discuss the factors which give rise to ownership-specific (firm-specific) advantages.

4 Compare and contrast the average annual growth rate of FDI inflows of developed countries with those of developing countries between 1983 and 1995.

5 Consider the figures given below (in millions of dollars) for Spain and Germany.

   Outward direct investment

	1992	1993	1994	1995
Spain	2192	2652	3831	3574
Germany	19670	15280	16690	34890

   Inward Direct Investment

	1992	1993	1994	1995
Spain	13276	8144	9359	6250
Germany	2640	1820	810	8940

   Source: IMF International Financial Statistics.

   (a) Which country is a capital exporter and which is a capital importer? Use the OLI framework to explain your answer.
   (b) How would you account for the trends in outward investment from Germany and inward investment to Spain?

6 During the period 1985–92, Germany had significant outward investment in the chemicals industry, but no inward investment. Spain had significant inward investment but very little outward investment in this industry. Use the OLI framework to explain this pattern.

7 During the period 1985–92, the two largest sectors in terms of inflows of direct investment into Spain were transport equipment and finance/insurance. For Germany, they were finance/insurance and other services. The two largest sectors in terms of outward investment from Spain were finance/insurance and other manufacturing and from Germany they were also finance/insurance and other manufacturing.

(a) Use the OLI framework to explain why these sectors were important for these countries.

(b) How would you explain the prevalence of intra-industry FDI (i.e. outward and inward FDI in the same industry and sector for the same country) in these cases?

8 In 1991, France was a capital exporter, with outward flows of FDI greater than inward flows. In 1995 the situation had reversed with inward flows exceeding outward flows. How would you explain this change in the situation of France with regard to FDI?

9 Why do you think that Britain attracts so much more extra-EU FDI than any other EU country? How would you explain the fact that Britain does not have the same dominance with regard to intra-EU FDI?

Main reading

Cantwell, J. (ed.) (1992) *Multinational Investment in Modern Europe*, Edward Elgar.

Caves, R. (1996) *Multinational Enterprise and Economic Analysis*, OUP.

Dunning, J. (1993) *The Globalization of Business*, Routledge.

Dunning, J. (1997a) The European Internal Market Programme and inbound foreign direct investment: Part 1, *Journal of Common Market Studies*.

Dunning, J. (1997b) The European Internal Market Programme and inbound foreign direct investment: Part 2, *Journal of Common Market Studies*.

Additional reading

Agarwal, J. P. (1997) European integration and German FDI: implications for domestic investment and Central European economies, *National Institute Economic Review*.

Baker, S. (1990) *An Introduction to International Economics*, Harcourt Brace Jovanovich.

Barrell, R. and Pain, N. (1997) The growth of foreign direct investment in Europe, *National Institute Economic Review*.

Block, J. and Dunning, J. (eds) (1982) *International Capital Movements*, Macmillan.

Buckley, P. (1989) *The Multinational Enterprise*, Macmillan.

Buckley, P. and Artisen, P. (1988) Policy issues of intra-EC direct investment: British, French and German multinationals in Greece, Portugal and Spain, with special reference to employment effects, in Dunning, J. and Robson, P. (eds) *Multinationals and the European Community*, Blackwell.

Buckley, P. and Casson, M. (1985) *The Economic Theory of Multinational Enterprise*, Macmillan.

Cantwell, J. (1988) The reorganization of European industries after integration: selected evidence of the role of multinational enterprise activities, in Dunning, J. and Robson, P. (eds) *Multinationals and the European Community*, Blackwell.

Cantwell, J. and Sanna Randaccio, F. (1992) Intra-industry direct investment in the European Community: oligopolistic rivalry and technological competition, in Cantwell, J. (ed.) *Multinational Investment in Modern Europe*, Edward Elgar.

Casson, M. (ed.) (1983) *The Growth of International Business*, George Allen & Unwin.

Casson, M. (1986) General theories of the MNE: their relevance to business history, in Hartner, P. and Jones, G. (eds) *Multinationals: Theory & History*, Gower.

Casson, M. (1987) *The Firm and the Market*, Blackwell.

Davies, S. and Lyons, B. (1996) *Industrial Organization in the European Union: Structure, Strategy and the Competitive Mechanism*, OUP.

de Jonquieres, G. (1997) Britain doubles share of EU inward investment, *Financial Times*, 14 July.

Dunning, J. (1981) *International Production and the MNE*, George Allen & Unwin.

Dunning, J. (1983) Changes in the level and structure of international production: the last one hundred years, in Casson, M. (ed.) *The Growth of International Business*, George Allen & Unwin.

Dunning, J. *et al.* (1986) The theory of international production: some historical antecedents, in Hertner, P. and Jones, C. (eds) *Multinationals: Theory and History*, Gower.

Dunning, J. and Cantwell, J. (1991) Japanese direct investment in Europe, in Burgenmeier, B. and Mucchielli, J. L. (eds) *Multinationals and Europe 1992*, Routledge.

Garrahan, P. and Stewart, P. (1992) *The Nissan Enigma: Flexibility at Work in a Local Economy*, Mansell/Cassell.

Graham, E. and Krugman, P. (1989) *Foreign Direct Investment in the United States*, Institute for International Economics.

Hood, N. and Young, S. (1979) *The Economics of MNE*, Longman.

Hunt, E. Y. and Sherman, H. J. (1990) *Economics*, Harper & Row.

Hymer, S. (1976) *The International Operations of National Firms: A Study in DFI*, MIT Press.

Jackson, P. and Barry, V. (1989) Women's employment and multinationals in the Republic of Ireland: the creation of a new female labour force, in Elson, D. and Pearson, R. (eds) *Women's Employment and Multinationals in Europe*, Macmillan.

Julius, D. A. (1990) *Global Companies and Public Policy*, Pinter/RIIA.

Julius, D. (1993) Foreign direct investment: Is the boom bust? A paper presented at the South Bank University, Centre for International Business Studies, London, 4 March 1993.

Lindert, P. H. (1991) *International Economics*, Harper & Row.

Molle, W. and Morsink, R. (1991) Intra-European direct investment, in Burgenmeier, B. and Mucchielli, J. L. (eds) *Multinationals and Europe 1992*, Routledge.

OECD (1989) *International Direct Investment and New Economic Environment*.

Oliver, N. and Wilkinson, B. (1992) *The Japanization of British Industry*, 2nd edition, Blackwell.

Pain, N. and Lansbury, M. (1997) Regional economic integration and foreign direct investment: the case of German investment in Europe, *National Institute Economic Review*.

Pearson, R. (1989) Women's employment and multinationals in the UK: restructuring and flexibility, in Elson, D. and Pearson, R. (ed.) *Women's Employment and Multinationals in Europe*, Macmillan.

Peel, Q. (1990) Sticky time for a valuable resource, *Financial Times*, 26 October.

Savary, J. (1992) Cross-investments between France and Italy and the new European strategies of industrial groups, in Cantwell, J. (eds) *Multinational Investment in Modern Europe*, Edward Elgar.

Servan-Schreiber, J. (1968) *The American Challenge*, Hamilton.

Sleuwagen, L. (1988) Multinationals, the European Community and Belgium: the small country case, in Dunning, J. and Robson, P. (eds) *Multinationals and the European Community*, Blackwell.

Thomsen, S. and Nicolaides, P. (1991) *The Evolution of Japanese Direct Investment in Europe*, Harvester Wheatsheaf.

United Nations (1995) *Transnational Corporations and Competitiveness*, World Investment Report.

United Nations (1996) *Investment, Trade and International Policy Arrangements*, World Investment Report.

Van Den Bulcke, D. and De Lombaerde, Ph. (1992) The Belgian metalworking industries and the large European internal market: the role of multinational investment, in Cantwell, J. (ed.) *Multinational Investment in Modern Europe*, Edward Elgar.

Vernon, R. (1966) International investment and international trade in the product cycle, *Quarterly Journal of Economics*, Vol. 80 (May), pp. 190–207.

Foreign exchange rates

This chapter is intended to describe the operation of foreign exchange markets. There is much reference to exchange rates in economic commentary published in both the press and financial bulletins. The different calculations of foreign exchange rates have implications for business decisions, in particular for competitive pricing and export profitability.

What is the foreign exchange market?

The foreign exchange market is a market in which large volumes of mainly bank deposits denominated in foreign currency are bought and sold in exchange for bank deposits denominated in other currencies. Most individuals' contact with the foreign exchange market occurs when they are buying foreign bank notes and coins for the purpose of a holiday or business trip. In fact, the transactions in currency amount to fairly trivial sums compared with the transactions in bank deposits. For most individuals and firms the main agents in the transfer of money are the banks, and it is indeed the banks, authorised to deal in foreign currency, which comprise the foreign exchange market.

The foreign exchange market is in fact a worldwide market. Banks in the major financial centres are able to buy and sell foreign currency virtually throughout the 24 hours of the day. Thus, when the Hong Kong foreign exchange market has just closed at 9.00 GMT the London foreign exchange market has been open for half an hour, and by the time the London market has closed at 16.30 GMT the San Francisco market has also been open for half an hour; the New York market overlaps with London by about four hours. Obviously, the eastern markets are operating in the early part of the day (by GMT) and as the day progresses, Frankfurt, London, New York, etc. are opening and closing. London, Frankfurt and New York account for most of the trade in foreign currencies. Clearly there is no single location for the foreign exchange market, and it is really a global market united by efficient telecommunications and computer systems. Since the bulk of transactions in foreign currency involve the US dollar, it is hardly surprising that large US banks are important operators.

The daily turnover in foreign currency deposits, converted to US dollars as a standard measure, is well over US$1.3 trillion. Three centres account for 60 per cent of turnover – the UK, the USA and Japan. Notwithstanding the heavy use of the US dollar, London is the major foreign currency centre and this is, perhaps, not surprising in view of the large number of banks operating from London. In 1994, of the Bank of England's authorised banks, over 60 per cent were foreign in origin.

This is a highly active market: on Reuter's electronic dealing system as many as 40 000 electronic 'conversations' occur per hour and 4000 banks worldwide are linked via *c.* 18 000 terminals. In 1992, 60 per cent of daily transactions were cross-border and 80 per cent of foreign exchange turnover in London was by foreign banks. Some 50 per cent of gross foreign exchange transactions were non-local currency on both sides of the transaction. The growth of the market has been more rapid than the increase in trade, so suggesting speculation.

How is the exchange rate measured?

When buying or selling foreign currencies the bank will quote two prices: one at which it will sell and one at which it will buy. Indeed this is one of the most familiar ways in which foreign currency prices are quoted. For example, on 18 March 1998 the average prices quoted during that day for the French franc against the pound sterling were:

£1 = Ffr9.9336/10.6236

This means that the selling rate for French francs was Ffr9.9336 for £1 and the buying rate was Ffr10.6236 for £1. (Banks buy currency at a lower price and sell for a higher price.) The difference between the two prices is called the spread and in the example above the difference between the buying and selling price was 0.935, or as a percentage of the selling price:

$(0.935/9.9336) \times 100 = 9.413\%$

The difference between the two prices is required to provide the banks with a profit on their dealings, as well as to cover them for their administrative costs and any risks they may run in such transactions.

Nominal exchange rates

In fact there are several ways in which exchange rates might be expressed. The presentation just discussed represents a bilateral rate, i.e. the price of one currency expressed in terms of one other currency. Since foreign currency deposits are traded freely in several financial centres simultaneously during each working day, once the quoted rate of exchange of the pound is known, for example, against the US dollar and the pound against the Deutschmark, the exchange rate of the US dollar against the Deutschmark can be worked out. The average exchange rates for the pound on 16 March 1998 in London were

£1 = US$1.6655
£1 = DM3.0325

It is a matter of arithmetic to work out that the exchange rate of the US dollar against the Deutschemark must have been 3.0325/1.6655 = 1.8208, i.e.

US$1 = DM1.8208

and this was indeed the case. If this were not the situation on that day then it would have been possible to switch from one currency to another to make a profit based on any inconsistency between their prices. Suppose the exchange rates had been:

£1 = US$1.6655 (in London)
£1 = DM3.1 (in Frankfurt)
$1 = DM 1.8208 (in New York)

This set of rates cannot hold because the last two exchange rates quoted would require, for consistency, a £/$ exchange rate of £1 = US$1.7025 and not US$1.6655. The pound is therefore set at too high a price in London or conversely the dollar is cheap. A bank in Frankfurt could therefore buy £10 million for DM31 million and then buy, in London, US$18.613 million. Using these US dollars the bank could then immediately sell them in New York for DM33.89 million. Such inconsistencies in the exchange rates could therefore produce a profit of £932 258 for a few minutes work. Clearly, such profitable opportunities would be visible to all banks operating in foreign currency markets and this would lead immediately to a substantial increase in the demand for US dollars in London. The effect of this would be to raise the price of dollars until it ceased to be profitable to switch from currency to currency. The only £/$ exchange rate in London that would satisfy this condition in our example is £1 = US$1.7025. The mechanism which ensures that the various cross rates (the price of one currency in terms of several other currencies) are consistent, and which has just been described above, is called arbitrage. Table 12.1 shows a set of cross rates prevailing on 16 March 1998. Are these rates consistent with each other?

The exchange rates given above are called spot rates. This is because they are prices quoted for the delivery of foreign currency immediately; the deal is done then and there, and the currency is expected to be available after the transaction. It is also possible to buy and sell foreign currency in the future (the reasons for this will be discussed below) and foreign exchange rates are quoted for future delivery at, say, one month or three months in the future. These rates of exchange are called forward rates, and correspondingly one can refer to the spot market and the forward exchange market. For example, on 14 October 1996 a bank could have bought spot Italian lira at a rate of £1 = L2405.00, but one month forward the corresponding exchange rate was £1 = L2410.09. This means that on October 14 one could have undertaken to buy lira for delivery in one month's time at the quoted forward exchange rate.

Table 12.1 Exchange rates against sterling and US dollars on 16 March 1998

£1 = $1.6655
£1 = DM3.0325
£1 = ¥215.940
$1 = DM1.529
$1 = ¥111.7

Source: Financial Times, 17 March 1998.

Effective exchange rates (EER)

Most European countries are at present in the Exchange Rate Mechanism (ERM) with the exchange rates fixed against each other and moving towards EMU. However, these rates do vary against other currencies.

In such circumstances it makes little sense to refer to one particular bilateral rate intended to represent the foreign exchange value of that currency. What is clearly needed is some kind of average foreign currency value, of, say, the pound or Deutschemark against several other currencies, and indeed this is what is currently computed for all major currencies. These 'average exchange rates' are termed effective exchange rates and are calculated as an index. Table 12.2 shows the recent movement in the effective exchange rates for sterling, US dollars, the Deutschemark and yen.

Real exchange rates (RER)

Both exchange rate definitions looked at so far try to measure the rate at which one currency exchanges for another. For a country which relies heavily on trade to maintain living standards (as most EU countries do) it is arguable that the exchange rate that is important is not the rate at which our currency exchanges for another but the rate at which our goods exchange in international trade. One such calculation of this is termed the real exchange rate (RER). This relates the effective exchange rate to the price of domestic goods relative to the price of foreign goods.

Suppose all goods were priced in a common currency, say, the pound sterling; in this case there would be no difficulty in establishing the rate at which UK goods exchanged for foreign goods. One could see immediately whether UK goods were more or less competitive, since foreign goods are imports into the UK, competing with home-produced goods, as well as being goods against which the UK competes in world markets.

Table 12.3 provides a simple illustration and shows the price of a representative bundle of goods priced in pounds: UK-produced goods and foreign-produced

Table 12.2 Effective exchange rates (1991 = 100)

	Sterling	US$	DM	Yen
1985	107.4	130.6	81.2	68.3
1986	99.5	113.9	89.8	89.9
1987	97.9	105.2	96.0	97.5
1988	103.8	100.1	95.8	106.5
1989	100.6	102.8	95.1	99.9
1990	99.1	101.0	100.4	91.8
1991	100.0	100.0	100.0	100.0
1992	96.5	98.6	103.8	105.4
1993	88.4	100.7	107.9	126.6
1994	89.2	100.1	109.7	136.3
1995	85.4	101.0	116.8	143.9
1996	87.3	107.6	115.0	125.5

Source: adapted from OECD (1997).

Table 12.3 Real exchange rates

	(1) Price (P_F) of a 'bundle' of goods (foreign-produced)	(2) Price (P_{UK}) of a 'bundle' of goods (UK-produced)	(3) $\dfrac{P_{UK}}{P_F}$	(4) Price index (foreign)	(5) Price index (UK)	(6) EER	(7) PP-ER	(8) RER (5)/(4) × (6)
Year 1	£100	£100	1.00	100	100	100	100	100.0
Year 2	£105	£115	1.09	105	115	108	91.3	118.3
Year 3	£110	£130	1.18	110	130	92	84.6	108.7

goods. In Year 1 both sets of goods sell for £100. By the end of Year 2 the foreign goods have risen in price by 5 per cent because of inflation, but UK goods have risen in price by 15 per cent. By the end of Year 3 inflation has raised the price of both sets of goods but inflation is presumed to be faster in the UK. The effect of this differential inflation rate can be seen in column 3: by the end of Year 2, UK goods are about 9 per cent more expensive than identical foreign goods, and by the end of Year 3 they are about 18 per cent more expensive than in Year 1. An alternative way of looking at this is to note that by Year 3, £100 buys about 10 per cent fewer foreign goods but about 30 per cent fewer UK goods. UK competitiveness has obviously diminished. It is this kind of relationship that the real exchange rate (RER) tries to measure.

The complication is that goods internationally are not priced in a common currency and movements in exchange rates change the observed price of goods when converted into, say, one's own currency. To take this into account, the average price of foreign goods must be converted into domestic currency by applying the effective exchange rate. Since the effective exchange rate is itself an index then price indices need to be converted as well. Columns 4 and 5 are price index numbers for foreign goods and UK goods, respectively, and it is clear how these index numbers have been derived from columns 1 and 2. It is essential to use index numbers for the respective price levels because there is no one exchange rate that would enable us to convert the average price of foreign goods into a sterling equivalent. The formula that we can use to calculate the real exchange rate is clear.

When considering the relationship between only two countries then the real exchange rate for the UK against, say, the German mark would be

RER = (£ price of UK goods/DM price of German goods) × (DM/£ exchange rate)

The appropriate calculation is contained in column 8. Thus, for Year 2 the calculation is (115/105) × 108 = 118.3. (Column 6 is the EER index and the numbers chosen are arbitrary.) The real exchange rate has risen by 18.3 per cent. What has really happened though and what does this really mean? This can be understood by considering the components of the RER:

RER = Price ratio × EER

Columns 4 and 5, respectively, show that the price of foreign goods has risen by 5 per cent but the same bundle of goods produced in the UK has risen by 15 per cent; clearly UK competitiveness has diminished because the relative price of UK goods has increased by almost 10 per cent. In addition to these changes, column 6 shows that the average value of the pound against foreign currencies has risen (appreciated) by 8 per cent. This latter change on its own would make UK exports less competitive and foreign imports more competitive with home-produced goods. So, the imaginary numbers selected for Table 12.3 show that in Year 2 there were two forces at work, both of which were making UK goods less competitive; that is, the rise in the relative price of UK goods and the rise in the EER (columns 3 and 6) and therefore the overall figure, captured by the calculation of the RER, shows that competitiveness has fallen by about 18 per cent. In Year 3, in contrast, UK inflation continues to rise faster than foreign inflation but in this year the average foreign currency value of the pound falls from 108 to 92 and this, of itself, would tend to make UK goods more competitive. The overall effect, combining the two forces (relative inflation and the movement in the average exchange rate (EER)) results in a movement of the RER from 118.3 to 108.7, i.e. UK goods in Year 2 have become more competitive than in Year 3.

To illustrate the significance of the RER some UK data can be used. Figure 12.1 shows the movement in relative export prices for the UK. Between 1985 and 1986 both the relative export price and the EER fell. Thereafter the relative export price was on a rising trend, whilst the EER was falling. On balance, therefore, what happened to UK competitiveness? Figure 12.2 plots the RER and shows that the balance of forces resulted in a falling RER between 1985 and 1986. It then rose between 1986 and 1988 and thereafter fell from 1988 to 1995. It can be said therefore that in the 1990s the UK has generally seen improved competitiveness as a result of the sustained decline in the effective exchange rate.

Fixed and floating exchange rates

Between 1973 and 1990 and between 1992 and the present time, people in the UK – whether business people or tourists – became accustomed to quite consid-

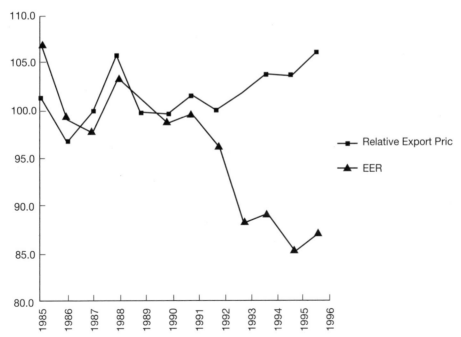

Figure 12.1 Effective exchange rate and relative export prices (UK) (*source: Economic Trends Annual Supplement* (1997) and OECD)

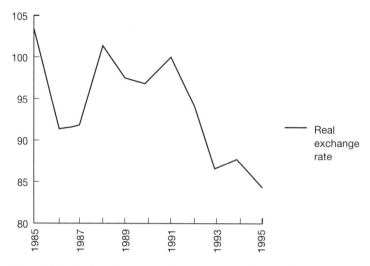

Figure 12.2 Real exchange rate (*source: Economic Trends Annual Supplement* (1996) and OECD)

erable movements in the foreign currency value of the pound. Such an exchange rate environment is often termed a free-floating exchange rate system because the price of the currency is determined almost entirely by the market forces of supply and demand. This means that the price of currencies can float up or down as market forces determine. During this period it was the case, however, that governments would sometimes choose to intervene in the foreign exchange markets to 'manage' the exchange rate, preventing it from either rising or falling unacceptably. This form of 'managed floating' was adopted by governments either because they wished to push the exchange rate in a particular direction for purposes of economic policy or to allow the exchange rate to appreciate or depreciate in an orderly way, thus preventing excessive oscillations in the exchange rate around a trend movement determined by market forces. Distinguishing in practice between these two motives is not always easy.

Conversely, various countries from time to time have chosen to move away from a system of market-determined exchange rates and adopt a fixed rate system whereby an administrative system is established which tries to prevent changes in exchange rates. The European exchange rate mechanism (ERM) is such a system. Twelve of the members of the European Union (except the UK, Greece and Sweden) belong to the ERM at present; ten have agreed to prevent the foreign exchange value of their currency moving by more than ±15 per cent beyond an agreed exchange rate against the other currencies of the Union, although Germany and the Netherlands have a smaller degree of flexibility of ± 2.25 per cent either side of the agreed exchange rates.

A similar, though distinct, fixed exchange rate mechanism existed in the period after 1945. The International Monetary Fund (IMF) was responsible for upholding a fixed exchange rate system, the Bretton Woods system, which survived more or less until March 1973. Today, however, the worldwide position shows variety in foreign exchange rate arrangements. For example, some countries adopt a fixed-rate arrangement with one other currency but free float against others.

Generally, under a fixed exchange rate regime the short-term position is determined by government administrative action and, of course, the intention is that there should be no change in the exchange rate against specified currencies despite market movements. However, in a free-floating system the price of one currency in terms of another will be determined by the forces of supply and demand.

Floating exchange rates

Taking the floating system first, what forces lie behind the demand and supply of a currency? A simple approach to this is to ask *who* buys and sells foreign currencies? The answer to that question is businesses, individuals and governments. Business demand and supply is from two sources:

1 non-financial companies such as BP and Gillette, Remy Cointreau, or Volkswagen, which need foreign currency to buy raw materials or equipment from foreign firms;

2 financial companies, mainly banks, which buy and sell foreign currencies for the clients and also for their main business of lending.

Individuals buy and sell foreign currencies for business reasons but also for purposes of foreign travel, and immigrants often send money back to their country of origin. Table 12.4 represents an approximate summary of these various reasons for buying and selling foreign currencies from a UK perspective.

There is, of course, a corresponding demand for sterling by foreigners. Many of the items in Table 12.4 are self-evident: 37 per cent of the demand for foreign currency in 1996 was for the purchase of such tangible items as basic materials,

Table 12.4 UK purchases of foriegn currency, 1996 (£ million)

Imports of goods		178 938
finished manufactured goods	100 805	
semi-manufactured goods	46 576	
food, drink and tobacco	16 644	
basic materials	6 528	
fuels	6 621	
Purchases of foreign 'invisibles'		151 560
services	43 665	
transfers	11 581	
to EU	6 720	
foreign aid	917	
private transfers	2 258	
interest, profits and dividends	86 419	
Purchases of foreign assets		144 840
direct investment	28 560	
portfolio investment	60 691	
loan by UK banks	55 589	
		475 338

Source: UK Balance of Payments Pink Book (1997).

manufactured goods, food, etc. Almost as important, UK residents and businesses bought 'invisible' items of various kinds such as services (e.g. tourism, shipping, insurance and banking), as well as buying foreign currency in order to transfer funds abroad. Most of these 'transfers' take the form of budgetary contributions to the European Union and the repatriation of funds by private individuals, e.g. UK citizens who have relatives living abroad. By far the largest single item under the heading of invisibles is 'interest, profits and dividends', and the largest item in this is caused by the payment of interest to foreigners and foreign financial institutions such as banks that have placed funds on deposit with banks in the UK. The rest are transfers of profits earned by foreign-based companies operating in the UK and transfers of dividends on shareholdings held by foreigners in UK companies – a total of £86.4 billion in 1996.

It is also clear from Table 12.4 that UK residents buy substantial amounts of foreign currency in order to buy foreign assets. These assets are of two kinds:

1 direct investment by UK companies in their overseas branches, subsidiaries or associated companies, including not only the purchase of fixed assets but also additions to working capital, and

2 portfolio investment, which represents the purchase of financial assets in the form of securities issued by overseas-registered companies or securities issued by overseas governments. Foreign currency loans by banks to foreign borrowers also generate a demand for foreign currency by the banks.

One formal framework which can be used to analyse short-term movements in exchange rates is the familiar supply and demand apparatus. If one assumes that foreign currencies are like other goods and services, then if the price of foreign currency is low a higher demand will result, but less will be supplied. Conversely, if the price of foreign currency is high then a lower demand will result, but more will be supplied. This can be shown by considering again the purpose of buying foreign currency – it is usually to buy foreign goods, services or assets. In that case if, say, the foreign exchange price of the DM declines in terms of pounds then this means that German goods are cheaper when converted into pounds. This is illustrated in the top part of Table 12.5.

Table 12.5 Illustrations of the effects of the exchange rate

(a) *Price of German cheese (exported to UK, prices in DM)*	*Exchange rate*	*Price of German cheese in UK shops*
DM20 per kg	£1 = DM2.8	£7.14 per kg
DM20 per kg	£1 = DM1.8	£11.11 per kg
DM20 per kg	£1 = DM3.0	£6.66 per kg
(b) *Price of UK porcelain*	*Exchange rate*	*Price of UK porcelain in German shops*
£100 per set	£1 = DM2.8	DM280
£100 per set	£1 = DM1.8	DM180
£100 per set	£1 = DM3.0	DM300

As the exchange rate changes so the price of the German cheese in pounds changes. If the pound falls in value (depreciates) from DM2.8 to DM1.8 (i.e. the price of a mark rises from 36p to 55p; a rise of 52 per cent) so the sterling price of German cheese rises from £7.14 per kg to £11.11; a rise of 55 per cent. If the price of sterling rises (appreciates), however, from DM1.8 to DM3.0 (i.e. the price of a mark falls from 55p to 33p; a fall of 40 per cent) the sterling price of cheese falls to £6.66 per kg. We can also view the effect of changes in the exchange rate from the UK side, as shown in the bottom part of Table 12.5.

Plainly, changes in the exchange rate can and *do* have an effect on the price (in home currency) of both exports and imports. One would expect, for example, that shoppers in the UK would vary their demand for German cheese as its price changes, switching to UK cheese as the prices rises.

A depreciation of the pound, which raises the price of German cheese, would cause a fall in demand and that in turn would cause a fall in the demand for marks. Correspondingly, for German citizens that same change in the exchange rate reduces the price of UK porcelain sold in Germany from DM280 per set to DM180. This would presumably cause a rise in the demand for UK porcelain and with it a rise in the demand for pounds by German citizens, who would be offering (supplying) marks in order to buy pounds. Figure 12.3 represents this situation.

The curve DD represents the varying level of demand for marks (by UK residents) at each possible price of marks. The curve SS represents the supply of

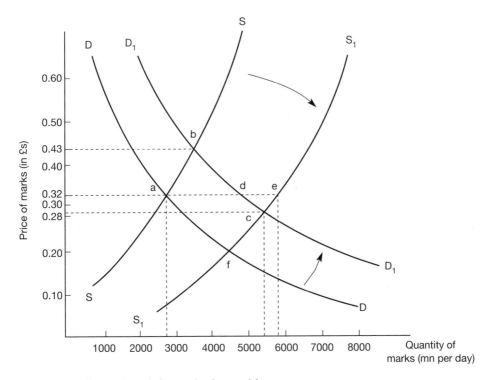

Figure 12.3 Illustration of change in demand for currency

marks from German residents at different possible prices of the mark. Given the demand (DD) and supply (SS) conditions represented by the diagram, the exchange rate (price of marks) must settle at or around DM1 = £0.32; only at that exchange rate would the demand for and supply of marks be equal to each other (point a). An overall increase in the demand by UK residents for German goods, services or assets would lead to a shift in the demand curve for marks to the right (D_1D_1). Such an increase in demand for marks would lead to a rise in their price to DM1 = £0.43 (point b). On the other hand, if German residents then wished to buy more UK goods, services or assets, this would correspond to a greater willingness of German residents to supply marks in exchange for pounds – in the diagram, a shift in the supply curve of marks to S_1S_1, and with that shift the price of marks falls to DM1 = £0.28 (point c).

Fixed exchange rates

As mentioned earlier, fixed exchange rate systems rely on administrative action to ensure that foreign exchange rates do not change. How might such a system work? Suppose that the UK government decided that it would agree to fix the value of the pound against the mark at DM1 = £0.32 (or £1 = DM3.12), where demand curve DD and supply curve SS cross. Here the demand and supply of marks is DM2800 million per day. Now suppose the demand curve shifts to the right (D_1D_1). Under free-market conditions the price would rise to £0.43. To keep the rate fixed, the UK government would have to restore the balance of supply and demand in the market. The problem is that at exchange rate DM1 = £0.32 the free-market supply of marks is DM2800 million per day but when the new level of demand is DM4900 million per day (represented by point d on demand curve D_1D_1) there is excess demand for marks of DM2100 million per day (a to d). Unless this excess demand can be met, the strength of market forces will simply move the exchange rate toward DM1 = £0.43 (at point b). The only response available to a government is to arrange that its central bank (e.g. the Bank of England or the Bundesbank) intervenes in the foreign exchange market and sells in this case marks to satisfy the excess demand. The marks would be obtained from the central bank's own foreign currency reserves. In contrast, if there were an increase in the supply of marks (a shift in the supply curve to S_1S_1) then there would be an excess supply of marks in this case. Assuming that demand curve DD is the relevant one, then the position would be represented by point e on S_1S_1. Demand for marks by UK residents is DM2800 million per day but supply is DM5900 million per day (point e). Without central bank intervention the price of marks would begin to fall towards £0.185 (point f). The central bank therefore would buy the surplus marks from foreigners through the foreign exchange market and in return supply pounds. Any system of fixed exchange rates requires such kinds of intervention by central banks. The European Monetary System (EMS) operating within the EU provides a system of assistance to EU central banks through the European Monetary Co-operation Fund (EMCF). The EMCF is able to provide foreign exchange assistance (through different kinds of credit arrangement) to a central bank which needs to intervene in the foreign exchange market to stabilise its exchange rate, and needs additional financial assistance to do so.

Why would businesses prefer such a system of fixed over floating exchange rates? The basic answer is stability. UK exports go mainly to Europe (especially Germany and France) and the USA, and similarly approximately half of UK imports come from Germany, France, the Netherlands, the USA and Japan. Obviously, under flexible exchange rates, what happens to the exchange rates of these countries is vital to trading firms. The exchange rate can affect prices, sales and profits, therefore knowledge of whether the pound is stable, falling or rising with regard to these currencies is vital.

Figure 12.4 shows the movements of the pound against the Deutschmark, the dollar and the yen. It can be seen that the pound has fallen consistently against the dollar and early on this was true against the Deutschmark. However, the period of 1985–92 shows the effect of fixing one currency to another. The early period 1986–90 shows the attempt by Nigel Lawson to shadow the Deutschmark to prevent the pound falling against the Deutschmark and therefore strengthening it. The period of stability between 1990 and 1992 reflects the UK's brief period in the ERM. Otherwise the pound rate has fallen and been very volatile, that is until 1996/7, when the uncertainty about European Monetary Union (EMU) and the raising of interest rates in the UK relative to other countries by the Bank of England as a means of controlling inflationary pressures in the UK has seen the pound rise appreciably against many European countries.

Let us take an example to illustrate. Say the UK sells cars to Germany in 1990. The average exchange rate in 1990 was DM2.87, and assume that the UK car ex-factory price is £15 000. The car with a mark up of 20 per cent for profit would

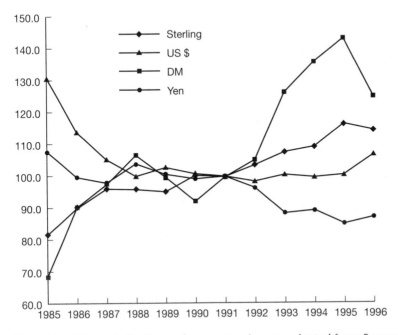

Figure 12.4 Selected effective exchange rates (*source:* adapted from *Economic Trends Annual Supplement* (1996) and OECD)

cost DM51 660 in Germany (£15 000 + £3000 = £18 000 × 2.87). The company would be expecting profits of £3000, but a year later when these profits would be repatriated they would bring only £2948.63. Furthermore, any new cars sent out would now cost £18 000 × 2.92 = DM52 560. So the fall in exchange rates has reduced profits and the competitiveness of the cars.

Variability of an exchange rate therefore exposes exporting firms to additional risks: (1) the profitability of exporting is made more uncertain, and (2) firms' pricing policies become more difficult. Considering the latter point more fully, if a firm chooses to invoice its products in sterling then variations in the exchange rate can alter the foreign currency price of its products and therefore cause a change in sales (in the above illustration one might presume that the appreciation of the Deutschmark made UK-manufactured cars less attractive from the point of view of price). On the other hand, if UK firms invoice in Deutschmarks – thus ensuring that the company knows for certain the price that will be charged by German car dealers – any variation in the exchange rate will change the profitability of operations in Germany. Although a UK firm can cover the exchange risk against its profits by selling Deutschmarks in the forward exchange, such an operation would only reduce the uncertainty of their trading operations in Germany. It would not eliminate the damage done to its profits by longer-term exchange rate changes.

Having seen the relative movements of fixed and floating systems, what lies behind such changes in exchange rates?

Movements in exchange rates

From the above it is easy to argue that the exchange rate for, say, the pound will simply be the result of day-to-day movements in supply and demand for currencies. Obviously this is true but we must also ask what other fundamental factors are at work which help to explain movements in foreign exchange rates? Figure 12.4 shows that the sterling EER has fallen since 1985 in a sustained way, whereas, in contrast, the EER for the Deutschemark has risen almost continuously since 1985.

What lies behind these movements? Various theories have been put forward to explain this.

The balance of payments

Assume that the demand curve for dollars shifts to D_1D_1 (in Fig. 12.3), perhaps because of a rapid rise in incomes and spending within the UK, but that the supply curve remains unchanged. At the mark price of £0.32 the balance of payments would, in a sense, be in deficit, as the demand for marks is DM4900 million per day whereas the supply is only DM2800 million. An alternative view might be that UK residents wish to spend abroad £1568 million per day (DM4900 million × £0.32), whereas German residents wish to spend only £896 million in the UK (DM2800 million × £0.32). UK residents clearly wish to spend on German goods more than they are currently receiving from Germany. However, as seen above, the effect of the excess demand for marks under a floating exchange rate system is to push up the price until the demand and supply of marks are once again in equilibrium (and equality). At that position (DM1 = £0.43), spending on German goods is matched by receipts from Germany. Not only is the exchange rate in equilibrium but so is the balance of payments: outflows exactly match inflows.

A simplified version of the UK balance of payments in 1996 is presented in Table 12.6. The accounts for 1996 show that during that year, residents of the UK spent more abroad on goods, services and transfers than foreign residents were prepared to spend in the UK: to the extent that the current account was in deficit by £435 million. The deficit on the current account was offset by an inflow of funds as result of foreign residents buying UK assets (with foreign currency exchanged for sterling). The balance of payments accounts also reveal the nature of this foreign inflow to the UK. We can see that UK investment overseas

Table 12.6 UK balance of payments, 1996

	Balance of payments (£ million)	
Current account		
Balance of exports and imports (visible)		−12 598
Balance of invisibles		+12 163
Services	+7 142	
IPD	+9 652	
Transfers	−4 631	
Current balance	−435	
Transactions in external assets or liabilities		
Transactions in assets		−219 293
UK investment overseas		
Direct	−28 560	
Portfolio	−60 691	
Lending to overseas residents by UK		
banks	−63 326	
Other deposits and lending	−66 572	
Central government	−653	
Official reserves	509	
Transactions in liabilities		217 095
Overseas investment in UK		
Direct	20 758	
Porfolio	27 701	
Borrowing from overseas residents by UK		
banks	74 725	
Other borrowing from overseas	94 703	
Government	−792	
Capital account balance		2 198
Balancing item		2 633

Source: UK Balance of Payments Pink Book (1997).

and foreign investment in the UK were not matched (£219 293 million compared with £217 095 million, respectively). Similarly, the respective borrowing and lending by the banks were not balanced. Lending overseas to foreign residents amounted to £66 326, whereas UK banks' and other borrowing from overseas totalled £74 725 million (in addition, see Table 12.6).

In summary, the proposition is that those influences which are tending to push the balance of payments into deficit would lead to exchange rate depreciation of sterling, whereas factors tending to cause balance of payments surpluses would lead to sterling exchange rate appreciation. The fall or rise in the sterling exchange rate would eventually ensure that the inflows and outflows of funds matched and therefore the balance of payments 'balanced'. A variation of this approach which finds favour amongst some 'city analysts' is that it is sustained imbalances in the current account which provide a clearer indication of likely movements in the exchange rate. Thus, for example, sustained current account deficits would be expected to lead ultimately to a depreciation of the exchange rate. Certainly the UK current balance deteriorated in the 1980s and on that basis one would have expected a decline of the EER in the 1980s. Figure 12.4 does indeed show such a decline. On the other hand, although the USA has experienced a current deficit since 1982, the US dollar EER increased after 1979 and continued to rise by 48 per cent until its peak in 1985 – notwithstanding ever-rising current accounts deficits (although these deficits have subsequently declined). Nevertheless, the dollar EER did not fall back to its 1979 value until mid-1990, even though the USA continued to run a current account deficit.

Purchasing power parity (PPP)

A more rigorous approach – not unconnected with the 'current account approach' above – is the purchasing power parity approach, which is based on the idea that in a world of free trade, exchange rates will change to ensure that the prices of (identical) goods must be equal in all countries. If this were not so, trade would occur to take advantage of apparent price differences between countries and the resultant changes in demand and supply of currencies would then cause exchange rates to adjust, thus eliminating this particular motive for trade. In effect, the purchasing power of a unit of currency is equal (or parity) in all countries. This simpler version of the approach (absolute purchasing power parity) may be represented as shown in Table 12.7.

The presumption in Table 12.7 is that there is a representative bundle of identical goods which can be compared between the UK and the USA. In Year 1, both sets of goods sell for an identical price when measured via the exchange rate, e.g. £1 = $2. By Year 2, however, it is assumed that inflation in both countries has occurred (5 per cent in the USA but 14 per cent in the UK). If the exchange rate were to remain at £1 = $2 then the bundle of goods produced in the USA could be purchased in the USA by UK residents for £52.50 ($105 ÷ $2) and in that case there would be commercial gain from importing these goods from the USA. Such import demand would generate a demand for dollars and this would then push up the price of dollars. In Year 2(b) the exchange rate for

Table 12.7 Absolute purchasing power parity

	Price of a bundle of goods in UK	Price of a bundle of goods in USA	Exchange rate	Price of US bundle in £s (via the foreign exchange market)
Year 1	£50	$100	£1 = $2	£50
Year 2(a)	£57	$105	£1 = $2	£52.50
Year 2(b)	£57	$105	£1 = $1.9	£55.26
Year 2(c)	£57	$105	£1 = $1.842	£57

the pound has depreciated to £1 = $1.90 but this would still permit profitable importation of goods from the USA since the goods could still be bought in the USA for £55.26 ($105 ÷ $1.90) compared with £57 in the UK. Further depreciation of the pound would occur, therefore, until the exchange rate approached £1 = $1.842. At this rate of exchange the US-made goods could be bought in the USA for £57 ($105 ÷ $1.82), i.e. the same price as UK goods in the UK. The excess demand for dollars would thus disappear since it would no longer be profitable to buy these goods in the USA and import them to the UK. In this situation purchasing power parity would have been re-established since £1 or $1 would buy, proportionately, the same amount in both countries because relative prices would have been equalised by virtue of the change in the exchange rate.

This example can also be used to identify the method of exchange rate 'adjustment' – at least in principle – on the basis of purchasing power parity. Table 12.7 shows that the price level in the UK had risen by 14 per cent in Year 2, to a level of 1.14, compared with Year 1 as 1.00, whereas in the USA it had risen to 1.05. Relatively, therefore, the value of the pound had fallen by 1.05 ÷ 1.14 = 0.921 of its original value and the appropriate adjustment of the exchange rate to re-establish purchasing power parity would have to be £1 = $2.00 × 0.921 = $1.842.

This latter illustration represents a variation on the 'absolute' purchasing power parity approach, which is that relative purchasing power parity operates; namely, that exchange rates will adjust to accommodate relative inflation between countries, i.e. changes in the exchange rate will represent the difference between the domestic inflation rate and 'rest-of-world' inflation. In the above illustration, the relative inflation between the USA and the UK was 8.57 per cent (1.14 ÷ 1.05) and therefore in order to establish purchasing power parity the exchange rate would need to depreciate by the same amount, i.e. from $2.00 to $1.842.

More than half of UK exports go to the EU countries and almost 13 per cent to Germany alone. In view of the importance of this trade relationship it is interesting to consider the way in which the Deutschmark (DM) and sterling (£) exchange rate has changed in recent years.

Figure 12.5 charts the movement of the nominal (actual) exchange rate, the movement in the real exchange rate, and the PPP-adjusted exchange rate. It is

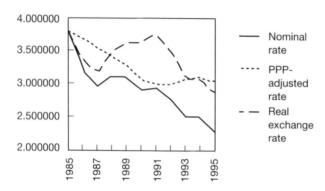

Figure 12.5 Deutschmark and sterling exchange rates: PPP-adjusted, real and nominal (*source*: adapted from *Economic Trends Annual Supplement* (1996))

clear from the data that in these ten years the nominal exchange rate has moved similarly but just below the PPP exchange rate and this has meant, of course, that the real exchange rate has been generally below the real exchange rate of 1985. Thus, the real exchange rate in 1995 was £1 = DM2.260, which is well below the rate in 1985, which was £1 = DM3.784. In other words, UK competitiveness *vis-à-vis* Germany improved during this period. One might expect, therefore, that UK exports to Germany would have risen significantly.

This approach can be extended to the general trading performance of the UK by calculating the RER and PPP-adjusted exchange rates based on the effective exchange rate of sterling (i.e. consider the exchange rate for sterling against *all* the major currencies and not just the Deutschmark).

Figure 12.6 provides estimates of the sterling effective exchange rate which has been adjusted for purchasing power parity and for changes in relative consumer prices. The figure also displays the effective exchange rate. These graphical data suggest that between 1985 and 1990 the real exchange rate depreciated by 30 per cent, which means that the UK's competitiveness

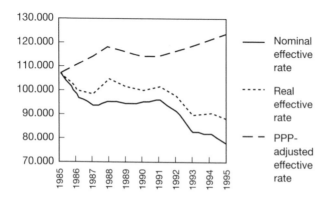

Figure 12.6 UK sterling exchange rate: real, nominal and PPP-adjusted (*source*: adapted from *Economic Trends Annual Supplement* (1996))

increased. This is similar to the Deutschmark relationship. The PPP rate, how-ever rose, during the period. This suggests that the fall in the relative EER was not sufficient to counter other factors raising the PPP.

As an explanation of movements in exchange rates, the purchasing power parity approach does not in fact have a great deal of statistical success. The diffi-culties of providing a satisfactory statistical test of this view do not, of course, invalidate the approach to exchange rate determination. Other, quite powerful factors can have a substantial influence on the movement of exchange rates and this may overlie or dominate any underlying shifts based on purchasing power parity. Some of these other factors will now be considered.

Capital movements

The purchasing power parity approach suggests that exchange rate movements will, in the long run, be heavily influenced by absolute differences in prices or relative differences in inflation rates. It is an approach which focuses on the goods and services aspect of economic activity, and in turn presumes that flows of funds across the foreign exchange markets are dominated by demand and supply of foreign currencies for purchases of goods and services. Taking a fairly long period, e.g. 1968–89, by 1989 the flow of funds across the UK foreign exchange market for purposes of transactions in assets had increased substan-tially: transactions in goods (exports) had certainly increased – from £6432 million to £92 831 million – but so had the transactions in assets: £1773 million to £90 255 million.

In October 1979 the UK government abolished restrictions on capital move-ments and the growth in capital transactions accelerated rapidly. In the past 15 years there has been an extensive relaxation of controls on movements of funds between countries for capital purposes and an important consequence of this has been the increasing importance of the demand (worldwide) for assets – real assets and financial – and the corresponding demand for foreign currencies to purchase such assets. The extent of this demand in respect of the UK is evident from Table 12.8.

One can argue in general that most capital flows, whatever their precise nature, are influenced by the potential rates of return in relation to the risk associated with that investment. Nevertheless, one can identify different imme-

Table 12.8 UK capital flows (foreign currency) in balance of payments (£ millions)

	1989	1996
UK direct investment overseas	19 365	28 560
UK portfolio investment	36 781	60 691
Foreign direct investment of the UK	18 344	20 758
Foreign portfolio investment in the UK	10 860	27 701
UK bank lending overseas	24 378	63 326
UK bank borrowing from overseas	32 841	74 725

Source: UK Balance of Payments Pink Bank (1997).

diate motives for the three kinds of capital flow identified in Table 12.8, not least because they are undertaken by different agencies having somewhat different time scales.

Direct investment

Direct investment, which is undertaken by non-financial businesses, such as manufacturing and trading companies, is likely to be of a long-term nature. The establishment of foreign operating units and equipping such units is, by its nature, a long-term decision not least because the capital assets set up or bought are likely to have a long life and are not easily liquidated. Such decisions may well be influenced by strategic objectives, e.g. the need for access to the markets of the European Union.

Portfolio investment

This form of investment concerns investment in securities by overseas-registered companies other than that classed as direct investment, and in securities issued by overseas governments, and as with any investment these will be influenced by perceived risk and rates of return. One needs to qualify this statement to the extent that the act of foreign portfolio investment may, of itself, change the total risk experienced by the holder of wealth in this form. The reason for this is that the ability to undertake the purchase of foreign securities allows an investor (whether an individual or an institutional investor) to diversify the whole portfolio of assets and by such diversification, reduce risk. To take a simple illustration: if two countries experience boom and recession at different times, then buying shares in companies operating in the two countries (even if one chooses companies producing the same goods or services) allows one to reduce the risk of variations in the total value of one's wealth. This is because as one of the countries experiences recession (and associated decline in share prices) the other country, experiencing boom conditions, will generate rising share prices. Overall the value of one's portfolio is stabilised. The same argument applies to an assessment of the return on such investments in the form of interest and dividends. One would expect such returns to decline in a recession and expand in a boom. The demand for foreign assets and therefore a demand for foreign currency will be determined partly by this strategy of diversification as a device for risk reduction. It will also be influenced by the changing perception of relative risk in different countries and the anticipated return on associated investments.

Furthermore, the relationship between the demand and supply of such assets will, in turn, affect the exchange rate. Suppose, for example, that investors in country A have achieved a particular balance of their portfolio, not only between their holdings of different kinds of financial assets (shares, bonds, etc.) but also between domestic and foreign assets. What might be the consequences of an increase in the supply of, say, domestic assets in general (perhaps the government is issuing more debt in order to finance a budget deficit or companies may be choosing to raise additional funds by issuing more shares or loan stock)? If it is assumed that asset-holders were holding their ideal mix of assets before the change in supply then it may be reasonably concluded that the additional supply of assets would not be willingly held because to do so would distort the portfolio and make it more risky. For asset-holders to be persuaded to increase their holding would require a higher return on such assets and additionally, they would try to re-establish their original mix of assets. Re-establishing the original mix of domestic and foreign assets would require, however, an increase in the holding of foreign assets and in turn would generate a rise in the demand for foreign currency. The effect of this increase in demand for foreign currency would be a rise in the price of foreign currency; the domestic currency would therefore depreciate. It is this kind of mechanism that may link the demand and supply of domestic and foreign assets with the movements in the exchange rate.

Bank lending and borrowing

It is clear from Table 12.8 that the flows of bank deposits between the UK and other countries are considerable. These bank deposits are largely short-term and are highly mobile, and it should be noted that these figures do not reflect the turnover of the deposits during a year. The data are a summary for these years – a snapshot.

Since these deposits are placed for very short periods, it enables the holders (mainly banks) to move them out of one currency into another in response to interest rate changes. Interest-rate differentials which emerge between financial centres are therefore likely to cause movements of these deposits from one currency to another and with such movements a change in the exchange rate.

Assume that rates of interest on identical bank deposits in London and New York were 8 per cent with a spot rate of £1 = $2.00. Suppose the rate of interest on sterling bank deposits in London changes to 10 per cent and for identical bank deposits (dollar-denominated) in New York the rate falls to 6 per cent. If the exchange rate did not change then it would clearly be highly advantageous for US dollar deposit holders to convert, say, $1 million into £500 000 and over 1 year earn interest of £50 000 (£500 000 × 10 per cent). Converting the capital and interest back into dollars would thus provide $1.1 million whereas $1 million invested in a New York bank would have provided only $1.06 million over the same period. So clearly, if there were no risk attached to future movements in the exchange rate then the response would be for dollar bank deposits to be converted to sterling deposits in order to benefit from the interest rate differential. Such a flow of dollars into sterling, and then at the end of the period out of sterling back into dollars, is likely to affect the exchange rate. A simple possibility might be that $1 million is converted into £500 000 at the initial exchange rate of £1 = $2.00 but as the switching takes place initially there will be a slight appreciation of the pound – making sterling bank deposits more expensive. At the end of the period it is likely there will be a slight depreciation of the pound, thus making dollar bank deposits slightly more expensive. As a matter of arithmetic, it would be profitable to undertake switches from dollars into sterling and back until the exchange rate fell to £1 = $1.927. At that exchange rate the £500 000 (principal + interest) would convert into $1.06 million. In other words, it is no longer profitable to switch into sterling. The movement in the exchange rate has eliminated the interest rate differential. There is, in effect, interest rate parity in the two financial centres.

The disadvantage with such movements of funds is that the holders may well be 'caught' by an untoward movement in exchange rates, which cause the deposit-holder to make a capital loss when converting the deposit back into the home currency. However, it is possible in practice to reduce the uncertainties by operating in the forward market at the same time as the spot market. To illustrate how this might work the previous illustration can be used. Assuming that the interest rate differential has opened up, which attracts dollar deposits, converted into sterling, holders of these dollar deposits may wish to know with certainty the exchange rate that will apply to the reverse operation when they convert the principal and interest back into dollar bank deposits. This can be done through the forward exchange market by obtaining a contract with a bank for the conversion of the £550 000 into dollars at the end of the period. It is plain that any $/£ exchange rate which is only slightly better than £1 = \$1.927 would be worth accepting. In fact we can take this further and suggest that market forces will ensure that the forward exchange rate will tend towards £1 = £1.927 (assuming there are no other factors at work in the market) because at that forward discount on the pound, effective interest rate parity is achieved and equilibrium in the market for bank deposits and the foreign exchange market has also been achieved. There is no further opportunity for gain by changing behaviour. The forward discount on the pound is equal to the interest rate differential.

This relationship has been the subject of much research. If the only consideration was the movement in the exchange rate at the end of the period, then we would expect the forward discount on the pound to equal exactly the interest rate differential as above. However, if the data showed that, for example, the forward discount on the pound exceeded the interest rate differential, what might this indicate? It might indicate that for international investors and dealers in foreign currency there is an additional risk which has to be faced: the possibility that in the future the exchange rate might depreciate by more than the interest rate differential. If that were so, the forward discount on the pound should take account of not only the interest rate differential but also include a premium for bearing foreign exchange rate risk.

Exchange rate adjustment

It has been observed by economists that under a system of flexible exchange rates, the volatility of exchange rates appears to be much greater than the theoretical approaches might suggest. One of the reasons put forward for this is that not all the economic variables relevant to the determination of the exchange rate (and especially its long-term equilibrium rate) move at the same speed in response to external changes. Broadly speaking, output of economies, and structural change within economies, as well as prices, are able to vary or adjust only fairly slowly. In the case of prices, for example, the real world is not that of the textbook model of perfect competition in which price adjustments respond swiftly to excess demand or excess supply. Most of the industrial output of the world is in the hands of relatively few business enterprises, and such organisations may well operate as monopolies, near-monopolies or oligopolies. In that case price adjustments would be expected to take place slowly and cautiously, being the result of administrative decision-making. Exchange rates and interest rates, on the other hand, can and do move quickly.

In other words, external disturbances which 'require' adjustments of, say, output or prices will not take place quickly and therefore it is the more flexible variables, such as exchange rates, which have to 'take the strain'. Of course the accompanying movements in these variables may well need to be substantial initially whilst waiting for output and prices to begin their adjustment. As an analogy, one might return home during the winter after a few days away to discover that the central heating system had, inadvertently, been switched off. In order to raise the temperature of the house quickly one would re-set the thermostat control well above the required 20°C in order to prevent the boiler continually cutting out on each occasion the water in the boiler temporarily reached 20°C. Gradually, as the temperature in the house rose, one would re-set the thermostat at lower levels as the house interior approached 20°C.

Similarly, suppose two countries (A and B) which trade with each other have at the present time a trade balance, i.e. exports = imports, and also capital inflows and outflows are balanced. Let us introduce a shock to this equilibrium relationship: country B undertakes political union with another, smaller, state which is very impoverished and has a fairly large unskilled population. What might be expected to happen to the exchange rate between A and B? It might be that the competitive performance of country B would decline, that its demand for imports may well rise dramatically and continue well into the foreseeable future, and that its export performance would deteriorate. The speculative expectation by banks and international investors would therefore be that the long-run exchange rate would have to incorporate a substantial depreciation of country B's currency. In that case, the rational response now (assuming completely free movement of funds) would be for a switch of investment funds away from B to A, in anticipation of, and to avoid, a future depreciation of the exchange rate. However, in that case, there would have to be a very large depreciation of the exchange rate now (much larger than that required in the future to re-establish equilibrium in the trade position between countries A and B) to establish a balance of demand and supply of currencies in the foreign exchange market. The spot price of B's currency would have to fall sufficiently to wipe out any benefits from selling B's currency now, hoping to buy the currency back later when it had fallen to the level expected by speculators. Subsequently, as country B's trade position with country A gradually recovers then the exchange rate would move upwards towards its long-term value, albeit lower than the previous exchange rate.

Various explanations exist, therefore, to indicate that deviations from the purchasing power parity exchange rate path can occur. Of particular importance are the size and speed of capital movements between countries: long-term capital movements as well as short-term movement of funds. Interest rate differentials could also bear significantly on exchange rates. All of these factors can be regarded as possible influences on exchange rates. Further, exchange rate movements appear much more flexible than changes in other variables, and because of this, exchange rates could overshoot their long-term equilibrium value. How can we relate this to what occurred with the ERM crises between 1992 and 1993?

The ERM is a system of exchange rates somewhere between the fixed and floating systems. Prior to 1993, this consisted of fixing the exchange rate between ±2.25 per cent of a set rate, with a wider band of ±6 per cent for the UK, Italy, Spain and Portugal at varying times. All rates are set to the ECU and therefore all other ERM currencies. In 1992, however, turmoil hit the ERM.

The fact that the ERM is to a very large extent a Deutschmark zone has meant that the fortunes of other currencies in the system have been closely tied to the state of the German economy. Throughout the 1980s the ERM currencies all gained credibility from their links to the low-inflation German economy: Britain, for example, was able to reduce interest rates and inflation significantly in the first year of its membership of the ERM. However, in the early 1990s the advantages of being linked to the German economy became less obvious as the costs of reunification fuelled inflation, making the Bundesbank extremely reluctant to reduce interest rates.

Meanwhile, the rest of the world was getting ever deeper into recession. Those countries, such as Britain, whose currencies were at the lower end of their permitted bands in the ERM found their options severely constrained as any cut in interest rates would have jeopardised the position of their currency within the ERM. None the less, across Europe there appeared to be a widespread consensus that governments were right to pursue policies which targeted inflation and thereby accepted the short-term pain of high interest rates rather than risk inflation with an expansionary growth policy. No country – including countries which were formally outside the ERM such as Sweden and Finland but which had linked their currencies informally to the Deutschmark – was prepared to call for devaluation. The rules of the ERM permitted a general currency realignment but even this appeared politically impossible.

In Europe, the future of monetary union, which had seemed unstoppable up until early 1992, was put in doubt by the narrow Danish rejection of the Maastricht Treaty in the referendum of June 1992. The immediate response of the French president, Francois Mitterrand, to hold a referendum on the Treaty in France in September 1992, which was intended as a calming measure, had the opposite effect as it became clear that the political mood in France meant that the outcome of the referendum could not be relied on.

Speculators on the money markets, knowing that the rules of the ERM obliged the central banks to support the weaker currencies, began to smell blood. Moreover, money could easily flow around the financial centres of Europe since the Single European Act had reduced the frictions on capital flows within the EU. The protestations of political leaders in countries whose currencies had come under attack that they were willing to take whatever action was necessary (i.e. raising interest rates) to safeguard their ERM parities were heard with growing cynicism by the money markets. Britain and Italy were forced to suspend membership of the ERM in September 1992. The turmoil did not end there. Between September 1992 and July 1993, the Spanish peseta, Portuguese escudo and Irish punt were devalued, and the Danish krona and French franc were also put under severe pressure (the reserves of the Bank of France were practically wiped out). In fact, the dramatic decline towards their floors of the French franc, Belgium franc, Spanish peseta, Portuguese escudo and Danish krona on 29 July 1993 led to the biggest crisis (to date) of the ERM. An emergency meeting of finance ministers was called over the weekend of 31 July–1 August 1993 and various options to 'save' the ERM were considered: suspension of the Deutschmark and guilder, a floating of all currencies, suspension of ERM, a float of some currencies, moves to wider bands (Germany suggested 6 per cent, France 15 per cent), improved intervention methods, devaluation, capital controls introduction and finally a move straight to a single currency. The decision had to be made before the currency markets in Tokyo opened (late Sunday EU time). After heated debate and at almost the last minute, the decision was taken to widen the bands to ±15 per cent for all but Germany and the Netherlands who kept to the narrow band of ±2.25 per cent. Many viewed this widening as virtually suspending the ERM. However, this is how it has remained to date and crises have so far been avoided. So what brought this second crisis?

As in the 1992 crisis, many blamed the refusal of Germany to cut its interest rates. This had led to a strong Deutschmark and weakened the other currencies. Its high interest rates had prevented others cutting theirs, despite suffering from unemployment and recession. Is it sensible for a country such as France, where in January 1993 inflation stood at 2 per cent (the bottom end of the EC average), to have interest rates of 12 per cent, giving real interest rates of 10 per cent at a time of recession and approaching 10 per cent unemployment? The use of high short-term interest rates during a world recession is not the usual medicine advocated to get an economy moving again! Advocates of further integration draw completely opposite conclusions, arguing that events show the urgent need for a European Central Bank capable of making monetary policy in the interests of the whole European economy rather than the rest of Europe having to fall in with German policy and a single currency.

Single currency

Obviously, with a single currency across the whole of the EU, many problems of exchange rate fluctuations would be solved for businesses. Admittedly rates would still vary for outside the EU, especially in the USA and Japan. However, approximately 65 per cent of UK business, for example, is done with EU countries, so these represent the most important markets for business.

So what is the likelihood of a single currency existing in the EU and what exactly are the costs and benefits? The Maastricht Treaty sets out the criteria to be met before a single currency can occur and the stages towards which monetary union will follow. These are as follows:

- Stage 1 (July 1990–31 December 1994). Completion of the internal market, including totally free movement of goods, capital and persons (before 31

December 1992). Countries would begin their economic convergence programmes and would be expected to enter the narrow band of the exchange rate mechanism.

- Stage 2 (1 January 1994–between 1997 and 1999). The establishment of a new **European Monetary Institute** which would enhance co-operation between European Union central banks, co-ordinate monetary policy and prepare for the setting up of a European Central Bank. The European Monetary Institute would seek to establish the convergence of the European Union member economies. The convergence criteria as set out under Maastricht are as follows:

  - Price stability: the inflation rate should not exceed, in any one country, the average inflation rate of the three countries with the lowest price increase by more than 1.5 percentage points.
  - Currency stability: the exchange rate should not have been subject to devaluation within the narrow band of the exchange rate mechanism of the European Monetary System during the last two years before the date of entry into EMU.
  - Public deficits: the budget deficit of any country seeking to enter EMU must not exceed 3 per cent of its GDP.
  - National debt: the public debt must be lower than 60 per cent of GDP.
  - Interest rates: the nominal long-term capital interest rates should not deviate by more than two percentage points from the average of the long-term interest rates of the three countries with the lowest price increases.

The Maastricht Treaty dictates that the European Monetary Institute should have specified, by the end of December 1996, the regulatory, logistical and organisational framework for the European System of Central Banks. Also, it should set a date for the beginning of the third stage and if this date is not set before the end of 1997, then EMU would automatically begin for those countries fulfilling the criteria set out above on 1 January 1999.

- Stage 3 (starts 1999). Founding of the European System of Central Banks and the European Central Bank; and replacement of national currencies of the member states admitted to the EMU by the euro (the currency of monetary union). The European System of Central Banks will be made up of the ECB and the national central banks, the latter being responsible for the implementation of the monetary policy set by the ECB.

Table 12.9 indicates the degree to which countries were likely to fulfil the Maastricht criteria of entry into a single currency in 1997.

Although a number of countries had moved close to the various targets there were still problems faced by some countries as regards the targets for budget deficits and public debt. However, the drive towards meeting the targets for entry into a single currency has surprised many observers and by 25 March 1998, 11 out of the 12 countries which sought entry in the first wave, i.e. 1 January 1999, were deemed to have satisfied the entrance criteria. The only country failing to meet the criteria is Greece. Although Sweden, Denmark and the UK meet most, if not all, of the criteria they have chosen not to be members

Table 12.9 Convergence situation of potential EMU members, 1997

	Inflation rate			Budget balance as % of GDP			Debt as % of GDP			Long-term interest rate 1997[a]	ERM band
	1996	1997	1998[b]	1996	1997	1998[b]	1996	1997	1998[b]		
Reference value	2.5	2.7	3.0		-3.0			60.0		7.9	
Germany	1.2	1.6	1.5	-3.8	-3.3	-2.9	60.7	62.4	62.9	5.8	±15%
France	2.0	1.1	1.4	-4.2	-3.3	-3.0	55.4	57.8	58.2	5.7	±15%
Italy	4.0	1.9	2.1	-6.8	-3.0	-2.9	123.8	122.6	121.5	7.5	±15%
UK	n.a.	2.1	2.4	-4.1	-2.0	-0.6	54.8	52.8	50.6	7.5	free-floating
Spain	3.6	1.9	2.4	-4.4	-3.0	-2.7	69.3	68.2	66.9	7.0	±15%
Netherlands	1.5	1.9	2.3	-2.3	-2.1	-2.0	77.9	73.9	72.1	5.7	±15%
Belgium	1.8	1.6	2.0	-3.2	-2.8	-2.5	127.4	124.5	120.9	5.9	±15%
Sweden	0.8	1.7	1.9	-3.3	-1.5	-0.5	77.7	75.9	73.6	7.0	free-floating
Austria	1.8	1.4	1.9	-3.8	-3.2	-2.9	70.0	67.0	66.0	5.8	±15%
Denmark	1.9	2.1	2.4	-1.6	0.2	0.3	70.2	66.9	83.8	6.5	±15%
Finland	1.0	1.1	1.7	-2.6	-1.5	-0.8	58.7	58.6	57.0	6.2	±15%
Portugal	2.9	2.2	2.5	-3.2	-2.9	-2.8	65.6	64.1	63.2	6.9	±15%
Greece	7.9	5.5	5.2	-7.4	-5.2	-3.8	111.3	108.6	104.8	9.4	free-floating
Ireland	1.7	1.8	3.5	-1.1	-0.8	-0.4	76.7	71.8	87.2	6.6	±15%
Luxembourg	1.2	1.4	1.9	1.8	1.5	1.0	6.4	7.5	7.7	5.9	±15%
Other European countries											
Switzerland	0.8	0.6	1.2	-3.0	-2.7	-2.6	50.1	51.9	52.8	3.7	free-floating
Norway	1.3	2.4	2.0	5.9	7.3	7.5	31.0	27.8	25.0	6.2	free-floating

[a] 12 months to August
[b] predicted

Source: The Observer, 14 September 1997.

of the first wave. At first inspection of their reported positions in Table 12.9, it could be said that some of the countries have come a long way. What has happened is that the entry criteria have been interpreted in the way the Maastricht Treaty always intended they should, rather than in the strict way Germany had envisaged. In fact, Germany at one stage appeared to be willing to fudge its own position with regard to government expenditure by selling Bundesbank gold. There is no doubt that some leniency has taken place; for example, both Italy and Finland have not been in the exchange rate mechanism for two years, and countries such as Belgium have been allowed to proceed in the first wave even though their government debt is above the target value (because their government debt is *approaching* the target value). Critics suggest that taking the less strict interpretation of the entry criteria will weaken the euro and that it will increasingly come under speculative attacks. Moreover, it is not whether countries meet the entry criteria that is important; the real issue may be to ensure sustainable convergence over the longer term.

Given that European Monetary Union will go ahead, what are the main advantages and disadvantages for Europe and European business of a single currency? From a purely economic standpoint, a single currency appears to be attractive for at least some of the larger countries within the European Union. It is anticipated that there would be low inflation and interest rates, participation in setting of these interest rates (rather than following German interest rates), and belonging to a currency area that may have more equal power with those of Japan and the United States. In addition, a single currency removes the **transaction costs** and uncertainties of operating in different countries. These are estimated to average out at 0.4 per cent of EU GDP. For example, the Bureau Européen des Unions Consommateurs (BEUC) in 1988 estimated that if a visitor went to ten of the EU's capitals, starting with 40 000 Belgian francs and converting his/her money in each state, then they would be left with only BFr21 300 without spending anything (a loss of 46.75 per cent) (Emerson 1992). The saving in transaction costs, however, would be lower for those countries which undertook a greater proportion of their business activities with countries outside of the single currency bloc. In this respect the UK in particular would find that it benefits less from transaction cost savings as it undertakes a higher proportion of its trade with the USA and the Commonwealth.

A single currency also makes it easier to compare prices between two countries and individual nations will not be able to use competitive devaluations as a way of enhancing their export performances.

Although the uncertainty of changing exchange rates within the single currency bloc is eliminated, it still leaves the uncertainties of exchange rates for dealing with trade outside the bloc. None the less, one of the main benefits from a single currency comes through the greater development of intra-EU trade and through its greater certainty this could boost investment (FDI and domestic) and growth. In the case of FDI a single currency should lead to greater market size/potential and this should encourage larger amounts of FDI.

Set against the benefits outlined above are a number of potential costs following from the establishment of a single currency. Firstly, there are the costs of transition. Machines and other appliances which take money, such as cash-points, parking meters and the like, will have to be adapted to take the euro. Also during this transition period 'double bookkeeping' and dual-currency price tags and invoices will be required. This could be administratively expensive. For example, in Germany more than half the accounting software cannot deal with more than one currency (DIHT 1995).

Monetary policy would then become the concern of the European Central Bank rather than being the responsibility of each nation's monetary authority. This means that any individual country will not have the ability to use interest rates for any other economic requirement. For example, with interest rates under the control of the ECB any individual nation cannot use interest rates to reduce domestic unemployment or control domestic inflation. Conversely, to what extent would a country that is not within the single currency have the ability to set interest rates which diverge greatly from those set by the single currency bloc? It was notable that during the ERM crisis in the early 1990s, UK interest rates were forced to respond to those being set at that time in Germany. Thus even if a member of the EU stays out of a single currency its interest rates may need to respond to those being set by the ECB.

Although monetary policy would be lost as a management tool, for each of the individual monetary authorities this would leave fiscal policy as the only form of discretionary economic policy available. The Maastricht agreement sets out targets for fiscal policy expenditure as a prerequisite for joining the single currency and the worry about fiscal mismanagement resulted in 1996 in a proposal to establish a new EU '**Stability Council**', which would monitor individual nations' fiscal policy expenditure after entry into a single currency to make sure that fiscal policy guidelines were not breached. If these fiscal policy guidelines were breached then the Stability Council would have the power to impose fines on any individual country if it takes more than 12 months to address its fiscal policy difficulties. Without such a stability pact it is possible that excessive borrowing by one or more of the members of the EMU could force interest rates up for all other members.

A third problem with a single currency is that a member country faces a loss of **discretionary exchange rate policy**. Before a single currency comes into existence a country could use its exchange rate as a 'safety valve' if its economy became uncompetitive say due to some internal shock, such as a rapid decline in competitiveness of one sector of its economy. Critics argue that some countries have been using exchange rate variations too often, not always as a means of dealing with internal shocks but as a means of gaining a competitive trading advantage. Under a single currency an internal shock of this type could only be solved by the use of massive EU fiscal transfers (regional policy).

There could also be costs for countries not joining EMU when it goes ahead. Some of these are shown in the case study.

Case study: UK tractor maker fears EMU opt-out

If the UK fails to join a single European currency, future investment could be put at risk in one of the country's best-regarded manufacturing sites, the Essex plant of New Holland. Mr Umberto Quadrino, chief executive of the company, the world's second biggest tractor manufacturer, majority-owned by Fiat of Italy, said yesterday he was 'seriously worried' by the prospect of sterling not being part of European Economic and Monetary Union.

A decision by Britain to opt out of the single currency might make New Holland reconsider future investment in its plant at Basildon, which makes about 40 per cent of the company's tractor output.

The factory, with production worth approximately £1bn a year at distributor prices and with a workforce of 1600, is one of the world's biggest tractor plants.

Mr Quadrino is the latest in a series of executives in multinational groups to raise questions over the UK's attractiveness as a business location should it stay out of a single currency. In recent weeks senior figures at Toyota and Unilever have voiced concerns.

If monetary union went ahead without the UK, 'for sure' New Holland would suffer, Mr Quadrino said. Referring to future investment in Britain, 'at the end of the day, we might refrain from suffering any more,' he added.

New Holland – in which Fiat has a 69 per cent stake with the rest owned by public investors – is investing $40 million (£24.5 million) at Basildon over the next three years. This investment is likely to go ahead whatever the UK's decision on EMU.

The effect of the pound's strength over the past year had caused revenues from New Holland's Basildon operations to be $20 million less than they would have been, Mr Quadrino said.

A floating pound would make planning difficult and impede efforts to complete the Single European Market. Mr Quadrino said he hoped 'common sense would prevail' and Britain would join the single currency.

The Basildon plant makes some 30,000 tractors a year, 85 per cent of them for export. In recent years it has introduced new work practices which devolve responsibility to plant operators and encourage suppliers to deliver components on a 'just-in-time' basis.

It is also among the leaders in 'mass customisation', in which mass production is combined with more responsiveness to individual user requirements.

Source: Financial Times, 4 March 1997.

Questions

1 What advantages does Mr Quadrino see in a country being a member of the European single currency?

2 Are there any disadvantages that the company, New Holland, may face on entry into a single currency?

Impact of EMU on business

The impact of EMU on business can be looked at from a number of perspectives: firstly, from the point of view of businesses in countries within EMU; secondly, from the perspective of businesses in European countries which stay outside of EMU, such as UK or Swedish businesses; and thirdly, from the position of businesses from countries which are non-European but which are active in European markets.

In terms of merger and acquisition behaviour, because the UK is not in the first wave of countries entering monetary union there may be important consequences for foreign acquisition activity in the UK. Marsh (1997) suggests that while many US executives stress concern about Britain's lack of entry in the first wave, they expect the UK to join eventually and therefore this is not affecting their behaviour on acquisitions of UK firms. However, for some investors the greater costs of being outside the euro bloc could lead to some FDI being switched to countries within the euro bloc. This has been mooted as being one of the factors that has led to Toyota undertaking new investment in France rather than expanding its activities in the UK. British companies will also face exchange rate risks not experienced by those in countries in the euro area. In fact, it is possible that the pound may become more volatile. For those countries within the euro bloc there will be, however, additional pressures to improve competitiveness as price transparency occurs and this will almost certainly lead to more bids and mergers both within and between countries in the euro bloc. Price transparency will also lead to organisations reviewing their business strategy.

Moreover, price transparency will force companies to put an end to differential pricing across the EU. For the airline industry and travel firms there will also be greater price transparency of air fares and hotel rates. At present the same airline often charges more for flying from, say, Frankfurt to London than in the opposite direction. It may also charge different fares on two routes of similar length. The travel industry will see some elements of price instability reduced with the development of the euro. Tour operators which booked hotel rooms without knowing the conversion rate of the local currency and therefore the impact on package holiday prices will have this problem diminished. However, the ECTAA (European Association of Travel Agents and Tour Operators) puts the changeover costs from investment in new technology and finance at between 1.8 and 3 per cent of a travel company's turnover. This is a significant cost for a low-margin industry. It is also possible that destinations such as Spain and Italy, which have had relatively weak currencies in Europe, could find themselves at a competitive disadvantage compared with Turkey, Greece and North Africa, if the euro is strong. Along with price transparency there will also be wage transparency. Therefore, employees will know whether companies in the same sector but in different countries are offering higher wages.

The euro could also alter things such as the basic design and size of a product. A marketing price of say, £45.99, when changed into euros, such as 55.73 euros, may make the product unattractive psychologically. Should the product be rounded up or rounded down? To achieve an acceptable price point, retailers may have to ask suppliers to alter the way the product is manufactured.

With the UK on the outside, the ECB is likely to adopt minimum reserve requirements, which UK officials regard as damaging to the City of London. These in effect act as a tax on financial transactions. The City of London can expect, therefore, greater pressure on its position as the leading financial centre in Europe. In terms of futures exchanges (see Chapter 13), Deutsche Terminborse, the German futures exchange, announced a link-up in November 1997 with other European futures exchanges. This positions it within the EU grouping head-on against the London futures market. Dealing in euro assets will also disadvantage the City of London. Barclays' and Natwest's withdrawal from these capital markets means that London dealing is now wholly based around foreign banks. When they deal in euro assets they will look for the best terms for their clients, and these will be in Frankfurt, Amsterdam and Paris. Therefore, business is likely to be moved there.

EMU might also bring about changes in the way in which companies behave. Mid-sized companies have traditionally relied on commercial banks, often local ones, for equity and debt finance. A single currency will allow a sufficiently liquid capital market in corporate bonds to develop, which even mid-sized companies may find attractive sources of finance. For multinational companies too, banking relations may alter. They will no longer need to have banks in each country – one bank in the euro bloc will be enough. Thus for commercial banks some traditional customers may be lost. Moreover, commercial banks will be further squeezed since lending margins will come down as a result of increasing cross-European competition. For the pensions industry, the most significant changes with regard to the euro are likely to take place in asset allocation. Currency risk and pension rules demand that funds cover their liabilities with investments in the same currency. A single currency will mean that funds can match their liabilities with assets held anywhere in the euro bloc, so Dutch pension funds can cover part of their payments with shares in German companies. The cross-border money flows resulting from this change could be huge.

Many UK companies are still unprepared for EMU. Even though the UK is not in the first wave, some foreign companies, notably Siemens and Daimler-Benz, are planning to force their UK suppliers into accepting the euro as the sole means of payment. UK bankers too are expecting that the euro will be pushed through the supply chain, as the affected suppliers might hedge against the resulting currency risk by forcing their own suppliers to accept euros. Marks & Spencer will even accept the euro at its cash desks, which means that it will accept cheques denominated in euros. Thus non-participation will not shield the UK from the effect of EMU. So companies will prepare irrespective of the UK government's strategy – in terms of their technical systems, financial systems and even corporate strategy. Moreover, UK companies will be affected by the way in which their European competitors change their strategy. For example, if Ford Europe or BMW change their pricing strategy so that cars carry a single pre-tax price tag in euros, this will have major effects on the UK car market.

The single currency is meant to provide lower interest rates, thus companies in countries outside the euro bloc may face a competitive disadvantage in the cost of borrowing. The euro is also meant to encourage better integration of national markets and in some industries this will mean restructuring.

Of course, for many companies computer systems will require overhauling and treasury operations will need to be reviewed. Commercial banks will lose their ability to make money on currency transactions within the euro bloc. In particular, the biggest losers will be big banks in small markets. At present they have an effective monopoly of a number of lucrative businesses, such as currency transactions and local debt issuance. For many of these banks, these businesses contribute a disproportionate share of profits and after EMU they will be much more vulnerable.

Once the euro is in operation it is likely to lead to further co-ordination of economic policies, most likely in the areas of tax harmonisation. Corporation taxes, indirect taxes and excise duties would be the most likely cases. This may not result in unified rates of tax but in common tax bands and rules. Thus the UK would be expected to adopt whatever the prevailing rules are among the Euro-11. The development of a single currency for Europe, therefore, poses many opportunities and threats for businesses, the outcome of which will not be borne equally by all sectors of the business community (Marsh 1997).

Optimum currency areas

Further criticisms lie in whether Europe is actually designed for a single currency: is it an **optimum currency area?** i.e. an area where the use of a common currency implies no loss of economic welfare. This can be understood as an area in which imbalances in levels of activity and employment will be removed as a result of 'natural' movements of capital and labour (into and out of an area) without the need to resort to changes in the exchange rate. The seminal work on optimum currency areas was developed by Mundell (1961). His work stressed that an area was only an optimum currency area if there was **factor mobility**. The reason for this was that if shocks occurred to certain areas rather than to the whole, factors would need to move to counter these. For example, if there are changes in the price of oil then the UK will feel the impact of these disproportionately. Before being in a single currency the UK may have been able to alter its exchange rate, for example, or alter interest rates so that its economy may be protected from this external shock. Such a policy is not an option under a single currency. The impact of the SEM (see Chapter 9) has improved mobility within the EU factors, especially with regard to capital, but there is still a lot to be done with regard to improving factor mobility for both labour and enterprise. For example, with labour there is low mobility within nations due to both culture and family ties, and barriers make labour even less mobile. The failure to get labour mobility between factors within any one economy within the EU is self-evident when you examine the differences that exist between unemployment levels in the north and in the south of both England and Italy. Even where adjustments do take place between countries, the time-frame can be rather large, indicating that wage and price flexibility is rather sluggish.

Normally **asymmetric external shocks** bring problems for a single currency. It is possible that different policy instruments will have different impacts in different nations. For example, changes in interest rates within a European single currency may have a much bigger impact on UK consumers through the impact of higher home ownership via mortgages than in Germany, where the rental sector is much larger.

Does all this mean that the EU is not an optimum currency area? It has been suggested that the EU is not like other countries that are optimum currency areas, e.g. the United States. However, it is possible that labour mobility is endogenous to the setting-up of a single currency area – that many currencies are preventing labour mobility. Bini-Smaghi and Vori (1993) noted that the founding EC-6's growth rates varied by a smaller proportion from the EU average growth rate than most US states from the US average. They also noted that the EU national economies were much more alike than US states. Thus their conclusion was that at least the EC-6 countries were less likely to suffer from asymmetric shocks than US regions (states). Gros (1996) goes further in his examination of the EU-15, suggesting that only large asymmetric shocks matter. Pelkmans (1997, page 293) sums up the debate:

> it would seem that such an EMU without much re-distribution and no stabilisation at central level, is possible and may well be stable. There are costs in terms of employment but similar costs are already incurred at the national level. Although cross-border labour migration is very low, the social and economic costs of higher intra-EU labour mobility mitigate the potential of the adjustment system.

Finally, major concerns have been expressed regarding the whole process of moving towards EMU. Concern has been voiced that the financial and monetary elements of the economy have been prioritised and very little emphasis has been given to unemployment. In fact, as seen above, in an attempt to hit the targets set out at Maastricht, the European economies have been operating tight fiscal policies, which have resulted in growing levels of unemployment and labour unrest, e.g. the general strike in Greece in 1997. In addition, for some countries privatisation has taken on a higher profile as they seek to balance their government accounts. If countries need to be more convergent in their performances as expressed through the Maastricht criteria then any fudging of the criteria for entry will make the member countries of a single currency less convergent and thereby weaken the strength of the euro. As Desai (1997) notes, the euro could be a severely deflationary currency. Countries may have to continue tight fiscal stances and if entry is too broad in the first instance then the euro will be seen as a weak currency. It is this view, and the notion that the UK will not be amongst the first wave of countries into the single currency, that has led to a large revaluation in the pound sterling during 1997/98. It is probably in everyone's interest that the euro bloc is made up of strongly convergent countries. It is certain that the run up to and working of the single currency provides a big challenge for the EU nations in their attempt to strengthen their trading position.

Conclusion

There are different definitions of a foreign exchange rate, and the one used should be suited for the purpose (nominal exchange rates, effective exchange rates, real exchange rates). Changes in these various rates have implications for both businesses (exporters and importers) and governments. Movements are influenced by day-to-day demand and supply of foreign currencies for trade, transfers and transactions in both real and financial assets. The latter may also be influenced by perceptions of risk and return on investment (including the risk of unforeseen movements in exchange rates) and also interest rate differentials between countries. Adjustment of exchange rates (and interest rates) can be seen as an equilibrating process and, if this is stopped perhaps by a country choosing to adopt a fixed exchange rate regime or single European currency, then it has implications for that country's international competitiveness as well as the way economic adjustment takes place internally and in its balance of payments.

The move towards a single currency within the EU provides the EU nations with a further stage in co-ordinating economic activity following on from the SEM. A single currency provides both costs and benefits to the individual nation-states. The real issues centre around whether the European economies have converged sufficiently for a single currency to work, whether fudging of the convergence criteria will weaken the euro, whether the correct convergence criteria have been operated, and whether the EU is an optimal currency area. If a single currency works as it is envisaged, then European business will benefit from increased competitiveness, economies of scale and improved growth. Conversely, if a single currency area is seen to be weak then the euro will come under pressure, the ECB will be forced to raise interest rates and the European economy will suffer from deflationary conditions. Going into a single currency at the right time for each country rather than on a specific date specified under the Maastricht criteria may prove to be the better long-term solution.

Questions for discussion

1 The following exchange rates were quoted for 14 October 1996.

£1 = US$1.5795
£1 = SFr1.979
US$1 = L1523

(SFr: Swiss franc; L: Italian lire)

Calculate: (a) the sterling/lire exchange rate;
(b) the US dollar/Swiss franc exchange rate;
(c) the Swiss franc/lire exchange rate.

2 What might be the effect on the exchange rate, within a flexible exchange rate system, of the following:

(a) income and spending within a country rising faster than that in the rest of the world;
(b) a government choosing to tighten monetary policy by raising interest rates;
(c) a government choosing to relax fiscal policy by permitting a growth in government spending financed by sales of government bonds;
(d) a country experiencing a sharp and sustained increase in the growth rate of productivity compared with the rest of the world.

3 What might be the consequences of such changes for a country which was part of a fixed exchange rate system?

4 Is the EU an optimum currency area?

5 What are the potential costs and benefits to be gained from a single currency by:

(a) large organisations, and

(b) small and medium-sized enterprises?

Main reading

Begg, D. *et al.* (1991), *Economics*, 3rd edition, McGraw-Hill.

Emerson, M. (1992) *One Market, One Money – An Evaluation of the Potential Benefits and Costs of Forming an Economic and Monetary Union*, Oxford University Press.

Additional reading

Bank of England Quarterly Bulletin (1991) February.

Bank of England Quarterly Bulletin (1984) September.

Barber, L. (1996) Mad dash for the line, *Financial Times*, 20 September.

Bini-Smaghi, L. and Vori, S. (1993) Rating the EC as an optimal currency area, *Temi di Discussioni*, No. 187, Rome, Banca d'Italia, January.

Burda, M. and Wyplosz, C. (1997) *Macroeconomics: A European Text*, 2nd edition, Oxford University Press.

Desai, M. (1997) Better late than never; strong enough to cope, *The Observer*, 17 August, p. 2.

DIHT (1985) Survey among 733 German companies, September.

Griffiths, A. and Wall, S. (1997) *Applied Economics: An Introductory Course*, 7th edition, Longman.

Gros, D. (1996) *A Reconsideration of the Optimum Currency Area Approach*, CEPS Working Document No. 101, Brussels.

Financial Times (1997) UK tractor maker fears EMU opt out, 4 March.

Marsh, P. (1997) US engineers invest in EMU, *Financial Times*, 31 December.

Midland Bank Review (1985) Exchange rate determination: the dollar – a case study, Winter.

Mundell, R. A. (1961) A theory of optimal currency areas, *American Economic Review*, Vol. 53 (1), pp. 657–64.

Pelkmans, J. (1997) *European Integration: Methods and Economic Analysis*, Longman.

13

International banking and capital markets

Introduction

One of the major features of markets since the war has been their increased interdependence. This is particularly true for international capital markets, where money flows from one country to another, seeking the greatest possible return or reduced risk. It is no accident that markets have developed in this way since countries have become increasingly linked via trading relations, and monetary restrictions placed upon capital flows have generally been reduced. In addition, it can be argued that capital markets have grown simply because of the demands placed upon them.

In the light of these developments this chapter considers the growth of the **Eurocurrency market**(s) and other financial instruments over the last fifty years, and discusses the role of these in the ensuing debt problems of the less developed countries. As a measure of capital markets responding to external factors we consider the behaviour of the banking and insurance sectors in the EU in the light of the development of the Single European Market and the further liberalisation of financial services. Finally, the chapter considers the growth and development of new financial instruments and **derivatives** and examines their importance both to the banking sector and to industry.

The growth of international capital markets

The period since the 1950s has seen unprecedented growth in the activity of the banking sector and international capital markets. Many reasons have been put forward, but all could be linked to a single factor: a growing demand for bank services in general and bank credit in particular. In addition we could look to the trade problems of the UK economy and regulatory banking framework in Europe and the USA, which also led to the banks becoming more efficient in their approach to lending.

The early 1950s saw sterling as the predominant vehicle for the invoicing of world trade flows. Concurrently, however, the huge trade surplus of the USA led many countries to experience periods of dollar shortages, the result of which caused these countries to impose controls on the import of goods. This picture was to change dramatically by the end of the decade. The foreign exchange crisis in the UK resulted in the UK government imposing restrictions on the use of sterling in external transactions and coupled with the disappearance of the US trade surplus, foreign holding of dollars rose, as did foreign capital inflows into the USA. With the growing availability of the dollar in Europe and elsewhere and the restrictions on sterling, the dollar's role as an international reserve currency grew.

British banks, restricted in their external use of sterling, began more actively to seek dollar deposits for use in their external operations. These dollars were readily available and by mid-1958 a European market in dollar deposits and loans had become established. The reasons why investors would wish to hold their dollar balances in Europe rather than in the USA include the lower transaction costs and the structure of regulations in the uniform asset world, as well as different attributes of markets whose assets are perfect substitutes.

There were also political factors to consider. Eastern European banks with dollar deposits did not wish to have these placed in the USA, since they might be impounded if a political crisis should occur between East and West; they therefore kept their dollar working balances in London or Paris. There were also structural and economic factors to consider. By 1958 Western Europe had removed many of the remaining foreign exchange restrictions on the conversion by non-residents of current earnings in Western European currencies and returned to full convertibility of currencies. With this, a more active and integrated foreign exchange market emerged which provided links between the emerging market in dollar deposits, other foreign currency deposits and national money markets. Moreover, some of the major European central banks encouraged dollar borrowing to supplement domestic credit and to finance trade, and of course the banking system was always aware that this growth could become a very profitable activity. The scope of this internal market began to broaden and deepen, and by the early 1960s it had become known as the Eurodollar or Eurocurrency market, one of the most important developments in post-war international banking.

Eurocurrency markets

The nature of Eurocurrency and the Eurocurrency markets

A Eurocurrency deposit can be defined as a deposit taken by a bank in a currency other than the 'local' currency. In any particular international banking centre, e.g. London, it is quite simply a foreign currency bank deposit. An important feature of such deposits is that they escape any controls imposed by the relevant central bank in the domestic money markets. For example, Eurodollar deposits are dollar deposits that escape control by the Federal Reserve. The nationality of both the bank and the depositor is unimportant. A German company, for example, may hold dollar deposits in an account with a Japanese bank in London: such deposits form part of the Eurodollar market. If Deutschmarks (DM) were deposited with a British bank in London then these would form part of the market in Euro-DM.

Since the original development of the Eurodollar market in London, Eurocurrency business has extended across both currencies and countries. The most important international banking and Euromarket centres are London, Tokyo and New York. Other important centres for Eurocurrency business include Frankfurt, Paris, Hong Kong, Bahrain and Singapore. The markets are spread right across the globe and are important both inside and outside Europe.

Although the dollar is clearly the most important single Eurocurrency, its relative market position inevitably deteriorated with the development of markets in many other currencies. These include Euro-DM, Euro-yen, Euro-French francs and Euro-Swiss francs. The Euro-sterling market, with its principal centre in Paris, while of particular interest to the UK, is a relatively small one.

Some appreciation of the enormous size of the Eurocurrency markets can be gained from inspection of Table 13.1. This shows that for banks operating in the UK between 1991 and 1996, the volume of foreign currency deposit liabilities comfortably exceeds the volume of sterling deposit liabilities in each year. In other words, in one of the principal Euromarkets, the UK, the volume of Eurocurrency deposits easily surpasses the value of the major component of the broadly defined domestic money supply.

Eurocurrency deposits tend to be very large in size, with individual depositors often holding accounts with deposits worth the equivalent of millions of pounds sterling. This is hardly surprising given that multinational companies are important depositors in these markets. The deposits held by these participants are mainly short-term in nature with typical maturities ranging from 0 to 6 months.

The creation of Eurocurrency deposits, or the expansion of an existing volume of deposits, depends on the switching of funds by depositors from domestic money market bank accounts to alternative accounts held with international banks. A simple example can best illustrate the point. Suppose a German company switches funds from a domestic bank account in Germany into an account with an international bank in London, possibly because the latter offers a marginally more favourable rate of interest. This transfer of Deutschmark deposits immediately augments the volume of Euro-DM. An important point to note, however, is that this transfer of deposits by the company does not reduce the volume of DM deposits held with banks in Germany. This is because the London bank accepting the DM deposits will, in turn, hold the acquired funds with a bank in Germany. There is merely a transfer of ownership of deposits. Such switching of deposits in favour of Euro-DM means that more than one bank can now lend on the strength of the same Deutschmark deposits and that the velocity of circulation of Deutschmark increases. The argument developed in the example above holds for any other Eurocurrency.

Table 13.1 Deposit liabilities of banks in the UK, June 1991–96 (£ million)

	1991	1992	1993	1994	1995	1996
Total sterling deposits	521 670	523 365	528 905	545 605	607 232	698 628
Total other currency deposits	689 794	577 121	764 737	807 532	901 436	1 023 211
Total	1 211 464	1 100 486	1 275 642	1 353 137	1 508 708	1 721 839

Source: Bank of England Quarterly Bulletin, June, various issues.

The credit creation possibilities in Euromarkets are also of relevance. The extent of credit creation possibilities in any banking system depends on the scope for leakages of deposits. The greater the scope for leakages, then the smaller the redeposit ratio following loans made to customers. While for individual banks in any system redeposit ratios are inevitably low, the domestic banking systems of different countries tend to enjoy high redeposit ratios. Leakages tend to be largely restricted to currency transactions (e.g. to finance the purchase of imports or foreign financial assets), the purchase of newly issued government debt and cash withdrawals. Now while cash withdrawals are not of any significance in the Eurocurrency markets, it is quite likely that much of the funds loaned by international banks will not return to the Euromarkets in the form of deposits. For example, when an international bank lends dollars to a multinational company, the latter may well use these funds to purchase goods from US companies. These companies may hold accounts with banks in the domestic US banking market, in which case none of the loaned dollars will be redeposited in the Eurodollar market. However, in practice, some funds are likely to be redeposited since some of the US companies in question are likely to hold at least some dollar funds with international banks. So, credit creation possibilities exist but on a considerably reduced scale compared with domestic banking systems. Of course, redeposit ratios and credit creation possibilities are likely to have increased to some extent, following the rapid growth of the Euromarkets in the 1970s, but still they compare unfavourably with those relevant to domestic banks.

Regardless of technical matters concerning credit creation possibilities, it is important to note that it is the growth of demand for Eurocurrency loans on the one hand, and the supply of Eurocurrency deposits on the other, that determines the size and strength of the Euromarkets.

The development and growth of the Euromarkets

Although the origins of the Eurocurrency markets are not known for sure, an important factor stimulating their early development was the introduction of **Regulation Q** in the USA in 1958, which limited the rate of interest that banks could offer depositors. This interest rate restriction stimulated the business of **'offshore' banks** (mainly European), which were not subject to the regulation and could therefore offer higher rates of interest on Eurodollars. Furthermore, since these international banks were not subject to reserve requirements imposed on banks in the US domestic market by the Federal Reserve Board, they could profitably lend a larger proportion of any funds deposited. This, in turn, meant they could operate on finer interest margins than US domestic banks and therefore lend dollars to customers at competitive rates of interest.

An important market growth factor in the 1960s was the series of US balance of payments deficits which were partly attributable to the financing of the Vietnam War. The deficits created an important flow of dollars across foreign exchange markets and this stimulated the dollar business of 'offshore' banks and thus the growth of the Eurodollar markets.

Following the collapse of the Bretton Woods system of fixed exchange rates in 1971 and the general move to flexible exchange rates after this date, currencies other than the dollar assumed increasing importance as international reserve currencies. This development helped to stimulate market growth in a variety of Eurocurrencies, the Euro-DM being especially important. The easing of exchange controls following the general move to flexible exchange rates significantly increased the international mobility of capital and removed some important market impediments to the growth of business in non-dollar Eurocurrencies.

The most staggering period of growth in the Euromarkets, especially the Eurodollar market, followed the oil crisis of 1973, when oil prices quadrupled in less than a year. Since oil is priced in dollars, oil-consuming countries not producing their own oil in any significant quantity (i.e. nearly all the developed countries) were in effect transferring large quantities of dollars to the OPEC countries. The massive inflow of dollars into OPEC countries could only be absorbed for development purposes relatively slowly, so that most of the OPEC surpluses were saved. A large volume of the petro-dollars were invested in money markets around the world. Apart from dollar investments in the USA, a significant quantity of funds flowed into the Eurodollar market, especially Eurodollars in the London international money market. Much of the demand for this influx of Eurocurrency deposits initially came from the countries now running large current account deficits. These countries needed to borrow in order to finance their deficits, thus preventing large unsustainable drains on official reserves. The Eurocurrency markets provided a vital source of international liquidity and this bought time for balance of payments adjustment policies to work. The international banks performed an essential role in the recycling of the petro-dollars, and the Eurodollar market was of major significance to the European countries.

By the late 1970s the real price of oil had fallen considerably from its 1974 level and most of the developed countries had implemented successful balance of payments adjustment policies. The demand for Eurocurrency loans from this particular source fell significantly. Developing countries were, however, keen to borrow money from the international banks and in considerable quantities. To maintain a good level of loan business, banks were keen to lend to developing countries with reasonable political stability.

An increase in oil prices of more modest proportions in 1980 was quickly adjusted to by most of the developed countries via deflationary policy measures. Nevertheless, for many developing countries the combination of dearer oil, reduced export demand and dearer credit following the rise in dollar interest rates in 1981 meant severe balance of payments problems and a mounting burden of debt. The ensuing debt crisis (see later in this chapter) brought a response from the international banks of severely restricting new lending to many of the developing countries and of tying new loans to policy reform packages which these countries had to agree with the **International Monetary Fund (IMF)**.

Naturally, the banks have been prepared to lend only very modest amounts of new money to many of the middle-income debtor countries since 1982 through fear of debt defaulting. This fact, combined with the successful development of some Asian countries (such as South Korea, until recently) has considerably reduced the demand for Eurocurrency loans and dampened the growth of the Eurocurrency markets.

One possible explanation for the growth of banking Euromarkets in the mid-1970s that has since received little support is that Eurobanking involves a significant credit multiplier process. It was suggested that a movement of deposits from domestic to Euromarkets led to a total increase in deposits that was a multiple of the original movement. The current view is that there is very little if any multiplier effect. Thus the existence of Eurocurrency markets does not undermine the ability of central banks to control money rates. None the less, as money supply targets or indicators are often defined in terms of domestic deposits, the movement of Eurocurrency deposits, which can act as a substitute for the former, may play a role in complicating the interpretation of monetary conditions.

The development in the 1980s that did dampen the growth of Eurocurrency business was the deregulation of the international stock market. This market deregulation has helped to stimulate **disintermediation** in the international money markets through a process known as securitization. The process involves some shifting away from bank loans by borrowers in favour of increased issues of marketable securities. It should be noted, however, that significant **re-intermediation** occurred following the stock market crash of 1987, leading to stronger growth of Eurocurrency business. Fluctuations in the growth of the Eurocurrency markets are to be expected if the stock market shows any marked volatility, and there has been further interest in Eurocurrency markets following the stock market fluctuations of 1997. None the less, for all the different reasons discussed above, only modest trend growth, at best, can be expected for these markets in the remainder of the 1990s. One explanation for this concerns the extent to which non-banks choose to hold deposits as Eurocurrency rather than as domestic currency deposits. High reserve requirements, for example, force banks to offer lower interest rates on domestic as opposed to Eurocurrency deposits. The reduction in reserve requirements in several countries noticeable during the 1990s is one reason why the proportion of Eurocurrency deposits in international banking markets has fallen from 90 per cent to just under 80 per cent during the past decade.

Of course, there will always be major borrowers and lenders wanting to use the Eurocurrency markets, with many bank borrowers enjoying high status in terms of creditworthiness, as do multinational companies, nationalised industries and other public sector bodies. As long as banks exercise sound prudential judgement concerning loan exposure to customers, maturity transformation, credit risk and bad debt provision, then an international banking crisis should not occur. This, in turn, should mean the avoidance of any serious instability in the Euromarkets in the 1990s.

The major lenders and borrowers in Eurocurrency markets

The major lenders and borrowers fall into roughly the same groups: industrial and commercial companies, banks, other financial institutions, governments and public sector enterprises. The commercial banks lend to and borrow from each other in active **inter-bank** markets and will be dealt with separately.

The motives of industrial and commercial companies in depositing funds in the Eurocurrency markets can obviously vary considerably. These would include the following:

- the convenience to a customer of transacting in a foreign currency with a local bank instead of one overseas;
- the ability to follow daylight hours across countries;
- as a way of assembling very large loans through syndication;
- as a way to reduce the tax burden;
- the ability to separate currency from political risk.

For example, a multinational manufacturing company based in Britain may well conduct important export and import business with many countries both inside and outside Europe. Payment for exports may be made in a variety of currencies by customers, and the company will need to hold some quantity of foreign currency to purchase imports. So, for mere transaction purposes, it may be convenient to hold some internationally acceptable currencies such as dollars and Deutschmarks. This can be most conveniently done by depositing the funds with one or more of the international banks operating in London. Such deposits are, by definition, Eurocurrencies. The terms of the deposits in this case will depend on both the timing of the relevant export receipts and import payments, and the amounts of money involved. Quite clearly, some deposits may only be lodged for days, while others may be lodged for months. The longer-term deposits will usually earn the company a higher rate of interest if appropriately invested, although this rate of interest will be marginally below the appropriate inter-bank rate. For example, if the company placed dollar deposits with a bank for one month, then the rate of interest received would be marginally below the inter-bank rate on one-month Eurodollars in the London money markets.

In the interests of effective cash management the company may seek to optimise risk-free returns on its **liquid asset portfolio**. If Eurocurrency interest rates are attractive relative to domestic money market rates, then this could induce currency switching backed by **forward cover** in the foreign exchange market. Of course, switching out of Eurocurrencies is to be expected if covered returns are favourable in the domestic money market.

The motives for holding Eurocurrencies, discussed above, are relevant to other major depositors such as central banks, governments and public utilities. Two important government accounts are managed by the Bank of England: the exchequer account and the exchange equalisation account. Tax revenue and the proceeds from government borrowing and the sale of state assets are paid into the exchequer account, whilst foreign currency reserves are held in the exchange equalisation account.

The exchequer account finances government expenditure but, since revenue received is not immediately spent, the government can invest some of the proceeds in interest-bearing liquid assets. Tax receipts, especially, are subject to seasonal variation, so when there is a clear surplus of revenue the government has the opportunity of investing considerable sums of money. In turn, the investments can be drawn on to help finance expenditure when there is a revenue shortfall. The government can, and does, transfer some of the exchequer account funds into Eurocurrency. The essential motive for doing this could be the relatively attractive rate of interest offered on Euro-sterling, which is a liquid asset for the government.

Any build-up of foreign currency reserves due to net inflows on the balance of payments provides the government with profitable investment opportunities. It will wish to keep some of the funds in a relatively liquid form yet still want to earn relatively attractive interest returns. The Eurocurrency markets can satisfy the government's liquidity requirements and dollars, Deutschmarks and other foreign currencies are deposited with banks operating in the London-based international money market.

As regards borrowers in the Eurocurrency markets, it is convenient to start with governments. There are two principal reasons for governments borrowing foreign currencies from international banks: (1) to boost official reserves in the interest of financing balance of payments deficits, and (2) for foreign exchange market intervention to defend the exchange rate. The importance of the latter activity depends to a large extent on exchange rate policy. The Bank of England, as agent for the government, often intervenes to support sterling, and despite the buoyancy of official reserves, intervention can partly be financed through Eurocurrency loans.

The most dramatic government borrowing from the Eurocurrency markets has been undertaken by the middle-income developing countries. This has been to finance balance of payments problems and allow some prospect of development. International banks have been prepared to lend for periods of well over ten years but at flexible rates of interest related to the relevant inter-bank rates. In practice, only the international banks have had the resources to lend on the scale required and the successful development of some of the developing countries (e.g. South Korea) is in no small way due to the finance provided via Eurocurrency loans.

Industrial and commercial companies are major borrowers in the Eurocurrency markets and can often borrow at rates of interest at least marginally below those ruling on the relevant currency in the domestic money market. For example, suppose a French car manufacturer wanted to finance the building of a new plant in Germany. It might wish to finance at least part of the investment by means of a bank loan. As an alternative to raising funds in the German money markets it may be marginally cheaper to borrow Euro-DM in the international money markets. It may, for example, borrow Deutschmarks from an international bank based in Paris or any other international banking centre, perhaps London.

While the majority of deposits are short-term (up to six months), much of the lending is for periods of up to two years. Some loans, however, are for much longer periods, such as ten years or more. The business is unsecured and interest rates offered to depositors and charged on loans are flexible, varying with the relevant inter-bank rates.

Inter-bank business in the Eurocurrency markets is important. It accounts for a sizeable proportion of the total lending and borrowing but cannot in itself, of course, increase the overall size of the markets. Funds are merely being transferred from one bank to another. Much of the inter-bank business is short-term, up to six months, and lending rates are referred to as inter-bank rates. The value of the interest rate depends on the currency in question and the term of the lending. Inter-bank business is vital to the smooth functioning of the markets, helps boost provision for bank liquidity and enhances the profitability of banks. To fully appreciate its importance it is necessary to consider the market positions of different banks. At any given time, there will be both surplus and deficit banks in relation to any particular Eurocurrency. For example, a particular bank in Milan may find that it is attracting more dollar deposits than it can profitably lend to non-bank customers. However, another bank may find that it cannot attract sufficient deposits to satisfy the dollar loan demand of its customers. Both banks can profit if the bank with surplus dollars lends to the bank that is short of dollars. The surplus bank is able to earn interest on these dollar deposits, while the deficit bank can profitably on-lend the funds acquired at a higher rate of interest. This channelling of money from surplus to deficit units helps to match smoothly the supply of funds with the demand for them and thus helps to stimulate the development and growth of business generally. So, inter-bank business is just as important to the Eurocurrency markets as it is to domestic banking markets.

Another feature of inter-bank business in Eurocurrencies is that chains of inter-bank lending may occur, involving several banks. Banks can profit marginally from the business since some small degree of maturity transformation is involved, allowing very small interest gains on the large sums of money involved. Such chains of inter-bank lending also contribute to the general balance sheet management of international banks.

At the end of the inter-bank lending chain, banks lend to corporate customers, governments and other bodies. Some of the Eurocurrency loans made to multinationals or governments can be very large, perhaps in excess of 100 million dollars. To spread the risk of loan exposure to individual customers the loan might be syndicated among a number of banks. Another reason for **syndicated** bank lending is simply that the size of the loan involved might be beyond the lending capacity of a single bank.

A final point worth noting is that unlike domestic money markets there is no 'lender of last resort' in the Eurocurrency markets. Indeed, it is difficult to see who could perform such a role, or would have the capacity to do so. This makes it especially important for international banks to exercise good prudential judgement in relation to both liquidity and capital adequacy. This has not always been the case, especially in relation to LDC loans. Although debt defaulting on any major scale by the developing countries has been averted, it is easy to see how a real crisis of confidence by depositors could cause a major international banking crisis that would seriously undermine the Eurocurrency markets. It is not before time that formal regulation with respect to the capital adequacy of international banks has been approved by the major banking countries.

Eurocurrency interest rates

Table 13.2 shows inter-bank rates, ranging from one-month to six-month, on alternative currencies in the London money markets in early March 1998. Apart

Table 13.2 Money market interest rates, March 1998

	1 month	3 months	6 months
Sterling	$7\frac{1}{2}$	$7\frac{9}{16}$	$7\frac{9}{16}$
US dollar	$5\frac{5}{8}$	$5\frac{5}{8}$	$5\frac{21}{32}$
Deutschmark	$3\frac{1}{2}$	$3\frac{1}{2}$	$3\frac{5}{8}$
French franc	$4\frac{3}{16}$	$3\frac{19}{32}$	$3\frac{5}{8}$
Swiss franc	$\frac{7}{8}$	1	$1\frac{5}{32}$

Source: Financial Times, 2 March 1998.

from sterling, of course, these are Eurocurrency interest rates. For most of the currencies shown it can be seen that the inter-bank rates tend to increase marginally with the maturity term. This reflects the normal relationship between term rates, although changes in relative supply and demand conditions can disturb the maturity pattern, at least temporarily.

The pattern of international money market interest rates

Inspection of Table 13.2 reveals that there are substantial differences between some of the Eurocurrency interest rates. For example, a comparison of one-month money rates reveals a difference of over six percentage points between sterling and the Swiss franc. Such differences in international money market interest rates tend to reflect different economic conditions and policy objective priorities in the various countries whose currencies are under consideration. To some extent, at least, a country's choice of **policy instruments** must also have an influence on the level of short-term interest rates associated with its currency. For example, in recent years Britain's inflation rate has been significantly higher than the rates of its major competitors, especially Germany. Furthermore, unlike many other European Community countries, Britain has not operated any form of direct monetary controls or formal bank reserve ratios in the last 15 years. Such measures, along with a more active use of fiscal policy, would have served to ease pressure on the single major policy instrument employed, the rate of interest. Within the EU countries the move towards monetary union for those countries entering in the first wave in 1999 has seen interest rates coming closer together as economic policies, via the Maastricht criteria, converge.

But aside from what is happening in Europe, given the mobility of international capital flows, especially with the progressive dismantling of exchange controls, the question arises as to why these flows do not largely eliminate these differences. After all, the liquid assets in question would appear to be very close substitutes. The problem, of course, concerns the risk of capital losses if market transactors adjust their preferred portfolio positions merely to take advantage of uncovered differences in international money market interest rates. Moving out of one currency and into another involves **exchange rate risk** and, by definition, only market speculators will wish to incur this in the hopes of making a capital gain on currency transactions. Many transactors will only switch funds from one currency to another after covering against exchange rate risk in the forward market. For example, investors looking for a safe return on their money must balance the cost of forward cover against the uncovered interest differential before switching between currencies. Only if the latter exceeds the former is it profitable to do so, meaning that differences between the various Eurocurrency interest rates are an expected feature of the international money markets.

For a better understanding of the relationships involved, the nature of forward cover and the forces that tend to restore market equilibrium following any given change in market circumstances, see the Appendix (page 365).

There are many different factors that can cause equilibrium changes in these markets and trigger major capital flows across foreign exchanges. Indeed, the market can never settle for long as, for example, fickle market sentiment can have a profound influence on the short-term behaviour of exchange rates. Changes in bank base rates and currency speculation are two major disequilibrium factors. Adjustment towards new equilibrium positions is, however, typically very rapid following market disturbances and this reflects the highly competitive nature of the Eurocurrency markets with well-informed players acting on high-quality information. Indeed, it is rare for more than a trivial difference to emerge between covered interest rates at the close of any particular day's trading. Even the development of major speculative runs on currencies will be largely countered by market arbitrage activities that keep covered interest differentials reasonably small. By way of example, to demonstrate that differences between Eurocurrency rates very largely reflect the cost of forward cover, it is worth considering the information shown in the Appendix which relates to sterling and dollars. It would be a worthwhile exercise to perform similar calculations on randomly selected dates. This will help to demonstrate that returns are very similar once the cost of forward cover has been taken into account (also see Chapter 12).

Other developments in the capital and banking sectors

During the 1970s banks began experimenting with floating-rate bonds or notes (FRNs), which allowed the interest rate to vary along with short-term interest rates, unlike conventional fixed-rate bonds, on which the interest rate is fixed for life when the bond is issued. Floating-rate bonds are linked to a fixed margin usually over the six-month **LIBOR** (London Inter-bank Offer Rate). The LIBOR is the interest rate at which banks lend between themselves on the London Eurocurrency market. A general feature of this inter-bank lending is the movement of large amounts of funds between markets and currencies in response to even small interest rate differentials.

Fixed-rate bonds and syndicated loans (see page 327) are only two of many ways in which international capital markets have grown during the last 20 years, and we must now turn to Eurocredit, **swap markets** and the like, as shown in Fig. 13.1.

In general, the Eurocurrency, Eurocredit, **Eurobond** and international stock markets have evolved to allow for the international transfer of funds from sectors which have excess funds to those which are deficient in funds. The use of an individual market is often dependent on the time factor of the loan: the

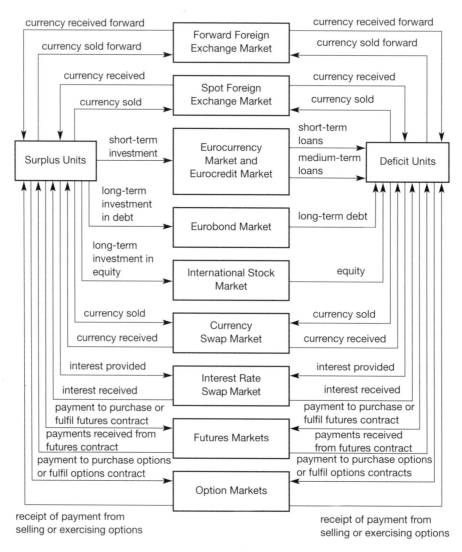

Figure 13.1 International capital markets (reproduced from Tucker *et al.* (1991))

Eurocurrency market deals with short-term loans; the Eurocredit with medium-term loans; and the Eurobond market facilitates the transfer of long-term funds. As with the Eurocurrency market, the commercial banks also serve as intermediaries in the **Eurocredit market** although often through syndicated loans. The Eurobond (a bond issued internationally mainly in markets other than those of its currency of denomination) market facilitates the transfer of long-term funds, usually in large denominations and in various currencies. Some commercial banks participate in this market by purchasing Eurobonds as an investment. However, their primary role is to make the placement of bonds issued by corporations and governments easier. The growth in this market derives largely from the benefits of globalisation, plus the ability of the banks to operate simultaneously, and with increased freedom of movement, in a number of financial markets free from the rules and regulations which govern issues of foreign bonds in that currency. By the mid-1990s about half of international borrowing was in the form of bonds, and about 80 per cent of this ($368.4 billion) was in Eurobonds. About four-fifths of Eurobond issues are said to be swapped into another currency in some years. As Eurobonds are unregistered 'bearer' bonds, from which withholding tax is not usually deducted, they also offer tax benefits. Even though the disadvantages of domestic bonds have reduced, the share of Eurobond issues in international borrowing has continued to grow, from 20 per cent in 1980 to over 45 per cent by 1996. Eurobonds now account for three-quarters of the total stock of international bonds. This growth has been helped by the standardisation of issue arrangements such as the form of the issue document and interest payment and clearing arrangements, which has helped to keep costs down. The Eurobond issue market is a flexible and competitive one, free from the high **transaction costs** typical of cartelised markets such as France, Germany and Switzerland, and of highly regulated markets such as those of New York and Tokyo. London is believed to have three-quarters of the trading in the secondary market, which is usually an over-the-counter market, in which banks act as dealers.

To compensate for the risks associated with the bond market, the commercial banks have produced the **floating-rate note** (FRN), whose interest yield is adjusted in line with market rates. Although interest in this area has remained relatively quiet, it is growing. The international stock markets also facilitate the transfer of long-term funds between borrowers and lenders, yet these funds represent an equity investment rather than a credit.

One variant on the FRN is the '**droplock' bond**, which allows the investor to convert to a **fixed-rate coupon** whenever the LIBOR rate falls to some predetermined level. The market also offers bonds that have been defined in terms of the ECU or the SDR (special drawing rights). Being 'basket' currencies these allow the investor some degree of diversification of exchange risk.

The above understates the flexibility of the international capital market. Loans can be tailored to almost anyone's need. For example, during the 1980s the market moved from Eurobonds, to internationally syndicated loans, to 'bought deals', where the lead bank is the only bank, and back to bonds again. For example, the Euro-yen market was very popular in 1986 due to deregulation in the Japanese market but has since faded in popularity.

The international transfer of funds in international capital markets often exposes a lender or a borrower to exchange rate risk, interest rate risk and market risk. The swap, **futures**, **options** and forward markets have evolved to alleviate these risks. Commercial banks and securities firms serve as the key intermediaries in the swap markets, whilst the latter handle most of the futures and options transactions.

During the 1980s and 1990s several developments occurred that have affected the internationalisation of financial and capital markets and blurred the distinctions between international banking, bond markets and the role of banks as either investment banks or commercial banks.

1 Bank deregulation: this includes the removal of interest rate ceilings, the removal of barriers to entry, and increased freedom on the types of deposits and financial services a bank can offer. This final point continued to distinguish the banking and securities industries in Europe and the USA. Deregulation has eliminated many of the artificial barriers to global finance, and technology has lowered the barriers imposed by nature. Advances in computing, information processing and telecommunications have boosted the volume of business by reducing transaction costs, expanding the scope of trading, and creating information systems that enable institutions to control their risk more efficiently.

2 Uniform capital requirements: if banks are required to maintain a different amount of capital as a cushion against losses in different countries, then some banks, which have lower targets, have a competitive advantage. The imposition of uniform bank capital adequacy requirements by 1992 in all the major industrialised countries has increased the globalisation of banking.

3 EU integration: the Single European Market and the move towards monetary union has, by reducing financial barriers, enabled countries' financial transactions to increase substantially (see Chapter 9).

To some extent there still appears to be a distinction in the role of the banks in the various markets: sometimes they are acting as commercial banks, whilst in the case of Eurobonds, the banks arrange placements and as such are acting as investment banks. This distinction between activities has become more and more blurred, however, due to three factors: the involvement of banks in the floating-rate notes market (a medium-term liability which has costing characteristics resembling short-term liabilities), the interest rate swap market, and note insurance facilities. Arbitrage risk differences of interest rate 'swaps' are embodied in the pricing of Eurobonds and bank loan instruments, and allow borrowers from banks to have indirect access to the securities market. Euronote facilities provided by the banks bridge maturity differences between bank loan and short-term securities markets, and back up their bank customers' direct access to securities markets.

The derivatives market

As a way of reducing market risk, one striking development of financial markets and other areas of commercial management, since the 1980s, is the use of derivatives. A derivative is an asset or obligation whose value is dependent on some asset from which it is derived. As such, any asset could be the subject of a derivative and it includes assets such as commodities (e.g. coffee, grain, copper) and financial instruments such as shares in companies, loans and foreign currency. So a derivative could be the option to buy or sell a specified asset, on a specified date or within a specified range of dates (the exercise date), for a specified price (the exercise price). For example, a Swedish manufacturer of instant coffee may buy the right to buy a specified quantity of coffee beans from a supplier in Brazil in six months time for a specified price per tonne. It is important to note that this is a right to buy rather than an obligation. If the actual price in six months time for coffee beans is below the price specified in the option, the Swedish manufacturer will forgo the right to buy and use the current market price. Alternatively, if the market price in six months time is in excess of that negotiated under the option then the manufacturer will take up the option. The reason why the manufacturer enters such a contract is that he requires a set amount of coffee at a maximum price. Entering into the option contract eliminates risk as far as the manufacturer is concerned. In fact, the risk is transferred to the other party (the counterparty). Of course the manufacturer has to pay to enter the option contract, but this is a charge they are willing to face to reduce the risk. In the case of the coffee example, the seller of the coffee option (the counterparty) might be a coffee trader, or an organisation that trades in options.

The example of options as a derivative is only one approach to the derivatives market. It is important to consider what have been the 'normal' types of derivative, the development of new instruments, the size of the market, and the operators in that market. The traditional approach to derivatives included not only options but also other straightforward transactions, futures and currency and interest rate swaps. As such their existence is not new but their development has been fuelled by the growth in currency risk following from the breakdown of the Bretton Woods relatively fixed exchange rate system, and the interest rate instability that followed from the two oil price rises of 1973/74 and 1980/81. A further factor in the growth of derivatives markets is the role of information technology, which helps the transfer of information on a global scale and allows the computations and control mechanisms needed by companies involved in these markets to be on a large scale. In addition, the standardisation of instruments has helped to increase volumes and so bring down transaction costs. Modern financial institutions, especially banks, have to be aware, therefore, of the potential use of derivatives both for their own use and for use by their customers.

The volume of transactions in derivatives markets has grown appreciably, especially in the area of financial futures on organised futures exchanges, where transactions outnumber those in the underlying security, and in swaps, where there are no formal organised markets but where banks act as market makers through their large-scale '**over the counter**' (OTC) operations. Of the organised futures exchanges, The Chicago Board of Trade (CBOT), Chicago Mercantile Exchange (CME) and London International Financial Futures and Options Exchange (LIFFE) are the largest, with the French derivatives market (MATIF) and Germany's (DTB) growing rapidly. At the end of 1996 the amounts of exchange-traded interest rate futures were 24 per cent of their OTC equivalents (US Swaps Monitor). This is down from 31 per cent a year earlier and 40 per cent in the first quarter of 1995. Whilst some futures exchanges have shrunk, others such as LIFFE appear to be growing and have the potential in the near future to overtake the CME. One reason for the shrinkage in some of the European markets is monetary union. As currencies become stabilised for entry into monetary union there is less need to reduce exchange rate risk. At the same time the development of the euro will lead to a reduction in some European currency derivatives. In anticipation of these changes what has been noticeable is the formation of alliances between separate European exchanges and alliances between European exchanges and American exchanges. For example, in 1996 LIFFE and MATIF announced alliances with CBOT and CME. As the scheduled launch of the euro comes into place there is increasing competition between LIFFE, MATIF, CBOT and CME to improve their market positions in anticipation of the consolidation of Europe's derivatives market. At the same time there has been the development of a range of new derivative instruments. These include **insurance derivatives, credit derivatives** and **equity derivatives.**

Although the big European and Chicago derivatives exchanges still dominate world markets, there is increasing evidence that emerging countries are entering this field. One of the biggest is the São Paulo Commodities and Futures Exchange (BM&F), whose financial volume was $4743 billion in 1996, placing it fourth in the list of commodity exchanges, whilst commodity exchanges in Singapore, South Africa, Hong Kong and Hungary show increasing amounts of business.

The use of derivatives by organisations has also been growing as a means of reducing risk. Their overall use is difficult to assess but a recent study by the Wood Gundy-Weiss Centre in 1995 of US firms revealed some important trends. Just over 40 per cent used some form of derivatives to reduce risk, with larger companies more likely to do this as were those based in either the primary or manufacturing sector. From their survey, the Wood Gundy-Weiss Centre found that 76 per cent of all derivatives users managed foreign exchange risk using foreign currency derivatives and of this type of derivative the forward contract was the most popular choice. Other types of derivative used to manage foreign exchange risk were OTC options, swaps and futures.

As a way of controlling interest rate risk, the swap was the most popular, followed by structured derivatives, OTC options and futures. Finally, around 37 per cent of companies in the sample managed commodity price risk through derivatives, with futures and swaps the two most popular types of derivative used. Although this survey was based on US firms there is little reason to suspect that European firms are any different.

Case study: Pulp futures

Two schemes aim to hedge risk and moderate ups and downs in profitability. Forward planning has never been the forestry industry's strongest characteristic. For years, companies have displayed an impetuous approach to investment in this most cyclical of sectors.

Typically, the pattern goes something like this. When prices rise, producers seek to take advantage by boosting capacity. New plants take a couple of years to build; by the time they come on stream, prices are often past their peak. The extra capacity floods an already-softening market with excess stocks, turning a slowdown in prices into a steep descent.

The inability of paper companies to co-ordinate new factory starts has pushed pulp and paper prices up and down. The price of long-fibre pulp – the key raw material of paper and packaging – rose from $390 a tonne in late 1993 to $1000 a tonne by the end of 1994, only to fall back to $500 by the end of that year. Prices are now on their way up again, currently at just over $600 a tonne.

This sort of volatility was the trigger behind the launch this year of two schemes for trading forward contracts in pulp.

The schemes, in Helsinki and London, see pulp futures as a way of helping producers, traders and buyers to hedge their financial risk and smooth out the ongoing peaks and troughs in profitability.

The Finnish Options Exchange offers forward contracts based on cash settlement. Prices are calculated using an index compiled weekly from information supplied by more than 30 companies.

At the UK Pulpex bourse operated by OM, the Swedish derivatives exchange operator – via its London Securities and Derivatives Exchange – settlement is based on physical delivery.

For pulp industry watchers, the two schemes have brought one immediate benefit. They have resulted in publication for the first time of an authoritative market price for pulp.

Producers have in the past been secretive about disclosing their exact prices of the commodity. Many disclose their official list price, which has only a loose correlation with real market prices because of large discounts given to big customers.

But while the two exchanges have aided industry transparency, they have so far proved less than a roaring success. An average of just 10 to 20 contracts a day are traded in Helsinki. Anders Lindeberg, the exchange's president, admits trading is not continuous.

Moreover, the exchange has only one market maker, Merita Bank, and just three active brokers. This is partly due to Finnish restrictions on domestic brokerages trading derivatives, but is none the less a considerable handicap to achieving a broad market.

Despite the fact that it was launched after the Helsinki scheme, Pulpex has proved more popular. Knut Lillienau, project manager, says an average of 70 to 80 contracts a day have been traded since the expiry of the first three-month future contract on September 17.

'We are aware that this is a long process, as it was in the oil industry when they introduced a future contract,' Mr Lillienau says. 'As long as we get new participants into the trading and they set up strategies, we feel we are going forward.'

He says that Pulpex had 20 industrial participants in September and now has close to 40, although only three or four companies trade regularly. Of these, two are North American and one is Scandinavian.

Herein lies the nub of the challenge facing the two exchanges. While many companies have been happy to test the water by making a few trades, none is as yet using pulp derivatives to hedge risk on a significant scale. Ulla Nilsson, head of capital markets at Enskilda Futures in London – one of Pulpex's four market makers – puts this down to the conservatism that pervades the executive boardrooms of pulp and paper companies internationally.

'It is a very conservative industry . . . many companies don't have treasury departments as such. Even if they do, the people there have to convince their managements to grant approval to carry out trades,' she says. Proponents of pulp derivatives stress that hedging against price fluctuations ought to be an integral part of companies' financial management.

'I find it astonishing that an industry as big as the forest industry can't predict its profitability like other blue chip industries,' Ms Nilsson states.

'They always blame the cycle (for variable profitability) but that is no longer viable in today's modern world,' she adds. The increasing stress on shareholder value convinces her that pulp derivatives trading will catch on. But it will take time.

Advocates of forward contracts stress they can be used not just by net producers of market pulp, but by companies that produce little pulp or are integrated producers (manufacturing pulp only for their own products) as part of managing volatility in prices of paper and packaging grades. But the companies, it seems, remain unconvinced. The chief executive of one big European paper producer says: 'For companies which are very dependent on pulp sales or purchases it might be useful, but we are self-sufficient in pulp and I don't think it will play an important role for us.' There is some way to go, it seems, before pulp derivatives graduate from interesting experiment to essential industry tool.

Source: McIvor, G. (1997) Pulp futures: smoothing out the peaks and troughs, *Financial Times*, 8 December.

Questions

1 How have pulp futures helped the forestry industry?

2 What prevents companies making full use of the new derivative market?

●●●

●●●●●●●●●●●●●●●●●●●●● ## Case study: Derivatives

Who says derivatives are divorced from the real economy? They are likely to facilitate Deutsche Telekom's upcoming privatisation, the second-largest ever arranged. An employee stock ownership programme arranged by Union Bank of Switzerland has been structured, using derivatives, to allow Deutsche Telekom employees to benefit from five times any gains in the share price, while protecting them from any decline. Unlike some previous deals, employees will benefit from the full extent of any share price appreciation during the six-year scheme.

This should help bolster demand for the deal and help to compensate for the lack of a domestic investor base in Germany and the current glut of telecom privatisations. Similar features have proved effective before: a one-year guarantee against losses on Repsol, the Spanish oil company, helped entice retail investors who had been badly burnt in previous offerings. More importantly, the programme is a sweetener for Deutsche Telekom employees, for whom privatisation signals the loss of more than 40 000 jobs in the next five years. This type of scheme is likely to gain currency: such sweeteners could help pave the way for the rationalisation of many state-owned European companies, which, as recent events in France have illustrated, can meet strong resistance. In fact it has already been used in France, for example by Rhône-Poulenc. The downside protection, rather than the positive effect of the gearing, has unfortunately proved necessary in most of France's privatisations.

Source: Financial Times (1995) Deutsche Telekom, 18 December.

Questions

1 How can derivatives reduce the risks associated with privatisation?

●●●

Has the growth in traded derivatives made financial markets more volatile? This does not appear to be the case from the evidence. In both the USA and the UK the volatility of equity markets has fallen since the 1987 stock market crashes, and share prices in countries without a futures market appear to behave in much the same way as those that have them. It may not be volatility that is the issue but the need for regulation following the Barings crisis in 1995. The Barings crisis indicated two important consequences: firstly, that financial failure can spread round the world very quickly, and secondly, that fragmented regulation of institutions dealing in multiple markets increases the risk of failure. For example, the problems in 1996 with Sumitomo, which lost approximately £2 billion from copper trading, impacted markedly on the London Metal Exchange.

One positive outcome from the Barings crisis was that there was an improvement in international co-operation between regulators. This began with the Windsor Declaration of 1995, where international regulators agreed to share information on institutions that had accumulated substantial market exposures. The main market through which market information is shared is the International Organisation of Securities Commission (IOSCO). At the same time, links between IOSCO and the Basle Committee of the Bank for International Settlements (see later in this chapter) have attempted to address the problem of global financial groups which operate in many different markets. However, regulation of the derivatives market is problematic, not least because of the fact that while individuals might be willing to consider some control over commodities derivatives, control over professionals who deal in financial contracts is more difficult. Moreover, a number of exchanges are concerned that if regulatory control is too harsh in their market then business will just reassemble in less regulated exchanges.

Who borrows in these capital markets and why?

On the whole, borrowers in these 'new' international money instruments are similar to those involved in the Eurocurrency markets. As seen earlier, such markets have been of particular importance both for governments as a means to raise finance for their budget deficits or to stimulate growth, and for businesses as a way of raising finance for growth, expansion or as a source of capital free from regulations.

Borrowing by governments and firms permits investment over and above that which could normally be obtained from the domestic market and can lead to higher levels of growth or profit. In the context of the general economy, Matthews *et al.* (1982) produced a study showing the importance of capital stock (investment) for a country's economic growth.

$$\Delta Y/Y = \alpha \Delta K/K + \beta \Delta L/L + \Delta TFP/TFP$$

where K = capital stock, L = labour, Y = output, and

$$TFP = Y/(\alpha K + \beta L)$$

where TFP = total factor productivity.

In other words, the growth in output is related to the growth in capital, labour and productivity, which indicates further that it is not only the quantity of capital stock but also the quality of capital stock that is important. We could also add that the efficiency with which this capital is used is vital, and a more market-orientated society would point to the fact that the private sector uses capital more efficiently than societies which are encumbered with large public sectors or those which are centrally planned. Thus societies that wish to achieve relatively high growth rates, a greater development of their economies, and a more equitable distribution of income, for example, often require access to a variety of capital markets. LDCs, therefore, which do not have well-developed capital markets but wish to achieve higher growth rates for the potential benefits they eschew, would logically turn to Western governments or the international capital markets as a source of funding.

In the context of the LDCs, the lack of a highly developed capital market in their own countries has resulted in an explanation of their slower growth and led to them borrowing externally. In other words, various 'gaps' exist in these countries which may not fill the discrepancy between income and expenditure. These gaps can be viewed as follows:

1 The savings gap: economic theory suggests that LDCs have been unable to save enough to finance the necessary investment for self-sustained economic growth. To make up the difference they can fill the savings gap with external borrowing. In theory the growth achieved in this way increases domestic savings and eventually generates a surplus over investment, which can then be used to repay the original borrowing.

2 The foreign exchange gap: for many LDCs their slow growth is the result of a lack of investment or of inappropriate investment. This investment gap is met by foreign sources rather than domestically, in order to finance plant and equipment and to provide missing expertise. If export earnings are insufficient to earn the foreign exchange necessary to finance this investment, overseas borrowing is seen as the best alternative. Such investment should lead to rapid growth, rising output and increased ability to produce sufficient exports to pay back the earlier debt.

3 The **marginal efficiency of capital** argument: in countries where capital is relatively scarce, the marginal efficiency of capital (MEC) tends to be higher than in the developed world, where capital is relatively abundant. If interest rates are equated broadly to reflect MECs, it follows that lending rates in developed Western financial centres will be generally below those prevailing for LDCs. In theory, therefore, capital should flow from the relatively less profitable 'first world' to the relatively more profitable 'Third World'.

If LDCs are not to get into debt then they would require (1) that the savings gap be reversed in the future (i.e. that MPC > APC); (2) that the foreign exchange gap be reversed either by causing exports to rise or by causing imports to fall; and (3) that money borrowed externally be invested in projects for which the return exceeds the rate of interest on the debt. The factors outlined above give us some insight into why some countries may get into debt-servicing difficulties. If, for example, an LDC does not allow domestic interest rates above the rate of inflation, then real interest rates will be negative and saving will be reduced. Additionally, some LDCs have not developed their capital markets sufficiently to take advantage of potential savings ability. Many LDCs have also attempted to keep their exchange rates above the true market rate. In so doing, domestic imports may be increased but exports may become internationally uncompetitive, therefore balance of payments problems ensue, leading to growth difficulties (see earlier in this chapter). Finally, some LDCs have borrowed money that has not been used to finance growth but has been put towards military expenditure, or prestige capital projects favoured by special interest groups (see Olsen 1983), which have not been successful, or has been used to sustain an overvalued currency. This last factor has allowed the higher-income groups to import many luxury goods and/or to export their savings (capital flight).

Nevertheless, there are external factors too which we must consider. If there is a deterioration in the price of primary goods, usually the main export goods of LDCs, due to the developing countries 'dumping' their overcapacity on world markets, then this is likely to depress world commodity prices (see Chapters 5 and 7). Similarly, if the developed countries use a combination of tight monetary and fiscal policies to constrain demand in their countries, or if the developed countries raise interest rates on overseas borrowing, then all these can have far-reaching effects on the LDCs' capacity to service any debt.

The role of the international banks in world debt

One of the most important developments in the 1970s, which had a major impact on international banking flows, was the oil price rises of 1973–74 and 1979–80. Their most obvious impact was to create a major disturbance in countries' balance of payments accounts. Between 1973 and 1974 the oil exporters' current account surplus increased from $6 billion to $68 billion, whilst oil-importing countries, particularly those of the industrialised West and non-oil developing countries, ran up huge balance of payments deficits. As we have seen, it proved impossible for the OPEC countries to spend all this new-found wealth and a very large proportion of this money found its way into foreign exchange reserves. In particular, the international banking system, through the Eurodollar market, was responsible for rechannelling the OPEC surplus to countries that ran huge balance of payments deficits. Of particular importance in this process was the role of syndicated banking through medium-term Eurocredits, which allowed for large amounts of the surplus to be recycled while the risks of lending to foreign borrowers were shared across the international banking system.

At first the international banks lent mainly to developed countries such as the UK and Italy, but soon they began to lend to the LDCs and other Central and Eastern European Countries (CEECs) (see Chapter 14).

LDC debt

As Table 13.3 shows, at the end of 1973, LDCs owed $130 billion to all creditors and their debts to the banks were about $17 billion. Three years later their debts totalled $228 billion, with bank debt at $49 billion. At the time the loans were made, the LDCs appeared to be reasonable credit risks. The prices of their export commodities were high and no one could see any sign of an international recession. Creditor banks fully expected the loans to be repaid out of borrowers' export earnings. Moreover, the international banks believed that the existence of 'lender of last resort' arrangements with their central banks meant that this facility would be on offer to them should the LDCs be unable to pay their debts. Knowing that such a facility was in existence in the case of LDC debt allowed the commercial banks to take on riskier portfolios in return for higher returns.

Although commercial bank lending contracted after 1982, commercial banks were still becoming over-exposed. Bank regulators in most industrialised countries became concerned by weaknesses in some banks' portfolios and took measures to improve the soundness of national banking systems. Therefore banks have since been very reticent in lending new money to LDCs and in fact, led by Citicorp in 1987, they have rapidly increased their loan-loss reserves. This approach has allowed the international banks to 'wash their hands' of the debt, either by writing it off or by selling it on the secondary market.

Table 13.3 Debts of LDCs, except major oil exporters, 1973–87 (billions of dollars)

Item	1973	1976	1979	1982	1985	1987
Total debt outstanding	130.1	228.0	439.1	708.0	846.5	995.9
Short-term debt	18.4	33.2	75.0	147.1	127.2	129.0
Long-term debt	111.8	194.9	364.1	560.9	719.3	866.9
To official creditors	51.0	82.4	150.6	222.5	302.5	399.2
To commercial banks[a]	17.3	49.0	116.6	190.0	283.8	330.4
To other creditors[b]	43.5	63.5	96.9	147.6	133.4	137.3

[a] Includes public and publicly guaranteed debt to banks and other financial institutions.
[b] Includes all unguaranteed debt.

Source: International Monetary Fund, *World Economic Outlook*, various issues.

The establishment of loan-loss reserves has been aided in a number of countries by flexible tax regimes allowing the commercial banks to have the option to reduce LDC debt through the tax deductibility of such provisions. This process has also allowed the commercial banks to establish a cushion against any potential losses on LDC debt. Another factor that has helped in the banks' attitude to debt–debt service relief is the link between loan-loss provision and capital. This is being modified in the context of convergence towards a common measurement of capital adequacy in the context of the new Basle Agreement.

For UK banks, the Bank of England set up a 'country scoring system' in 1987 (and modified in January 1990) to get the commercial banks to examine their provisions against country risk. This system, known as '**the matrix**', sets a score (the higher the value, the worse the problem) against a whole range of criteria applied to individual country loans. For example, a country that appears to be unwilling or unable to meet its debt obligations, or for which there are current difficulties in meeting debt repayments, gets high scores. For countries which receive a score greater than 145, then a commercial bank must have put aside 100 per cent provision against the debt.

In countries such as France, where reserves are included in regulatory capital, banks are unlikely to want to take losses and write down reserves. Table 13.4 indicates the ratio for total capital requirements as a proportion of risk-weighted assets, and it is worth noting that in 1989 the figure for France had almost reached the level that will be required in 1992 by the Basle Committee.

The other major factor concerning the banks' position is the variation in the regions in which the banks have provided money. US banks in particular, and to some extent UK banks, have debts biased towards South America, whilst the European banks face heavy debts from Eastern European countries, and France has a heavy concentration of claims in Africa. Resolving the **debt crisis** is, therefore, different for the various countries' banks. French claims are in the lower-income countries, whose debts were not serious until the mid to late 1980s, whilst the US claims have been on higher-income developing countries, whose debts have been serious since the early 1980s.

Table 13.4 Estimated average Basle G–10 committee ratios, end 1989 (total capital requirement as % of risk-weighted assets)

Belgium	8.0
Canada	7.6
France	7.5
Germany	> 8.0
Italy	7.5
Japan	9.0
Netherlands	> 8.0
Sweden	8.0
Switzerland	> 8.0
UK	8.9
USA	8.0

Minimum Basle ratio (for 1992) 8.0.
Minimum Basle ratio (for 1990) 7.25.

Source: Griffith–Jones (1991) page 277.

The process of protecting the banking sector has to some extent worked, as Table 13.5 indicates. The amount of debt owed to the commercial banks has stabilised and been compensated by debts to official sources and other private sources. In addition, the policies to change short-term debt into long-term debt also appear to have been successful.

The ways of resolving world debt

The various methods of and approaches to reducing debt have tended to concentrate on measures to reduce LDC debt. However, rather than concern themselves with the debtor countries, governments' initial focus was biased towards the banking system, which had lent too much, rather than the LDCs, which had borrowed too much. For example, in the USA at the end of 1982, the nine major US banks had lent 176.5 per cent of bank capital to Latin American countries and 287.1 per cent of bank capital to all developing countries; thus if the claims on developing countries 'went bad', many major US banks would have become insolvent. Aside from the problems facing US commercial banks, Table 13.5 indicates that the total debt facing the banking sector in general is a significant proportion of total debt. In the UK, between 1989 and 1990, UK commercial banks made provisions in their accounts in excess of £5 billion against bad debts in the developing countries. In other words, initial policies were aimed at keeping the pressure on debtor nations so that the debt could be serviced, whilst at the same time looking for ways to relieve the pressure on the banks. Some of the proposals which have been suggested, and even tried, include the following:

1 **Rescheduling the debt**: rescheduling of debt refers to renegotiating the terms of the loan; in other words, postponing and extending the repayments of principal and interest. One of the most important arenas for this to take place has been the '**Paris Club**', and between 1982 and 1987 it rescheduled some $48 billion of debt for 39 countries. During the 1990s the Paris Club has been very active in reducing CEEC debt (see Chapter 14).

2 **Multi-year rescheduling agreements** (MYRA): a MYRA involves the rescheduling of a number of years' maturities over a longer term, often

Table 13.5 Developing countries' external debt, by maturity and type of creditor (billions of dollars)

	1989	1991	1993	1995	1997	1998
Total debt	1117.5	1250.8	1451.0	1698.0	1790.8	1875.4
By maturity						
Short-term	166.9	223.1	285.6	318.6	309.9	302.2
Long-term	950.6	1027.6	1165.4	1379.4	1480.9	1573.2
By type of creditor						
Official	528.2	603.3	721.4	761.7	729.0	731.3
Banks	398.5	404.9	394.8	415.2	432.4	447.6
Other private	190.8	242.6	459.9	521.1	629.4	696.5

Source: World Bank (1997) table A39, page 208.

incorporating a significant 'grace' period. One of the features is to ensure that covenants, events of a default, and other clauses are linked into such arrangements with other creditors so as to build in as much protection as possible.

3 **Debt/equity swaps**: commercial banks have also become involved in exchanging developing countries' debts for equity in commercial projects in these debtor countries. The existence of these debt/equity swaps has stimulated the growth of a 'secondary' market where creditor commercial banks may sell their developing country debt. The buyers in this market can then trade this debt for an equity position in the debtor country. Alternatively, the foreign currency debt can be exchanged for domestic currency debt. The market for this arrangement, however, is still small, accounting for 5 per cent of the total LDC debt held by the international banks.

4 **IMF**: the IMF has been an important source of funding for debtor nations experiencing repayment difficulties. The funding is not given without 'ties'. The IMF requires borrowers to adjust their economic policies to reduce their balance of payments difficulties and improve debt repayments (structural reform policies, which are to stimulate growth). The conditions usually involve targets for macro-economic variables, such as money supply growth or the reduction in government borrowing, the abolition or liberalisation of foreign exchange and import controls, devaluation of the official exchange rate, the control of wage increases, dismantling price controls and the opening of the economy to international commerce.

The IMF policy to reduce indebtedness by targeting imports has meant that reductions are normally in the form of capital and industrial supplies, which are easier to sacrifice, rather than essential imports such as fuel and food. This has an adverse effect on LDC export performance due to the damage caused to industrial capacity and, therefore, growth. The implementation of this policy has been widespread.

5 **Debt cancellation**: initially, at the onset of the debt crisis, it was suggested that some debt be cancelled, thereby increasing the ability to service the remainder of the debt and also allowing the debtor nation to retain more money for its own development. It was thought that across-the-board arrangements could be made. However, the credit-worthy, middle-income countries, which were planning to borrow more funds in the future, disavowed themselves from such a proposal. Before long, therefore, it was fairly obvious that the request for debt relief was confined to official loans to low-income countries.

6 **Buybacks**: in a buyback, the debtor country uses cash reserves, either its own or money borrowed externally, to repurchase some of its debt from its creditor banks, but at a large discount price using the secondary market for debt (see example earlier).

7 **Debt conversion**: using this tool, some of the existing debt is converted into new assets. For example, a country might convert some of its existing debt,

which carries a floating market interest rate, into a new debt which carries a fixed interest rate below market interest rate with some, if not all, future interest payments guaranteed. This new asset would have a lower contractual debt service burden and it would be safer than the original debt by backing it with guarantees or collateral.

8 **Debt-for-debt swaps**: a bank not wishing to make a loss on a loan sells it to an investor, keeps the original amount on the books, but changes the terms to make it considerably more favourable to the debtor country. The bank does not have to show a loss, and hopes that the new paper will be worth more than the old, whilst the debtor country has reduced the cost of servicing the foreign debt.

9 **Relending**: a bank awaiting payment from an LDC of money in local currency, which has to be converted into foreign currency, chooses to relend it locally to a client of its choice. The bank makes an extra profit locally, and the debtor does not have to use up its scarce foreign exchange reserves. In addition, such lending may well be more remunerative for the creditor due to extra earnings from fees, higher margins or because of tax advantages.

10 **On-lending**: a bank agrees to put some new money into an LDC but in order to make sure it is spent wisely, selects who will receive the money.

11 **Cofinancing**: a bank agrees to lend new money as long as it is tied to a project that has received other banking support, e.g., a **World Bank**-supported project.

12 **Exit bonds**: here a bank that wishes to pull out of lending converts its foreign currency bonds into new ones with a lower interest rate, or bonds that are worth less but guaranteed by a third party. The bank earns less but thinks it has a better chance of being paid off, and the debtor country reduces its stock of outstanding debt.

13 **Bridge finance**: if there is a short-term crisis, bridge finance may be required to 'bail out' a country whilst a more long-term solution is sought. Such bridge finance may come from official sources exclusively, from the banks or from a combination of both.

14 **Interest capping, relief and capitalisation**: a debtor could agree to defer payments above a certain maximum interest level. Amounts above this would be debited to the country's account to be paid off when interest rates fall below the cap, or the extra may be rolled up into an additional payment at the end. Alternatively, the loan maturity may be extended to allow interest to be stretched, with provisions for recontraction of the loan maturity if rates fall.

15 **Securitisation/long-term instruments**: on a small scale, certain Latin American banks have sought to convert short-term inter-bank loans into longer-term instruments such as floating-rate notes, commercial paper and certificates of deposits. Both debtors and creditors can gain. The debtor is more secure about funding, the creditor has on the books a security that

could be traded if an active market develops, and less time is wasted in renegotiating the loan.

16 **The World Bank**: the World Bank aided the moves towards debt reduction by the commercial banks, IMF and governments through its lending of a wider range of currencies to debtor nations. Its 'debt relief initiative' in 1996 provided additional funding if countries met a range of conditions (such as the targeting of specific economic variables) for periods of between three and six years. The cost of this initiative has been estimated at between $5.6 billion and $7.7 billion. This debt relief initiative was developed in conjunction with the IMF, the main commercial lenders and most governments.

Apart from these responses from the banks, more 'official' government-backed plans have been forthcoming in the shape of the Baker, Bradley and Brady plans, which were US proposals to reduce the debt burden of LDCs and CEECs.

The extent to which these policies have reduced the debt burden can be seen in Table 13.6. One measure of indebtedness is the ratio of external debt to GDP. For less developed economies this has fallen since 1988, though for Africa, and sub-Saharan Africa in particular, the debt crisis has far from receded.

Is the debt crisis over?

For many in the West the debt crisis appears to be over. Almost 80 per cent of the outstanding debt owed to commercial banks by the most heavily indebted countries (Mexico, Argentina, Brazil and Venezuela, amongst others) has been restructured. With the signing of the Brady-type restructuring deals with Argentina and Brazil in 1992 the commercial banks could begin to worry less about debt problems. However, as Table 13.6 indicates, the crisis for the countries themselves, in particular those in Africa, appears to be worsening. Their debt payments comprise almost 20 per cent of export revenues for some countries. So although the commercial banking sector has benefited from IMF-type policies, the squeeze is still on a number of developing countries.

Table 13.6 Developing countries: ratio of external debt to GDP, 1988–97

Country/area	1988	1990	1992	1994	1996	1997[a]
Africa	60.2	60.3	62.0	70.5	65.8	64.9
Asia	23.2	22.5	22.9	24.1	22.3	22.1
Middle East/Europe	36.6	35.3	33.6	32.0	25.6	22.0
Sub-Saharan Africa	80.4	89.4	100.0	132.7	114.8	107.0
Four newly industrialising Asian economies	12.5	9.7	9.5	10.6	13.7	14.4
Less developed economies	76.3	72.4	59.4	49.4	41.0	35.5

[a]Estimated

Source: *World Bank Report* (1997) table 13.5, page 212.

Developing countries now stand a better chance of attracting capital. The prospect for an increase in international capital flows into the developing world is a bright one.

The pool of capital offered by private international securities markets, official financing, and private foreign direct investment should satisfy in large part the thirst for investment from the rapidly growing developing countries.

Meanwhile, reform of the way governments and multilateral institutions treat the very poor nations is helping to ensure that these countries receive more public money and stand a better chance of attracting private sector capital in the future.

Several important developments have occurred in the area of official financing for developing countries in recent years. Perhaps the most important was the agreement in December 1994 – and subsequent implementation for selected countries – of the so-called 'Naples terms' for low-income countries by Paris Club creditors.

This agreement, which allows up to 67 per cent debt relief for selected poor countries, has enabled many poor states to finally resolve their outstanding debt problems and prepare for a re-entry into the world financial community and, potentially, the world's capital markets.

One important initiative being debated in the international arena at present is a plan to raise the 67 per cent limit allowed under the Naples terms to about 90 per cent for selected countries, although not all debt is eligible for relief.

A second important development has been the increasing focus on the issue of multilateral debt. Governments have come to recognise more clearly the burden placed on countries by the debt they owe to institutions such as the World Bank and the International Monetary Fund.

There are proposals to alleviate a large part of the burden of this multilateral debt. The World Bank's proposed Trust Fund and the plan to sell off a proportion of the IMF's gold reserves would be used to finance this objective.

Such initiatives would not only lessen the burden imposed on poor countries of large debt interest payments, but they would also greatly increase these countries' ability to attract new capital from the private financial markets.

A third important development in official financing was the support provided by official creditors in early 1995 to Mexico and the subsequent efforts by the international policy-making community to put in place safeguards to ensure that a financial crisis such as that in Mexico is less likely to happen again.

These safeguards – such as better financial supervision and data standards, larger emergency credit arrangements and recommendations to ensure a fairer deal for creditors in the event of a crisis – represent an attempt to set up a framework of checks and balances in which countries can operate without government interference and more effectively attract sustainable investment flows.

On the securities front, in spite of the world bond market reversal of 1994, the Mexican crisis of late 1994 and the turbulence in financial markets at the beginning of this year, 'net issuance of international securities by borrowers in developing countries has been highly resilient', according to the Bank for

International Settlements. These events had 'no more than a temporary and localised influence on issuance,' the BIS said.

The flow of capital via securities into the developing world even managed to withstand the sharp rise in US long-term interest rates at the beginning of this year.

Rises in US interest rates have in the past been associated with a decline in investment flows into developing countries as investors are typically attracted back to higher yielding and more credit-worthy US assets. But this time round, the flows were sustained. As a result, securities issued by developing countries had already by the end of the first quarter of this year exceeded the previous record issuance in 1994.

The optimism about rising capital flows into the developing world extends to foreign direct investment.

The share of worldwide foreign direct investment inflows going into countries outside the OECD area has been increasing since the late 1980s.

However, its share still remains below that achieved in 1982 before the Third World debt crisis and the recessions that followed it in many debtor countries.

However, since 1985, once the effect of the debt crisis had diminished, flows into developing countries increased every year to reach about $80 billion in 1994, according to the OECD.

Deregulation, privatisation and liberalisation, including the dismantling of trade barriers in these countries, have been some of the factors behind this growth. They have created an environment more conducive to inward investment.

But another significant factor has been the rapid economic growth in many of the developing countries. As their economies have grown, the incentive for foreign companies to locate in these growing consumer markets has increased.

In the past, the absence of suitable domestic economic policies meant that the benefits of much of the investment which did flow into many poor countries were diluted.

However, the past few years, according to the OECD, have been marked by a sea-change in attitudes towards inward investment, as well as a corresponding rise in the levels of flows. Investment in the 1990s has been very different from that in previous decades in terms of quantity and quality.

As the removal of trade barriers continues in the developing world, as more and more of national economies are privatised, as political instability declines, and as economic growth gathers pace, the flow of foreign direct investment into the developing world looks set to continue to grow. More importantly, economic reforms in these countries are creating the environment which will help ensure that these increased flows generate greater gains for poor countries.

Source: Bowley, G. (1996) World economy and finance: prospects brighten, *Financial Times,* 27 September.

Questions

1 Why does the future look brighter for the debt-ridden developing countries?

2 What economic packages have been used to improve the developing countries' debt positions?

None the less, for those countries where a satisfactory deal has been struck, the problems of debt can easily resurface. In early 1995, Mexico was forced to devalue its currency. Its debt had been growing and it was due to repay in that year 35 per cent of its total debt. Because many felt that Mexico would find it difficult to repay its loans, almost half of the private **portfolio investment** capital that had flowed into Mexico during the early 1990s was withdrawn. The USA came to Mexico's assistance through a range of loan guarantees in exchange for Mexico pledging its oil revenues in exchange. Thus, although the problems facing the commercial banks have been greatly reduced, external debt issues may still be a problem of the future.

Banking and insurance in Europe

One of the areas that has seen dramatic developments in the 1990s has been that of financial services, especially in the fields of banking and insurance. Sometimes, however, the distinction between these at corporate level is blurred, with banks owning insurance companies and insurance companies having substantial shareholdings in banks. Thus not only are the individual sectors experiencing considerable changes but national companies are increasingly diversifying on both a geographic and a product basis.

The forces that are creating these changes are global in nature, through the globalisation of business, which has been further enhanced by the development of new technologies. New technology has encouraged both retail and investment banks to respond quickly to customers and market changes. It has also led to new channels of distribution in banking such as banking via the Internet, which, although currently a small part of the banking interface, is likely to have an increasing impact in the future and will call into question the role of the branch banks.

The Single European Market has also had an impact on the sector, not only in terms of banking directives, which have sought to open up some of the traditionally protectionist national markets, but also in terms of focusing the minds of banks on the need to compete internationally, rather than just relying on the domestic market. This has been reflected in the considerable merger and acquisition activity in the sector, particularly in the acquisition of investment banks by the **retail banks**. This has been supported by increased deregulation in many European countries, where governments have (in some cases) loosened their grip on their control over the banks or their direct shareholdings in them in an attempt to further competition in the sector.

Many of the proactive banks and insurance companies are also beginning to address the strategic significance of European Monetary Union, and the introduction of the euro, for bank use in 1999 although not general use until 2002, which will have further repercussions in these sectors.

The structure of banking and insurance in Europe in the 1990s

An inspection of the leading commercial and savings banks in Europe shows that there are a significant number of major players on a global level. Table 13.7 shows the top 20 European banks based on 1996 revenues. As an indication of the rapid changes that are taking place in this sector, the leading position of Deutsche Bank in the table has already been overtaken in its own country by the merger in June 1997 of Bayerische Vereinsbank and Bayerische Hypobank and the even bigger merger in December 1997 of the Swiss giants UBS and SBC, which both have substantial **investment banking** arms. Although the data in Table 13.7 reflect retail banking, many banks are involved with private banking, investment banking and asset management, which substantially increases their asset base. Thus on these criteria the greatest assets are held by HSBC Holdings, followed by the new Swiss giant, which will be called the United Bank of Switzerland.

Despite all this merger activity, the retail banking sector has stubbornly retained its national dimension in that most of the mergers in the sector have been within countries, where there has been significant activity, but the record of cross-border mergers has been less impressive despite all the pressures pushing banks in that direction. France, for example, has a number of large banks but very little overseas ownership of them.

Table 13.7 Leading commercial and savings banks in Europe, 1996

Rank[a]	Name	Country	Revenue ($millions)
1 (2)	Deutsche Bank	Germany	39 413
2 (3)	Credit Agricole	France	34 620
3 (5)	GAN	France	32 260
4 (7)	HSBC Holdings	UK	28 860
5 (9)	ABN-AMRO	Netherlands	27 651
6 (10)	Credit Suisse	Switzerland	27 647
7 (12)	Société Générale	France	26 010
8 (13)	Credit Lyonnais	France	25 180
9 (14)	BNP	France	24 125
10 (17)	National Westminster	UK	22 784
11 (20)	Dresdner Bank	Germany	21 489
12 (21)	Paribas	France	21 212
13 (23)	Westdeutsche Landesbank	Germany	20 474
14 (26)	Lloyds–TSB Group	UK	20 373
15 (27)	Barclays	UK	19 692
16 (28)	Commerzbank	Germany	19 691
17 (29)	UBS	Switzerland	18 902
18 (30)	Bayerische Vereinsbank	Germany	17 598
19 (35)	Swiss Bank Corporation	Switzerland	15 709
20 (37)	Banco di San Paolo	Italy	15 269

[a]Figures in brackets denote global ranking.

Source: *Fortune* (1997) Global 500, page F17.

From Table 13.7 it can be seen that France has some of the biggest banks in Europe, with Credit Agricole, GAN, Société Générale and Credit Lyonnais well up in the league of leading banks. There has been a tradition of government involvement in the running of banks in France (e.g. Credit Lyonnais has six government representatives on the board of directors), which has sometimes made change difficult, although under the Chirac government in 1986, Société Générale was privatised, along with two big merchant banks, Banque Indosuez and Paribas.

Despite their traditional conservatism, the French banks have invested heavily in new technology, especially automatic cash dispensers and computerisation, throughout all their networks. However, government involvement through supervision of the banks has not always been strong, as has been seen with the recent example of Credit Lyonnais. During the 1980s, Credit Lyonnais had sought to develop a global presence through acquisition and global lending through a rapid expansion of its offices world-wide, and by the end of the decade it had become the world's largest non-Japanese financial institution. Unfortunately, it then lent money to a number of doubtful sources such as supporting the acquisition of the loss-making MGM studios; the result of which was that it had to be saved by a rescue plan in 1997. EU Commissioner Karel van Miert estimates its losses to be around $25 billion (roughly equivalent to half the amount paid annually in income tax in France). As a result of this state aid support package, Credit Lyonnais has been forced to sell assets in Germany, Spain and Belgium.

In Germany there has for a long time been a cosy oligopoly between the dominant firm Deutsche Bank together with Dresdner Bank and Commerzbank. The banks have carried considerable influence in the country, not least because of the special relationship between banks and industry in Germany, with many bankers being on companies' advisory boards (*aufsichtrat* – see Chapter 3), where they often have significant votes through their shareholdings or have proxy votes which they can use to influence the company's strategy. Deutsche Bank, for example, owns 22.6 per cent of the shares in Daimler-Benz (1996 figures) and also 10 per cent in both of the insurance giants Allianz and Münchener Ruck. The views of the banks are usually welcomed rather than resented as they tend to take a long-term supportive position and thus there is less of the short-term pressure on dividend payments which is so common in the UK. One of the main challenges facing the German banks has been supporting the development of eastern Germany, which initially meant substantial bad debt provision, although it has led to a substantial increase in their customer base.

There is less concentration in the German banking market than in many other countries, with the top five banks in 1996 controlling 27 per cent of the market (compared with 84 per cent in the Netherlands and 41 per cent in France), although the recent (1997) merger between Bayerische Vereinsbank and Bayerische Hypobank has created a new banking giant in Bavaria and suggests a move towards more concentration. However, the German banks have embraced credit cards and automatic cash machines much less than most other European countries. Many of the German banks are trying to move towards having a wider range of financial services, especially insurance, and this is bringing them into more competition with large insurance companies.

The UK banking market has also been oligopolistic in nature with the 'big four' – Barclays, National Westminster, Lloyds and Midland – dominating the scene. This oligopoly remained fairly intact despite the acquisition of the Midland by the Honk Kong and Shanghai Group and the merger between Lloyds and the Trustee Savings Bank. Currently (1998), there is speculation about a merger between National Westminster and Barclays, although regulatory problems would be anticipated in this case.

The main change faced by UK banks has been the increased competition from the old building societies, which were allowed to operate as licensed deposit takers, the result of which has seen two of them (the Abbey National and the Halifax) changing their structures to public limited companies and to all intents and purposes operating as retail banks whilst maintaining their other financial services (approaching the *allfinanz* model in Germany). This has led to much more competition in the sector, with the 'big four' moving to widen their range of financial services to compete more directly with the new 'banks', which in turn has led to significant restructuring and downsizing in the sector. For example, in February 1998 it was announced that Lloyds–TSB was to close 800 branches and lose 10 000 jobs over the next five years, although this should improve efficiency and reduce costs. The retail banks have also faced competition in the credit card market with the development of store-based credit cards.

Italy has a different situation in that there is a proliferation of banks but many of these have a regional bias and thus only one Italian bank falls in the top 20 (Table 13.7). There is not too much competition, despite the large number of banks, because many of the banks are either state-owned or have a significant political dimension in that many of their management appointments are based on political criteria and the patronage of political parties. This has resulted in a high level of bureaucracy and inefficiencies within the system (e.g. delays in clearing cheques). There is also overmanning. For example, when the merger between Banco di Roma, Banco di Santo Spirito and Cassa di Risparmia di Roma took place in 1993 there were no job losses, compared with 13 000 jobs lost in a similar-sized merger between UBS and SBC in Switzerland in 1997.

Some of the most efficient banks in Europe are found in the Netherlands and Scandanavia, where cross-border mergers are taking place. The Netherlands has long been dominated by three banks – ABN-AMRO, Rabobank and ING – which have all developed substantially into investment banking and international diversification. ABN-AMRO, for example, has built up its presence in the United States over twenty years, and recently (1996) purchased Standard Federal Bancorporation, the largest savings bank in the Midwest of the USA. It also improved its range of European operations by setting up a joint venture with Rothschilds to develop its international investment banking. ING is also seeking to develop outside the Dutch market by the proposed (1997) merger with the Belgian bank Banque Bruxelles Lambert, which is the largest cross-border deal in retail banking that has hitherto been proposed. This suggests the possible development of a Benelux regional market. Thus rather than dramatic international restructuring in retail banking, we could be moving towards regional groupings of banks, where there might be greater synergies and fewer cultural problems in mergers and alliances.

This is supported by the possible beginnings of a Nordic market in banking and other financial services. The Swedish banks have recovered well from the crisis of the early 1990s and there has been a clear move to consolidation and the provision of a wider range of financial services. Svenska Handelsbanken, the country's largest bank, has acquired Stadshypotek, the country's largest mortgage lender; whilst in Norway in 1997 the merger was announced between the country's second bank, Christiana, with the country's largest insurer, Storebrand. There have also been cross-country mergers with Den Danske Bank of Denmark acquiring the Swedish bank Ostgota Enskilda Bank, and Sweden's Nordbanken acquiring Finland's Merita in October 1997.

Case study: Restructuring in Swedish banking

Sweden's bankers and financiers may feel more in need of a holiday than usual as they set off this week for their country cottages at the start of the traditional July summer break. A blaze of restructuring in the last six months has set pulses racing across the financial services sector, consuming the energy of executives and investors. As they peer into the future, few foresee much slackening of the consolidation trend. The beckoning challenge of a single European currency, and ever-increasing competition for business between banks and insurers, suggests pressure for rationalisation will remain intense.

Only a few years ago, in the early 1990s, obituary writers were out in force as Swedish banks staggered under the weight of massive losses. Today, the crisis has been left behind. Tough management medicine has streamlined the banks, transforming them into among the most profitable and cost-competitive in Europe. Balance sheets have been rehabilitated and profits last year hit record levels.

Symbolising the turnaround, Securum, the state 'bad bank' created in 1992 to manage distressed assets of Nordbanken and the now-defunct Gota Bank, was wound up last week. It has recouped nearly SKr13 billion through asset sales in one-third of the time and at half the cost to the taxpayer originally forecast. Indeed, the state stands to claw back almost all of the SKr65bn it expended to bail out the banking system in 1992 – if dividends, privatisation revenues from Nordbanken and values of existing holdings are included.

Economic conditions have supported the banks' strong progress. A depreciation of the krona has boosted demand for investment capital, particularly from Sweden's big export-focused corporations, while low interest rates have also encouraged borrowing – reflected in a 4 per cent increase in house prices this year.

Nevertheless, overall growth across the banking market is anaemic. Interest margins are under constant pressure as banks and insurers thrust deeper into each other's territories. Meanwhile, increasing numbers of foreign banks are establishing operations in Sweden.

Foreign banks have, until now, gained only small market shares. This may change, however, as European Monetary Union approaches. Faced by strongly negative public opinion, Sweden's Social Democratic government has opted out of participation in EMU's first wave. For the banks – and for Stockholm as a financial centre – this poses problems.

Most economists agree that staying out will confer a higher premium on the issuance of government bonds. Nor will Sweden be any more able to pursue looser fiscal policies outside the union than inside. On the contrary, says Mr Anders Nyren, a senior vice-president at Nordbanken, 'We are even more dependent on adhering to the EMU convergence criteria if we stay out than if we go in.'

Inside or outside euro territory, Swedish financial institutions face growing competition from foreign rivals. A European-wide trend of integration and concentration of business in large financial centres is in progress. 'Competition is going to increase with EMU, that is for sure. The euro will become the main invoicing currency for large companies and that will make it necessary for the banks to move into the continental arena,' says a foreign banker in Stockholm.

Having pruned costs and seen credit losses drop to normal levels, Sweden's banks are turning to mergers and acquisitions to boost revenues and market shares. In little more than six months, the banking landscape has been transformed into a near-oligopoly. Svenska Handelsbanken, the country's largest bank, has acquired Stadshypotek, the leading mortgage lender.

Swedbank and Foreningsbanken, two retail-based banks, have merged to form the country's second biggest bank, and Den Danske Bank of Denmark has purchased Ostgota Enskilda Bank, a regional bank – marking the first significant incursion by a foreign bank into the retail market. This dizzying round of deals would have been capped by a merger between Skandinaviska Enskilda Banken and Nordbanken, the other two remaining big banks, had it not been for a failure to agree on ownership structures. But so substantial are the prospective synergy benefits that many analysts believe the two managements will eventually return to the negotiating table. Certainly, Mr Lars-Eric Petersson, chief executive of Skandia, Sweden's largest insurance group, is in little doubt that more activity is pending.

'I believe we will see more inter-bank mergers and mergers between insurers in the next two to three years,' he says. 'In the wave after that, we will have banks and insurers getting together both on a national and Nordic level.'

This is looking ahead. Current reality is that while the banks set a scorching pace in the restructuring race, insurers are still on their starting blocks. Skandia did try to take over Stadshypotek before being outbid by Handelsbanken, and Trygg-Hansa, the second largest insurer, has been rebuffed in its attempt to acquire Wasa, a smaller competitor.

None the less, both groups look exposed as the dividing line between banks and insurers blurs. The banks have been more successful in growing their life assurance operations than the insurers have been in attracting customers to their banking products. Niche banks launched by the insurers in the past three years have had some impact on pricing and distribution, but their growth is tapering off.

Mr Lars Thunell, Trygg's chief executive, admits 'the banks have been very successful with some insurance products' but emphasises his company still managed to gain market share last year owing to rapid growth in the savings market. That growth is underlined by a sharp increase in the popularity of unit-linked funds, as savers have moved money into products offering higher returns than low-interest rate bank deposit accounts.

This trend has created a strong rise in liquidity on the Stockholm stock exchange – a phenomenon which will be accentuated if the government allows big state pension funds to invest more in equities. Whether this will go ahead is uncertain because of political factors. The main conservative opposition Moderate party is opposing the initiative on the grounds that it would increase state ownership of Swedish companies.

The stock exchange itself is at the centre of a radical restructuring of financial market infrastructure. Last month it launched a joint equities trading market with the Danish bourse, the first cross-border move of its kind in Europe and seen as a possible first step to the creation of a joint Nordic market embracing Norway and Finland. It is also exploring a link with the OM Swedish derivatives exchange to create a combined market for equities and derivatives trading, although a planned merger between the two recently foundered on disunity over the proposed ownership structure.

Underpinning such ambitions is the rapid development of technology. Swedish banks are among the global leaders in areas such as telephone and Internet banking, reflecting a high level of personal computer penetration and high staff costs. Trygg Bank, Trygg-Hansa's niche bank, launched its Internet banking service in April. Some 16 per cent of its customers have already used it to pay their bills.

In this light, it is unsurprising that some question whether branches are an asset or a liability. 'I think branches will continue to be an important contact point with clients, but they are being partly replaced by information technology,' says Mr Jacob Wallenberg, new chief executive of Skandinaviska Enskilda Banken.

As technology develops, so the argument for rationalisation becomes more compelling. With frontiers being dismantled across Europe, Sweden's banks and other financial institutions are moving into exciting – and unsettling – times. No longer can they measure themselves merely against Swedish competitors; they increasingly must compete against large-scale international interests.

The level of structural manoeuvring already seen in 1997 demonstrates a strong degree of alertness to the challenges ahead. More will need to be done to remain competitive. The restructuring race is not yet won.

Source: Brown-Humes, C. and McIvor, G. (1997) Swedish banking and finance: rivals merge for a competitive edge, *Financial Times*, 1 July.

Questions

1 What factors can be put forward to explain the restructuring that has been occurring in the Swedish banking sector?

2 What role has technology played in the restructuring process?

The impact of the single market

The impact of the single market on the banking sector was undoubtedly a stimulus towards more consolidation and indicated that retail banking needed a wider European dimension. A number of directives have been passed aimed at widening competition on a European basis through freedom of establishment and the freedom to provide services throughout Europe. The Second Banking Directive, which came into operation in January 1993, was seen as particularly significant with the development of the Single EU Banking Licence, which meant that banks could operate throughout the EU.

However, the actual impact on European consumers has been smaller than anticipated. It was hoped they would be able to 'shop around' European financial institutions for the best deal in financial services. One factor behind the sluggish implementation of more than fifty directives in the field of financial services has been the complex tax, legal and social security systems that make it difficult for cross-border activity. There is also the tendency to stick with national providers, especially in the field of retail banking. The European Commission is currently (1997) actively encouraging cross-border operations by removing technical barriers and making it easier to set up telephone banking operations. The Commission says that the number of cross-border retail branches has increased by 50 per cent since the Second Banking Directive (albeit from a fairly low base) and it has issued guidelines defining where a cross-border bank is based for legal purposes.

Strategic responses by retail banks

Given the many factors in the business environment that are affecting this sector, many banks are having to develop new strategies in order to maintain competitive advantage and market share. Some of the identifiable strategies have been (1) growth through acquisition, either domestically or cross-border, (2) diversification, (3) rationalisation and (4) increased technological innovation. The move towards acquisition and merger has already been observed when looking at banking trends in Europe. The rationale behind these moves seems to be to increase physical presence within a European perspective and to achieve synergies through economies of scale and developing a larger capital base from which to offer corporate finance. Herman Wijffels of Rabobank and Jan Kalff of ABN-AMRO have identified the likelihood of further cross-border link-ups and mergers, partly spurred by the arrival of the single currency from 1999. None the less, they have identified the difficulty of finding the right partner without losing their own bank's identity. For some the record of cross-border activity has not always been smooth, with both Barclays and NatWest pulling back from expansion into Spain and France through technical and cultural problems.

Another strategic response has been to move towards diversification away from retail banking. Some retail banks have sought to expand their banking interests by acquiring investment banking arms, as has been seen by ING's acquisition of

Barings after the Leeson fiasco and Deutsche Bank's acquisition of Morgan Grenfell. These acquisitions have not always proved successful because of different corporate cultures between retail and investment banking and in 1997 Deutsche Bank fully incorporated Morgan Grenfell into its operations with substantial cuts in its workforce. Some banks have diversified into other areas of financial services as has been the case in Scandanavia or with the Royal Bank of Scotland and its thriving Direct Line Insurance subsidiary for car insurance.

Along with the move towards consolidation has come rationalisation. Banks have been seeking ways of cutting costs as the level of competition has squeezed profit margins. One way has been to restructure the organisations into flatter organisations following a merger, in order to reduce bureaucracy and make the bank more responsive to its customers. For example, following the 1997 merger between the Swiss banks UBS and SBC it was announced that 13 000 jobs would be going through restructuring, and Deutsche Bank is carrying out a programme to reduce its workforce by 9000. Despite this, many banks still remain bureaucratic with tall organisational structures and large headquarters, and have generally resisted dramatic change, although this does reduce their efficiency

A further strategic response by banks has been a move into new technology, particularly in new areas such as telephone banking and banking by the Internet. Both these forms of banking may prove significant in the future as they are easier to operate across borders and do not encounter the same problems as cross-border mergers of retail banks. Swedish banks have been at the forefront of these developments, reflecting a high level of personal computer penetration in the country and the fact that computer-driven banking may be cheaper to operate than branches with high labour costs. Trygg Bank launched its Internet service in April 1997 and already 16 per cent of its customers have used it to pay their bills.

The impact of EMU on retail banking

The Dublin Summit in December 1996 successfully concluded with agreements on the shape of the future exchange rate mechanism and the proposed euro. The successful development of negotiations on monetary union has led many banks to assess the likely impact of EMU on their operations. Herman Wijffels, the Chairman of Rabobank in the Netherlands, has argued that the implications of monetary union for the retail banks may be mixed. On the positive side, it is likely that the euro will become an important international currency which should attract more business in financial markets, and as EMU is eventually meant to lead to more economic growth, the banks should ultimately benefit. The negative aspect of the introduction of the euro will be that most banks will lose income from currency trade and that it will encourage further competition in the sector, which will put interest rate margins and commission income under pressure. He further argues that the potential winners will be the retail banks with strong investment banking arms, and also those which have already rationalised, have lower costs and can withstand the narrower margins.

In theory the introduction of the euro should remove some of the technical problems for cross-border mergers (although the cultural barriers may well remain) and it should also encourage further diversification into a wider range of financial services. Perhaps the ultimate beneficiaries will be the banks' customers as competition drives down prices but much will depend upon how the structure of the industry evolves in the next five years.

Insurance in Europe

There are a number of substantial insurance companies in Europe and, as Table 13.8 shows, they are global leaders in both life and health insurance (ING Group) and property and casualty insurance (Allianz).

The insurance sector reflects the banking sector in terms of movements towards greater consolidation through merger and acquisition and also in terms of offering wider services through shareholdings in banks, such as in Allianz's substantial shareholding in Dresdner Bank. Some of the insurance companies have been much more active internationally than the retail banks. For example, the French group Axa has expanded considerably so that less than a third of its income comes from its French base. It owns Equitable Life, one of America's biggest insurers, Canada's Boreal Assurances and the UK's AXA Equity and Law. Its major move, however, came in 1996 with the takeover of France's UAP to create a bigger insurance conglomerate than the then current leader Allianz, although Allianz responded in November 1997 with a

Table 13.8 Top European insurance companies, 1996

Rank	Name	Country	Revenue ($ millions)
Life and health insurance			
1 (1)	ING	Netherlands	35 913
2 (2)	Prudential	UK	27 834
3 (3)	CNP Assurance	France	25 400
4 (5)	Fortis	Belgium/Netherlands	22 646
5 (6)	Assurance Générale	France	19 062
6 (10)	Aegon	Netherlands	14 522
7 (11)	Aachener and Münchener	Germany	13 533
8 (15)	Skandia Group	Sweden	9 861
Property and casualty insurance			
1 (1)	Allianz	Germany	56 577
2 (2)	Union des Assurances	France	40 737
3 (3)	AXA	France	32 681
4 (4)	Zurich Insurance	Switzerland	30 761
5 (5)	Assicurazioni Generali	Italy	29 619
6 (8)	Münchener Ruck	Germany	24 192
7 (9)	Winterthur Group	Switzerland	23 574
8 (11)	Royal and Sun Alliance	UK	20 310
9 (13)	Commercial Union	UK	18 355
10 (15)	Swiss Reinsurance	Switzerland	14 130

*a*Figures in brackets denote global ranking.

Source: *Fortune* (1997) Global 500, page F22.

proposed merger with the French company AGF, which would again make it the market leader.

It must be remembered though that most insurance is still domestically based; there is room for more cross-border activity in areas like car insurance but demand for life assurance tends to be driven by national tax regulations and thus remains domestic in nature. These legal and fiscal differences between countries often distort markets. Thus it is too expensive for a British insurer to offer services on the Belgian market because it has such high costs and is a relatively small market. Several directives have been passed on insurance at EU level, but again the problem has been in implementation at national level, especially with life assurance.

Case study: Cross-border deals in insurance

The proposed merger between the German insurance giant Allianz and French insurer AGF is being billed as a preparatory move for the euro and the single market. No doubt other moves in European financial services will be justified on similar grounds. Yet past experience suggests room for scepticism about such mega-deals. Could it be that the dinosaurs of the industry are huddling together for comfort as a tide of liberalisation and new technology undermines traditional ways of doing business?

There are, of course, circumstances in which cross-border mergers will make sense. In financial services the euro will transform capital markets. Asset allocation will be done on a pan-EMU basis and it will possible to match pension liabilities with assets from anywhere within the monetary union without incurring exchange risk. There will thus be synergies in fund management.

Euro-induced price transparency will also add to pressures for consolidation in banking and insurance. Yet cross-border deals are not necessarily the best way to restructure. Surplus capacity in banking, for example, offers cost-cutting opportunities chiefly on a domestic basis since foreign acquirers have few overlapping branches.

In insurance, meantime, most retail business is purely domestic. Standardised products such as motor insurance may lend themselves to genuine cross-border economies of scope and scale. Demand for life assurance, by contrast, is driven by national tax breaks, while distribution is subject to varying regulatory arrangements.

There is room for efficient suppliers to compete out of existence some very costly, low-return European insurance and pensions products. But this is more likely to come through competition in the marketplace than via bids and deals.

A more active market in corporate control now provides great opportunities for managers to feather their nests. Size provides a defence against hostile takeovers, yet size-driven deals can readily be justified with vacuous babble: critical euro-mass. A cross-border merger may offer an easy escape from competition policy problems at home – only to become a headache when it comes to melding disparate national and business cultures.

Note, too, that currently fashionable bank–insurance mergers release fewer cost cuts than bank–bank mergers, while leaving senior managers in place. Cross-border deals should be more rigorously justified. Sadly, shareholder activism in Europe is too frail a growth to restrain ego-tripping management when a poor case is advanced.

Questions

1 What factors appear to be leading to the growth in cross-border deals between insurance companies?

2 What problems may arise in cross-border arrangements?

International financial and capital markets in the 1990s and beyond

This chapter has looked at the development of international capital markets throughout the post-war period, their involvement in the world debt crisis, the attempts to resolve the crisis from official and banking positions, the relationship of economic growth and capital markets, and the development of banking and insurance within Europe. How then will capital markets change in the remaining part of the 1990s and into the next decade? One of the most striking and important developments of the last quarter of a century has been the increasing interdependence of world financial and capital markets and this move is set to continue. The stock market fall in October 1987 and the problems on international stock markets in 1997 have illustrated the strong links between the main equity markets in the world, but this is only one of the international connections. Traders and investors now have to concern themselves with international portfolios. It is not simply a choice between a US Treasury bond or some other US instrument, but a choice between US, European and Japanese Treasury bonds. There are three essential ingredients to this globalisation.

- **Demand for the product**. The increase in demand for international capital has come partly from the expansion of international trade and foreign investment (both direct and portfolio), which increases the demand for foreign exchange transactions, for hedging instruments (such as futures and options) and for foreign currency borrowing – either from banks or in the form of bond issues.

- **Supply side factors**. Technological advances in communications and computers have significantly lowered the costs of supplying and analysing information as well as meeting the demands for more sophisticated and diversified financial products. As financial intermediaries expand abroad there may also be cost savings through economies of scale.

- **The liberalisation of capital markets**. Whilst the regulation of markets was one of the factors in the growth of the Eurocurrency markets, subsequent liberalisation, especially the abolition of exchange controls, has removed distortions, reduced inefficiencies and enabled suppliers of financial services to meet the upsurge in demand, whilst at the same time increasing competition and reducing costs to borrowers and investors.

So where does Europe stand in this ever-changing world of international capital markets? It is likely that the 1990s will see a convergence between the use of bank finance and capital markets finance in corporate restructuring. There is an important distinction currently between US/UK and continental Europe restructuring. In continental Europe, corporate finance has traditionally been heavily bank-orientated, and this has given the banks considerable influence over management decisions. This has not been the position in the UK and the USA. Here capital markets play a large role in industrial finance. **Corporate debt financing** has relied much more heavily on the securities markets, with bond-holders exerting limited influence on managerial decisions.

Both systems have merits and demerits. Bank-orientated systems are likely to be less crisis-prone, to favour a longer term view in decision-making, and to provide superior continuous monitoring of corporate performance, leading to pre-emptive structural adjustment. Market-orientated systems, on the other hand, are credited with greater efficiency, financial innovation, dynamism, superior resistance to conflicting interests between stakeholders and less susceptibility to major uncorrected industrial blunders.

In the 1990s there has been a move towards convergence between the two approaches. Continental firms will make wider use of the securities market, whilst UK organisations will allow banks to play a larger role in industrial restructuring transactions. The view that US and UK companies are short-termist because of the role of stock markets and that Germany's and Japan's bank-based systems take a longer-term perspective is challenged by Marsh (1997). He finds little evidence to suggest that **short-termism** *per se* is a major factor in the worse performance of UK/US industry. In fact, he points to situations in the 1990s where the performance of UK companies has matched, if not bettered, the performance of many German and Japanese companies.

However, although national financial markets have become more integrated through the decline in the costs of communication and the globalisation of financial services, these markets in the future may still remain segmented because of concern about the losses from unanticipated changes in exchange rates, which in turn reflect differences in inflation rates and changes in monetary policy. Whilst in one scenario, EU markets may come closer, there will still be separation of EU markets from those in Japan and the USA. However, although there are reasons why financial markets between countries may still diverge within countries, there have been moves during the 1990s in eroding the boundaries between commercial and investment banking. In the UK this separation ended in 1986 when the rules of the stock exchange were altered so as to allow the full ownership of securities houses by banks, foreign as well as British. There may still be legal separation between the two in other countries but competition from the expanding securities markets will bring these sectors closer together.

At the same time, in the UK there has been a dissolution of the boundaries between building societies and banks, and similarly in the USA the boundaries between banks and savings and loan companies have diminished. The traditional market of banks has also been invaded by non-financial companies. For example, retail stores offer credit cards, insurance and the like. Multinational groups operate in wholesale money markets in a way similar to that of banks, and banks and insurance companies have joined together, as they have done in Germany, to provide a better financial package to customers.

The spectacular growth seen in financial markets over the past 15 years has also been paralleled by changes in the composition of financial markets. The share of banks in total recorded financial assets has tended to fall, while that of securities markets and derivatives such as swaps, futures and options has greatly increased. This has been most noticeable in the UK and USA but is also under way in France, Germany and Japan. So is the commercial bank as we know it dead? It could be argued that the traditional bank which offered loans and demandable deposits is declining, but banks have responded to the impact of technology and deregulation by emerging into new firms which offer a wider range of opportunities. Some banks will become universal banks offering a wide range of both commercial and investment banking, whilst at the same time moving into areas of derivatives and insurance. Not all commercial banks will want to make this move, nor will all commercial banks be successful. Those that do not are likely to see their traditional markets under threat and unless they can find further comparative advantages they will be subject to decline.

As for stock exchanges, what has been seen during the 1990s is that a hiccup in one exchange, say Hong Kong, has important consequences for stock exchanges elsewhere. But will these exchanges come together? Changes that have occurred in the way exchanges operate have often been due to external forces, and there appear to be too many diverse and conflicting interests within institutions for them to change from within. However, securities trading operates more effectively when it is concentrated in a single market, thus the long-term impact would be moves towards a global organisation satisfying a global market.

Much of the restructuring in financial and banking markets appears to be under way with the current merger boom in Europe and, given the growth in European financial markets, these European organisations should no longer rely largely on bank lending or on arranging their capital market finances in non-European currencies or in non-European markets. Given the elimination of all barriers to cross-border transactions for both issues and investors in the coming years, it could be hypothesised that a single European capital market will emerge. This integrated market will reflect the consolidation of previously separate domestic capital markets, serviced mainly by local banking institutions, with the existing Eurobond and European 'foreign bond' market structures.

This emerging consolidated European market is likely to be characterised by a high degree of competition and financial innovation with the proliferation of sophisticated financial services. Although dominated by European issuers, Japanese and US issuers will be attracted to this market. It will be expected that financial firms will extend their activities beyond the familiar 'blue chip' organisations to some of the middle-sized firms, which were previously believed not capable of capital market access.

The 1990s will also see further developments in international money market instruments, which will place further pressure on the traditional Eurocurrency markets. Before the year 2000 there may well be some profound changes in the nature of the Eurocurrency markets due to the process of economic and monetary union (EMU) in Europe. Ultimately, EMU will involve a single European currency, so only three major currencies will be traded in world markets: the dollar, the yen and the euro. Once again, the dollar would become the all-important Eurocurrency in the European international banking centres since, by definition, a Euromarket in euros can only exist outside Europe (e.g. in New York). Once a single European currency is established then some of the Eurocurrency markets in London which are important now, such as Euro-DM, Euro-Swiss francs and Euro-French francs, will simply cease to exist. Furthermore, if Britain is stubborn over EMU, then there is the considerable danger that Frankfurt will eventually become the major international banking centre in Europe, at London's expense. While the future of the Eurocurrency market seems assured, the shape of other financial markets and the operators in these may well change dramatically over the next ten years.

Conclusion

The growth and development of capital markets has been staggering over the last forty years. Moreover, the speed with which new instruments are being developed and the level of activity in these markets shows no sign of diminishing. Part of the explanation can be related to the growth of international trade, but equally the relaxation of exchange controls, the reduction in trade barriers, the development of the SEM within Europe, and the desire to cater for increasingly exotic demand for instruments have all played their part. Some of these developments have not been costless. The development of the Eurocurrency market and the participants therein could be partially to blame for the debt crisis of the 1980s. The development of new instruments or derivatives can be seen as a factor in the demise of Barings Bank. Moreover, the growth in new financial instruments has led countries to examine whether freedom in these capital markets needs to be controlled.

On one level there is no doubt that the distinction between financial markets is becoming blurred, and in this respect the merger and takeover activity by banks and insurance companies indicates this. At the same time capital markets are becoming more international as multinational companies seek to obtain finance when and where they desire. International exchange markets are also not immune to these globalisation effects, and this has resulted in associations and partnerships between a number of these derivative exchange markets. Although stock markets can be viewed as individual there are also forces at play here to form more globalised arrangements. Even if they remain apart, the inter-relationships between markets have been seen once more during the 1990s as collapses in one market are transmitted very quickly to others. It is quite possible that the changes that have taken place in the past decade through the development of technology and the coming together of trading blocs are just the beginning of even greater changes that will take place in financial markets during the next millennium.

Questions for discussion

1 Account for the sharp decline in the growth of the Eurocurrency market since 1980.

2 For what reasons might a government deposit funds in, and borrow funds from, the Eurocurrency market?

3 Explain why, despite 'highly mobile' international capital flows, the pattern of Eurocurrency interest rates is characterised by substantial differences between some of the alternative currency rates.

4 Who are the main users of derivatives markets? Why have they become increasingly important over the last decade?

5 Describe how debt–equity swaps can enable commercial banks to reduce their LDC debt.

6 To what extent has the separation between investment banks and commercial banks been removed during the 1980s?

7 How successful has the banking system been in alleviating the debt crisis?

8 Are financial markets likely to become more or less integrated in the future? Explain.

9. Identify the essential difference between a retail bank and a merchant bank and assess which of these would be likely to be used by (a) a business contemplating a move into Europe, and (b) a business already established in a particular country.

10 Within Europe why have the distinctions between retail banks, investment banks and building societies become more blurred?

11 Discuss the major advantages and disadvantages for a bank or insurance company of expanding by means of merger, strategic alliance or co-operation agreement.

Main reading

Demirag, I. and Goddard, S. (1994) *Financial Management for International Business,* McGraw-Hill.

Griffiths, A. and Wall, S. (1997) *Applied Economics: An Introductory Course,* 7th edition, Longman.

Hill, C. W. L., (1997) *International Business: Competing in the Global Marketplace,* 2nd edition, Irwin.

Mclaney, E. J. (1997) *Business Finance: Theory and Practice,* 4th edition, Pitman.

Madura, J. (1995) *International Financial Management*, 4th edition, West, St Paul, Minnesota.

Todaro, M. P. (1997) *Economic Development*, 6th edition, Longman.

Additional reading

Austin, J. (1990) 1992: The single European market and the British financial services industry, *European Business Review,* Vol. 90 (2).

Bank of England (1989) The market in currency options, *Bank of England Quarterly Bulletin*, May, pp. 235–42.

Bank of England (1996) The over-the-counter derivatives markets in the United Kingdom, *Bank of England Quarterly Bulletin*, February, pp. 30–8.

Beecham, B. J. (1988) Eurocurrency markets, in *Monetary Economics*, 2nd edition, Pitman, pp. 191–201.

Bowley, G. (1996) World economy and finance: prospects brighten, *Financial Times*, 27 September.

Brown-Humes, C. and McIvor, G. (1997) Swedish banking and finance: rivals merge for a competitive edge, *Financial Times*, 1 July.

Cameron, D. (1997) No bank is safe, *The European*, 11 December.

CBI/National Westminster Bank plc (1989) *Finance for Growth*, Mercury.

Chevrillon, M. (1991) Mauvais temps sur les banques, *Nouvel Economiste,* 26 April.

Colchester, N. and Buchan, D. (1990) *Europe Relaunched: Truths and Illusions on the Way to 1992*, Hutchinson.

Corden, M. (1991) The theory of debt relief: sorting out some issues, *Journal of Development Studies*, Vol. 27 (3).

Dale, R. (1990) 1992–2002 The future evolution of financial markets in Europe, *Royal Bank of Scotland Review*, March.

Dow, J. C. R. (1984) *The Management of the British Economy 1945–60*, Cambridge University Press.

Eaton, J., Gersovitz, M. and Stigler, J. (1986) The pure theory of country risk, *European Economic Review*, Vol. 30.

EC Commission (1990) *A Single Insurance Market: State of Play and Future Work*, EC Commission.

The Economist (1991) The IMF and the World Bank, 12 October, p. 32.

Financial Times (1995) Deutsche Telekom, 18 December .

Financial Times, (1997) Euro-shuffle, 19 November.

Financial Times (1998) Money market interest rates, 2 March, p. 35.

Fortune Magazine (1997) The Fortune global five hundred – the world's largest corporations, 4 August.

Frost, L. (1996) Big is beautiful as takeover fever grips insurance world, *European*, 21 November.

Goacher, D. J. (1990) UK financial markets, in *The Monetary and Financial System*, Bankers Books, pp. 115–22.

Griffith-Jones, S. (1991) Creditor countries' banking and fiscal regulations. Can changes encourage debt relief? *The Journal of Development Studies*, Vol. 27(3), p. 17.

Grilli, V. (1989) Europe 1992: issues and prospects for the financial markets, *Economic Policy*, October.

Hawkins, P. (1997) Debit Lyonnais, *The European*, 4 December.

HM Treasury (1990) Economic reform in Eastern Europe, *Economic Progress Report*, April.

Husted, S. and Melvin, M. (1990) *International Economics*, Harper & Row.

IMF *World Economic Outlook*, various issues.

Kaldor, N. (1966) *Causes of the Slow Rate of Growth of the UK*, Cambridge University Press.

Lines, T. (1989) British policy and the cancellation of commercial debts, *Development Policy Review*, Vol. 7 (3), p. 215.

Marsh, P. (1997) Myths surrounding short termism, Mastering Finance, No. 6, *Financial Times*, pp. 6–7.

Matthews, R. C. O., Feinstein, C. H. and Odlin-Smee, J. (1982) *Economic Growth, 1956–1973*, Stanford University Press.

McIvor, G. (1997) Pulp futures: smoothing out the peaks and troughs, *Financial Times*, 8 December.

Mitchell, D. (1990) The single European market for financial services, *European Business Journal*, Vol. 2 (1).

Olsen, M. (1983) The political economy of comparative growth rates, in Mueller, D. C. (ed.) *The Analytical Economy of Growth*, Yale University Press.

Quelch, J., Buzzell, R. and Salama, E. (1991) *The Marketing Challenge of Europe 1992*, Addison-Wesley.

Randlesome, C. *et al.* (1990) *Business Cultures in Europe*, Heinemann.

Romer, P. (1986) Increasing returns and long-run growth, saving and government, *Journal of Political Economy*, Vol. 94, pp. 1002–37.

Stanyer, P. and Whitley, J. (1981) Financing world payment imbalances, *Bank of England Quarterly Bulletin*, Vol. 21 (2) June.

Tucker, A. L., Madura, J. and Chian, T. C. (1991) *International Financial Markets*, West Publishing Company.

Wijffels, H. (1997) Dutch take courage from experience, *The Banker*, March.

Wood Gundy-Weiss Study (1995) derivatives as a way of reducing risk, in Bodnar, G., Marston, R. and Hayt, G. (eds) *Mastering Finance*, 9th edition, *Financial Times*.

World Bank (1997) *Financial Statistics*, Washington.

Appendix: The relationship between money market interest rates associated with alternative currencies

Example using data from the *Financial Times*, 27 June 1997.

$$R_f \approx R_d + [\ 100 ([F - S] / S) X \ ]$$

R_f = rate of interest on foreign currency, e.g. rate of interest on three-month Eurodollars = 5.75 per cent.

R_d = rate of interest on domestic currency (or more generally some currency other than R_f), e.g. rate of interest on three-month sterling = 6.875 per cent.

F = forward exchange rate, e.g. \$ price of £ in the three-months forward market = \$1.6621.

S = spot exchange rate, e.g. \$ price of £ in spot market = \$1.6662.

$F - S$ = three months forward discount on sterling against the dollar, expressed in \$ = 0.0041.

X = number of interest rate term periods in a year, e.g. four (i.e. four quarters in the year).

$5.75 \approx 6.875 + [100([1.6621 - 1.6662]/1.6662)4]$

$5.75 \approx 6.875 - 0.9842$

$5.75 \approx 5.8908$

From the above, it can be seen that the covered interest differential is very small (0.1408 per cent) and it amounts to just over 1 per cent of the relevant Eurodollar rate. The entire term in the square brackets basically reflects the cost of forward cover. In equilibrium the values on the left- and right-hand sides will be almost identical. Only minor market imperfections and brokerage costs (normally minimal due to the scale of transactions of many of the players involved) will typically prevent complete equality.

14

Central and Eastern Europe

Introduction

The changes that have taken place in Central and Eastern Europe since the fall of the Berlin Wall in 1989 have tremendous significance for all the peoples of Europe, both in the East and the West. They are also vitally significant for the process of integration centred on the European Union and for the strategies and prospects of Western European businesses. In this chapter we will review these developments and their implications for European business.

Central and Eastern Europe is not a homogeneous area. The countries of the region differ widely with regard to income levels, industrial structures and economic policies, as well as embodying broader political, social and cultural differences. At the risk of oversimplifying, three main groups of countries can be distinguished. Firstly, there are the Central European countries, which have relatively high income levels, a strong orientation towards economic integration with the West and fairly stable political systems. These countries include the so-called '**Visegrad Four**' (named after an agreement signed in the Hungarian city of Visegrad in February 1991) of Poland, Hungary, the Czech Republic and Slovakia, as well as the former Yugoslav republic of Slovenia, and possibly Croatia. The Baltic states of Lithuania, Estonia and Latvia are also often included in this group. Secondly, there is the rest of Eastern Europe, typified by lower income levels, a more volatile political environment and a more protracted and difficult transition process towards a market economy. Relevant countries here are Bulgaria, Romania and Albania, as well as the remaining Yugoslav republics, notably Serbia. Thirdly, there are the 'European' parts of the old USSR; most importantly Russia, but also the Ukraine, Belarus and Moldova. In this chapter we will concentrate on the first group, and in particular on the Visegrad countries, since these have the closest links with the European Union and are almost certain to be the first Central and Eastern European countries to join the EU.

Trade in Central and Eastern Europe before 1989

Under Communist rule the Central and Eastern European countries (or CEECs) showed two main characteristics with regard to trade and foreign relations. Levels of trade were low, and were very much centred on the Eastern

European region, with little integration into the world economy. This is shown in Table 14.1.

Note that the intensity of a country's trade with another country (or region) is defined as the share of the country's total trade with the other country divided by the share of the second country in world trade (excluding trade with the first country). If the **trade intensity ratio** is greater than unity it means that the trade of the two countries is more centred on each other than we would expect given the pattern of world trade. If it less than unity the reverse is the case (compare the FDI intensity ratios given in Chapter 12). Intensity ratios are taken to be better indicators of trade patterns than simple trade shares because they are not affected by factors like size of country and income. For example, we expect trade within North America and in Africa to be relatively low compared with Western Europe because in the first case there are only two large countries, and in Africa the countries are poor and cannot afford large import bills.

The data in Table 14.1 show that the intra-regional trade intensity for Eastern Europe in the late 1970s was considerably higher than anywhere else in the world, while the intensity of Eastern European trade with the rest of the world (extra-regional trade) was lower than elsewhere. At the same time, trade in Eastern Europe was relatively limited in total size. In 1990, Eastern Europe (including the USSR) had only a 5 per cent share of world trade, as compared with 46 per cent for Western Europe, 16 per cent for North America and 21 per cent for Asia (Anderson and Norheim 1993).

The reasons for this pattern have been extensively analysed. It has been argued that centrally planned economies are by their nature less inclined to trade than market economies (Lavigne 1991). Trade is seen in such systems primarily as a way of overcoming difficulties in achieving nationally determined plans: plans are not drawn up with international considerations in mind. In addition, the Eastern European countries were limited in their trade by the fact that much of what they produced was not competitive in Western markets. During the late 1970s and the 1980s, Hungary and Poland, in particular, faced problems in foreign trade relations as a result of their high levels of external debt. Political problems also played a role in limiting trade, especially the 'Comecom' restrictions on export of military or technologically sensitive materials to the East (Gowan 1990).

Table 14.1 Trade statistics for various regions in 1979

	Intra-regional trade share (%)	Intensity of intra-regional trade	Intensity of extra-regional trade
Eastern Europe	54	7.88	0.49
Western Europe	66	1.57	0.58
North America	30	3.63	0.76
Latin America	20	3.80	0.84
Asia	41	2.77	0.69
Africa	6	1.24	0.99
Middle East	7	1.17	0.99

Source: Anderson and Norheim (1993).

Despite the fact that trade within Central and Eastern Europe was very much centred on trade within the region, no successful multilateral trading framework was developed prior to 1989 between these countries. The Eastern European trading organisation, the Council for Mutual Economic Assistance (CMEA or Comecon), remained essentially a framework for bilateral trading relationships between its members. Of these relationships the most important were those between the individual Central and Eastern European countries and the USSR. These took various forms, but generally involved the supply of manufactured products to the Soviet Union in return for fuel and raw materials; with Soviet oil exports to the CEECs in particular being fairly heavily subsidised.

Various attempts to deepen the Comecon machinery to encourage economic integration did not succeed. The level of political involvement in the planning process made such integration an intensely political matter, subject to fierce disagreements. This was made worse by the requirement that Comecon decision-making be unanimous. In addition, Comecon members had markedly divergent interests along two main lines of division. One division was between those countries implementing economic reform, particularly Hungary, which saw integration as involving a greater use of market mechanisms in foreign trade, especially in the area of currency convertibility, and those countries such as the USSR, which saw integration as being based on extending the planning mechanism across national frontiers. A second division was between countries whose trade was primarily orientated towards Eastern Europe and those with wider international links, which were more sceptical of integration. For example, in 1980 the share of trade with socialist countries in total trade (the average of the share of exports and the share of imports going to socialist countries) was 74.8 per cent for Bulgaria, 69.9 per cent for Czechoslovakia, 53.1 per cent for Hungary, 55.7 per cent for Poland and 41.2 per cent for Romania (Wallace and Clarke 1986). Comecon did not appear institutionally strong enough to handle these differences and was finally dissolved in June 1991.

Foreign investment in Central and Eastern Europe before 1989

Not only trade but also foreign investment was rather limited in the CEECs before 1989. The extent of FDI in the region is shown in Table 14.2.

As can be seen, despite increasingly favourable conditions for joint ventures from 1971 onwards, the sums invested were relatively small. Lavigne (1991) quotes the Soviet author Rodina as finding for the period 1972–87 that for Eastern Europe (excluding the USSR) FDI amounted to only $0.5 billion, i.e. 0.1–0.2 per cent of total capital invested in those countries. For the USSR the sums were larger, with approximately $500 million being invested in 1987–88. In the first seven months of 1989, immediately before the collapse of the Communist regimes, more Western money was invested, but this money still amounted to only 22.3 per cent of the investments in question (Lavigne 1991). In Poland, 500 investment authorisations were granted in the first nine months of 1989, compared with 52 in the previous two and a half years, but the total FDI inflow was only $110 million (Kilmister 1990).

Table 14.2 Foreign investment in Eastern Europe in 1989–90

	Stock of FDI 1989 (\$ million)	Number of joint ventures: 1 March 1990
Bulgaria	N/A	30
Czechoslovakia	256	60
Hungary	550	1000
Poland	100	1000
Romania	N/A	5
USSR	837	1400

Source: data on the stock of FDI from Schmidt (1995). Data on number of joint ventures from Lavigne (1991), page 375, and Schmidt (1995) table 12.3, page 278.

Problems involved with setting up joint ventures included the complexity of legislation, an insecure environment (shortages of materials due to planning problems and labour unrest in the Polish case), relatively high taxes, the requirement to pay wages at more than local levels, confusing accounting systems, and poor communications and infrastructure. Against this the CEECs offered both a large market and a highly trained workforce.

Trade relations between East and West after 1989

The magnitude of change required by the transition to a market economy involved major disruption of trading relationships for the CEECs after 1989. This was accentuated by two further developments. Firstly, in their eagerness to underline the depth of the changes taking place, the new Central and Eastern European governments dismantled the old trading arrangements in the region, such as the Comecon structures, with considerable speed. Secondly, the economic crisis in the USSR from 1990 onwards and the break-up of the Soviet Union into its constituent republics after August 1991 had a dramatic impact on the CEECs. The effect of all these factors was to reorientate Central and Eastern European trade decisively towards Western Europe. This both opened up important opportunities for Western European producers, as a result of the new markets, and posed major challenges stemming from the possibility of a new source of cheap imports competing with EU countries. The structure of trade between Eastern Europe (excluding the USSR) and the West at the start of the transition period is given in Table 14.3.

It can be seen that Central and Eastern European exports tended to be concentrated in a number of areas where Western European producers were facing quite severe difficulties in the 1980s, notably agriculture, steel, chemicals, textiles and clothing. Indeed, most observers agreed that Eastern European trade would have been even more centred on those areas had there not been protectionist barriers, notably in textiles. At the same time, Central and Eastern Europe offered new markets for a number of industries where market growth was relatively low in the West and where consumer demand was previously pent-up in the East, e.g. motor vehicles and food, drink and tobacco.

Table 14.3 Commodity composition of Eastern European trade with the West in 1990 (% of total trade)

	Eastern European exports	Eastern European imports
Primary products	28.5	15.1
Food	16.9	10.0
Mineral fuels	10.7	3.2
Manufactures	60.0	79.9
Iron and steel	7.2	2.8
Chemicals	9.3	14.4
Road vehicles	1.6	4.0
Transport equipment	6.8	11.2
Specialised machinery	4.8	21.5
Textiles	3.4	6.4
Clothing	9.8	1.9

Source: Lavigne (1995) (reprinted with permission from EBRD) table 5.2, page 85.

The potential extent of trade between East and West

There have been a number of attempts to estimate the likely potential growth of trade between Eastern and Western Europe. One very influential approach has been to use what is known as the '**gravity model**' to estimate the expected growth of trade flows. This model stems originally from work done by Linnemann (1966); the application of it to Eastern Europe is due to a number of writers, such as Hamilton and Winters (1992), Baldwin (1994) and Winters and Wang (1994). The account below is based on Hamilton and Winters (1992), which has been widely adopted as a benchmark study in this area.

Hamilton and Winters used a version of the gravity model which stipulated that for any two countries the level of trade between the two countries would depend positively on the level of GNP of each country, the existence of a common border between the countries and the existence of trade preferences between the two countries; and negatively on the population of each country and the distance between the two countries. Using data for 76 market economies accounting for about 80 per cent of total world trade averaged over 1984 to 1986, they estimated coefficients for this model. They then applied the estimated model to data for the USSR and the CEECs for 1985 to derive estimates for potential trade with other regions of the world (on the assumption that the transition to a market economy would mean that these countries would follow the pattern of the gravity model), which they then compared with the actual situation obtaining in 1985. Some of their results are shown in Table 14.4.

It can be seen that, according to this approach, the potential growth in trade is very significant. The largest absolute predicted growth is between Germany and the CEECs; however, in proportional terms this is not so large because of the existing high level of trade between Germany and the East. When the Soviet Union is added to the picture the results are even more striking. Hamilton and Winters found that in 1985 for the Soviet Union and Eastern Europe taken

Table 14.4 Potential increase in Eastern European trade (excluding the USSR) with selected Western European countries

	France	Germany	Italy	UK
Potential minus actual $bn				
Exports	10.0	18.1	8.3	7.3
Imports	9.3	16.8	7.6	7.1
Increase as multiple of current trade				
Exports	9.7	2.5	7.4	7.7
Imports	8.1	3.4	4.3	5.9
Increase as percentage of total actual trade of Western country				
Exports	9.8	9.9	10.6	7.0
Imports	8.6	10.6	8.3	6.5

Source: Hamilton and Winters (1992) table 6, page 87.

together, actual exports to the European Union were $27.2 billion and imports from the EU were $22.2 billion; while the gravity model predicted that exports could have reached a potential level of $132.6 billion and imports could have reached a potential level of $141.7 billion. Other estimates using the gravity model have been similar in magnitude.

The gravity model has been criticised for lacking an explicit theoretical underpinning. An alternative approach is that followed by Collins and Rodrik (1991), who estimated aggregate equations for exports and imports based on levels of GNP and population and then applied these to the CEECs to obtain an overall estimate of trading potential. They then estimated the breakdown of this overall potential between particular countries by updating a trade matrix for 1928. They did this by looking at a sample of six countries (Austria, Finland, Germany, Italy, Portugal and Spain) and by using their experience to estimate a relationship between the trade flows recorded in 1928 and 1989 trade flows. They then applied these estimates to the CEECs, and to the USSR.

The results arrived at by Collins and Rodrik are fairly similar to those based on the gravity model. In the medium term, exports from the Czech and Slovak Republics to the 12 EU member states were predicted to rise from $3.8 billion in 1988 to $12.6 billion (the study was carried out before the break-up of Czechoslovakia). For Hungary the predicted rise was from $2.4 billion to $5.9 billion, and for Poland from $4.3 billion to $20.1 billion (Baldwin 1994). However, the study has been criticised for assuming that one can predict on the basis of the changes that have taken place elsewhere in 1928 trading patterns. Hamilton and Winters argue that the countries used as a reference group by Collins and Rodrik have all been strongly affected by the process of Western European integration. Using their experience as a benchmark leads to an exaggeration of the extent to which Eastern European trade will centre on Western Europe.

Both the Collins and Rodrik results and those based on the gravity model predict dramatic increases in trade between Eastern and Western Europe as a result of the transition to a market economy in the East. However, they remain at an aggregate level and do not distinguish between different sectors. One study which does attempt to do this is that by Landesmann (1995a). Landesmann's approach is to take a group of new EU members or neighbouring countries outside the EU as a reference group. This group includes Austria, Switzerland, Finland, Sweden, Denmark, Spain, Portugal, Greece and Turkey. Landesmann starts from the hypothesis that by 2010 Eastern European countries could be expected, other things being equal, to have reached similar levels of trade with the EU to that reached by the countries in his sample group in 1986/87. He refers to estimates based on this projection as his 'naive' long-term projections. He then examines the extent to which selected Eastern European countries can actually be taken to be comparable with this group, making adjustments for product quality in specific sectors, size of country, distance from EU markets, and for estimates of speed of 'catching up' with the EU and for political instability. Using this exercise to modify his naive projections he arrives at more sophisticated estimates of trade between the CEECs and the EU.

Landesmann predicted that for Eastern Europe and the USSR as a whole, market penetration in the EU will rise from 2 per cent in 1987 to 8.5 per cent in 2010. Of the Central European countries the largest rise will be that for Hungary, from 0.2 per cent to 1.4 per cent. However, these aggregate figures conceal significant differences between sectors. On his most optimistic set of assumptions, Landesmann sees the six industries with the highest prospective growth in market penetration as being paper, chemicals, mechanical engineering, metal products, mineral extraction and mineral products. On average, their share of EU markets is projected to rise from 2 per cent to 11 per cent, with paper rising the fastest, to a share of over 20 per cent. On the other hand, the six industries projected to grow the slowest in terms of entering EU markets from Central and Eastern Europe are instrument engineering, office equipment, leather, motor vehicles, transport equipment and other goods. Landesmann attributes the problems faced by the Eastern European countries in these areas to issues of product quality and competition both from within the EU and from the rest of the world.

Trade policy and the 'Europe' agreements

The high estimates for potential East–West trade in the above studies, including in some troubled industries and sectors, underline some important policy questions for the European Union. The main framework governing trade relationships between the CEECs and the EU is a set of agreements known as the '**Europe' agreements**, which give the CEECs associate status with the EU. The Europe agreements are broader than simple trade agreements; however, interim agreements covering their trade provisions were implemented before final ratification. The interim agreements with Czechoslovakia, Hungary and Poland came into effect on 1 March 1992, with Romania on 1 March 1993 and with Bulgaria on 31 December 1993.

The agreements immediately abolished all quantitative restrictions on industrial imports from the CEECs, except for textiles and coal, and removed tariffs on over 50 per cent of the EU's imports from the East (Faini and Portes 1995). Other tariffs were to be abolished over a two- to five-year period, except for textiles and clothing. No new duties or quotas could be introduced by the European Union. The 'sensitive' sectors for which tariff removal would be slow included some important East European industries – iron and steel, chemicals, furniture, leather goods, footwear, glass and vehicles. However, the 1993 Copenhagen European Council did accelerate the process of trade liberalisation for these sectors. The agreements include a rule-of-origin provision, which effectively requires that CEEC exports have a 60 per cent local content to qualify for inclusion under their scope. Agricultural trade remains restricted and the agreements include an anti-dumping clause.

Assessments of the Europe agreements vary significantly. The European Commission wrote in 1994 that 'The Europe Agreements constitute a very substantial trade liberalization package, the scale and pace of which is without precedent in the EU' (quoted in Faini and Portes 1995, page 3). On the other hand, Winters and Wang write that

> throughout the agreements one finds the stamp of the EC's powerful internal enemies of change. Despite the parlous state of the CEEC economies, the EC will maintain agricultural protection, keep quantitative import restrictions on textiles and clothing for six years, leave EC chemicals and iron and steel producers free to harass CEEC suppliers through anti-dumping law, keep tariffs on sensitive labour-intensive products for five years, and discourage the CEECs from processing inputs from other countries. . . . The restrictions in the Europe agreements undermine the recovery of the CEEC's economies and ultimately even their reform programmes.
>
> (Winters and Wang 1994, pages 47–8)

There have been a number of analyses of the likely effect of free trade between East and West in the so-called 'sensitive' sectors. The general message from these studies is that removing trade restrictions would benefit both the CEECs and the EU. Winters (1995) looked at the steel industry. He found that removing restrictions would lead to a fall in steel output of just 1.6 per cent in the EU and 3 per cent in EFTA, while output in the CEECs would rise by 18 per cent. There would be net welfare gains of over ECU100 million in both the EU and the CEECs. In addition, since the comparative advantage of the CEECs is in lower-quality steel, they will increase demand for higher-quality Western European steel as their consumer goods production rises.

Corado (1995) looked at the textiles and clothing industry. She found that trade with Eastern Europe benefited Western European textiles producers in two ways. Firstly, they were able to exploit niche markets in those areas where they did hold a comparative advantage, namely textile goods and high-quality clothing products. Secondly, by transferring labour-intensive operations to the CEECs they were able to face up to competition coming from the rest of the world. This **outward processing trade** (OPT), where EU firms transfer fabric to CEEC firms and contract operations with them, is more important for East–West trade, according to Corado, than either domestic CEEC production or FDI in the textiles and clothing industry. For example, in 1992, for clothing covered under the Multi-Fibre Agreement, while 10 per cent of overall imports into the EU from outside were made up of OPT, the figure for Poland was 77 per cent, for Hungary 72 per cent and for the Czech and Slovak Republics 49 per cent.

Movements in East–West trade since 1989

The period since 1989 has seen significant shifts in the direction of Eastern European trade, as shown in Tables 14.5 and 14.6.

While trade between the EU and the CEECs has grown quite strongly since 1989, the pattern and extent of trade has been subject to quite strong changes within that period. At the risk of oversimplifying, three main sub-periods can be distinguished.

The first few years after 1989 saw EU exports to the CEECs increase more strongly than Eastern exports to the West, as the Eastern European countries imported capital goods to reconstruct their economies and as pent-up demand for consumer goods was expressed. From 1989 to 1992, CEEC exports to the EU grew by about 50 per cent, while EU exports to the CEECs grew by about 70 per cent (figures in money terms including the former Soviet Union, calculated from Cadot and de Melo 1995, page 90). For the CEECs as a whole, including the former USSR, the trade surplus with the EU dropped from $4.3 billion to $1.05 billion during this period. For the Visegrad countries a trade deficit of $132 million in 1989 widened to one of $2.46 billion in 1992, with the value of trade in both directions more than doubling (Cadot and de Melo 1995).

The mid-1990s saw the Eastern European countries achieving something of an export boom in trade with the West. In 1994, for example, exports from the post-Soviet world grew by 18 per cent in dollar terms, twice as much as imports, with the region's current account deficit narrowing from $8.3 billion in 1993 to

Table 14.5 Percentage of Eastern European exports and imports which go to/come from Western industrial countries

	1989	1993
Czech Republic		
Exports	37.0	69.9
Imports	37.3	73.1
Hungary		
Exports	44.1	67.6
Imports	49.6	64.9
Poland		
Exports	49.1	75.1
Imports	53.0	76.2
Slovenia		
Exports	67.6	69.6
Imports	77.6	73.4
Bulgaria		
Exports	8.0	43.1
Imports	17.1	42.6
Romania		
Exports	39.3	48.0[a]
Imports	11.5	54.0[a]

[a] 1992 figures.
Source: Landesmann (1995b) table 7.1a, page 118.

Table 14.6 Percentage of Eastern European exports and imports which go to/come from the EU

	1989	1993
Czech Republic		
Exports	26.3	54.6
Imports	26.5	51.4
Hungary		
Exports	24.8	46.5
Imports	29.0	40.1
Poland		
Exports	32.1	63.2
Imports	33.8	57.2
Slovenia		
Exports	51.3	57.4
Imports	56.9	55.7
Bulgaria		
Exports	5.5	28.1
Imports	10.3	30.2
Romania		
Exports	25.2	32.6[a]
Imports	5.7	37.5[a]

[a]1992 figures.

Source: Landesmann (1995b) table 7.1, page 119.

$3.4 billion (Robinson 1995). Much of this represented intra-industry trade: the *Financial Times* reported that

> Fiat, for example, already sources its Europe-wide sales of the Cinquecento small car from plants in Poland, while General Electric, through its Tungsram subsidiary, has made Hungary its springboard for expansion in the entire European market. Asea Brown Boveri is also reaping the benefits from its far-sighted forays into the former communist world from where it sources growing volumes of increasingly sophisticated but relatively low-cost parts and products from a growing network of plants in Poland, Hungary, Ukraine, Russia and elsewhere.
>
> (Robinson 1995, page 13)

The last two years, however, have seen the trade performance of the Eastern European countries worsen once more. In 1996 the Czech trade deficit rose to 7 per cent of GDP, and for Central Europe as a whole the trade deficit rose from $19.9 billion in 1995 to $31.6 billion (*Business Central Europe* 1997). The Polish deficit for 1997 is predicted to be $9.6 billion. A number of factors have been suggested as possible causes for this development. Among them are weaker Western demand owing to slow growth in the EU, high currency values in the East as a result of anti-inflationary policies, concentration of Eastern European exports in very competitive areas (such as textiles, steel and heavy machinery), high investment in the East, the prevalence of OPT with consequent high imports of inputs, and large wage rises. Public sector wages were estimated to be up by almost 20 per cent in the Czech Republic in 1996 compared with the preceding year (Boland 1996). Despite the problem of the Czech trade deficit, the koruna continued to rise, presenting the government with a difficult problem of economic policy. In 1997, however, the koruna 'bubble' burst. By August 1997 it had fallen 10 per cent since April and 15 per cent since the start of the year. The ensuing political arguments over economic difficulties eventually brought down the Czech prime minister, Vaclav Klaus (Harris 1997).

Data on changes in the structure of trade are quite hard to obtain. Sheehy (1995) calculated **coefficients of structural change** (defined as the sum of changes in the trade shares of each sector over one-year intervals) for Central and East European exports to and imports from the EU, from 1988 to 1992. His finding was that the sectoral pattern of EU exports to the East had changed significantly more than that of Eastern exports to the EU. The implication was that the Eastern European countries had been relatively unsuccessful in reorientating trade from East to West after the collapse of Comecon. Sheehy estimates that only about 19 per cent of the increase in Hungarian trade with non-Comecon countries over this period could be attributed to such reorientation of trade flows. Dobrinsky (1995) looked at changes in the structure of trade between 1984/85 and 1991/92. In absolute terms, the CEECs continued through this period to specialise in their exports to the EU in products of high energy content, low skill content and very low R&D content. In part this was the legacy of former cheap energy imports into Eastern Europe from the Soviet Union.

Dobrinsky also looked at a more sophisticated measure of export specialisation. This is the **export specialisation index** (or ESI). This is defined as the share of a commodity in a country's total exports to a particular region divided by the share of that commodity in total imports for that region. So, for example, if the ESI for a particular commodity and Eastern European country, defined relative to the EU as an importing region, is greater than unity, this means that the Eastern European country is relatively specialised in that commodity in its trade with the EU. If it is less than unity the reverse is the case.

In most cases the results using the ESI measure were similar to those using absolute shares of exports. However, there were some important differences. In particular the sectors in Hungary with the highest ESI had a relatively high R&D content and a low energy content and capital intensity. Dobrinsky writes that 'this indicates a process of successful industrial restructuring in prospective manufacturing branches (for example in electrical engineering industries and, lately, in components for motor vehicles), which Hungary had started quite a few years ago. Although these sectors are not the leading exporters yet, their future prospects seem to be good' (Dobrinsky 1995, page 108).

Landesmann (1995b) carried out an econometric study of changes in export structures for the CEECs with regard to the EU from 1989 to 1993. He found a significant movement away from capital- and energy-intensive exports towards labour-intensive exports. There was also some evidence of a shift towards more R&D-intensive exports for Czechoslovakia and Hungary and away from skill-intensive exports for Bulgaria. The movement away from capital-intensive exports and towards labour-intensive exports was more pronounced and longer-lasting for Bulgaria and Romania than for the Visegrad countries.

Havlik (1995) found that in 1992 the industries with the biggest shares in the EU market were, for Czechoslovakia, clay, cement and concrete, brewing and malting, wood manufactures, glass, structural metal products and boilers; for Poland, cement, wood manufactures, structural metal products and boilers, wooden furniture and salt extraction; and for Hungary, manufacture of bodies for motor vehicles, meat slaughtering and preparation, asbestos, electric lamps and lighting, and insulated wires and cables. He concluded that:

> it is interesting to note that the combined market share of the three CEECs in some of these industries is extremely high. Thus, for instance, the combined market share in cement and lime is almost 52 per cent, in clay it is 37.2 per cent, in boilers 27.5 per cent, in other wood manufactures 26.2 per cent, in wooden containers 24.9 per cent, in structural metal products 23.5 per cent. This means that the three CEECs have become important EU suppliers of selected industrial products.
>
> (Havlik 1995, page 151)

Trade within Eastern Europe after 1989

As discussed above, the initial effect of the collapse of communism led Eastern European countries to trade much less amongst themselves and more with the West in general and the EU in particular. However, in recent years there has been a modest revival in trade within Central and Eastern Europe. One factor that has encouraged this has been the formation of the **Central European Free Trade Agreement (CEFTA)**. CEFTA was founded by Czechoslovakia, Hungary and Poland in 1992. Slovenia joined at the end of 1995. Romania and Bulgaria have been negotiating membership. The Ukraine, Croatia and the Baltic states have also expressed interest in joining CEFTA.

The aim of CEFTA is to abolish all mutual tariffs by 1 January 2001. However, at present it consists of a group of bilateral trade agreements, reviewed twice yearly. Most industrial goods and about half of farm products are free of tariffs, but there is no CEFTA bureaucracy and no proposals to harmonise product standards or liberalise capital flows (Lyons 1997). Including Romania, CEFTA represents a market of 89 million people with a combined GDP of just $280 billion. However, if all prospective members do actually join, the market could increase to 160 million people.

Intra-regional trade is rising. Polish exports to CEFTA rose from 3.6 per cent of its total in 1993 to 5.8 per cent in 1996. The corresponding figures for Hungary were 5.2 per cent and 8.8 per cent. In total, in 1996 about 15 per cent of CEFTA exports and about 10 per cent of imports were intra-regional. It has been predicted that this could rise to around 20 per cent for exports and imports over the next two decades (Lyons 1997). On the other hand, trade within CEFTA is dominated by trade between the Czech Republic and Slovakia. In 1994, Czech exports to Slovakia totalled $2.4 billion and Slovak exports to the Czech Republic were $2.1 billion. Each of these flows was over four times as large as the next largest set of trade flows within the CEFTA region for that year (that between the Czech Republic and Poland).

In 1996, over 40 per cent of Slovak exports and about 30 per cent of Slovak imports were with the CEFTA region. For the Czech Republic the corresponding figures were over 20 per cent and around 15 per cent. If Czech–Slovak trade is excluded then only around 6–10 per cent of CEFTA trade is intra-regional. In addition, there have been strong disagreements over trade policy within CEFTA. The April 1997 CEFTA meeting saw accusations that Poland and Slovenia were delaying the removal of tariffs (Lyons 1997).

Foreign direct investment in Central and Eastern Europe since 1989

The period immediately following 1989 saw tremendous optimism in Central and Eastern Europe about the potential for FDI. However, such investment proved relatively slow to materialise. By 1 October 1992 the total investment in the region (including the former USSR but excluding the Yugoslav republics) was just $12.4 billion (Radice 1995). Of this the Czech and Slovak Republics accounted for $1.7 billion, Hungary for $3.2 billion, Poland for $1.2 billion, the former Soviet Union for $5.5 billion, Romania for $0.5 billion and Bulgaria for $0.3 billion. Reasons put forward for the slow pace of investment included the persistence of complex regulations and instability, uncertainty over ownership structures and the slow pace of privatisation programmes in some countries, disputes over the assignment of the bill for dealing with ecological problems, the depth of the recession in Eastern Europe and the problems of valuing enterprises.

One of the most detailed analyses of motivations for FDI in Eastern Europe during this period is that of Radice (1993, 1995). He points to two main strategic objectives for investment: market growth and low-cost production.

The importance of the Eastern European market as a factor attracting FDI is fairly obvious: the region was typified by shortages of both consumer and producer goods before 1989. Radice points to branded consumer non-durables as a key area; for example, cigarettes (BAT, RJR, Philip Morris), detergents (Henkel, Proctor and Gamble, Unilever), jeans (Levi-Strauss, VF), razor blades (Gillette) and food (Nestlé, Parmalat, Unilever, United Biscuits). However, in consumer durables, with the exception of cars, ownership levels are too high and income levels too low to permit extensive market growth. The motor industry has been an important area for FDI, however, including the largest single investment in the early years of transition, the Volkswagen purchase of Skoda in the Czech Republic, and further investments by General Motors, Fiat and Suzuki.

Potential market growth is also significant in the service sector; for example, in insurance (Aegon, American International, Allianz, Sedgwick), airlines (Alitalia), retailing (Delhaize, k Mart, Tengelmann), advertising (Lintas, Leo Burnett, Ipsos) and fast food outlets such as McDonald's.

The producer goods sector includes areas of likely growth as well, owing to the lack of infrastructure investment under communism. Areas where FDI took place in the early 1990s included power engineering (ABB, Siemens), lifts (Otis, Schindler), steel (Voest-Alpine), glass (Glaverbel, Pilkington), chemicals (Cabot, Columbian Chemicals, Rhône-Poulenc) and trucks (MAN, Renault, Scania). Most recently, with the progress of privatisation schemes in the East, there has been a significant growth of FDI in telecommunications and in the big utilities, notably electricity. There has also been investment from abroad in environmental improvement projects.

A second key motive for FDI is the search for low-cost production. This can apply to labour-intensive production in areas like furniture (Ikea, Schieder), white goods (Electrolux, Whirlpool), consumer electronics (Philips, Samsung) and car components (Audi, Ford, Loranger). As mentioned above, however, in one important labour-intensive area, that of textiles, clothing and footwear, contractual arrangements between Western and Eastern companies are used more than direct investment.

In addition to cheap labour, the use of spare Eastern capacity can also help to lower costs. Examples here are acrylic fibres (Dow), steel (Voest-Alpine), ball-bearings (SKF) and machine tools (Dorries Scharmann). Cheap raw materials have also attracted investment in areas like non-ferrous metals (Alcoa) and construction materials (Wimpey, Ciments Français).

In addition to these two main motives for FDI, Radice also points to what he terms as the 'opportunists', trading companies and financial consultancies who essentially provide services directly related to the process of transition, often exploiting contacts or connections with officials of various kinds in the CEECs.

Finally, there are a number of sectors or companies in Eastern Europe which are particularly attractive for FDI since they are potentially competitive on world markets. Radice terms these the 'crown jewels'. Skoda is one such example, and was the subject of intense rivalry between bids from Volkswagen and from Volvo and Renault. Another such company is the Polish FSO car plant, now in alliance with the South Korean company Daewoo. The Czech heavy truck companies and the Hungarian light bulb company Tungsram, which was bought by General Electric, can also be mentioned in this context.

There has been some controversy about the motives for foreign investment in some of the more successful Eastern European companies. A few years after the GE takeover of Tungsram, which had an 8 per cent share of the Western European light bulb market, there was a fairly widespread view in Hungary that the company was being starved of investment by its new owners, and that part of the motive for the investment was to eliminate a potential competitor. This was denied by GE, which however did step up its investment programme in Tungsram.

Patterns of FDI in Central and Eastern Europe

The last few years have seen an acceleration in the pace of foreign investment in the CEECs, partly encouraged by large privatisation deals. In 1995, for example, investment into the Czech Republic grew by 86 per cent (Williams 1996). In 1996 Poland was the most favoured recipient of FDI in the region, attracting over $3 billion. Hungary, which in the early years of the transition obtained by far the largest amount of FDI among the CEECs, has found inward investment growing more slowly in recent years, partly due to slow output growth and currency problems in 1995. However, per capita investment remains highest in Hungary for the region, apart from the rather special case of Slovenia, which has a population of just two million. Cumulative levels of FDI for the region are shown in Table 14.7.

The source countries for FDI into Central and Eastern Europe are quite varied but Germany is the largest investor in the region, with a stock of about $4.9 billion (20.3 per cent of the total) in January 1995 (Sinn and Weichenrieder 1997). This has been explained by cultural, historical and linguistic links as well as the strength of the German economy within the EU. In addition, German unification allowed Germany to use the contacts and experience of dealing with the other Eastern European countries built up by East German companies and individuals during the communist era. Following Germany in importance for FDI in the CEECs are the USA with about $3.9 billion (16.3 per cent) and Austria with about $2.8 billion (11.8 per cent). A breakdown of investors in the Visegrad countries is given in Table 14.8.

Despite the recent acceleration of FDI to Central and Eastern Europe, the absolute values of investment remain relatively low. Sinn and Weichenrieder point to the fact that the accumulated stock of FDI in the region of $43 billion by January 1996 was lower than the $47 billion of FDI received by just Argentina and Mexico between 1989 and 1996. In per capita terms the FDI received by the CEECs over this period was just one-third of the figure for Argentina and Mexico and less than 1 per cent of that received by eastern Germany, if one includes West German investment there.

The reasons for a relatively low supply of FDI for the CEECs have been outlined above. Sinn and Weichenrieder argue further that the Eastern European

Table 14.7 FDI to Central and Eastern Europe, cumulative to January 1996

Country	Total ($m)	Per capita ($)
Albania	270	81
Belarus	331	32
Bulgaria	517	58
Croatia	1 200	252
Czech Republic	5 587	542
Estonia	646	409
Hungary	13 740	1 334
Latvia	485	181
Lithuania	352	94
Moldova	87	20
Poland	7 843	204
Romania	1 597	68
Russia	5 875	39
Slovakia	726	138
Slovenia	2 762	1 399
Ukraine	891	17
TOTAL	42 911	130

Source: Sinn and Weichenrieder (1997) table 1, page 181.

Table 14.8 Major investors in the 'Visegrad 4' (cumulative FDI to January 1995, $ million)

Source	Host country			
	Czech Republic	Hungary	Poland	Slovakia
Austria	216.6	1961.2	123.5	113.6
Belgium	188.6	205.9	60.8	0.9
Canada	n.a.	86.2	25.2	6.6
China	n.a.	1.2	0.9	0.1
Croatia	n.a.	n.a.	0.3	0.2
Finland	n.a.	21.6	21.8	0.0
France	355.6	507.7	105.3	38.5
Germany	1113.0	2197.1	631.3	123.5
Greece	n.a.	8.4	14.3	0.2
Italy	92.5	465.8	166.3	14.1
Netherlands	n.a.	1111.1	371.3	36.9
Poland	n.a.	n.a.	–	0.6
Russia	n.a.	n.a.	21.5	0.3
Sweden	n.a.	110.2	75.9	17.4
Switzerland	136.7	383.1	154.2	4.2
United Kingdom	n.a.	419.1	147.8	14.6
USA	651.1	1331.4	653.1	79.7
Other	323.3	1097.7	266.2	100.4
TOTAL	3077.4	9907.7	2839.7	551.7

n.a. = Not available. Albanian figures refer to 1994.

Source: Sinn and Weichenrieder (1997) table 2, page 183.

countries exhibit a relatively low demand for FDI. The optimism about the transfer of technology and expertise that typified the first years of transition has, they claim, been replaced in large measure by feelings of resentment in the East, particularly with regard to the privatisation programme and its effects (see later in this chapter). However, it is certainly the case that the Eastern European countries have become more selective and careful about some of the partnerships into which they enter with foreign investors. *Business Central Europe* (1995) points to a detailed rethink of FDI in the Czech Republic beginning in mid-1992, prompted by the failures of CKD's joint venture with the German engineering firm Deutsche Babcock and Mercedes Benz's withdrawal from a deal to buy the truck makers Liaz and Avia. And further, the need to reconsider FDI also followed from the collapse of the CSA deal with Air France and the scaling down of the Volkswagen investment plans for Skoda in November 1993. It is argued that as a result of this more sceptical approach to FDI, the Czech government was able to get a better deal when privatising the telecommunications company SPT Telecom than the Hungarians were when selling their equivalent company, Matav (Papp 1995). The TelSource consortium of Swiss Telecom and PTT Nederland beat four rivals for a 27 per cent stake in SPT Telecom, with a bid of $1.45 billion. In order to do this it promised to double line density to 40 per 100 inhabitants by the year 2000, to reduce promptly a waiting list of between 600 000 and 1.5 million people and ensure that in the first year of operation at least 30 per cent of new applicants were satisfied, and to improve the 'successful call rate' for SPT from 65 per cent to 98 per cent within three to five years.

The issues affecting FDI in Central and Eastern Europe are explored further in the case study.

Asea Brown Boveri

Asea Brown Boveri (ABB), the Swiss–Swedish engineering combine, has been one of the most active investors in Central and Eastern Europe since before 1989. By 1996 it had built a network of 60 companies in the region, the largest manufacturing operation of any Western group. Details of ABB's operations in Eastern Europe are given in Tables 14.9 and 14.10.

ABB began negotiating with the Polish government about possible investments in 1988 and completed its first acquisitions in 1990. These were of Zamech, the only turbine maker in Poland, and of Dolmel, the largest generator manufacturer in the country. This was the basis for further expansion in the region, especially in the area of power engineering, particularly the renewal and replacement of out-dated power stations. ABB bought a large power engineering complex in Brno in the Czech Republic. Orders in the region grew from $225 million in 1990 to $1.65 billion in 1994 and are expected to double by the year 2000. By 1996 ABB employed almost 30 000 people in Eastern Europe, out of a total of 211 000 world-wide.

Eastern Europe is an attractive location for ABB because of both cost considerations and market-related factors. Components like turbines and switchgear are up to 40 per cent cheaper there than from Western suppliers. Acquisition costs are kept low; the company rarely spends more than $20 million on a single

Table 14.9 ABB operations in Eastern Europe 1996

Country	Number of subsidiaries	Number of employees
Poland	13	7000
Czech Republic	6	7000
Russia	14	3000
Romania	4	2000
Ukraine	5	1500
Hungary	4	600
Slovakia	4	500
Croatia	2	500
Latvia	2	400
Estonia	4	100
Bulgaria	2	100
Kazakhstan	2	50
Lithuania	2	25

Source: Business Central Europe (1996).

Table 14.10 ABB in the Czech Republic and Poland

Company	Operation	Date of Investment
Czech Republic		
Asea Brown Boveri	Country holding company	10/91
ABB Lummus	Process engineering	12/92
ABB Energo	Protection relays	9/92
ABB PBS	Boilers, turbines, power plants	4/93
ABB EJF	Switchgear	1/93
ABB Elektro-Praga	Installation material	11/93
Poland		
Asea Brown Boveri	Country holding company	7/91
ABB Zamech	Turbines	5/90
ABB Dolmel	Generators	10/90
Dolmel Drives	Drives	10/90
ABB Elta	Transformers, switchgear	4/92
ABB Zwus Signal	Railway signalling	12/91
ABB Ind. Components	Sales	12/92
ABB Rail Engineering	Railway engineering	12/92
ABB Centrum	Power plant control	12/93
ABB Elwy	Switchgear	3/93
ABB Instal	Switchgear	12/93
ABB Elmont	Switchgear	4/94
ABB Industry	Industrial products	4/94

Source: Business Central Europe (1996) page 44.

company and its whole Eastern network is estimated to have cost just $300 million. In the first nine months of 1996, ABB reported a 47 per cent increase in net profits, to a figure of $651 million.

While costs are important, they are not the sole reason for ABB investment in the East. After all, while revenue per worker in the company's Czech plants doubled between 1994 and 1996 it remained four times lower than the ABB average, as a result of lower productivity and lower value-added production. In some ways more important than costs are growing markets as the region builds up the infrastructure of railways, airports, factories and energy supplies.

The group has had some problems; it lost $1 million when a joint venture in Russia had to be abandoned when the partner company was found to be involved in criminal activities. More importantly, the Eastern European activities have demanded a large commitment of management time and energy. The chief executive of ABB, Percy Barnevik, is estimated to spend about a fifth of his time in the region and ABB has had to train thousands of Eastern managers and technicians. In 1994, for example, ABB trained 17 000 workers in Poland and the Czech Republic. It has founded training centres in both Brno (Czech Republic) and Warsaw.

The company has committed itself to a common level of quality in both Western and Eastern plants, and to managing its Eastern factories with managers from the region. Eastern European managers were paired individually with Western counterparts (known as 'coaches') to learn management and marketing skills. This approach has now been developed so that Polish and Czech employees of ABB are training Russians and Ukrainians. In addition to management expertise the company has transferred technology, such as machine tools, computer programs, technical drawings and sales manuals.

There has been some suspicion within the company about the Eastern European policy, focusing on claims about the 'export of jobs' from the West. Between 1990 and 1994 the Western European workforce of ABB decreased from 141 000 to 125 000, with further large job losses in North America. At the same time the Czech and Polish subsidiaries have taken over production work from factories in Germany and Switzerland. The ABB Kraftwerke plant in Mannheim, Germany, orders at least DM35 million of supplies from ABB plants in Poland, while the company has replaced an engine-starter production line in Germany with one in Brno and has moved the production of air-cooled genera-tors from Switzerland to Gdansk (Poland). ABB management argues that this was inevitable anyway and that the Eastern investment safeguards jobs through-out the company by making it more competitive. Around half the components in the Asian power plants built by ABB come from Central Europe.

It is also the case that ABB plants in the East have seen restructuring and cost-cutting. At Zamech in Poland the workforce was cut from 4300 to fewer than 3200 by 1993 through retirements and the outsourcing of services such as cleaning to new private companies. Production costs fell as labour, raw materials and factory space were used more intensively. In the early years of the Zamech investment, funds were concentrated on computerising and modernising exist-ing equipment. By 1996, however, total investment in the subsidiary had risen to $70 million and the workforce was rising once again. Between 1992 and 1996 Zamech increased its profits from $2000 per employee to $16 000.

Source: adapted from Wagstyl, S. (1996) Woven into the fabric, *Financial Times*, 10 January; Business Central Europe survey on Foreign Investment, April 1996.

Kraft Jacobs Suchard

Kraft Jacobs Suchard (KJS) was a relatively late investor in Eastern Europe. During the early 1990s the company was being taken over by Philip Morris and consequently was focused on other issues while competitors like Nestlé, Unilever and Danone moved into the region. However, from 1992 onwards the company began an ambitious strategy of investment in Eastern Europe, amount-ing to about $300 million by late 1995. The pattern of KJS investment is shown in Table 14.11.

As a result of the relatively high investment by other Western food companies in Central Europe KJS has not restricted itself to that region but has been pre-pared to invest further east in Bulgaria, Romania and the former USSR. It has opted to manufacture in each country, arguing that high tariff barriers and unstable currencies make importing difficult. It has focused on confectionery and coffee both because of market considerations and because of the availabil-ity of local companies for sale.

KJS has to a large extent avoided extensive restructuring of its East European acquisitions. It has chosen companies which did not need immediate dramatic changes and has negotiated with plant managers before approaching govern-

Table 14.11 Kraft Jacobs Suchard investments in Eastern Europe, October 1995

Date	Company	Country	Operation
Sep 92	Figaro	Slovakia	Confectionery
Dec 92	Osemege	Hungary	Confectionery/Coffee
Apr 93	Olza	Poland	Confectionery
Jul 93	Dadak	Czech Rep.	Coffee
Oct 93	Lietuva	Lithuania	Confectionery
Nov 93	Chorzele	Poland	Cheese
Dec 93	Svoge	Bulgaria	Confectionery
Jan 94	Poiana	Romania	Confectionery
Feb 95	Ukraina	Ukraine	Confectionery
Jun 95	Petroconf	Russia	Confectionery

Source: Financial Times (1995) page 20.

ments. Among the main problems which it faced after acquiring East European firms were poor hygiene and quality, weak accounting and stock systems and shortages of raw materials. In this context improvements in purchasing and production line management yielded rapid results. In the first six months of KJS ownership, for example, the plant in Trostanec (Ukraine) saw output rise by 26 per cent, with 45 new products being launched.

Important problems include the supply of raw materials and energy. In Romania, KJS has had to import milk powder, and it has seen large rises in sugar prices in Ukraine. Good-quality packaging is hard to obtain locally. In Trostanec the local authorities threatened to cut off electricity supplies because residents could not afford a large price increase – KJS ended up paying the bills for the whole town! It also bailed out the generating plant with an advance payment of $100 000 each quarter when it ran out of cash to obtain fuel.

Other problems have included high inflation, which results in a complicated pricing policy, and the necessity of building a local distribution network. KJS has responded to this issue by assigning exclusive territories to local entrepreneurs. In Romania it has invested heavily in advertising to support its locally developed chocolate brand.

In 1995 KJS had total annual sales of $600 million in Central and Eastern Europe and averaged a 16 per cent return on investment in the region. In Lithuania it recovered its initial investment in two years. However, its performance in Hungary was disappointing. The company intends to continue with an ambitious investment programme in the future in order to modernise plant and expand further. However, with wages at about one-tenth of those in its Western factories it is unlikely to invest in extensive automation.

Source: De Jonquieres, G. (1995) Bittersweet taste of expansion, *Financial Times*, 2 October.

Questions

1 What are the main factors that ABB and KJS have had to take into account when making decisions about investing in Eastern and Central Europe? In

what ways are these factors different from those which have to be considered by companies making investment decisions in Western Europe?

2 How successfully do you think that ABB and KJS have managed the process of investment in the East? Are there any ways in which they could have improved their approaches?

3 What are the main similarities and differences between the approaches of the two companies to investment in the East? To what extent do you think these can be explained by the fact that ABB makes producer goods while KJS makes consumer goods?

• •

Privatisation in Central and Eastern Europe

The growth in FDI into the CEECs can come through a variety of means: the establishment of greenfield sites, the development of joint ventures and strategic alliances between Western companies and those in the CEECs, and through the process of privatisation.

For the CEECs privatisation could be seen as an important step towards the creation of a market economy. It allows state monopolies to be broken up, creates a property-owning middle class, provides the motivation for managers, increases external funding, brings in new technology and new management where the company privatised is sold to Western businesses, and develops a share-owning society. The process of privatisation is not without its difficulties, however. Firstly, there is a need to consider how the process of privatisation will take place. It is possible that free shares can be distributed to everyone. Although this returns state assets to the private sector it does so without providing the state with new money. A variation on this approach is for the free shares to be in large investment trusts or funds, which in turn hold shares in many different state-owned companies. This is an approach adopted by the Polish government. Alternatively, shares could be given or sold to employees and managers in organisations, thus providing an incentive for employees to make sure that the business operates effectively. This approach has been adopted in Russia. The use of vouchers is another approach adopted by the Czech Republic and Russia. These may be given to individuals, as was the case in Russia, or sold to them as in the Czech Republic. Foreign investors are also encouraged to purchase vouchers. A similar voucher system has been used in both Poland and Romania.

The privatisation process could also include the restoration of assets to previous owners, and this has been important in East Germany. Hungary has also used cheap loans, repayable over five years, as a means of encouraging share ownership. Finally, privatisation in the CEECs can also follow the approach adopted by Western European governments where shares are sold, at a fixed price, to both domestic and foreign investors. This method was used by former East Germany and Hungary.

One thing that distinguishes the state sector in the CEECs from that in the West is the sheer size of the sector and the speed with which privatisation was anticipated to take place. In many Western economies it took a number of years for privatisations to take place and this was with sophisticated financial and legal institutions. In the CEECs the process of privatisation has not been as rapid as expected, and on a number of occasions, the privatisation process itself has been halted. The Czech prime minister, Vaclav Klaus, has explicitly warned against selling the 'family silver'.

> In Hungary, opposition to privatization through foreigners has been growing. Polish privatization minister Gruszecki warned against giving foreigners too much preference in the privatization process; former prime minister Pawlak argued that he had tried his utmost to prevent foreign investors taking over Polish companies. Polish trade unions accuse foreign investors of employing 'slave labour' and taking away the 'family silver'. Russia has restricted the shares of assets that can be sold to foreigners and has made little attempt to withdraw discriminatory regulations that exclude foreign investors.
>
> (Sinn and Weichenrieder 1997, page 182)

It can be argued that this is a rather one-sided view of the current attitudes in Eastern Europe, given the prevalence of large-scale privatisation programmes and the expressed desire to join the EU. In fact, as Tables 14.12 and 14.13 indicate, the role of state ownership has diminished somewhat in the CEECs.

Before considering some of the CEECs in detail, it is important to note that the process of privatisation can be divided into small scale and large scale. The privatisation of small-scale enterprises has been fairly successful, transferring ownership to the private sector of small state-owned enterprises or co-operatives. It is with large-scale privatisations that the problems have occurred. Because of the lack of financial markets in their countries, the lack of resources, and the lack of management expertise, large-scale enterprises either have been difficult to sell or the government has looked to foreign capital. As a result of these difficulties, privatisation in the various CEECs has advanced at different speeds.

Table 14.12 State ownership of industry by country, 1990

	Percentage of value-added
Czechoslovakia	97
USSR	97
Poland	82
Hungary	65
France	17
Italy	15
United Kingdom	12
USA	2

Source: Independent on Sunday, July 1991 and Welford and Prescott (1996) page 405.

Table 14.13 CEECs with private sector percentage share of GDP exceeding 50% in mid-1994

Country	Private sector share of GDP
Czech Republic	65
Estonia	55
Hungary	55
Latvia	55
Poland	55
Slovakia	55
Albania	50
Lithuania	50
Russian Federation	50

Source: Lavinge (1995) and Harris (1996) page 142. *EBRD Transition Report* (1994) reprinted with permission from EBRD.

Hungary

The Hungarian approach to privatisation is market-orientated, with the sale of companies by open tender. Although there have been legal delays in implementing privatisation legislation, significant progress in sell-offs was made in 1995 and 1996. By the end of 1996 the private sector accounted for 60–70 per cent of GDP and privatisation revenue of $5.5 billion accounted for almost one-third of FDI. Areas which have been subject to privatisation include the telecommunications sector and the oil and gas industry, and the privatisation of the banking sector is largely complete. However, in a number of companies the state still holds a 'golden share' to ensure that the government has a veto over important decisions. These sales of banks, industrial enterprises, power stations, water, sewerage and other utilities including telecommunications have led to a large section of control of important industries in foreign hands. Such a process is unprecedented in the CEECs and has enabled Hungary to replace obsolete machinery and improve the management of its industrial sectors in a way that would have been impossible under state ownership.

Poland

It was Poland's intention to sell off 50 per cent of its state enterprises in a five-year period starting from 1990. However, the programme got off to slow start, with the relevant legislation only being passed in 1993. The process was always going to be subject to problems because there were 8000 state companies involved. The legislation passed in 1993 set up privately managed national investment funds (NIFs) involving foreign expertise. Of the shares released through the privatisation process the majority are held by the NIFs and the NIFs themselves have now been listed on the stock market in 1996. The privatisation process to include the banking sector has met with some delays but moved towards completion in 1997.

The privatisation of small to medium-sized companies, on the other hand, has proceeded rapidly. However, in strategically important sectors such as fuel and power, coal mining and shipyards, privatisation has not as yet been carried through.

Russia

In Russia the privatisation process made every rapid progress during the early part of the 1990s, with over 100 000 enterprises being privatised through voucher schemes during 1993–94. However, the loans-for-shares programme of privatisation adopted was heavily criticised during 1995 due to the alleged low prices paid for companies and the lack of transparency. Even with these difficulties and the failure to use the privatisation process in the oil, gas, electricity and agriculture sectors, the private sector accounted for 70 per cent of GDP in 1996. One of the issues raised with the privatisation process in Russia has been that it has converted public sector monopolies into private sector ones. There has also been concern about the efficacy of the whole privatisation process. Thus the privatisation process has slowed during 1997 and a more selective privatisation process is being followed.

The Czech Republic

The first wave of privatisation began in 1992, and the use of a voucher scheme has meant that privatisation in the Czech Republic has added credibility to the privatisation process. A second wave of privatisations followed towards the end of 1993, involving a few thousand companies. The process through which privatisation took place changed, however. In this second wave management/employee buy-outs, auctions, tenders and direct sales were the preferred approach to privatisation. During the middle of the 1990s the pace of privatisation has slowed due to concerns over rising unemployment and increased foreign ownership in some sectors.

Whereas the countries considered above could be viewed as the success stories of privatisation, the case study indicates some of the problems faced by Bulgaria.

Case study: Bulgarian privatisation

After seven years of stopping and starting, privatisation is back on track. After seven years of on-again, off-again privatisation policies, Bulgaria is making a last-ditch effort to find buyers for about 30 big enterprises that have remained firmly in the grip of the state.

The aim is to avoid the delays, caused by inefficiency and corruption, that have plagued previous attempts at privatisation and discouraged investors.

Companies failing to find buyers in the next 15 months will be liquidated, says Alexander Bozhkov, deputy prime minister and industry minister, who holds overall responsibility for privatisation.

However, the timetable is less rigorous for selling controlling stakes in five state-owned banks and for disposing of smaller companies in mining, manufacturing and food processing.

The diverse group of companies for sale under Mr Bozhkov's fast-track privatisation programme include Soviet-era chemicals and pharmaceuticals manufacturers, a dilapidated Black Sea tourist resort and Balkan Airlines, the struggling state carrier.

For foreign investors, the main attractions of the fast-track programme will be the sale of a strategic stake in Bulgarian Telecommunications Company, the state telecoms monopoly, and the disposal of Neftochim, the biggest oil refinery in south-east Europe, based in the Black Sea port of Burgas.

Mr Bozhkov launched the programme early this year as Bulgaria struggled to overcome its worst economic crisis since the collapse of communism. A desperate need for hard currency to prop up the foreign exchange reserves and meet interest payments on external debt proved a catalyst in completing several much-delayed privatisation deals.

In the first big deal, Solvay of Belgium paid $150 million of the $160 million purchase price for a 60 per cent stake in Sodi Devnya, the Bulgarian soda ash manufacturer, on the day the contract was signed. Two other big cash privatisations involving Western European companies have also been completed. Marveks, a Spanish–Bulgarian joint venture, bought a 70 per cent stake in Devnya Cement, one of the biggest Bulgarian producers, for $44 million and undertook to invest $200 million in modernising the plant, situated outside Varna in the same industrial area as the Sodi factory.

Union Miniere, the Belgian non-ferrous metals producer, paid $80 million for 56 per cent of MDK-SPJSCo Pirdop, a copper smelter in central Bulgaria. The Belgian company agreed to invest $220 million over five years, including the construction of an ore processor and an environmental clean-up. A $25 million loan from the World Bank will finance the four-year clean-up project, designed to bring the plant into line with EU environmental standards.

The prospect of a fire-sale of Bulgarian assets has receded as the economy stabilises and funding from international agencies picks up, but cash from privatisations will remain important for cutting the budget deficit next year. And only foreign buyers can provide the investment to modernise enterprises designed in Moscow to supply not just the small Bulgarian market but much of the former Comecon trade bloc.

To improve transparency and increase the chances of finding investors from abroad, the European Union and US Aid, the US agency, are covering the cost of hiring international advisers for the fast-track privatisation programme.

Deutsche Morgan Grenfell, the international investment bank, has already been appointed as BTC's adviser for the telecoms offering under an agreement with the World Bank. Treuhand, responsible for privatisation in the former East Germany, and Speedwing, the consulting arm of British Airways, the UK carrier, are advising Balkan Airways.

The start of privatisation procedures for another 26 companies has been delayed because of the slow pace of disbursement of funds from EU programmes for aid to Eastern Europe. 'The procedures have been speeded up but we've been waiting for two months to get approval from Brussels to sign contracts with consultants,' says Mr Bozhkov.

However, potential investors are voicing interest in Neftochim. Despite a chronic lack of investment, the refinery is operating close to its full processing capacity of 27,000 tonnes of crude oil daily. Its strategic position at Burgas, expected to become an important transit point for oil reaching the Black Sea from Central Asia, is an additional incentive for investors.

Shell Petroleum, the Anglo-Dutch group, which operates a petrol station chain in Bulgaria, is mentioned as a possible investor. But the main contender is Rosneft, the Russian state oil company, which supplies Neftochim with crude oil and already operates a joint venture, Rosbulneft, with the Bulgarian refiner for transporting oil and selling downstream products in international markets.

'Rosneft will certainly be bidding,' says Valentin Zlatev, Rosneft's export director. 'We would bring in considerable investment. We have already prepared a five-year programme for modernising the refinery, which would be carried out in co-operation with a Western engineering company.'

Source: Hope, K. (1997) Privatisation: last attempt to dispose of assets, *Financial Times*, 21 October.

Questions

1 Why has there been renewed interest in the privatisation process in Bulgaria?

2 What are the problems faced by the Bulgarian authorities in their move towards privatisation?

• •

Central and Eastern European banking

Economic growth is a major goal in the transformation that is taking place in CEECs and privatisation is a step in that direction, but the creation of a real market for capital and, in particular, a well-developed banking sector where resources are allocated efficiently, is an essential component of the economic transformation.

In particular, banks in Eastern Europe need restructuring so that they can identify the extent of their capital positions. Moreover, with Western resources being transferred to CEECs, the potential is there for their misuse, unless existing banks are restructured. Banking reforms in the East would also create an institutional framework for effective control of the money supply by the central bank. There is a need to free commercial and central banks from their traditional roles as financiers of both fiscal deficits and the losses of state-owned enterprises.

Privatisation also requires a capital market, and a capital market cannot be created unless a thorough reform of the banking system is enacted. If privatisation occurs without banking reform, capital may not be allocated efficiently and this will hamper the hoped-for supply side response which is essential for economic growth. In addition, firms may not face effective financial discipline if the banks cannot refuse them loans (Brainard 1991). Finally, the banking system is a serious source of economic disequilibrium in some CEECs. For example, in 1987 Yugoslavia's budget indicated a small surplus, but losses recorded by its National Bank of Yugoslavia accounted for 8.5 per cent of GDP. These losses resulted from loans made to loss-making state enterprises through the banking system.

Eastern European banking model

A traditional banking model in a CEEC consisted of a central bank and several purpose banks – one dealing with individuals' savings and other banking needs, and another focusing on foreign financial activities, etc. The central bank provided most of the commercial banking needs of enterprises in addition to other functions. During the late 1980s, the CEECs modified this earlier structure by taking all the commercial banking activities of the central bank and transferring them to new commercial banks. In most countries the new banks were set up along industry lines, although in Poland a regional approach has been adopted.

On the whole, these new state-owned commercial banks controlled the bulk of financial transactions, although a few ***de novo* banks** were allowed in Hungary and Poland. Simply transferring existing loans from the central bank to the new state-owned commercial banks had its problems, since it involved transferring both 'good' and 'bad' assets. Moreover, each bank's portfolio was restricted to the enterprise and industry assigned to them and they were not allowed to deal with other enterprises outside their remit.

As the central banks would always 'bale out' troubled state enterprises, these commercial banks cannot play the same role as commercial banks in the West. CEEC commercial banks cannot foreclose on a debt. If a firm did not wish to pay, the state-owned enterprise would, historically, receive further finance to cover its difficulties – it was a very rare occurrence for a bank to bring about the bankruptcy of a firm. In other words, state-owned enterprises were not allowed to go bankrupt, primarily because it would have affected the commercial banks' balance sheets, but more importantly, the rise in unemployment that would follow might have had high political costs.

What was needed was for commercial banks to have their balance sheets 'cleaned up', perhaps by the government purchasing their bad loans with long-term bonds. Adopting Western accounting procedures might also benefit the new commercial banks.

This picture of state-controlled commercial banks has begun to change during the mid- to late 1990s as the CEECs began to appreciate that the move towards market-based economies required a vibrant commercial banking sector. There are still a number of issues to be addressed in this sector, however. For example, in the Czech Republic the government has promised to privatise the banking sector beginning in 1998. Currently the banking sector suffers from a number of weaknesses. A number of the smaller banks appear to be facing difficulties as money market competition picks up, highlighting their under-capitalisation and the greater amount of higher-risk business in which they are involved. There have also been issues concerning banking sector regulation and the control mechanisms that are available. This has resulted in the government's proposal for an independent securities commission to regulate capital markets.

The privatisation package for the Czech Republic's four largest banks, which currently control about 60 per cent of the sector's assets, will also allow foreign banks into a highly developed market where their influence has been marginal until now. It is anticipated that each of the four banks will be sold to a single bidder in an attempt to create a regional hub of a foreign bank's network. One problem with all four banks is that inspection of their balance sheets may throw up problems which could reduce the size of any bid. All four banks have at least 20 per cent of their loans as classified – where no interest has been paid for 30 days or more. Banks could make provisions to reduce these loans by collateral held against them, but in some cases the loans exceed the collateral. Moreover, getting an accurate picture of the value of the collateral is difficult since bankruptcy legislation is ineffective. The ability to write off these bad debts was not permitted until 1996, but even if this route is taken then this will eat into the banks' assets, leaving them very close to the lower limit of 8 per cent capital adequacy ratio. In addition, the 'commercial' banks have been influenced by the action of the national bank, which in early 1997 caused bond prices to fall, leading to a fall in the commercial banks' bond portfolios. Thus the banking sector in the Czech Republic still has a long way to go.

In Hungary the privatisation of the banking sector is almost complete. However, a state rescue package had to be agreed at the beginning of 1997 for the second-largest state bank, Postabank, owned indirectly by the main social security bodies and the post office, and this indicates the fragility of this sector. Outside of the difficulties experienced with Postabank, the Hungarian banking system has been transformed. The rapid move towards privatisation resulted from the problems experienced by the state-owned banks, which the government had to bail out, costing it around 7 per cent of GDP. At that stage it was possible that the banking system could collapse and government funding, although saving the banks, did not solve the problems of corporate governance or moral hazard. Thus the privatisation process was started in earnest. Magyar Kulkereskedelmi Bank (MKB) was sold to Bayerische Landesbank and the EBDR in 1994. Budapest Bank was bought by GE Capital and Magyar Hitel Bank was bought by ABN-AMRO. In November 1997 the state completed the last stage of the sale of the state savings bank (OTP), Hungary's largest bank. The state, which dominated the banking system three years ago, now only retains a majority stake in two specialist banks, the Hungarian Development Bank and Eximbank.

The move towards, and success of, privatisation can be seen in the balance sheets of the banks, which showed an increase in post-tax profits of 45 per cent in 1996. These banks are also seeing higher savings and deposits and a strong rise in demand for corporate and retail lending. In addition, the growth in competition in the banking sector has led to a narrowing of the spreads between lending and deposit rates, and the further knock-on effect of mergers and small-bank closures. Over 50 per cent of Hungarian bank assets are controlled by foreign-owned banks, and this has led to Hungarian banks offering services similar to those expected in many Western European countries. Most of the foreign-owned but mainly Hungarian-managed banks were recapitalised after their acquisition and they have spent heavily on staff training and new information technology systems. From 1998, foreign banks will be free to open branches in Hungary, thus opening up the domestic banking market to full competition.

As a whole, the CEECs have come a long way since the early 1990s in dealing with their banking problems. For some countries the process of privatisation still has a long way to go but others such as Hungary have moved quickly along the process of transforming their banking systems in readiness for their entry into the EU.

Central and Eastern European external debt

The debt crisis (see Chapter 13) has not passed by the CEECs. Poland was one of the first countries which could not meet its debt obligations (in 1982) and requested the rescheduling of its debt. Most of this debt is owed to Western governments with only around 20 per cent owed to Western banks, mostly Western European ones.

For the region as a whole the external debt situation of the CEECs deteriorated rapidly in the late 1980s. The total gross debt of the region reached $142 billion at the beginning of 1991, with the most heavily indebted countries being the then Soviet Union, Poland and Hungary. Bulgaria ran into debt service problems in early 1990, and was forced to reschedule its debt. Given that a debt service ratio of 25 per cent is a critical figure, the figures for 1990 for Bulgaria, Poland and Hungary of 77 per cent, 71 per cent and 65 per cent, respectively, show the extent of these countries' difficulties. In addition, by early 1990 the Soviet Union began to accumulate sizeable amounts of external debt.

The strategies used to overcome the debt problems in the CEECs included measures by Western creditors to reduce their exposure to debt together with increased direct and equity investment. For specific countries the period of the early 1990s saw both Poland and Bulgaria continuing to seek debt relief measures, increased borrowing from international financial organisations by Poland, the former Soviet Union and Bulgaria, and debt rescheduling by Bulgaria.

Within the CEECs it has been appreciated that their debt issue problems cannot be solved in the short term. The transformations that have been taking place with these countries require greater export growth, and growth in their economies. At the same time the question needs to be raised concerning the creditworthiness of these countries. So how has the process of debt rescheduling worked in some of these CEECs and has the overall debt pressure been reduced?

Poland

Poland reached an agreement in 1991 with the **Paris Club** of creditor nations and in doing so reduced its official debt by 50 per cent or around $33 billion.

The final stage of the Paris Club arrangements was agreed in 1994, which was linked to IMF approval of Poland's budget deficit of that year. Subsequently the **London Club** of commercial bank creditors restructured a further $13 billion of the debt into long-term bonds, reducing debt by a further 43 per cent. These agreements improved Poland's creditworthiness and reopened international capital markets. As Table 14.14 indicates, these agreements have allowed Poland's medium- to long-term external debt to fall to $42 billion. At the same time there has been a fall in both Poland's debt/GNP ratio and its debt/export gross sales (XGS) ratio since 1991.

The Czech Republic

Table 14.15 indicates that the Czech Republic has relatively low external debt, which at the end of 1996 was estimated to be $18.3 billion though this figure has been rising over the last five years. An indication of its outward-looking economy is that its debt/export ratio has stayed fairly constant, though its debt/GDP ratio has been rising. Debt servicing issues are not expected to be a

Table 14.14 External debt for Poland

	1991	1992	1993	1994	1995
External debt (US$ billion)	53.6	48.7	45.3	44.0	43.9
Short-term	7.6	4.5	2.7	1.0	1.7
Medium–long-term	46.0	44.2	42.7	43.1	42.2
Debt/XGS (%)	287.4	250.6	246.7	198.4	166.6
Debt/GDP (%)	68.7	57.7	52.7	45.9	35.2
Debt service/XGS (%)	5.4	7.8	9.2	13.3	15.2
Interest payments/XGS (%)	3.3	4.9	5.5	7.9	6.9
Current account/GDP (%)	−2.8	−3.7	−6.7	−2.7	−1.6

Source: *Barclays Country Reports*, March 1996, page 10.

Table 14.15 Debt indicators for the Czech Republic

	1992	1993	1994	1995	1996[a]
Foreign debt (US$ billion)	7.6	9.2	10.7	16.6	18.3
Short-term	1.8	2.0	2.9	5.1	5.5
Medium–long-term	5.8	7.2	7.8	11.5	12.8
Debt/exports (%)	66.7	50.2	54.2	56.4	59.2
Debt/GDP (%)	27.1	29.4	29.7	35.1	35.0
Debt service/exports (%)	14.7	7.6	12.7	8.7	9.1

[a]Estimated.

Source: *Barclays Country Reports*, May 1997, page 7.

problem and the Czech Republic has received one of the highest investment grades in the region from international credit rating agencies.

Russia

In 1993 Russia agreed to take over sole responsibility for the foreign debt of the former Soviet Union. Loan rescheduling by the Paris Club occurred in 1993, 1994 and 1995. A further rescheduling of around $40 billion of Soviet-era debt occurred during 1996. By the end of 1995, total foreign debt amounted to $106 billion compared with $94.2 billion in 1994, with IMF borrowing accounting for a large proportion of the increase (Table 14.16). Debt ratios are expected to remain relatively favourable over the medium term with a debt/GDP ratio of under 30 per cent and a debt/service ratio of approximately 10 per cent.

Hungary

Table 14.17 indicates that the foreign debt in Hungary was estimated to have declined in 1996 to $27.5 billion. The debt/export and debt/GDP ratios both

Table 14.16 External debt position for Russia

	1991	1992	1993	1994	1995
External debt (US$ billion)	67.6	79.0	83.9	94.2	106.1
Short-term	12.6	13.1	8.3	10.0	10.0
Medium–long-term	55.0	65.9	75.6	84.3	96.1
Debt/XGS (%)	189.4	244.6	184.0	117.5	107.9
Debt/GDP (%)	8.8	92.4	48.5	33.8	29.7
Debt service/XGS (%)	33.8	4.0	5.1	4.6	9.2
Interest payments/XGS (%)	10.3	1.1	1.7	1.7	5.9
Current account/GDP (%)	0.8	−6.6	2.5	4.1	3.4

Source: *Barclays Country Reports*, November 1996, page 10.

Table 14.17 Debt indicators for Hungary

	1992	1993	1994	1995	1996[a]
Foreign debt (US$ billion)	22.0	24.3	28.1	31.2	27.5
Short-term	2.3	2.0	2.4	3.2	3.5
Medium–long-term	19.7	22.2	25.7	28.0	24.0
Debt/exports (%)	157.8	212.3	245.5	174.3	134.7
Debt/GDP (%)	59.1	63.0	67.9	71.5	61.2
Debt service/exports (%)	35.7	38.7	49.3	39.1	34.6

[a]Estimated.

Source: *Barclays Country Reports*, September 1997, page 7.

fell in 1996 and are estimated to further improve during 1997/98. However, the ratios are still high relative to some of the other CEECs.

EU enlargement

Part of the transformation of the CEECs has come about through adopting Western European practices. However, the CEECs do not see themselves as simply following their larger Western European neighbours but envisage that they will play a full part in the future development of Europe and the EU. As such, a number of them have made applications to join the EU. As a response to this the European Commission published *Agenda 2000* in July 1997. This dealt with three main issues:

- the future shape of the Union's main policies;
- the EU's financial perspectives for the years 2000–2006;
- the enlargement of the Union.

With regard to the latter the EU set out a number of criteria for future membership of the EU, which included the following:

- political issues, *viz.* the stability of democratic institutions, the rule of law, the respect for human rights and the protection of minorities;
- economic issues, e.g. the Copenhagen European Council suggested that these economic issues required the existence of a functioning market economy as well as the capacity to cope with competitive pressure and market forces within the Union;
- the ability to take on the obligations of membership (the *acquis communautaire*), including adherence to the aims of political, economic and monetary union.

If the economic issues are examined in more detail, the functioning of the market economy requires a number of conditions to be met:

- equilibrium between demand and supply should be established through the role of market forces; this requires prices as well as trade to be liberalised;
- significant barriers to market entry and exit should be absent;
- the legal system, including the regulation of property rights, needs to be in place so that laws and contracts can be enforced;
- there needs to be macro-economic stability, including adequate price stability and sustainable public finances and external accounts;
- there should be broad consensus about the essentials of economic policy;
- the finance sector should be sufficiently well-developed so that savings can be channelled towards productive investment.

In the area of competitive pressure, the criteria have been constructed to consider the capacity of each of the CEECs to withstand the competitive pressure and market forces within the Union. The elements taken into account include the following:

- the existence of a functioning market economy which has sufficient macro-economic stability so that economic agents can make decisions that are predictable;
- an appropriate amount of both human and physical capital, including infrastructure, education and research;
- the desire that firms can adapt, tapping into investment finance, skills and technology, from both home and abroad.

As an indicator of the degree of competitiveness, the EU considered the degree of trade integration of the country with the EU before enlargement, and the proportion of small firms. In considering where the countries are now it is also important to bear in mind the positions expected of the countries by the year 2005/6. In the Commission's view, Hungary and Poland come closest to meeting the two economic criteria taken together, whilst close behind come the Czech Republic and Slovenia. Estonia meets the first criterion, but has still got some way to go to meet the second. Slovakia meets the second criterion but is not regarded, at present, as a functioning market economy. In addition to these transitional economies, Malta (if it so wishes) and Cyprus have also been included in the first-wave group. Thus Slovakia, Romania, Bulgaria, Latvia and Lithuania are considered as countries in the second wave of entry together with those still waiting for an invitation to apply for EU membership.

For the successful applicants the move towards full membership of the EU is somewhat different to the accession issues faced by earlier Western European economies. They are poorer, they are in a transitional phase to a market economy, they face an EU that is undergoing change, and they may have to accept agreements, such as monetary union, which are far greater than those experienced by other applicant countries before. For those countries unsuccessful in the first wave there is a need for the EU to make sure that they are not sidelined and that a major distinction should not be drawn between those that are 'in' and those that are 'out'.

The costs and benefits of a wider EU

The costs and benefits from enlargement can be viewed from both an East and a West perspective. Before these are considered, however, it is important to note the differences that currently exist between the two blocs.

The CEECs are at present twice as agricultural as the EU15 and two and a half times poorer in terms of GDP per capita. In addition, the five Eastern European economies taken together amount to only approximately 6 per cent of the EU15 economy. Thus East–West integration should expand the CEECs' opportunities much more than those of the EU15.

In the area of trade the EU15 and CEECs are almost balanced, with the exceptions being in 'chemicals and rubber and plastic goods' and in capital goods, where the EU is a net exporter. For the EU15, trade with the CEECs is distributed disproportionately, with Germany accounting for over 40 per cent of EU exports. Austria, Belgium, France, Italy, the Netherlands and the UK account for approximately 5 per cent each. In addition, whereas CEEC exports to the EU amount to approximately 60 per cent of total CEEC exports, EU exports to the CEECs are only approximately 5 per cent of total EU15 exports.

In the area of protection the tariff rates for many goods indicate that the CEECs are on average more protectionist than the EU. However, the EU is far more protectionist than the CEECs when it comes to agriculture. Thus as the CEECs enter the EU there will be increased protection against third countries' agricultural goods. Overall, when the CEECs enter the EU there will need to be a great deal of tariff cutting in the CEECs, but very little tariff cutting in the EU, particularly since imports from the CEECs account for only approximately 5 per cent of EU imports.

There have been a number of studies which have attempted to examine the possible impact of membership of the EU by the CEECs (see Brown *et al.* 1995; Baldwin *et al.* 1997). Not all of them are comparable, however, since some consider the establishment of a free trade area between the CEECs and the EU, whilst others consider full membership under a range of different scenarios. Furthermore, other studies of the impact of enlargement were undertaken with a group of CEECs which are different to those being considered by the EU in the first wave. There are areas of commonality, however, between the studies. Membership of the EU would have a risk premium effect. Joining the EU will make the CEECs a far less risky place in which to invest. Furthermore, if this is coupled to improved growth and lower rates of inflation then investor confidence in these countries is improved.

As for costs, the emphasis of many studies has focused disproportionately on the budgetary issues of EU enlargement. *Agenda 2000* proposed tight budgetary management, holding EU spending until 2006 to 1.27 per cent of EU GDP, the level expected to be reached by 1999. This budgetary constraint is seen by some countries, such as Spain, as likely to reduce the expenditure that they currently receive from the centre. At the same time, the Netherlands is adamant that there should be no increase in individual member states' contributions to the overall budget to compensate for the first-wave entrants from the CEECs.

Case study: EU enlargement – a Spanish view

Spain is bracing itself for what could be its biggest conflict with the European Union since it joined 12 years ago.

The conflict arises from the tension between the EU's enlargement plans and Spain's claims on the structural grants designed to reduce inequalities between different parts of the EU.

'The debate has hardly begun,' Ramon de Miguel, state secretary for Europe, said. But he warned in an interview that the issue of finding the financial resources for expansion risked provoking 'serious clashes' between partners.

'We cannot expand at the cost of dissolving fundamental principles,' he said.

The centre-right government of Jose Maria Aznar has taken a firm view that the accession of new members should not be paid for by making the poorer members of the current 15 forgo 'cohesion' funds and other structural grants they currently receive.

The line from the prime minister's office is that Spain is ready to pay its share of the cost but not part of others' share as well. Mr de Miguel denied Spain was threatening to block the enlargement negotiations, due to begin next year, or was setting preconditions. It wanted to keep to the spirit of *Agenda 2000*, the European Commission's blueprint programme, by taking 'one step at a time'. If the different processes became entangled, the result could be 'total gridlock'.

Madrid remained 'totally in favour' of widening the EU, although not out of its own economic interests. 'We are not going to gain from enlargement,' Mr de Miguel said. It was a matter of continuing to show solidarity between European countries.

But solidarity among existing members would be in jeopardy if current support funds were sacrificed. He said some European Commission officials were backing German proposals to cut off 'cohesion' funds for countries joining the single currency in 1999.

These funds, launched five years ago at Spain's demand to ease the monetary union process, are destined for transport and environment investment in the four countries with per capita income levels below 90 per cent of the EU average. Spain, because of its size in relation to Greece, Portugal and Ireland, gets more than half – to date, some Pta600 billion (£2.4 billion).

'This is not a debate we want to open,' Mr de Miguel said. Challenging the cohesion payments 'would imply such an injustice that Spain would not be willing to accept it.' Spain deserved recognition for its 'special effort' in tightening its national budget to meet the convergence targets for monetary union. This was at the cost of 'real' convergence – the process of bridging the 22–23 per cent gap between average income in Spain and the EU as a whole. Spain still needed big investments in infrastructure, he said, arguing: 'It is in the interests of the more prosperous parts of the EU that Spain should catch up with them.' He hoped the future of support funds would be agreed by the end of next year, but it was hard to tackle budget issues with Dutch and German elections looming.

Commission financing proposals for 2000–2006 foresee spending of ECU275 billion (£196 billion) on structural measures, including ECU21 billion on cohesion payments. Of the remainder, ECU45 billion would be set aside for the future new members, with part of the money coming from savings made as some regions cease to qualify for special regional funds.

Most of Spain's regions have up to now obtained 'Objective 1' funding, destined for areas with income levels below 75 per cent of the EU average. Madrid accepts that some – notably the Valencia region – are likely no longer to qualify, but insists aid should be phased out over a period. It is also keeping a wary eye on proposals for channelling some structural funds into employment initiatives.

'We are running the risk of not putting up enough money to finance our ambitions,' Mr de Miguel said. Spain agreed there should be spending limits, but the plan to keep to a maximum of 1.27 per cent of EU GDP should be 'indicative', not a fixed ceiling. This might be sufficient as long as the EU sustained 2 per cent real growth over the period, as envisaged, and ordered its finances better. The package should cover the needs of new members, since for the first part of the period negotiations would not have been completed. 'Another question is what happens from 2007,' he warned.

'What we do not want is to discover halfway through that 1.27 per cent is not enough, and to have to find the money,' he said. Spain wanted the EU to have the courage to strengthen its funding, changing the basis of members' contributions and gearing them to per capita income levels as well as national GDP. But it realised this idea was 'very unpopular', he said. 'It is easier to take away cohesion funds and reduce structural funding.'

Source: White, D. (1997) Spain prepares to fight for EU grants: Madrid fears accession of new members will be paid for by cutting 'cohesion' funds, *Financial Times*, 18 November.

Questions

1 Why is Spain concerned about EU enlargement?

2 What solutions does Spain put forward to the potential crisis? What further difficulties does Spain envisage in the next decade over the budget?

● ●

Two main items dominate the spending side of the EU budget, the CAP and structural spending (the structural fund and the cohesion fund). In fact, the interest lies in the CAP, cohesion and contributions. At present there is little debate about the area of contributions – all countries have committed themselves to approximately 1 per cent of GDP. In terms of cohesion expenditure, the greatest part goes on Objective 1 regions (approximately two-thirds of all structural spending) (see Chapter 7). If the expenditure on the two poorest nations in terms of structural funding expenditure is extrapolated to the CEECs and noting the Edinburgh Summit desire to double this figure by 1999, then structural funding would cost in excess of ECU26 billion for the CEECs (Courchene *et al.* 1993). However, this figure is seen as an overestimate since structural funding needs to be matched by equal funding from the state's government and this does not always occur. None the less, the entry of the CEECs will lower the average GDP of the EU and because Objective 1 status requires the per capita income of region to be below 75 per cent of the EU then there will be some regions in the current EU states that are receiving structural funding but which will lose this after the entry of the CEECs. A more conservative estimate for the amount of increased structural funding that is needed is given by Baldwin *et al.* (1997) at ECU13 billion.

When the CAP is considered, estimating the cost is difficult for three reasons. Firstly, Franz Fischler, the farm minister, has called for massive agricultural reform, which may reduce the burden of the agricultural budget; secondly, there has been a lack of accurate data on CEEC farms; and thirdly there has been continued change in the farm sector in these countries. In addition, the effect of the CAP on the CEECs and any further budgetary commitments is bound up in an EU rule – in effect since 1988 – which limits CAP spending to rising not faster than 74 per cent of the Union's GDP growth. For the CEECs there is also the issue that entry into the EU will mean changes in the export behaviour and protection of their agricultural sector since the EU signed up to different agreements on agriculture following the completion of the Uruguay Round of trade talks compared with the CEECs.

Overall a conservative estimate of the costs to the CAP of CEEC membership lies anywhere around ECU10–15 billion (Baldwin *et al.* 1997).

Case study: EU enlargement – the effect on the sugar industry

The expansion of the European Union to include Central and Eastern European countries – the first wave of which might join in 2002 – will mean a large-scale shake-out of the enlarged EU's sugar production, delegates to a London sugar conference heard yesterday.

As well as a consolidation of the industry, the accession of Eastern and Central European states to the EU will also require transitional mechanisms to help iron out large price differences in agricultural products – which in the case of sugar beet are as much as 50 per cent – between original and new EU member states, said Simon Harris, corporate affairs director of British Sugar.

Mr Harris told those attending the London-based International Sugar Organisation's conference on European sugar that 'the distorted nature of world markets for sugar . . . and the capital intensity of the sugar industry' meant that sugar producers faced an unusually testing time both before and during the EU's enlargement.

The first wave of Eastern and Central European new members may include the Czech Republic, Estonia, Hungary, Poland and Slovenia. Their inclusion would almost double the number of people employed in agriculture in the EU, to perhaps 17 million.

Mr Harris said the process of factory rationalisation and financial concentration in Europe's sugar industry still has far to go, even though the EU has seen the number of its beet factories halved since 1968 – from 312 to 155 – when the EU sugar regime was introduced.

Delegates also heard that Russia expects to import 'not less than 2.3 million tonnes' of raw sugar in 1998, the same as in 1996 and 1997, according to Vasiliy Severin, chairman of the country's Union of Sugar Producers.

In its latest report, sugar analyst Czarnikow forecast that Russia faces a poor sugar beet harvest in 1997–98, with sugar production down to 1.48 million tonnes, compared with 1.87 million tonnes in 1996–97.

Mr Severin said that in spite of current production problems – 17 new sugar mills need to be built and 54 out of the currently existing 95 require upgrading – Russia intended producing 5.2 million tonnes of sugar by 2005, with the aim of eliminating the need for imports.

Source: Mead, G. (1997) Bigger EU a test for sugar, *Financial Times*, 26 November.

Questions

1 Why does European enlargement pose problems for the EU sugar industry?

∙∙∙

So what does the final picture look like for the EU and CEEC first-wave membership? Both the EU and the CEECs get benefits from reduced risk premiums. The EC15 are expected to face net costs of around ECU8 billion, which is less than 1 per cent of EU GDP. Of the costs the largest contributors will be the big four – Germany, the UK, France and Italy – with Germany paying the greatest proportion. The CEECs are also expected to benefit greatly. Real incomes will rise, they will benefit from transfers of money from the other EU members, and if the additional transfers from structural funding and agriculture are included then estimates are for an increase in the region of anything between ECU23 billion and ECU50 billion. These are expected to be the long-term gains in real incomes. In addition, the CEECs are expected to benefit from the large improvements in their economic performance through their transitional stage to EU membership.

Conclusion

The past decade has seen major changes in the economies of many CEECs as they have moved from centrally planned economies through transitional phases and on towards the market-based economies of the West. This move has been brought about by the demise of communism and the realisation that in terms of economic development and sound finances the Western European model for all its deficiencies has much to offer. Part of the move towards transition was prompted by the level of external debt accrued by some of the Eastern Bloc countries. In addition to debt issues, the last decade has seen the CEECs become more heavily integrated with the EU, not only through trade but also through the role of Western FDI and the selling-off of state-owned assets. Many CEECs now perceive that they would like to take the next step to greater integration with the West by becoming members of the EU. Integration into the EU is not without its problems for both the CEECs and current EU members. If all proceeds to plan, by the year 2010 the EU will be seen to cover a region from the Arctic to the Mediterranean and from the Atlantic to the Baltic.

Questions for discussion

1   For each of the factors mentioned in the gravity model, explain why it affects trade in the way described in the text. Can you think of any factors

omitted in the analysis by Hamilton and Winters? What problems are there in using the gravity model to analyse the potential levels of trade between Western and Eastern Europe?

2　How justified do you think the criticisms of the Europe agreements given by Winters and Wang are? In what ways might these agreements be altered to help the countries of Eastern and Central Europe?

3　To what extent do changes in trading relationships between Eastern and Western Europe represent a threat to workers and companies in the West and to what extent are they an exciting opportunity?

4　Do you think that the main obstacles to foreign direct investment in Eastern and Central Europe are concerned with the supply of investment from the West or the demand for investment from the East? Can you think of any policy measures which might increase the flow of investment?

5　How significant do you think the CEFTA grouping is for the future trading relationships within Eastern Europe and between Eastern and Western Europe?

6　Can you think of any motives for Western investment in Eastern Europe that have been omitted from the analysis of reasons for investment by Radice which is described in the text?

7　How would you explain the differences in the pattern of sources of investment for the four Visegrad countries as shown in Table 14.8?

8　For both the current EU members and the CEECs, what are the costs and benefits of EU enlargement?

9　Why has privatisation proved to be so problematic in the CEECs?

10　Have the external debt problems of the CEECs started to recede?

Main reading

Dobrinsky, R. and Landesmann, M. (eds) (1995) *Transforming Economies and European Integration*, Edward Elgar.

Faini, R. and Portes, R. (eds) (1995) *European Union Trade with Eastern Europe: Adjustment and Opportunities*, Centre for Economic Policy Research.

Radice, H. (1995) 'The role of foreign direct investment in the transformation of Eastern Europe, in Chang, H.-J. and Nolan, P. (eds) *The Transformation of the Communist Economies: Against the Mainstream*, Macmillan.

Additional reading

Anderson, K. and Norheim, H. (1993) History, geography and regional economic integration, in Anderson, K. and Blackhurst, R. (eds) *Regional Integration and the Global Trading System*, Harvester Wheatsheaf.

Baldwin, R. (1994) *Towards an Integrated Europe*, Centre for Economic Policy Research.

Baldwin, R. E. François, J. F. and Portes, R. (1997) The costs and benefits of eastern enlargement: the impact on the EU and central Europe, *Economic Policy*, April 1997, pp. 127–76.

Boland, V. (1996) Heavyweight currency squeezes Czech trade, *Financial Times*, 18 October.

Brainard, L.J. (1991) *Amex Bank Review.*

Brown, D., Deardorff, A., Djankov, S. and Stern, R. (1995) An economic assessment of the integration of Czechoslovakia, Hungary and Poland into the EU, AIGGS Economic Working Paper No. 8.

Business Central Europe (1995) September.

Business Central Europe (1996) Foreign Investment, April.

Business Central Europe (1997) July.

Cadot, O. and De Melo, J. (1995) France and the CEECs: adjusting to another enlargement, in Faini, R. and Portes, R. (eds) *European Union Trade with Eastern Europe: Adjustment and Opportunities*, Centre for Economic Policy Research.

Collins, S. and Rodrik, D. (1991) *Eastern Europe and the Soviet Union in the World Economy*, Institute for International Economics.

Corado, C. (1995) The textiles and clothing trade with Central and Eastern Europe: impact on members of the EC, in Faini, R. and Portes, R. (eds) *European Union Trade with Eastern Europe: Adjustment and Opportunities*, Centre for Economic Policy Research.

Courchene, T., Goodhart, M. G., Majocchi, A., Moesen, W., Prud'homme, T., Schneider, F., Smith, S., Spahn, B. and Walsh, C. (1993) Stable Money – Sound Finances, *European Economy*, No. 53, European Commission, DG 2, Brussels.

European Commission (1997) *The EU and its Enlargement – Agenda 2000*, July.

de Jonquieres, G. (1995) Bittersweet taste of expansion, *Financial Times*, 2 October.

Dobrinsky, R. (1995) Economic transformation and the changing patterns of European East–West trade, in Dobrinsky, R. and Landesmann, M. (eds) *Transforming Economies and European Integration*, Edward Elgar.

Gowan, P. (1990) Western economic diplomacy and the new Eastern Europe, *New Left Review*, No.182, July/August.

Hamilton, C. and Winters, L. A. (1992) Opening up international trade with Eastern Europe, *Economic Policy*, No. 14.

Harris, F. (1997) Poisoned chalice, *Business Central Europe*, July/August, pp. 19–20.

Havlik, P. (1995) Trade reorientation and competitiveness in CEECs, in Dobrinsky, R. and Landesmann, M. (eds) *Transforming Economies and European Integration*, Edward Elgar.

Hope, K. (1997) Bulgaria 97: privatisation: last attempt to dispose of assets, *Financial Times*, 21 October.

Kilmister, A. (1990) Poland: Courting Western Capital, *International Labour Reports*, No. 37, January/February.

Landesmann, M. (1995a) Projecting East–West trade integration, in Landesmann, M. and Szekely, I. (eds) *Industrial Restructuring and Trade Reorientation in Eastern Europe*, Cambridge University Press.

Landesmann, M. (1995b) The Pattern of East–West European integration: catching up or falling behind?, in Dobrinksy, R. and Landesmann, M. (eds) *Transforming Economies and European Integration*, Edward Elgar.

Lavigne, M. (1991) *International Political Economy and Socialism*, Cambridge University Press.

Lavigne, M. (1995) *The Economics of Transition: From Socialist Economy to Market Economy*, Macmillan.

Linnemann, H. (1966) *An Economic Study of International Trade Flows*, North Holland.

Lyons, R. (1997) Not even a poor man's EU, *Business Central Europe*, June.

Mead, G. (1997) EU a test for sugar, *Financial Times*, 26 November.

Papp, B. (1995) Equal footing, *Business Central Europe*, September.

Radice, H. (1993) Western investment in Eastern Europe, *Labour Focus on Eastern Europe*, No. 44.

Robinson, A. (1995) Region emerges as a supplier, *Financial Times*, Exporter Supplement, 18 April.

Schmidt, K. D. (1995) Foreign direct investment in Eastern Europe: state-of-the-art and prospects, in Dobrinsky, R. and Landesmann, M. (eds) *Transforming Economies and European Integration*, Edward Elgar.

Sheehy, J. (1995) Economic interpenetration between the European Union and Central and Eastern Europe, in Dobrinsky, R. and Landesmann, M. (eds) *Transforming Economies and European Integration*, Edward Elgar.

Sinn, H. W. and Weichenrieder, A. (1997) Foreign direct investment, political resentment and the privatization process in Eastern Europe, *Economic Policy*, No. 24.

Wagstyl, S. (1996) Woven into the fabric, *Financial Times*, 10 January.

Wallace, W. and Clarke, R. (1986) *Comecon, Trade and the West*, Frances Pinter.

White, D. (1997) Spain prepares to fight for EU grants: Madrid fears accession of new members will be paid for by cutting 'cohesion' funds, *Financial Times*, 18 November.

Williams, F. (1996) Eastern Europe investment grows strongly, *Financial Times*, 17 July.

Winters, L. A. (1995) Liberalization of the European steel trade, in Faini, R. and Portes, R. (eds) *European Union Trade with Eastern Europe: Adjustment and Opportunities*, Centre for Economic Policy Research.

Winters, L. A. and Wang, Z. K. (1994) *Eastern Europe's International Trade*, Manchester University Press.

15 Conclusion

The 1990s have witnessed great changes in the world of international business in general and European business in particular. Within the EU, the results of the SEM are still reverberating around the EU economies and have been observed to improve the efficiency and competition in many markets. At the same time the move towards market-based economies is well under way in many CEECs through the introduction of private capital, privatisation and the development of capital markets. The full effects of the Uruguay Round of GATT are still working their way through the international economy and such has been the importance paid to the freeing of trade that a new trading body, the WTO, has come to replace GATT. The United States remains as the sole superpower, both in political and in defensive terms, and this has led to its leading role in both economic and political decisions.

Europe has increasingly been at odds to improve its competitiveness. This was partly achieved through the establishment of the EU and could improve further through additional expansion. The SEM took this agenda further and the establishment of a single currency within the 11 member states which have achieved the entry criteria continues the process not only towards increased competitiveness but also towards even greater European integration. A United States of Europe appears to be getting closer and the size of its market and level of economic activity will be greater than that of the USA. Meanwhile, one of the new powerhouses of world economic activity is being developed: the Chinese economy, growing at an average rate of 7–10 per cent per year, is expected to become a major economic force in the new millennium.

Whereas forty years ago it was possible to talk about French products produced by French firms and Swedish products produced by Swedish-owned firms, the world today has altered. There are still brand names which are associated with their country of origin but now ownership of the company may well be in foreign hands. The owners of these companies are true transnational enterprises, using global financial markets when and where they need them. In addition to takeover and merger activity there have also been large amounts of activity within the area of FDI. Some of this has been to overcome barriers to entry into markets, but in addition some has been developed to take advantage of flexible and/or cheap labour. Given that it is increasingly difficult to talk about domestic companies and their international activities, since many domestic companies are foreign-owned, does this pose any problems for the domestic economy?

In the UK, foreign investment amounted to £160 billion at the end of 1997, more than three times that of 1986. The positive aspects of this activity have been to improve management techniques and introduce innovative technologies, but at the same time foreign ownership may 'starve' the UK of research and development, which may still take place in the home, rather than host, economy. In addition, a large proportion of profits will be repatriated, and since many of these global corporations could be viewed as 'footloose', if global profits are squeezed it is possible that operations in satellite countries – the UK in this case – will be the first to be shut down. In addition, global corporations reduce the number of suppliers since MNEs often utilise the same suppliers everywhere they operate. None the less, does ownership of the company really matter? Surely it is better to have the 'best' management? If this argument is true, foreign ownership should see the foreign-owned company flourish. Profits will increase, the workforce will grow, and consumers will get higher-quality goods at lower prices. In the case of the UK, the motor industry, consumer electronics and televisions fit into this category. For example, in the television industry the UK produced one out of every three televisions produced in the EU, although the last UK-owned factory closed in 1988. The four biggest manufacturers in Britain are Sony, Matsushita and Toshiba of Japan and Samsung of South Korea, and their contribution to the UK's trade balance was £540 million in 1997. But in other sectors outside manufacturing there have also been increases in foreign ownership, such as utilities and banking. It is true that many of these sectors are highly profitable, but not all earnings from foreign-owned plants will be reinvested in the domestic economy. Moreover, many governments still keep 'golden shares' in a number of companies which they view as strategically important. It may also be less politically sensitive for a Japanese multinational to close down its production facilities in another country rather than ones in Japan.

The greater globalisation of companies suggests that problems elsewhere in the global economy will have repercussions for economic and business activity within Europe. A good example of such problems are those currently being seen in Asia. There is a view that the Asian crisis will have only a minor impact on Europe's economy. For example, it is a recipient of only 7 per cent of European exports, compared with 20 per cent of the USA's and more than 40 per cent of Japan's; none the less, the linkages to Europe are much wider. Companies which have a large amount of their business activity in the region have seen their share prices fall and outward investment has been curtailed since profit forecasts are much lower. More importantly, the Asian crisis is also a banking crisis. Many Asian banks are over-exposed and as much as the IMF has stepped in to relieve their over-exposure to bad debt provision, there will no doubt be further banks that cease trading. The fragility of some of the Asian economies will also lead to an economic slowdown, which is likely to lead to further difficulties for the commercial bank sector. At the same time, as a condition for receiving IMF help, many countries such as South Korea, Thailand and Indonesia will have to restructure their economies. The problems within Asia may at one level reduce globalisation of business activities but at the same time might encourage some non-Asian businesses to purchase the relatively cheap Asian firms which were once considered to be rivals.

In some sectors too it would be expected that the developed world is likely to face intense competition from some super-competitive Pacific Rim organisations, which will be in a position to exploit the fall in their currencies and which have excess capacity because of the fall in demand at home. The knock-on effect from this could be increased trade deficits with Asia and a greater move towards calls for increased protectionism. The problems within Asia have also affected the Japanese economy. Its banking system is under pressure, particularly after the collapse of Yamaichi Bank, and its growth has slowed. Western governments have long been encouraging Japan to open up its markets further and to embark on a programme of stimulating domestic growth. A weakening of the yen–dollar exchange rate would help Japanese exports but would at the same time lead to higher trade imbalances between the USA and Japan, and could lead to a call for greater protectionism.

At the same time, Europe in general and the UK in particular through Samsung and Daewoo have been important sites for inward investment from Asia. The Asian crisis has resulted in some inward investment being curtailed, notably that by Hyundai and Samsung of South Korea. This does not spell disaster for the UK, since over half its inward investment comes from the USA. None the less, there are signs that the path of inward investment is switching within Europe. Decisions by Toyota, IBM, Motorola and Fedex to build in France, despite having to negotiate with more than a single union, higher labour costs, a maximum on hours of work per week and higher corporate taxes suggest that there are other factors that are resulting in location decisions. Pro-Europeans suggest that it is membership of the EMU which has led to some organisations expanding or settling in continental Europe rather than in the UK; however, government grants may also be a factor. None the less, the explanation could lie in the strategic plans of MNEs in that they do not want all of their European investment in one country. For some companies, expanding to other countries outside of their original European site may be one of the ways in which they can achieve further European market share. This process of expansion elsewhere within Europe can be explained by the need to be closer to other geographical markets, and that as a company expands, its original site loses its competitive advantage as the pool of skilled labour is reduced. Thus what Europe may see during the next decade is some expansion at existing sites but new greenfield investment will go to other sites within Europe. Countries should not rely on a continued flow of foreign investment just because they were successful in the past. It may be more worthwhile for Europe to encourage home-grown firms rather than to rely on attracting foreign investment.

It was noted in Chapter 2 that although Europe has improved its performance in a number of sectors, it still lags behind Japan and the USA in others. One way of achieving improved competitiveness is through direct government intervention to reduce market failure. Another approach is to argue that Europe has lost competitiveness through having too much government intervention in markets. These conflicting sides of the argument can be seen with the approach Europe has taken towards its labour market. There is a group of countries, of which the UK is a leading exponent, which argue that labour markets should be flexible. Labour markets should be deregulated, making it easier to hire and fire workers, workers need to be more flexible (see later in this chapter), and the labour input should be organised to be responsive to changes in demand through the use of temporary and part-time staff. Conversely, there are other countries, such as France and Germany, which say that freeing labour markets encourages employers to take advantage of workers and reduces training, and therefore some element of social protection is required. The European Union needs to address these issues and in particular the way in which changes in labour markets can enhance the efficiency and competitiveness of organisations.

Within Europe one feature has been noticeable during the 1980s and 1990s, and that is that unemployment has been rising relative to that in the USA. Both economies have been subjected to massive external changes such as the rise of the newly industrialised countries (NICs), rapid changes in technology, changes in the way production is organised, structural reforms and the like. However, while the USA has reduced its unemployment rate to under 6 per cent in March 1998, a number of EU countries such as Spain, France and Germany have a rate easily double that figure. Explanations for these differences are numerous. It could lie with the move towards monetary union in the EU, which has resulted in demand-dampening policies. Secondly, there is the insider–outsider condition. The greater strength of trade unions in the EU means that they pay little attention to those unemployed, using their position to gain higher pay awards, rather than showing restraint in order to enhance the job-creation prospects for others. Alternatively, the outsiders – the unemployed – once outside of the job market for too long have redundant skills, and the longer individuals are out of the labour market, the more reticent employers are about taking them on. Thirdly, some employers in the EU may not take on more labour, because of the high costs of firing their workforce.

Until recently, Spain was used as an example, where high firing costs and high unemployment have gone hand in hand. Bean (1994) also suggest that the level of capital stock in countries such as Germany, France and the UK is at a sub-optimal level, thereby lowering the marginal productivity of labour in these countries. When demand rises in these countries then unemployment will only fall as capital stock is built up.

But what of the arguments that EU labour markets are less flexible and thus EU companies are losing out in the global marketplace? Many countries as well as the EU have minimum wage legislation. Minimum wages, it is argued, increase labour costs and thereby reduce competitiveness. There have been a number of studies to suggest that the setting of a minimum wage in a competitive labour market does not necessarily raise unemployment (Card and Kreuger 1994; Machin and Manning 1994). There are also issues about the level at which a minimum wage is to be set (the UK still has not announced its figure but should do so by the end of 1998) and the degree to which labour costs, due to the process of downsizing (see Chapter 2), are a significant proportion of overall costs for some organisations. Within the EU, France, the Netherlands, Portugal, Spain and Luxembourg have statutory minimum wages, while in Belgium and Greece a national minimum wage is set by collective bargaining. In Germany, Italy and Denmark, pay minima for individual sectors are set by binding collective agreements covering a large proportion of the workforce, while in Ireland legal minimum rates are set for certain low-wage sectors such as hotels and catering. Of the EU countries, only the UK has no minimum wage protection at either national, regional or sectoral level, having abandoned minimum wages set by wage councils in 1993. It has been argued that the lack of a minimum wage in the UK explains its unemployment level, which is lower than that of many of its partners in Europe, during the 1990s. Moreover, the US minimum wage is set lower than those in Europe, explaining the lower unemployment rate in the USA. But it is still not clear whether higher minimum wages in Europe can explain the higher unemployment in the EU. Dolando *et al.* (1996) note that it is surprisingly hard to find strong evidence of any adverse unemployment effects resulting from minimum wages, and the presence or absence of a minimum wage will not be the difference between economic success and failure.

However, it may not be in the minimum wage area that European competitiveness is being lost, but through higher 'other labour costs'. A distinguishing feature of most EU economies is the high level of social protection provided by the state. To fund this, social protection charges are made on businesses, and it is felt that these extra costs for each unit of labour are putting European organisations at a competitive disadvantage and discouraging them from employing individuals. If these additional costs differ between states then employers could also look to relocate themselves to areas where these extra costs are lower. The impact of increased social cost can affect organisations in a number of ways. They may be able to pass on higher costs to the consumer by raising prices, they could absorb these costs through reduced profits, or the cost may be borne by the employee through reduced wages. For those at the minimum wage level, wage costs may not be reduced, so they may end up losing their jobs as organisations substitute capital for labour. Thus European organisations may react differently to the social costs attached to labour. Moreover, for some European organisations these extra social costs may not be considered as part of a social contribution package but as part of the overall salary package offered to their employees.

When the term flexible working is discussed it is worth noting that flexible working can mean different things in different countries. It could mean

- wages or earnings flexibility;
- labour mobility;
- functional flexibility: reducing the demarcation lines between different occupations;
- flexibility in the pattern and organisation of work: this includes flexibility in the place of work, flexibility in hours, and greater use of part-time, temporary and self-employed (subcontracted) workers.

Between 1992 and 1996, the number of temporary workers within the UK rose by nearly a third, with fixed-term contracts and agency temping increasing by a similar amount. But does flexible working improve the performance of the organisation? According to Guest *et al.* (1997), some aspects of flexible working are counter-productive. It appeared to be the case that subcontracting could work. For example, working 'outsourced' from say a weak IT department to a major external supplier may provide more job security, and part-time arrangements may suit some employees. None the less, new arrangements could meet resistance from the workforce and where the new arrangements are voluntary, it is possible that it is the best employees that go freelance. The result is that they can offer themselves to competitors and can, therefore, push up the price for any contract. Thus although flexibility might be able to reduce fixed costs, it is not always clear as to whether it yields overall savings. For example, flexibility leads to a more rapid turnover of the workforce, which entails added costs of recruitment, training and management time. Moreover, line managers have found themselves at a distinct disadvantage with experienced negotiators. Using fixed-term contracts as a means of encouraging individuals to work harder may not work if managers are not experienced negotiators. Organisations have found it easier simply to renew the contracts. In addition, part-time workers often receive less training than full-time workers and this reduces long-term competitiveness. It could be argued that if long-term contracts between organisations and their suppliers and customers appears to be the best approach, organisations should similarly undertake long-term commitments with their employees if organisations are to become more competitive.

There are other areas, too, where the EU needs to address labour market issues during the next millennium. These include issues associated with skill deficiencies, the changing age structure of the population and therefore the use of older workers, and the greater use of women in the labour market.

Outside of labour market developments and their importance for improved efficiency and competitiveness, EU industry is likely to see further moves towards merger and takeover activity. Part of this is being triggered by deregulation of markets such as telecommunications and air passenger traffic, the need to restructure an industry because of changes in demand (e.g. the European defence industry), and the role of the single currency in Europe as differentiated pricing strategies are reduced. In fact, the world airline passenger market is likely to spawn a number of major cross-border mergers such as that proposed between British Airways and American Airlines. Within the banking sector and the insurance sector (discussed in Chapter 13), the proposed merger between Citicorp and Travelers (April 1998) will create the largest financial services group in the world. Such a move to create an organisation to cater for every financial services need, if successful, would lead to a further wave of such deals. However, in the past, success of mergers in the financial services sector has proved to be more elusive.

Areas where success has been more forthcoming have been in the defence industry. The American defence firms began a process of merger shortly after the Berlin Wall was torn down in 1989. European defence firms, however, have tended to remain more separate. The result has been that US firms are leaner and fitter, and coupled with the downturn in sales in their own economies they have proved to be highly competitive against the unmerged European firms. Thus what we are likely to see in the future is a greater degree of cross-border co-operation between European defence firms.

If there is a further wave of merger activity within both a European and a global framework to create ever-increasing global companies then what may occur is a further round of de-merging and divestment. This process will lead to organisations focusing on successful areas, reducing their involvement in non-core operations. For those companies which experience successful mergers and takeovers there may be a greater need for some form of global control mechanism since they may lie outside of most current nations' or trading bloc control. In Europe there is a tension between encouraging competition and developing national champions. Even where successful national champions have occurred there has been a tendency for them to behave in a similar fashion to other non-European MNEs. For example, Fiat ignored directives from the Italian government to develop the Mezzogiorno region and expanded production in Brazil, and Michelin reacted to French indicative planning by building plants outside France in a ratio of three-to-one to those built within its domestic economy. Conversely, if policies are used to inhibit indigenous organisations from expanding abroad while their international rivals have greater flexibility then it tends to weaken domestic organisations, making them less competitive. Foreign MNEs might be regulated, however, if they are in sensitive or strategic areas. What has been witnessed over the last decade is the development of more global corporations and as markets become more globalised, domestic and regional MNEs are being replaced by global MNEs. National or even regional governments may not be in a position to prevent these global MNEs dividing economic rent in their favour. Somewhere along the way a global body may be required to oversee the behaviour of global corporations.

For a number of European organisations the new millennium will throw up a further problem. The move towards monetary union provides both opportunities and threats (see Chapter 12), yet once in place the EMU members will follow a stability pact, keeping inflation under control and government expenditure as a proportion of GDP within the levels set by the Maastricht Treaty. Thus, periods of rapid growth seem unlikely in the short term. European businesses may therefore seek to invest abroad to enhance profits or further examine their own cost bases, leading to higher levels of unemployment. In the long term employment may rise as long-run competitiveness improves, but in the short term the impact is less optimistic.

For Europe and for European organisations the changes that have taken place in the 1990s and are due to take place with the development of a single European currency suggest that successful organisations are those that can adapt to situations more quickly. At the same time markets are becoming more globalised and this means that situations that arise in one market can get transmitted very easily to others. The situation in South-East Asia has shown this. However, the South-East Asian crisis also shows problems with the direction of economic policy taken by governments; deregulating capital markets can lead to huge speculative capital flows. This has been partly to blame in the collapse in the Mexican peso during 1994, the ERM crisis of 1992/3 and the South-East Asian crisis of 1997/98. This had led to a call for a revision of the world financial system to fit the needs of the current global environment.

One approach may be to introduce restrictions on capital flows. An alternative might be the introduction of a new form of fixed exchange rates similar to that operated under Bretton Woods, which saw the largest improvement in growth performances by the developed economies after the Second World War. What appears to be the case is that deregulation of capital markets as it stands can lead to abrupt changes in economic activity, especially where this activity has been based on bad loan provision.

For the next millennium, there are a number of uncertainties that are facing European business if it wishes to improve its competitiveness. The Europeans have been concentrating on their own market and have been trying to improve the conditions under which European business operates. At the same time they are aware that in some sectors European business has fallen behind that from the USA and Japan. If the predictions are correct, the single currency will make European firms leaner and fitter, and with the added expansion into Eastern Europe will provide a great many opportunities for business. However, there is often a large gulf between a forecast and out-turn and European business will need to be ready to take advantages of rapid changes in its economic environment.

Main reading

Bean, C. (1994) European unemployment: a survey, *Journal of Economic Literature*, Vol. XXXII, No. 2, June, pp. 573–619.

Card, C. and Kreuger, A. (1994) Minimum wages and unemployment: a case study of the fast food industry in New Jersey and Pennsylvania, *American Economic Review*, Vol. 84 (4) pp. 772–93.

Dolando, J., Kramatz, F., Machin, S., Manning, A., Margolis, D. and Teulings, C. (1996) Minimum wages: the European experience, *Economic Policy: A European Forum*, Centre for Economic Policy Research, October, pp. 319–72.

Guest, D., Mackenzie-Davey, K. and Smewing, C. (1997) Innovative employment contracts: a flexible friend? *Birkbeck College Report.*

Machin, S. and Manning, A. (1994) The effects of minimum wages on wage dispersion and unemployment: evidence from the UK wages councils, *Industrial and Labour Relations Review*, Vol. 47 (2), pp. 319–29.

Glossary

Absolute advantage: This is when a country is better (more efficient) at producing certain goods compared with others.

Acquis communautaire: The acceptance by all member states (and states wishing to join) of the entire body of community law, and the obligations implicit therein.

Additionality: The process by which funds from the EU are matched by equivalent funds from the member states.

Ad valorem **tax**: A tax which is a certain percentage on top of the price.

Agglomeration economies: These are reductions in costs that occur by having activities concentrated in one area.

Agglomeration factors: Factors which encourage FDI into a region and which are related to the effects of previous FDI decisions.

Agreement on Government Procurement (GPA): There are various GPAs involving EU member states and other governments to try to open up public procurement procedures and processes to foreign firms.

Anti-trust: The US term for competition policy.

Asymmetric external shocks: A shock to a group of countries, such as a rise in oil prices, which has greater impact on some countries than others.

Autarky: The position at which an individual nation can maximise its welfare but in the absence of trade.

Barter: Exchange of goods with no money involved.

Beggar-thy-neighbour trade policies: Trade policies based on the view that one country's gain implies another country's loss. There are no mutual gains from trade in this theory. Exporters gain 'bullion' from those they sell to; thus exporting countries 'win' and importers 'lose' by having to sacrifice 'bullion'.

Bilateral quotas: Agreements to allow equal access between two member states.

Bilateral trade: Trade between two countries.

Bilateral trading agreements: Trading arrangements agreed between two countries.

Buy-ins: The ownership of an organisation is transferred to a new set of shareholders who are a management team external to the organisation.

Buy-outs: The ownership of the organisation is transferred to a new set of shareholders, among whom the incumbent management is a significant element.

Cabotage: An agreement to allow non-domestic freight hauliers access to haulage services in the domestic market of another member state.

Cadres: Managers in France who have emerged from the top management schools.

Capital arbitrage: Transactions to take advantage of differences in the 'rate of interest'.

Central European Free Trade Agreement (CEFTA): An Eastern European grouping originally founded in 1992. It includes the Czech Republic, Slovakia, Hungary, Poland

and Slovenia. Romania is due to join very soon. It consists of a set of bilateral trade agreements together with a commitment to abolish all mutual tariffs by 2001.

Coefficients of structural change: A measure of changes in the structure of imports and exports for a country. They are defined as the sum of changes in the trade share of each sector over a one-year interval.

Commercial policy: Government policy regarding external trade matters.

Common external tariff: The same tariff rate in all the member states against a given commodity from outside the union.

Common good: A good with a characteristic of non-excludability in consumption.

Common market: The next stage from a customs union, where not only commodities move freely between member states but so do factors of production.

Comparative advantage: Where a country has a higher degree of superiority in the production of a good compared with others.

Comparative disadvantage: Where a country has a lower degree of superiority in the production of a good compared with others.

Competition policy: Policy designed to promote competition in business and often specifically to limit or prohibit the abuse of monopoly (or 'dominant firm') power and to prohibit restrictive trade practices such as price fixing and collusive tendering.

Core countries: Dunning's grouping of key EU countries with regard to FDI. This includes Belgium/Luxembourg, France, Germany, Italy, the Netherlands and the UK.

Corporate debt financing: One way in which organisations have financed their demand for investment funds, that is, through the issue of debt rather than equity.

Corporate networks: Patterns of company organisation caused by restructuring through the use of FDI, according to Cantwell. Such networks can be either horizontal or vertical in nature.

Council for Mutual Economic Assistance (CMEA or Comecon): The pre-1989 trading organisation linking the Eastern European countries and the Soviet Union. Comecon was essentially a system of bilateral trading arrangements.

CPV: Common Procurement Vocabulary. The European Commission has proposed a set of standard terms for use in the public procurement process to encourage further openness and transparency.

Credit derivatives: This is where the entire economic risk attached to an asset is transferred to a counterpart without actually moving the asset itself.

Customs duties: Duties payable on imports.

Customs union: A free-trade area with a common external tariff.

Debt crisis: The difficult or inability of countries to pay back international loans from private sources, the commercial banks or international institutions.

Debt equity swaps: A process by which creditors return debt to debtors in exchange for an equity interest in assets owned by debtors.

Demergers: The break-up of a previously merged organisation into separate parts.

De novo banks: New commercial banks which can be either state or privately owned and managed.

Deregulation: A process under which government restrictions on markets are reduced.

Derivative: A derivative is an asset or obligation whose value depends on some asset from which it is derived.

Derogation: Modification of a law.

Devaluation: A reduction in the value of a currency against other currencies in a fixed exchange rate system.

Direct investment: Inward capital flows to plant or other productive capacity.

Direct taxes: Taxes paid directly to the government, i.e. income taxes.

Discretionary exchange rate policy: The ability of an individual country to alter the value of its currency.

Discretionary financial regional support: Regional support that is not automatic but at the discretion of the government.

Diseconomies of scale: Increasing long-run average total cost as output increases.

Disintermediation: The diversion of business away from financial institutions which are subject to controls.

Divestment: The sale of non-core parts of the organisation.

Division of labour: To divide production into various tasks, and labour then specialises in the particular tasks.

Droplock bond: A bond which is flexible enough to allow conversion into another type of bond at a predetermined interest rate.

Dumping: This occurs where a good is sold in an overseas market at a price below the real cost of production.

Eclectic theory: A theory which brings together the different strands of various hypotheses in one comprehensive theory.

Eco-labelling: A scheme introduced in the EU for products which cause the least environmental damage in all stages of production.

Economic union: The next stage from a common market, where there is a high degree of integration of fiscal, monetary and commercial policies.

Economies of scale: As production increases, costs per unit fall.

Economies of scope: The reductions in costs that can be attained from the joint production of two or more products.

Environment action programme: A series of programmes introduced in the EU to tackle environmental matters.

Equity derivative: These are derivatives arranged to take care of the risk involved in holding shares, in particular the risks associated with new share issues.

Equity markets: These are markets for equities such as stocks and shares.

Euro: The official name of the single currency within Europe.

Eurobond: A bond placed in countries other than the one in whose currency the bond is denominated.

Eurocredit market: A market designed to provide medium-term funds (in various currencies) to deficit units, whereby commercial banks serve as intermediaries.

Eurocurrency market: A market designed to facilitate the transfer of short-term funds (in various currencies) from surplus units to deficit units, and in which commercial banks serve as intermediaries.

Europe Agreements: A set of agreements between the EU, and a number of Central and East European countries. These agreements give the Eastern European countries associate status with the EU. They cover trading arrangements and other broader political questions.

European Central Bank (ECB): The central monetary authority of the EU, which will operate the single currency.

European Coal and Steel Community (ECSC): The forerunner of the EEC. An agreement between France, Italy, West Germany, Belgium, the Netherlands and Luxembourg for free trade in coal and steel, with a central 'high authority' to regulate the opening of the market and provide assistance to distressed areas.

European Investment Bank: This was a bank established under the Treaty of Rome to channel funds at competitive rates of interest to member states with the task of contributing to the balanced and steady development of the EU.

European Monetary Institute: An institution set up to guide the European economies towards monetary union.

European Payments Union: A grouping set up in 1950 to encourage trade in Western Europe. Member countries agreed to accept payment in each other's currencies, rather than just gold or dollars, up to a certain amount.

Eurosclerosis: A term used in the 1970s and 1980s to describe the relatively poor growth performance of the EU and its job-creating ability.

Exchange controls: Controls on the amount of foreign currency that can be bought with domestic currency.

Exchange rate: The price of one currency in terms of another.

Exchange rate risk: The risk that an exchange rate will vary in the future and make profitable contracts loss-making.

Export Specialisation Index (ESI): The share of a commodity in a country's total exports to a particular region divided by the share of that commodity in total imports for that region. This measures the extent to which, in its trade with another region, a country is specialising in exporting a particular commodity.

Extra-EU FDI: FDI entering the European Union from outside, notably from Japan and the USA.

Extra-EU trade: Trade taking place between EU countries and countries outside the EU.

Factor endowments: The quantity of factors of production a country possesses.

Factor intensity reversal: This occurs when wage–rent ratios differ across countries and goods.

Factor mobility: The degree to which factors of production such as labour are free to move from one country/occupation to another.

Factors of production: Factors which are used in the production of goods, e.g. land, labour, capital.

Fifth Freedom: The right of an EU air carrier to offer services between two other member states.

Fixed-rate coupon: A piece of paper entitling the owner to a money payment, which in this case is at a fixed rate.

Floating-rate bonds or notes (FRNs): A bond or a note where the interest rate varies in line with short-term interest rates.

Footloose MNC: A firm is considered to be technically 'footloose' if its location decisions are largely unaffected by cost at different locations.

Foreign direct investment: The flow of foreign money into the domestic or European economy from countries outside Europe.

Forward cover: When two parties agree to exchange currency and execute a deal at some specific time in the future.

Free-rider problem: Where a consumer benefits from a commodity without having to pay for it.

Free trade area: Where tariffs are eliminated between member countries but each applies its own tariff policy regarding the outside world.

Futures: Contracts made in a 'future market' for the purchase or sale of commodities, currencies and the like for delivery at a specified future date.

Game theory: An attempt to explain economic and business interdependence by analogies with games, like poker. Some games may be 'zero sum' so that what winners win they get at another 'player's' expense; or games may have more than one winner.

GDP: Total value-added (income) created within the boundaries of a country.

GFCF: Creation of physical capital including depreciation in a year.

Global Triad: The increasing role of three trading regions – North America, Europe and East Asia – to account for world trade and FDI flows.

Golden Triangle: An area of activity within the EU between London, Turin and Frankfurt in which there lies the region of the EU with the greatest level of economic activity.

Gravity model: A model which attempts to predict the extent of trade between any two countries or regions on the basis of a small number of factors.

Green rate of exchange: The rate at which one ECU exchanges for the national currency regarding agricultural goods.

Heckscher–Ohlin theory: That countries should specialise in the goods which use intensively the factor of production which they have in abundance.

Home country: The destination of FDI.

Host country: The source of FDI.

Human capital: The skills obtained by labour.

Internalisation-specific advantages (ILA): Advantages accruing to a firm when transaction costs of market solutions are too high.

Imperfect competition: This is when there are a number of firms in an industry, each producing a differentiated product.

Income elasticity of demand: Responsiveness of quantity demanded to changes in incomes.

Increasing returns to scale: A situation where an increase in output is associated with decreases in the long-term average total cost.

Industrial policy: A term with different shades of meaning. Most simply IP can be viewed as government policy (other than fiscal or monetary macro-policies) to try to encourage business success and to increase competitiveness.

Insurance derivative: Derivative which insurance companies use to reduce the risk of insurance being taken up because of some possible catastrophe.

Intensity ratio: A measure of the extent to which FDI from one country or region is concentrated in another.

Inter-bank business: The level of activity in financial markets that takes place between banks.

International Monetary Fund (IMF): International institution set up to maintain order in the international monetary system.

Intra-EU FDI: FDI flows from one European Union member state to another.

Intra-EU trade: Trade flows from one EU state to another.

Intra-industry trade: The trade between two similar sectors in different countries, e.g. the trade in cars between European countries.

Investment banking: This is the process of underwriting and selling shares and bonds to investors, making markets in these securities for the investors who want to buy them, and selling all manner of advice to large organisations and governments.

Joint venture: An agreement between two or more firms to co-operate in some way, whilst typically maintaining the separate identities of each of the partners in the joint venture.

Labour theory of value: The value attributed to a good by the amount of labour embodied in it.

Laissez faire: To allow the market to work alone, with no government interference.

Law of comparative advantage: Each country should specialise in producing the good(s) in which it has a relative (comparative) advantage and trade for other good(s).

Leontief paradox: An attempt to prove the Heckscher–Ohlin theory using US data which actually showed the opposite.

LIBOR: London Inter-bank Offer Rate. This is the interest charged on inter-bank dollar loans.

Liquid asset portfolio: A collection of assets which can be turned very easily into usable funds.

Local content: A method introduced to encourage foreign direct investment to use a proportion of domestic suppliers.

London Club: A group of commercial bank creditors whose purpose is to restructure the debt of highly indebted countries.

Location-specific advantages (LSA): Certain advantages which a firm has due to its location.

Marginal efficiency of capital: This is equivalent to the internal rate of return; that is, the rate of return that just makes the present value of a future income stream equal to zero.

Market concentration: The share of a market controlled by a given number of firms.

Matrix: A method of assessing bank loans based on their level of risk.

Mercantilism: The belief that the aim of trade is to increase wealth in terms of precious metals and so increase exports and reduce imports by various means.

Merger or acquisition: Often called 'concentrations' in EU terminology. A situation where two or more independent businesses come together to form one new legal business entity.

Multi-fibre agreement: An agreement between countries on the quotas that are set for the import of textiles and fibres.

Multinational enterprises: These are enterprises which own or control production or service facilities in more than one country.

Neo-functionalism: A view of European integration which sees it as mainly governed by institutional developments, which acquire their own momentum when integration first begins. Ernst Haas is a leading exponent of this view.

Neo-realism: A view of European integration which sees it as mainly governed by national economic priorities. Alan Milward is a leading exponent of this view.

New protectionism: These are non-tariff barriers to trade, which have replaced tariffs as the major obstruction to the free flow of international trade.

Niche markets: These are specialist markets.

Non-discrimination: A country should treat all its trading partners alike.

Non-tariff barrier: In the wider sense these are barriers to trade which are not tariffs and would include quotas, health and safety regulations and the like.

Offshore banks: Banks that have been developed because of their trading advantages such as lower tax rates or lower regulatory control in countries outside the domestic economy.

Opportunity costs: The cost of opportunities not undertaken.

Optimum currency area: A region where the use of a common currency implies no loss of welfare.

Option: An agreement between a buyer and a seller permitting the holder to buy or sell, if he/she chooses to do so, at a given price within a given period.

Ownership-specific advantages (OSA): A certain type of know-how which is specific to the firm.

Ossified industries: Those that have not changed or adapted to new trends.

Outward processing trade (OPT): A contracting arrangement where firms in one country transfer inputs to firms in another country (normally where labour is cheaper).

Goods are assembled in the second country and then exported back to the first via intra-firm trading arrangements.

Over-the-counter derivatives: These include currency swaps and options, forward rate agreements (FRAs), interest rate swaps, options on traded securities, interest rate options, equity forwards, swaps and options.

Paris Club: A group formed by representatives from industrialised creditor nations with substantial debt owed to them by developing and Third World countries. Their purpose is to restructure the debt of highly indebted countries.

Partial equilibrium analysis: Equilibrium conditions examined in a given market.

Policy instruments: The type of actions such as changes in government expenditure, changes in taxation levels or interest rate changes that can be used by a government to control the economy.

Portfolio investment: Creation or transfer of financial capital.

Price elasticity of demand: Responsiveness of quantity demanded to price changes.

Prisoner's dilemma: A special case of game theory based on the idea of two arrested people being interviewed by the police. If neither confesses, they will go free; but it may be that because of uncertainty and risk, they both do, in fact, choose to confess.

Private costs: The costs to the market of producing an output or charging for a product.

Producer subsidy equivalent (PSE): A measure of the total payments made to a farmer as part of the agricultural support system of the CAP.

Production subsidy: A subsidy to producers to lower the cost of production.

Public procurement: The purchase of goods and services by governments and state-owned organisations, often by contract or by tender.

Qualified majority voting: Each EU member is given a number of votes (according to the size of population) and a set number is required to achieve what is seen as a majority vote.

Quota: An upper limit to the level of imports allowed into a country.

Reciprocity: If one country makes a reduction in a trade barrier with another then this other country should also respond with an equal-sized reduction in trade barriers.

Regressive tax: A tax which takes a higher proportion of the income of the poor than that of the rich.

Regulation Q: A US regulation which limited the rate of interest commercial banks in the USA could offer.

Re-intermediation: The moving of financial business back towards financial institutions.

Reserve assets: Assets held by banks as contingency against calls on their funds.

Retail banks: These consist, in the UK, of the 'big four' banks, i.e. Barclays, NatWest, Lloyds and the Midland. They operate both deposit and current accounts and undertake the provision of loans.

Revaluation: An increase in the value of a currency against other currencies in a fixed exchange rate system.

Schengen Agreement: An agreement to remove all checks on travellers at internal borders.

Screwdriver operations: A situation where a foreign-owned company in the domestic economy brings in the parts for a product from abroad and they are assembled in the domestic economy. Little skill or expertise is required.

Set-aside policy: The policy of withdrawing agricultural land from production.

Short-termism: A belief that some organisations set very short time horizons by which time investment projects or other investments are required to achieve a profitable income stream.

Social Charter: Alternatively titled, 'the Community Charter of Fundamental Social Rights' was developed to establish a minimum set of conditions which all member states should implement to ensure that social dumping does not occur.

Social costs: These are the costs of some activity or output which are borne by society as a whole, and which need not be restricted to the costs borne by the individual or firm carrying out the activity or producing the output.

Social dumping: Unfair competition based upon low wages and poor working conditions.

Social Protocol: The operation of the social provisions of the Maastricht Treaty from which the UK negotiated an opt-out until 1998.

Specific tax: A tax of a set or specific amount.

Specialisation: To choose to produce certain goods and not others.

Stability Council: A policing body which will oversee fiscal policy in the member states after entry into a single currency.

Stakeholders: The internal and external groups which have relationships with an organisation.

State aid: Financial assistance given by governments to home-based firms, or even to home-based industries.

Strategic alliances: An association between two or more organisations, which may be either formal or informal, enabling an organisation to gain access to an external market without having to expand its operations there.

Strategic trade policy: A means by which a government can undertake trade policies so as to improve its own welfare and obtain a comparative advantage in the production of a product.

Super levy: A punitive tax imposed upon those farmers who exceed their allocated production quota in the CAP system.

Swap markets: These are markets for the simultaneous purchase and sale of a given amount of foreign exchange for two different value dates.

Syndicated loans: Loans which are developed through involving a number of banks as a means of reducing the risk facing any bank.

Synergy: Positive synergy is the effect of two or more firms merging or co-operating so that the end result or performance of the whole is greater than the sum of the parts, or, more simply, when $2 + 2 = 5$.

Tariff: A tax on imports as they enter the country. These taxes may be a proportion of the value of the product (*ad valorem*) or related to size or weight (specific).

Tariff escalation: The process by which tariffs on products increase the greater the product is developed.

Tariffication process: The process by which non-tariff barriers are converted into their equivalent tariff barriers.

Terms of trade: The price or rate at which goods exchange.

Trade creation: Domestic production is replaced by imports from a customs union partner.

Trade diversion: Extra-union imports are replaced by intra-union imports.

Trade expansion: The growth of trade due to a reduction in prices (from tariff reductions) from joining a CU.

Trade intensity ratio: The share of a country's trade with another country or region divided by the share of the second country or region in world trade (excluding trade with the first country). This ratio measures the extent to which the trade of a country is 'centred' on a particular region.

Trade-related investment measures (TRIMs): These are the performance requirements imposed on multinational firms which engage in foreign direct investment.

Trade-related property rights (TRIPs): These are the ways in which the creators of intellectual property – patents, copyrights and trademarks – can enforce their rights outside of the country of origin.

Trading bloc: General name for a group of countries which are linked by trade agreements of varying depth.

Transaction costs: The costs of changing one currency into another.

Transaction cost theory: The cost of using the market.

Transparency: The replacement of disguised barriers to trade with more overt ones.

Visegrad Four: The Central European countries of Hungary, Poland, the Czech Republic and Slovakia; so-called as a result of an agreement in Visegrad in February 1991.

Voluntary export restraint: An agreement by an exporting country to set an upper limit on the amount of goods it will export to other countries.

World Bank: International institution set up to promote general economic development in the world's poorer nations.

World Trade Organisation (WTO): An international grouping set up to promote and regulate trade. All major economies except for China, Russia and Taiwan are members. The WTO is the successor organisation to the General Agreement on Tariffs and Trade (GATT).

Index